HISTORY OF
THE SECOND WORLD WAR

UNITED KINGDOM MILITARY SERIES

Edited by J. R. M. BUTLER

A

The authors of the Military Histories have been given full access to official documents. They and the editor are alone responsible for the statements made and the views expressed.

ALLIED MILITARY ADMINISTRATION OF ITALY

1943–1945

BY

C. R. S. HARRIS

LONDON : 1957

HER MAJESTY'S STATIONERY OFFICE

First published 1957

Published by
HER MAJESTY'S STATIONERY OFFICE
To be purchased from
York House, Kingsway, London W.C.2
423 Oxford Street, London W.1
13A Castle Street, Edinburgh 2
109 St. Mary Street, Cardiff
39 King Street, Manchester 2
Tower Lane, Bristol 1
2 Edmund Street, Birmingham 3
80 Chichester Street, Belfast
or through any bookseller
Price £2 2s. od. net

Printed in Great Britain under the authority of H.M. Stationery Office
by Bradley & Son, Ltd., Caxton Street, Reading; and London

CONTENTS

APPENDICES

MAPS AND DIAGRAMS

EDITOR'S PREFACE

UNDER INTERNATIONAL LAW the commander of a force occupying territory hitherto subject to the enemy's authority assumes certain rights and duties; but even if it were not so he would need, in his own interests, to provide for the control of the civil population and the exploitation of the country's resources. This need has always been recognised, but it has never before presented a problem on the scale of the war of 1939–1945 or involved so large an expansion of organization, and it has attracted little attention from military historians. It is therefore proposed to include a few volumes on this subject, Military Government, as part of the United Kingdom Military Series of the History of the Second World War.

In planning for the administration of that country with which the present volume is concerned the Allies were faced with a task of particular difficulty and delicacy. The country was inhabited not by African tribes or, as in the Far East, by communities formerly under Allied rule, but by one of the most gifted peoples the world has known, and one from which the Allied nations had largely derived their own civilization. On the other hand this great nation had for twenty years been governed by a regime which cared little for personal freedom and rejected many of the accepted canons of civilised humanity. Mr. Harris' book is a military, not a political, history, but he has been bound to devote considerable space to the political happenings which influenced the successive phases of military government in Italy.

The book has further the peculiar interest of showing how this inherently difficult task was complicated by the fact that the campaign was jointly conducted by two Great Powers; it describes the formation, the functioning, and the remarkable success of an Anglo-American organization 'integrated' to a degree unknown in previous history.

Mr. Harris enjoys the advantage of having himself played a part in this organization, having served with AMGOT in Sicily as Controller of Property and later in Italy as Head of the Property Control Sub-Commission in the Control Commission from June 1943 to July 1944.

As has been explained in the prefaces to former volumes of the history, the practice has been adopted of not giving in the text detailed references to sources not open to public inspection; they are printed however in a confidential edition.

J.R.M.B.

AUTHOR'S PREFACE

To compose the history of an administration after wading through its innumerable files is in some respects a hazardous undertaking, even when the author has some personal knowledge of the working of the machine with which he is dealing, since in the welter of detail the perspective of the whole is so easily distorted. Nor is this particular hazard diminished, when the perusal of the files has been unavoidably far from complete. This work has been based directly not on the original files of the Allied Commission, which are not in this country but in Washington, but, as it were second-hand, on the records of its higher echelon, Allied Force Headquarters of the Mediterranean theatre, a circumstance which automatically effected a primary sifting of the vast quantity of papers lying in the basement of the Pentagon. But on a short visit to Washington in 1949 I had the privilege of examining certain files which were freely placed at my disposal, and photostatic copies of some of them were sent to me in London. Shortage of time and dollars, however, rendered a complete examination and reproduction of the material in the Pentagon quite out of the question. To have made a really exhaustive investigation of all of the Allied Commission's files would have been the labour of several years, the value of which could hardly fail to be quite disproportionate to the effort. It is very unlikely that any important facts relevant to this history will have escaped my notice for this reason, since it may confidently be assumed that they would have found their place in the records of A.F.H.Q., though it must be confessed that these appear to reveal some rather surprising gaps, particularly in connection with the very rapid process of the liberation of the North.

In connection with my visit to Washington I should like to record my thanks to the Historical Section of the U.S. War Department, and in particular to Lieutenant Kenneth Munden.

My thanks are also due among others to many officers of AMGOT and the Allied Commission on both sides of the Atlantic, who have given me the opportunity of discussing my problems with them and at great trouble to themselves have read in whole or in part my manuscript in its most voluminous and crude condition. First and foremost to Admiral Stone, the Chief Executive of the Commission, whose notes and comments have been of great value in assessing the work of that body; secondly to Colonel R. H. Wilmer of Washington, to whose indefatigable corrections and criticisms this work owes a great debt; thirdly, to Lord Rennell, whose revision of the first four chapters has saved me from many errors. I am also indebted to the Duke of Wellington for some valuable notes on his experiences as S.C.A.O., Catania, immediately after the Allied landings in Sicily; to Commander Frank Southard Jr. for some stimulating comments and to Brigadier-General Charles M. Spofford for many illuminating side-lights on the working of the Commission, as well as to Colonel (Mr. Justice) Willmer for many helpful suggestions. I have received also much help from officers of the Army A.M.Gs., many of whom contributed the kind of information not to be found in any official files. My thanks are due in particular to Air-Commodore C. E. Benson, Group-Captain Trevor Beer, Colonel E. B. Mayne, Major Peter Clarke, Major A. Negretti and Major (Professor) Deane Keller of Yale University, who placed at my disposal the manuscript of a history of A.M.G. Fifth Army which has unfortunately never been published.

I should like also to express my thanks to three persons not directly connected with the Commission, who have read my manuscript and given me the benefit of some helpful criticism, namely, Professor Sir Llewellyn Woodward, Professor A. P. d'Entrèves and Mr. R. J. Stopford, and to Sir Frederic Bovenschen, whose comments on my first draft have, I hope, enabled me to correct some errors of perspective.

In dealing with specialist subjects I have received valuable help from the former officers of the Commission: Finance, Brigadier A. Grafftey Smith, Major F. W. Cook and Major T. Gilbertson; Public Safety, Colonel A. E. Young, Lieutenant-Colonel C. Francis, and Lieutenant-Colonel T. W. Walters; Military Courts, Colonel Ian Campbell; and Public Health, Colonel G. M. Frizelle. Last, but not least, I am greatly indebted to Sir Harold Caccia and Sir Noel Charles for some illuminating side-lights on the political side of the Commission's work.

These acknowledgments of assistance must not be taken to involve their generous givers in any responsibility either for the accuracy of the facts related, or for the correctness of the comments made on them: that belongs wholly to the author.

C.R.S.H.

Abbreviations and Code Names

A.A.I.	Allied Armies in Italy
A.C.	Allied Commission
A.C.C.	Allied Control Commission
A.C.I.	Army Council Instruction
A.C.M.F.	Allied Central Mediterranean Force
A.C. of S.	Assistant Chief of Staff
A.F.A.	Allied Financial Agency
A.F.H.Q.	Allied Force Headquarters
A.F.L.R.S.	Allied Force Local Resources Section
A.G.	Adjutant General
A.M.	Allied Military
A.M.F.A.	Allied Military Financial Agency
A.M.G.	Allied Military Government
AMGOT	Allied Military Government of Occupied Territory
A.P.B.	Allied Publications Board
AVALANCHE	Code designation for planned invasion at Salerno
BAYTOWN	Code designation for the invasion of Calabria
BRASSARD	Code designation for invasion of Elba
B.M.A.	British Military Administration
C.A.	Civil Affairs
C.A.D.	Civil Affairs Division, War Department (Washington)
C.A.O.	Chief Administrative Officer
C.A.O.	Civil Affairs Officer
C.A.P.O.	Civil Affairs Police Officer
C.C.A.C.	Combined Civil Affairs Committee
C.C.A.O.	Chief Civil Affairs Officer
CC.RR.	*Carabinieri Reali*
C.C.S.	Combined Chiefs of Staff
C.E.A.I.S.	Italo-Slovene Citizens' Executive Committee
C.E.M.	Captured Enemy Material
C.G.I.L.	*Confederazione Generale Italiana del Lavoro*
C.I.C.	Counter-intelligence Corps
C.I.L.	*Corpo Italiano di Liberazione*
C.I.P.	*Comitato Italiano Petroli*
C.L.N.	*Il Comitato di Liberazione Nazionale*
C.L.N.A.I.	*Il Comitato di Liberazione Nationale per l'Alta Italia*
CORKSCREW	Code designation for invasion of Pantelleria
C.S.D.I.C.	Combined Services Detailed Interrogation Centre
C.V.L.	*Corpo Volontari della Libertà*
D.A.D.L.	Deputy Assistant Director of Labour
D.C.C.A.O.	Deputy Chief Civil Affairs Officer
D.M.E.	Director of Mechanical Engineering
D.W.	Director of Works
E.M.	Enlisted Men
ENAC	*Ente Nazionale Auto-Trasporti Cose*
ENDIMEA	*Ente Nazionale Distribuzione Medicinali degli Alleati*

ENDSI . .	*Ente Nazionale Distribuzione dei Soccorsi per Italia*
E.T.O.U.S.A. .	European Theatre of Operations, U.S. Army
F.E.A. . .	Foreign Economic Administration
FLAMBO . .	Code designation for A.F.H.Q. Advanced Administrative Echelon in Italy
FORTBASE .	Supply District for Eighth Army
F.S.P. . . .	Field Security Personnel
GAP . . .	*Gruppi Azione Patriottica*
G.N.R. . . .	*Guarda Nazionale Repubblicana*
G.O.C. . .	General Officer Commanding
HOBGOBLIN .	Code designation for Pantelleria
HORRIFIED .	Code designation for Sicily
HUSKY . .	Code designation for invasion of Sicily
I.A.F. . . .	Italian Air Force
I.B.S. . . .	Island Base Section
ICE . . .	*Istituto Nazionale per Commercio Estero*
I.G.C.R. . .	Intergovernmental Committee on Refugees
INC. . . .	Information and Censorship
INT . . .	*Istituto Nazionale Trasporti*
IRI . . .	*Istituto di Ricostruzione Industriale*
I.W.T. . . .	Inland Water Transport
J.A.G. . .	Judge Advocate General
J.I.C. . . .	Joint Intelligence Committee
L.C.T. . . .	Landing Craft Tanks
L. of C. . .	Lines of Communication
M.A.A.F. . .	Mediterranean Allied Air Forces
M.A.C. . .	Mediterranean Air Command
MEDBO . .	Mediterranean Shipping Board
M.E.F. . .	Middle East Forces
M.F.A. & A. .	Monuments, Fine Arts and Archives
M.G.S. . .	Military Government Section, A.F.H.Q.
M.M.I.A. . .	Military Mission to the Italian Army
M.R.S. . .	Military Railway Services
M.T. . . .	Motor Transport
M.T.O.U.S.A. .	Mediterranean Theatre of Operations, U.S. Army
N.A.A.F.I. . .	Navy, Army, Air Forces Institute
N.A.E.B. . .	North African Economic Board
N.A.T.O.U.S.A. .	North African Theatre of Operations, U.S. Army
O.C. . . .	Officer Commanding
O.R. . . .	Other rank
O.S.S. . .	Office of Strategic Services
P.B.S. . . .	Peninsular Base Section
P.M. . . .	Provost Marshal
P.O.L. . . .	Petrol, Oil and Lubricants
P.O.W. . .	Prisoner of War
P.R.B. . .	Public Relations Branch
P.W.B. . .	Psychological Warfare Branch
P.W.E. . . .	Psychological Warfare Executive
Q.M. . . .	Quartermaster

Q. (Mov.) . .	Quartermaster (Movements)
R.A.C. . .	Royal Armoured Corps
R.A.M.C. . .	Royal Army Medical Corps
R.A.O.C. . .	Royal Army Ordnance Corps
R.D.L. . .	Royal Decree—Law
R.E.M.E. . .	Royal Electrical and Mechanical Engineers
S.A.C. . .	Supreme Allied Commander
S.A.C.M.E.D. .	Supreme Allied Commander Mediterranean Theatre of Operations
SAP . . .	*Squadre d'Azione Patriottica*
S.C.A.O. . .	Senior Civil Affairs Officer
S.C.A.P.O. . .	Senior Civil Affairs Police Officer
S.H.A.E.F. . .	Supreme Headquarters Allied Expeditionary Force (North-Western Europe)
SIAP . . .	*Società Italiana Petrolio*
S.O.E. . . .	Special Operations Executive
S.O.M.T.O. .	Subversive Operations, Mediterranean Theatre of Operations
S. & T. . .	Supply and Transport
T.O. . . .	Tables of Organization
TORCH . .	Code designation for invasion of North Africa
UNPA . .	*Unione Nazionale Protezione Anti-Aerea*
U.N.R.R.A. .	United Nations Relief and Rehabilitation Administration
U.S.N. . .	U.S. Navy
W.E. . . .	War Establishment

CHAPTER I

PLANNING FOR 'HUSKY'

THE INVASION of Sicily as a joint Anglo-American operation was decided upon at the Casablanca Conference in January 1943, and was given the code name 'Husky'. The operation, like the invasion of North Africa ('Torch'), was from the first conceived as a combined operation of armies, navies and air forces under the supreme command of General Eisenhower, while the command of the invading land forces—the American Seventh Army and the British Eighth Army—was entrusted to General Sir Harold Alexander, G.O.C. Fifteenth Army Group. Among the innumerable problems connected with the operation, two questions arose quite early in the mind of General Eisenhower; what kind of Military Government was to be set up in the island? and who was to be responsible for this function? In connection with 'Torch' the question of Military Government had not arisen because the Darlan-Clark agreement enabled North Africa to be treated as 'friendly liberated', as opposed to 'enemy', territory. Moreover the arrangements concerning the relations between the occupying forces and the French authorities had, for political reasons, been handled by the Americans, who had throughout been treated by Mr Churchill as senior partners in the joint undertaking.[1]

But the invasion of Sicily presented an altogether different situation. The institution of a Military Government in the occupied enemy territory was clearly unavoidable, and the political repercussions of its character would obviously be far reaching, since 'Husky', as General Eisenhower pointed out to General Marshall in a telegram dated 8th February, constituted the first United States operation involving the invasion and occupation of enemy territory, and the first British operation involving the occupation of any but colonial enemy territories. The precedents established would therefore be far reaching in scope and importance, and would set the pattern for later operations in Europe.

General Eisenhower from the outset wisely determined to guard against the proverbial difficulties which beset those who serve two masters. He therefore insisted on the necessity of laying down well in advance a single Allied policy, in order to arrive at a joint and single attitude with respect to the civil and military authority and the civil population of the territory occupied. He left his Government in

---

[1] See Winston Churchill, *The Second World War*, Vol. IV, Ch. 35.

no doubt as to the character of the Military Government which he wanted to establish. From the outset he recommended a policy of 'joint Anglo-American responsibility and joint conduct of Military Government' under an agreed 'single effective' system to be jointly planned and to function under the Allied Commander. This implied an altogether new venture in the history of military government, an integrated Anglo-American administration working neither by national zones (an American zone for the area occupied by the American Seventh Army and a British zone for that occupied by the Eighth Army) nor by executive diarchy (British and American 'opposite numbers'), but by a complete fusion of personnel divided between the two nationalities on a fifty-fifty basis.

The creation of this novel instrument of international administration, and the determination by mutual agreement of the policy which it was to execute, led to prolonged negotiations between the various interests involved. These included the Foreign departments of both nations, besides the two War departments, upon which in both countries rested the formal responsibility for the administration of occupied territories in accordance with joint policies worked out by the Combined Chiefs of Staff. These negotiations, which were not concluded without the direct personal intervention of the heads of the two Governments, will not be dealt with in this volume. Here we are concerned only with the planning in the theatre of operations.

As a first step towards developing an operational plan, General Eisenhower sent an American officer, Lieut.-Colonel Spofford, to Tripoli to study the organisation of British military administration established in that Italian colony under the Middle East Command. As a result of this visit an 'Appreciation and Outline Plan' was prepared by him and submitted on 24th March to the Chief of Staff at Allied Force Headquarters (A.F.H.Q.)[1] by Colonel Julius Holmes, head of the Liaison Section, the staff branch then responsible for Civil Affairs. This plan, which received the tentative approval of Lieut.-General Bedell Smith, was then submitted to General Alexander's Chief of Staff at Force 141, the nucleus of Fifteenth Army Group, and transmitted to Washington and London for approval. During this period no senior British officer with military government experience had been available for planning, and it was not until 6th April that Major-General Lord Rennell, who had been Chief Political Officer in the East African Command, was able to take charge of the work in Algiers. Lord Rennell approved the Appreciation and Outline Plan (generally known as the 'Spofford Plan') with certain comparatively unimportant amendments, and it became the basis for the development in detail of the military government plans for Sicily.

---

[1] For a table of abbreviations, see p. xiii.

British and American ideas on the nature of military government were, speaking generally, for the most part in agreement. Differences of emphasis on the immediate measures to be taken for the destruction of Fascism did however raise a principle of fundamental practical importance, the issue of direct versus indirect rule. Opinion in Washington at first took the view that all Prefects and Mayors of important communities should be removed[1] and replaced by military officers of the occupying forces. The impracticability of this plan was pointed out by Lord Rennell, who had no difficulty in convincing General Alexander and General Eisenhower that, though the heads of the various departments would most of them have to be dismissed as too tainted with Fascism, the Italian administrative machinery should be maintained intact and local substitutes found for the dismissed chiefs, and he received verbal instructions from General Eisenhower to continue planning on that basis.

The imposition of direct rule, even if it had been practical, would have been most undesirable from the strictly military point of view, since it would have required a very much larger number of Allied officers to be employed in military government. For there were in Sicily, besides nine provinces whose prefects would have to be replaced, some seventy-two towns with more than 10,000 inhabitants, of which three contained more than 100,000. Under direct rule each of these would require one and, in many cases more than one, Allied Officer to administer them, whereas under indirect rule a single Allied officer could supervise the municipal administrations of several towns of moderate size. Moreover, it had to be asked where a sufficient number of Allied officers could be found who were possessed of the requisite local knowledge to take over the functions of Italian chief officials. Their intrusion into the official hierarchy would certainly be resented, and might well have given rise to tactics on the part of their Italian subordinates which would have led to complete administrative chaos.

It was perhaps natural enough, in the light of experience in French North Africa and the criticism—as Sir Winston Churchill has shown, not altogether just[2]—to which the War Department in Washington had been subjected over the agreement with Darlan and the subsequent arrangements with various French political interests, that the replacement of Fascist officials by other Italians should have been regarded as a possible source of undesirable political complications which might be avoided by direct military government, but in principle the idea underlying it was wrong. The disagreement between British and American views on the question of direct *versus*

---

[1] See Robert E. Sherwood, *The White House Papers of Harry L. Hopkins*, Vol. II, p. 719–722, for some American plans for A.M.G.

[2] Churchill, *op. cit.*, Vol. IV, Ch. 34 and 35.

indirect rule took a considerable time to straighten itself out, and even as late as 1st June, when the agreed directive was transmitted to the Supreme Allied Commander, policy had not been finally settled. Indeed, it was only at the end of June that a formula was found which left General Alexander free to decide the issue at his own discretion, and removed from his shoulders the incubus of a mandatory dismissal of Prefects and Mayors of the important communities irrespective of the actual conditions discovered upon occupation.[1]

Under an Administrative Memorandum of A.F.H.Q. dated 1st May the Allied Military Government of Occupied Territory (AMGOT) was set up and placed under the direct supervision of the Commanding General, Force 141, later to become Fifteenth Army Group. General Alexander was designated Military Governor of Sicily—and, as such, made responsible to General Eisenhower for the conduct of the Military Government of the territory. Major-General Lord Rennell was appointed head of AMGOT, with the title of Chief Civil Affairs Officer (C.C.A.O.). A month later an American officer, Brigadier-General F. J. McSherry, was appointed Deputy Chief of AMGOT, with title of Deputy Chief Civil Affairs Officer (D.C.C.A.O.). May and June were spent in elaborating in detail the plans for the constitution and establishment of AMGOT, which were embodied in a document (known colloquially as the 'AMGOT Bible') issued to all officers concerned; in integrating these plans with 'Husky' operational planning for the assault; and in assembling in North Africa, and instructing, the officers, about 400 in number, whom the Military Government of Sicily, even on the basis of indirect rule, was calculated to require—one per 10,000 of the population.

In the AMGOT Plan, which became the model for the military administration of successive portions of the mainland as they were liberated, the province was chosen as the administrative unit. Each province was placed in charge of a Senior Civil Affairs Officer (S.C.A.O.) whose function it was to direct and supervise the administration of the Prefect. Under his command were a number of Civil Affairs Officers (C.A.O's), responsible for the general supervision of the various municipalities, and 'specialist' officers of the six divisions, Legal, Financial, Civilian Supply, Public Health, Public

---

[1] The text of the final version of the Directive on this point was as follows: 'The replacement of any Prefects and Mayors of important communities who may be removed will rest with the Military Commander. He will decide whether the functioning of Military Government is better served by the appointment of officers of the occupation forces or by the use of the services of Italian officials. No actual appointment of Italians to important posts, as distinct from their temporary use, will be made until it has been approved by the two governments through the Combined Chiefs of Staff'.

Safety and Enemy Property, under which AMGOT headquarters had been organised. Assuming the C.C.A.O. to be analogous to a Commander-in-Chief, the heads of divisions were more or less the functional equivalents of his chief staff officers (A.G., Q.M.G., etc.), the provincial S.C.A.O. corresponding to a divisional commander.

Of these special divisions the Legal occupied what was in some respects a central position during the planning stage. It was responsible for the drawing up of the Proclamations of the Commander-in-Chief establishing his Military Government and the instruments under which it operated; for the setting up and administration of Allied Military courts and the supervision of the Italian law courts; and, last but not least, for advising the C.C.A.O. on the nature and limits of his powers under the Hague Rules and other conventions of international law.

Under a system of indirect rule the responsibilities of the Public Safety Division were particularly important, since on it depended the maintenance of law and order in the rear of advancing troops in the most critical phase. In North Africa, the employment of the Italian police forces had been impracticable, and a special native force had been organised under British officers. But conditions in metropolitan Italian territory were wholly different, and the only alternative to employing the local police forces would have been to import a ready-made Allied military police corps, which, quite apart from the obvious disadvantages such an alien body would have to face, would have been contrary to one of the primary purposes of military government, the preservation of public order with the least possible diversion of military manpower. It was therefore decided that the risk must be taken of relying on the local police, of which the principal force was the *Carabinieri Reali* (CC.RR), notwithstanding the fact that this corps was formally a unit of the Italian army. To supervise the administration and operation of this potentially hostile force, a large number of Allied officers with police training, including some sixty-five London Metropolitan Police officers, was assigned to the Public Safety Division. The decision to employ local Italian police forces in maintaining law and order in the island was amply justified in the event, and the Civil Affairs Police Officers, of whom the large majority were British, rendered admirable service as the right-hand men of the provincial military administrators.

The task of the Finance Division may be considered under four headings. In the first place, it had to supervise the Italian machinery for the collection of revenue and the control of expenditure. It was known that a very small proportion of Italian budget expenditure was being met from taxation and, since Sicily was poor in comparison with central and northern Italy, it was anticipated that, even when all items of war expenditure had been eliminated, local receipts from taxation would almost certainly fail to cover disbursement. Hence special arrangements would have to be made for covering deficits. In the second place, regulations would have to be drawn up to control banking houses and other financial institutions, in order to ensure that, under the stress of invasion and probable panic, the banks, almost all of which would be cut off from their head offices, would not be called upon to meet sudden withdrawals of deposits—a delicate task of nicely calculated less or more. Here the first essential was to provide an adequate and mobile currency reserve. In the third place, the Division was charged with the responsibility of organising supplies of a locally accepted military currency, to be placed at the disposal of Army paymasters in any quantity required for purposes of paying Allied troops and meeting all forms of local currency expenditure, after the emergency currency supplies with which the invading troops had been provided had been exhausted.

In order to equip itself to perform these three tasks, all of which pivoted on a single essential requirement, the provision of currency in practically unlimited quantities, the Finance Division set up an Allied Military Financial Agency (A.M.F.A.) whose chief function was the issue and distribution, for both military and civilian purposes, of Allied military lire, which were printed in the United States after D-day and transported to Sicily, some by air within a few days of the Allied landings. A.M.F.A. was intended to fulfil some of the functions normally performed by a bank of issue, and was 'the lender of last resort'. Besides issuing Allied military lire to the troops for their pay and local expenditure, it provided the currency required by AMGOT to finance its own administrative expenditure and that of Italian governmental agencies, in so far as this was not covered by taxation receipts. It was also empowered to make loans to municipalities, public utilities and such business enterprises as were considered to have public importance. Finally, the Division was made responsible for keeping the accounts of the currency issued by A.M.F.A. to the forces and to other borrowers, as well as those of the receipts and expenditures of the military government, in order to establish the liabilities to be subsequently charged to the Italian Government.

The invasion of the island in high summer, involving heavy possible damage to water supplies and drainage systems and the destruction of a large number of dwellings, made it appear more than probable that severe outbreaks of epidemic disease would occur. Hence the necessity for a Public Health Division, staffed by medical officers from both sides of the Atlantic with experience of these problems. In addition to the control of venereal disease, the Public Health Division was made responsible for welfare matters. These comprised the care of refugees, child welfare, the supervision of social insurance, mass feeding and relief in general, all of which were placed under Public Health, in view of the acute problems certain to arise out of war damage and destruction and the general social dislocations and distress which must entail acute danger to the health of the population.

The Civilian Supply Division, as originally planned, was something of a maid of all work. It was recognised that, to begin with, its primary function would be to plan for the procurement and importation of essential requirements for the first 90-day period after invasion. Orders were placed with the supply authorities at A.F.H.Q. early in June for an emergency stock of foodstuffs to meet immediate requirements after the invasion. This stock was to consist of some 13,000 tons of flour, evaporated milk, meat and sugar—a quantity calculated to be sufficient to maintain on existing ration scales some 500,000 persons for three months. It was hoped that after about a month normal supply channels in the island would be reopened. If, however, there was a harvest failure or large destruction or removal of foodstuffs by the enemy, supplies would be needed on a larger scale. It was therefore recommended that a stockpile of 32,000 tons of wheat flour should be set aside in North Africa. AMGOT planners also placed orders for (*Americane* 'requisitioned'—a useful technical term which will be employed in this sense throughout this volume) a small stock of medical supplies, consisting of 94 tons of soap and 150 American drug and dressing units, as well as considerable quantities of anti-tetanus, anti-typhus and small-pox vaccines. As the invasion was to take place just about harvest time and Sicily was during normal years considered to be self-sufficient in bread grains, the estimation of long term requirements was left to be made after occupation. The Division was responsible for supervising the rationing system in the island, for arranging for the transport of essential civilian supplies and for the survey, development and control of local resources for both military and civilian needs. It was also to be given charge of agricultural policy (including fisheries) and labour relations, as well as public utilities, including railways, as soon as the control of these should be relinquished by the military authorities.

The Enemy Property Division, which had exercised an important function in occupied Italian African territories under British military administration, where the custodianship of Italian Government property had been dominated by a very strict idea of stewardship in accordance with the Hague Rules[1], had no counterpart in American practice of military government; and it was realised that, in the circumstances created by the invasion of Sicily by large Allied

[1] See Lord Rennell, British Military Administration in Africa, 1941–47, Ch. XVII; also Appendix III; and the article *British Stewardship in the Colonies, an Account Rendered*, by D. C. Cumming in International Affairs Vol. XXIX No. 1, January 1953.

armies, a Custodian of Enemy Property could not be expected to hold even a watching brief, where the employment by the invading forces of Italian Government property was concerned. His trusteeship could therefore be extended only to those portions of the Italian and other enemy Governments' property which were not occupied or utilised by some other branch of the Allied forces, and to property found abandoned or property belonging to absentee owners. State-owned businesses and enterprises in which the state had full or substantial control, following the British practice in Africa, were also to be placed under his control. An entirely new function was superimposed on these activities. Following on the declaration of war, the Italian Government had submitted practically all the property belonging to subjects of the Allied nations to the process of sequestration, in accordance with the practice now usual among all belligerents. It was decided that such property on occupation should be taken into custody on behalf of its Allied owner by the Enemy Property Division, which in consequence added the adjective 'Allied' to its title, and it was found that most of the Division's activities were in fact concerned with Allied property.

The C.C.A.O.'s staff also included an Educational Adviser, and an Adviser on Fine Arts and Monuments—an appointment which indicated a civilised recognition on the part of the Allies of the importance of preserving, as far as war conditions allowed, the artistic patrimony of the island. The activities of these various divisions were coordinated under a Chief of Staff—a post occupied after the invasion by Colonel Spofford—who had also under him a number of administrative officers concerned with 'A' and 'Q' functions of AMGOT in its capacity as a unit under the command of Fifteenth Army Group.[1]

We must now consider briefly the shape of the organisation set up at A.F.H.Q. to deal with the Civil Affairs of the campaign; it was settled only after prolonged discussion, revealing a good deal of initial disagreement between American and British views. All that is appropriate here is a brief description of the form of organisation eventually arrived at. Since AMGOT with Lord Rennell at its head was serving under General Alexander on a different continent, there was obviously the need for some machinery of liaison on Civil Affairs between the Supreme Allied Commander and his chief subordinate in the field. A.F.H.Q., after the landing in North Africa, had dealt with Civil Affairs, which had never entailed Military Government in the proper sense, through a mixed military and civilian organisation, of which the head had been Mr Robert Murphy, the personal representative of President Roosevelt, who

[1] The provisional lay-out of AMGOT H.Q. Staff, as laid down at the end of May, will be found in Annexe III to this chapter.

occupied a position at Algiers closely analogous to that of the British Resident Minister, Mr Harold Macmillan, though he was not a member of the President's Cabinet.

For 'Husky', General Eisenhower was anxious to establish a purely military chain of command leading back directly to the Combined Chiefs of Staff—now to be provided with an appropriate organ, the Combined Civil Affairs Committee—and through them to the War departments of the two countries, each of which had evolved an organisation to deal with Civil Affairs, the Civil Affairs Division at Washington and the Civil Affairs Directorate in London. A new section of the staff was consequently set up at A.F.H.Q., the Military Government Section (M.G.S.), known later under the denomination of G-5, the head of which was to be an assistant Chief of Staff, the adviser of the Supreme Allied Commander on Civil Affairs, a position first held by Colonel Julius Holmes. The creation of this new position raised some misgivings in the mind of Lord Rennell who was anxious to avoid the tendency of staff branches of the higher echelons to intervene in the operations of the lower. These misgivings were however to some extent assuaged by the verbal instructions given to Colonel Holmes by General Bedell Smith in Lord Rennell's presence, that the new staff section would not interfere in political and administrative matters in Sicily and would act only as a channel of communication for the Commander-in-Chief with the Combined Chiefs of Staff in such matters as the Commander-in-Chief could not himself settle. Though these instructions were in fact adhered to as far as AMGOT in Sicily was concerned, subsequent events, as we shall see, shifted the centre of gravity to Algiers, with not altogether happy consequences. Nevertheless, even if, as will be shown later, it resulted in a good deal of unnecessary duplication, the creation of the G-5 branch must be regarded both logically and practically as a necessary development of military organisation—the inevitable consequence entailed by the impingement of political considerations upon military decisions. Marlborough rather than Moltke is the model for the modern supreme commander. Meanwhile the creation of the new military chain of command left both Mr Murphy and Mr Macmillan somewhat in a backwater. It was therefore arranged by Mr Churchill with President Roosevelt that, though all formal correspondence connected with 'Husky' should pass from General Eisenhower to the Combined Chiefs of Staff, the Supreme Commander should keep in close touch with both Mr Murphy and Mr Macmillan, enabling them to continue to give to the heads of the two Governments 'intimate information about what happens in the civil and political sphere', and thus preserving for 'Husky' more or less the same relations between them and himself as had been evolved after 'Torch'.

The policy laid down in the Combined Chiefs of Staff's directive for the Military Government of Sicily was embodied in Political, Monetary and Fiscal, and Economic guides. The first of these began by laying stress on the Allied and exclusively military nature of AMGOT:

> There shall be a military administration which will show every characteristic of an Allied undertaking. Both American and British flags shall be displayed at Headquarters and Posts of Military Government, the administration shall be identical throughout the area . . . The military administration of HORRIFIED (code word for Sicily) shall contain no political agencies or political representatives of either Government.

Representatives of the civilian agencies of neither Government were to participate in AMGOT in the initial stages, their later participation being subject as to both time and extent to the decision of the Combined Chiefs of Staff.

With respect to the civilian population the administration was to be benevolent—as far as was consistent with military requirements. It was to be made clear to the Sicilian population that the military occupation was intended to deliver the people from the Fascist regime which led them into the war, and to restore Italy as a free nation. The Fascist party organisation was to be dissolved immediately and the entire Fascist 'hierarchy', from the top down to local secretaries, was to be removed from all posts of authority. The Fascist militia and the Fascist youth organisations were to be abolished and Fascist leaders and pro-Nazi partisans arrested. It was however realised that these stringent provisions, if taken *au pied de la lettre*, might seriously hamper the putting together of any workable administration, as well as depriving the population of much that they valued. They were therefore qualified by the injunction that the first objective must be to get and keep a local government working smoothly, so as to relieve the Commander-in-Chief of all trouble and anxiety as to the civil population. A distinction was also drawn between 'Fascist' organisations; e.g. between the Party itself with its militias and security police and all purely Fascist accretions grafted onto the local government system, and those institutions which were of direct benefit to the people, the removal of which would adversely affect the efficiency of the administration. The former were to be suppressed, while there was a *prima facie* case for preserving the latter. But Fascist doctrine and propaganda in any form were to be prohibited and no political activity whatsoever was to be countenanced.

All laws discriminating on the basis of race, colour, or creed were to be annulled, the special Tribunal for the Defence of the State abolished, and political prisoners promptly released, but warned that political activity on their part during the period of military government would not be tolerated. It was also strictly laid down that neither individual politicians nor organised political groups, however sound in sentiment, should have any part in determining the policies of the administration. Commitments of any kind to, or negotiations with, any local political elements were to be avoided and Italian political leaders in exile were to have no part in the administration. But in so far as military interests were not prejudiced, freedom of the press and freedom of speech were to be instituted. War criminals charged by the United Nations (a list of whom was to be communicated to the Supreme Commander) were to be imprisoned and held until further direction, and a plan was to be prepared to prevent the dispersal by Fascists of their property with the intention to 'defeat, evade or avoid the responsibilities, fines or punishments to be imposed on them.'

The Monetary and Fiscal guides laid down the arrangements to be made in respect of military currencies, and the exchange rates to be observed between them and the lira. For reasons of military security the production of military lira notes had to be postponed until after the invasion. Invading troops had therefore to be provided with some substitutes to act as 'spearhead' currencies. The currency used by the U.S. forces was the 'Yellow Seal' dollar. British forces were provided with two alternatives—Italian lire which had fallen into British hands as the result of the African campaigns, and British Military Administration notes denominated in sterling, which had also been used in Africa. The use of these 'spearhead' currencies was to cease as soon as possible, and Allied military lire were to replace them as soon as they were available. A.M. lira currency was not intended to replace the lira in normal circulation, but merely to supplement the existing circulation for the use of the Allied forces and AMGOT. Provision was also made for the withdrawal of all 'spearhead' currencies as soon as this could, in the opinion of AMGOT, be successfully accomplished.

'Spearhead' and Allied military currencies were to be declared legal tender by a proclamation requiring all persons to accept these at the agreed exchange rates, but holders of local Italian lire were not entitled to exchange them for 'spearhead', dollar or sterling currencies. The following rates of exchange were laid down: between the Yellow Seal dollars and the B.M.A. notes, four dollars to the pound; between the dollar and the lira (Italian or Allied Military), 100 lire to the dollar; between the B.M.A. pound and the lira 400 lire to the pound. Transactions at any other exchange rates were to be forbidden by the proclamation. All foreign financial and foreign trade transactions and all imports and exports of currency were to be prohibited, except under regulations to be issued by AMGOT.

The issue of Allied military currency was to be the business of the Allied Military Financial Agency (A.M.F.A.), which had charge of the military currency reserve. The Finance officers of both the Allied Armies and other services were to draw their currency requirements from this source, currency drawn being recorded against the service concerned. A.M.F.A. was also empowered to accept deposits from the Finance officers or cashiers of both Armies. AMGOT was to draw its currency requirements from the reserve, these being debited to an AMGOT account. It was not however intended, if this could be avoided, that A.M.F.A. should set up an independent banking business of its own. The idea of setting up an Allied Military Bank to transact the business of AMGOT, which had originally been proposed in Washington, had been abandoned on British suggestion. It was therefore laid down that, if found practicable, the Bank of Sicily, the only Italian bank whose head office was in the island, should be appointed as agent for A.M.F.A., 'under the direct control of the Military Governor'. AMGOT and other Allied military authorities, when satisfied that the Bank was under adequate control, should be empowered to use it for official business, to make credits available to it by providing it with A.M. lira notes, and thus to place it in a position to finance other banks in the island for the conduct of business approved by the Military Government.

In order to prevent panic withdrawals of deposits and the diversion of financial resources into enemy hands, Allied military authorities were directed immediately upon occupying any locality to close all banks and financial institutions and to place them under military custody, to declare a general moratorium, to impound or block the funds of all enemy government and Fascist agencies, to seal all vaults and safe-deposit boxes, and to take an inventory of the assets of the banks as quickly as possible. Holdings of gold, foreign currencies and foreign securities and the funds of Fascist political organisations were to be taken into custody as quickly as possible and deposited either with A.M.F.A. or with banks designated by AMGOT. The closing of the banks was only a temporary emergency measure; they were to be encouraged to reopen for business, under AMGOT control, as soon as they were able to do so without risking excessive withdrawals of deposits, arrangements being made before they reopened for the reconstitution of their reserves by loans from the Bank of Sicily or other agencies designated by the Military Governor. Access to safe-deposits and vaults was to be permitted only when a proper supervision had been instituted, but gold, foreign currencies and foreign securities were to be withheld from their owners against accredited receipts. Except by special permission from AMGOT, local banks were only to hold lira accounts, but they were to be allowed to accept, at the decreed rate of exchange, Yellow Seal dollars and B.M.A. notes, which they were to surrender to A.M.F.A. in exchange for A.M. or Italian lire.

With regard to fiscal matters, the Military Governor was given authority to maintain the existing taxes and, where the proceeds derived from them were inadequate, to raise such contributions for the civil administration of the country as were consistent with international custom and usage. All tax receipts were to be deposited with A.M.F.A. or in banks designated by AMGOT. All branches of National Insurance were to be placed under military control and their revenues made available to the Military Government. Railways, postal and telegraph services, radio, and all government monopolies were also to be placed under military control and their revenues, when their operation by Allied military forces was relinquished, made available to the Military Government. With regard to expenditures no rule was laid down in the directive, except the provision that no tax or other revenue should be used for the payment of principal or interest on Italian Government securities.

In the matter of economic guides the directive was not very illuminating. Beyond general instructions to make the island as self-supporting as possible, to establish maximum prices of rationed or imported staple commodities, and to punish severely hoarding and black marketing, no concrete measures were laid down. It was however specified that all supplies, whether imported or domestically produced, should be sold as far as feasible through commercial channels under rigid control, and that relief in kind should only be given when absolutely necessary. The responsibility for procuring materials deemed essential to the re-establishment of the various public utilities and the maintenance of agricultural production through 'requisitions' on A.F.H.Q. was also specifically laid down. AMGOT was also given the task of preserving such strategic materials for export as the United Nations might require. Hence a system of control for imports and exports was to be established immediately, shipments being only permitted under licences. In determining what exports should be permitted, paramount consideration was to be given to the needs of the military forces and the local population. With regard to labour matters and the institutions of the 'Corporative State' established under the Fascist regime, definite instructions were given to abolish the corporations and subordinate organs, but some of the local machinery of the corporative organisation might temporarily be preserved in the shape of the Provincial and inter-Provincial Associations of Employers and Employees, after they had been purged of their objectionable Fascist features and personnel, if so found necessary by the military authorities, in order to avoid the sudden disruption of the internal economy. AMGOT was instructed to 'give careful attention to the matter of sound, fair and voluntary labour relations'—a conditional mandate for the revival of free Trade Unions—and was also specifically empowered, 'if necessary', to fix hours of labour and wages. To implement these economic guides laid down in the directive, two measures obviously suggested themselves, the preservation of the existing rationing system in force at the time of occupation, and the regulations for the collection and storing (*ammassi*) of bread-grains and olive oil; and the 'freezing' of all wages and prices at the level which they had reached at the time of invasion.

On the political side it might appear at first sight that this directive in many respects transgressed the letter of the Hague Rules which, in Article 43, require the military authority occupying hostile territory to do all in his power to restore public order and safety 'respecting at the same time, unless absolutely prevented, the laws in force in the country'.[1] How far the abrogation, even of the most unjust laws of the Fascist regime prescribed in the directive, must be regarded as a contravention of a ratified international compact, may be left to the international lawyers to decide. Professor Lauterpacht, in his edition of Oppenheim's treatise on International Law, deals briefly with this question. The principle which he lays down, in connection particularly with National Socialist laws in Germany, is that in exceptional cases in which the law of the occupied state is such as to flout and shock elementary conceptions of justice and the rule of law the occupying state must be deemed entitled to disregard it. It may be said, without unduly straining the interpretation of Article 43, that the wartime powers 'were absolutely prevented' from administering laws and principles, the application of which within occupied territory was utterly opposed to modern conceptions of the rule of law.[2] It will be interesting to see whether the views of reputable international lawyers in Germany and Italy will be found of the same opinion.[3]

Be that as it may, the political justification for the breaking up of the Fascist party and the annulment of legislation which offended the moral conscience of western demoscracies was overwhelming. The most obvious conclusion to be drawn from the dilemma would appear to be that the provisions of the Hague Conventions requiring the occupying authorities to respect existing laws must be interpreted in the light of modern political developments, as imposing

---

[1] *L'autorité du pouvoir légal ayant passé de fait entre les mains de l'occupant, celui-ci prendra toutes les mesures qui dépendent de lui en vue de rétablir et d'assurer, autant qu'il est possible, l'ordre et la vie publics en respectant, sauf empêchement absolu, les lois en vigueur dans le pays.*

[2] Oppenheim, *International Law*, 7th Edition, Vol. II, p. 446–7.

[3] For some recent Italian opinions maintaining that these instructions did exceed the limits laid down by international law, see Marino Bon Valsassina, *La decadenza dell' ordinamento statuario* and Elio Ladolini, *La illegittimità del Governo Badoglio.*

no duty to retain laws which violate fundamental human rights. The rules laid down trace their origin, no doubt, to the practice of the wars of the French revolution, when Napoleon and other French military authorities were in the habit of setting up local republics, 'liberating' the occupied territories and annulling the legislation of the 'legitimist' sovereigns. In these days of totalitarian dictatorships, the restoration of the *status quo ante* would seem to entail something very like the exercise of temporary 'sovereignty', which would therefore appear to need some juridical sanction. As Dr Lauterpacht points out, the authors of the Hague Rules did not envisage dictatorial regimes of the modern type. But that would seem to imply an admission that they need to be reinterpreted, or even amended, in a sense which will definitely permit a military occupant in certain closely defined circumstances to annul particular laws of the occupied state for reasons other than military necessity, if these laws are incompatible with basic standards of humanity and justice.

For the rest, it seems a little difficult to reconcile the institution of freedom of speech and freedom of the Press enjoyed in the directive with the complete prohibition of all political activity. For it should have been anticipated that a liberated public opinion would abhor a political vacuum. Yet the distrust of emigré politicians, and the desire to avoid every possible occasion of inflaming the feelings of a populace in a way which might lead to disorder behind the lines, were natural enough. The only question was, how far the prohibition of political activity among a people expert in underground activities could be made effective. To forbid major political demonstrations may have been all to the good, but the potential danger of clandestine political movements in the country of the *Mafia* soon manifested itself in the shape of Sicilian Separatism. It was perhaps fortunate that the repressive measures imposed on AMGOT by this directive were reversed as the result of the armistice.

A brief description of the principal legal instruments establishing Allied Military Government, the proclamations by the Commander-in-Chief of the two occupying Armies, which with certain amendments and modifications were employed in successive stages of the 'liberation' of the whole of the mainland, may help to make clearer to the reader the plan evolved for the establishment of AMGOT.

By Proclamation No. 1 General Alexander, as Military Governor, assumed in his own hands all powers of government and jurisdiction in occupied territory, and established AMGOT as his administrative organ. Care was taken in the preamble to explain that it was not the policy of the Allied forces to make war upon the civilian inhabitants of the occupied territory, but to protect them in the peaceful exercise of their legitimate pursuits in so far as exigencies of war and their own behaviour would permit. Assurance was given that personal and property rights would be fully respected and that existing laws would remain in force, except in so far as it might be necessary for him, in the discharge of his duties as G.O.C. and Military Governor, to change or supersede them. All administrative and judicial officials and municipal functionaries and state employees—except those removed by the Military Governor—were required to continue in the performance of their duties, subject to the direction of such Allied military officers as might be deputed for that purpose. Finally, as a temporary measure, all Italian civil and criminal courts and all universities, schools and educational establishments were closed until further order.

Proclamation No. 2 detailed War Crimes, i.e. offences against the Allied forces.[1] Annexed to it was an order requiring all civilians to surrender arms, weapons and explosives, as well as all wireless transmission sets, under pain of death or imprisonment, and a notice imposing curfew, which prohibited persons to circulate outside their houses between sunset and sunrise without a pass from AMGOT. Other security regulations were promulgated in Proclamation No. 11, which rendered compulsory the declaration of wireless receiving sets, cameras, photographic supplies and telescopes, and forbade the taking of photographs without permit from AMGOT, prohibited the publication of printed matter without a permit, and the holding of meetings and assemblies, rendered compulsory the possession of an identity card, and enforced black-out regulations.

The war crimes specified in Proclamation No. 2 were divided into two categories, those punishable by death and those punishable by fines and imprisonment. The former category included all those actions which under military law have traditionally been punishable by death, such as spying, communication with the enemy, assisting the escape of prisoners, etc., and included *inter alia* the forging of passes, permits and identity cards issued by the Allied forces, and the counterfeiting of coins or notes made legal tender under AMGOT [illegible]gulations.[2] The latter included the large majority of the offences [illegible] which persons were actually arraigned before military courts, like [illegible]tions of curfew, stealing or wrongful possession of property b[illegible]ging to the Allied forces, wilfully disobeying orders given by th[illegible]ied forces or AMGOT officers.

I[illegible]dition to prescribing war crimes, the proclamation contained an a[illegible] providing that persons violating Italian laws could be

---

[1] This pha[illegible]ust not be confused with that of 'War Criminals', i.e. offenders against the internati[illegible]laws of war.

[2] The lists o[illegible]se two categories are given in Articles I and II of the Proclamation, the text of whic[illegible]ll be found in Appendix I.

brought for trial before a military court and punished as provided by Italian law, if convicted. It also empowered the Military Governor to levy fines on communes, where it was established that these were collectively responsible for the commission of offences against his proclamations or orders. The power to try offences against Italian law was necessary for two reasons. In the first place, Italian courts were to be suspended pending an examination of the records of the existing judicial officials, in order to ascertain whether they could be relied upon to dispense justice impartially; in the second place, occasions might arise in which political prejudice, or the pressure of public opinion, might prevent Italian courts from functioning satisfactorily.

Allied Military courts were established by Proclamation No. 4 which constituted three grades of courts, according to the gravity of sentence they were permitted to impose, namely, General Military, Superior Military and Summary Military courts. The first of these was competent to try all offences and to impose all penalties, including the death penalty. These courts were to consist of not less than three officers of the Allied forces, appointed by the Military Governor, of whom at least one had to be a judicial officer of AMGOT, defined as any AMGOT officer who was a qualified lawyer. Superior Military courts were competent to impose any sentence, except death and imprisonment for more than ten years; they were to consist of one or more officers of whom at least one was to be an Allied Military Government officer. The lowest grade of Summary courts was not empowered to impose sentences of imprisonment exceeding one year or fines exceeding 50,000 lire, and was constituted by a single officer, who need not be a judicial officer of AMGOT, but any AMGOT officer available, or indeed any Allied officer. The appointments of General and Superior Military courts, during the operational phase when AMGOT was functioning under the command of the Task Force commander, were to be made by the Task Force commander, or by any officer delegated by him not lower than a divisional commander. In areas where AMGOT was functioning under the orders of the Chief Civil Affairs Officer, General courts were appointed by the C.C.A.O., or his deputy, acting on the advice of the Chief Legal Officer, whereas Superior Military courts could be appointed by the Senior Civil Affairs Officer of a province. It was laid down in the proclamation that proceedings in military courts should be held in public, except where otherwise ordered by the C.C.A.O. or by the court—a necessary qualification in matters affecting military security—that defendants should be entitled to receive in advance a copy of the charges on which they were to be tried, and to be defended by counsel unless the Chief Legal Officer or the court prohibited this—another necessary precaution for military security.[1] In any case they were to be entitled to consult a lawyer for their defence, before trial. Persons convicted were given the right to file a petition for appeal[2], and all sentences of death had to be confirmed in writing by the C.C.A.O. or any officer, not below the rank of Brigadier or Brigadier-General, to whom he delegated this power.

The closure of Italian courts was only intended as a temporary measure, and it was laid down that they should be reopened as soon as possible, beginning with the lower courts, first criminal and then civil, but certain safeguards for the public were to be instituted. The right of attendance at any court was to be given to any Civil Affairs officer or Legal officer, and the right of reversing any sentence to AMGOT. The right of recourse to the Military Governor was granted to all defendants who could claim that the judgment against them was affected by hostility towards the Allies, or was prejudicial to the interests of the Allied forces. In order to eliminate the long-standing Italian practice of holding prisoners for many months without trial—a practice which had been greatly aggravated under Fascism—Proclamation No. 13 was issued after the occupation. This enacted that no person should be imprisoned by an Italian official, unless he was charged with the commission of specified crime, and that no person should be detained in prison without trial, trial to take place as promptly as the circumstances permitted. It also abrogated all powers to impose fines and imprisonment vested in any Italian official by the Law of Public Safety of 1931, or any other law passed by the Fascist regime.

Financial and fiscal measures were laid down in Proclamation No. 3 which declared military 'spearhead' currencies legal tender at the official rate, in Proclamation No. 5 which closed financial institutions and established the moratorium, in Proclamation No. 10 which prohibited transactions in gold, silver or foreign exchange, and in Proclamation No. 12 which made Allied Military lire legal tender. Proclamation No. 6 annulled all measures affecting Allied property introduced by the Italian Government as the result of the war and required all Italian officials administering such property to surrender it into the custody of the Controller of Property, who was likewise empowered to take into his custody such property belonging to the Italian State as was not in the occupation of other branches of the armed forces, including State-owned or State-controlled businesses, as well as abandoned property, the control of which was

[1] In spy trials Italian counsel were in practice nearly always excluded, but great care was taken to give the accused the assistance of the most competent A.M.G. Legal officer available.

[2] In practice all cases were reviewed quite apart from any petition by the accused. All sentences involving imprisonment of over two years or a fine of 50,000 lire (£125) and above, were automatically submitted for review to the Chief Legal Officer.

in the opinion of the C.C.A.O. essential to the needs of the Allied forces or the inhabitants of occupied territory. He was also required to take into his charge the private property of any individual, corporation or institution whose activities were deemed to be prejudicial to the safety of the Allied forces or to public order.

In addition to these proclamations a number of administrative instructions were prepared for Civil Affairs Officers, Civil Affairs Police Officers, Finance Officers, Legal Officers, etc., laying down procedure for the installation of military government. This was envisaged in two phases: the first, while the area in question was still the scene of military operations, was described as, rather curiously in view of the controversy referred to earlier in this chapter, the imposition of direct control; the second, dealing with the measures to be taken when the permanent administrative needs of the island as a whole could be met by a unified and stable organisation, as the imposition of indirect control. During the first phase Civil Affairs officers were to be attached to the staffs of the tactical commanders under whose command they served, and the commander's authority on all Civil Affairs matters was final, though a direct channel of communication from C.A.O's with the C.C.A.O. was to be maintained. This meant that there were two AMGOT headquarter organisations, one with each Task Force headquarters, in addition to the central AMGOT headquarters at Fifteenth Army Group. As soon as circumstances permitted, the two Task Force headquarters would merge into the main headquarters. When the whole of the island, or at any rate the larger part of it, had been occupied, its administration would be conducted by the C.C.A.O. from his central headquarters. This second phase was to be inaugurated by the Commander-in-Chief, Fifteenth Army Group, and Military Governor, who assumed direct control of AMGOT united under his C.C.A.O., Lord Rennell.

During the first phase Military Government officers were divided into two groups, one attached to the American Seventh Army and one to the British Eighth Army, each headed by a Senior Civil Affairs Officer, to act under the Task Force Commander. These were known later as the Army A.M.G's and constituted the spearheads of military government advancing up the Italian peninsula. The number of Military Government officers taking part in the invasion was necessarily very small, consisting almost entirely of Civil Affairs Officers and Civil Affairs Police Officers, and their distribution was arranged on a tactical rather than a territorial basis, officers being attached to army, corps or division. Only after considerable areas had been occupied would it be possible to organise the civil administration on a provincial basis. Care was taken in Administrative Instruction No. 1 to C.A.O's to emphasize the fact that their first task was to assist the invading troops in their operations:

> It may therefore be less important to formally take over a centre which has been by-passed than to go forward with the combat troops . . . The rule of 'first things first' must be remembered . . . the 'first thing' therefore is to help the combat units even if this is at the expense of efficient administration.

The way in which Military Government officers were to help the combat troops was by maintaining law and order in the rear, by assisting to prevent civilians from getting in the way of their advance, by providing food for them in the stage immediately following an assault before the regular commissariat arrangements had been organised, by arranging with the local authorities for the provision of billets, and by cooperating with the military security organisations in their task of arresting and interning undesirables.[1]

The first task of a Civil Affairs officer serving with the assault troops, when he had entered or occupied a town, was to make contact with the local authorities, instructing them to remain in their posts, to establish his office in the *Casa del Fascio* or town hall and to get posted—in prominent places, but not on the walls of churches—the first three proclamations, establishing the Military Government of the Commander-in-Chief, detailing war-crimes, and establishing as legal tender the 'spearhead' currencies used by the Allied forces, and their obligatory rate of exchange. Where possible, arrangements were to be made with the combat units, before entering a town of any size, to close and mount guard on all bank premises, and to guard power stations and other public utilities, and, last but not least, to prevent access of troops to churches, monasteries, convents, and national monuments or warehouses containing valuable goods. Meanwhile the Civil Affairs Police Officers (C.A.P.O's), at least one of whom was where possible to accompany the C.A.O., were to keep in close contact with the military police, security, and intelligence organisations. But it was realised that in the first stages a clear distinction between the duties of C.A.O's and C.A.P.O's, etc., would be difficult to draw, since AMGOT officers would be so few on the ground that each and all of them must be prepared to do any of each other's jobs. Indeed, in practice, the C.A.P.O's frequently had to act as C.A.O's. Perhaps the C.A.P.O's most important police function in the initial stages was to persuade the local *Carabinieri* (CC.RR.), and later the other non-Fascist police forces, to

---

[1] The assistance to be given to combat troops was in practice interpreted somewhat elastically. Thus, for example, while the battle was raging in front of Catania the acting C.A.O. of Lentini was called upon to purchase for a G.O.C. of very exalted rank a cage full of canaries. He wanted them because they kept him in a good temper.

cooperate with the invading forces in keeping public order, and it was laid down that CC.RR. officers who would not give an undertaking to cooperate should be taken into custody by the military authorities and treated as prisoners of war. If the senior officer was not prepared to cooperate, he was to be replaced by the next senior officer prepared to do so. Similar steps were to be taken to obtain the cooperation of prison officials and fire-fighting services. The C.A.P.O's next task was to obtain quickly as much information as possible on the status of law and order in the community, the condition of the *Carabinieri* organisation, the location of police establishments available for duty, of civil defence organisations, jails, concentration camps, etc., the numbers of prisoners under detention, the details of arrangements for traffic control and registration of vehicles, and pass these on to the Provost-Marshal and the S.C.A.O. Another important function was the issue of passes and permits to civilians needed for essential services, e.g. to enter prohibited areas, or to circulate during curfew hours. The arrest, internment, or detention of civilians for 'security' reasons was in the first place the responsibility of the Task Force commander and his security organisations. But apart from this, C.A.P.O's were instructed that they should not rely on the possibility of obtaining detachments of military police to assist them in carrying out their duties of maintaining law and order.

When the immediate requirements of the invading forces had been attended to, the work of organising the civilian administration of the occupied areas, in accordance with the policy laid down in the directive described above, would be undertaken. It was planned to organise this on the basis of the province as a unit, as soon as possible after the area had been occupied. Hence the 'spearhead' parties of officers attached to the invading forces included a number of provincial Senior Civil Affairs Officers (S.C.A.O's), to take over the administration of the provinces as soon as the Armies had passed on. The chief factor in avoiding disease and unrest was to keep the populations in the towns properly fed, by assuring the transport and distribution of essential foodstuffs. C.A.O's were instructed that one of their most important duties was to help make the occupied area self-supporting, that they would have for the first two or three months to rely entirely on local resources for civilian supplies, and that only in the most urgent cases could they request their tactical commander to release army stocks.

A tentative time-table was drawn up for their operations in this connection. Within forty-eight hours of their arrival in a town, they should have placed all food warehouses, enemy food dumps, wholesale food concerns and other major food stocks under guard, have notified municipal and government officials that they were responsible for continuing the existing rationing and price control system, and have secured an estimate from the local food distributors of the numbers of days' food supplies in hand. Within a week, they should have cleared any demand for food needed by the Allied Armies, making sure that such purchases did not curtail critically supplies available to the civilian population, secured from every major food distributor a statement of his inventories and daily sales, and reported to the director of Civilian Supplies on the position, giving a statement of the estimated shortages or surpluses.[1] Guards were to be placed, if this had not already been done by combat troops, over the *ammassi* (grain and oil deposits) and other places where agricultural products were stored. Movement from these was to be controlled by permit from the C.A.O.

In keeping the large urban centres supplied, the question of transport was realised to be vital. In the Spofford Plan it had been assumed that civilian transport would for the most part either have been removed or destroyed by the enemy and that, accordingly, for the movement of essential civilian supplies, transport would have to be provided by the occupying forces. In the later planning it was realised that military vehicles would not be easily obtained for this purpose. C.A.O's were therefore instructed that, though they might be able to secure transport from the local transportation officer, military vehicles should be requested for the movement of essential food supplies only when no other sources of transport were available. All local lorries were therefore to be declared by their owners and permits to operate granted only for essential civilian services. Freight was to be given priority over passengers, and a priority list of freight movements was detailed. In this, however, the first place was given to the requirements of the occupying forces, agricultural products and foodstuffs for civilians coming only second on the list.

In order to keep the machinery of government working, plans had to be made for ensuring the necessary finance. Under the Hague Rules (Article 48) the occupant, if he collects taxes, is obliged to do so as far as possible in accordance with the legal basis and assessments in force at the time, defraying the expenses of the administration 'to the same extent as the National Government had been so bound'. C.A.O's were therefore instructed that existing arrangements for effecting and controlling expenditures were to be maintained. But it was planned to suspend certain items, namely the payment of contributions to the workers' and employers' syndicates, the payments of interest and principal on funded and unfunded government debts, and the payment of family-allowances to dependents of members of the Italian armed forces, unparoled

[1] For guidance in estimating the number of days supply of various foodstuffs a table of weights was given. A week's supply for 10,000 persons of flour was reckoned at 6¾ metric tons.

prisoners of war, or Italian workers in Germany or Axis-occupied countries. Other normal expenditures would be authorised, to the extent of 1/12th per month, of the total annual expenditure laid down in the existing Italian budget.

But normal expenditure would certainly have to be increased by a large number of emergency expenses, some of which might have to be met by the C.A.O. before the Finance Officer's approval could be obtained. Authority was therefore given to C.A.O's to incur emergency expenditure. Permission was also given to make advances to authorised private relief agencies, such as the Red Cross or the Church, in cases of emergency, for the maintenance of public health, the relief of destitution and the maintenance of refugees, where it was found that there was no satisfactory method of including such expenditure in communal budgets. Meanwhile, the whole machinery of municipal and local government would have been paralysed by the closure of the banks and the moratorium, unless plans had been made for exempting it from this 'freezing' operation. It was therefore arranged that before the banks could open for general purposes payments should be permitted from the accounts of provinces and communes, if the bank in which these funds were held had the quantity of cash required, and from the accounts of private persons and companies for the payment of sums due in respect of municipal and governmental taxes. Even so, expenditure immediately accruing had to be provided for, especially during the operational phase. C.A.O's were therefore entitled to draw the sums required in 'spearhead' currencies from Army paymasters, until the regular machinery of drawing from A.M.F.A. through Finance Officers had been established.

During this planning period, which was inevitably short, considering the complicated nature of the eventualities to be provided for, full use was made of every source of information which could be tapped. But, as Colonel Spofford pointed out in his report to the War Department, the amount of information available concerning the Italian machinery of government and administration, local and economic conditions, etc., was extremely meagre and much of the 'intelligence' collected quite inaccurate. Nevertheless it was possible to plan in some detail the functions to be carried out by the Civil Affairs officers and the specialist officers of the six Divisions, though plans had often to be amended on the ground at short notice by innumerable improvisations. In spite of this deficiency, the machinery of AMGOT was able to establish itself and get to work without any major disasters, though at the cost of a good deal of initial confusion which better information might have eliminated.

The next problem was to collect a mixed Anglo-American staff, assemble it, and give it a minimum of instruction in the two months that remained before D-day. A provisional War Establishment on the British side had been laid down by the War Establishment committee of A.F.H.Q. at the beginning of April, for 196 officers and 243 other ranks, with estimated transport requirements of 63 cars and 15-cwt trucks and 35 motor cycles, but it was not until much later that an American equivalent emanated from H.Q. NATOUSA, consisting of 192 officers, 3 warrant officers and 166 other ranks.[1] The principle of division on a fifty-fifty basis between British and American officers could not be applied with mathematical exactitude, but it was arranged that of the heads of the six specialist divisions, three should be American and three British, seconds-in-command, in each case, being of the opposite nationality to the chief. Under this arrangement the heads of the Legal, the Civil Supply and the Public Safety Divisions were American, those of the Financial, Public Health, and Allied and Enemy Property Divisions, British. In subordinate posts division between the two nationalities was approximately equal, though most of the C.A.P.O's were British.

In filling the various positions in AMGOT, two kinds of qualifications were called on. Officers to serve in the Legal, Financial, Public Health and Public Safety Divisions had to be specialists qualified by practice in their particular professions. But C.A.O's did not require specialised professional experience. What was needed here was the type of ability which in any walk of life enables a man to become an efficient administrator. The British had the advantage of being able to draw on a number of officers who had had personal experience of military government in Africa, and these, both in the planning and, later, in the operational stage, were a considerable source of strength. The Americans had only about thirty officers in the North African theatre who had suitable qualifications, but in drawing on their resources in the United States they had an advantage which the British lacked, a large supply of Italian-speaking officers—many of them of recent Italian origin—especially among the lower ranks. This fact, though it by no means proved to be an advantage in every instance—since the existence of close relations among the enemy population to be governed opens a way to obvious abuses—certainly facilitated the initial stages of getting administrative work started.

Most of the officers of this new experiment in military government—in which all but the C.C.A.O., Lord Rennell, and his deputy General McSherry found themselves with officers of the opposite nationality both above and below them in the chain of

---

[1] By the time the Sicilian operation started the initial W.E./T.O. of AMGOT had been stepped up to nearly 440 officers and 460 other ranks, in order to make provision for subsequent landings on the mainland.

command—had to be recruited from Britain and the United States, with only the barest minimum of training for the jobs they were to undertake, provided by courses in the Military Government Schools of Charlottesville and Wimbledon. Quite a number of them, before being commissioned for this purpose, had had no military experience whatsoever. In these circumstances the solid contingent of sixty-five London Metropolitan Police officers, whose tact, common-sense, and resourcefulness amply compensated for any lack of knowledge of the country or the language, formed a tower of strength, if such a metaphor may be applied to activities dispersed, both geographically and administratively, over many fields.

A planning and training centre was set up in May at Chrea, a delightful mountain resort above Blida, some thirty miles south of Algiers, 5,000 feet above sea level. To this centre began to dribble in detachments of officers from the United States, the United Kingdom, North Africa and the Middle East. A large contingent of over 100 American officers arrived at Chrea on 2nd June, a contingent of ninety-four British officers on 27th June, and a further American contingent of about forty officers at the beginning of July. Three courses of instruction[1] were organised, divided into four parts, (a) Study of the Italian language, (b) Lectures and talks on Military Government with particular reference to conditions in Italy and Sicily, (c) Committee work in the particular field in which the officers were to be specialists, and (d) Physical training. A number of British officers with practical experience of military government in Tripolitania assisted in the instruction, and some talks were given by military commanders of high rank, including General Eisenhower.

But instruction was not the most important function of the training centre. What had to be learned was the more subtle and intimate lesson of establishing a spirit of cooperation without reserves between individuals of two nationalities who, although they spoke (more or less) the same language, had inherited very different national traditions and prejudices. How this was accomplished would be impossible to explain, but accomplished it was. And few of those who partook in this interesting experience are likely to forget the 4th of July 1943, when the Americans were marched off, apparently on the customary route march, only to be brought after a circuitous route to a clearing in the Algerian mountains where they were confronted with a formal parade of their British

[1] The first course, which ended on 25th June, included approximately 50 British and 120 American officers. The second, which started at the end of June and lasted until 14th July, included about 40 American and 100 British officers. The third course (which took place, not at Chrea, but at Tizi Ouzou, which had by then been established as a Military Government Holding Centre) was reduced to about a week and comprised 37 American and 10 British officers.

allies who, with hand and voice, saluted the 'Star-spangled banner' before entertaining them to well-deserved refreshment, in which incidentally the 'Scotch' element was not lacking. After that no more was heard of Americans versus British. AMGOT had indeed become one, and so it remained until, after the occupation of Sicily, it became again divided, but this time not on national lines.[1]

While the detailed planning of AMGOT's general administration and special Divisions was being carried out at Chrea, plans for the two Military Government organisations with the Task Forces had to be worked out at the widely separated headquarters of the two invading Armies—Forces 343, the American Seventh Army, at Mostaganem in Algeria, and Force 545, the British Eighth Army in Cairo. It was laid down that the Senior Civil Affairs Officers and two-thirds of the staff of the two Army A.M.G's should be of the same nationality as their commanders. Lieut.-Colonel Charles Poletti, who had been deputy-Governor of New York State under Governor Lehman, was selected to be head of the Seventh Army A.M.G. detachment, and Group-Captain Benson, R.A.F., to be head of Eighth Army A.M.G.

The organisation of these two Army A.M.G's was planned on slightly different lines. In the American Army, Military Government officers were attached to tactical units. A number of officers were sent to join each of the four divisions composing the Seventh Army, and officers were assigned to II Corps and to the 2nd Armoured Division. The balance joined the main and rear Headquarters of the Army to reinforce the divisional teams as their activities expanded. The Military Government officers with the tactical units were generally assigned to the Judge-Advocate General's staff section of their respective divisions, since according to American Army tradition the business of ensuring law and order in the rear of troops was regarded as part of the Provost Marshal's functions. The practice in the British Eighth Army was somewhat different. Generally A.M.G. officers were not attached to divisions—though four A.M.G.

---

[1] The official inspiration of unity was incorporated in General Administrative Instruction drafted by Lord Rennell himself, which contained the following paragraph:
'The formation commander to which you, as a British or American officer are attached, may at any time be either an American or British officer. Your superior Civil Affairs Officer may equally be either American or British. You must understand that there are differences in procedure, custom and outlook between the two Armies of which you form a part. It will be for you to see that these differences do not affect the efficiency of your work and in no circumstances form the subject of complaints or gossiping. A serious view will be taken by your superior officers of any idle chatter or criticism of any member of the other Forces. This administration constitutes the first attempt at a Joint Allied Administration and it is your work, your efficiency, and your attitude of mind which will make the Administration a success or a failure and will serve as a model or a warning for the other administrations which will have to be built up in other parts of the world'.

officers came out with the Canadian Division from England, and landed with it. A small number of A.M.G. officers were attached to each assault force, and the remainder were held in two pools, so as to make them available to step in and take over towns and areas for which they were responsible, as soon as they were occupied—an arrangement which was a good deal more flexible than that employed in the Seventh Army.

In practice neither system was permitted to work satisfactorily in the 'Husky' landings, since landing schedules of neither Army gave the requisite priority to Civil Affairs officers, and still less to the transport without which they were practically helpless. The main reason for this was the complete ignorance of most of the military commanders of tactical units of the functions, or even the existence, of Military Government. In the Seventh Army, in particular, the presence of Lieut.-Colonel Poletti and his Civil Affairs staff was, to begin with, strongly resented. Nor were conditions in this respect much better at the highest headquarters. As Lord Rennell remarked:

> Seventh Army and Allied Force Headquarters seem to have regarded my requirements generally as nothing but an unmitigated nuisance to be met only when nothing else could be done in the face of direct orders from the Chief of Staff.

The last month before D-day was vividly described by him as

> a nightmare on the A/Q side. American officers were arriving or due to arrive on unknown dates from U.S.A. and the North African theatre as far west as Casablanca. British officers were being collected from Madagascar, Kenya, the Somalilands, Ethiopia, Eritrea, Egypt, Palestine, Cyrenaica, Tripoli, the North African theatre and the United Kingdom. Most of the officers of both armies were unknown quantities to any of us. They then had to be selected and posted to a provisional and varying WE/TO and despatched for mounting to ports ranging from Akaba to Oran, together with such vehicles as could be extracted, with great difficulty, from Allied Force Headquarters, Tripoli, Cairo and Oran.

These tasks could have been rendered a good deal easier had AMGOT been provided with an adequate A/Q staff of experienced regular officers, the need of which was repeatedly felt in Sicily during the following months.

The reluctance to give any priority to the shipment of A.M.G. personnel and transport was even more pronounced at Force 343 than at Force 545, since at the former it was reinforced by definite resentment at A.M.G's very existence. The 1st United States Division bluntly stated that they were quite capable of looking after Civil Affairs themselves in their sector, and wanted no British or American officer for the purpose. Indeed, as we shall see in the following chapter, they did in fact temporarily set up a Military Administration of their own in at least one Sicilian district. And it was only as a result of direct orders from Allied Force Headquarters that Civil Affairs officers and a few vehicles were embarked with the assault parties at all. In the event, Colonel Poletti only succeeded in embarking seventeen officers with Seventh Army assault forces on D and D + 1 days and reinforcements of this quite inadequate band were very long delayed.

But even at Force 545, where experiences in North Africa of Civil Affairs administration had resulted in a more friendly atmosphere, similar difficulties were experienced. Lord Rennell's proposal to attach some thirty officers in small parties to the beach-assault forces was rejected, and Group-Captain Benson was informed that only four of his officers would be allowed to be embarked in the second line of the assault wave; the remainder were to be called forward by air and sea-transport 'as required' from Tripoli, Malta and the Tunisian loading ports. This, as Lord Rennell pointed out, would in fact have meant that Civil Affairs officers would never have been available to take over territory as occupied, and would in all probability have been marooned for weeks at embarkation ports. Fortunately in the end wiser counsels prevailed, and Group-Captain Benson was able to land over thirty of his officers in Sicily between D and D + 2 days, followed by a further fifty officers in the succeeding ten days, so that by D + 16 he had succeeded in landing eighty officers. But the embarkation of A.M.G. transport was quite another matter. In the Instruction to the Task Forces issued by 141 Force on AMGOT administration (Instruction No. 3), it was definitely laid down that Civil Affairs officers with the assault formations would only be provided with a nominal scale of transport, and that the balance would arrive with the following convoys. Civil Affairs officers would therefore have to depend in the initial stages on locally requisitioned vehicles, and the use of combat units' M.T. And, though Assault Commanders were given instructions to assist Civil Affairs officers in the execution of their duties, including, at any rate by implication, the provision of transport, the arrangement did not work satisfactorily, as will be shown in the following chapter.

In planning the invasion of Sicily the propaganda side was not neglected. Though this was in no sense a responsibility of AMGOT, but was assigned to an entirely separate branch of A.F.H.Q. staff, the Psychological Warfare Branch (P.W.B.) whose functions and operations can only be briefly alluded to in this volume, a summary must be given of General Eisenhower's message to the Italian people. In this message, which was delivered in the name of both Allied Governments, the attempt was made to reconcile the Italian people to the invasion of their territory and to the Military Government which was to be installed there. General Eisenhower stated

that the Allied forces were not acting as enemies of the Italian people, but as their liberators from Fascism and German tyranny, with the intention of restoring Italy after the war to the position of a free nation. They had no intention of changing or undermining the traditional laws of the Italian people, but they would take all the measures necessary to eliminate the Fascist system, by dissolving the organisation of the Party and its appendages, like the Youth organisation and the Fascist militia. Fascist propaganda in all forms would be prohibited, nor would any form of political activity of any kind be tolerated during the period of Military Government. Steps would immediately be taken to stop the operation of all laws which discriminated on the basis of race, colour or creed. Freedom of religious worship would be upheld and freedom of speech and of the press instituted in so far as military interests allowed. Political prisoners would be liberated, and the Fascist 'Star-Chamber', the Tribunal for the Defence of the State, abolished. Copies of this declaration, the full Italian text of which will be found in Annexe I to this chapter, were placed in the hands of the assaulting troops for posting, together with Proclamation No. 1 establishing Military Government.

A further message from President Roosevelt and Mr Churchill to the Italian people was also prepared, to be broadcast as soon as the military situation was sufficiently advanced to assure the success of operation 'Husky'. This was actually delivered on the morning of 16th July—less than a week after D-day. In this joint message the heads of the Allied Governments laid upon the shoulders of Mussolini's shameful leadership the responsibility for dragging Italy into the war as Hitler's satellite, a war fought by Italian soldiers not for the interests of Italy, but for those of Nazi Germany. The sole hope of Italy's survival, it continued, lay in honourable capitulation to the overwhelming power of the Allied forces. The time had therefore come for the Italian people to take counsel for their own self-respect, their own interests, and their own desire for a restoration of national dignity, security and peace. The English text of this joint message will be found in Annexe II to this chapter.

ANNEXE I

Italian text of General Eisenhower's message to the Italian people.

AL POPOLO ITALIANO!

Nella mia qualità di Comandante in Capo delle Forze Alleate vi trasmetto questo messaggio a nome dei Governi degli Stati Uniti e della Gran Bretagna:

Le Forze Alleate stanno occupando terra italiana. Agiscono non da nemici del popolo italiano, ma in conseguenza ineluttabile della loro guerra che ha lo scopo di distruggere la forza dominatrice della Germania nell'Europa. La loro meta è di liberare il Popolo d'Italia dal regime fascista che lo ha trascinato in guerra e, ciò compiuto, di ristorare l'Italia come nazione libera.

Le Forze Alleate non hanno l'intenzione di cambiare o di menomare le leggi e le usanze tradizionali del popolo italiano. Verranno prese, nondimeno, tutte le misure necessarie per eliminare il sistema fascista in qualsiasi territorio italiano occupato dalle loro forze. Quindi, verrà scolta l'organizzazione del Partito Nazionale Fascista; le appendici del partito quale la Milizia Volontaria per la Sicurezza Nazionale, e le cosidetta organizzazioni della gioventù abolite.

La dottrina e la propaganda fasciste in qualsiasi forma verrano proibite. Nessuna attività politica di qualsiasi genere verrà tollerata durante il periodo di Governo Militare. Conformemente alla politica dei Governi Alleati verranno prese immediatmente le misure necessarie per porre fine all' effetto di tutte le leggi le quali fanno distinzione in base a razza, colore o fede. La libertà di culto verrà mantenuta; e purchè gli interessi militari non vengano pregiudicati, verrà istituita la libertà della parola e della stampa.

Verranno prese misure per l'immediate liberazione di prigionieri politici. Il Tribunale Speciale per la Difesa dello Stato verrà abolito.

Il Governatore Militare del Territorio Occupato prenderà le disposizioni per mettere in vigore, mediante proclama, od altrimenti, le misure di cui sopra non appena le esigenze militari le permettano.

Ciò porterà testimonio ai principi, ai quali gli Alleati aderiscono, e per il ristabilimento dei quali essi combattono spietatamente. Tali sono i principi ai quali i capi dell'Asse sotto il dominio della Germania si oppongono. Voi sarete i beneficiari della lora sconfitta. Come figli di padri che hanno combattuto per la loro libertà, sta nel vostro interesse di non resistere alle Arme Alleate, anzi, di facilitare la missione degli Alleaticon una pronta e totale vittoria Alleata di liberare l'Europa dal giogo nazista.

DWIGHT D. EISENHOWER,
General,
Commandante in Capo delle Forze Alleate.

luglio, 1943

ANNEXE II

Text of President Roosevelt and Mr Churchill's message to the Italian people. Delivered 16th July 1943

At this moment the combined armed forces of the United States, Great Britain, and Canada under the command of General Eisenhower and his deputy, General Alexander, are carrying the war deep into the territory of your country. This is the direct consequence of the shameful leadership to which you have been subjected by Mussolini and his Fascist regime. Mussolini carried you into this war as the satellite of a brutal destroyer of peoples and liberties.

Mussolini plunged you into a war which he thought Hitler had already won. In spite of Italy's great vulnerability to attack by air and sea, your Fascist leaders sent your sons, your ships, your air forces, to distant battlefields to aid Germany in her attempt to conquer England, Russia and the world.

This association with the designs of Nazi-Controlled Germany was unworthy of Italy's ancient traditions of freedom and culture-traditions to which the peoples of America and Great Britain owe so much.

Your soldiers have fought *not* in the interests of Italy but for Nazi Germany, they have fought courageously, but they have been betrayed and abandoned by the Germans on the Russian front and on every battlefield in Africa from El Alamein to Cape Bon.

Today Germany's hopes for world conquest have been blasted on all fronts. The skies over Italy are dominated by the vast air armadas of the United States and Great Britain. Italy's sea coasts are threatened by the greatest accumulation of British and Allied sea power ever concentrated in the Mediterranean.

The forces now opposed to you are pledged to destroy the power of Nazi Germany—power which had ruthlessly been used to inflict slavery, destruction and death on all those who refuse to recognise the Germans as the master race.

The sole hope for Italy's survival lies in honourable capitulation to the overwhelming power of the military forces of the United Nations.

If you continue to tolerate the Fascist regime which serves the evil power of the Nazis, you must suffer the consequences of your own choice. We take *no* satisfaction in invading Italian soil and bringing the tragic devastation of war home to the Italian people. But we are determined to destroy the false leaders and their doctrines which have brought Italy to her present position.

Every moment that you resist the combined forces of the United Nations—every drop of blood that you sacrifice—can serve only one purpose: to give the Fascist and Nazi leaders a little more time to escape from the inevitable consequences of their own crimes.

All your interests and all your traditions have been betrayed by Germany and your own false and corrupt leaders; it is only by disavowing both that a reconstituted Italy can hope to occupy a respected place in the family of European Nations.

The time has now come for you, the Italian people, to consult your own self-respect and your own interests and your own desire for a restoration of national dignity, security and peace. The time has come for you to decide whether Italians shall die for Mussolini and Hitler—or live for Italy and for civilization.

CHAPTER II

AMGOT–SICILY

WHILE the finishing touches were being put at Chrea to planning for AMGOT Sicily, the first actual experiment in Allied Military Government was already being carried out in Pantelleria and the nearby Pelagian Islands, Lampedusa, Linosa and Lampione, which lie between Sicily and the North African coast. Pantelleria was taken on 11th June, Lampedusa on the 12th and Linosa and Lampione—the latter found deserted—on the 13th. Four islands, as General Eisenhower remarked in his despatch, in three days. Major-General Clutterbuck, O.C. British 1st Infantry Division, was in command of the land forces in this combined operation and was appointed Military Governor of Pantelleria, but since the principal Allied aim in the occupation of the island was to use it as an airbase for the coming attack on Sicily, he was quickly succeeded in this office by Brig.-General Strickland, of the U.S. Air Corps. An American officer, Lieut.-Colonel Monfort, was selected to be the Senior Civil Affairs Officer. Only three of the AMGOT proclamations were employed, Proclamation No. 1 setting up the Military Government, Proclamation No. 2 detailing war crimes, and Proclamation No. 4 setting up Military courts. For reasons of security, the 'spearhead' military currencies were not used, lest these should give away the plans for the forthcoming invasion of Sicily, the needs of the occupying forces being provided for by a supply of Italian lire, which had been obtained from the Civil Affairs Branch of the Middle East Command. The operation did not come under the command of 141 Force, but it was specifically laid down that the S.C.A.O. was to be free to consult AMGOT 141 Force on any technical matter.

The Military Government of these islands raised few problems, except those raised everywhere by extensive war damage caused by aerial bombardment. The civilian inhabitants were friendly, sometimes almost embarrassingly so, and the local machinery of government was of the simplest, though even this had broken down under the combined influence of Italian military occupation and Allied bombardment. *Faute de mieux*, the existing municipal administrators were continued in office and proved co-operative, whatever their Fascist past may have been. In spite of the fact that none of these islands produced more than a fraction of their civilian food requirements, immediate hunger, the spectre that was to haunt the early days of Sicilian AMGOT, provided no terrors, thanks to Italian military stocks. Of these a considerable quantity had been looted in Pantelleria by the population of the port town, so providing at least a proportion of the civilian population with some hidden reserves. On Pantelleria the chief staple product was the grape, from which, besides wine, raisins of a high quality were produced. The whole output was purchased for the services by A.F.H.Q. Fishing was another important source of livelihood and this, for reasons of naval security, had to be severely restricted. It was however found possible at an early date to issue a number of limited permits in certain areas. The maintenance of public order provided few problems, except in Pantelleria, where the establishment of a military zone entailed the evacuation of a considerable portion of the population.

This initial essay in military government hardly provided a fair sample of the difficulties and complications soon to be encountered by AMGOT. Hence the lessons to be derived from the experiment were comparatively few, except for the revelation of certain characteristic deficiencies, such as the absence of co-ordination between the operating forces and A.M.G. officers, and the complete lack of any material equipment with which to provide for the establishment of military government, such as paper, ink or typewriters.

On the night of 9th–10th July the first contingents of the British and American Armies landed in Sicily, and before D-day (10th July) came to a close the British and Canadians were in possession of Syracuse and the country west of it as far as Palazzolo, and the Americans of Gela and Licata. The following day the British had taken Augusta and begun their advance northwards into the plain of Catania, but here their progress was checked by the stubborn resistance put up by the German forces in the island for about three weeks, and the town of Catania did not fall till 5th August. Meanwhile the progress made by the Seventh Army under General Patton was much more rapid. Palermo was entered on 22nd July and by the end of the month the whole of the western half of the island was clear of the enemy. After reaching the north coast the Seventh Army turned east, and the last enemy stronghold, Messina, was entered by combined American and British forces on 17th August, leaving the whole of Sicily in uncontested possession of the Allies.

The Eighth Army landings were concentrated into two groups (XIII Corps and XXX Corps), one on the beaches a little south of Syracuse, and the other round Cape Passero. Within the first three days Group-Captain Benson succeeded in landing some thirty AMGOT officers, most of whom had not been detailed on the loading schedules but were smuggled on board, in spite of Army H.Q.'s refusal to include them in the assault quotas. These were reinforced during the course of the next fortnight by about fifty

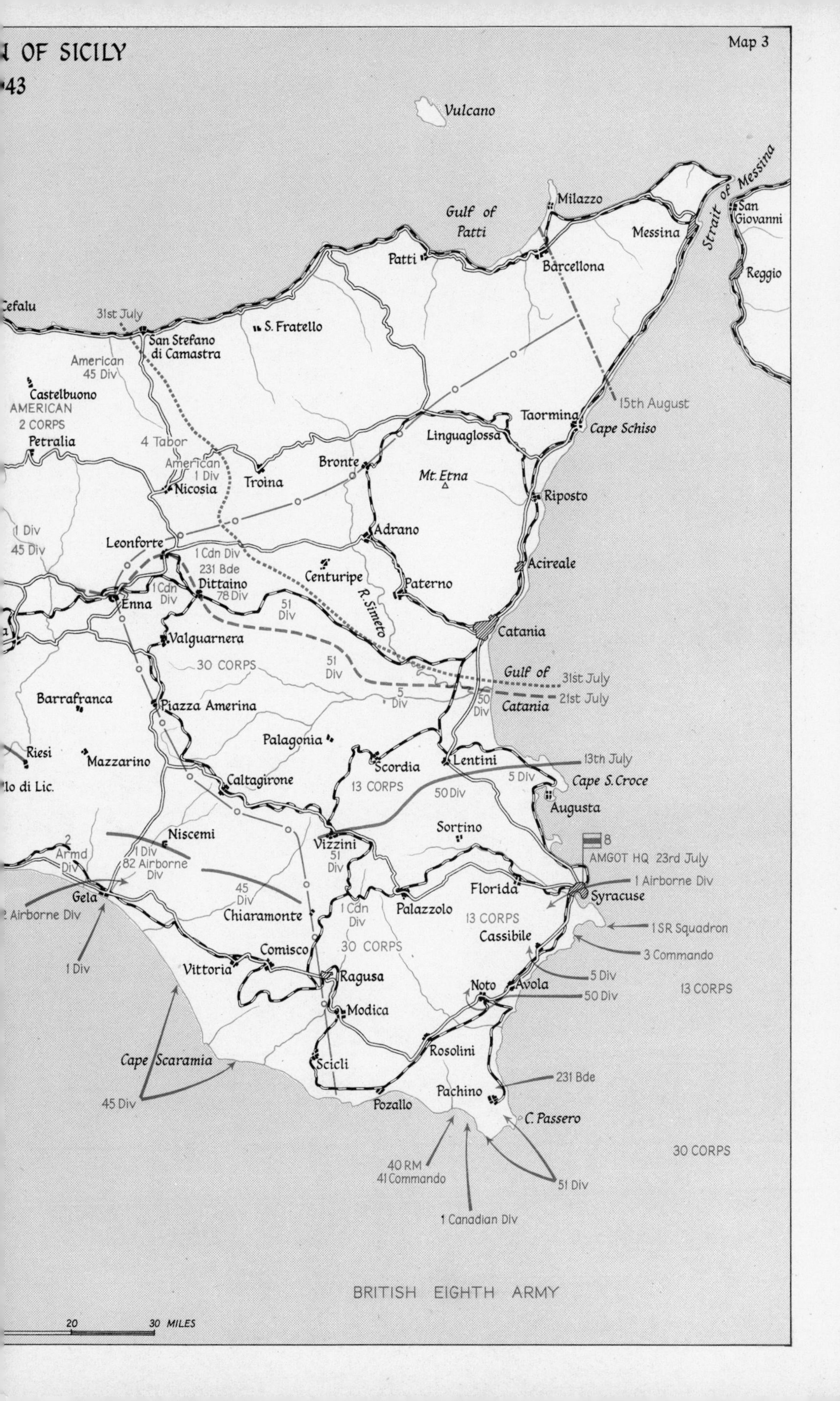
OF SICILY
43
Map 3
Vulcano
Gulf of Patti
Milazzo
Strait of Messina
San Giovanni
Messina
Reggio
Patti
Barcellona
Cefalu
31st July
San Stefano di Camastra
S. Fratello
American 45 Div
Castelbuono
AMERICAN 2 CORPS
15th August
Taormina
Cape Schiso
Linguaglossa
Petralia
4 Tabor
American 1 Div
Nicosia
Troina
Bronte
Mt. Etna
Riposto
1 Div
45 Div
Leonforte
Adrano
1 Cdn Div
231 Bde
Acireale
Centuripe
Dittaino
78 Div
1 Cdn Div
Enna
R. Simeto
Paterno
51 Div
Catania
Valguarnera
30 CORPS
51 Div
Gulf of Catania
31st July
21st July
Barrafranca
5 Div
50 Div
Piazza Amerina
Palagonia
Riesi
Mazzarino
Scordia
Lentini
13th July
5 Div
Cape S. Croce
13 CORPS
50 Div
Caltagirone
Augusta
Sortino
Niscemi
Vizzini
51 Div
8
AMGOT HQ 23rd July
2 Armd Div
1 Div
82 Airborne Div
1 Airborne Div
Gela
45 Div
Florida
Syracuse
Airborne Div
Chiaramonte
1 Cdn Div
Palazzolo
13 CORPS
1 SR Squadron
Cassibile
30 CORPS
3 Commando
Comisco
1 Div
Vittoria
Ragusa
5 Div
Noto
Avola
50 Div
13 CORPS
Modica
Cape Scaramia
Rosolini
Scicli
231 Bde
45 Div
Pachino
Pozallo
C. Passero
30 CORPS
40 RM
41 Commando
51 Div
1 Canadian Div
BRITISH EIGHTH ARMY
20
30 MILES

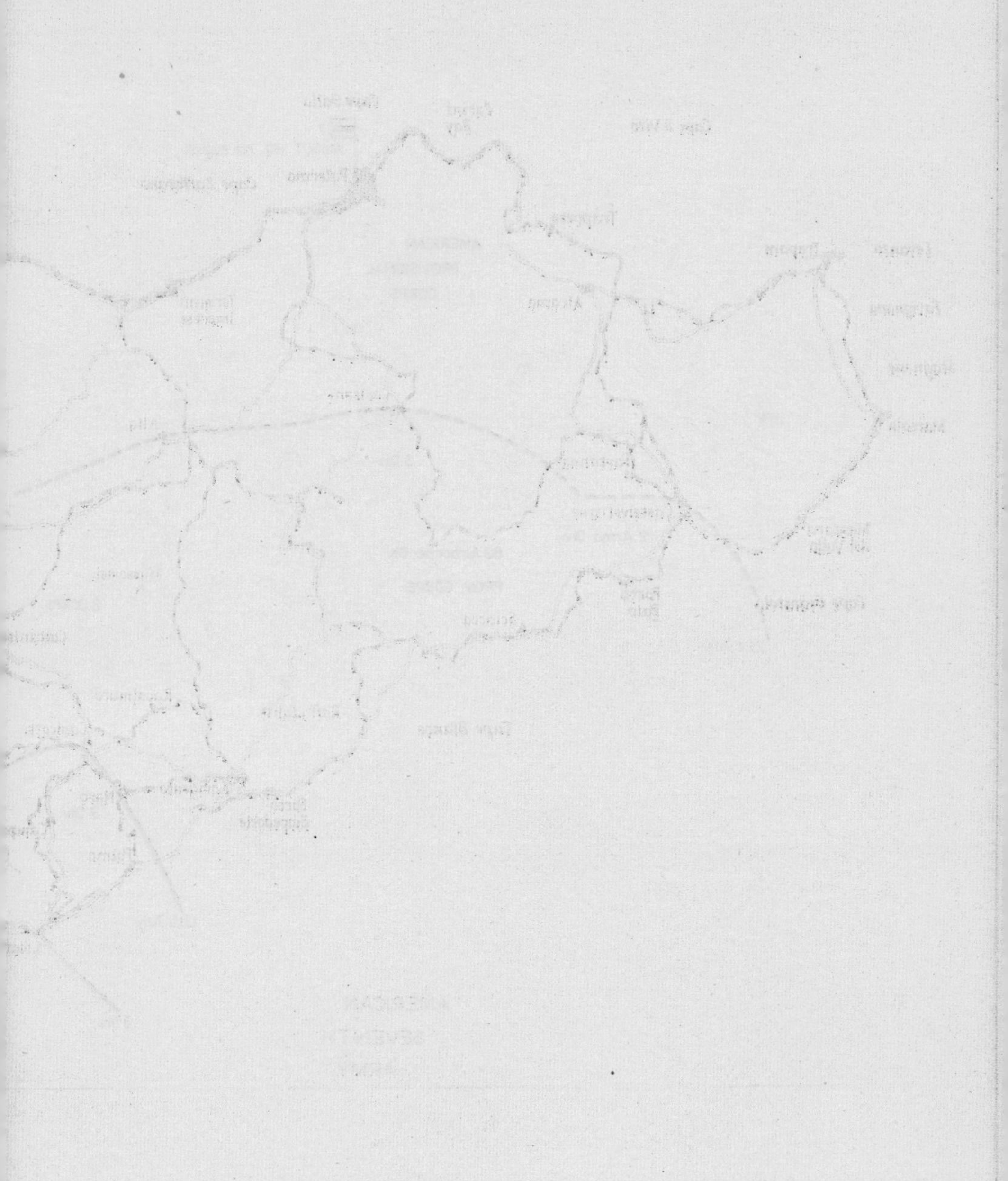

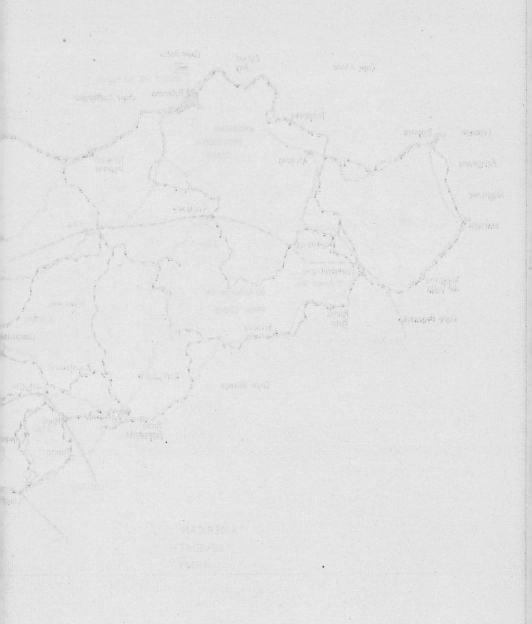

officers who had been assembled in pools—one at Malta and one at Sousse to deal with the immediate post-assault requirements, and a third at Main Army H.Q. in Tripoli. On D-day, 10th July, the towns of Avola, Noto and Pachino were entered, and to each of them a C.A.O. was despatched. Syracuse was captured on the night of 10th and early in the morning of 11th three AMGOT officers, who had landed the previous day on the beaches with the assault troops, were installed. Immediately after its capture they secured a lift into the town on a Signals lorry, and had taken over the administration of the Commune and Province by ten o'clock. Within less than a fortnight from D-day it was possible to organise a complete AMGOT provincial administration for two provinces, Syracuse and Ragusa, with C.A.O's, C.A.P.O's and Legal, Finance and Public Health officers, in spite of the fact that Group-Captain Benson had been obliged to part with some of his staff in order to reinforce A.M.G. Seventh Army.

The decision of H.Q. Eighth Army, already referred to, not to include A.M.G. officers in its early loading schedules was soon found by its Commander to be inconvenient. Complaints quickly began to reach AMGOT headquarters of the lack of A.M.G. officers and the G.O.C. himself complained strongly to Lord Rennell that his XXX Corps had never had a sufficient number of Civil Affairs officers to take over towns as they were occupied. But even more crippling, from the A.M.G. point of view, than the shortage of Civil Affairs officers was the shortage of transport. In the first place, the quantity of transport allocated to AMGOT was quite insufficient for its internal needs, and, what was still more important, such transport as AMGOT had been able to procure was accorded a very low order of priority in the loading schedules. Nor were the effects of the shortage at first sufficiently understood by the higher tactical commanders.[1]

The shortage both of personnel and of transport made the task of A.M.G. Seventh Army even more difficult. Ten Civil Affairs officers had originally been detailed to accompany each of the three infantry divisions taking part in the assault, and two each to the 2ndArmoured Division and to II Corps; but numbers were drastically cut, so that only two landed with the 1st Division and four each with the 3rd and 45th Divisions. In consequence by 11th July (D+1) only seventeen A.M.G. officers had been landed, and there was much delay in landing the first reinforcement group of fifty officers, owing to the unwillingness of Seventh Army H.Q. to accommodate any reserve

---

[1] A remark on this subject, attributed to General Montgomery himself, is perhaps worth quoting. When his complaint of the absence of Civil Affairs officers to take over towns immediately on occupation was met by Lord Rennell with the explanation that this was due to lack of transport, he is reported to have replied 'Why can't they get cracking on a bicycle?' But the lesson had been learned, and transport arrangements for A.M.G. in the Calabrian landings were enormously improved.

of Civil Affairs personnel in the advanced embarkation areas. Indeed it was not until 28th July that the much needed reinforcement group of sixty-two officers reached Palermo, though by that time the Army had occupied the provinces of Trapani, Agrigento and Caltanissetta as well as Palermo, with the result that Colonel Poletti and his second-in-command found themselves obliged, without any assistants, to undertake the administration of Palermo City, as well as the direction of the Seventh Army A.M.G. as a whole. And it was only by arranging with Group-Captain Benson that Eighth Army C.A.O.'s should take over the western part of Ragusa province, that even the vestiges of an AMGOT administration could be made to cover this very large territory. In part of the north-western portion of the province of Palermo, American combat troops had for about a week found themselves obliged to maintain a civil administration of their own, pending the arrival of an AMGOT officer.

The allotment of Civil Affairs officers to commands of corps and divisions did not work very satisfactorily. Some commanders tended to keep military government, in the initial stages, in the hands of their Judge-Advocate-General, using their Civil Affairs officers merely as liaison with the civil authorities. Moreover, since tactical movements bore no relation to civil administrative divisions, it was not easy to get any A.M.G. administration going beyond the municipal level. Finally, as Colonel Spofford pointed out, since the officers were attached to armies or smaller tactical units, it was erroneously assumed that they would be provided with rations, enlisted personnel and above all, transport, by the unit to which they were attached, and units were too prone to feel that they had none to spare. The system employed by the Eighth Army of organising AMGOT officers in a pool and leaving only single liaison officers with tactical units was recognised by Colonel Spofford to have its advantages, as well as the practice—not followed sufficiently early or thoroughly enough, though initiated by the Eighth Army—of instructing units, even down to platoons, on the nature and work of military government. These lessons were quickly learned and, in respect of both personnel and equipment, A.M.G. attached to the American Fifth Army in the Salerno landings was accorded the requisite priorities.

It was certainly fortunate that during this initial phase, when it was still beset by every kind of teething trouble, AMGOT did not have to encounter the most difficult of all the problems facing the Military Government, that of dealing with a hostile civilian population. Had that occurred, it is difficult to see how it could have succeeded in performing its essential functions, that of relieving the Commander-in-Chief of the necessity of devoting time or resources to the maintenance of law and order behind his advancing troops.

Indeed, as Lord Rennell remarked to General Alexander in a semi-official letter—'I am frank enough to think we shall get away with things here more by good luck than by good management.' Civilian hostility to the invaders was nowhere seen. On the contrary, the genuine friendliness with which Allied troops were everywhere greeted, in spite of the immense amount of suffering caused by Allied bombardments, was astonishing to many of those who had arrived, as they supposed, in the capacity of enemies. In this matter General Eisenhower's announcement, made at the time of the invasion, certainly exercised a powerful influence—more powerful in the opinion of some competent observers than that of the later joint announcement of President Roosevelt and Mr Churchill. There was thus no difficulty in obtaining the co-operation of civilian elements either official—even Fascist official—or unofficial, and the plan of relying on existing police forces, particularly the *Carabinieri*, to maintain law and order was amply justified. Though their authority was somewhat shaken by the initial treatment they received at the hands of the invading forces, it was quickly restored, even in the somewhat turbulent sulphur-mining districts, as for example at Sommatino, where municipal buildings had been occupied by a local group which proclaimed a Communist regime.

The chief problems facing AMGOT officers were of quite a different nature—material problems, which raised in some cases almost insuperable difficulties. Generally speaking, the first tasks of an AMGOT officer on entering a captured town might be summed up, in the epigram of Lieut.-Colonel Lord Gerald Wellesley, S.C.A.O., Catania, as being 'to bury the dead and to feed the living'. The first, a most essential task in the heat of a Sicilian July, was comparatively simple, even if it sometimes proved more difficult than expected where material destruction had been heavy and resulted in much debris, or where the civilian population had fled, as for instance in Augusta. One S.C.A.O. even had to cope with a phenomenon undreamed of by Hamlet, a grave-diggers' strike. The second task was the central problem which persistently haunted, not only AMGOT Sicily, but every detachment of Military Government in Italy till the end of the campaign. And during the early days it naturally presented itself in its acutest form, owing to the disorganisation caused by the tide of battle.

Under the stress of the forthcoming invasion the rationing system of the island had all but broken down. Owing to the reluctance of the grain-growing farmers to deliver their corn to the *ammassi*, and the progressive growth of a vigorous black market, the actual bread-ration distributed in the weeks before invasion varied from district to district, from about 125 gms (just over a quarter of a pound) to 200 gms (about seven oz) daily per head, and some of the eastern coast towns had been supplied for some months from the mainland. The official ration had been fixed at 150 gms (less than six oz) of bread, plus a weekly ration of pasta of 60 gms (just over 2 oz) a day. Stocks were low, as the recently gathered harvest—a poor one—had not yet been brought into the *ammassi*. Indeed some of it had not yet been gathered and had been destroyed by military operations. The Germans too, wherever they had the time and the opportunity, had removed such stocks as they could find. Moreover the reluctance of farmers to bring in their crops to the *ammassi* had been reinforced by the seizure of local transport by two invading armies. What the canker-worm had not eaten, the palmer-worm had devoured. All means of transport may legitimately be taken by an occupying army, and when the Allied forces had exhausted what the Germans had left in the way of motor transport, they started availing themselves of mule transport and wagons—a decorative speciality of the Sicilian peasants. As Lord Rennell remarked in his first situation report to General Alexander, on many occasions AMGOT officers organised trains of mule carts only to find this form of transport seized by troops. And even when grain and transport had somehow been procured, the problem was not yet solved, since practically all the mills were worked by electric power, and electric power in the early days following the invasion was cut almost everywhere. The feeding of the larger urban centres was thus extremely difficult, and that of some of the medium-sized towns little easier.

A typical picture of the problems facing the Civil Affairs officer immediately on invasion is that presented by the conditions discovered in Licata, which was captured on D-day. The officer administering Licata found that the whole of the municipality had disappeared, and all public utility services ceased working. To add to his troubles, he had found that a bomb had destroyed the main sewer, and he spent his first thirty-six hours ashore collecting enough people to mend it. He then turned his attention to rounding up further civilian labour and mules, and began collecting enough wheat to start up the town flour mill, but he discovered that the mill was run by electricity and there was no current. So he went to a neighbouring village where he was told that there was a flour mill driven by steam. This was put into working order, to mill wheat brought from Licata. Here the shortage of transport proved critical, but eventually the town hearse was discovered and did excellent work transporting flour. In another town in the vicinity the local ambulance was the one vehicle which enabled the starving population to be fed.

At Palermo the situation was saved by the discovery of a reserve stock of 1,600 tons of flour belonging to the Italian Army. The food position in Catania caused A.M.G. a good deal of anxiety in the first few weeks. Within twenty-four hours of its capture fifty tons of grain had been rushed into the town from Lentini, but the only mill where it could be ground was still under shell fire, so that the S.C.A.O. did not consider it proper to risk the borrowed military lorries which were conveying it. The grain had therefore to be transferred to horse carts for the last part of the journey. When Catania was entered, there were only about 60,000 of its 245,000 inhabitants left in the town, but almost immediately afterwards the refugees began to come streaming back, thus adding enormously to the food problem. By 21st August about twenty-seven tons of wheat were needed daily and three weeks later requirements had risen to about 100 tons.

In order to assist AMGOT in coping with this problem, General Alexander had given orders to both Armies that seized transport was to be returned, but in the heat of the battle administrative orders from higher headquarters are not always complied with, and it was a long time before any of the seized Sicilian transport was given up. Moreover emergency imports from the little stock-pile collected in North Africa, which had been scheduled to be brought in on the convoys D+15 and D+30 to provide an emergency reserve at Catania and Palermo, were much delayed in arriving, and had finally to be diverted to Messina and Calabria. In the early days therefore the bread ration which could be distributed, in spite of the fact that the amounts of grain available outside the town were considerable, was extremely low. In spite of this fact AMGOT, with a somewhat mistaken optimism according more with the exigencies of propaganda than with realism, had increased the standard ration to 300 gms of bread a day—a level which, as will be seen, could not be maintained.

Even more critical was the food situation of Messina, the hinterland of which produced practically no grain. The town—whose occupants had been reduced by the ravages of Allied bombardments from nearly 200,000 to 55,000—had been largely dependent on the mainland for supplies, and under the stress of war had for some months before the invasion received a ration of only fifty gms per person per day. Here, under the stress of hunger, a good deal of looting occurred, which the Italian police were unable to prevent. An immediate supply of flour was sent from Palermo by road—a considerable part of it in borrowed Seventh Army trucks—and later by sea in an L.C.T., as well as in small Italian coastal craft,[1] and a certain amount of grain was provided from the neighbouring province of Enna; but it was a long time before the average daily

[1] Here considerable difficulties arose, as the Naval authorities would not permit these craft to move without Allied personnel on board. Consequently the 'other ranks' clerical staff, small as it was, had to undertake sailing the high seas as an additional portion of their duty.

distribution of bread attained 100 gms per head. By the middle of September—about a month after its capture—civilians were still getting less than 100 gms (3½ oz). Thanks to these efforts an increase to 150 gms was made possible.

In spite of these acute shortages there was no starvation, since fortunately the supply of fruit, nuts and vegetables was nearly everywhere plentiful, though among the poorer urban population there were in places definite signs of malnutrition. Moreover, in the first few days after the capture of bigger towns particularly, the fact that a large proportion of their population had taken refuge in the country certainly made the food problem less acute; since in the country friends and relations would keep these town-dwellers fed, even if later they aggravated the problem by employing all the available transport in carrying their domestic effects back to the town, when it should have been used for carrying grain.

After food, perhaps the most immediate preoccupation of the Civil Affairs officer on taking over a town was the avoidance of any outbreak of disease due to the destruction of buildings, and particularly of water mains and sewers, at the height of summer. The bigger jobs—such as the repair of aqueducts supplying large towns—were the responsibility of the Engineer units of the combat troops, but the repair of water mains in the towns and of the sewers had to be organised by the Civil Affairs Officers, using local labour and resources. Except at Marsala and Gela damage to water supply installations in the western half of the island was comparatively small, but in Catania the main aqueduct supplying the town had been badly damaged. This was quickly repaired by Eighth Army Engineers; but in many places water supply was severely restricted by the lack of electric power to work the pumps. In Syracuse, for example, water-supply to houses was for some time cut off, the limited supply available being distributed at water-points in the town. Severe restriction of the water supply during the height of the summer had not been unknown in Sicily in peace-time, but under war conditions it gave rise to a good deal of anxiety, since in Syracuse, Catania and Messina thousands of people were living in grottoes, caves or air-raid shelters, under sanitary conditions which beggared description. The clearing up of these places therefore was a problem of the second, if not the first, importance to the C.A.O. Thanks to the efforts of the Public Health officers, who received the willing co-operation of the Italian Public Health officials and doctors, the calamity of large epidemic outbreaks was avoided. Indeed the only definite outbreaks of disease, which could even remotely be attributed to war conditions, were local epidemics in three comparatively small towns, Avola, Rosolini and Scordia, of typhoid, a disease which is endemic in Sicily and has never been eliminated in peace time.

But disease and destitution were not the only problems presented by the refugees. Their movement was extremely difficult to control, and their carts tended to obstruct the roads already used to their maximum by military convoys. They also rendered all but impossible the strict enforcement of the ten kilometre limit to circulation, which had been imposed for security reasons, since the number of road blocks which would have been required was far greater than combat troops were willing or able to provide.

Except in very badly damaged places, like Marsala, for example, Civil Affairs officers found no difficulty in getting some sort of administration working. Instances of refusal to cooperate were few, if any. Of the Prefects some, like his Excellency of Catania, had fled to the mainland, while others were almost immediately arrested by Field Security organizations, without waiting for any failure of cooperation. Of the nine heads of provinces only two career civil servants, the Prefects of Agrigento and Enna, had been given a clean bill of health by the intelligence organization of the Psychological Warfare Executive. The former was somewhat peremptorily removed by Seventh Army Counter-Intelligence Corps, while the latter was after some time removed by AMGOT for incompetence. In most provinces the sub-Prefects were, in the first instance, left in charge. Some proved satisfactory, others the reverse, but no instance of deliberate failure to cooperate in carrying on the administration was encountered. Of the *Podestàs* (Mayors), those whose Fascist past was most deeply compromising had also fled to the mainland, like the Mayors of Palermo and Catania, but in most cases the *vice-Podestàs* were, to begin with, permitted to carry on. Some *Questori* (Chief Constables) and municipal officials were arrested, and others deposed, by Civil Affairs officers. The heads of the communes were usually replaced, either by their immediate subordinates or by prominent citizens whose anti-Fascist records seemed unexceptionable. The decision to maintain the local administration in the towns proved remarkably successful, and in a number of places councils of prominent citizens and officials were nominated at an early stage to advise the Civil Affairs officers and the Italian heads of the communes. Cases occurred when the zeal of security authorities in arresting Fascists or suspected Fascists made the resuscitation of local administration rather difficult, but, as Lord Rennell reported, in the Eighth Army area the security intelligence authorities were, in the initial stages, careful to avoid doing anything which would cause a complete breakdown in the administration which AMGOT was trying to get running.

At first the employment of the *Carabinieri*, who, as already explained, were part of the Italian Army and wore uniforms almost indistinguishable from those of combatant units, led to a certain amount of confusion. They were in many instances taken as prisoners of war and shipped off to North Africa. One of the earliest tasks of the Civil Affairs Police Officers often was to get them released, dress them in mufti and provide them with special civil-police armbands or, where such was available, to dress them in the well known blue swallow-tail peace-time uniform, with which all travellers to Italy must be familiar. Of civil disorder, except for all too plentiful looting, there was very little; and though the prestige of the CC.RR. suffered rather severely in the eyes of the civilian public from disarmament and internment, it was in most cases found possible to rearm them and get them to resume their business of maintaining public order, as well as to secure their active cooperation in enforcing the law against war crimes promulgated in Proclamation No. 2.

In these circumstances General Alexander decided at an early date to transfer responsibility for Civil Affairs from the tactical commanders to Fifteenth Army Group over a large portion of the island. On 31st July the 'settled' provinces of Syracuse, Ragusa, Agrigento, Trapani and Caltanissetta, the southern part of Catania and all but the most easterly portion of Palermo were removed from the administrative control of the Army Commanders and placed under the direct administration of the Chief Civil Affairs Officer, who had set up his headquarters for a few days on the hill overlooking the south of Syracuse harbour, en route for Palermo, where AMGOT headquarters were organised during the first days of August. Lieut.-Colonel Poletti was installed as S.C.A.O. of Palermo province, and A.M.G. Seventh Army was dispersed, a nucleus remaining with the combat-troops, to become on the capture of Messina the provincial administration of that province. A.M.G. Eighth Army meanwhile prepared to continue its functions in the invasion of the mainland (Calabria and Apulia); but since a new formation, the American Fifth Army commanded by General Mark Clark, which included a large British contingent, was to undertake the landings at Salerno, a new unit of Allied Military Government officers, A.M.G. Fifth Army, was formed.

The centralised AMGOT administration included under its headquarters at Palermo nine provincial units, of which five of the commanding officers (S.C.A.O's) were American and four British. Each province is divided under the Italian system into communes or townships—for there are practically no villages—with their surrounding rural areas. The general administration of these towns was the responsibility of the Civil Affairs Officers (C.A.O's) of whom there might be one or more in the larger towns, while the smaller were grouped together, sometimes as many as six or seven, and placed under the administration of a single officer. In the larger towns the Civil Affairs Officer was assisted by a Civil Affairs Police

Officer, but in the smaller this proved to be unnecessary, as the Sicilian police contingents could be more efficiently administered from provincial headquarters. Indeed the number of Police officers, thanks to the cooperation obtained from the Sicilian police forces, was rather larger than was required for strictly police duties. But the talents of Police officers were by no means wasted. The Metropolitan Police contingent proved itself astonishingly versatile in the role of Civil Affairs Officers, Supply Officers and in any other administrative job on which they were employed. It would be no exaggeration to describe them as more responsible than any other element for such practical success in military government as AMGOT undoubtedly achieved. Provincial headquarters contained, besides the S.C.A.O. and his deputy, a number of 'specialist officers' from each Division to take charge of their particular branch of the administration: Public Safety and Legal to maintain public order; Finance, all pervading, to activate the sinews of peace; Public Health, Civilian Supplies—before long broken up into a number of separate divisions, Agriculture, Economics and Supply, Transportation, Communications and Public Utilities, and Labour—Education, Fine Arts and, finally, Property Control.

The task of headquarters in coordinating the activities of the various branches of administration in the nine provinces was in any case not easy, and it was made ten times more difficult by the absence of efficient means of communication and shortage of transport. The initial restriction of postal and telegraph facilities made it essential for officers at headquarters to do a great deal of travelling, and it was here that the absence of conveyances, public, private and official, made itself most acutely felt. The result was sometimes an involuntary decentralisation which did not always entail the advantages claimed for this type of organisation. In fact for a long time each province remained, in a way not always desirable, a law unto itself. But considering that AMGOT had had no previous administrative experience as a unit and had been thrown together out of varied elements of two nationalities, the important thing was to create provincial teams which would work together, and this was, on the whole, accomplished with remarkable success. The straightening out of anomalies, however essential, was after all a secondary consideration.

The Military Government of Sicily was dominated by one central problem, how to keep the people fed in the towns, while the rationing system was threatening to break down under the additional stresses placed upon it by an acute shortage of transport and progressive monetary inflation. The former affected distribution even more than collection, since after grain had been collected at the *ammassi* it had to be distributed to the mills for grinding and thence to the consumer. It was felt most acutely in the earlier stages after the invasion. Later, improvisations like cannibal reconstruction of damaged vehicles, the surrender of seized vehicles by the Armies, the emergence of hidden vehicles and the re-opening of the railways to civilian traffic, considerably eased the situation. But the pressure of inflation steadily increased, paradoxically enough, as an incidental effect of the complete success of the financial arrangements which had been planned, and this vitally affected the problem of collection, since it strongly reinforced the farmers' tendency to hoard.

The financial arrangements laid down in the AMGOT Plan worked almost without hitch. There was no difficulty in getting people to accept the 'spearhead' currencies and, later, Allied Military lire at the official rate of exchange, to evade which no serious attempts were made. Nor had the shock of invasion greatly shaken public confidence in the existing banks and other financial institutions. Only in Palermo and Ragusa had there been any burning of Italian currency, of which a considerable reserve stock was discovered in Caltanissetta. It therefore became possible to reopen banks at a comparatively early date—6th September in Palermo and 18th September in the rest of Sicily—first for withdrawals subject to a limit of 5,000 lire, which was cancelled the following month. Cash ratios to the volume of deposits only fell slightly and then quickly recovered, soon reaching a height beyond the pre-invasion level. The moratorium was ended and on the surface conditions had reverted to normal. Though badly shattered by the impact of war, the financial machinery of tax collection was also gradually rehabilitated after several months' suspension. In spite of the prevalent wishful-thinkng that the 'four freedoms' inscribed upon the A.M. lire note included also freedom from taxation, revenue began slowly to trickle in, but it covered only an exiguous percentage of AMGOT expenditure, the deficit of which was financed by A.M.F.A. issues of A.M. lire. The situation caused no visible anxiety to the public, since budget deficits on an enormous scale, rather naively camouflaged, had been Mussolini's normal practice ever since the beginning of the Abyssinian War.

But though public confidence appeared to have been so quickly re-established, it was not long before a certain fundamental distrust in the value of currency began to make itself felt in an important class of the community, the farmers, whose tendency to hoard grain was greatly increased by the general rise in prices, which began to make itself felt within a few days of the invasion. This rise in prices, which, in the circumstances, could hardly have been avoided, was due to a number of different causes. War finance in every country in the world produces a highly inflationary situation, however much this may be concealed by government regulations and restrictions, and Italy was no exception to this rule. Indeed the suppressed inflation had been going on for several years before the outbreak of the Second World War. To this inflationary pressure was now added the spending power of the invading British, and still more the American, troops with their higher rates of pay—a pressure which was made all the more powerful by the low rate of exchange; since in terms of the slender stock of consumable commodities existing in the island it gave the soldier a disproportionately large amount of pocket money. For, with the exception of agricultural produce, the proportion of consumers' goods produced in Sicily was very small, the vast majority being derived from the mainland. And now this dwindling stock of consumers' goods began to be competed for, not only by the existing four million civilian inhabitants, but also by two armies of Allied soldiers whose pockets were stuffed with A.M. lire. Nor, with certain notable exceptions, was the purchasing power in the hands of the civilian inhabitants correspondingly reduced. Industry, it is true, came practically to a standstill, but the industrial workers of Sicily were only about a quarter of the employed population, and the enormous volume of employment offered by the Armies soon absorbed such unemployment as had begun to appear. The wage scale drawn up for army use by the Civilian Supplies Division had been constructed on rather a liberal scale, partly because detailed information was lacking, and partly because no risk could be taken by the Armies of paying rates not competitive with those of civilian industry. This scale was in general observed by the Seventh Army, though the equation of the lira with the cent encouraged a certain liberality in the minds of the 'liberators', and by the Eighth, with certain improvised modifications. It was however greatly exceeded by some other branches of the armed forces, with the result that a good deal of competition arose, which pushed up the general level of wages paid and, as prices rose, the pressure on the wage-level was increased.

Under these conditions the policy of keeping wages and prices to the level existing on 9th July quickly broke down. The official price of wheat at the time of invasion of 330 lire a quintal had already been too low to induce farmers to deliver to the *ammassi* their full quotas of grain, with the result that increasing quantities had been finding their way on to the black market. At an early stage after the invasion one of the S.C.A.O's of a grain-growing province, anxious to gather in the grain quickly to the *ammassi*, had raised the price of wheat—without authority—to 700 lire a quintal. This to some extent forced Lord Rennell's hand. Immediate action was therefore taken to raise the official price of grain throughout the island on a sliding scale designed to stimulate early delivery, payments being made at 500 lire a quintal for grain delivered by the end of August, at 450 for that delivered by the end of September, and 400 lire for that delivered by the end of October. At the same time the ration was raised to 300 gms a day and 280 gms of pasta a week. These two measures had some effect in diminishing the farmers' hoards, and for a while it was possible to maintain the new ration in most districts, with certain ominous exceptions—the Province of Trapani and the larger urban centres of Palermo and Catania.

And now the influence of inflation began to make itself felt in two ways. As black market prices soared, the temptation to make hay while the sun shone was difficult to resist, but the hoarding instinct was even stronger. Official prices had already risen, and might rise again, and it was therefore safer to hold grain than money. Moreover the 1943 crop was a poor one, drought and war operations having greatly diminished the yield. The grain-producing provinces began to fear that they themselves would go short and deliveries fell off, since the supplies which had been promised by Allied propaganda to liberated territories conspicuously failed to appear. Food conditions on the mainland, now invaded by the Allies, were critical; it was believed that the Allies might divert Sicilian grain to meet this emergency. In October AMGOT was faced with a serious food crisis as conditions in the three large towns were growing tighter, and hunger even led to some rioting on the outskirts of Palermo and in some of the small towns in Catania province.

By the middle of November things began to look desperate. Catania had just one day's supply left when a ship arrived on 20th November, and in Palermo the average daily ration was 112 gms. On 18th November General Patton informed General Eisenhower that the situation in Sicily due to shortage of flour was very serious 'and may become critical with resulting riots and bloodshed', and that he considered the immediate shipment of 10,000 tons of flour necessary. Meanwhile the American Island Base Section (I.B.S.) had provided AMGOT with a small supply of flour out of military stocks for immediate issue 'to prevent actual conditions of starvation'. Thanks to emergency borrowings from military stores enough grain to prevent the spreading of serious disorder was made available.

But the crisis should and might have been avoided altogether, if A.F.H.Q. had shipped, when called upon, the small stockpiles of food—13,000 tons emergency stock and 32,000 tons reserve of flour—that it had been arranged to accumulate in North Africa, as related in the previous chapter. Though instalments of these little reserves were bid for in plenty of time by AMGOT—the whole of the emergency stock and 2,000 tons from the flour reserve—very little actually arrived. By 30th October the amount was less than

7,000 tons.[1] The failure to ship these comparatively small quantities asked for must not be attributed in the first place to any reluctance on the part of the 'Q' authorities. Though it is true that administrative changes in the staff channels of Fifteenth Army Group and A.F.H.Q., may have added to the difficulties, the chief cause of the failure must be attributed to the Military Government Section at A.F.H.Q., which had accumulated much of the stockpiles at ports at which normal convoys did not load, and had failed to persuade the French to collect together—much less to mill and bag—the emergency reserve of 32,000 tons of flour.

The Italian rationing system *qua* system was not a bad one, but the *ammassi* had from the beginning been very unpopular with the farmers, and the administrative machine in its dealings with both millers and bakers was extraordinarily corrupt. In Catania it was found that the only course was to close almost all the bakeries, a measure which led to long bread queues and caused a good deal of unpopularity. In Palermo it was discovered that the reserve of ration books had been looted, with the result that there were at least 25,000 illegitimate ration books in the hands of the public. Hence AMGOT by November had to bring out a new issue. But, however corrupt and unpopular, the existing rationing system had to be preserved. There could be no question of introducing a new one, and the only practical course for AMGOT was to try and make it work, by organising as efficient transport arrangements as the circumstances permitted, and by taking steps to suppress the black market, a field of action in which, as will presently be seen, very little success was secured. The hopelessness of trying to maintain the innumerable price controls, which existed, at any rate in theory, during the last years of Fascism, induced AMGOT to dispense with a large number, retaining only those on grain, sugar, meat and oil. And though the rationing of oil caused difficulties scarcely less than that of bread, in spite of occasional localised failures the people of Sicily were somehow kept fed. In the larger towns particularly they often went short; there was certainly a good deal of undernourishment and sometimes even hunger for a while; but of starvation there was no question, of disease attributable to lack of food practically none, and of unrest, nothing that from the military point of view could be regarded as serious.

Compared with this problem of feeding four million people, one tenth of whom were concentrated in the single city of Palermo, the other administrative tasks facing the C.A.O's were relatively easy.

---

[1] Actually some 9,000 tons arrived in Sicily, but of the first shipment of over 3,000 tons, which came by coaster to Catania, all but a small quantity had to be diverted to Reggio Calabria. These figures do not include 5,000 tons of sugar which, *mirabile dictu*, arrived at Palermo on 10th October.

Nor did AMGOT's prime political objective, the destruction of Fascism, present any difficulties. Fascism, notwithstanding any attraction the association of its name with the homonymous but wholly different Sicilian '*Fasci*' of the nineteenth century may have possessed, had never been popular in the island, and under the stress of defeat had become odious. Hence most of the important members of the 'hierarchy' had fled to the mainland before the Allies arrived. A number had been arrested by military security agencies immediately on arrival, and though everywhere there were party members galore—for in practically all professions and callings membership had been the *sine qua non* of success—convinced Fascists were few. The downfall of Mussolini killed the remainder. Fascism was not only dead, there was no body to bury—nothing left to 'go underground'. Even the discovery of a small clandestine group of Fascist youths at Trapani—whose trial incidentally was attended by M. Vyshinski—caused no tremors. But the dismantling of Fascist legislation and administrative machinery and the removal from office of those whose reputation had been badly compromised was not quite such an easy matter. If genuine enthusiasm for the party had in Sicily been small, lip service to it had been all but universal among officials, the professional classes and the well-to-do. Many of the best elements in the country had at one time been drawn to it and, for fear of worse, had often given it their passive support.

The assumption that mere membership of the Fascist Party had to be treated as a crime was wholly unrealistic, and the dismissal of all party members from office would have involved complete administrative chaos. The question was how to judge between the 'harmless' Fascist and the Fascist who had to be eliminated. As soon as the destruction of Fascism was known to be the official policy of the occupying forces—and it had been emphasised in General Eisenhower's announcement—every party member set out to prove that he had never been a real Fascist, while everyone who had a personal grievance against his neighbour at once denounced him to AMGOT or the Security Services as a dangerous Fascist. Amid the double smoke-screen of self-excuse and delation, the truth was particularly difficult to discover for the invading stranger, and no doubt a good deal of folly and injustice was committed. But a rough and ready method of distinguishing the sheep from the goats was finally evolved. This consisted of a questionnaire called a *Scheda Personale*, which all officials and teachers were required to fill up. The answers were designed to elicit exact details of the party activities in which the person in question had been engaged during his career, and the various party offices which he had held. The sanction of dismissal for holders of certain qualifications was usually automatic[1]—a

[1] See below, pp. 147-49, pp. 165-66.

method which became the pattern for the process of 'defascistisation' pursued on the mainland. Under this procedure the percentage of officials actually dismissed proved comparatively small; even that of teachers not very large. But the mayors of most communes were removed and their title *Podestà*, with its Fascist association, was changed back to that of *Sindaco*.

The destruction of Fascism was a task in which AMGOT had to work in very close cooperation with the Intelligence-Security services of the Armies. It is important to distinguish two processes, the arrest and internment of 'dangerous' Fascists, who for general reasons of military security had to be put out of circulation, whose names had as far as possible been incorporated before invasion in a 'black list', and the purging or 'epuration' of the public services from Fascist influence. The first of these was primarily the business of the military security organisations, but even here it had been laid down beforehand that no arrests should be made, except in cases of urgency, without reference to the nearest C.A.O. In all rather over 1,500 Fascists were arrested and interned, but a large number of these were released after varying terms of confinement.

'Epuration' was of course essentially an AMGOT responsibility, though here too cooperation with Intelligence and Security services was highly desirable. Collaboration at the time of the invasion was far from perfect. Security officers were frequently far ahead of any Military Government officers on entering a town, and took the first steps in the establishment of Military Government, posting the essential proclamations enforcing curfew and the surrender of arms and ordering municipal authorities and *Carabinieri* to continue to perform their duties; they could hardly be expected always to await opportunities of consulting C.A.O's before arresting black-list persons. On the other hand, the initial caution in interning Fascists quickly disappeared, and the indiscriminate zeal of the younger Field Security personnel and Counter-Intelligence Corps officers led to a great deal of unnecessary trouble.

One of the first measures following the dissolution of Fascism was the liberation of Italians who had been put in prison for political reasons, and of citizens of countries at war with Italy, who had been interned. In Trapani and probably Catania[1], through excessive zeal, jails had been opened by Allied troops, and their inmates, who were practically all of them common criminals, liberated. It was therefore essential that a careful examination of prison records should be made before releasing these victims of Fascist tyranny—a work which was immediately undertaken by the Public Safety and Legal Divisions. In all, some 669 political prisoners were released.

[1] In his report on Catania Lt.-Col. Lord Gerald Wellesley, the S.C.A.O., leaves the matter in doubt, but in Trapani it was certainly the action of the liberating troops.

In certain cases it had been the habit of the Fascist regime to confine political prisoners together with other criminals in isolated islands off the coast. One of these, Ustica, some thirty miles north of Palermo, was captured at the end of July, single-handed, by a British Police officer, Major Hickinbotham, who arrived in a British naval vessel, and accepted the formal surrender of the island. Among the *confinati* were discovered not only Italian political and other prisoners, but, also a number of Yugoslav and Greek civilian internees, Their condition was shocking. They stated that they had been most brutally tortured and starved, and many of them were alleged to have died of their treatment. The island was only too closely living up to its evil reputation of classical days.[1] Investigation showed, to quote the report submitted for information to the Combined Civil Affairs Committee in Washington by Lieut.-Colonel Chanler, Chief of the Legal Division,

> that the prison officials had for some years been conducting a ghoulish racket: they received about 12 lire per day from the Government to feed the prisoners but spent only 2 or 3 lire on feeding them, keeping the rest as graft . . . When prisoners complained, they were viciously tortured, many being alleged to have been killed in this process.

It was finally laid down by the Combined Chiefs of Staff that the Italian officials responsible for this treatment of Yugoslav civilian internees should be tried as war criminals. Since it had been decided at the Moscow Conference that all war criminals were to be tried after the war was over, the officials in question were imprisoned, and, in order to take all the evidence before the necessary witnesses were dispersed, a commission was organised to do this and despatched to Palermo. But bad as the conduct of the officials was, it was found that there was not sufficient case for classifying them as 'war criminals', since Italians were equally affected, and the motives inspiring it had nothing to do with the war. The civilian internees were, of course, released and a camp for them was prepared near Palermo, where about 120 persons were fed and sheltered, including 63 Yugoslavs and 9 Greeks.

Though the dissolution of the Fascist Party and its institutions entailed no political difficulties, the administrative complications to which it gave rise were numerous, since a large proportion of Italian welfare legislation and institutions, including social insurance, had become inextricably intertwined in the web of Fascist measures. Moreover, the dissolution of the machinery of the Corporative State left a vacuum in the sphere of relations between capital and

[1] According to Diodorus Siculus, *Bibiliotheca Historica*, V, 11, this island was called Osteodes, 'bony', because during the war between Syracuse and the Carthaginians, one of whose chief settlements was Palermo, the latter had confined on it a large number of mutinous mercenaries who had died there of starvation.

labour which had to be filled immediately, since the labour demands of the Armies, both direct and indirect, were of fundamental importance. In the initial stages of the invasion labour matters were handled by Civil Affairs officers. Proclamation No. 8, which froze wages and prices, was posted in every occupied town, employment offices were opened, usually in the Fascist syndicate building, in places where the occupying forces needed labour, and notices were put up inviting the public to register for work. At this earlier stage the question of labour had to be dealt with more or less impromptu as military necessities presented themselves. The C.A.O's were not responsible for providing the military forces with labour, since these had their own organisations for labour recruitment, but their function was to assist the forces in meeting their requirements. The Armies had no difficulty in procuring all the labour they wanted, since the wage-scale prepared by AMGOT before the invasion was in many cases as much as seventy per cent above the existing wage-level.

After the consolidation of AMGOT as a single unit, a labour policy embracing the whole island had to be developed. It was found that all the higher officials of the Fascist workers' and employers' organisations had fled, but their subordinate staff and records remained. It soon became clear that the 'corporate' labour organisation, both on the workers' and the employers' sides, was so inextricably interwoven with the party-machine that the system could not be adapted to changed conditions. Practically the only part of it which could be kept working was the social insurance funds. These, and the workers' and employers' contributions to them, were continued, and Allied military units paid the employers' contribution on the same scale as Italian employers. But the whole elaborate four-tier machinery of 'Syndicates', 'Unions', 'Federations', and 'Confederations', which had constituted the 'Corporative state', was abolished. Existing labour exchanges were re-formed on a voluntary basis, workers were invited, no longer compelled, to register, and the preference given to members of the Fascist party was abolished. It was laid down that preference should instead be given to those who had been imprisoned for anti-Fascist activities. These labour exchanges, which were constituted in all the larger towns, were not normally used by the Armies as their source of labour recruitment, but their location was communicated to the Allied forces, and they often were able to assist them, especially in matters where specialised labour was concerned. Indirectly they were also of value to the military effort, since a considerable volume of work was given out by the Armies to civilian contractors.

In order to deal with all labour questions, provincial Labour offices were set up whose policy was directed by the Labour Section of the Civil Supply Division, until it became a separate division. Existing contracts between employers and employed were maintained, pending their revision by negotiation. The 'Fascist' principle of the illegitimacy of strikes had to be adopted, and some machinery put together to adjust labour disputes. This was improvised by the Labour Division at headquarters, later to become the Regional Labour office, working through the provincial Labour offices, since the organisations through which this had been accomplished under the Corporative system had been abolished. A number of strikes nevertheless did occur in the autumn. They were quickly settled by the AMGOT organisation, which was able to avert others, which were threatened in the railways, power companies, and other essential industries, owing to food shortage and the rise in the cost of living. The workers were permitted and encouraged to form independent unions of their own and, before Allied Military Government in Sicily came to an end, the authority of the Combined Chiefs of Staff had been obtained for the appointment of shop-stewards and other representatives of the workers for the purpose of collective bargaining. In the meantime a large number of unions had been organised by the workers themselves, their activities being tolerated by AMGOT pending the reception of official authorisation.

But the 'freezing' of existing wage contracts could not long be maintained. Though industry was practically at a standstill, agriculture and commerce were both active, and with the exception of the 40,000 sulphur miners, most workers could be provided with employment, either by the Armies or by the municipalities in 'clean-up' projects. Since the Army was by far the largest single employer of labour, and different branches of the Service often competed with each other, a uniform wage-scale was worked out under the auspices of AMGOT to be applied by all the Services, containing rates of pay classified for over 170 jobs. As the result of this revision a large number of rates originally paid by various branches of the Allied armed forces were considerably cut down. But by this time the economy of the island was already caught in the vicious spiral of inflation, and the wage rates of both civilian and government workers had soon to be increased.

The restoration of the morale of the *Carabinieri* was the notable achievement of the Metropolitan Police officers, who managed to command not only the professional respect but, what was even more important, the personal loyalty of their Italian colleagues. The initial behaviour of the Allied forces, already described, had considerably damaged their morale, but, thanks to the tactful handling of the Civil Affairs Police Officers, this quickly recovered. Moreover the police authorities of the Allied Armies soon realised that they could benefit from their cooperation. An important step was therefore taken to restore the prestige of the *Carabinieri* in the eyes of the Sicilian public, by arranging with the military police authorities that town patrols should be combined, consisting of British or American Military Police and *Carabinieri* working together.

The maintenance of law and order was thus successfully accomplished, in the one essential respect that General Alexander had to devote neither time nor resources to the suppression of civil disorders. But below the surface the situation was not quite satisfactory. The other national police force[1], the Agents of Public Safety (*Agenti di Sicurezza Pubblica*), which corresponded roughly to the British Criminal Investigation Department, had been much more corrupted by Fascism than the *Carabinieri*, and therefore took longer to bring to a state of even moderate efficiency. A number of their chief officers, *Questori*, had to be interned. The respect for the law had been considerably diminished. This showed itself in a number of ways at first, in a considerable increase in crimes of violence and of robbery, and an enormous increase in the whole range of black market offences, and, later, what was much more significant, in a revival of the *Mafia*, which had to all appearances been really stamped out by the energetic measures of the Prefect Mori in the early days of Fascism. The paying off of old scores in a land where vendetta had been for centuries a national characteristic was only to be expected. The removal of the heavy hand of Fascism gave rise to a freer use of the dagger and the pistol—which Allied Military Government was wholly unable to prevent. For the surrender of civilian fire-arms was often compensated for by the acquisition of military weapons, which had been left behind or thrown away in the precipitation of retreat. Thus, though the surrender of weapons was enforced to the degree which would have rendered an armed rising, or even guerilla warfare, against the Allies impossible, it was certainly not sufficiently thorough to prevent their occasional use for private murder.

The suppression of the black market might be cited as an example of a definite failure of indirect rule, though it is difficult to imagine how direct rule could have achieved any better results. Here the cooperation of the two Italian police forces, *Carabinieri* and *Agenti di Sicurezza*, was, to say the least of it, only partial. With the cost of living soaring month by month, till the men's pay, low even under normal conditions, was quite inadequate to sustain their families, it was small wonder that the temptation to graft was often irresistible. Nor was it common-sense to risk too much unpopularity at the behest of the foreigner. As a result of police connivance, it was

---

[1] Besides these, there were other national forces with highly specialised duties like the Finance Guards and Forest Militia, as well as the various Fascist militias.

often impossible to enforce charges in the law courts. Even the stiff sentences imposed in the more serious cases, which were transferred to Allied Military courts, wholly failed to suppress, or even seriously to diminish, this class of offence.

Even more disturbing was the resuscitation of the Mafia, that characteristically Sicilian institution with its mysterious name[1], a secret society whose activities have been described as cooperative brigandage blended with the vendetta, the origin of which probably dates from the period of exile of the Bourbon court at Palermo during the Napoleonic wars. The society had definitely been stamped out, as far as appearances go, by the measures taken in 1925; its revival can be accounted for by the emergence from prison, after long sentence, of old members or by their return after many years from America. Be that as it may, unmistakable signs of its activity showed themselves very soon after Allied occupation. There were several murders, the perpetrators of which were concealed and protected by the unwritten code of *omertà*, which made it all but impossible to trace them. In one instance however, the murder of a landowner in the province of Agrigento, where the suspects were arrested by the very commendable efforts of a *Carabinieri* officer, both defendants were found guilty and sentenced to death, thanks to the foresight of Lord Rennell in transferring the case to be tried by an Allied Military tribunal, and the death sentences were duly carried out.

Offences against Proclamation No. 2 were on the whole more numerous than serious. Actions inspired by definite hostility against the Allied armed forces were very few, and the motive of the crime of cutting military signal wires was found in nearly every case to be loot rather than sabotage. Besides this, the graver offences were pilfering, or being in possession of stolen property of the Allied forces, and concealing arms. But the majority of cases were furnished by more trivial offences, which were tried in Summary Military courts. These kept the Legal and Police Officers extremely busy. By the end of August nearly 1,300 cases had been tried, many of which involved an enormous amount of time owing to the necessity of using interpreters. Of these only about 100 needed to be tried in General or Superior courts. Thanks to the work of the Metropolitan Police officers, the help of the *Carabinieri* in detecting and arresting persons guilty of these war offences was in most cases readily

[1] Nobody nowadays accepts the derivations from the French word *Mauvais* or the incredibly convenient attribution *Mazzini Autorizza Furti, Incendi Avvelenamenti;* since the Mafia certainly existed long before Mazzini's day and is generally thought to have been, in its original form, composed of elements from the private armies of feudal lords which were suppressed under the constitution of 1812. A more plausible derivation is from a dialect used by Western Sicily, *mafiuso*—'handsome'. Members of the society were certainly called *mafiusi*.

obtained. The Military courts on the whole worked satisfactorily. It had been emphasised in the initial Administrative Instructions that it was as important that justice should seem to be done, as it was to do it, and the decision to hear cases publicly made a very good impression, as well as the rules of procedure with their fundamental implication of the innocence of the accused until proved guilty. But the moral effect of this display of fairness by enemy military tribunals was not always accompanied by sufficient respect for the majesty of this foreign law, since, certainly to begin with, sentences tended to be much too light to deter offenders, and in black market cases even heavy sentences did little to deter. But the fact that, despite the number of crimes which under Proclamation No. 2 could legitimately have been made the subject of the death penalty, the actual number of death sentences pronounced during the whole of the Military Government of Sicily could be counted on the fingers of a single hand, is an eloquent testimony to the forbearance in the enforcement of military law.

It was found that the Italian judiciary had been much less affected by the corruption of Fascist influence than had at first been feared. In accordance with the plans made at Chrea, Criminal courts were reopened before Civil courts and Lower courts before the higher, and, before any court was started, all its officers were carefully 'vetted' and outstanding Fascists eliminated. Some of the higher judicial officials had fled before the invasion, and in these cases the Chief Civil Affairs Officer had to fill the vacancies. Committees were formed at the seat of each court of appeal to assist Legal officers in supervising the operation of the Italian Courts, and relations with both bench and bar were good. The Bar associations, which had been controlled by the Fascists, were dissolved, and new free associations formed in their place. Considering the lack of communications, which made the service of papers and documents extremely difficult, and the dispersal of witnesses many of whom were refugees or prisoners of war, the restarting of the Italian courts was a very creditable achievement. Once they had got started, efforts were made to transfer to them as many cases as possible of offences under Proclamation No. 2, which did not directly involve the Allied armies. By the end of September criminal courts were in full operation in all provinces except Messina.

One of the more difficult problems with which the Legal Division had to contend was the overcrowding of the jails with prisoners awaiting trial, a large number of whom had been detained for months without the formulation of any charge against them, and with persons confined for political reasons. The dissolution of the Fascist regime naturally led to a large number of requests for release, all of which needed careful investigation. Many accused were released, either because there was no case against them at all, or because they had already been in jail for as long a time as the longest sentence they would have received had they been found guilty. In order to prevent any recurrence of this undesirable state of affairs Proclamation No. 13, the improvised habeas corpus act referred to in the previous chapter, was issued on 17th August, defining the legal rights of the Italian people and enacting that no person should be imprisoned by any Italian official without trial. By these measures much was done to diminish overcrowding of the jails, but the success achieved in this direction was only partial, since many of the jails had been rendered unserviceable by bombing, and the conditions in those which survived were in many cases extremely bad owing to lack of sanitary arrangements, aggravated by shortage of water, food and clothing. Among the worst jails was that on the Aeolian island of Favignana, a criminal penal settlement where starvation added to the horrors of a lack of hygiene. The work of the Prison section of the Public Safety Division in cleaning up conditions in Sicilian jails earned the special commendation of Lord Rennell.

In spite of the terrible sanitary conditions resulting from the devastation caused by Allied bombardments, public health, once the tide of war had passed on, gave A.M.G. little cause for anxiety. Though the incidence of certain diseases, e.g. tuberculosis, was found to be distressingly high, there was no evidence to show that the conditions produced by the invasion had caused any noticeable deterioration; except for small quickly mastered outbreaks of typhoid at Messina, Trapani and Centuripe, which occurred some time after the occupation, following on the earlier outbreaks of the same diseases already mentioned. The health of the Sicilian public remained more or less normal. Medical staffs of hospitals which, where they had been depleted by war absentees, were filled up with Italian army doctors released on parole, carried on without great disturbance, though in certain cases their hospital accommodation had temporarily been greatly reduced, mostly by bombing, but partly also by requisition of hospital buildings for Allied hospital use. AMGOT gave priority to hospital reconstruction and emergency improvisation of hospital accommodation where required. The distribution of essential medical stores was also undertaken by AMGOT, partly from a small stock of imported supplies which had been accumulated before the invasion, but mostly from captured war material—Italian army medical stores which were made over to it by the Allied military authorities. A central medical store was set up at Caltanissetta from which all the provinces drew their requirements, each province receiving initially a twenty-ton 'brick' for distribution to hospitals and later to selected pharmacies.

But there were two kinds of disease which, if they did not disturb unduly the Sicilian public health authorities, caused much anxiety to Allied army medical staffs, namely malaria and venereal disease. Largely owing to defective anti-malarial discipline, casualties from this source in both Allied Armies were exceedingly high, higher in fact than the battle casualties.[1] One of the most important tasks of the Military Government Public Health division was therefore to re-organise the Sicilian malaria-control administration, which had been split up between a large number of different authorities, and to concentrate the work under a single authority in each province. Mosquito control by dusting with Paris Green was rapidly restarted and at a later stage ditching and steam channelling projects were re-organised—all this before the use of D.D.T. as an anti-malarial agent, which was not employed in Italy till April 1944, had become known. In Palermo province work was carried out in combination with the Seventh Army 20th Malarial Control unit. By the beginning of October at least 2,000 civilians were engaged on various anti-malarial projects. The system of distributing suppressive and curative drugs for this disease, much of them provided from Allied sources, was also reorganised.

The problem of venereal disease was far more difficult, owing to the virtual impossibility of dealing with the enormous volume of clandestine prostitution provoked by the invasion—a phenomenon not wholly unconnected with economic causes, such as the shortage of consumer goods and the general rise in the cost of living resulting from growing inflation. A concerted attempt to tackle this problem, which met with some, though by no means unqualified, success, was made in Trapani province, as a result of a joint conference called by the S.C.A.O. and attended by representatives of the local medical officers of the occupying troops, the police, the Chief Public Health officer of the province (*Medico Provinciale*) and the A.M.G. Public Safety officials. Vice-squads of discreet *Carabinieri* and *Agenti di Pubblica Sicurezza*, working, where possible, in concert with the Military Police, were formed to detect clandestine prostitutes and persons soliciting for an immoral purpose and to investigate complaints respecting the contraction of venereal disease. Offenders detained on suspicion were subjected to a medical examination, and to compulsory medical treatment, if found suffering from disease. The Italian courts on the whole cooperated satisfactorily in imposing sentences, where these offences could be proved, for clandestine, as opposed to licensed, prostitution was an offence which could be severely punished under Italian law.

---

[1] During the third quarter of 1943 casualties from primary malaria in the Eighth Army amounted to 12,500, while battle casualties were only about 6,400.

The medical profession in Sicily had been comparatively free from Fascist influence and the medical and public health authorities knew their business, so that indirect government in this field was highly successful and gave rise to comparatively few problems. Hence the most important task which the Public Health Division was called upon to perform was on the welfare side. Here there were two different sets of problems to be faced, the special problems for individuals raised by homelessness and destruction due to war devastation, and the general problem of the administration of the social services under war conditions and in the chaos resulting from the dissolution of the Fascist party. The first set of problems was complicated not a little by the perfectly natural decision, made before the armistice, not to pay the Italian allowances to dependants of Italian soldiers, and the decision to stop any payment due on the Italian National Debt. Both these created a class of persons wholly dependent on public relief, the soldier's wife and the small rentier. The machinery for paying relief was immediately set working, and the allowance fixed initially for public relief was adequate; but this condition did not survive very long, as the cost of living was constantly pushed up by inflation. Relief scales were never able to catch up with prices and a good deal of hardship must have resulted.

The problems caused by the dissolution of the Fascist party were much more complicated, since a large number of welfare activities, if not inspired, had at any rate been used by Fascism to secure the party hold on the public, not only in the shape of the Youth Movement, *Gioventù Italiana Littorio* (G.I.L.), and the various recreational activities connected with the *Dopolavoro* (After Work) organisation, in which party propaganda and welfare activities and facilities were inextricably confused, but also in a number of the social services like maternity and child welfare and the care of the aged poor. It became the task of the Welfare Section to supervise the reassembling of the *disjecta membra* of these institutions—some of which had lost a good deal of property from loot, not to mention military requisition, often unauthorised—under the aegis of the Provincial and later the Regional Social Welfare office, *Ufficio di Assistenza Sociale*. These offices were created by AMGOT to supervise the granting of family relief under a means test on a communal basis through the existing machinery of the *Enti Communali di Assistenza*.

In the relief of destitution and the performance of welfare work AMGOT was greatly assisted by the American, and later by the British, Red Cross organisations. Mr Norman Davis, the chairman of the American Red Cross, paid a visit to Sicily early in September, and arrangements were made for American, and later British, Red Cross workers to come to Sicily to work under AMGOT's supervision. The American Red Cross also provided a considerable quantity of clothing and medicines for the relief of the destitute, who included not only Sicilians but Yugoslav and Greek internees, and a number of refugees. A programme was worked out under which Red Cross workers were made available in Sicily and on the mainland to distribute clothing, food and medical supplies, to help to register, re-locate, re-house and repatriate refugees, and to help running camps for the temporary care of homeless Sicilians, released political prisoners and internees, and Allied nationals. After the application of a suitable 'purge' the Italian Red Cross was re-organised. This institution was responsible for a far wider field of activity than the Red Cross in the United Kingdom or the United States. Under the Italian system, its functions included the care of civilian hospitals, the training of nurses, a good deal of malaria-control work, and first-aid work in air-raid shelters, as well as communications with prisoners of war and refugees. The financial aid necessary for carrying out these essential services, which had been supplied from Rome, was provided by AMGOT. Steps were immediately taken to improve the working of the prisoners-of-war clearance centre.

The political vacuum created by the dissolution of the Fascist party soon began to fill itself, in spite of the refusal of AMGOT, in accordance with the directive issued by the Combined Chief of Staff, to countenance any form of political activity. The first political movement to show its head above ground was that of the Separatists, who within a few days of the Allied occupation began to hold meetings and, contrary to Proclamation No. 11, posted handbills in the streets, which were taken down by Lord Rennell's orders. The Separatist movement in Sicily has a very long history. It can be traced at least as far back as the eighteenth century, when the Sicilian feudal lords tried to resist the 'enlightened' centralising policy of the Bourbon monarchy at Naples. It received a vigorous encouragement from the occupation of Sicily by the British in the Napoleonic war, and the granting of a separate constitution devised on what was supposed to be the British model. It embodied miscellaneous currents of discontent during the reigns of the last Neapolitan Bourbons, which broke out into open revolt in Palermo in 1848, though on this occasion the ideals of the leaders of the revolt were Federalist rather than Separatist, in that they did not want complete independence. Since the unification of Italy under the crown of Piedmont, it had continued to exist. Though it was a movement which had traditionally received the support of some of the large landowners—and Sicily was by tradition one of the strongholds of the *latifondisti*—it had derived its main strength from middle-class elements, who shared the belief, held by many Italians in Calabria, Apulia and Campania, that the backward south had been consistently exploited under the House of Savoy in favour of the northern industrialists. There were in Sicily three Separatist leaders of some standing, Signor Finocchiaro Aprile and two great landowners, the Tasca brothers. The interests of the *latifondisti* had been seriously threatened by Fascism, which had begun to put into execution plans for breaking up the large estates, and the Tasca family had been associated with the movement in its more extreme form since before the first World War. And just as the occupation of Sicily under Lord William Bentinck in the early nineteenth century had given a great stimulus to aspirations for an independent Sicily under British protection, so in 1943 the Separatist leaders attempted to use the Allied occupation for their own ends, needless to say with very little success.[1] The notion of an independent Sicily, though it appeared to receive a certain amount of superficial popular favour in the days of enthusiasm which followed the overthrow of Mussolini, never succeeded in stirring the imagination of the Sicilian people as a whole. Though the movement still continued to cause some anxiety after the administration of the island had been handed back to the Italian Government, it never became a real menace to Italian unity, and in the eyes of the Italian Government it cannot have possessed much more than a 'nuisance' value. But the idea of administrative decentralisation and a far wider degree of local autonomy received strong popular support, and was embodied in the new constitution of the Italian republic.

Apart from Separatism, which in the early stage was the most active political movement, groups belonging to a number of other parties came to the surface, notably the Communists (whose influence was strongest in the sulphur mining districts, and had managed to survive, in cellular form, thoughout the Fascist domination), the Action Party, and the Christian Democrats, the successors of the Catholic *Partito Populare* which had been founded by a Sicilian priest, Don Sturzo. These various groups held clandestine meetings, but no popular demonstrations of any size were organised. But after the fall of Mussolini, the Allied recognition of the Badoglio Government as co-belligerent, and the pronouncement of the three Allied Foreign Ministers at the Moscow Conference[2], it was really no longer practicable to forbid the resumption of all political activity. Rather

---

[1] For the historical background of Sicilian Separatism in the eighteenth and the first half of the nineteenth century see Rosario Romeo's, *Il Risorgimento in Sicilia,* and J. Rosselli's, *Lord William Bentick and the British Occupation of Sicily, 1811-1814.*

[2] Lord Rennell records that he twice personally warned Finocchiaro Aprile that his Separatist propaganda must cease, and adds: 'I need hardly say that he and his friends had at an early date informed me that they desired to see created a Sicily independent of Italy under British protection, while at the same time informing certain of my American officers that they desired the same development but under American protection'. Lord Rennell also forbade the inter-provincial meeting which the Separatists tried to organise in August.

more repressive measures were taken against the Separatists than against the other parties, since the political complications that Separatism might have led to were obvious. But the dangers of underground political activity were clearly much greater than any danger which would result from a resumption, under control, of ordered political activity. Meetings of political groups were therefore overlooked, if not tolerated. Indeed, it would hardly have been in the power of AMGOT to prevent them without reverting to the police state. Formal permission for the resumption of political activities from the Combined Chiefs of Staff was not, however, given until January 1944, only a few weeks before the handing back of the administration of the island to the Italian Government.[1]

The influence of the Church did not play a great part in determining the attitude of the Sicilian people to their invader/liberators. There was no necessity for the clergy to engage in any active anti-Fascist propaganda, since Fascism was not popular in the island, nor did they see fit to undertake any definite mission in favour of the Allies. But within the circle of this neutrality they were both helpful and friendly. The bishops did their best to assure the tranquillity of their flock, and the general trend of preaching from the country pulpit was to exhort the people to obey the behests of the Allied Military Government. But they refused to take any part in denouncing either *mafiusi* or prominent Fascists. The influence of Cardinal Lavitrano in Palermo and two other important prelates was rather engaged in endeavouring to persuade the Allied authorities to release interned Fascists and let bygones be bygones.

The ban on the countenancing of political activity did not however mean that the Allied Military Government was content to neglect the education of public opinion, or to prohibit its legitimate expression within the limits imposed by the circumstances of belligerence. The control of the Sicilian press was, it is true, left in the first place to the Psychological Warfare Branch of A.F.H.Q., but this branch was directed to work in close co-operation with AMGOT, whose influence was exerted, on one or two reasons quite decisively, in favour of permitting as much freedom as possible in the expression of ideas not positively injurious to the Allied cause, including criticism of AMGOT itself.

An attempt was also made to restore to the organs of local government something of the democratic character they had possessed before they were perverted by Fascism, which had virtually eliminated all elements of a representative nature. In pre-Fascist Italy central control of local Government was much closer than in the United Kingdom, the powers of the Prefect, the local representative of the central government, who has no administrative counterpart in

[1] See below, pp. 136-37.

Britain or the United States, being extensive and in most cases paramount. But elective bodies based on a wide franchise did exist both in the Province and in the Commune. The *Consiglio Provinciale*, which may be compared (though not too closely) with the English County Council, worked through an executive Committee called the *Deputazione Provinciale*, whose chairman was called the *Presidente*. The Council of the Commune (*Consiglio Communale*), corresponding to Town or Rural District Council, which chose the Mayor (*Sindaco*), also had an executive committee (*Giunta Communale*). Moreover the administrative board of the Prefect (*Giunta Provinciale Amministrativa*), which was responsible for supervising and controlling the operations of the communes, also contained an elective element, of which the members were chosen by the Provincial Council (*Consiglio Provinciale*). The elective councils had been abolished by Mussolini. The place of the *Deputazione Provinciale* was taken by the *Rettorato*—a body appointed by the central government—while in the commune an advisory council (*Consulta Communale*) had been set up, whose members were appointed, from names submitted by the Fascist Syndicates, by the Prefect.[1] The Communal councils had been made purely advisory and the mayor, renamed by the ill-omened appellation of *podestà* and appointed by the Minister, could carry on without it. So too in the *Giunta Provinciale Amministrativa*, the former elected members had been replaced by nominees of the local Federal Secretary of the Fascist Party.

It was not considered possible in the emergency conditions created by the Allied occupation to restore the elective councils, though this was expressly recognised as the ultimate goal to be aimed at. In the meantime the Fascist-appointed members of the *Giunta Provinciale Amministrativa* were replaced by prominent citizens of untainted reputation chosen from various walks of life. The *Rettorato* was abolished and the *Deputazione Provinciale* restored, its members being appointed from prominent anti-Fascist citizens by the Prefect, after consultation with and approval of AMGOT, the same procedure being followed in the appointments to the restored *Giunta Communale*. These arrangements, which were tentatively introduced in Sicily, were subsequently embodied in a local government decree of the Badoglio Government, and so extended to the whole of liberated Italy.[2]

The central administrative machine represented by the professional civil servants was able to function reasonably well, after removal of the Prefects and a quite small number of convinced Fascists, except in the field of food rationing, and even here, thanks

[1] In communes with a population of over 100,000 inhabitants by the Minister of the Interior.

[2] See below, pp. 174-75.

to the strenuous efforts of AMGOT, there was no actual breakdown. But it was hardly to be expected that the experiment of indirect government in municipal and communal affairs should prove in every case successful. The replacement of the existing mayors, more than half of whom were removed, was no easy matter, since Civil Affairs Officers did not have the requisite local knowledge, even where they had the requisite degree of discretion. The situation was picturesquely summed up by Lord Rennell in the following sentences:

> More than half the adult population of Sicily is illiterate and the choice of candidates for an unpaid office was small in many of the remoter communes. Moreover the Sicilians of any standing, whatever their political views, who were ready to cooperate by work and responsibility, as opposed to advice and criticism, were singularly few. The majority of communes are rent by personal jealousies and feuds and found it difficult to agree in suggesting a name or names. With the people clamouring to be rid of a Fascist *Podestà*, many of my officers fell into the trap of selecting the most forthcoming self-advertiser, or following the advice of their self-appointed interpreters who had learned some English in the course of a stay in the U.S.A. The result was not always happy. The choices in more than one instance fell on the local Mafia 'boss', or his shadow, who in one or two cases had graduated in an American gangster environment. All that could be said of some of these men was that they were as definitely anti-Fascist as they were undesirable from every other point of view. The difficulty in early days of an occupation for a foreign element to weigh up the value or danger of local characters must be clear to any one who has given the subject a moment's thought.

Mistakes such as these are inevitable in any system of indirect government. They only go to show how much greater might have been the mistakes which would have occurred, had a system of direct government been attempted. AMGOT's mistakes were more often than not due to the tendency among its officers, constantly criticised by Lord Rennell, to do too much by way of direct government. As may well be imagined, Anglo-Saxon standards of efficiency were often different from, though not always, perhaps, in the ultimate resort superior to, the traditional Italian way of doing things, and the temptation to interfere could not always be resisted.

The administrative lessons to be learned from this first experiment in Allied Military Government were quickly recorded in a report submitted to the Chief Administrative officer at A.F.H.Q., and some, at any rate, of the mistakes which occurred in operation 'Husky' were avoided in subsequent operations on the mainland. The original handicap of AMGOT was that its *raison d'être* and functions were not understood by lower formations. Nor was it in many cases possible to attach A.M.G. officers to the units of the assault forces with which they were to operate, sufficiently long before D-day to enable them to 'sell' military government to their colleagues, or to co-ordinate their activities with the units of the Counter-Intelligence Corps and the Field Security Officers with whom they would have to cooperate closely in action. The importance of these considerations was immediately realised, and the problems solved, by the attachment to each Army of a permanent cadre of A.M.G. officers which advanced with the combatant troops installing military government in the areas immediately to their rear.

For the invasion of Calabria the cadre already operating with Eighth Army under Group-Captain (later Air-Commodore) Benson accompanied the assault up the Italian peninsula. A similar cadre under Colonel (later Brigadier-General) Hume was attached to the American Fifth Army, which landed at Salerno and proceeded step by step up the west coast of the mainland. Colonel Hume was able to profit by the experience gained in Sicily. His initial relations with Fifth Army were on a much happier footing than those of Lieut.-Colonel Poletti with the Seventh Army. And later the very carefully coordinated planning between Fifth Army A.M.G. and the various combat formations which were employed in the capture of Rome showed that the lessons of 'Husky' had not been forgotten.

The second important lesson learned from the Sicilian landings was that Civil Affairs officers were needed immediately invaded towns had been captured, and that they must be provided with their own transport to get them there. In the stress of battle, reliance on transport belonging to the combat units to which they were attached or on captured or requisitioned indigenous transport was shown to be quite impracticable. Combat units had no transport to spare, and locally requisitioned transport was unobtainable, since tactical units requisitioned every vehicle they could lay hands on. Moreover local vehicles, even where they could be found, were often not in sufficiently good condition to perform the strenuous work required of them.

Another handicap from which AMGOT suffered during the first phase of the invasion was the shortage of Enlisted Men/Other Ranks to act as clerks, interpreters and guards. Shortage of subordinate personnel heavily handicapped AMGOT officers in their attempts to prevent looting and to enforce the proclamations, particularly the curfew. Experience showed that in the early stages of occupation the provision of some small detachments of Military Police could have rendered very useful services in the protection of warehouses of foodstuffs, and in some instances of national monuments and works of art. In cases where the advance of the combat troops was particularly rapid, it often occurred that a town was left completely denuded of troops, so that an AMGOT officer frequently found himself the sole Allied person in uniform in a captured town. A great improvement both as regards the provision of transport and subordinate personnel was made in the Calabrian and Campanian landings, though the proposal for the provision of AMGOT with military police detachments did not take effect.[1]

In the planning for 'Husky' perhaps the least satisfactory point, as the event subsequently proved, was the organisation of the Civil Supply Division, which was conceived on much too small a scale for the bundle of diverse responsibilities which were finally thrust upon it. Although the lack of transport for maintaining the essential civilian requirements of the island had been foreseen in the Spofford Plan, the original AMGOT team contained no officer who was a specialist in road transport. It was some time before the necessity was realised for immediately immobilizing all civilian vehicles, and for 'marrying' all permits with the petrol rationing system. Nor were sufficiently prompt steps taken to locate and guard all dumps of captured enemy equipment, with the result that many arms and much ammunition passed into undesirable hands, and much petrol and fuel oil, on which AMGOT depended for civilian supply purposes, was stolen. The initial assumption, too, that military formations would be responsible for handling electric power, railways and communications and that AMGOT would consequently not concern itself with these, also required some modification. During the initial phase immediately following invasion the complete monopoly of means of communication by the armies is no doubt essential, as well as the control of supplies of electric power. But this phase may pass very quickly, and, in order to avoid disease and unrest, some provision has soon to be made for civilian needs. As Colonel Spofford pointed out, it is a mistake to rely entirely on the military formations to handle electric power, railways, communications and the like, as they do not have time to think about, and still less to organise, a transport system for the benefit of the civilian population. It is therefore essential that at an early date A.M.G. specialists in these fields should be brought on the scene of action, to work with the military formations in order to make certain that the civilian population's essential needs are met. In Sicily AMGOT personnel was not provided for these purposes, and the military technical services, as Lord Rennell pointed out in his despatch, had in practice shown themselves very jealous of allowing AMGOT to have anything to do with such public utilities. But as soon as the landings in Calabria, Apulia and Campania took place they decided, practically without warning, to hand them over to AMGOT, which was at that moment not equipped with the specialists

[1] After the consolidation of the Allied Armies on the mainland the police needs of the Army A.M.G.s were provided for by the organisation of units of mobile *Carabinieri*. The shortage of transport made available to A.M.G. officers once the Regions were consolidated caused continual trouble.

required to assume this responsibility. A considerable improvement in this matter was effected on the mainland, where members of the Transportation Sub-Commission were attached to the Military Railway Services.

In order to coordinate military requirements in the matter of local resources with the needs of the civilian population, and to provide a clearing house for settling local policy where Service interests conflicted with civil requirements, Local Resources Boards were set up, on the insistence of General Sir Brian Robertson, commanding 'Fortbase', the organisation which was subsequently transformed into the Advanced Administrative Echelon of A.F.H.Q. These boards consisted of AMGOT officers and representatives of the 'Q'/G-4 services of the Eighth and Seventh Armies. The first of them was instituted at the beginning of August in Syracuse, for the two provinces of Syracuse and Ragusa, even before Catania had fallen. It worked by means of sub-committees on Supply, Engineering and Labour. A similar organisation was set up in the Seventh Army area in September, and the two Resources Boards were finally amalgamated under the chairmanship of the C.C.A.O. This system of Local Resources Boards had been used in the occupied territories in North Africa, and had proved very useful in reconciling the competing claims of Service formations and Military Government. It was transplanted to the mainland, where the military side of the composition of the boards was heavily increased. In Sicily the Boards did a useful piece of work in straightening out the muddle caused by the indiscriminate competition in the procurement of labour and the different wage rates offered by the various branches of the Services.

CHAPTER III

INVADING SOUTHERN ITALY

THE DECISION to invade southern Italy, following the success of the Sicilian campaign, raised the question of the organisation of Military Government as the Allied armies advanced up the peninsula. The lack of communications made it impossible to adopt the province as the unit to be controlled from a single central headquarters, which was the existing system of Italian Government. It was therefore necessary to group provinces round some intermediate centre, thus creating some form of regional decentralisation. For this purpose the most obvious unit to choose was the *compartimento*. Though the 'compartment' was in fact little more than a geographical expression, since it did not constitute a separate Italian administrative entity, it did correspond to some of the ancient historical divisions into which the country, which had only achieved unity for about three-quarters of a century, had been divided since the sixteenth century. And in many cases it embodied a real unity of regional public opinion. It was therefore planned that Allied Military Government should be decentralised into a number of 'Regions' to be activated successively as the Allied armies advanced up the peninsula. Each of these 'Regions' was to embrace one, or in certain cases two or three, of the *compartimenti*.

The actual form which this successive regional division finally assumed does not concern us for the moment. We are concerned here only with the regional structure adopted in connection with the landings in Calabria and Apulia and the Bay of Salerno by the Eighth and Fifth Armies. As in operation 'Husky' Military Government was organised into a 'spearhead' group landing with the assault troops, to be followed, as the territory was occupied, by a territorial organisation based on the province and finally united in a single AMGOT, so the 'spearhead' A.M.G. groups landing with each Army were to expand into provincial organisations which were finally to be united under a single regional headquarters. Only in this case the territory of each region would include only one army area, whereas AMGOT, Sicily, covered the areas of both Armies. The two regions to be constituted in the first stage after the landings were named Region II and Region III. The first of these was to include three *compartimenti*, Calabria, Lucania and Apulia, the second only Campania—a sufficiently large unit with its huge urban population round the Bay of Naples. Meanwhile AMGOT, Sicily, was to be transformed into Region I.

The complications introduced into the higher echelons of Allied Military Government by the armistice and the formation of the Allied Control Commission will be explained in a later section of this chapter; the first two sections will deal with the organisation and composition of the groups of A.M.G. officers who participated in the landings, the story of the part played by them in these operations, and the constitution of Regions II and III in the weeks immediately following.

The detachment of Allied Military Government officers to follow behind the Eighth Army in its Calabrian and Apulian landings and to constitute AMGOT, Region II, behind its advance, was known as AMGOT Eighth Army and was placed under the command of Group-Captain Benson. It consisted of a nucleus of his staff who had taken part in the 'Husky' landings, supplemented by officers taken from AMGOT, Sicily, and by another group from the Middle East. Its international composition was approximately one-third American and two-thirds British. In order to coordinate movements with the tactical forces, A.M.G. liaison officers were appointed to the three formations concerned with the Calabrian landings, namely XIII Corps, 1st Canadian Division and 5th Division, and also to the 78th Division and V Corps which landed at Taranto. The deployment of the remaining body of A.M.G. officers was planned in four detachments, (a) eight officers to land with the Canadian Division and to cover Reggio town and area, (b) seven officers to land with 5th Division, (c) 'follow-up' and (d) 'reserve' detachments, each of seven officers, and an advanced 'tactical' Regional Headquarters. Profiting by the lessons of 'Husky', arrangements were made for officers to be accompanied by their own transport[1], and commanders of the various units of the Army had been particularly requested not to disarm *Carabinieri*. These arrangements on the whole worked very well. There were no complaints heard of A.M.G. officers landing without transport or equipment, and when the first A.M.G. Police officer entered the town of Reggio, he found ninety *Carabinieri* at their posts[2].

The first landings took place early in the morning of 3rd September, some hours before the actual signature of the armistice at Cassibile in Sicily, and five days before its announcement to the

[1] For the landings in Calabria the 'spearhead' (including liaison officers) consisted of 35 officers and 43 O.R's, two 3-ton lorries, four 15-cwt lorries, 16 Jeeps and 16 motor cycles.

[2] He had, however, to rescue a considerable number from the P.O.W. cages, and the request to abstain from taking *Carabinieri* prisoners was not always complied with, but the position was very much easier in this respect than it was in Sicily.

Italian people. The first A.M.G. detachment arrived in Reggio on D-day and immediately established the Civil Affairs administration of the Province. By the end of the day twelve officers had landed on the mainland, twenty-five arrived the following day, eight more on the day after that, and a Regional H.Q. was set up in Reggio immediately. Enemy resistance was negligible, and in spite of the intense bombardments from land, sea and air, which had taken place since the beginning of the German withdrawal from Sicily to the mainland, the town of a normal population of about 120,000 inhabitants was found to be less damaged than had been expected. Water supply at about half the normal rate was available from the beginning, and some electricity on the third day after its capture. The A.M.G. Police officer (C.A.P.O.) on entering the town found only about 17,000 of its inhabitants in residence, the remainder having taken refuge in the countryside; but the refugees soon returned, bringing with them the immediate problem of feeding them, since there was very little food left in the town. The amount of hoarding was insignificant and very little looting had occurred, as this had been promptly stopped by the arrival of the C.A.P.O. and his direction of the *Carabinieri*. Stocks of flour were immediately taken into custody and protected, bakeries set working, and a bread ration of 150 gms per day established. The small existing stocks of grain were supplemented by the diversion of a coaster from Catania to Reggio, laden with 2,000 tons of wheat from North Africa. But the transport situation was not so easy, as some forty-five civilian cars, fire engines and tenders, an ambulance and many civilian lorries had been removed by the Canadian troops.

The advance of the Eighth Army up the Calabrian toe was rapid, thanks to successful landings by sea at Bagnara and Pizzo. Cozensa was entered on the 14th, and advance patrols reached as far north as Sapri and on the same day established contact with outposts of the Fifth Army, which had landed in the Bay of Salerno. On the same day Eighth Army units, which had landed in Calabria, made contact with the Eighth Army troops who had landed at Taranto. The whole foot of the Italian peninsula was now in Allied hands, and the Eighth Army was immediately concentrated on the Adriatic side of the Apennines in order to prepare its advance up the eastern coast. Eighth Army A.M.G. was therefore divided into two sections—a 'spearhead' detachment under Group-Captain Benson, which went forward with the Army administering the territory it occupied in its advance, and a regional detachment under an American officer, Lieut.-Colonel Harvey Gerry, to organise and take charge of Region II. The advance of the Eighth Army up the Calabrian coasts had been rather more rapid than had been anticipated and, when this division of AMGOT took place, the staff of Region II was scarcely more than a handful. The regional establishment had not been completed by the time that the Calabrian operations started, and though some reinforcements were sent from Sicily and later from the Middle East, A.M.G. Region II was for many weeks very thin on the ground. A skeleton staff was however organised for the three Calabrian provinces of Reggio, Cosenza and Catanzaro and the two provinces of Lucania—Matera and Potenza. On 3rd October General Alexander established the two *compartimenti* of Calabria and Lucania as a static area, and the responsibility for its administration therefore passed out of the control of General Montgomery, G.O.C. Eighth Army, and his S.C.A.O., Group-Captain Benson, and was assumed by Fifteenth Army Group and its C.C.A.O., Lord Rennell.

Military Government presented fewer difficulties in Region II than in Sicily, since there was not the continually urgent problem of feeding very large towns, the only town in the Region containing over 100,000 inhabitants being Reggio Calabria. The *compartimento*, it is true, did not produce sufficient food to feed this town and many of the other scattered communes, and the problem of transport was a perpetual difficulty, but supplies in the northern province of Catanzaro were adequate, and the neighbouring *compartimento* of Lucania actually produced a surplus of grain, which in normal times had been used to feed both Calabria and Apulia. Thus, though rations were sometimes short in the outlying communes and up in the hills, and there was some initial difficulty in getting supplies to the coast towns such as Palmi and Locri, there was during the first few weeks never any real danger of hunger on a large scale. In Catanzaro the Civil Affairs officer was able to make a very satisfactory arrangement with the G.O.C. of the Italian XXXI Corps, which had been organised as a Labour Corps to follow up behind the Eighth Army, by which the distribution of food in the province and the neighbouring districts was undertaken with Italian army lorries.

But these comparatively easy conditions did not last very long. Before the middle of December no flour or grain was left in the three Calabrian provinces, and the ration had been reduced to 100 gms per day. This desperate situation was caused in part by the acute shortage in Sicily in November, as a result of which 1,200 tons had been diverted from Reggio to the island, but the main reason was the fact that, of the 22,000 tons called forward by AMGOT for the two Regions, nothing had been received. The immediate crisis was eventually relieved by the transfer of about 1,500 tons from Sicily and about 3,800 tons from the Middle East. But, to maintain Calabrian consumption at a daily ration of only 150 gms per head, much more was needed. And during this period something approaching famine conditions was prevailing in Naples and Salerno, so that it was some time before the standard ration of 200 gms could be distributed.

With the exception of Reggio only two towns, Cosenza and Potenza, had been damaged at all severely, so that the interruption in public utilities, like water-supply and electricity, was not of long duration. For the retreating Germans had no time to sabotage thoroughly the main hydro-electric station of the Sila, though the damage done to the Apulian aqueduct led to considerable shortage of water in Matera province. The passage of the tide of war was so rapid that conditions of life in many of the towns, especially those off the main routes, were practically undisturbed. So normal did they remain that in a number of places in the Region neither the banks nor the law courts were closed—a development not perhaps quite so much the result of deliberate policy, as of the scarcity of Finance and Legal Officers.[1] Nor did the maintenance of public order entail any special difficulties. No organisation comparable to the Mafia raised its head—the Camorra had been dead long before the birth of Fascism. The only disorders of any significance were outbursts of anti-Fascist, or so-called anti-Fascist, riots which broke out at two small towns in the province of Potenza. Public health caused no anxieties, except for a small outbreak of typhoid at Scilla, and the existing public health organisation continued to function without any disturbance worth recording.

New problems for A.M.G. did however present themselves in connection with the self-dissolution of the Italian Army, and the influx of refugees and displaced persons. As a result of the armistice many units of the Italian Army immediately disintegrated, and the roads became cluttered with soldiers—many of them armed—going back to their homes, or else trying to find somewhere to live. The Eighth Army, perhaps naturally enough at this stage, did not feel inclined to cope with this problem, nor were they much concerned with the disbandment of units—except those providing labour for them—so long as they were not called upon to feed them. A considerable number of these disbanded soldiers were Sicilians, who wished to avail themselves of the ruling given by General Alexander in Sicily that Italian prisoners of war of Sicilian domicile were to be released; and their conveyance by fishing craft, and even by Allied landing craft, across the Straits of Messina raised obvious dangers from the point of view of security. But the majority of them were

---

[1] It is interesting to note Colonel Spofford's comments on this policy: 'Banks and courts were permitted to remain open if they were already open when the C.A.O. entered the town. This practice proved to be entirely sound and perhaps if it had been carried out in those parts of Italy where there had been little fighting, it would have taken a much shorter time to restore the normal life of the areas'. It was not, however, considered a safe policy to apply during the advance from Naples and the Sangro to the Gothic line, and banks continued normally to be closed for a short period, on occupation, though the interval before their reopening was, except under special conditions, cut down as far as possible—often to about a week or even less, until in the autumn of 1944 currency shortage induced a prolongation of the period of closure.

probably not prisoners of war but deserters. Arrangements were made by Lord Rennell with the General commanding the Italian XXXI Corps to establish a post at Reggio to intercept Italian stragglers, but many of them dispersed into the country-side and, having no civilian ration books, were forced by devious means to live on the country.

The refugee problem was first encountered by the 'spearhead' A.M.G. with the Eighth Army. The first big flow of Italian refugees through the Eighth Army lines began in November, when the Germans deliberately started driving hordes of frightened and destitute civilians across their lines in a southward direction. By the end of that month they were coming over at the rate of about 500 a day, creating an enormous problem in transport and feeding for the Army A.M.G.

A.M.G's first contact on any large scale with the problem of displaced persons took place in the big internment camp of Ferramonte di Tarsia, near Cosenza, which came under the administration of A.M.G. Region II very soon after liberation. The majority of the inmates were Jews, including 350 refugees from Yugoslavia, most of whom had arrived in Italy in the spring of 1940; there were also a considerable number of Czechs, Austrians and Poles. As a result of the military operations which led to the occupation of Cosenza, a general dispersal from the camp had occurred. Many of the internees took to the roads and the hills, some of them even finding their way to Sicily; but once they had learned that the Allies had definitely driven the Germans out of the province, they started coming back. A group of camp leaders, under the direction of a Yugoslav orchestral conductor, Mr Mirski, took over the administration of the camp, which was desperately short of food. An appeal for food made to the commander of the Eighth Army troops in the vicinity was promptly granted, but feeding the camp became the responsibility of A.M.G. as soon as it arrived on the scene. Mr Mirski was appointed camp director, responsible directly to A.M.G. Rations were called up from Reggio and, pending their arrival, an emergency load from Taranto from army stocks. A.M.G. Region II remained in charge until the camp was taken over by the Displaced Persons Sub-Commission of the newly formed Allied Control Commission.

The problem of reconstituting an administration after the removal of a large number of its Fascist chiefs also proved rather easier than it was in Sicily. In the six weeks following the fall of Mussolini Marshal Badoglio had replaced most of the prefects and some of the mayors of the larger towns like Reggio. The majority of the prominent Fascists had managed to escape into German-occupied territory, and the number of persons arrested and interned by the military security organisations was much smaller than in Sicily, amounting to less than 300, of whom the large majority were subsequently released. But while a beginning had been made by Badoglio of the 'purging' of the central administration, the 'defascistisation' of the local administrations had to be done by A.M.G., which removed most of the mayors from office, 93 out of 152 in the province of Cosenza, 100 out of 154 in that of Cantanzaro, 70 out of 89 in that of Reggio, 27 out of 32 in that of Matera and 70 out of 91 in that of Potenza. In the latter province two committees consisting of A.M.G. officials and leading anti-Fascists citizens were set up, one to investigate complaints against Fascists who had escaped punishment for crimes they had committed before occupation, and the other to examine persons alleged to be dangerous Fascists. But the progress of 'defascistisation' in some of the more remote communities was slow and, as in Sicily, there was a good deal of criticism aimed at A.M.G. on account of its alleged employment of Fascists.

Apart from the acute shortage of staff, especially in the earlier months, the gravest administrative difficulty encountered by Region II was the lack of communications—very little transport, no railways, no telephones and no telegraph—a defect which was felt acutely because of the very large distances from one end of the Region to the other. These two factors led to considerable modifications of the Sicilian administrative arrangements. Owing to the large number of communes spread over a very large area, and the small number of towns even of quite a moderate size, C.A.O's and C.A.P.O's were not assigned to particular communes: all C.A.O's and C.A.P.O's worked from the provincial headquarters and covered an average of about twenty communes apiece. An attempt was also made to substitute the '*compartimento*' for the province as the lowest unit of administration, but this did not prove a success, since under the Italian administrative system the province was the only unit where effective responsibility could be exercised.

The conclusion of the armistice on 3rd September brought about a sudden change in the Allied military plans. General Eisenhower decided to occupy Taranto and Apulia in conjunction with the Eighth Army's operations in Calabria. The troops involved were entirely British, consisting of the 1st Airborne Division, followed by other troops from the Middle East grouped under the headquarters of (British) V Corps under the command of Lieut.-General C. W. Allfrey. Attached to the landing brigades of the Airborne Division, which came ashore on 9th and 12th September, was a group of Allied Military Government officers under the command of Lieut.-Colonel Monfort, who had been in charge of Military Government in Pantelleria. Meanwhile a military mission headed by Lieut.-General Sir Noel Mason-MacFarlane, whose chief function was to transmit the instructions of the Supreme Allied Commander to the Italian Government, was formed in Algiers and landed by air at Brindisi, where the King of Italy and Marshal Badoglio had established themselves, on 13th September. The mission immediately made contact with General Ambrosio, the Italian Chief of the (joint) General Staff, and the Prime Minister. In order to preserve such remnants of dignity for the new regime as had survived the ignominious (though necessary) flight from Rome, it was decided by General Mason-MacFarlane, in agreement with Mr. Macmillan and Mr Murphy, that the imposition of Allied Military Government on the four Apulian provinces forming the heel of Italy should be avoided. Major-General Lord Rennell and Brig.-General Holmes were summoned to confer with the Italian Government in order to arrange a *modus vivendi*, pending the receipt of definite instructions from the Combined Chiefs of Staff. Agreement was reached with Marshal Badoglio that Allied Military Government should continue as before in the 'occupied'' provinces, but that in the provinces of Taranto, Bari, Brindisi and Lecce the Government should remain in the hands of the King and the Marshal, subject only to such control under the armistice terms as might be imposed by the Military Mission. In these four provinces no proclamations establishing Military Government were posted, but Allied Military Government officers were installed in the office of each of the four prefects as liaison officers. The Civil Affairs staff were placed directly under General Mason-MacFarlane's command, and the S.C.A.O. was instructed to act as his liaison officer for Civil Affairs between the Military Mission and the Italian central authority. The province of Foggia, though part of the *compartimento* of Apulia, was not included in this arrangement, as it was still the scene of active hostilities, Allied Military Government being carried on there, as in other occupied territories, by the 'spearhead' A.M.G. formation commanded by Group-Captain Benson. These *interim* arrangements were envisaged as the preliminary stage of the policy, subsequently adopted, under which Allied Military Government was confined to a comparatively narrow area behind the Allied Armies; the territory to the rear being handed back progressively, as the Allies advanced up the peninsula, to the administration of the Italian Government, under the supervision of the Allied Control Commission. This policy was described by General Holmes in the following terms:

> 'General Rennell and I made a visit to Brindisi last week and with General MacFarlane worked out an ad interim arrangement with Marshal Badoglio, under the terms of which we agreed not to proclaim military government in the four southern provinces of Apulia. In the circumstances it seemed inadvisable to give public notice of our control of sovereignty

> right under the nose of the little King and the old Marshal. Instead of establishing military government, we agreed to allow the Marshal to govern these four provinces with A.M.G. officers established in prefectures and other appropriate places as liaison officers, but with the distinct understanding that they were to exercise substantial influence on local administration. Badoglio was perfectly agreeable to this, as he and all concerned were abundantly aware that any reluctance on the part of the Italians to do things we require in getting on with the campaign might quickly result in the establishment of complete military control . . .
>
> I personally believe that we can make some political capital out of the transfer of occupied areas to Italian jurisdiction, by telling the world that we install military government only where it is necessary for military operations and that, as soon as conditions permit, we hand the territory to appropriate civil authorities. It might even be useful propaganda-wise to have public interment of AMGOT; as AMGOT is, I believe, destined to become a comparatively small unit to operate immediately in the rear of tactical forces and moving north as the line moves north. Areas cleared and settled would in the circumstances be turned over to the Italians, subject to the control we would exercise through the Allied Commission'.

While these negotiations were proceeding, the position of the Civil Affairs officers who had landed at Taranto with the first detachments of the Airborne Division was far from comfortable. The first AMGOT officer to arrive in the town had a distinctly cool reception. When he went to explain his mission to the vice-Prefect—he had not then been informed that AMGOT was not to carry on according to the normal directive, since the Civil Affairs personnel for Apulia had been despatched direct from North Africa without the knowledge of Group-Captain Benson's headquarters—he was told that the Italians were allies, that they had never heard of AMGOT, and did not intend to recognise it.

In spite of some initial confusion, the decision to permit the Italian Government to continue to administer the four Apulian provinces and the island of Sardinia—the first instalment of 'King's Italy'—which set the pattern for subsequent operations of the Control Commission, worked reasonably well. The system of A.M.G. liaison officers under the Military Mission enabled the Allied forces to obtain all the facilities and assistance they required from Italian local officials; though at the beginning it was not always easy to make them understand that outside this limited territory they were under the command of A.M.G. and that the King's writ did not run. But these temporary misunderstandings were soon straightened out, and no major difficulties subsequently disturbed this division of administrative authority.

The emergence of 'King's Italy' meant that only one Apulian province, Foggia, which was at one time included in Region II, came under Military Government. This province was subsequently attached to Region IV, and later transferred to Region V, which included the *compartimento* of Abruzzi and Molise immediately to the north[1]; but until nearly the end of the year it was administered by A.M.G. Eighth Army under the command of Group-Captain Benson. By the beginning of the last week in September the forward troops of the Eighth Army were well clear of the province of Bari, whose northern boundary was the limit of 'King's Italy', and the city of Foggia was captured on 27th September. Allied troops advanced quickly northwards. By 1st October armoured patrols had reached Serracapriola and Canadian troops had reached Lucera, while two days later, as the result of a combined Commando operation, Termoli was captured. By the middle of October the whole of the province was in Allied hands. The possession of Foggia with its very large airfields was one of the important strategic objectives of the campaign, since from these airfields, which became the headquarters of the Strategic Allied Air Force in the Mediterranean, extensive attacks not only on the Balkans but on southern Germany could be undertaken. From the point of view of AMGOT its importance was also very great, since it was the centre of the largest grain producing area of southern Italy, upon which the feeding of Naples as well as of Apulia depended.

The town, whose normal population was rather over 60,000, had suffered enormously from Allied bombardment, and all but a very small proportion of its population had fled into the surrounding countryside. Public utilities had been sabotaged by the Germans, who had blown up power-transformer stations and severely damaged the Apulian aqueduct, upon which not only Foggia but many towns in the south of the *compartimento* were dependent for their water supply. This was repaired comparatively quickly by the help of Allied Engineers, but sewers had been badly damaged by bombing, and from 1,500 to 2,000 bodies of civilians were estimated to have been buried under the debris of destroyed or damaged buildings. There were thus present in an acute form all the usual problems facing AMGOT on entry into a heavily damaged town, and they were complicated by an extraneous factor.

In order to organise Foggia airfield with the least possible delay as a base for offensive operations, the advance unit of the Allied Air Force (XII U.S. Bomber Command) proceeded immediately to requisition every habitable building, including the *Municipio*, and

[1] Region IV was originally designed to embrace the two *compartimenti* of Lazio and Abruzzi—Molise, but they were subsequently separated. Abruzzi—Molise was coupled with the Marche to make Region V and Lazio was eventually united in Region IV with Umbria.

it was only with the greatest difficulty that some accommodation could be found for AMGOT. Meanwhile the branches of the provincial administration had been dispersed, under the influence of Allied bombing, into various towns in the province, the Prefect being installed in the castle of Bovino, some thirty miles away, and the problem of reassembling these scattered fragments of the provincial administration was not easily solved. For a considerable time a number of the branches of the Italian administration had to be accommodated in AMGOT headquarters. The resulting chaos can readily be imagined. The American Air Force finally decided to evacuate the whole civil population from the town and turn the area into a military cantonment—so great was their demand for space and for requisitioned furniture. From the administrative point of view this was at any rate a logical solution. Orders were consequently issued forbidding the evacuated townsfolk to return even to fetch their belongings, but these could not be enforced. This decision was finally revised by A.F.H.Q. and a halt was called to the requisitions of the U.S. Air Force, with the result that AMGOT and the municipal administration, which was being turned into the streets, eventually obtained sufficient accommodation to carry on. A house was finally found also for the provincial administration. Since the shortage of accommodation was almost equally acute in the other towns of the province on the direct line of the Eighth Army's advance, the attempt to instal the administration of the province in another town had to be abandoned.

AMGOT, Eighth Army, was not greatly worried in the province of Foggia by the problem of food, though in the outlying communes the question of distribution gave rise to some difficulties owing to the shortage of transport. The machinery of rationing somehow kept functioning, however imperfectly, and there was enough grain in the province to provide small stocks for the provinces of Campobasso and Chieti to the north, and to make some, albeit a small, contribution to the feeding of Naples and Salerno. The most serious immediate problems were those concerned with public utilities, water, electricity, sanitation, and above all refugees—a problem which became increasingly urgent with every advance up to the Winter Line. That advance was comparatively rapid up to Campobasso, occupied on 14th October. Vinchiaturo was occupied the following day, and after a pause of about a fortnight it continued northwards. But it was contested inch by inch by severe fighting, notably in the battle of the Sangro at the beginning of November. Not till close on the end of the year was it finally bogged down by weather conditions on the line Ortona-Orsogna.

Thus from the provinces of Chieti, Campobasso and Foggia a stream of refugees began to flow southwards. The evacuation of civilians from the Army area had to be organised by AMGOT. The elements of which this stream was composed were roughly the following: civilians and soldiers who had come from the other side of the German lines, *sfollati*, i.e. persons who had been bombed out, and civilians who had been turned out of their homes by the armed forces—no small number, since in most towns lying in the route of the Eighth Army's advance the scale of war damage was very heavy and the remaining accommodation was often required for military purposes. Moreover in many of the towns the destruction of public utilities and sanitation made it desirable to evacuate the population. The stream of evacuees also included non-Italian displaced persons, mostly aliens interned in concentration camps by the Italians as the result of the war and liberated by the Allied advance.

The evacuation of this miscellany of people created a number of different problems. First, 'screening': all persons, whether military or civilians, coming across the enemy lines had to be carefully scrutinised and interrogated by the Field Security authorities for obvious reasons. To help 'screen' refugee soldiers, a staff of Italian officers was sent up from 'King's Italy'. Next, assembly and transport: the scarcity of accommodation in the area made it necessary to use prisoners-of-war cages for assembling and staging, transport being provided in army lorries. Next, feeding: supplies for these destitute persons while in army areas had also had to be provided from army sources. Finally, arrangements had to be made for the treatment of casualties, wherever possible in Italian civilian hospitals, often desperately short of essential medical supplies, though arrangement had been made by which forty tons of medical supplies were sent up from Naples. Quite apart from refugees, civilian casualties in Eighth Army area were very great, often quite beyond the capacity of existing civilian hospitals, with the result that serious emergency cases had to be treated in the British military hospitals. In Campobasso, a civilian hospital was for some time actually taken over by Eighth Army medical officers and run by them for the benefit of the local inhabitants.

Some idea of the size of the refugee problem may be gathered from the statistics of the numbers of persons evacuated from the Eighth Army area during the month of November, which amounted to at least 8,500.[1] During this month the southward flow of refugees, etc., increased from 100 to over 500 a day. From September 1943 to the end of January 1944 the recorded movement on the Eighth Army front amounted to over 30,000 persons. The equivalent total on the Fifth Army front was only about 1,800, but thereafter the relative

[1] This figure probably represents a considerable under-estimate, since it is based only on the rations issued at railhead and a considerable number of refugees must have moved southwards by other routes.

position on the two fronts was reversed, the major flow occurring on the west coast. In order to deal with this problem a special organisation under the command of the S.C.A.O., Eighth Army, was built-up as a sub-division of the Public Health and Welfare Division of A.M.G., Fifteenth Army Group,[1] to work in cooperation with the Displaced Persons Sub-Commission.

In Foggia and Campobasso provinces the administrative machine continued to work without any great disturbance. The Prefects of both cooperated well, though it was a little difficult at first to make clear to the Prefect of Foggia, a General appointed by Marshal Badoglio, the limits of his authority, a matter which was certainly not rendered any easier by a visit from the King of Italy on 30th September. Nor was it altogether easy to make the Italian Government understand that its authority ended at the northern boundary of Bari province.[2] Difficulties of this kind were however rapidly solved after the organisation of the Allied Control Commission.

But political difficulties of quite another character soon began to appear, as the result of the refusal of the renascent political parties to co-operate with the King and the Marshal. These looked like developing into an underground left-wing opposition in territory under A.M.G., until the ban on open political activity contained in the directive of the Combined Chiefs of Staff was removed. This underground activity showed itself in various ways, for example, by the organisation of demonstrations, not of an openly political character, but disguised as meetings of protest by women against the stopping of military family allowances to dependents of Italian soldiers in German-occupied territory, and by the refusal of relief payments substituted for them, though these were on a higher scale; by the invasion of a *municipio* and the destruction of municipal records, and by the sudden appearance of crowds to demand salt, or to complain of difficulties in respect of rationing, or of getting wheat milled—all manifestations of public unrest suspected by Lord Rennell as being of political origin. Another form was the denunciation of officials as Fascists to the Allied authorities. During the few weeks preceding the armistice the Badoglio Government had changed most of the Prefects, but the 'defascistisation' of the other ranks of the administration and of the municipal services had for the most part been suspended owing to the influence of the King. Consequently a large number of persons on the Field Security Services' black-lists were still in office. Moreover such new appointments as had been made by the Marshal were scarcely of a nature to appeal to the left-wing

---

[1] For the constitution of this unit, see below, pp. 96-97.

[2] Thus on 12th November the Prefect of Foggia was appointed by the Chief of Staff of the Italian Army to be Commander-in-Chief of the CC.RR., the same letter replacing him as Prefect by another General.

parties. It cannot be doubted that this opportunity was used by the Communists and other left-wing cliques to denounce as Fascist any officials whom they disliked, and it is difficult to resist the conclusion that the Field Security authorities often unwittingly lent themselves to intrigues of this nature.

During the advance up the Adriatic coast to the Winter line the technique was developed of installing static Military Government progressively as the Eighth Army moved forward. A.M.G. Eighth Army was essentially a mobile organisation. It consisted of groups of 'spearhead' C.A.O's and C.A.P.O's working in touch with corps and division liaison officers, but under direct command of the S.C.A.O. who was responsible for their deployment, and a H.Q. staff divided into two sections—a small mobile staff, including the S.C.A.O., who lived in caravans, advancing with main Army H.Q., and the main body which remained at Army Rear H.Q., together with the Control Commission's regional teams that were to stay permanently in the areas taken over after the Army had moved forward. The 'spearhead' officers formed a permanent mobile cadre, which meant that the C.A.O's remained with their formations and moved on with them. Arrangements had therefore to be made for a permanent administration to take their place as they advanced. In order to minimise the administrative change involved by the moving on of the 'spearhead' A.M.G., permanent C.A.O's were introduced from the regional organisation before the 'spearhead' officers moved forward.

The 'spearhead' phase may be considered as divided into two stages. During the first stage, immediately after the capture of a town, the communal administration was the point of immediate impact upon which the C.A.O's were set to work. As this became organised, and when the provincial capital fell into Allied hands, it became possible for the 'spearhead' team to organise a rudimentary provincial organisation of all the communes under a 'spearhead' S.C.A.O. During this phase the call-forward of officers from the regional staff took place. When this was completed, and the moment came for the 'spearhead' organisation to move on, the Regional A.M.G. officers were already *in situ*, though they remained under the command of Group-Captain Benson until the rear army boundary moved forward. The purpose of this system was to ensure that the heritage of locally acquired knowledge, so essential to an improvised administration, was passed on without loss. Thus Foggia commune was entered by the Allies on 27th September and a 'spearhead' A.M.G. officer followed next day. Before the last week in October the province had been organised under a provincial S.C.A.O., who handed over to the future Regional S.C.A.O. of the province by the beginning of November. But the administration of the province was not handed over by A.M.G. Eighth Army to Region IV until December.

Thanks to the system of liaison officers the relations between A.M.G. and the combat forces quickly improved. The higher formations, particularly, began to appreciate its functions and its difficulties. Thus, whenever operational considerations allowed, they were prepared to help A.M.G. with its perpetual problem of transport for the distribution of food-stuffs. But operational considerations in a hardly-contested advance frequently did not so permit. Transport remained the principal problem of A.M.G. administration throughout the campaign. Relations of A.M.G. with lower formations were not always so easy. The conduct of the troops in the matter of looting civilian property was often anything but exemplary, and the reports of some of the 'spearhead' officers on this subject make most unpleasant reading. Nor was the task of A.M.G. made any easier by the repeated mishandling by combat troops of the *Carabinieri*, the employment of whom as messenger boys by combat units was bitterly complained of by one C.A.P.O.

The contingent of A.M.G. officers to accompany the Fifth Army in its landings at Salerno, and to constitute Region III in its rear after the capture of Naples, was organised by General McSherry in Algiers. Its international composition was approximately two-thirds American and one-third British, and its personnel was derived chiefly from the Military Government School and Holding Centre at Tizi-Ouzou, stiffened with a few experienced officers from Sicily. Command of the detachment was given to Colonel Hume, an officer of the American Army Medical Corps, who had been Colonel Cheyne's assistant in Sicily. His previous experience of pestilence and famine in charge of relief organisation in Serbia after the First World War, and earlier as medical director of the American Relief Expedition to Italy after the Avezzano earthquake of 1915, was singularly appropriate in view of the chief problems to be encountered by Region III in Naples during its early days. The deputy S.C.A.O. and Chief of Staff A.M.G. Fifth Army/Region III was a British officer, Colonel J. O. M. Ashley. The total strength amounted to 150 officers and 225 E.M./O.R's, with approximately 80 vehicles.[1] The detachment had to be organised in a considerable hurry, as officers attached to the tactical units started to leave Tizi-Ouzou for various embarkation areas stretched from Tunis to Oran as early as 20th August. Tables of organisation and equipment were received too late to enable anything

[1] 1 Staff car (British), 2 C and R cars (American), 23 Jeeps, some with trailers, 10 British utility cars and about 40 lorries, British and American, varying in condition from new (very few) to very old.

but a very few items, which were immedately available, to be drawn. A.M.G. officers took with them little else besides their personal kit, flags, proclamations, armbands for civil police, a little stationery and some cash. 'Provided that they had a jeep and a trailer with spare petrol and water cans, they asked for little or nothing more except a tent and a typewriter'.

In 'Avalanche' (the Salerno landings) the great defect of A.M.G. 'Husky' operations—'too few, too late'—was actually reversed. Owing to the slow initial progress made by the invading forces, the number of Civil Affairs officers landed during the early stages of the operation appeared to be in excess of local requirements. Living mainly on or near the beaches, in open fields and orchards, and frequently in slit trenches, these 'Aged Military Gentlemen On Tour'—to use the irreverent nickname given them in Sicily by some of the more supercilious operational units—shared the lot of the combatant troops in every respect. (One British officer was posted missing, believed killed, several others and some O.R's were wounded.) The first landings in the bay took place in the early morning of 9th September, and A.M.G. officers were ashore in various places only a few hours later. The C.A.O. for Salerno city landed on the beaches on 10th September and entered the town on the day of its capture, shortly before 35 Field Security Section, who after their arrival immediately contacted AMGOT in the *Municipio*, where it had installed itself. Region H.Q. was set up a little later at Agropoli. At this centre, under very difficult conditions, various drafts of A.M.G. specialist officers were collected, after landing at various points in the bay during the second and third weeks in September. Since the distances from extreme points in Region III were very much smaller than those in Region II, there was no need to distinguish between a 'spearhead' and a 'regional' Civil Affairs officer. The officers entering a town immediately on liberation were the 'static' A.M.G. contingent destined to remain there as part of Region III. There was no necessity to keep Army A.M.G. and Regional H.Q. as separate entities, and the actual separation was not made until nearly three months after the occupation of Naples.

With the enemy up in the hills only about three-quarters of a mile away, Salerno was for a week or more continually under fire, and a large proportion of the population had fled, leaving only a few thousand people in the town. A.M.G. had therefore immediately to tackle the problem of keeping roads clear for the Allied forces from a stream of returning refugees. All public utilities were out of action. The Germans had removed as much food and transport as they could lay hands on, and the population in the town itself and the neighbouring town of Vietri were verging on starvation. Owing to the continued fighting round the bridgehead, it was impossible to introduce supplies for civilians while maintenance of the troops was still being carried out over the beaches. But AMGOT Supply officers were able, after the first few days, to arrange for the movement of stocks which were discovered hidden in the hills, and thus to avoid the occurrence of any actual famine, since vegetables and fruit in the area helped to stave off starvation. There was considerable looting by the population in the earlier phases, which the *Carabinieri* were unable to control. Their treatment by the troops—they were frequently arrested—left much to be desired and greatly hindered their efficiency. Looting by Allied troops also added to the difficulties.

One of the first tasks of AMGOT on its establishment in Salerno was to organise the recruiting of a supply of labour for the troops, to work on the beaches and handle cargo off the convoys and at the dumps. It was impossible at the outset to reorganise the existing labour exchanges, as the offices of the various provincial 'Unions' of workers were destroyed and the personnel almost entirely dispersed. After the Allied advance towards Naples, they began to return and report for duty, and when the Prefect, who had been absent through illness at the time of the landings, returned he was able to assist in putting them back into action. Arrangements were made with him to take over the provincial 'Unions' and run them as labour exchanges under the control of the Provincial Economic Council (*Consiglio Provinciale dell' Economia*), of which he was president, for the supply of labour for civilian needs and to assist the military when required. In the meantime D.A.D.L. of X Corps (British) had already improvised arrangements for supplying army needs, in which A.M.G. participated. In areas outside the director's sphere of operation, the Civil Affairs Officers found labour for military needs through the mayors of the various communes.

The other task in which AMGOT was able to offer considerable direct assistance to the army was the handling of refugees, who crowded the roads in vast numbers and constituted an obvious danger to security. No Refugee Officers had been allowed for in the original A.M.G. table of organisation, and there had been no time to plan the handling of refugees beforehand in co-operation with the Military Security Services. As the southern flank of the bridgehead was practically open, there was nothing at first to prevent the stream of individuals from the south trying to reach Naples. During the advance on that city there was an even larger stream from the opposite direction, from evacuated forward divisional areas towards the rear. These could not be allowed out of the Army areas, as they might get round the flank, back through the hills, and carry information to the enemy. Both streams of refugees contained civilians, but they consisted mostly of Italian soldiers dispersing as the result of the announcement of the armistice. There was considerable doubt as to how these should be treated. Efforts were made to collect them and form them into labour companies, but legal difficulties regarding the Allied right to use compulsion in the new circumstances, and the disorder caused by shell-fire and bombing, prevented these enterprising efforts of the Army Labour officers from being effective. Considerable irritation was caused to Allied troops by the sight of British and American soldiers working on the roads, while able-bodied Italian ex-soldiers looked on.

AMGOT did what it could to help to remedy this disorderly state of affairs. The Regional C.A.P.O. laid out a programme for establishing control points in appropriate stations, at which all refugees were handled, questioned, and, after proper investigation by the military security authorities, given cards of identification. But the feeding of these refugees constituted a very difficult problem, in view of the shortage of supplies for ordinary civilian needs, as well as the provision of shelter. Many of them had temporarily to be put in gaols.

In the general confusion following the landings in Salerno Bay, AMGOT came in for a good deal of criticism from other branches of the Services for their tardiness in coping with these problems. Accusations of ineptitude were certainly not lacking, but in spite of all the initial chaos no major disorders among the civilian population occurred such as to necessitate the diversion of the attention of the Army Commander from his tactical tasks. Though a much ampler provision of transport had been made for A.M.G., shortage of vehicles continued to hamper the efficiency of its operations. The outstanding difficulty was the lack of the jeep-type of vehicle. Nearly all the four-wheel-drive vehicles had to be kept with the C.A.O's in Corps area, and specialist officers could not be fully employed because of this shortage, even after Naples was reached and many civilian cars had been requisitioned. Another shortage was motorcycles, of which there were only five, not nearly enough to supply an adequate despatch-rider service. This was urgently required, since the normal army systems of communications, which could only give AMGOT a low priority, were both too complicated and too slow.

But the difficulties encountered by AMGOT in the Salerno area were mere child's play compared with those which were awaiting it at Naples. Alarming reports about the conditions which would be encountered in that city, with its close on a million inhabitants, had begun to trickle in from various sources ever since the beginning of September. The town was reported to be on the verge of starvation, and cholera and typhus were stated to have broken out. The Duchess of Aosta was said to have reported from Naples that the whole city was in complete disorder, without doctors, drugs or communications, and that the administration had completely broken down. Lord Rennell therefore sent a message to the Military Government Section

(M.G.S.) at A.F.H.Q. asking them to reinforce Region III medical personnel immediately, and to send adequate additional medical stores as well as food. M.G.S., after consulting the Chief Surgeon, replied that stocks of cholera, typhus and typhoid vaccines within that theatre were sufficient, and could be flown to Naples in case of need, but in view of the reported break in the chief aqueduct he considered typhoid more probable then typhus or cholera. As an emergency food supply, 1,200 tons of flour, 650 tons of dehydrated soup, 175 tons of milk and 75 tons of army biscuit had been loaded with Fifth Army maintenance for A.M.G., as well as several 'Civil Affairs Division' (C.A.D.) units of medical stores which had been prepared in America for A.M.G. use. A Naval Situation Report on 19th September stated that refugees reported cholera and typhus rampant in the city, but ten days later A.F.H.Q. informed the Combined Chiefs of Staff that intelligence reports indicated that there was no foundation for the rumour of epidemics in the city—a judgment which proved to be rather optimistic.

On 1st October Naples fell to the Allies. Brigadier-General McSherry and Colonel Hume formally received the surrender of the city from the Italian civil authorities, proceeding thereafter to the *Municipio*, where contact was made with the provincial and municipal authorities. The full A.M.G. staffs intended for the city, which had been billeted at Castellamare, were brought in on the same day, and the headquarters staff of Region III was called forward from Agropoli. AMGOT headquarters moved into the city on 2nd October. Though it was discovered on entry that the rumours of plague, pestilence and famine had been somewhat exaggerated, conditions were serious enough. Food was extremely short, but the most acute trouble was the almost complete absence of water, which in a city of a million inhabitants, more than a half of whom were still in the town, portended serious trouble. In addition to some damage from Allied bombing, the main aqueduct supplying the city had suffered from deliberate German sabotage, which had blown up the main bridge and demolished it in no less than seven places, and all reservoirs, except one small one, had been drained. That one had only been saved from German sabotage by the action of an Italian, who had cut the fuse intended to demolish it after the Germans had actually set it alight. When Allied troops entered, there was only a small trickle of water from a few hydrants, besieged by queues of people with pails and water jugs, many of whom were unable to receive enough to quench their thirst. This situation was relieved by the prompt action of Fifth Army engineers, who established distribution points for water distilled from the sea-water of the bay, and placed guards at these points to prevent the larger and stronger of the inhabitants from denying access to women and children.

AMGOT immediately took charge of the secondary aqueduct, which was still functioning and by severe rationing of long queues made the supply go as far as possible, but the suffering caused was considerable. With the assistance of Army engineers the work of restoring the supply was started immediately. In four days some supply was obtained from the main aqueduct, but it was a fortnight before all the districts of the city could be provided even with a moderate quantity.

Great damage had been caused to the main sewers, and the sabotaging of the electric power-mains and sewage pumping machinery was so extensive that, even if water had been available, the sewers could still not have functioned, since the sewage system was in large part so constructed as to require pumping from low levels. Efforts were made by articles in the newspaper published under the control of the Psychological Welfare Branch of A.F.H.Q. (P.W.B) and by notices posted to instruct the public in the elementary sanitary precautions to be taken, but, considering the habits of large numbers of the population, it was something of a miracle that no outbreak of water-borne typhoid or dysentery occurred. Fortunately, before the month was far gone the rainy season had started. Hard downpours enabled people to collect water in pans and helped to flush out most of the sewer system. Meanwhile the pumping machinery had been given emergency repairs by Fifth Army engineers in record time—the main reason why no epidemics of typhoid or dysentery occurred—and by the end of the month a limited amount of electric power for pumping was available.

The head of the Public Health service reported to General Mc Sherry, on his entry, that there was no cholera or typhus. The latter statement, as events subsequently showed, was quite incorrect. On 5th October General Eisenhower informed the Combined Chiefs of Staff that his Director of Medical Service had visited Naples and had discovered only thirteen cases of typhus, and for some weeks it was still possible for the inhabitants and the local medical authorities to conceal the presence of this disease. In the end, it was the absence of soap rather than of water which gave rise to this louse-borne epidemic. The initial public health arrangements for Region III were inadequate, the number of Public Health officers being much too small, but even so, according to one competent opinion, steps might have been taken earlier to counter the conditions leading to the outbreak. Here, as in Syracuse, a considerable portion of refugees to escape from Allied bombing had taken to living in shelters in the caves, and it was these troglodyte conditions which were largely responsible for the propagation of the typhus epidemic.[1]

---

[1] As a Senior A.M.G. Officer remarked, 'The typhus scare might never have developed had senior Civil Affairs officers paid more visits early on to the poorer quarters, and especially the air-raid shelters'.

Electricity was another initial shortage. On arrival no electric current was available, since German sabotage had completed very thoroughly the work begun by Allied bombing. The principal thermal generating station had been demolished beyond possibility of immediate repair, but two of the three high-voltage sub-stations were in better condition, some of the hydro-electric installations in the vicinity were found virtually intact, and ways were found to make immediate repairs in the transmission system. By these means it was possible before the end of the month to furnish the city with a small regular supply of power, which was carefully rationed according to strict priorities, first and foremost military needs, then hospitals, flour mills, and the water system. In the meantime an emergency supply for the port area and for pumping some water into the city was produced by using the engines of two Italian submarines lying in the harbour.

Food was in very short supply, but on the day following the occupation AMGOT officers succeeded in discovering certain stocks which had been hidden in the surrounding country to save them from the Germans. These were distributed by the rationing authorities, but the amount was very small. And though port facilities were restored by the U.S. Base organisation so quickly that six days after the capture of the city shipments of flour and milk for the civilian population were being unloaded at the rate of 200 tons a day, this quantity was not enough to enable AMGOT to distribute a daily ration in Naples of more than 100 grams—a quantity insufficient for proper nutrition. Conditions in Salerno were no better. The competition of the military services for shipping and for the limited berthing facilities of the port did not allow imports for civilian purposes on any adequate scale. But even such imports as had been agreed in the planning for 'Avalanche' failed to arrive, since the arrangements which had been made to procure food-stuffs from the United States broke down badly, owing to the mishandling by the Military Government Section at A.F.H.Q. of the process of calling forward. Emergency supplies planned for the period immediately following the Salerno landings and the capture of Naples arrived according to schedule, but the bids for supplies called forward by Lord Rennell to arrive in November were never dealt with at all by the Military Government Section. Nothing came, not even an acknowledgement from A.F.H.Q. that the bids had been received, or that arrangements were in progress. And worse was to follow. Owing to some error, for which it would appear that the Military Government Section was ultimately responsible, the civilian supplies which had been called forward were not included in two of the three convoys from the United States due to arrive in December. These had been notified to Lord Rennell as conveying some 40,000 tons of flour, of which over 10,000 tons had been earmarked, prematurely as it turned out, for the feeding of Rome. But even though the allowance set aside for Rome was available for other places in southern Italy, actual arrivals left AMGOT still over 15,000 tons short on expected arrivals. The situation was only saved, in the sense that real starvation was avoided, by the delivery of some 6,000 tons of wheat from the Middle East, and the borrowing—against replacement—of 20,000 tons of breadstuffs from French North Africa. Even so, for about three months the population surrounding the Bays of Naples and Salerno went very short of food, to the point of severe malnutrition.[1]

Nor was the failure of imported supplies the only problem. The whole machinery of distribution throughout the Region was almost brought to a standstill by the lack of civilian transport. In Naples the Germans had removed or destroyed practically all mechanical transport, even that used by city authorities for the removal of refuse. A similar policy had been applied in the other provinces of the Region. And since railways were not available, it was not possible to move into the city in any quantity even such small surpluses as could be extracted from the stocks existing in the Foggia district and in the province of Matera. Naples, which consumed more than the Campanian plain produced, was therefore largely dependent upon imports brought in by the Allies, and it was clear that the position of Rome would be no better. There was thus the most urgent need to ensure that in the competition for supplies and shipping the needs of AMGOT and the civilian population should be kept in the picture, in respect of both food and military transport.

By the middle of December the position had become so critical that military action on the highest level was taken. The confusion arising out of the administrative relations between A.M.G. and A.C.C., which had not yet organised a Food sub-commission, made a drastic change imperative. Responsibility for feeding the Italian people was taken out of the hands of A.C.C. and temporarily transferred to General Robertson, who was put in charge of a Central Economic Committee, whose chief executive officer was controller of civilian food. This arrangement—never intended to be permanent—only lasted for a few weeks, but it filled a dangerous gap while the Allied Control Commission was organising a Food sub-commission, with which it ought originally to have been provided; and it performed a useful service by compelling at any rate some staff officers to recognise that civilian needs are an essential element of operational requirements. The immediate result was that military transport was made available to A.M.G. for food distribution on a

[1] There was even some evidence of actual starvation in one or two isolated instances.

substantial scale, and that in the theatre generally the significance of civil supplies began to acquire a truer perspective. Pressure was also brought by A.F.H.Q. on the Combined Chiefs of Staff in Washington.[1]

Meanwhile the necessity for feeding the civilian population was clearly recognised as a military responsibility by General Eisenhower, who frankly accepted the conclusion that this might involve, with the limited resources at his disposal, some sacrifice in military build-up and maintenance. Shortly before leaving the theatre to assume the supreme command of the invasion of northern Europe, he laid down the following principle in an administrative instruction dated 19th December:

> The primary interest of this headquarters in meeting the minimum food requirements in Italy is to avoid interference with military operations. It may be an over-riding military consideration that the civil population be fed. In emergencies where the consideration involves direct interference with military build-up and maintenance the decision of the General Officer Commanding-in-Chief Fifteenth Army Group will govern.

In the face of the not unnatural tendency of the lower, and not only the lower, military formations to consider the needs of AMGOT as marginal, i.e. to be sacrificed in case of difficulties, this statement by the Supreme Commander, as Lord Rennell remarked 'put the supply of civilian requirements in its right perspective'. After the reorganisation of the supply arrangements in the Military Government Section at A.F.H.Q., following on the failures related earlier in this chapter, the position improved somewhat, so that a 200 gm (7 oz.) bread-ration for the whole of southern Italy could be established in February and distributed. But, as will appear in later chapters, imported civilian supplies still too often tended to be looked upon as 'marginal', especially when the pressure in world shipping resources made itself felt with increasing weight in the Mediterranean theatre towards the end of the year. The margin of safety for A.M.G. was often indeed a narrow one.

In the midst of these initial difficulties AMGOT Fifth Army/Region III in Naples, as in Salerno, had lost no time in embarking on one of its more important, though less spectacular, functions of helping to procure labour for the use of occupying forces. The head of the Labour Section arrived in Naples on the day following its capture and opened up a Labour Exchange immediately with sections for dealing with clerical workers, skilled and unskilled

---

[1] Cf. the message sent by A.F.H.Q. on 14th December 1943. 'Conditions in Southern Italy and Sicily are such that unless reasonable quantities of food are supplied very promptly we will experience sabotage, unrest and a complete cessation of those activities necessary to our advance'.

manual workers and port labour. Meanwhile an independent exchange for recruiting labour was set up by the Navy, for port and naval installations, with which AMGOT cooperated, supplying office personnel, interpreters, engineers, etc., and meeting emergency calls for common labour. Labour demands from the Peninsula Base Section and for 57th Area in Naples City were entirely dealt with by AMGOT exchange.

The reception of the Allied forces by the Neapolitans left nothing to be desired. The Germans, who naturally enough regarded the conclusion of the armistice as a piece of bare-faced treachery on the part of their ally, had behaved accordingly, and had provoked a rising on the part of certain sections of the populace against their retreating rearguard. There was thus no difficulty to be apprehended from a hostile resistance movement. The difficulties in maintaining public order, in spite of the initial absence of both light and water, were not great, and the cooperation of the *Carabinieri* was quickly obtained. But as in Sicily the problem of the black market proved insoluble. There were cases, too, in which the *Carabinieri* found themselves exceedingly unpopular when they attempted to enforce certain A.M.G. orders. Thus, for example, at Centola in the province of Salerno a riot broke out at the end of November, on the attempt by the *Carabinieri* to enforce the A.M.G. Regional Order requiring farmers to deliver to the *ammassi*, on loan, forty per cent of the amount of corn they were permitted to retain themselves for seed and the feeding of their families—an emergency order which had been made for the purpose of feeding the hungry city of Naples. Some *Carabinieri* were attacked, wounded and disarmed, but next day reinforcements led by the C.A.O., assisted by a small party of twelve men under a corporal of the Royal Air Force, restored order.[1] But riots even on this small scale were rare and isolated instances. The chief difficulties in connection with the maintenance of public order came from quite a different source, the behaviour of the members of the Allied forces, particularly in Naples, where the temptations of drink and women were apt to lead to trouble. But troubles of this sort occur in every military occupation.

The financial arrangements planned for 'Avalanche' were practically identical with those of 'Husky', except for detailed improvements suggested by Sicilian experience. One important modification was the decision to make use immediately of the existing central banking machinery of the *Banca d'Italia*, helped out by A.M.F.A. as lender of last resort. Here too they worked without a hitch. Emergency cash needs for the Salerno operations were provided by 16,000 yellow-seal dollars, supplemented a few days after the landings by

[1] This was one of the very few instances in which Allied forces were requested to come to the aid of A.M.G. to restore public order.

nearly 100 million A.M. lire brought in by the deputy Regional Finance Officer. Cash reserves of the banks in Naples were rather better than had been expected, since the *Banca d'Italia* had only a fortnight before the capture of the city received from Rome 250 million lire in cash; but reserves were not considered sufficient to enable banks to be opened for anything but very restricted withdrawals before a supply of A.M. lire, amounting to almost a thousand million, had been received from Palermo. This arrived on 21st October and 600 millions were placed into an account in the Bank at Naples for the purpose of making advances to other banks, to enable them to cover their cash requirements. Banks were re-opened for unrestricted withdrawals and the moratorium was withdrawn on 30th October. Meanwhile earlier in the month special arrangements had been made for certain large industrial companies to withdraw from their own safe-deposit boxes sufficient cash to meet their payrolls. Banks in Naples borrowed over a hundred million lire from the *Banca d'Italia* for the purpose of re-opening, but deposits soon exceeded withdrawals and by the end of November all but a few millions had been repaid.

In Naples, no less than in Sicily, the impact of the Allied occupation was immediately and intensely inflationary, and the attempt to hold prices at the existing level broke down completely, not without a considerable diminution in the prestige of AMGOT, which found itself quite unable to enforce its regulations. With the official rate of exchange at 400 to the pound sterling and a military wage-rate often more than twice the existing rate for civil labour, the task was hopeless. As Colonel Ashley remarked, the possibility of enforcing a list of maximum prices depends on the fulfilment of three conditions, the availability of the goods, an efficient rationing system, and a police force capable of enforcing the law, none of which were in fact in existence in Naples at the time of its capture. It might perhaps have been better, as he suggests, to have attempted to control only one or two commodities like flour and olive oil, and to have ensured the provision of adequate supplies of these to meet the diminished ration, a task in which for some months A.M.G. was only partially successful. Instead, the attempt was made, in order to protect the Allied soldier and sailor from exploitation, to control, besides the prices of many of the necessities of civilian life, also those of luxury articles like jewelry and silk stockings—an attempt which only ended in driving these commodities also underground into the black market.

Thanks to the excellent relations established by Colonel Hume with Lieut.-General Clark and his staff at Fifth Army Headquarters, the initial tasks of AMGOT were enormously facilitated by the immediate decision of the Commanding General to divert military engineers, with all the necessary materials—including temporary bridging to carry it over a valley—to the repair of the sabotaged main aqueduct, and in many other ways to assist in the restoration of public utilities. Relations with lower formations, especially static formations like the Peninsula Base Section and the 57th Area, were not so good, largely owing to the lack of opportunity for common planning. A number of misunderstandings took place, some of which might have had disastrous consequences. One of these arose from the occupation by British A.A. gunners and R.A.F. other ranks of the principal hospital for infectious diseases, just at the time when the typhus epidemic was developing, and their refusal to evacuate it until pressure was put upon them from the highest quarters. Nor were relations with the Field Security Services and the Counter-Intelligence Corps in the early stages very satisfactory. As in Sicily, prisons were filled with individuals against whom nothing was known, Italian police officers were promiscuously arrested, public officials were removed by Security officers on hearsay from discontented local inhabitants—a phenomenon which also occurred in the Eighth Army area—and C.I.C. officers in the early days were too apt to do A.M.G. 'spearhead' work on their own. In Naples in particular, liaison with the military security staff was not as good as it should have been, the blame in many cases lying equally on both sides[1], and there was at first no adequate machinery to effect any reasonable compromise between witch-hunting and administrative efficiency. But these were after all mostly teething troubles. Some of them might however have been avoided, had the Military Government Section in Algiers arranged for a sufficient number of AMGOT officers with actual experience in Sicily to be posted to Region III.

The initial organisation of A.M.G. Fifth Army/Region III differed considerably from that of the Eighth Army A.M.G., owing to the different nature of the territory occupied. Eighth Army had moved fast through a mainly rural area with a few big towns, while Fifth Army had only moved the comparatively short distance from Salerno to the Volturno, and later the Garigliano, its main interest being concentrated on the large urban area of the Bay of Naples, whose port remained the principal import centre of the Army's supply axis until the capture of Leghorn in the summer of 1944, and the main political focus of liberated Italy until the occupation of Rome. A.M.G. Fifth Army and A.M.G. Region III consequently operated as a single unit, Colonel Hume, the S.C.A.O., concentrating on the administration of Naples and liaison with the Army Com-

[1] Security officers often wanted to remove Italian personnel with high technical qualifications who were absolutely essential to AMGOT administration. For example, they arrested one of the most prominent bankers on his way home from an important meeting with AMGOT officers. On the other hand, some divisions of AMGOT, in their zeal to create an efficient administration in their particular department, often had no compunction in employing obvious Fascists.

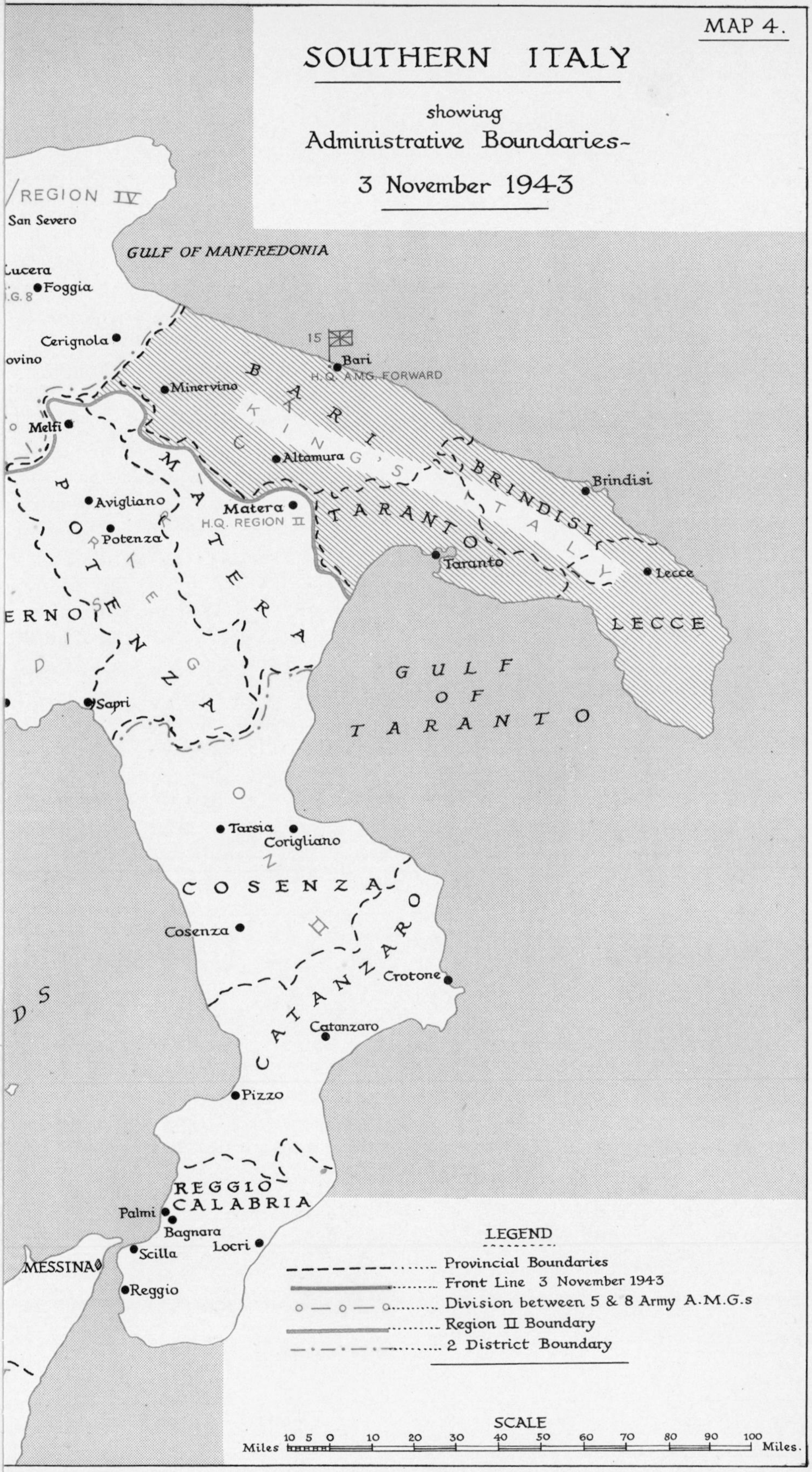

MAP 4.

SOUTHERN ITALY

showing

Administrative Boundaries–

3 November 1943

REGION IV
San Severo
GULF OF MANFREDONIA
Lucera
Foggia
Cerignola
Bari
H.Q. A.M.G. FORWARD
Minervino
Melfi
BARI
KINGS ITALY
Altamura
Brindisi
BRINDISI
Avigliano
Matera
H.Q. REGION II
TARANTO
Potenza
POTENZA
MATERA
Taranto
Lecce
LECCE
Sapri
GULF OF TARANTO
Tarsia
Corigliano
COSENZA
Cosenza
CATANZARO
Crotone
Catanzaro
Pizzo
REGGIO CALABRIA
Palmi
Bagnara
Locri
Scilla
MESSINA
Reggio

LEGEND

- Provincial Boundaries
- Front Line 3 November 1943
- Division between 5 & 8 Army A.M.G.s
- Region II Boundary
- 2 District Boundary

SCALE

Miles 10 5 0 10 20 30 40 50 60 70 80 90 100 Miles.

mander, and his deputy, Colonel Ashley, on Military Government in the Army areas and in the provinces. It was not until December that A.M.G. Fifth Army and Region III were officially separated and a Regional S.C.A.O. appointed, Colonel (Brigadier-General) Hume remaining S.C.A.O. of Fifth Army A.M.G. with Colonel Ashley as his deputy.

After its separation from Region III, A.M.G. Fifth Army, except for the Rome unit, became, like A.M.G. Eighth Army, an essentially 'spearhead' formation. General Hume's organisation differed somewhat in detail from that of Group Captain Benson. In accordance with the American tradition, the 'spearhead' officers were assigned to formations. Each Corps had a Senior Civil Affairs Officer, with Civil Affairs Officers under him attached to each division. A.M.G. Corps headquarters also contained a Public Safety Officer and a Supply Officer. In the summer of 1944 IV Corps A.M.G. was enlarged so as to include an Engineering Officer, a Finance and Legal Officer—a curious combination—and a Public Health Officer. The chain of command ran down from A.M.G. Army through Corps to division, whereas in Eighth Army A.M.G. officers attached to corps and divisions were only liaison officers, the deployment of the whole spearhead detachment being made on the 'pool' basis originally employed in the invasion of Sicily, by Army A.M.G. headquarters. The same principle of introducing teams of officers from the Regional establishment to take over the provincial administration while the province was still under the command of the Army A.M.G. was adopted, but provincial administrations were not usually brought forward into Corps area until the larger portion of the province was already behind Corps boundary. A.M.G. attached to the French Expeditionary Corps incorporated two French officers, while A.M.G. Fifth Army Engineer Officer had under his command two Italian engineer officers, a diversification of nationality which found no place in Eighth Army A.M.G.

Before the operations of A.M.G. described in this chapter had even begun, events had occurred which completely changed the relations between Italy and the Allies, and consequently led to a recasting of the role of military government. On 25th July Mussolini was overthrown by a double conspiracy, one led by the General Staff and supported by the King, the other by the leading members of the Fascist Grand Council. Marshal Badoglio, who succeeded him as Prime Minister, after some hesitations proceeded to make contact with the Allies with a view to negotiating an armistice. He was met with an uncompromising demand of unconditional surrender, which *faute de mieux* had to be accepted, and the 'short terms' were signed at Cassibile on 3rd September, a few hours after the invasion of Calabria across the Straits of Messina had started.

Some time before the armistice, plans had been evolved at A.F.H.Q., under the auspices of Colonel Holmes, head of the Military Government Section and an Assistant Chief of Staff to General Eisenhower, for the extension of Allied Military Government to the Italian peninsula up to the Po basin. These plans included a national government headquarters of about 400 officers to take over direction of the central government, in case there should be no Italian Government in Rome with which the Supreme Allied Commander could deal, and it was assumed that the whole of the country south of the Apennines would be administered by Military Government. Under this scheme Allied Military Government was to be decentralised on a regional basis, the territorial division being in most cases, as has already been explained, the *compartimento*. The Regions were to be the following: (I) Sicily; (II) Calabria; Lucania and Apulia; (III) Campania; (IV) Abruzzi-Lazio; (V) Marche -Umbria; (VI) Sardinia; (VII) Rome-Central Government; to which were later added (VIII) Tuscany and (IX) Emilia. On 21st July General Eisenhower was authorised by the Combined Chiefs of Staff to extend AMGOT as far as Rome. This involved the immediate collection of personnel for Regions II, III, IV and VII, and the drawing up of provisional war establishments for all these entities.

This was done without reference to Lord Rennell, who, as C.C.A.O. Fifteenth Army Group, was no longer regarded as having any responsibility for the planning at A.F.H.Q., carried out by the Military Government Section. Moreover his subsequent criticisms of such details of the plans as were communicated to him were left entirely unheeded. Officers required to fill up the bloated regional establishments contemplated in this plan were meanwhile assembled at the Military Government Training School and Holding Centre established at Tizi Ouzou in Algeria, where they proceeded to plan military government of the regions *in vacuo*. No attempt was made to post them to Sicily in order to give them actual experience of military government before they assumed their responsibilities. A more practical course would have been to dilute the Sicilian AMGOT progressively with officers from Tizi Ouzou, while at the same time providing each Region, as it was brought into action, with a nucleus of experienced officers drawn from AMGOT. But this was not to be.

The basic assumption on which these plans were built was completely changed by the armistice. The recognition of the government of King Victor Emmanuel and Marshal Badoglio, symbolised in the abstention from proclaiming Military Government in the four Apulian provinces constituting 'King's Italy', was followed by the formal conferment of the status of 'co-belligerent'. The constitution of a 'friendly' Italian Government made the imposition of Allied Military Government quite unnecessary, except in the comparatively restricted zones actually occupied by the combatant armies. But though this fact was recognised in theory by the planners in Algiers, the elaborate and cumbersome regional machinery designed by the Military Government Section for the imposition of Military Government was allowed to survive in the structure of the Allied Control Commission, the constitution of which forms the subject of the next chapter.

It was immediately realised that the need for maintaining Allied Military Government in the static areas behind army boundaries had disappeared, and that, as already explained, these territories should therefore be handed back to the administration of the Italian Government. Sicily had become No. 1 Military District at the end of September and by the middle of October it had been decided to create a second Military District (No. 2) on the Adriatic side. This was to embrace the four Apulian provinces of 'King's Italy' the *compartimento* of Lucania and the province of Salerno.[1] It was therefore contemplated that these territories, as well as Calabria, would be handed back almost immediately to the Italian Government, perhaps even as early as the middle of November, to be administered by Marshal Badoglio, under the advice and supervision of the Allied Control Commission in the process of formation. But in the meantime their administrative position was rather anomalous, since the territories of the Military Districts were no longer under the command of Fifteenth Army Group, but depended directly from A.F.H.Q. in Algiers.

The results to AMGOT of this territorial division of military authorities were by no means fortunate. General Alexander moved his headquarters to the vicinity of Bari and Lord Rennell, as his chief staff officer on Civil Affairs, decided that he must remain at his side. Meanwhile the headquarters staff of AMGOT were stationed in Palermo, and negotiations of the most important kind affecting Military Government had to be carried out by A.F.H.Q. with the Italian Government at Brindisi. The distances between Palermo, Bari and Naples, to say nothing of Algiers, were very great and communications notoriously bad. In these circumstances not even the aeroplane could confer on Lord Rennell the indispensable administrative attribute of omnipresence. Some division of AMGOT was therefore inevitable. This division might logically have been made by an administrative separation following the chain of command, making a static AMGOT under command of A.F.H.Q. entirely

[1] But not Calabria: the whole of that 'compartment' was to be evacuated by Allied troops, since after the capture of Naples neither Reggio nor Crotone had any further military interests as ports.

separate from AMGOT Fifteenth Army Group under the command of General Alexander. But such a complete division had political drawbacks, quite apart from the routine difficulties of constituting two separate headquarters. Had it been made, General Alexander would have ceased to be Military Governor of Sicily—a step which might have been interpreted, according to Lord Rennell, as favouring the Separatist movement, while the institution of a new AMGOT on the mainland might have given rise to the suspicion that the proposals for the return of territory to the Italian Government, which had already been put before Marshal Badoglio, were not sincerely intended. In these circumstances Lord Rennell, to meet what was a purely transitory phase pending the transfer of the territories in question to Italian administration, proposed a formal division of AMGOT into two parts, both to remain under General Alexander as Military Governor. These were Forward AMGOT in the Army areas, of which Lord Rennell was to assume direct command, and AMGOT Rear Areas, to be placed under the command of his deputy, General McSherry, who would administer Regions I and II and depend administratively on A.F.H.Q., though General Alexander remained titular Military Governor. This situation was merely intended as an *interim* arrangement to tide over the interval which must elapse before the Allied Control Commission could assume such a degree of control as it was considered necessary to exercise over the Italian administration in these areas.

The proposal was accepted by General Eisenhower. On 24th October, the day on which Military District No. 2 came into being, A.M.G. Forward and A.M.G. Rear[1] were formally divided. Forward A.M.G. consisted of three commands; A.M.G. Fifth Army and A.M.G. Eighth Army, which were placed under the Army Commanders, as the 'spearhead' A.M.G's had been in the invasion of Sicily, and A.M.G. Fifteenth Army Group, which was responsible for administering both them and the regional units following up behind them—Regions III and IV. A.M.G. Rear consisted of an H.Q. at Palermo administering two Regions, namely I, Sicily, and II, Calabria, Lucania and the Campanian province of Salerno, originally part of Region III, which was joined to it because it was included in Military District No. 2.

The establishment of Forward A.M.G. was worked out by Lord Rennell on an economical scale. The Army A.M.G's were essentially 'spearhead', mobile formations equipped with their own transport, consisting of 'general purpose' officers with a sprinkling of 'specialists' such as Finance, Public Health, Supply and Legal Officers to be responsible for the routine work in these departments. The higher direction of the specialist divisions was concentrated in A.M.G.

[1] AMGOT was officially re-designated as A.M.G. on 24th October.

Fifteenth Army Group under Lord Rennell's direct supervision. The establishment of Fifth Army A.M.G. consisted of fifty-six officers, that of Eighth Army A.M.G., which had a much larger territory to cover, of sixty-eight officers, and that of A.M.G. Fifteenth Army Group of twenty-eight officers. The division of officers as regards nationality followed in general lines the principles laid down for operation 'Husky'. A.M.G. Fifteenth Army Group was divided between British and American officers roughly on a fifty-fifty basis, while in the Army A.M.G's, so far as the higher ranks were concerned, the preponderance followed the nationality of the Army Commander. In the Fifth Army detachment there was a higher proportion of American officers of all ranks, while in the Eighth Army detachment there was a higher proportion of senior British officers, but an equal or greater number of junior American officers, owing to the difficulty experienced in finding a sufficient number of young British officers.

The War Establishments of all three detachments were considered as a single entity, so as to enable transfers and attachments to be made between the three detachments without cross-posting. The manner in which the officers of the region lying immediately behind the advancing Army A.M.G's were 'infiltrated' into the territory as occupied has already been described. The regional administration, which was to come into active existence as the rear army boundary moved forward, was intended to come under the command of A.M.G. Rear. This was amalgamated with the Allied Control Commission, a formation administratively dependent on A.F.H.Q., which came into being on 10th November. This logical arrangement however had to be modified; for, while army boundaries moved forward, the territory handed back to Italian Government administration was not correspondingly enlarged. It was for several months limited to that lying south of the northern boundaries of the provinces of Salerno, Potenza and Bari. This meant that Regions III and IV formed a no man's land between rear army boundaries and King's Italy. It was consequently decided that A.M.G. Fifteenth Army Group should take control of these two Regions as separate units under its command.

The separation of A.M.G. Forward from A.M.G. Rear, though it was an administrative necessity, led to considerable complications in regard to supply matters, since the military channels of supply did not correspond with this division. In order to expedite the maintenance of Fifteenth Army Group, which possessed no A/Q machinery of its own, an Advanced Administrative Echelon of A.F.H.Q. was set up in Naples, immediately after its capture, under Major-General Sir Brian Robertson. This organisation, which was known to everyone through its telegraphic address FLAMBO—a convenient appellation which will be used frequently in this volume—was responsible for calling forward shipping to the mainland ports for supplies for all troops on the Italian mainland, as well as civilian supplies, since it had been from the beginning laid down that these should pass through military channels. But FLAMBO was not responsible for the procurement of these supplies, i.e. of seeing that they were despatched to the theatre—that was the business of the Q/G-4 branch of the staff at A.F.H.Q.—nor for their distribution on arrival in the theatre. Nor was FLAMBO responsible in any way for supplying No. 1 District, Sicily, or A.M.G. Region I, which was done by A.F.H.Q. through separate channels. It was however responsible for the shipment of supplies for No. 2 District, and therefore for Region II, administered by A.M.G. Rear H.Q. in Palermo. In order to avoid confusion Lord Rennell found himself obliged to undertake the co-ordination of all civilian supplies for the Italian mainland, including those for Region II, now no longer under his command, since General Robertson did not wish to complicate his task by having to deal with two A.M.G. headquarters. These civilian supplies for the whole mainland, including 'King's Italy', as well as all A.M.G. areas, were co-ordinated at A.M.G. Fifteenth Army Group headquarters at Bari through a liaison officer attached to FLAMBO in Naples. Complicated as these arrangements certainly were, they did in fact work reasonably well, as far as calls forward through FLAMBO were concerned, since Lord Rennell's demands for shipping were practically all accepted by General Robertson. Nor did the question of distribution raise any extraordinary difficulty, except for the chronic shortage of transport. Arrangements were worked out with FLAMBO for the breaking of bulk cargoes at Naples and their distribution in schooners or small coastal craft to Salerno, Reggio and Crotone.

For the severe shortage in food supplies which affected practically the whole of southern Italy during the winter months of 1943 neither FLAMBO nor Lord Rennell was responsible. The trouble, as has already been noted, lay further back at A.F.H.Q. But the division of A.M.G. and the relations of its constituent parts with A.F.H.Q., Fifteenth Army Group, the Italian Government, and the nascent Control Commission, constituted an administrative nightmare of which some description must be given in the next chapter.

ANNEXE

Civil Affairs Sardinia[1]

To A.M.G. Forward and A.M.G. Rear a third section of Civil Affairs was added in the island of Sardinia, which after the armistice maintained its loyalty to King Victor Emmanuel. Sardinia at the time contained a large force of Italian troops under General Basso, including the 'Nembo' Parachute Division, which was comparatively well equipped and contained elements strongly pro-Fascist in feeling, and a number of units of Fascist militia, as well as a German armoured division under General Lungerhausen. The relations between the German and Italian commands appear to have been very cordial, and the German General messed with the Italian command. When the armistice was announced, General Lungerhausen made overtures to General Basso to induce him to throw in his lot with the Axis, but this was refused. In order to avoid unnecessary bloodshed between persons who had till then been Allies, General Basso, who does not appear to have been at all sure of the attitude of his troops[2], agreed to permit the German General to evacuate his forces to Corsica and fixed a date for the completion of this operation, namely 17th September. It was not apparently until 13th September that orders reached General Basso from Brindisi that the Germans were to be treated as enemies and that their evacuation to Corsica was to be prevented. Though there was some fighting, the Germans managed to leave the island practically intact, but more effective action was taken by Admiral Brionesi, in charge of the naval base at La Maddalena, who opened fire on the ferry boats. The Germans, as the event proved, had merely jumped from the frying pan into the fire. In Corsica they were met by Free French troops, sent from North Africa, to expel them and by the beginning of October their resistance on that island came to an end with the capture of Bastia.

Meanwhile the Allies lost no time in making contact in Sardinia with General Basso. On 15th September an American officer landed by parachute on the island; three days later a military mission under the command of Brigadier-General Theodore Roosevelt arrived by sea at Cagliari. The island was of very great strategic importance to the Allied Navies and Air Forces, and to it was despatched an Allied force including a contingent of the American Air Force and a Civil Affairs detachment under Brigadier P. K. Boulnois, to whom I am indebted for much of the information contained in this note. As General Basso had demonstrated his loyalty to the King and received and obeyed the orders from the Italian General Staff, it was decided that Sardinia should not be regarded as occupied territory but as a part of 'King's Italy'. No form of Military Government was therefore established in the island and no proclamations were posted. In the planning which had been taking place in Algiers,

---

[1] I am largely indebted for this note to a memorandum compiled by Brigadier Boulnois.

[2] See *Tamaro, Due Anni di Storia*, Vol. 1, pp. 509–510, and General Basso's book *L'Armistizio del Settembre 1943 in Sardegna.*

Sardinia had figured as Region VI and a regional organisation on the standard pattern had been drawn up, with regional headquarters and provincial staffs.

Brigadier Boulnois, with the skeleton of this regional headquarters, including Public Safety, Finance, Civil Supply and Public Health officers, arrived on the island on 29th September and made contact with General Basso, who, though never officially appointed as High Commissioner by the Italian Government, had in fact assumed complete control of the civil administration of the island. Brigadier Boulnois, in his instructions from A.F.H.Q. dated 28th September, had been appointed Regional Commissioner for Sardinia under a not yet existing Allied Control Commission, and had been ordered to place himself in contact with a not yet existing High Commissioner of the Italian Government. His business was not to govern but to control, transmitting the instructions of the Commander-in-Chief and seeing that they were carried out. His mission was two-fold. On the military side, as agent of General Eisenhower and successor to General Roosevelt as head of the Allied Military Mission, he had to deal with General Basso concerning the evacuation of the Italian garrison from Corsica to Sardinia and the despatch of mules, guns and troops to the mainland, and, on the civil side, with the general administration of the island. Since General Basso had assumed a similar duplicate role, this arrangement worked easily enough, but afterwards, when Brigadier Boulnois was relieved of the military side of his work by the appointment of an Allied garrison commander, the position was not so easy, since his authority was limited to Civil Affairs, while the Italian Military Commander remained in charge of the civilian administration, the appointment of a civilian High Commissioner by the Italian Government being long delayed. Brigadier Boulnois was not under the command of General Alexander's Fifteenth Army Group. He was therefore completely independent of Lord Rennell; nor was he under the command of the H.Q. A.M.G. Rear.

Brigadier Boulnois immediately established friendly relations with General Basso, but this co-operative attitude was not so completely maintained by his successor, General Magli, who had commanded the Italian troops in Corsica and was at first suspected of anti-Badoglio and anti-Allied leanings, probably not altogether justly. Only one of the prefects of the three provinces into which the island was divided had fled, the prefect of Cagliari, the largest town, which had been heavily bombed by the Allies and from which over nine-tenths of the population had dispersed. The local administrative machine was otherwise intact, but, in the absence of communications with the embryonic government of Brindisi, all sense of direction had been lost. General Basso created a Civil Affairs Section of his own staff to co-ordinate the activities of the provincial administration. This suffered considerably from the lack of understanding of civilian problems.

On the civilian side there were two problems which immediately engaged Brigadier Boulnois's attention, the feeding of the Sardinian population, amounting to nearly a million and a quarter, and the reactivation of the Sardinian coal industry—the only important source of

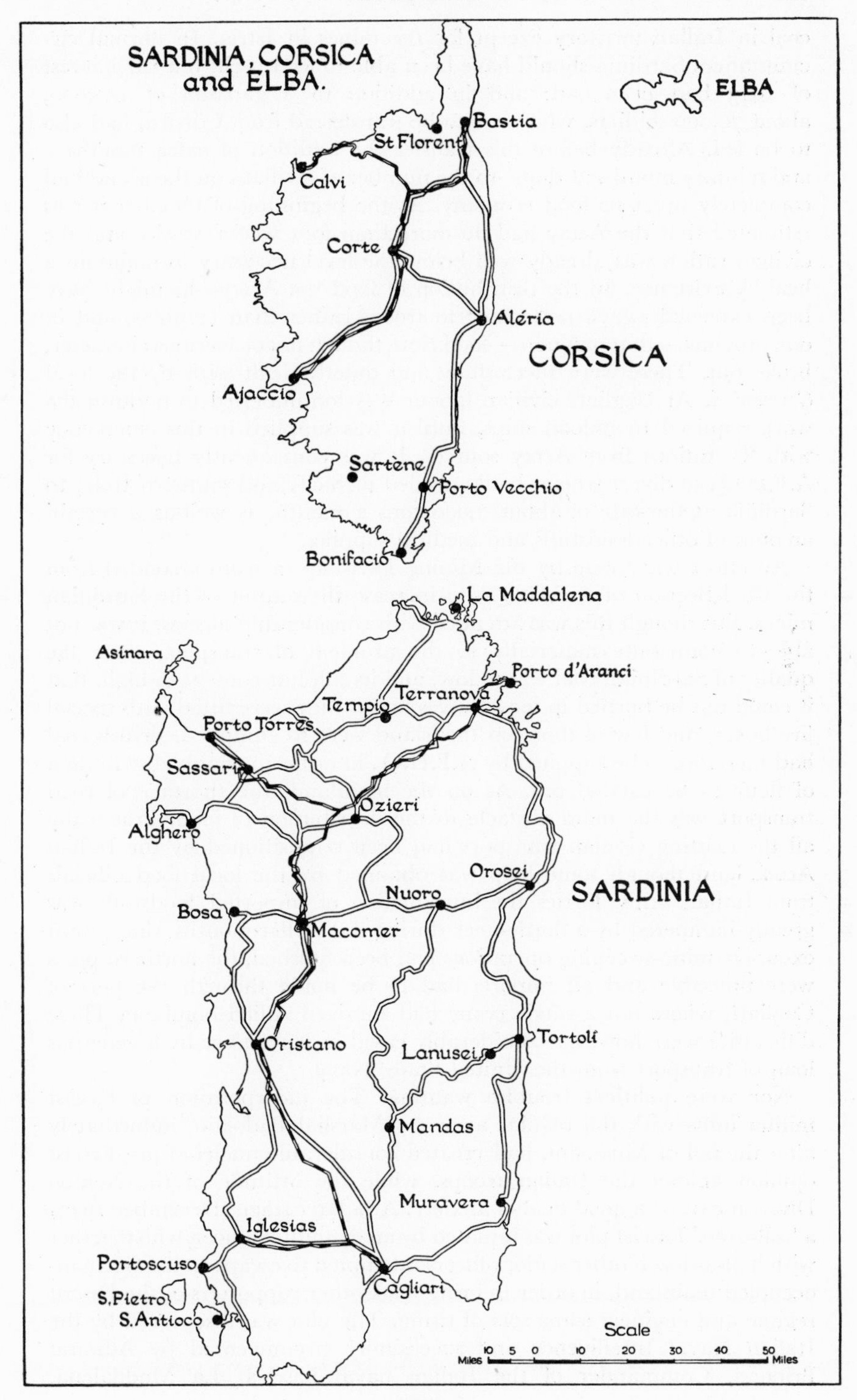
SARDINIA, CORSICA
and ELBA.
ELBA
Bastia
St Florent
Calvi
Corte
Aléria
CORSICA
Ajaccio
Sartène
Porto Vecchio
Bonifacio
La Maddalena
Asinara
Porto d'Aranci
Terranova
Tempio
Porto Torres
Sassari
Ozieri
Alghero
Orosei
SARDINIA
Nuoro
Bosa
Macomer
Tortolí
Oristano
Lanusei
Mandas
Muravera
Iglesias
Portoscuso
Cagliari
S. Pietro
S. Antioco
Scale
10 5 0 10 20 30 40 50
Miles
Miles

Map 5

coal in Italian territory except for the mines in Istria. In normal circumstances Sardinia should have been able to feed itself, but the harvest of 1943 had been bad; and in addition to a garrison of 150,000, about 70,000 soldiers, who were to be transferred from Corsica, had also to be fed. Already before this transfer the addition of extra mouths—and military mouths at that—to the number of civilians on the island had completely upset its food economy. At the beginning of October it was estimated that the Army had no more than four weeks' stocks, and the civilian ration was already well below the level necessary to maintain a healthy existence. In the distribution of food the Army—as might have been expected—gave preference to troops rather than civilians, and in one province—that of Nuoro—food riots, though not of a serious character, broke out. These were successfully and quietly dealt with by the local *Carabinieri*. At Cagliari civilian labour was too underfed to perform the work required to unload ships, until it was supplied in this emergency with 'C' rations from Army sources. It was consequently necessary for A.F.H.Q. to divert wheat, badly needed in Sicily and southern Italy, to Sardinia at the rate of about 7,000 tons a month, as well as a certain amount of other foodstuffs and medical supplies.

An effort was made by the Mining Division—a team seconded from the Coal Section of A.F.H.Q.—to increase the output of the Sardinian mines. But though this was attended with considerable success, it was not able to contribute materially to the problem of transport, since the quality of Sardinian coal was so low, and its sulphur content so high, that it could not be burned in locomotives unless they were fitted with special fire boxes, and few of those on the island were so equipped. British coal had therefore to be supplied by A.F.H.Q. in order to enable distribution of flour to be carried out. As on the mainland, the shortage of road transport was the main obstacle to the distribution of food. Practically all the existing civilian transport had been requisitioned by the Italian Army, and though some help was obtained by the local food officials from Italian army lorries the introduction of imported foodstuffs was greatly hampered by a bottle-neck during the earlier months, since, until extensive mine-sweeping operations had been finished, the northern ports were unusable and all imports had to be made through the port of Cagliari, where not a single crane had survived Allied bombing. These difficulties were however considerably eased in November by a generous loan of transport from the United States Navy.

Nor were political troubles wanting. The incorporation of Fascist militia units with the regular army by Marshal Badoglio, immediately after the fall of Mussolini, had created considerable nuclei of pro-Fascist opinion among the Italian troops, while the attitude of the Nembo Division caused a good deal of anxiety. At a later stage (December 1943) a 'full-dress' Fascist plot was initiated by an ex-militia officer, who together with half-a-dozen other senior officers attempted to escape to the German-occupied mainland, in order to bring back other supporters of the Fascist regime and engineer some sort of rising. The plot was discovered by the Italian Naval Intelligence and successfully circumvented by Admiral Brionesi, Commander of the Italian naval base at La Maddalena.

Certain *Carabinieri* officers, with full cognisance of Brigadier Boulnois and his Public Safety Officer, were dressed as sailors and put on board the small tug which the Fascist General had chartered to take him to the mainland. A few miles from the Sardinian shore the sailors happily discovered some iron pipes in their trouser legs, and the General and his accomplices were easily arrested.

Apart from this Fascist plot, which arose not from the civilian population but from the Army, the resurgence of political parties which followed the fall of Mussolini created no serious disturbance. As in Sicily, so in Sardinia, a Separatist party made its appearance, backed by some of the large landowners, who hoped to use it as a means of maintaining their semi-feudal position. But the Sardinian party did not aim at complete independence. What it wanted was a certain measure of home-rule under British or American protection. In each of the three provinces 'Committees of anti-Fascist Union' representing the newly-born parties, of which the strongest were the Socialists, Communists and Christian Democrats, made their appearance, and were enlisted into co-operation with General Magli's administration to assist the Prefect in an advisory capacity. Meeting together they formed a Regional Committee which was recognised by the General as an advisory body for affairs concerning the island as a whole. This arrangement contrasted very favourably with the relations of the parties with the Badoglio Government in southern Italy.

CHAPTER IV

SETTING UP THE CONTROL COMMISSION

On 3rd September, a few hours after the first Calabrian landings, the armistice, known as the 'short terms', was signed at Cassibile in Sicily. This brief document, consisting only of twelve clauses, provided for the immediate cessation of all hostile activity by the Italian armed forces, for the transfer of the Italian fleet and Italian aircraft to such points as might be designated by the Allied Commander-in-Chief, for Allied requisition of Italian merchant shipping, for the immediate surrender of Corsica and all Italian territory, both islands and mainland, to the Allies, for the immediate guarantee of the free use of all airfields and naval ports—these to be protected by the Italian armed forces from seizure by the Germans—for the immediate withdrawal of Italian armed forces from areas outside Italy, and for a guarantee by the Italian Government that, if necessary, it would employ all its available armed forces to ensure prompt compliance with all these provisions. The Allied Commander-in-Chief reserved to himself the right to take any measure which he thought necessary for the protection of the interests of the Allied forces for the prosecution of the war, while the Italian Government bound itself to take such administrative or other action as the Commander-in-Chief might require. In particular it was laid down that the Commander-in-Chief would establish Allied Military Government over such parts of Italian territory as he might deem necessary in the military interests of the Allied Nations, and he reserved to himself the full right to impose measures of disarmament, demobilisation and demilitarisation. In a final clause (No. 12), it was stated that other conditions of a political, economic and financial nature, with which Italy would be bound to comply, would be communicated at a later date. The signing of the armistice was kept secret for five days but announced from Algiers and Rome on 8th September, the day before the Salerno landings.[1] In the early hours of the following morning the King of Italy and

[1] A good account in English of the negotiations leading to the signing of the armistice terms and its announcement is contained in Wagg and Brown, *No Spaghetti for Breakfast*. For Italian accounts see Castellano, *Come Firmai L'Amistizio*, which is commended for its objectivity in Field-Marshal Alexander's despatch, *The Allied Armies in Italy, from 3rd September 1943 to 12th December 1944*, published as a supplement to the *London Gazette*, 12th June, 1950, p. 2889.

Marshal Badoglio left Rome for an unknown destination, finally arriving by sea at Brindisi, which for several months remained the seat of the Italian Government.

The longer terms were signed by Marshal Badoglio and General Eisenhower in Malta on 29th September. In the meantime a Military Mission had been despatched to Brindisi by General Eisenhower, as soon as the location of the Italian Government became known, under the command of Lieut.-General Sir Noel Mason-MacFarlane, Governor of Gibraltar, the advanced group of which arrived in Taranto on 13th September. This Mission was entrusted with a three-fold task, namely, to transmit the military instructions of General Eisenhower to the Italian Government, to collect and transmit intelligence, and to 'arrange for such co-ordinated action as the Italian armed forces and people can be induced to take against the Germans'. To it were attached the representatives in North Africa of the American President and the British Prime Minister, in the persons of Mr Murphy and Mr Harold Macmillan, in order to make the necessary diplomatic contacts with the Italian Government; but it was arranged that both should report to General Mason-MacFarlane and that all instructions from General Eisenhower, on political as well as on military questions, should be transmitted through him. The Mission was divided into four sections; Army, under Brig.-General Maxwell Taylor; Navy, under Vice-Admiral Power, R.N.; Air Force, under Air-Commodore Foster; and Communications, under Captain Stone (U.S.N.R.), who subsequently became the executive head of the Allied Control Commission. Most of this Mission's immediate business was concerned with the implementation of the military provisions of the armistice, but Civil Affairs, as already explained, also came under its jurisdiction.

The longer armistice terms were designed to effect three main objects: to give the Allies complete control over the Italian armed forces and all the facilities and material resources at their disposal; to ensure the maximum exploitation, consistent with international law, of the resources of the country for the Allied war effort, both as a base of operations and as a source of consumable commodities and services;[1] and to effect the final destruction of Fascism. The political implications of a surrender, originally termed unconditional, were not neglected. Under Clause 30 all Fascist organisations, including specifically the militia, the secret police and the youth organisations, were to be disbanded, and the Italian Government undertook to comply with all such further directions as the Allied Commander-in-Chief might give for the abolition of Fascist institutions

---

[1] Including, of course, exports of commodities needed by the United Nations for the war effort.

and the dismissal and internment of Fascists.[1] They also undertook in Article 31 to cancel all legislation involving discrimination on grounds of race, colour, creed or political opinions, to release persons detained on such grounds, as directed by the United Nations, and to comply with all further directions from the Allied Commander-in-Chief for the repeal of Fascist legislation and the removal of any disabilities or prohibitions resulting therefrom. They agreed in Article 29 to apprehend and to surrender Mussolini, his chief Fascist associates and all persons suspected of having committed war crimes or analogous offences, into the hands of the United Nations. On the financial side, besides breaking off all intercourse with countries at war with the United Nations or territories occupied by them, the Italian Government undertook in Article 23 to make available such Italian currency as the United Nations might require, as well as to redeem all holdings in Italian territory of currencies issued by the United Nations during military operations and occupation, thus making themselves by implication responsible for the redemption of A.M. lire. In addition they agreed to take such measures as might be required by the United Nations for the control of banking and business, foreign exchange and foreign commercial transactions, and for the regulation of trade and production, and to comply with any instructions regarding these and similar matters.

The arrangements described in the last chapter, by which the jurisdiction of the King of Italy was preserved in the four Apulian provinces and in Sardinia, were made by General Mason-MacFarlane, after consultation with his political advisers and with Lord Rennell and General Holmes. This division of liberated Italy into 'occupied territory' and 'King's Italy' was, as we shall see, of fundamental importance in distinguishing Military Government from Armistice Control, since in 'King's Italy' the role of A.M.G. officers was no longer to administer, but to transmit to the Italian Government the orders of the Allied Commander-in-Chief, and to see to it that they were effectively carried out. In the event of any failure to obey these orders, the Commander-in-Chief had ample means to enforce them, the ultimate sanction being the power reserved under the armistice to treat any portion of Italy as 'occupied territory' and to impose Allied Military Government under proclamations, general orders and instructions, which Italian public servants were obliged to carry out.[2]

Under Article 37 a commission was to be appointed by the Allies which would be charged with regulating and executing the instrument

---

[1] At A.F.H.Q. thoughts on 'defascistisation' appear to have gone considerably beyond considerations of military and political security. Among the problems selected for further study was 'the punishment in various ways of Fascist officials'.

[2] See 'Short terms', Clause 10; 'Long terms', Clauses 18 and 20.

of surrender, under the orders and general direction of the Allied Commander-in-Chief. Even before the Sicilian landings planning had been initiated in London for an armistice control commission to be brought into operation in the event of an Italian surrender. At this stage, naturally enough, the thinking was in terms of disarmament and control of a defeated Fascist enemy. The vision of a co-belligerent Italy had not yet dawned on the horizon. When the armistice was concluded unexpectedly early as the result of Mussolini's downfall, immediate action had to be taken to bring this body into being. The planning of its constitution was carried out between Washington, London and Algiers, where the detailed work on the Civil Affairs side naturally devolved on the Military Government Section which had been planning the extension of A.M.G. on the Italian mainland.

In the directive issued on 6th September, the functions of the Control Commission were envisaged as being, first, to enforce and execute the instrument of surrender, and secondly, to ensure that the conduct of the Italian Government conformed to the requirements of an Allied base of operations, especially in the matters of transportation and communications; but its activity was not confined to these military objectives; it was also to be the organ through which the policy of the United Nations towards the Italian Government would be conducted.

The interpretation given by the planners in Algiers, who could not count either practical experience of military government or first-hand knowledge of Italian administrative conditions among their qualifications, in terms of establishments and detailed directives, resulted in the creation of a top-heavy organisation, which had to be reformed and reduced within a few weeks of its creation. The implications of co-belligerency appear to have been most imperfectly realised, and detailed control of every branch of Italian administration was insisted on. One reason, no doubt, for this exaggerated supervision was the almost complete lack of elementary resources possessed by the Badoglio Government on its arrival in Brindisi.[1] But it is difficult to avoid the conclusion that, instead of thinking things out afresh, A.F.H.Q. merely trimmed the organisation which they had designed for the military government of the peninsula in the event of no acceptable Italian Government being available. The headquarters of the new body was the reproduction on a very slightly reduced scale of the National headquarters of 'post-Husky' planning, while the Regional staffs were rather more substantially reduced. In the planning of these arrangements neither Lord Rennell nor General

[1] The Marshal himself to begin with was even without a typewriter. His communications to General Mason-MacFarlane were written in long-hand and a typed copy made by the Allied Military Mission, which was then returned to Badoglio for his own use.

McSherry nor General Mason-MacFarlane was consulted and the arrangements appear to have been accepted in Washington and London on the principle that such matters must be left to the judgment of the man on the spot.[1] Nor was it understood, in London, that Lord Rennell had not been associated with the planning and that his criticisms had been ignored.

In designing the Control Commission no account was taken of the experienced body of AMGOT headquarters. All the senior posts, with one exception, were offered to newcomers with no experience of Italian administration. Even on the lower level of the headship of sub-commissions the claims of AMGOT experience were all but completely ignored. Lord Rennell was offered the Vice-Presidency of the Economic and Administrative Section, which he did not accept, owing to his disapproval of the constitution of the Commission. Having asked to be relieved of his position as C.C.A.O., he returned to London.

As initially brought into action, the Allied Control Commission was an integrated Anglo-American unit divided into four sections—Military, Political, Economic and Administrative, and Communications, each sub-divided into a number of sub-commissions. The Military Section was to contain six, namely, Naval Forces, Land Forces, Air Forces, Prisoners of War, War Material Factories, and War Material Disposal. The Political Section was to have three, Foreign and External Affairs, Internees and Displaced Persons, and Information, Press and Censorship. The staff of the Political Section was to be largely civilian—mostly Foreign Office officials—in contrast to that of the other three, which was to be formed of officers of military rank. The Economic and Administrative Section was to be sub-divided into two directorates, each embracing a varying number of sub-commissions. The first of these, the Economic Directorate, was to consist of eight sub-commissions, namely, Finance, Foreign Trade, Industry and Commerce, Public Works and Utilities, Fuel, Food and Agriculture (together with Forestry and Fisheries) and Labour. The Administrative Directorate was to comprise six sub-commissions, namely Interior, Legal, Public Safety, Public Health, Property Control, and Education, Monuments, Fine Arts and Archives. The Communications Section was divided into three sub-commissions, namely, Shipping and Ports, Inland and Air Transportation, and Posts and Telecommunications.

In order to coordinate this proliferation of twenty-six separate sub-commissions, of which all but four were actually brought to birth, a very clumsy superstructure was projected. The Supreme Allied Commander was naturally the president of the Commission,

[1] According to the statement made to Lord Rennell by Mr McCloy, Under-Secretary of the War Department.

but the effective head of the organisation was to be a deputy-president, a high ranking officer with four vice-presidents under him, each with a deputy of opposite Allied nationality, to take charge of each of the four sections. The directorates of the Economic and Administrative Section were each to be provided with a director and a deputy-director of the opposite nationality. In general the proportion of both nationalities was to be equal, and the deputy-heads of each sub-commission were also to be of the opposite nationality to their chiefs. In addition to this hierarchy of specialised officers, the Commission was to be provided with a large and variegated headquarters staff comprising a chief of staff, a vice-chief of staff, a deputy-chief of staff, an executive officer, a security intelligence staff, an industrial planning staff and a large secretariat.[1]

This top-heavy superstructure was accepted in London and Washington in deference to the principle of maintaining in every department the most scrupulous equilibrium between the two nationalities composing the integrated unit of the Commission. Negotiations between the two Government concerning the appointments to these more important posts were prolonged, and a large number of them were still unfilled when the Commission came into formal being on 10th November. Apart from the senior posts, the personnel required to staff this gigantic organisation was to be derived in part from the existing A.M.G. (rear), but mostly from the establishment planned for 'Post Husky' A.M.G.—described in the last chapter—which was being collected at Tizi-Ouzou. But this large headquarters was only to form part of the Control Commission. Beneath the central hierarchy were large regional teams of Civil Affairs Officers and specialist officers organised on AMGOT lines. These were intended to provide 'a thinly spread control over the local administrations in the field'. The regional organisations were regarded as a provisional stage, pending the establishment of the Italian Government and the headquarters of the Commission in Rome, after which they would be eliminated from the chain of command, headquarters of the Commission operating directly through provincial control officers. But, as we shall see, the regional controls, like the Marxist state, refused to fade away according to plan. It was calculated that the number of officers already agreed on 31st August by the Combined Chiefs of Staff for 'Post-Husky' AMGOT establishments, amounting to 990 when added to the 400 originally agreed for Sicily, would be sufficient to constitute the entire personnel needed by the Control Commission and the Army A.M.Gs under Fifteenth Army Group. But this calculation proved to be rather on the optimistic side; by October it was estimated that

[1] For the plan of the Commission as originally drawn up, see the chart in Annexe II to this chapter.

the Commission (including Army A.M.G's) would need a combined total of 1,479 officers, 828 American and 650 British, to cover Italy south of the Po valley.[1]

The assembly of a staff of these dimensions at short notice raised an almost insoluble problem. The only sources from which they could be drawn were the officers then in the theatre (who were already, it may be presumed, usefully employed elsewhere), officers in England and the United States who had taken courses in Civil Affairs at Charlottesville or Wimbledon, and civilians in both countries who had suddenly to be put into uniform. The selection of military officers in the theatre and in both countries tended to follow the same pattern. It was hardly to be expected that military commanders would be willing to part with any of their best talent, and the selection of civilians in considerable numbers on a sudden demand was none too easy. In these circumstances men of the requisite ability or experience were not to be found in sufficient numbers to create *ex nihilo* a very satisfactory unit—the more reason to train these raw recruits by giving them as soon as possible some practical experience in the field, and to associate experienced AMGOT officers with both the planning and the organisation of the nascent Commission. But unfortunately the Military Government Section of A.F.H.Q. did not follow these lines. Not only were officers held at Tizi-Ouzou planning *in vacuo* for several months on a different continent; but when the Headquarters of the Commission was amalgamated with A.M.G. (rear), little account was taken of acquired experience.[2] Nevertheless something of the AMGOT tradition of a harmoniously integrated bi-national administration soon penetrated the morale of the new body. Under General Mason-MacFarlane and Captain Stone Anglo-American cooperation, even if it did not quite attain the degree of perfection manifested in AMGOT, did show how remarkably coherent an integrated administration, hastily thrown together from miscellaneous British and American sources, could become. It was not here that the weakness of the commission's organisation lay.

Though it had been understood that General Mason-MacFarlane would become the effective head of the Commission, it was decided, on the advice of General Eisenhower, that the Deputy-President, the effective head of the new body—now formally named the Allied Control Commission—should be of the same nationality as the Supreme Allied Commander-in-Chief. An American officer, Major-General Kenyon A. Joyce, was consequently appointed acting

---

[1] These figures do not include the Military Section.

[2] The lack of experience of the nascent Control Commission was accentuated at the end of the year when a considerable contingent of A.M.G. (rear) was sent back to England to plan Civil Affairs for 'Overlord'.

Deputy-President and under him the Commission was formally brought into being on 10th November, headquarters being divided between Palermo and Brindisi.[1]

The relations between A.M.G. and the Control Commission provided a problem which was initially handled in a far from satisfactory manner. Opinion both in London and Washington was in favour of fusing both into a single organisation directly responsible to the Supreme Allied Commander at A.F.H.Q. The directive of the Combined Chiefs of Staff issued on 15th October laid down that the Deputy-President, the working chief of the Commission, should be the Military Governor of occupied Italy, while the Vice-President of the Economic and Administrative Section was to be his Chief Civil Affairs officer. Strong objection was taken to this proposal at A.F.H.Q. on the ground that it would have eliminated General Alexander from the picture. General Eisenhower consequently 'submitted most strongly' that only the responsibilities for A.M.G. in static areas should be placed under the Control Commission, and that General Alexander should remain as Military Governor of all occupied Italy—a rather illogical arrangement which was accepted by the Combined Chiefs of Staff. The implicit contradiction would have eliminated itself, if the arrangements originally planned could have been carried out[2], and the territories administered by A.M.G. (rear) transferred immediately to the Italian Government, since once transferred they ceased to be occupied territory under military government. But the dichotomy of liberated Italy into 'occupied territory' administered by Allied Military Government under Fifteenth Army Group, corresponding to Army areas, and 'restored territory' including the L of C areas administered by the Italian Government under the supervision of the Control Commission, could not in practice be translated into a clear-cut administrative separation. A delay of several months elapsed before the territories were actually transferred to the Italian Government. This left a strip of territory behind the forward Army areas organised as regions under Military Government in Fifteenth Army Group territory, in the shape of Regions III and IV, the Military Government of which remained under A.M.G. Fifteenth Army Group, while Military Government was still being exercised by the Control Commission in Sicily (Region I) and Region II (Calabria and Lucania).

---

[1] General Joyce's principal staff Officers were as follows: Chief of Staff, Brig.-General Maxwell Taylor; Vice-Chief of Staff, Brigadier Gueterbock; Deputy Chief of Staff, Colonel Spofford; Vice-President Military Section, Rear-Admiral R. R. McGrigor, R.N.; Vice-President Political Section, Mr Harold Caccia; Deputy Vice-President, Mr Samuel Reber; Vice-President Economic and Administrative Section, Air-Commodore Viscount Stansgate; Deputy Vice-President, Mr Henry F. Grady; Vice-President Communications Section, Captain Ellery W. Stone, U.S.N.R.

[2] See above, p. 96.

The anomaly, which had at first been accepted by A.F.H.Q., of two entirely separate organisations, A.M.G. Fifteenth Army Group and the Allied Control Commission, each conducting Military Government was not of very long duration. It was eliminated in the re-organisation of the Control Commission undertaken by General Mason-MacFarlane on his appointment as its Deputy-President. But while it lasted, it enormously complicated the task of administration during the critical period when the newly-formed Control Commission was trying to organize itself. The resulting chaos will be remembered by those who took part in it as an administrative nightmare, of successive and often contradictory policies, the details of which were circulated (or more often failed to circulate) between five headquarters and two continents—A.F.H.Q. at Algiers, Fifteenth Army-Group at Bari, the advanced Echelon of main H.Q. A.F.H.Q. (Flambo) at Naples, A.M.G./A.C.C. at Palermo, and the main H.Q. of A.C.C. beside the Italian Government at Brindisi.

Criticism of the nascent organisation was forcibly expressed by Lord Rennell:

> The unwieldy size and constitution of the Allied Control Commission in its present form makes me doubt of its utility at any time, even in Rome. The number of officers, and in many cases their training and background, leave me in doubt whether any Italian Government would ever survive being overlaid by such a nursery governess. The authority of the Prefectoral Government in the provinces will never survive so numerous a staff—as is proposed shall guide and control them when they become the executive of a Central Italian Government. The mere number of such officers is a guarantee that they will interfere in matters which will render any Italian Civil Service machine inoperable.

And Lord Rennell was not alone in regarding the Allied Control Commission, in the form in which it was constituted, with distrust. Mr Caccia, Vice President-to-be of the Political Section, commented to Mr Macmillan from Brindisi in almost identical terms.[1] Brig.-General Maxwell Taylor, the acting chief of the Mason-MacFarlane Mission, on 23rd October also expressed concern at the size of the new organisation, which 'far transcends what is considered necessary or even desirable on the basis of the knowledge and experience acquired by this mission'. It should consist of small liaison groups to contact each of the ministries. It should have no operative field forces, as such functions would be executed by agencies of the Italian Government.

[1] 'In the period after Rome has been reached and a broad-based government, we hope, got going, I doubt if an Armistice Commission of some six hundred officers' (an erroneous under-estimate of the actual figures) 'will be found a workable proposition. Certainly it is more than doubtful whether prominent Anti-Fascists will agree to service for any length of time in a government which will in effect be a Colonial administration'.

Mr Macmillan's own judgment, after witnessing the functioning of the Commission for its first two months, was sufficiently devastating:

> Planning of A.C.C. by academic methods thousands of miles from the scene of operation, without comprehension of the situation regarding transport, accommodation, light, communications likely to exist in conquered and largely devastated territory, has produced an organisation, especially in the case of A.C.C., ill-conceived, ill-staffed and ill-equipped for its purpose. The exaggerated insistence of exact Anglo-American parallelism has led to too much weight at the top. It is also overstaffed throughout.

As a result of the armistice and the cooperative attitude displayed by Marshal Badoglio, the conditions to be met had completely changed. Once Italy had become co-belligerent, all that was needed to ensure the enforcement of the terms of surrender was a comparatively small body to advise the central Government—including a small liaison staff in the provincial capitals, made necessary by the lack of adequate communication facilities—supplemented by an efficient supply organisation to arrange for the procurement, shipment and distribution of imports necessary to avoid disease and unrest, in addition to the comparatively small staff of the Army A.M.G's, each of which consisted of between seventy and eighty officers required to cope with the special problems of the forward areas.

The establishment of the Control Commission entailed a large expansion of the Military Government Section at A.F.H.Q. This development, according to the accepted pattern of military organisation, could scarcely have been avoided. From the simple 'post office' advocated by Lord Rennell, which was not perhaps really practical, the Section developed into a full grown staff branch with its own separate number in the 'G' series. Its most important function, from the point of view of A.M.G., was that of arranging for the procurement and shipping of civilian supplies. After the initial failures already mentioned, a competent procedure was evolved, under which the Military Government Section 'screened' the estimates for supply needs put forward by the Control Commission, previous to their submission to the scrutiny of G-4 and the various technical services, whose final approval was necessary in order to co-ordinate them with supply plans for the whole theatre. G-4 established for this purpose a special civilian branch, and phased requirements were transmitted to the Combined Civil Affairs Committee of the Combined Chiefs of Staff for approval and for allocation of the responsibility for procurement between the United Kingdom and the United States. At first a good deal of difficulty was experienced by the Military Government Section in securing the consideration by the other staff sections of requirements, which they tended to consider 'marginal'.

But supply matters, though first in importance, were only one part of the Military Government Section's activities, which were rapidly expanded so as to include every department of Military Government. The Section, after the manner of higher headquarters, began to exercise over the policy of the operational formation a detailed supervision which was certainly necessary, at any rate in the economic field, in order to coordinate the activities of the two A.M.G. headquarters and the Control Commission. Before the end of 1943 it had been divided into two branches, a planning staff and an Economics and Supply and Italian Affairs branch, with financial and legal advisers, making a total of forty-eight officers. But complications did not stop here. With the planning of operations in Southern France and the Balkans, the need for detailed coordination of policy increased. Consequently General Sir Henry Maitland Wilson, who had succeeded General Eisenhower as Supreme Allied Commander-in-Chief in the Mediterranean theatre, following the example of S.H.A.E.F., elevated M.G.S. to be a general staff section known as G-5, under an assistant Chief of Staff, in May 1944. G-5 was organised in two main divisions, Operations and Plans, Economics and Supply, but before the end of the year the Refugees and Displaced Persons section of the Plans and Operations division was made a third division, in view of the increased magnitude of its work in liaison with the United Nations Relief and Rehabilitation Administration (U.N.R.R.A.). By the end of 1944 the British component of G-5 had increased from ten officers, as at the end of 1943, to thirty-seven.

These complications of administrative machinery did not make for speed in arriving at decisions, or for the stimulation of initiative in the field. Reference back to Algiers and from Algiers to the Combined Chiefs of staff, which meant, before combined deliberation, a separate reference to the Governments in Washington and London, frequently took months to elicit a definite policy, much to the detriment of both prestige and administrative efficiency.[1] This was strikingly illustrated, as will be shown in Chapter VIII, in the long delays which occurred in issuing the directives of the 'New Deal' policy. That in matters of supply particularly reference back was essential, is not to be disputed; and accusations of excessive dependence are, of course, easy to make and difficult to refute. But the historian who has examined this vast volume of correspondence cannot fail to note the exasperation of the lower echelons, and to

[1] Mr Macmillan's comments on this point also are equally incisive: 'Italian organisations are hamstrung at every turn by excessive dependence on Algiers, which itself lavishly refers too many questions to the Combined Chiefs of Staff'.

wonder how far the application of this complicated procedure was really necessary.

G-5 and the Allied Control Commission were not the only bodies responsible for advising the Supreme Commander in his task of administering the policy of the United Nations towards Italy. At the Moscow Conference of October 1943 it was agreed that an Advisory Council to deal with matters pertaining to Italy should be established, composed in the first instance of representatives of the 'big three' and of the French Committee of National Liberation. Provision was also made for the addition of representatives of Yugoslavia and Greece. The Council was to be purely advisory, until such time as the Allied Commander-in-Chief considered it possible to bring direct military control of the Italian administration to an end. When this happened, he would relinquish the Presidency of the Control Commission, and the Advisory Council would assume the direction of that body. The Council was to have the duty, in particular, of watching the operation of the machinery of control which was enforcing the terms of surrender. It was to keep itself closely informed of current Italian affairs, its members being supplied by their respective Governments with all relevant information on political and military developments, and it was empowered to make joint or several recommendations, but possessed no authority to take decisions. It had no power of issuing orders of any kind to the Commander-in-Chief, and it was not to concern itself with his military functions, but was to advise him in his capacity as President of the Control Commission on general policy connected with the work of control, and to have the right to ask him for information or explanations on matters affecting the Council's work. It was also to maintain close touch with such other technical inter-Allied bodies as might be established in Italy. The first meeting of the Advisory Council was held in Algiers on 30th November, the members being Mr Murphy representing the U.S.A., Mr Macmillan the United Kingdom, M. Vyshinsky the U.S.S.R., and M. Massigli the French Committee of National Liberation.

But neither the Russian nor the French desire to participate in the Allied task of controlling Italy was satisfied by membership of the Advisory Council. The Soviet Government claimed to be entitled to appoint its representative to the Allied Control Commission itself—a claim which was admitted, on the ground that the instrument of surrender was signed in the name of the British, American and Russian Governments, a consideration which placed the Soviet Government in a separate category from other governments. M. Massigli made a similar claim for French representation on the Commission. Both the British and American Governments were anxious to avoid creating a precedent which would permit other governments of the United Nations to assert similar claims, and thus create a danger of making the Commission unmanageable, but as a result of the decision in the Advisory Council M. Vyshinsky sent a recommendation to Moscow that there should be both a Soviet and a French member of the Control Commission, whose functions would be consultative. The right to appoint members of the Commission should not be further extended. This solution to the problem was finally accepted at the beginning of February 1944, after General Wilson had cabled the Combined Chiefs of Staff in favour of French participation, since French troops were 'fighting gallantly and pulling their weight in the battle'. The French member of the Commission appointed was General De Sevin.

The Advisory Council, supplemented though it subsequently was by Greek and Yugoslav representatives, dealt only with Italian problems; but the Commander-in-Chief's responsibilities extended to the whole of the Mediterranean theatre, involving him in an enormous number of day-to-day decisions, either directly of a political nature or fraught with political implications. Some staff machinery was therefore necessary to deal with them, on the lines of the defunct Political and Economic Control established by General Eisenhower in North Africa early in 1943. General Wilson had created a similar body in the Middle East and, when he assumed Supreme Command of the Mediterranean theatre, he established, at the beginning of February 1944, a Political Committee, which normally met once a week. The Supreme Allied Commander himself or his Chief of Staff usually took the chair, and other members included, besides Deputy-SACMED, the Naval C.-in-C. Mediterranean, the C.-in-C. Mediterranean Allied Air Forces, the Chief Administrative Officer of A.F.H.Q., the American Political Adviser and the British Resident Minister. The membership of this body was quickly enlarged so as to include the Assistant Chief of Staff in charge of the Military Government Section (later G-5) and the Chief of the Psychological Warfare Branch.[1]

The departure of General Eisenhower at the beginning of January 1944 to take supreme charge of the Allied operations in northern Europe entailed a change in the nationality of the head of the Control Commission, since the principle had been accepted that the head of the Commission was to be of the same nationality as the Supreme Commander. It was consequently decided to recall Lieut.-General Sir Noel Mason-MacFarlane to Italy, to take charge of the Control Commission under the title of Deputy-President and Chief Commissioner. General Mason-MacFarlane took over from General

---

[1] The title and composition of this body were altered when General Alexander succeeded to the post of SACMED in December 1944. It was renamed S.A.C's Conference (Political) and its membership was further expanded so as to include the Chief Commissioner of the Allied (no longer Control) Commission.

Joyce on 16th January and immediately set to work to reorganise the Commission into a rather more manageable shape. The most important feature of this reorganisation was the abolition of the dual exercise of Military Government by Fifteenth Army Group and the Control Commission. This was made possible by the incorporation of the Advanced Administrative Echelon of A.F.H.Q. with Fifteenth Army Group into the formation first known as Allied Central Mediterranean Force (A.C.M.F.)—later called Allied Armies in Italy (A.A.I.)—which was placed under General Alexander's command and included all troops on the Italian mainland. General Alexander remained Military Governor, and the Deputy-President (later Chief Commissioner) of the Control Commission, which was placed under his command, became his C.C.A.O., though retaining direct access to A.F.H.Q. The Commission thus became the Civil Affairs branch of General Alexander's staff.[1] A.M.G. Fifteenth Army Group was abolished, and the Army A.M.G's, while still remaining operationally under the Commanders of the Fifth and Eighth Armies, were placed under the technical control of a new section of the Allied Control Commission, which took under its charge the whole of A.M.G., both in the forward and the static areas. This section, called the Regional Control and Military Government Section, was placed under Brigadier Lush, who was given the title of Executive Commissioner with the status of Vice-President. It was made responsible for all control work in the field, including, besides the technical direction and administration of the Army A.M.G's, the command of all Regional officers, not only in territory subject to military government, but also those in Regions which had been restored to the administration of the Italian Government. The section was also made responsible for many of the duties which had hitherto been performed by the Chief of Staff of the Commission, whose post was abolished.[2] Region VI (Sardinia), which had up till now been under the direct command of A.F.H.Q., was transferred to the Commission.

Other changes, the effects of which can perhaps be most clearly appreciated by comparing the tables of organisation given in Annexe II and Annexe III to this chapter, were as follows:

The Military Section was abolished. The three Service Sub-Commissions were made 'independent'. The direction of their operations lay, for all practical purposes, completely outside the Commission; their chain of command depended from the headquarters of each of the three Services. The Prisoners of War and War Material Factories Sub-Commissions were dissolved, and the administration

---

[1] This arrangement was subsequently modified after the transfer of A.F.H.Q. from Algiers to Caserta and its consequent reorganisation. See below, p. 256.

[2] The title was however revived later in favour of Brigadier Lush.

and repatriation of escaped Allied prisoners of war was eliminated from the functions of the former. The remaining sub-commission of the Military Section, War Material Disposal, was preserved as an 'independent' sub-commission, the duties of handling Italian prisoners of war being combined with it in July 1944.

The Political Section was confined to the function of supervising Italian foreign relations, and officials of the two Governments, Mr Caccia of the Foreign Office and Mr Reber of the State Department, were given the rank of joint Vice-Presidents. The Displaced Persons Sub-Commission was transferred to the Military Government and Regional Control Section, and the Information Sub-Commission was eliminated, its functions being performed by the Information and Censorship branch of A.F.H.Q.

The Economic and Administrative Section was split up into two distinct sections, the Administrative Section under Air-Commodore Lord Stansgate as Vice-President, and the Economic Section under President Roosevelt's nominee, a civilian, Mr Henry Grady, as Vice-President. Monuments, Fine Arts and Archives, which had been combined with Education, was made into a separate sub-commission.

The Foreign Trade Sub-Commission was eliminated, since during the campaign there was no Italian foreign trade. The Fuel Sub-Commission was also abolished, its functions being carried out by the Petroleum and Coal Sections of Allied Force headquarters. Another important change was the creation of a Food Sub-Commission. This had been included in the first directive of the Combined Chiefs of Staff, but had afterwards been eliminated on the ground that the sub-commissions should follow the pattern of the Italian ministries, under which food distribution and rationing was a function of the Ministry of the Interior. The responsibility for the rationing system had therefore been allotted to the Interior Sub-Commission. This arrangement aroused strong representations from the Ministry of Food in London, and the Food Sub-Commission was restored, becoming responsible for what was perhaps the most important single function of the whole Allied Control Commission.

The Communications Section of the Commission was also eliminated. Telecommunications became an 'independent' sub-commission; Inland Transportation was assigned to the Administrative Section. The control of Italian shipping was divided between the Allied Navies and MEDBO, the Allied shipping control in the Mediterranean. Only the management of the small volume of coastal shipping (schooners) reserved for Italian civilian needs was assigned to the Transportation Sub-Commission.

General Mason-MacFarlane also succeeded in reducing considerably the number of high-ranking posts. Deputy Vice-Presidents and the Directors and Deputy-Directors of the Economic and Administrative Sections were eliminated, as well as the Chief, Vice-Chief and Deputy Chief of Staff. A deputy to the Deputy-President was appointed in the person of Captain Ellery Stone, while the functions of the Chief of Staff and his deputies were coordinated under the Executive Commissioner in the Regional Control and Military Government Section, which included the Establishment Branch responsible for the A and Q work of the whole Commission. The other three sections, the Political, Economic, and Administrative, had as their function the control of the policy of the Italian Government, with which the sub-commissions dealt directly. They prepared the orders and directives on policy for the Chief Commissioner, which were passed to the Regional Commissioners in the field through the Executive Commissioner.

But the reorganisation of the Commission, though it eliminated some of its more patent organisational inefficiencies, did not really go to the heart of the matter. The Commission never wholly escaped the deformities arising from the confused conditions which attended its birth. These reforms did however enable it to get down to the task of organising its machinery, which had been impossible in the first three months of its existence, when most of the high posts had remained unfilled and its staff had been divided between Palermo and Brindisi, where the accommodation available for both the Italian Government and the Control Commission had been miserably inadequate.[1]

The problem of accommodation hampered the work of the Commission continuously from its birth, until it was able to take up its headquarters in the Ministry of Corporations in Rome. When the Italian Government was moved out of the very cramped quarters available to it at Brindisi, Salerno was chosen as its temporary seat. To maintain its prestige, it was essential that it should not be located in territory subject to Military Government, and in any event military considerations (including that of accommodation) made it undesirable to establish it at Naples. But the accommodation available at Salerno was insufficient to house both the Italian Government and the whole Control Commission. The Commission had consequently to be divided: its main H.Q., the Regional Control and Military Government and the Economic Sections were settled in Naples, only the Administrative Section being located at Salerno—an arrangement which certainly did not make for either comfort or co-ordination.

---

[1] At one time the small staff of officers of the Commission who were posted to Brindisi were 'commuting' daily by road from their living quarters in S. Cesarea, south of Otranto, about fifty miles distant from their office.

The unification of A.M.G. in both the forward and rear areas under the single control of the Allied Control Commission was certainly a great improvement, since it ensured for the first time a unity of policy, extending from 'King's Italy' into the forward areas, in matters where such unity was indispensable, if chaos was to be avoided. The nightmare of divided controls, which, particularly on the supply side, had led to serious trouble, was thus dispelled, even if the besetting sin of the Commission's administrative structure remained unredeemed. This unity of policy was maintained by the following arrangements. Legislation passed by the Italian Government for its own territory was applied by the Control Commission in the Regions for which it was responsible, including even Army areas, when conditions were considered suitable. This application was not automatic, but depended upon the decision of the Executive Commissioner, whose counter-signature was required. Similarly, when territories were handed back to the Italian Government, the Italian Government published in the Official Gazette decrees reproducing substantially the contents of A.M.G. Proclamations and General Orders.

The placing of the Commission under General Alexander's command, making it the Civil Affairs Branch of his headquarters, entailed his appointment as the representative in Italy of SACMED, the President, and the delegation to him of the authority to perform, on his behalf, certain of the functions which belonged to the President. In a memorandum issued on 28th January 1944 by General Wilson's Chief of Staff, Lieut.-General J. A. H. Gammell, it was stated to be the desire of A.F.H.Q.

> that so far as is practicable all problems of Civil Affairs arising in Italy shall be solved on the ground under the control of the G.O.C. A.C.M.F. and accordingly the Allied Commander-in-Chief empowers him to act for him in such matters.

But certain subjects were expressly excepted as requiring reference to A.F.H.Q., namely matters which called for high political guidance and raised issues not confined to Italy, as well as questions of civilian supply, where reference to A.F.H.Q.

> will often be requisite in view of the responsibility of the theatre commander to decide, if need be, between conflicting needs. There will however be questions other than the foregoing which because of their importance, intrinsically or as precedents, should be submitted to the Commander on whom the final responsibility rests.

The memorandum went on to point out that it was impossible to set up a rigid list of the matters in which action should in all cases be taken by the G.O.C.-in-C., A.C.M.F.;

> the result would be an inflexible system and this Headquarters might thereby preclude itself from acting on matters which, when they arose, would call for action here. The object of the present directive instead is to enable the G.O.C.-in-C., A.C.M.F., acting through H.Q., A.C.C., which will also be the Civil Affairs Branch of H.Q. A.C.M.F., to decide on the ground every question arising there, while leaving A.F.H.Q. free to act on all matters where it is found that action must or should be taken here.

In retrospect this attempt to attain flexibility might appear a trifle naive. The correct interpretation of its phraseology is not very clear, but it is difficult for the historian not to suspect that its meaning in practice at A.C.C. headquarters must have been taken to be 'when in doubt refer'. He can also scarcely help asking whether this detailed control of Italian administration at three levels was really necessary, in order to attain the fundamental purpose of the Commission, namely the devotion of the maximum of Italian resources, both in manpower and materials, to the Allied war effort, and the restoration to the Italian people of a democratic form of government through the destruction of Fascism, questions which will be discussed in a later chapter.

The first event of importance after the reorganisation of the Allied Control Commission was the handing back of territory, already proposed in the autumn of 1943, to the Italian Government. This territory to be handed back included Sicily (but not Pantelleria, Lampedusa and Linosa, which for strategic reasons remained under Allied occupation), and all Italy south of the northern boundaries of the provinces of Bari, Potenza and Salerno.[1] This event, which the Military Government Section had suggested should take place on 20th December 1943, did not in fact come about until 11th February 1944, owing in part to the difficulties experienced by Marshal Badoglio in forming a coherent administration—difficulties which were largely overcome by the formation of the so-called Government of Under-Secretaries in November—but even more to the prolonged discussion aroused in Washington and London by the proposed instruments of transfer.

Meanwhile the Italian Government had agreed to pass, before the date of transfer, certain legislation intended to incorporate into Italian law the decrees and orders of the Allied Military Government. This included a decree stabilizing wage rates and maximum prices as fixed by A.M.G. previous to the restoration, a decree defining the maximum quantities of grain permitted to be held by farmers as

---

[1] It would appear that the legal status of the four Apulian provinces and of Sardinia was regarded as being that of 'occupied territory' in the sense laid down in the Terms of Surrender, though Allied Military Government had never in fact been installed in them.

laid down by A.M.G., and a decree establishing the authority of the Allied Military courts. The proclamation announcing the restoration of Italian administration was signed by Marshal Badoglio. It contained clauses under which the Italian Government recognised the validity of all proclamations and orders issued by the Military Governor, and declared all official action taken by him as legal, valid and binding, including specifically, besides the sentences imposed by Allied Military courts, all appointments to, and removals from, office, public or private. These clauses were afterwards embodied in a Decree-Law (RDL 31). In addition the Italian Government undertook 'with all possible expedition' to pass certain other decrees of a financial character, barring transactions in land and buildings, so far as necessary to prevent inflation, restricting transactions in foreign exchange, bullion, etc., as well as empowering the competent minister, as a war-measure, to prohibit any type of business, and to block or take into custody any property containing a Fascist or enemy interest. Finally the Government was also requested to pass a decree conferring administrative power on the Commission's Director of Property Control in relation to the property belonging to nationals of Allied Nations and French nationals—a decree which was subsequently abandoned owing to a change in Allied policy. Simultaneously with the Marshal's proclamation an announcement was made by General Alexander, declaring the transfer of territory and recording the aims and achievements of Allied Military Government, laying particular stress upon the eradication of Fascism and the restoration of freedom of speech and of the press, which had been one of the fundamental aims of military government.[1]

The territory administered under Allied Military Government was thus reduced to a comparatively narrow strip stretching across the Italian peninsula, consisting of Campania—minus the province of Salerno—the provinces of Foggia and Campobasso and part of Chieti province. In the remainder of liberated Italy a new regime of 'advisory control' was inaugurated, under which the Italian Government through its various ministries was advised and controlled by the headquarters of the Control Commission, while Regional Commissioners were informed of the nature of this advice and instructed to ensure, in cooperation with the Italian provincial authorities, that it was carried out. It was realised that this task of advisory control was far more difficult than executive government, the more so, because the removal of many Italian administrative officers through 'defascistisation' had left the machinery of government without many of its cogs. But Regional officers were instructed to do everything in their power to uphold the authority of Italian officials and to abstain from executive action, exercising the greatest

[1] The text is given in Annexe IV to this chapter.

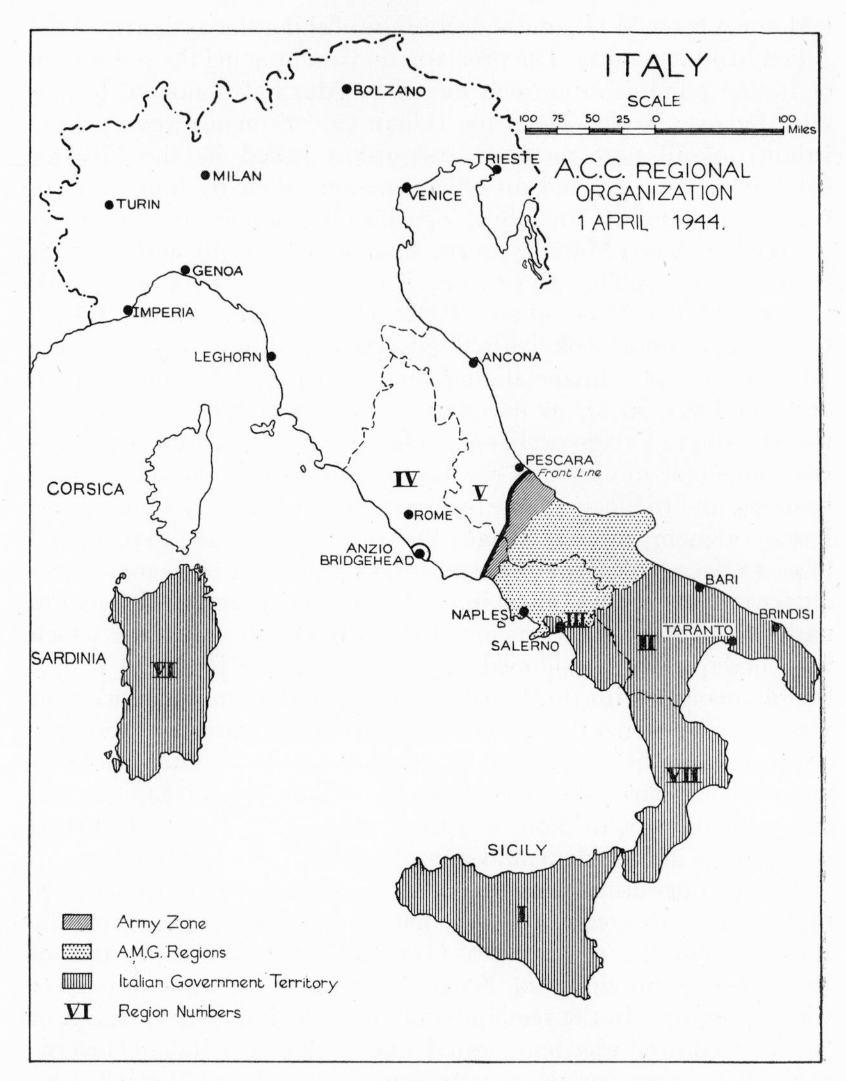

Map 6

care not to bring the administration into contempt, even when its officials seemed guilty of inefficiency and corruption, their function being to help to sort things out and to report any case of bad administration immediately. They were also informed that their numbers would be progressively reduced, since the tendering of advice was more likely to be successful when emanating from only a few key men than if every Italian official was bolstered up by the presence of an Allied officer.

All this was indeed very good sense, but it did not really touch the essence of the problem. So long as Allied military officers, either in headquarters or in the field, were in fact controlling the activities of Italian officials, even in an 'advisory' form, the ultimate responsibility lay with them and not with the Italian Government. Moreover advisory control by foreigners did not make for the speedy decision so necessary in war time. Under these new conditions the Italian official was too often inclined to take one of two attitudes. Either he was content from lack of initiative to let the real responsibility for his actions rest on the Allies, or he was inclined to regard Allied advice with suspicion, because he was not convinced that it represented the real opinion of his own Government. Here again this 'hedging' process could lead only to procrastination and the damping down of initiative. Nor with the best will in the world was it easy for the Allied Military Government officers to divest themselves of executive responsibility. The habit of command was not more easily changed than the habit of obedience. Hence the evacuation of Allied officers from transferred areas was much slower than was at first anticipated; the result was that the efficiency of the Commission was greatly hampered when the resources of its rigidly limited war establishment were strained by the taking over of large areas of newly liberated territory.[1] Nor was the position of the Italian Government—a government in leading-strings—either easy or dignified. The restoration of sovereignty to the Italian Government in unoccupied territory was in fact beset everywhere by the limits imposed by the Allied Commander-in-Chief through the agency of the Allied Control Commission. Until some time after the liberation of Rome and the installation of the Bonomi Cabinet, the accent remained strongly on the middle 'C' of A.C.C.

---

[1] See below, p. 177.

ANNEXE I

Moscow Resolution on the Advisory Council

1. An Advisory Council for Italy will be established forthwith, composed in the first instance of Representatives of the United Kingdom, the United States of America, the Soviet Union and the French Committee of National Liberation. Representatives of Greece and Yugoslavia will be added as full members of the Council as soon as practicable, in view of the special interests of these two countries arising from the aggressions of Fascist Italy upon their territory during the present war.

2. Each representative will be assisted, where necessary, by a small staff of technical advisers, civilian and military. The council will establish itself as soon as possible in Italy at the same place as the Headquarters of the Allied Commander-in-Chief.

3. The Council will keep itself closely informed of current Italian affairs and advise the respective Governments and the French Committee of National Liberation in regard to problems. The members of the Council will be supplied by the respective Governments and by the French Committee of National Liberation with all relevant information on political and military developments affecting their work. They will make joint or several recommendations to their Governments or to the French Committee, but will have no power to take final decisions. They will not, of course, concern themselves with the military functions of the Allied Commander-in-Chief.

4. The Council will have the duty in particular of watching the operation of the machinery of control in Italy which will be enforcing the terms of surrender.

5. The Council will advise the Allied Commander-in-Chief in his capacity as President of the Allied Control Commission on general policy connected with the work of the control. For this purpose it will maintain close touch with the Allied Commander-in-Chief as President of the Control Commission and will have the right to ask him for information or explanations on matters affecting the Council's work. It will maintain close touch with such technical inter-Allied bodies as may be established in Italy, and will be entitled to obtain information and explanations from them on matters effecting its work.

6. The Allied Commander-in-Chief will continue as in the past to receive instructions from the United Kingdom and the United States Governments through the Combined Chief of Staff in Washington.

7. When, in the opinion of the Allied Commander-in-Chief, it is possible to bring direct military control of the Italian administration to an end, the Commander-in-Chief will relinquish the Presidency of the Allied Control Commission. The Advisory Council for Italy will thereupon assume the direction of the work of the Allied Control Commission.

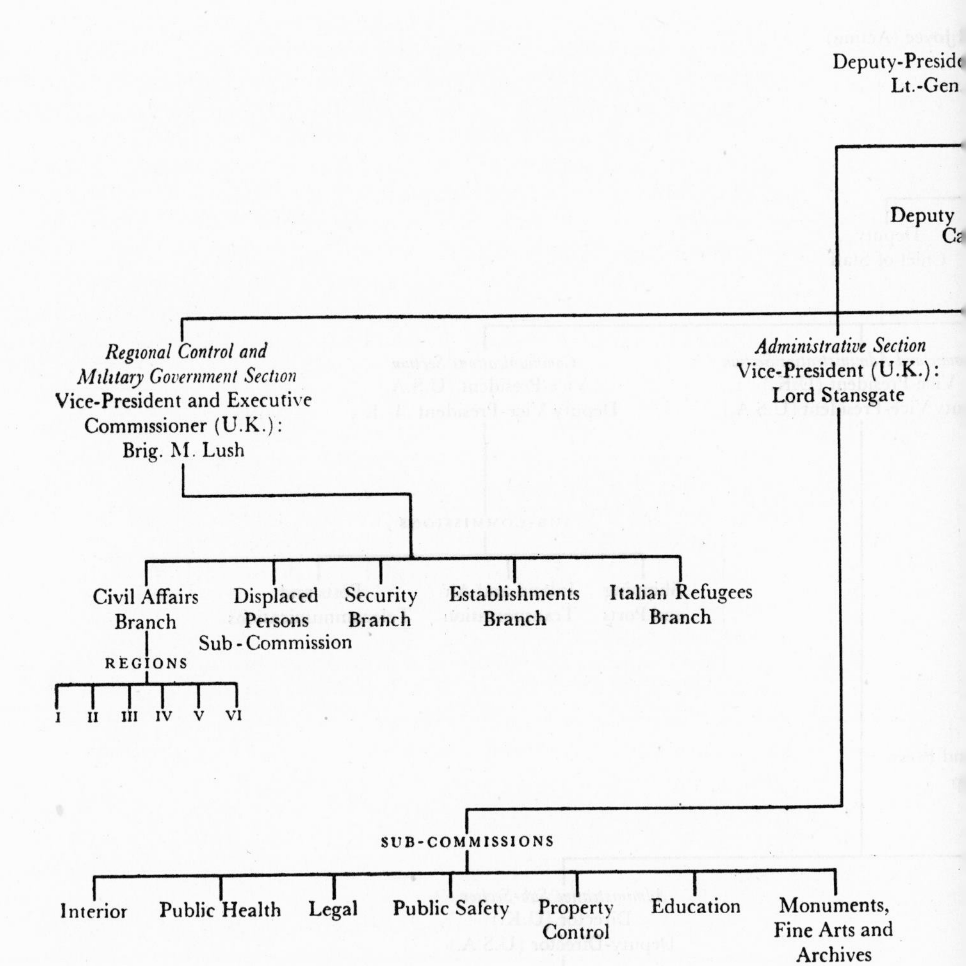
A
Allied Control Comm
President (U
Deputy-Presid
Lt.-Gen
Deputy
Ca
Regional Control and
Military Government Section
Vice-President and Executive
Commissioner (U.K.):
Brig. M. Lush
Administrative Section
Vice-President (U.K.):
Lord Stansgate
Civil Affairs
Branch
Displaced
Persons
Sub-Commission
Security
Branch
Establishments
Branch
Italian Refugees
Branch
REGIONS
I
II
III
IV
V
VI
SUB-COMMISSIONS
Interior
Public Health
Legal
Public Safety
Property
Control
Education
Monuments,
Fine Arts and
Archives

NNEXE III

ission as reorganised, February 1944

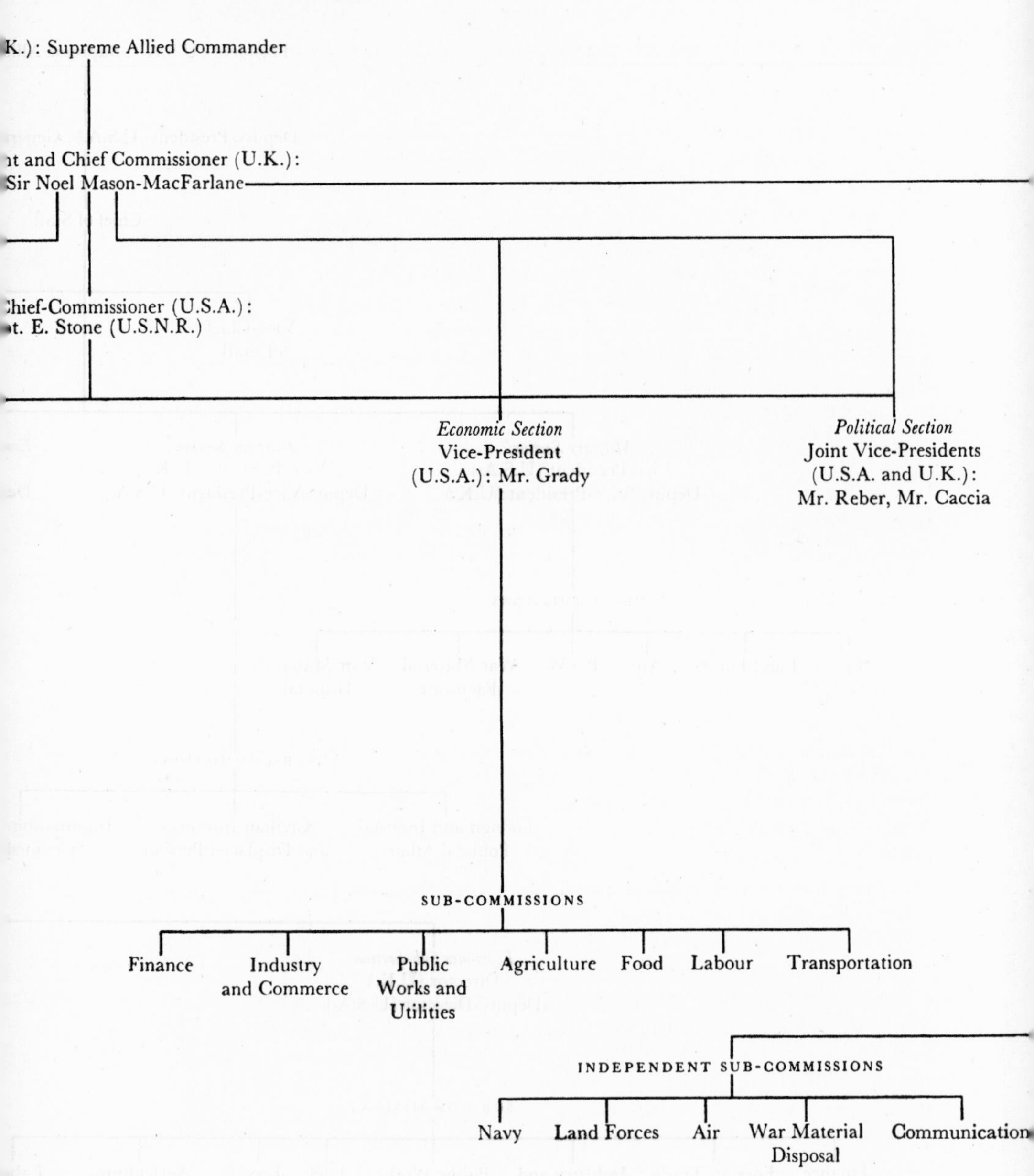

K.): Supreme Allied Commander
it and Chief Commissioner (U.K.):
Sir Noel Mason-MacFarlane
Chief-Commissioner (U.S.A.):
t. E. Stone (U.S.N.R.)
Economic Section
Vice-President
(U.S.A.): Mr. Grady
Political Section
Joint Vice-Presidents
(U.S.A. and U.K.):
Mr. Reber, Mr. Caccia
SUB-COMMISSIONS
Finance
Industry and Commerce
Public Works and Utilities
Agriculture
Food
Labour
Transportation
INDEPENDENT SUB-COMMISSIONS
Navy
Land Forces
Air
War Material Disposal
Communication

ANNEXE IV

Terms for Restoration of Territory to the Italian Government

WHEREAS, in the course of their conduct of the war against the Axis powers, the Allied Forces have occupied certain Italian territory and

WHEREAS, an Armistice has been concluded with the Italian Government pursuant to which the United Nations may take such measures within and in regard to such territory as they may deem necessary for the protection of the Allied Forces and for the successful prosecution of the war and to occupy such other portions of Italian territory as they may deem necessary, and

WHEREAS, the Italian Government has declared war on Germany and has become a co-belligerent with the United Nations and

WHEREAS, the Italian Government has requested that certain areas now occupied by the Allied Forces be restored to the jurisdiction of the Italian Government and

WHEREAS, it is the desire of the United Nations to comply with this request in so far as may be compatible with the successful prosecution of the war and

WHEREAS, it is necessary for the successful prosecution of the war that certain rights, powers and immunities in all Italian territories which has been liberated from German domination be retained by the Allied Forces,

NOW, THEREFORE, I, HAROLD R. L. G. ALEXANDER, G.C.B., C.S.I., D.S.O., M.C.,
General, Military Governor, by virtue of authority vested in me by General Sir Henry Maitland Wilson, G.B.E., K.C.B., D.S.O., A.D.C., Commander in Chief of the Allied Forces, hereby terminate Allied Military Government in the territory described below. The Italian Government will resume the government of that territory, subject to the terms and conditions hereinafter set forth.

Territory Restored: That portion of the Mainland of Italy south of the northern boundaries of the provinces of Salerno, Potenza and Bari, and Sicily and Adjacent Islands (but not Pantelleria or Lampedusa and Linosa).

Terms of Restoration: Without prejudice to any rights, powers and immunities of the United Nations under the Armistice terms heretofore granted to the Italian Government, all of which remain in full force and effect throughout all Italian territory, there is hereby reserved to the United Nations and to the Commander in Chief of the Allied Forces and to such officers or other representatives, including the Allied Control Commission, as he may designate, the rights, powers and immunities described below, in any part of the said territory and in all other Italian territory which has been liberated from German domination and is now under the jurisdiction of the Italian government, hereinafter referred to as 'the Unoccupied Territory':

1. There will be made available to the Allied Forces such facilities, utilities and installations as may be required by the Allied Commander

in Chief or his agents for such disposition, use or operation as may be determined.

2. To maintain and quarter troops in such parts of the Unoccupied Territory as they may see fit.

3. To hold or require the Italian Government to hold in custody prisoners of war and civilian internees as may be directed by the Allied Commander in Chief.

4. To declare any area to be a Military Zone and to exercise therein the rights of an occupying power or enforce such other controls as may be determined by the Allied Commander in Chief.

5. To convene Allied Military Tribunals for the trial of any person violating any order or regulation issued by the Allied Military authorities and of any person otherwise doing any act hostile to the Allied Forces or any member thereof, and to inflict such punishment upon such person as such Tribunals may direct.

6. To conduct and carry to ultimate conclusion the trial by Allied Military Tribunals of any person charged with an offense heretofore committed and cognizable under any proclamation or order heretofore issued by or on behalf of the Allied Military Governor.

7. To requisition private and public property and services.

8. To reoccupy the whole or any part of the Unoccupied Territory at any time or to take such other steps or exercise such other powers in any part of such territory as may from time to time be deemed necessary for the proper prosecution of the war.

9. To import and export and to control and supervise the distribution to the civilian population of such civilian supplies as the Allied Forces may determine without the payment of any impost, tax, charge, or duty of any kind whatsoever either to the Italian Government or to any of its political subdivisions or agencies.

10. To engage in such operations and import and export such military or other supplies or property of any nature as may be deemed necessary for the proper prosecution of the war, free from the imposition of any impost, tax, charge or duty of any kind whatsoever by the Italian Government or any of its political sub-divisions or agencies.

11. Any official or other representative or agent of the United Nations, civilian or military, may enter and remain within the Unoccupied Territory free from the imposition of any impost, tax, charge or duty of any kind whatsoever by the Italian Government or any of its political subdivisions or agencies.

12. No member of the Allied Forces or any official or other representative or agent of the United Nations, civilian or military, shall be brought to trial in any Italian Court for any cause whatsoever either civil or criminal without the consent of the Allied Powers.

13. All expenses and costs arising from the maintenance of Allied Troops or other personnel within the said territory will be chargeable to the Italian Government as a part of the costs of occupation.

14. Proclamations and Decrees in the form annexed hereto and made a part of these terms and conditions will be issued by the Italian Government at the time of transfer of the territory.

CHAPTER V

THE BADOGLIO GOVERNMENTS

THE INITIAL relations between the Allied Command and Marshal Badoglio could, in the circumstance, hardly have been inspired by a great degree of mutual confidence.[1] But the manner of the surrender of the Italian fleet, and the first encounters of the Military Mission of General Mason-MacFarlane with the Marshal at Brindisi, quickly convinced General Eisenhower that, whatever the motives which had induced the capitulation, cooperation with Badoglio was possible in the pursuit of the main Allied objective, defined by Mr Churchill the day following the announcement of the armistice (9th September) as 'the conversion of Italy into an active agent against Germany'.[2]

The attainment of this object did not appear to General Eisenhower to be entirely consistent either with the 'short terms' of the armistice signed at Cassibile, or with some of the provisions of the 'long terms', the signature of which he had been instructed to obtain. This document, though accepted by the U.S. Government, was from the beginning looked upon with a certain amount of reserve by the President. In seeking guidance from the Combined Chiefs of Staff on future relations with the Italian Government on 19th/20th September, General Eisenhower saw only two possible alternatives: to accept and strengthen the Government of the King and Badoglio by formally recognising it, not only as the sole legitimate Government of Italy, but also as co-belligerent; or to sweep it aside and set up an Allied Military Government over the whole of occupied Italy. Of these two courses he strongly recommended the first on military grounds, pointing out the considerable assistance already obtained from active Italian cooperation in Sardinia, Corsica and elsewhere. He also sketched the conditions subject to which such recognition should be accorded, including the strengthening of the national character of that government by the inclusion of representatives of the political parties to form a sort of national coalition, a decree restoring the former constitution and promising free election for a constituent assembly after the war, and, possibly, the abdication of the King in favour of his son or grandson—though this point, he insisted,

[1] The impressions left in the mind of General Alexander by the somewhat peculiar course of the negotiations leading to the conclusion of the armistice, are described in his despatch. See particularly *op. cit.* pages 2888 to 2890.

[2] Churchill, *The Second World War*, Vol. V, p. 119.

would require careful study, as it might prove more popular abroad than with the Italian people—and the acceptance of an armistice commission. In return for the fulfilment of these conditions, he requested some discretion in enforcing the stipulations of the 'long terms' and suggested that the Allies might agree to the suspension of certain rights under the armistice in favour of a reformed and liberated Italy.

The recognition of the Badoglio Government, though it was agreed by the President, was never popular with the American public, and misleading analogies between Badoglio and Darlan were only too easily drawn. Moreover the Secretary of State, Mr Cordell Hull, did not regard it with favour. In his opinion the Marshal 'was adequate for the purpose of signing the terms of surrender, but I did not think him adequate for the purpose of governing Italy'.[1] Mr Churchill, on the other hand, whose gaze was always focused on the paramount objective of defeating Germany, was inclined to stress the importance of Badoglio and the House of Savoy, not as an end in themselves, but as a vitally important factor in maintaining the loyalty of the Italian armed forces, in particular the navy, to the Allied cause.[2]

In spite of this difference in perspective on the two sides of the Atlantic, it was possible to agree on a concerted policy to support the Badoglio Government by recognising its claim to be the legitimate government of Italy, by treating it as a co-belligerent[3] in the war against Germany, subject to its working for the Allies on the basis of the armistice, and by recognising useful service performed against the enemy in the adjustment of the enforcement of the armistice terms, on the principle of payments by results. This support was to be based on the clear understanding that it would in no way prejudice the right of the Italian people to decide freely on their eventual form of government after the Germans had been evicted. In the meantime the King and Marshal Badoglio were to be requested to

---

[1] *The Memoirs of Cordell Hull*, (English edition), Vol. II, p. 1550.

[2] See Churchill, *op. cit.* Vol. V, Ch. XXVIII. See also his speech to the House of Commons on 22nd February 1944.

[3] The exact significance of this word—*parola bruttissima* in Italian opinion—is not very clear. It was used to denote the status conferred by the Allies on the Czecho-Slovak and Polish national insurgent forces, which came into being at the break up of the Austrian Empire in 1918, with the intention of preventing them being treated merely as rebels. See *Oppenheim's International Law* (7th edition) Vol. 2, pp. 251–299. In the second World War the term was specially chosen because it did not put an end to the juridical state of war existing between the Allies and Italy. See G. G. Fitzmaurice, *Hague Recueils* 73, (1948) (ii) pp. 272–274. 'There is no doubt that the term co-belligerency was employed both in the Peace Treaty and at the time of Italy's original declaration of war against Germany, to mark the fact that Italy did *not* thereby acquire Allied status. There is no doubt either, that Italy's co-belligerency was not intended to put an end (nor did in fact put an end) to the juridical state of war between Italy and the Allies. Nevertheless Italy's co-belligerency created a highly anomalous situation juridically, and one which to some extent defies legal analysis and classification . . .'

widen the basis of their government by building up the most broadly based anti-Fascist coalition, including all patriotic liberal and left-wing elements. This policy was accepted by Marshal Badoglio, who publicly expressed his intention to resign as soon as final victory over the Germans had been assured. It also received the adherence of the Soviet Government at the Moscow conference, in a three-power declaration of which the following extract gives the principal points:

> The Foreign Secretaries of the three Governments are agreed that the following measures are important and should be put into effect.
>
> (1) It is essential that the Italian Government should be made more democratic by the inclusion of representatives of those sections of the Italian people who have always opposed Fascism.
>
> (2) Freedom of speech, of religious worship, of political belief, of Press and of public meeting shall be restored in full measure to the Italian people who shall also be entitled to form anti-Fascist political groups.
>
> (3) All institutions and organisations created by the Fascist regime shall be suppressed.
>
> (4) All Fascist or pro-Fascist elements shall be removed from the administration and from institutions and organisations of a public character.
>
> (5) All political prisoners of the Fascist regime shall be released and accorded full amnesty.
>
> (6) Democratic organs of local government shall be created.
>
> (7) Fascist chiefs and Army Generals, known or suspected to be war criminals, shall be arrested and handed over to justice.

It should be noted that the declaration, besides withdrawing the ban on political activity, which had formed part of the AMGOT directive, announced a policy of 'defascistisation' and suppression of Fascist institutions without any of the reserves previously laid down.

Marshal Badoglio, after an initial protest, made no difficulties in accepting the 'long terms', which it was decided to keep secret because of the obvious use which could be made of them for propaganda purposes by Mussolini and the Germans. Only on one point did he enter a specific objection, namely, the very low official rate of exchange accorded by the Allies to the lira. This matter was also taken up in a personal letter addressed by King Victor Emmanuel to King George VI and President Roosevelt, in which the Italian Sovereign pointed out *inter alia* that his Government would be enormously strengthened *vis-à-vis* the neo-Fascist regime, if it were allowed to extend its jurisdiction over the remainder of occupied territory, since this would give him a greater choice of political leaders to carry out the political reconstruction of the country and the eventual return to parliamentary government which he desired. The return to parliamentary government was thus expressly laid down as the aim of the King's policy several weeks before the Moscow Conference.

Marshal Badoglio lost no time in opening negotiations for the broadening of his administration. He had arrived in Brindisi with no civilian ministers—only the Minister for Air, General Sandalli, and the Minister of Marine, Admiral De Courten. Even his Minister of War was left behind in Rome. But Signor Leopoldo Piccardi, Minister of Corporations in his first government—a Councillor of State uncompromised by Fascism, with liberal connections—had succeeded in escaping to Naples just before it fell to the Allies, and had already made contact with the political leaders in the city, before pursuing his way to Brindisi. The Marshal now sent him back to Naples to initiate negotiations with a view to persuading them to join his Government. Already during the period of the negotiations leading to the *coup d'état* of 25th July, Badoglio appears to have been anxious to include anti-Fascist political leaders in his Cabinet. Indeed, he was prepared to offer the post of deputy-premier to his ultimate successor, Signor Bonomi, but the King was adamant in refusing a government of politicians who had been out of office twenty years. He would have no 'ghosts' (*revenants*), to which the Marshal is reported to have replied, 'Sire, we two also are now ghosts'.

For some months before the fall of Mussolini clandestine groups had been organising the revival of the pre-Fascist political parties in Rome, Milan and other cities. Of these, five came to be reconstituted as important nuclei, namely the Communists, the Socialists, the Christian Democrats—a revival of the *Partito Popolare* founded by Don Sturzo—the Liberals, (who in British parlance would more appropriately be called conservative) and the Labour Democrats. A sixth party, inspired by Mazzinian ideals and founded on the anti-Fascist underground movement, *Giustizia e Libertà*, led by the Rosselli brothers, murdered by Cagoulards in France in 1937, completed the group. This called itself the Party of Action, and was composed largely of intellectuals but was without any mass following. When Badoglio left Rome after the declaration of the armistice, these parties constituted the Committee of National Liberation under the presidency of Signor Bonomi, which kept in touch so far as the circumstances permitted with similar committees in the larger cities, such as Florence, Milan, Turin; but the main body of the self-constituted group of party leaders in Rome was cut off from colleagues in southern Italy, where the most distinguished representative of renascent liberalism was the philosopher Benedetto Croce. Several other anti-Fascist political leaders of importance found themselves in southern Italy at the time of the armistice. Some had been liberated by Badoglio from forced residence (*confino*) or prison in the islands, some had succeeded in crossing the German lines. To these were added another group of anti-Fascist exiles, mostly from America, of which the leader was Count Carlo Sforza. Naples was the centre of this group of politicians.

Though the pre-Fascist politicians and their adherents were anything but united in their views as to general policy, there was one point on which nearly all were agreed, namely, in regarding the King as personally responsible for the institution and maintenance of Fascism. They therefore refused to take any part in the government so long as he remained on the throne, though many of them professed themselves perfectly willing to co-operate with Marshal Badoglio. The strongest advocate of this refusal in southern Italy was Croce, himself a convinced monarchist, though most of the other political leaders were ardent republicans.[1] Meanwhile feelers were put out from the Royal household towards another group of politicians in Naples, of whom the most important was Senator Enrico De Nicola, a former President of the Chamber of Deputies. This group refused to serve under Marshal Badoglio as Prime Minister, not apparently on any personal grounds, but because they considered it a violation of the Italian tradition of parliamentary government to serve under a soldier.

Such was the somewhat confused position of the negotiations when Count Sforza re-entered upon the Italian scene. On 23rd September Sforza, who had been for some twenty years an exile in America, had addressed a letter to Mr Adolf Berle, Under-Secretary of the Department of State, in which he declared it to be the first duty of all Italians independent of party to collaborate in unity in order to drive the Germans from Italian soil. As long as Badoglio was engaged in this task and acceptable to the Allies he considered it criminal to do anything to weaken his position and obstruct his work in fighting for the liberty of the Italian people. He was therefore ready to offer him his full support while engaged in this task. Questions of internal politics should be postponed for the period of the struggle, and the political as well as the military activities of Italians should be dedicated to helping those organised forces who were endeavouring to defeat the common enemy.[2] The undertaking given in the letter,

---

[1] Badoglio, *Italy in the Second World War*, p. 46. Badoglio understood clearly at the time of taking office the feeling against Victor Emmanuel among the politicians. Indeed he appears, in discussions with Duke Acquarone, the Minister of the Royal Household, either before or immediately after the 25th July, to have suggested that the King, realising that even in the most loyal regions of the country, like Piedmont, he was blamed by public opinion for continuing the Fascists in power, should follow the precedent of his ancestor Charles Albert after the disaster of Novara, and abdicate in favour of his son.

[2] The English version of this letter will be found in Hansard of 8th December 1944. An Italian version was printed in the *Gazzetta del Mezzogiorno*, published at Bari on 9th December 1943.

though it did not mention the King directly, certainly did so by implication, and was naturally interpreted by the Allies as a pledge of cooperation with him. Though Mr Churchill expressed some scepticism about the wisdom of permitting his return, it was agreed to send Sforza to Italy via London, where Mr Churchill had a long conversation with him, as the result of which the Prime Minister believed that they 'had reached an agreement whereby he was to work loyally with the King and Badoglio until we were in a position, following on the capture of Rome at the earliest moment, to form a broad-based non-Fascist government'.[1] Count Sforza's own interpretation of this pledge, by virtue of which he was permitted to return to Italy, was, to judge from actions, very different.[2]

Whatever may have been Count Sforza's original intentions when he landed on Italian soil, contact with the political leaders in Naples and Bari very soon convinced him that his role was to lead the opposition to the continuation of King Victor Emmanuel upon the Italian throne. He therefore declined the invitation made by the King to join Marshal Badoglio's cabinet as Vice-Premier. The insistence of Croce and Sforza on their refusal to collaborate in any government while the King remained on the throne was in these circumstances decisive. The attempts made by Badoglio to include them in his new cabinet had definitely failed, and the Marshal consequently felt that he had no alternative but to offer his resignation. But now a further complication was introduced. The King meanwhile had received a message from Bonomi, speaking on behalf of the underground Committee of National Liberation (C.L.N.) in Rome, requesting that no new cabinet appointments should be made until Rome was liberated, and promising the Committee's united cooperation on three conditions—namely, the reconstruction of the entire Ministry, the formation of a completely political government with a civilian head, and the election of a constituent assembly as soon as the whole country was free to determine the future form of government.[3] The King therefore refused to accept the Marshal's resignation and requested him to carry on until Rome was reached by forming an *interim* administration of suitable 'technicians' to operate in close collaboration with the Allied Control Commission.

Badoglio thereupon formed, early in November, the Government of Under-Secretaries, so-called because at its formation, in order to emphasize its temporary character, it contained, besides the Marshal himself, only two other ministers, Admiral De Courten, Minister of the Navy, and General Sandalli, Minister of the Air. The other departments were all placed in the hands of under-secretaries. These

---

[1] Churchill, *op.cit.* Vol. V, 175–6.

[2] See his account in his book on '*Italy from 1914 to 1944 as I saw it*'.

[3] Bonomi, *Diario di un anno*, p. 132.

included, besides the Sicilian Guido Jung, a former finance minister of Mussolini's, who on account of his Jewish origin had later become a victim of his racial legislation and in the opinion of the Allied authorities had thus redeemed his Fascist past, several members of pre-Fascist parliaments. But for the most part it was made up of persons chosen for their administrative ability, like Professor Epicarmo Corbino, who was given charge of the food rationing, Mario Fano, an able Jewish ex-director of the northern telegraph companies from Turin, who took charge of communications, and General di Raimondi, who was placed in charge of railways, though those on the mainland were for the most part still being operated by the Allied Armies. The appointment of the two last-named was of particular interest to the Allied High Command, who insisted on their retention in all the subsequent governments until after the conclusion of the campaign.

The formation of this interim Government enabled Badoglio to organise the rudiments of a central departmental machinery sufficiently stable to assume the government of the territories to be handed back to Italian administration. But, however acceptable to some members, at any rate, of the C.L.N. in Rome, this compromise found no favour in the eyes of the southern politicians. Both Sforza and Croce were determined to make the abdication of the monarch a *conditio sine qua non* of forming any alliance with Badoglio, and the winter of 1943–4 was spent by Count Sforza and his associates in devising various methods of bringing pressure to bear on him and on the Allies through Allied Press correspondents—and, it must be suspected, even representatives of the Psychological Warfare Branch of A.F.H.Q., responsible for controlling Italian radio news services and newspapers—in order to persuade them to force the King to abdicate. In these circumstances the Government of Under-Secretaries could only merit Disraeli's description of 'transient and embarrassed phantoms'[1].

Pressure on the Allies, no less than on Badoglio, was maintained by the creation and manipulation of the mysterious entity called public opinion. In obedience to the aim, reiterated in the Moscow declaration, of reintroducing freedom of expression and, within certain limits, freedom of the Press, the Allies had put into the hand of the political parties an instrument which was bound to be used against the King. For, however lacking these self-constituted parties may have been in popular support—a condition for which no standard of measurement could be devised, since no elections could take place—

[1] It was a Government of Under-Secretaries only in name, as special legislation was passed giving the Under-Secretaries practically all ministerial powers; as soon as Sicily and southern Italy were handed back to Italian administration in February it was officially transformed into a government of ministers, with a slight change in personnel, to terminate its brief existence about two months later.

the doings and sayings of the politicians were unquestionably 'news'; and the mere publication of their views, however impartially reported, did in fact help to create a public opinion against the Monarch. It was not surprising therefore that General Mason-MacFarlane should on occasions have found some reason to complain of the activities of P.W.B.—largely composed of pressmen—and that the King and Badoglio should have protested against the publicity given to their opponents. Nor could Allied Press correspondents fail to be struck by the politicians' opposition. For the opposition was led by persons of some distinction, whereas the support accorded to Badoglio and the King by the general public was largely passive, not to say apathetic.

Meanwhile, during the whole of this period of political controversy, Naples, the real political centre of gravity of liberated Italy, remained in Allied Military Government territory. A.M.G. officers were thus brought into close contact with the politicians, and it became increasingly obvious, especially after the Moscow declaration, that the 'Husky' directive forbidding all political activities was no longer applicable. The directive was therefore re-interpreted by A.F.H.Q. at the beginning of November, after consultation with Mr Macmillan, so as to permit expression of political opinion—including criticism of the Italian Government—and normal orderly political activity; except that in the Naples area public meetings and demonstrations, because of disturbed conditions and its proximity to the front line, continued to be prohibited. A congress arranged by the Neapolitan Committee of National Liberation, to be held on 20th December with delegates from Bari, Lecce, Brindisi, Foggia, Taranto, Avellino as well as Calabria and Sicily, was consequently forbidden on orders from Fifteenth Army Group.

The Committee thereupon presented to A.M.G. a formal letter of protest addressed to President Roosevelt, Mr Churchill and Marshal Stalin, which A.M.G., taking exception to its contents on the grounds that it insinuated that the Allied authorities were being misled by Badoglio and the King, refused to accept; but it was published in the Neapolitan Press.[1] Meanwhile it was explained to the Committee that the prohibition only applied to Fifteenth Army Group area, and that the meeting could take place either in Apulia or in Region II. A few days later (1st January 1944) the amendment to the political 'Husky' directive was received from the Combined Chiefs of Staff, giving the Military Governor discretion to permit the Italian people to participate in political activities, which did not lead to rioting and disorder, including among these the right of peaceful assembly,

[1] The publicity given to this affair had induced General Eisenhower to ask the Combined Chiefs of Staff for a revision of the directive in the form which was subsequently agreed.

attendance at meetings of political committees, and the publication and distribution of political writings. Permission was consequently given for the meeting to be held in Bari at the end of January—without Marshal Badoglio being consulted, though Bari was in King's Italy.[1]

The Congress of Bari can hardly have been a very welcome guest to the King's Government, which it was trying to upset; but, in fact, it created a good deal less commotion than had been anticipated in certain government circles. The revolutionary motion which was to have been proposed by the Action Party never reached the paper. This resolution, which was formulated under the influence of the Socialist delegate of the C.L.N. in Rome, called upon the congress to draw up a joint bill of indictment against the King for his violation of the constitution in supporting Fascism, to proclaim itself the representative assembly of liberated Italy, and to proceed to the formation of a government to prosecute the war and to safeguard the liberties of the Italian people. The Congress, which would continue to sit in the form of an executive committee, pending the convocation of a constituent assembly, should form an extraordinary government on a broad basis in which should be united the powers of the crown and the dissolved parliament. This motion was opposed behind the scenes of the congress by the Liberals, Christian Democrats and Labour Democrats, who were none of them prepared to accept a proposal which would in their opinion have meant the end of the monarchy. Largely owing to the influence of Croce, Arangio Ruiz and Rodino, the Congress managed to agree on a compromise resolution, which, while accepting the formation of a permanent executive committee pending the liberation of Rome, rejected this absurd attempt at a *coup d'état*.[2] It contented itself by affirming that, while prevailing conditions did not permit an immediate solution of the constitutional question, the immediate abdication of the King was an essential condition of the moral and economic reconstruction of Italy.

It was noted that the resolution made no mention of the Crown Prince. The reason was that the three centre and right-wing parties were awaiting the outcome of certain conversations which had been initiated with the King by Enrico De Nicola, who was attempting to persuade the monarch not to abdicate but to withdraw from public life, after appointing his son Umberto as his viceroy, Lieutenant of the Realm, to carry on his functions until such time as the constitutional question could be put to popular vote when the war was over. This form of withdrawal, which was first proposed as far back

---

[1] See Badoglio, *op.cit.* p. 125.

[2] See Croce, *The King and the Allies*, pp. 66–74. For the text of the Action Party motion see *Degli Espinosa, Il Regno del Sud*, p. 257.

as December 1943, was, with a fine understanding of the King's personal character, chosen by De Nicola as the alternative to abdication, because he was convinced that the King would in the end accept it, though he would refuse to abdicate. On 20th February the King, whose decision in the matter appears to have been influenced by Acquarone, decided to retire.[1] Before the end of the month General Mason-MacFarlane was informed that he had agreed to appoint the Crown Prince Lieutenant-General of the Realm, that an announcement to this effect would take place immediately, but that the actual transfer would only be made when the Allies had reached Rome. The Crown Prince would then proceed to form a new government on a broad base. But the acceptance of this plan by all six parties was not so easily procured.

In creating the conditions which at last induced the reluctant Monarch to accept these terms, the Bari Congress had been decisive. It had provided a focus for propaganda against the King and Badoglio, not merely in southern Italy but also in Allied countries, particularly in the United States. The long delay in the occupation of Rome had already convinced the State Department—though not the Foreign Office—that there should be no further delay in reorganising the Italian Government on a broad political basis, and that pressure should be brought on the King to abdicate in order to make this possible.[2] In the setting up of a permanent committee the congress had also created an instrument for bringing pressure to bear, first, on Marshal Badoglio, and through him on the Allied authorities in Italy.

As a first step, a letter was addressed by the executive committee to the King, dated from Naples 6th February, pressing upon him his duty to abdicate in view of the congress's resolution which 'expressed the unanimous sentiments' of the Italian people.[3] The next step was an appeal to all those in the service of the State to regard the King and his Government as rebels and not to take part in their rebellion against the Italian people. This move was immediately intercepted by the Control Commission, which succeeded in preventing any wide publicity being given to the appeal and warned the *giunta* that action on these lines would not be tolerated. The appeal, which had been drafted and distributed from A.M.G. territory, put the Allied authorities in something of a dilemma. If they took action against the political leaders by arresting them, an enormous protest would be raised; scarcely less protest would arise if they permitted Marshal Badoglio to take similar action in King's Italy.

---

[1] Croce, *op.cit.* p. 83.
[2] See Cordell Hull, *op. cit.* Vol. II, pp. 1552 seq.
[3] The text of this letter is given in Tamaro, *op. cit.* Vol. II, pp. 412 seq.

This action by the committee was supplemented by the submission to the Control Commission, for transmission to President Roosevelt and Mr Churchill, of an agreed programme of action. The King should abdicate immediately and be succeeded by the Crown Prince, who must, however, agree to delegate the exercise of his constitutional powers to a Lieutenancy of the Realm, consisting of one or more persons, of whom none should be either a soldier —thus excluding Badoglio—or a member of the House of Savoy. The Lieutenancy thus would have powers to proceed immediately to the constitution of a representative government of anti-Fascist parties. The delegation of powers would remain in effect until conditions permitted the calling of a constituent assembly, regularly elected by the whole Italain people, which would thereupon decide the form of the constitution. One of the reasons given for immediate action was the hint that the patriots and parties in the north of Italy were becoming restless at this unsatisfactory situation, and might therefore decide to have recourse to more radical solutions of their own.

In commenting on these proposals to the Combined Chiefs of Staff General Wilson pointed out that there were only two alternative courses, namely, either to bring pressure upon the King to abdicate in favour of his son, or to inform the political leaders that the Allied Governments would not tolerate any change in the political situation until Rome was reached, and that any attempt to interfere with the Badoglio Government would be ruthlessly repressed. Of these two courses General Wilson, from the local angle, favoured the former and recommended that the Allied Governments should at the earliest possible moment inform the King that they insisted on his bowing to the will of his people and abdicating in favour of the Crown Prince. This recommendation was made by General Wilson before he had been informed of the result of the negotiations between the King and Signor De Nicola.

No move could have been better calculated than these proposals to bring out into the open the latent divergencies between British and American views—though there is no direct evidence to show that the extent of this divergence was known to the Naples Committee. Mr Churchill and the Foreign Office, though less interested than Americans believed in the ultimate fate of the monarchy, disagreed with the American view on the question of timing; they thought that a new government might be more troublesome than that of Badoglio in regard to the fulfilment of the armistice terms. Above all, Mr Churchill was convinced that a change of horses in midstream was most undesirable—at any rate until Rome had been occupied. As he stated in the House of Commons on 22nd February:

> We signed the Italian Armistice on the basis of unconditional surrender with King Victor Emmanuel and Marshal Badoglio, who were, and up to the present are, the legitimate Government of Italy. On their authority, the Italian Navy, not without risk and loss, surrendered to us, and practically all troops and airmen who were not dominated by the Germans also obeyed the orders they received from the Crown. Since then these Italian forces have cooperated with us to the best of their ability, and nearly 100 Italian ships of war are discharging valuable services in the Mediterranean and the Atlantic. Italian troops have entered the front line in Italy, and although on one occasion they suffered severe casualties, they continue to fight alongside our men. Very much larger numbers are engaged in indispensable services to the Allied Armies behind the front. Italian airmen are also fighting at our side.
>
> The battle in Italy, for reasons which I have already explained, will be hard and long. I am not yet convinced that any other Government can be formed at the present time in Italy which would command the same obedience from the Italian Armed forces. Should we succeed in the present battle and enter Rome, as I trust and believe we shall, we shall be free to discuss the whole Italian political situation, and we shall do so with many advantages that we do not possess at the present time. It is from Rome that a more broadly-based Italian Government can best be formed. Whether a Government thus formed will be so helpful to the Allies as the present dispensation, I cannot tell. It might of course, be a Government which would try to make its position good with the Italian people by resisting, as much as it dared, the demands made on them in the interests of the Allied Armies. I should be sorry, however, to see an unsettling change made at a time when the battle is at its climax, swaying to and fro. When you have to hold a hot coffee-pot, it is better not to break the handle off until you are sure that you will get another equally convenient and serviceable or, at any rate, until there is a dishcloth handy.

This speech provoked a sharp reaction from the Naples politicians. The leaders of the Communist, Socialist, and Action parties issued a pamphlet calling for a ten-minute strike—to be compensated by fifteen minutes overtime—concluding with the following sentence: 'By paralysing for ten minutes the economic and administrative life of the city, the Neapolitans will tell Churchill what our country wants'. They were informed that such action would not be tolerated, and General Mason-MacFarlane ordered the pamphlet to be withdrawn. The strike was called off and the politicians contented themselves by holding a public meeting—with A.M.G's permission.

Strong as the pressure was from certain sections of American public opinion, and from his own State Department, President

Roosevelt held firm at this time in refusing to allow any open divergence between British and American policy.[1] Nor was this divergence as great as has often been represented. Mr Churchill's desire to maintain the Badoglio Government must not be interpreted as implying any prejudice in favour of the person of King Victor Emmanuel. The Prime Minister, whose support of the King was based entirely on the desire to maintain the loyalty of the Italian armed forces to the Allied cause, appears eventually to have been convinced that the King was too heavily involved in Fascism, that he should disappear from public life altogether, and that Prince Humbert should take his father's place, though he could not see any advantage in by-passing Prince Humbert in favour of a regency for his eldest son, which would have to include representatives of the political parties.

But now a new factor appeared in the intervention of the Soviet Government. On 8th March Signor Prunas, the Secretary of the Foreign Ministry, informed the Political Section of the Control Commission that M. Bogomolov, who had replaced M. Vyshinski as Russian member of the Advisory Council, had informed Marshal Badoglio that the Soviet Government was willing to re-establish diplomatic arrangements with the Italian Government, and to exchange representatives who would have all privileges and rights of ambassadors. Since this offer had come from one of the Allied Governments, the Italian Government felt that it must accept and was telegraphing to Moscow accordingly. This announcement came as a complete surprise to the Governments of London and Washington, who had not been consulted; nor had the matter been raised in the Advisory Council.

Marshal Badoglio, in his book on Italy in the Second World War[2], states that after a meeting of the council at Naples—presumably that held on 10th January 1944 at which he (Badoglio) had been invited to attend—M. Vyshinski had told him that the Soviet Government was anxious to establish direct relations between the two Governments. He adds that he immediately reported the subject of this conversation to General Joyce, who was also present at this meeting.[3] He also says that, on hearing M. Bogomolov's communication, he immediately told Signor Prunas, 'in order to behave with complete loyalty and correctness', to see General Mason MacFarlane giving

---

[1] See Cordell Hull, *loc. cit.* pp. 1555 seq.; Churchill, *op. cit.* Vol. V, pp. 444-447.

[2] *Op. cit.* p. 120–121.

[3] I have, however, been unable to find any record of this conversation, though General Joyce entertained Marshal Badoglio at dinner after the Council meeting. It seems on the face of it rather extraordinary that such important information, if it was received, should not have been transmitted to higher headquarters. But I have been told by Admiral Stone that Badoglio might have tried to convey this information in an indirect way, the real intention of which was perhaps not appreciated by General Joyce.

him the particulars of the interview with the Russian delegate and to remind him of the communication he had already made to General Joyce.[1] What he does not tell us is that he replied accepting the Russian proposal without consulting the Allied Control Commission, and that the news was released before Allied efforts to stop it could be brought into action.

In the circumstances it is easy enough to understand why Badoglio, in his effort to win Allied status for Italy, should have found himself unable to resist the temptation, so blandly offered, of playing off one Allied power against the others. He had, however, to submit to a rebuke administered by General Mason-MacFarlane on behalf of the Supreme Allied Commander, who informed him that in the interests of security the Italian Government was not entitled to enter into relations with any Power, Allied or neutral, without his previous consent given through the Allied Control Commission.

But the intervention of the Soviet Government was not confined to the mere establishment of diplomatic relations. Whatever its ultimate aims, which can only be conjectured, its influence was immediately directed to the solution of the deadlock between the King and the Italian politicians in the interest of the Allied war effort—a solution which prevented the development of any further divergence between British and American policy. It had been arranged with the Allies that one of the leaders of the Italian Communist Party, Signor Togliatti (known 'underground' by the pseudonym, Ercole Ercoli), who had been trained by long residence in Moscow, should be despatched to Italy. He arrived in the last week of March, to find that there were in fact two questions at issue. The first concerned the King. According to the agreement arrived at by De Nicola, the King pledged himself to withdraw from public life as soon as Rome was occupied, which would mean that the representatives of the parties, if they entered the government, would have to begin by serving under him for a limited period; the plan of the Executive Committee of the Bari Congress, on the other hand, demanded his immediate abdication. The second concerned the premiership. Were the representatives of the six parties prepared to serve under Badoglio? or would it be necessary to appoint one of themselves, or a person chosen by them from outside their ranks, as prime minister ? In answering both these questions the influence of Togliatti was decisive. He declared that, in order to obtain the maximum national effort in the struggle against the common enemy, he would be prepared to serve under Badoglio and the King. This course of action was, after

---

[1] Badoglio, *op. cit.* p. 127–8. In none of the accounts of Signor Prunas's communications which have come to my hand is any mention made of an earlier communication to General Joyce.

considerable discussion, followed by the leaders of the other five parties. The way was now clear for the immediate formation of a six-party Government under Marshal Badoglio's leadership.

Once the central issue had been decided there remained one important detail to settle, the timing of the announcement by the King of his proposed withdrawal. King Victor Emmanuel was bent on returning to his capital and making his announcement of withdrawal from the Quirinal. But it was felt, both by Badoglio and by the Allied authorities in Italy, that further delay would be most undesirable. After an audience on 10th April with General Mason-MacFarlane, Mr Murphy, Mr Macmillan and Sir Noel Charles[1], the King was persuaded to issue immediately on 12th April an announcement stating his intention to withdraw into private life as soon as Rome was occupied, and to delegate his powers to the Crown Prince Humbert as Lieutenant of the Realm.[2] When the moment for withdrawal came, the King expressed his desire to accomplish this act in Rome, but in agreement with Marshal Badoglio the Allied authorities were compelled to refuse this request, and the actual act of devolution was signed by King Victor Emmanuel at his temporary residence at Ravello.

Badoglio's six-party government, which was formed in the third week of April, was composed as follows: the Marshal remained Prime Minister and Minister for Foreign Affairs and the Service members of the previous Cabinet, Admiral De Courten (Navy), General Sandalli (Air) and General Orlando (Army) remained on unchanged. The five most prominent political leaders, Croce, Sforza, Rodino, Togliatti and Mancini, became ministers without portfolio, the other offices being divided up between the six parties in such a manner as to obtain a condition of equilibrium, with minister of one party and under-secretary of another. The two non-party 'technicians', General di Raimondi and Signor Fano, both members of the last administration and both specially chosen by the Allied Command, were retained as under-secretaries.

In accordance with a resolution passed by the Advisory Council Marshal Badoglio was required to give in writing two undertakings. First, that his new Government accepted all the obligations towards the Allies entered into by his previous Government; secondly, a definite pledge not to reopen the constitutional question, until such

---

[1] Sir Noel Charles had been appointed High Commissioner in Mr Macmillan's place, since the functions of Resident Minister at Algiers could no longer be combined with membership of an Advisory Council located in Italy.

[2] The manner of the persuasion is somewhat baldly described by Mr Cordell Hull, *op. cit.* Vol. II, p. 1558, where it is stated that Mr Murphy obtained the agreement of his British colleagues that he should 'inform the King personally and unequivocally that the time had come for him to retire'. For an Italian account of this audience, see *Degli Espinosa, op. cit.* p. 333–4.

time as the whole Italian people were in a position freely to express their views. Both these undertakings were required from all the successive Italian Governments which took office before the conclusion of the peace-treaty.

The new Government, which was destined to enjoy a life of barely six weeks, immediately announced its programme, which included, *inter alia*, the drafting of an electoral law for the choosing of a constituent assembly, under conditions of universal suffrage, to decide the constitutional question after the conclusion of the war; the creation of a small consultative body to be a symbol of Parliament and to maintain contact with the Committees of Liberation in Rome and elsewhere; and the energetic pursuit of the task of excluding Fascists from public life and administrative positions.

While the development of the constitutional controversy concerned chiefly the Political Section of the Control Commission, the other sections were engaged in feeling their way towards the establishment of workable relations with the Italian Government. The Control Commission had been brought into being only a few days before the appointment of the Government of Under-Secretaries, and the winter of 1943–4 was a period of experiment and adjustment during which these two newly-formed organisations, after a great deal of mutual confusion, some of which at least might have been avoided by wiser planning, evolved a technique of collaboration. The chief problem was to establish a routine of administrative procedure to implement the arrangements described in the previous chapter, under which liberated Italy was divided into two portions, one ruled by Allied Military Government and the other by the Italian Government.

The first difficulty to be encountered was merely geographical—to find a place which would accommodate the Italian Government, with its enlarged responsibilities, as well as the Allied Control Commission. Naples, as already explained, was ruled out by military considerations, as well as by the fact that it lay in A.M.G. territory. A compromise was therefore found in Salerno, which was transferred to Italian Government territory, having previously formed part of A.M.G. Region III, and the Italian Government moved there in February. This move resulted in some improvement in the administrative facilities of the Government, which had been fearfully cramped for accommodation at Brindisi, and had therefore been forced to distribute its offices over a number of different towns, the Ministry of War and a large part of the Ministry of the Interior being located at Lecce, the Ministry of Marine at Taranto, and the Ministries of Justice, Agriculture, Public Works and Air and the Under-Secretaryship of Railways at Bari. But at Salerno, too, the accommodation was insufficient to accommodate the whole of the

Italian Government and the Allied Control Commission, of which only the Administrative Section could be housed in that city. The Italian Service Ministries remained in their original seats at Lecce, Taranto and Bari, and the Ministry of Industry was accommodated at Vietri sul Mare, a suburb of Salerno, while the Under-Secretaryship of Railways was located at Naples, which also accommodated all but the Administrative Section of the headquarters of the Control Commission. These arrangements were thoroughly unsatisfactory. Not only were the headquarters of the Commission and the Italian Government in different towns, but the headquarters of the Commission itself was split. Geographical division inevitably led to divided counsels.

The next problem was to work out the relations in Italian Government territory between the officers of the Control Commission and the Italian Government officials, both in the field and at the centre. Though direct control of local affairs was abolished, the Civil Affairs Officer of the communes being eliminated, the prefects and other officials of each province were 'advised' by a staff, consisting often of the same officers who had given orders as A.M.G. executives. In these circumstances it was hardly surprising that the Government in Salerno should find reasons to complain of Allied interference.[1] For in the absence of adequate communications such interference was often quite inevitable. While in the field direct control of Italian officials was thus, in theory at any rate, abandoned, the central government itself was subjected to minute supervision by twenty-two sub-commissions. Not only was the approval of the Commission required for all higher appointments, but, in addition, all legislative and executive measures had to be submitted to the Commission for approval, with a view to determining whether they were consistent, first with the armistice terms and, secondly, with the furtherance of the Allied war effort. In most cases these measures had been drafted in cooperation with the sub-commission concerned. Indeed often it was the sub-commission that initiated the proposed decree. But in a good number of cases the Control Commission really had no direct interest. It was however considered necessary that before becoming law all decrees should be submitted to the Legal Sub-Commission, since Italian Ministries had sometimes enacted important decrees without the knowledge of the relevant sub-commission. The logical counterpart to this system of complete control was the application, wherever practical, of the legislation passed by the Italian Government to A.M.G. territory, unless the Regional Commissioner or the Commission's headquarters saw any special reason against it. In fact this application became the general rule, and the occasions when it

[1] Badoglio, *op. cit.* pp. 139-40, 159, 173.

was refused were quite exceptional.[1] It was also laid down that the Italian Government should normally be consulted when any new Regional or General Orders in A.M.G. territory were contemplated, in order that continuity of policy might be established against the time when the territory was handed back to Italian administration.

That some of the more intelligent sections of the Italian public bitterly resented the degree of control, is hardly surprising, but this resentment was certainly not shown by the mass of the people.[2] When all is said and done, it must be recorded that, whatever its mistakes—and there were many—the Control Commission made a genuine and disinterested effort to protect what it conceived to be the best interests of the Italian people, in so far as this was consistent with the paramount aim of defeating Germany. Ruthless exploitation of the Italian people is certainly not a charge which can be substantiated.

A short survey of some of the more important legislation passed by the Governments of Marshal Badoglio during the interval of less than eleven months which followed the overthrow of Mussolini on 25th July 1943 may perhaps help to make clear the evolution of the Italian internal political tendencies. During the period of the 'forty-five days' immediately following the *coup d'état*, some measures had already been taken to foreshadow an eventual return to parliamentary institutions. In addition to the abolition of the Fascist party and the dissolution of the Chamber of *Fasci* and Corporations, decrees had been passed before the armistice providing for the eventual election of a new Chamber of Deputies. The special Fascist Tribunal for the Defence of the State, the 'Star Chamber' of Fascist tyranny, was also abolished. A start, too, was made at 'defascistisation' by getting rid of the more notoriously Fascist officials, through the replacement of over fifty prefects, and by setting up a commission of magistrates to execute a decree confiscating the riches illicitly acquired by persons who had held public office since the institution of Fascism. The politicians imprisoned under Fascism were immediately set free, and all persons condemned for political

---

[1] Two cases worth recording were:

(a) the legislation for the expropriation of large landowners—a long term affair, the application of which could be postponed until territory had reverted to the Italian Government without prejudice to its ultimate application.

(b) D.L.L. 149 of 26th April 1945, passed without consulting the Commission, as an addition to the already complicated legislation on Defascistisation.

The Decrees of the Italian Government, published in the official gazette and implemented by A.C.C. in A.M.G. territory, were automatically applied after October 1944 in Fifth Army area, but not, for some reason of which I can find no record, in Eighth Army area where their application continued to depend upon the decision of the S.C.A.O.

[2] Some Italian writers, e.g. Tamaro, have greatly exaggerated the 'servitude' to which their Government was subjected, even where the facts do justify some criticism of unnecessary interference.

crimes by the Fascist regime (*reati politici*) were let out of prison. The entire body of provisions discriminating against bachelors in the public service and the armed forces were also revoked. But neither the freedom of the press nor the reconstitution of political parties had been looked on with favour.

Further steps were taken by the Government at Brindisi and Salerno to lay the foundations for a return to democratic practice. The right to express political opinions—with the exception of Fascist doctrines and propaganda—was restored. Civil and political rights were given back to Jews, and arrangements were made for the re-admission into public service of all those who had been dismissed in accordance with the racial laws or because of their refusal to take the oath of allegiance to the Fascist regime, and of all persons who could prove that their dismissal was due exclusively to political considerations. The central organs of the corporative structure were also abolished and the right to free organisation of labour unions was reintroduced. A new law was passed regulating the entire field of labour relations, adopting in substance the provisions laid down by Allied Military Government in regard to Regional and Provincial Labour offices and the procedure for the settlement of individual and collective labour disputes.

After the armistice Marshal Badoglio, in accordance with Article 30, took his cue in the matter of defascistisation from the Control Commission. He adopted, as A.M.G. had done in Sicily, the rough and ready method of 'epuration' by categories, based on the *scheda personale*.[1] The first decree dealing with this matter was not published till the last days of December 1943, but the general lines of the policy were announced in a communiqué from Brindisi the last week in November.[2] The principle of retroactive criminal liability, though not laid down in black and white, was at any rate implied by the announcement of 'sanctions' against those responsible for the Fascist revolution, and for the political and military situation of the country brought about by twenty years' government against the wishes and interests of the nation. All Fascists responsible for the suppression of political and individual liberties were to be deprived of the exercise of their civil rights. Arrangements were to be made to bring to trial, three months after the declaration of peace, all Fascists guilty of crimes whose prosecution had been omitted or suspended for political or party reasons. All appointments and promotions due to 'Fascist merits' were to be cancelled by eliminating from all branches of the public administration holders of Fascist distinctions, '*Squadristi*', '*Marcia su Roma*', and '*Sciarpa Littorio*', all

---

[1] See above, pp. 48–49.

[2] The text of this communiqué dated the 24th December 1943 is given in Tamaro *op. cit.* Vol. II, p. 194.

the Fascist 'hierarchs' and all Fascists known to be guilty of attempts against individual liberty. Fascists in public offices were also to be removed, whose 'political precedents do not correspond to the exigencies of the present situation and the state of war'. The neo-Fascists on the other side of the line were likewise threatened by the declaration that all those who had collaborated in any way with the Germans after the armistice, or had taken up arms against their countrymen, or committed acts of violence would be brought to justice before a military tribunal. Drastic as this declaration of policy may appear, its application was softened by a final sentence which exempted from sanctions all those who had redeemed their past in the struggle against the common enemy.

In the decree published at the end of December (R.D.L. 29/B), no attempt was however made to introduce retroactive criminal liabilities. Sanctions were confined to dismissal by categories. All Fascists of certain specified categories[1]—belonging to the Armed Forces, the Civil Service, Local Government Service, and other public bodies were liable to trial and dismissal—as well as those who, without holding any of the said offices, could be proved guilty of actions constituting an attempt on individual liberty (*atti costituenti attentati alla libertà individuale*). All persons who had held Fascist offices were obliged to communicate this fact to their superior officers and special authorities were set up to try the different categories of public servants. For the top grades (1 to 6) of the Civil Service the 'Cabinet' (*Consiglio dei Ministri*) was the body indicated; for the inferior grades of the Civil Service, the Executive Council (*Consiglio delle Amministrazioni*) or disciplinary commissions (*Commissioni di Disciplina*) of the various Government departments.[2] Persons dismissed under this procedure were allowed to maintain their pension rights, and those who were not qualified by their length of service for any pension were in certain cases awarded a small indemnity or subsistence allowance. Certain members of the objectionable Fascist categories were also exempted, for instance those whom, either from their tender age or for their technical competence and meritorious behaviour, it was judged desirable to maintain in the public service.

In Italian Government territory which had never been subject to Military Government, where desperate efforts had to be made to build up a technically efficient administrative machine, this decree was largely a dead letter. The attention of the Advisory Council was drawn by General Solodovnik, the Russian representative on the

---

[1] Art. I of the decree specified, besides *Squadrista*, *Marcia su Roma* and *Sciarpa Littorio*, ten other classes of the 'hierarchy'.

[2] Later (by decree-law of the 12th April 1944) these bodies were replaced by a special central commission presided over by a minister and peripheral commissions nominated by the Prefect of each Province.

Control Commission, to the unsatisfactory state of epuration in Sardinia. But the 'Government of Under-Secretaries', though it did institute a High Commission for sanctions against Fascism, was far from effecting any vigorous action. The body of Ministers never met to pronounce judgment on any of the higher ranks of civil servants, and the commissions appointed by the Prefects, partly from lack of transport, but perhaps even more from lack of enthusiasm, made comparatively few dismissals.

In A.M.G. territory, beginning with Region III, under the command first of Lieut.-Colonel Kraege and, later, of Colonel Poletti, the application of the sanctions embodied in this decree was carried out in a much more vigorous manner. Under a Regional Order dated 1st January 1944 all Fascists of the categories specified in the Italian Government's decree (but without the exceptions laid down in Article 4), were ordered to be 'removed from the position they occupy in the Government or any administration directly controlled by the Government'. All promotions 'which have been made principally because of activity on behalf of the Fascist cause' were annulled and all persons discharged or placed on unlimited leave because of their political views were reinstated. A Regional Commission of four prominent Anti-Fascists was appointed, of which the first president was Professor Arangio Ruiz, subsequently Minister of Justice in the last Badoglio Government. Its functions were to establish the procedure of epuration, under the Regional Order; to determine the procedure to be followed; to choose the members of the Provincial and 'Technical' (*Anglice* 'departmental') Commissions to be set up to purge the various departments; and to hear appeals from the Provincial Commissions. The number of Technical Commissions was fifteen. These dealt not only with the various branches of central and local administration, but also with schools, public welfare institutions, banks, public utility enterprises and industrial companies in which the Government had a financial interest. Their powers were widely drawn. They had to examine the personal situation of each employee, and to propose the names of persons to be eliminated as well as those of desirable substitutes. These were then passed on for revision to the Provincial Commissions.

In the meantime A.M.G. had already taken steps to secure a preliminary 'epuration' of the administrative bodies in the region. In Naples some twenty officials had been removed by Badoglio before the armistice; nearly forty had fled before the Allied forces arrived. By the end of the year A.M.G. had removed as many as 385. In the other provinces of the region the number of officials removed was much smaller, but nearly all the *Podestà's* were dismissed, either by A.M.G. or by the newly-installed Prefects. The above procedure, established by Colonel Poletti in Naples, set the general pattern for action by A.M.G. during the remainder of the campaign.

So far the emphasis of Marshal Badoglio's legislation had been mostly on the purging of public administration. With the resurgence of the political parties this emphasis changed. Now the punishment of Fascism, as such—quite apart from any criminal offences committed while in office under the Fascist regime—was to become the order of the day. The pressure on Marshal Badoglio and his colleagues—both from the side of the Allied Commission and from the newly resuscitated leaders of the political parties—for a more thorough measure of 'defascistisation' had already begun to exercise its effect before the democratic front was incorporated into Marshal Badoglio's Government. At the end of February the announcement was made of the appointment of a High Commissioner for Defascistisation—a position which was conferred on Signor Tito Zaniboni, a Socialist who had served long years in prison for an attempted assassination of the Duce and had acted as President of the Bari Congress.[1] Emphasis at this stage was still on crimes committed and illicit enrichment (*illeciti arrichimenti*) and wrongful profits (*lucri indebiti*). The underlying conception of 'epuration' was still as humane as in the circumstances could be expected.[2] But this humane programme was far from satisfying the leaders of the six parties who constituted the last Badoglio Government. The conception of 'epuration' underwent a profound change. Just before the liberation of Rome a new decree, drafted by a committee of representatives of each of the six parties, definitely categorised as retroactively criminal the action which brought the Fascist party into power, and to Fascism was now added the crime of collaboration with the Germans since the armistice. With the details of this decree, dated 26th May, we need not concern ourselves, since Rome fell before it could be put into action. Its importance lies in the fact that it set the not altogether happy juridical pattern for the subsequent legislation of the Bonomi Government.

In the field of foreign affairs the prime objective of Marshal Badoglio's Government, as of that of his successor, was to get rid of the armistice regime and co-belligerence by obtaining for Italy the status of an ally. Encouraged no doubt by the Russian gesture of resuming diplomatic relations, the Marshal directly approached President Roosevelt at the beginning of April with the plea for Allied status. No reply was sent by the President to this letter. On

---

[1] He was now expelled from his party for his collaboration with the Badoglio Government.

[2] Cf. the official announcement of the creation of the office of High Commissioner (*Gazetta del Mezziogiorno*, 25th February 1944), and Zaniboni's statement in the Gazette two days later quoted by Degli Espinoza, *op. cit.* p. 228.

24th April he wrote another letter to the President with the same request, now reinforced by his establishment of the six-party government.[1] This time an answer came, in the form of a message from Mr Cordell Hull to Mr Murphy, instructing him to inform the Marshal that the State Department, after exchanging views with Great Britain on this subject, had no intention of granting Italy the status of an ally. On 16th May, 'since the agitation for Allied status continued', Mr Hull once more cabled Mr Murphy that the State Department considered such a change in status premature, not only because such a step would have far reaching consequences towards breaking down the entire machinery of the Allied Control Commission and the armistice terms, but also because of the unfavourable impact it would have upon the other sufferers from Italy's aggression.[2]

But however great the desire of Marshal Badoglio to win the approval of the Allies, there was one question on which it was impossible to arrive at any agreement, namely, the treatment of the Italian prisoners of war. Of these there were by the time the armistice was signed a very large number in Allied hands, chiefly British, though the Americans in the course of the Tunisian campaign had also collected a considerable number. The total amounted to about 450,000 officers and men, distributed over a wide area, large numbers of them being in India, the Middle East, North Africa and Australia, and some of them in the United States and the United Kingdom, where they were employed on tasks permitted under the Geneva Convention of 1929, for the most part as agricultural labourers. The Convention, which had been ratified by Germany and Italy as well as Great Britain and the United States, forbids the detaining power to employ prisoners of war on any work having a direct connection with the operations of war, mentioning specifically the manufacture and transport of arms or munitions of any kind and the transport of material destined for combatant units[3], but does permit their employment on civilian work.[4]

After the armistice and the declaration of war on Germany by the Italian Government the question naturally arose as to what changes, if any, should be made in the treatment of these prisoners. The recognition of Italians as co-belligerents did not alter their status, which remained that of a defeated enemy. It was no intention of Allied policy to liberate them from this status, which might have entailed the obligation to ship them back to their own country—a commitment which could not have been undertaken without grave prejudice to the Allied war effort. The addition to Allied manpower

---

[1] The text of this letter is given in Tamaro, *op. cit.* Vol. II, pp. 569–70.

[2] Cordell Hull, *op. cit.* Vol. II, pp. 1559–60.

[3] Cf. Section III, Chapter 3, Art. 31.

[4] Cf. Section III, Chapter 1, Art. 27.

resulting from their compulsory employment could not be dispensed with. The question was therefore how to obtain from them the maximum contribution to the Allied cause by getting rid of the limitations imposed by the Convention on their employment, and by so improving their conditions of employment as to encourage them to co-operate voluntarily with the Allies, thereby eliminating the task of keeping them under guard.

The Geneva Convention was the embodiment of the fundamental principle of international law that the rules of war do not permit a belligerent state to force the subject of an enemy state to fight against their own countrymen. It hardly contemplated the situation arising when one of the belligerents changed sides in the middle of the war. The fact that the Italian Government had declared war on Germany did not justify the Allies in compelling Italian prisoners of war to fight against the Germans or against such of their own countrymen as had become members of the armed forces of Mussolini's Social Republic. But there was no reason why they should not volunteer to engage in any service to assist the Allied cause. Marshal Badoglio had in October issued an appeal to them to do so and made a verbal agreement with General Eisenhower by which Italian volunteers were allowed to do certain types of war work. Italian prisoners of war in North Africa and Sicily were consequently organised on a voluntary basis into various groups, first to dilute British units, and later as separate Italian service units, like as pioneer companies, transport companies, etc.

It was therefore decided by the two Allied Governments to regularise this practice by agreement with the Italian Government. A draft convention was submitted to Marshal Badoglio in January 1944, under which all prisoners of war under control of the Governments of the United States and the British Commonwealth should be given the opportunity—at the discretion of the detaining Government—to serve in units or formations organised on a military basis, or to be otherwise employed under United States or British Commands in any part of the world on such duties as might be considered appropriate in the interests of the common cause by the said Governments. While so serving they were to retain their status as prisoners of war, but their treatment was to be ameliorated, as the circumstances permitted. Volunteers were to be formed into units under Italian officers and N.C.O's, wearing Italian uniforms and badges of rank, but the United States and British Commonwealth Governments were to retain final control in all matters of discipline, promotion and internal administration. The provisions of the Geneva Convention limiting the types of employment in which these volunteer prisoners of war—afterwards officially christened "Co-operators' —might be used, were to be suspended (Articles 31 and

32) and all reference to them as prisoners of war was to cease. They were, in fact, to be Italian soldiers employed on service duties similar to those performed by some British and American troops, and they were again to come under the command of Italian officers.

The details concerning the negotiations of this agreement, and the amendments proposed to make it acceptable to the Italian government, do not concern this volume. There can be little doubt that, but for the retention of the status of prisoners of war, Marshal Badoglio would have been induced to accept it in the modified form in which it was finally presented. But that vital point was considered by all Italians as an essential point of national honour. No government, least of all that headed by a soldier, could explain away the glaring antithesis between the retention of prisoner status and the fact that Italians were dying in combat on the side of their detainers. And Badoglio firmly refused to sign. After making alternative proposals, which were not accepted, he broke off negotiations at the beginning of April.

The absence of any agreement did not however make much practical difference from the Allied point of view. Marshal Badoglio and his successor, anxious to 'work their passage', ceased to press the formal objections which could have been raised, and made no appeal to Switzerland the 'protecting power'. The practice of forming co-operator units continued; in spite of the humilitation of their prisoner status, 'cooperators' managed to serve side by side in Italy with their free compatriots without showing any resentment. The Allies placed no obstacle in the way of releasing to the Italian Government key men for its military services, e.g. *Carabinieri* and officers with special qualifications, as well as a considerable number of Sicilians, captured in the island, who had been released on parole after the Sicilian campaign and were engaged on agricultural work of importance. Releases were also made quite liberally on compassionate grounds. These exceptions were certainly of considerable assistance to the Italian Government. Nevertheless it is difficult to believe that the knowledge that nearly half a million of their countrymen were detained overseas as prisoners by the Allies, whom they were assisting to fight the German enemy, can have stimulated the war effort of the Italian people.

CHAPTER VI

GUSTAV TO GOTHIC

THE SUBJECT of this chapter is a brief account of Allied Military Government during the advance of the Armies from the positions reached in the winter of 1943, stretching just north of Naples from the River Garigliano in front of the Gustav Line to Ortona on the Adriatic coast, to the positions established in the winter of 1944, stretching from north of Pisa to north of Ravenna along the northern edge of the Apennines, after the piercing of the Gothic Line. The tasks set to the Army A.M.G's during this advance varied considerably in different localities, being determined not only by the physical and political character of the areas occupied, but also by the rate of progress of the Allied advance and the degree of enemy resistance encountered. The comparative stability for several months of the Winter Line of the Garigliano enabled a number of problems to be worked out. The main difficulty which had confronted A.M.G. since the occupation of Naples, the feeding of the large population of southern Italy, was gradually overcome, largely owing to the improvement effected by G-5 in Algiers in the methods of estimating and procuring foodstuffs to be imported as part of the Commander-in-Chief's military programme. Some improvement was also effected in the efficiency of the *ammassi*—for example in the province of Matera—by the action of A.M.G. officers. Throughout the winter food shortage remained acute, particularly in Naples and parts of Calabria, but before the end of February 1944 sufficient imported supplies had arrived to make it possible to maintain a standard ration for the whole of southern Italy equivalent to about 200 gms (7 oz) of bread per day. This standard, though by no means sufficient to maintain perfect health, did make it possible to avoid any severe degree of malnutrition. Failures to distribute this modest ration did occur in various places from time to time, but in general it was maintained adequately, and it soon became possible to supplement the rations of heavy workers, particularly those working for the Armies.

With the advance beyond the Winter Line the task of A.M.G. was complicated by the emergence of a number of problems which had not developed during the invasion of Sicily. The first of these was that of devastated areas. Apart from one or two small towns no wholesale destruction of urban centres had been encountered in Sicily at all comparable to the devastation caused by the fighting north of Naples and the deliberate destruction and sabotage which the Germans had plenty of time to plan and execute. On the west side of the Apennines destruction was greatest in the plain of Monte Cassino, in the zone lying between the Garigliano river and Rome, and in northern Tuscany. Towns in southern Tuscany and Umbria, on the other hand, were often practically undamaged owing to the rapidity of the German retreat. On the east side of the Apennines war damage was much more continuous, because of the character of the narrow coastal plain which, intersected at short intervals by rivers, permitted the Allied advance to be contested mile by mile, with the consequent destruction of large areas of nearly all the coastal towns; though here, too, the rapidity of the Allied advance from Pescara to just south of Ancona limited the extent of the destruction. A second legacy of German war operations was presented by extensive minefields which covered large areas of agricultural land. A third problem which kept the A.M.G's of both Armies exceedingly busy was that of the refugees, the beginnings of which were recorded in Chapter III. This was more continuous on the eastern side of the Apennines where the destruction of the coastal towns led to the wholesale evacuation of their populations on military grounds. But evacuation for military reasons on a large scale also took place in the Fifth Army area, notably in the case of the Anzio beach-head, the biggest single operation of this nature, and in the territory on both sides of the Arno. Finally, in their advance north of Rome the Army A.M.G's encountered a new and delicate problem of a specifically political character in the shape of the partisans—armed bands whose existence was an obvious danger to public safety—and the local Committees of National Liberation in which the Communists were more often than not the dominating element. These committees claimed the right to exercise wide powers of local government, and their political aspirations had to be given some measure of satisfaction in the constitution of local administrations.

In Italian—as opposed to Allied Military Government—territory, and even in the Regions subjected to Allied Military Government immediately behind the army boundaries, the functions of the Allied Control Commission became increasingly political. In this they differed considerably from those of the original AMGOT. Though AMGOT from the outset had been charged with the general mission of destroying Fascism, it was still primarily an instrument of military policy, designed to keep politics in cold storage for the duration of the campaign. And even after the armistice, which completely changed the basis of military government, the task of the army A.M.G's remained, to begin with, almost exclusively military. It was only north of Rome that the problem of partisans became really serious, and that the activity of the Committees of

National Liberation forced them to deal with immediate political issues.

To feed the living and to bury the dead was still their primary task. Their first pre-occupation was almost everywhere the organisation of the distribution of food. Owing to the destruction of electric power installations, this meant in all the larger towns the distribution of imported flour. Forward supply depots were set up in the Army area, from which the communes in the operational zones could be supplied. The creation of these depots was often delayed and hampered by the lack of transport, a shortage which constantly aggravated the problem of distribution to the forward consumers. The initial rations distributed therefore tended to be small in the forward areas where no stocks were found; they were usually limited to the equivalent of about 100 gms (3½ oz) per head per day. For example, on the Fifth Army front after the capture of Naples, the bread ration in the corps areas was not increased to 150 gms (5 oz) till the middle of January, though some of the communes had been occupied for many weeks.

As the Army moved northwards across the Garigliano up the Liri valley towards Rome meeting the most obstinate resistance, devastation made the feeding of the inhabitants even more difficult, owing to the destruction of mills and bakeries, so that 'spearhead' distribution often had to be made in the form of biscuits and tinned soup. Under these conditions, with the large number of civilian casualties, the distribution of medical supplies was often scarcely less pressing than that of food. These, too, were distributed wherever possible from forward supply depots, but in emergencies were supplied by the medical authorities of both Armies, whose co-operation with their A.M.G. colleagues was unstinted. And after immediate emergencies had been met, the assistance afforded by the American and British Red Cross teams, whose work was at first directed primarily, though not exclusively, to caring for refugees and displaced persons, was extremely valuable.

Next to keeping the people fed, the most important task of the Army A.M.G's was to ensure the maintenance of public order, under conditions which were frequently chaotic. This problem was solved by the organisation of mobile squadrons of *Carabinieri* who moved forward with the 'spearhead' Civil Affairs officers. A small number of these were attached to each 'spearhead' C.A.O. and moved in with him, while larger detachments followed behind with the provincial teams. The services rendered by these *Carabinieri* were of many kinds. They helped the 'spearhead' Civil Affairs officer by restoring order, where necessary, reorganising the local police, if any, posting proclamations, rounding up civilian doctors, reporting on the location of mines and booby traps and making an immediate survey of the food resources of the commune, as well as in starting to organise the cleaning of streets and the disposal of dead bodies. They were also told off to assist the Military Police and Field Security Services in the control of civilian movement and civilian traffic by establishing road blocks, as well as in the 'screening' of refugees. With the advance northwards into German-occupied territory, the importance of their services increased, since no reliance could be placed on the Social Republic's police, the *Guarda Nazionale Repubblicana* (G.N.R.). Indeed it would be hard to over-estimate the contribution made by the *Carabinieri* under the leadership of A.M.G. Public Safety Officers to the prevention of disease and unrest.

With the details of A.M.G's activities before the advance on Rome we have no space to concern ourselves, but one of the 'side-shows' of the Fifth Army A.M.G. is perhaps worth describing at some length, the administration of the isolated enclave of the Anzio beach-head. Here A.M.G. was detailed on the Fifth Army pattern, with a Senior Civil Affairs Officer and staff attached to VI Corps headquarters, which was in charge of the operation, and Civil Affairs Officers attached to each division. Attached to VI Corps headquarters under the S.C.A.O. was a Civil Affairs Police Officer, and four further C.A.P.O's came in with the mobile *Carabinieri*. One of them became the Corps Refugee Officer. A Civil Affairs Public Health Officer also arrived at an early stage, and ten Civil Affairs Officers some of whom had been destined for the towns of Nettuno and Anzio. These towns, however, did not need them, since nearly all their inhabitants had been evacuated by the Germans some months before the Allied landing, to a zone three kilometres from the coast. But in a rural belt between the roads to Rome and to Cisternia about 15,000 evacuees were living in nine clusters of shanties.

In spite of its diminutive scale the Anzio operation provided in miniature almost all the typical problems with which military governments of the forward areas had to deal: the selection of local officials and their supervision; the provision of funds to meet the necessary (mostly extraordinary) communal expenses; the distribution of the requisite food ration, so that no one should go without his 200 gms of bread a day, to populations constantly under shell fire, often widely scattered, and frequently changing their habitat; the restarting of essential civilian services; the rescue of civilians trapped in houses in battle areas, by leading groups out at night through minefields; the evacuation and treatment of civilian casualties and the organisation of civilian hospitals; the enforcement of security measures, including the curfew and prohibition on circulation; the assistance of military units in the procurement of civilian labour, materials and storehouses; even the curbing of prostitution and the illicit sale of wine. Added to these was the special problem of wholesale evacuation by sea to the Naples area, which had to be organised in minute detail in cooperation with the Army transport services and the Navy, so as to make full use, without any delay, of the return schedules of empty vessels.

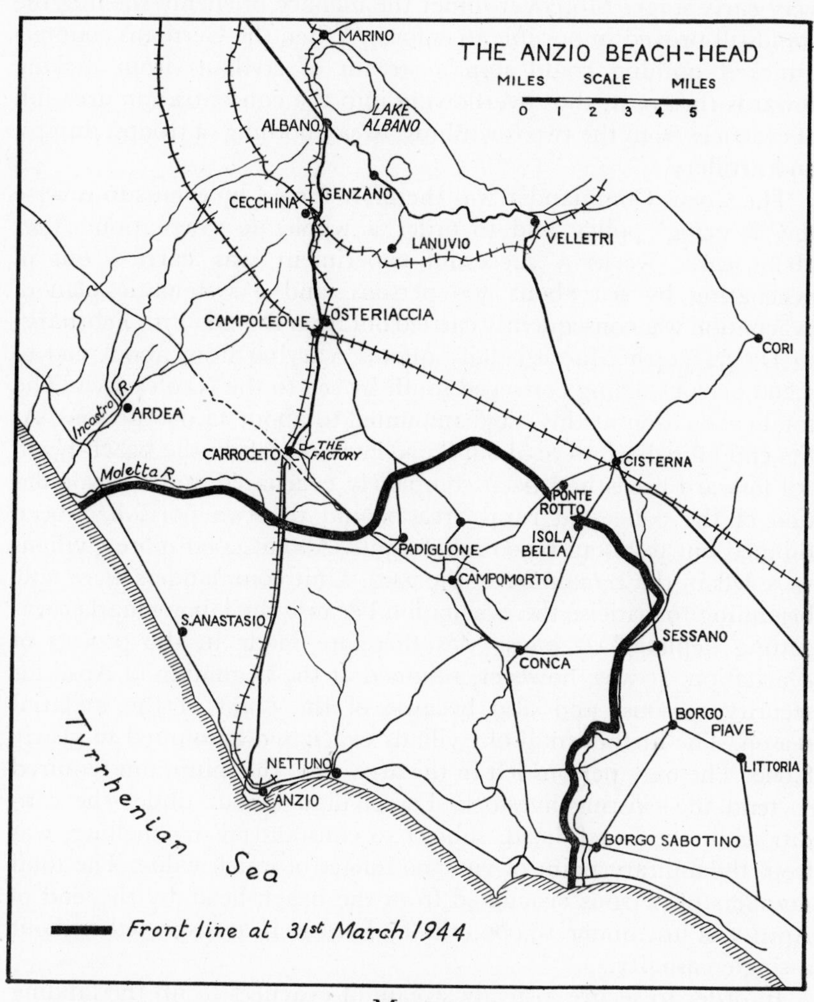

Map 7

The landings took place on 22nd January 1944, and the Corps Commander, in the hope that after about three weeks the main Fifth army would be able to get in contact with him—a hope frustrated by the failure of the first attacks on Monte Cassino—ordered the population to be 'frozen'. No civilians were permitted to enter the two towns, except essential workers provided with an A.M.G. pass, and tactical commanders were instructed to 'freeze' civilians, even in the most forward areas—an instruction which could not be complied with *au pied de la lettre* for security reasons, since some evacuation of local inhabitants was considered necessary in order to remove any danger of civilians passing information to the enemy. In the areas of the British divisions 500 persons were evacuated at a very early stage. Moreover under the menace of enemy shelling the standstill proved impossible to enforce. When the Germans counter-attacked nothing could stop a stream of civilians from making towards the coast, thus overflowing into the concentration area full of evacuees from the two townships, to say nothing of troops, dumps, and artillery.

The Corps Commander was therefore forced by events to reverse the 'freezing' policy and to order a wholesale evacuation. After about three weeks a successful experiment was carried out of evacuating by sea about 500 persons, and a systematic plan of evacuation was consequently carried out from D+26 (17th February) to D+52 (14th March), daily quotas, varying from about 200 to 1,200 persons, being conveyed south by sea to the Naples area. The total evacuation at this stage amounted to about 11,000 persons. At the end of it there were about 8,000 civilians left in the beach-head. All forward areas had been completely evacuated and the population of the congested rural area behind the two ports had been thinned out to about 6,000 inhabitants. About 2,000 more civilians were left in the remainder of the area. Unit commanders were now beginning to criticise the evacuation because the labour market was getting depleted. A pause was therefore made in the process of evacuation. It was, however, resumed at the beginning of April for security reasons, and also because of the onset of the malarial season. The further total of civilians evacuated amounted to nearly 8,000. The only persons left in the area were the minimum required to tend the existing livestock. For civilian labour under the conditions in the beach-head, subject to constant enemy shelling, was from the military point of view no longer of much value. The total numbers of persons evacuated from the beach-head by the end of April was just under 19,000, all of whom were transported without a single casualty.

In order to secure a steady stream of evacuees to fill the landing craft without any delay as they arrived and unloaded, collecting points had to be organised and a holding centre set up near the sea, where the evacuees could be fed and housed—for the availability of landing craft depended on the weather. This was established, with the consent of the priest, in a church near the port of Anzio, and evacuees were given meals made from 'C' rations as well as a 200 gm bread ration, which was sold to them each day. Nor was their welfare neglected. Infirmaries were set up in several places, and a civilian hospital organised at Nettuno. Severe wounds (e.g. from shell splinters) had however to be dealt with in army hospitals. In order to assist in the marshalling and discipline of evacuees as well as the general security arrangements, a detachment of mobile *Carabinieri*, selected from the party which was being assembled for the occupation of Rome, was despatched to the beach-head, where its services were very useful.

The two nightmares which haunted so many military government operations throughout the campaign were fortunately absent. There was a shortage neither of food nor of transport. Until A.M.G. flour arrived on D+15 there was some difficulty in effecting a proper distribution. But the armed forces were prepared to lend a hand, as proper distribution of food to the civilian population was a matter of first rate military importance. The wanderings of civilians in search of food on a crowded beach-head had at all costs to be avoided. By D+3 a mill had been established in Nettuno with a tractor supplying power, and another a week later in the forward area. Since the area was a food-growing country most families had some hoarded food-stuffs. Such transport as was necessary to bring corn to mills, flour to bakeries and bread to distribution points was supplied by the Quartermaster—the military function of transport for civilian purposes being clearly understood—since it was necessary to keep carts off the roads. The cooperation between the various military and naval authorities and A.M.G. throughout the operation was most satisfactory.

But the problem of evacuating refugees was not confined to the Anzio beach-head. Three towns in the Cassino plain were completely destroyed and the task of A.M.G. Eighth Army was to prevent the former inhabitants from returning to the ruins and to evacuate them from the district. Aquino, the birth place of the Angelic Doctor (St. Thomas Aquinas), had also been made practically uninhabitable. With the advance up the Adriatic coast north of Rome evacuation on a considerable scale had to be carried out, for military reasons, from the badly damaged coast towns. In the Fifth Army area too, during the fighting before the capture of Rome and later, when the battle front became relatively stable in the north of Tuscany, the evacuation of refugees became an important task assigned to A.M.G. But war was not the only agency to provide a problem of evacuation for the Fifth Army A.M.G. On 18th March Vesuvius erupted, necessitating the evacuation of several of the townships on its sides, an operation carried out by the A.M.G. staff of Naples Province, assisted by a number of officers brought in from the Regions. The necessary vehicles were supplied by the American Peninsular Base Section (P.B.S.) and the British 57 Area, as well as both the Allied Air Forces.

The occupation of Rome was planned and carried out by Fifth Army A.M.G. under Brig.-General Hume. Planning was started at

Caserta as far back as December 1943, in close collaboration with the Special Force of the Fifth Army, which was to occupy the city and become the Rome Area Allied Command. A special City Administration Section was formed, consisting of a Civil Affairs Administration branch and no less than sixteen specialist divisions, each of which co-ordinated its operation with one of the major staff branches (G-1, 2, 3 & 4) of the Fifth Army. The total staff consisted of 103 A.M.G. officers, four civilian members of A.F.H.Q. Petroleum Section, and seven British and American Red Cross workers. A staff of Political Advisers, including the two Vice-Presidents of the Political Section of the Allied Control Commission, were also attached to General Hume.[1]

In order to profit by the lesson of A.M.G. experience in Naples, the Public Utilities Division was made large, since it was assumed that German sabotage would probably have effected major destructions to water and electricity supply systems. This Division worked in very close cooperation with the Engineers of 'S' Force, the task force detailed to occupy the capital. The Public Safety Division was the largest of all, since it was known that in Rome the *Carabinieri* had been disbanded by the Social Republic and that their place had been taken by the *Polizia Africa Italiana*, a body with strong Fascist traditions, and neo-Fascist police forces which would have to be replaced immediately on entry. A mobile detachment of *Carabinieri*, some 2,000 strong, was therefore trained and equipped in Sardinia for this purpose, part of which was employed on the Anzio beach-head, as well as a detachment of about 300 Finance Guards.

The feeding of the capital was planned so as to entail the shortest possible road haulage. It was therefore decided to ship supplies by sea from Naples to Anzio, transporting them thence by road. G-4 Fifth Army agreed to provide the labour for unloading them as well as the trucks required to move them to Rome—an arrangement which nearly caused a break-down, since when the time came for this undertaking to be fulfilled 'more urgent military needs . . . made it impossible for G-4 to fulfil the necessary requirements'. The detachment of Finance Guards, however, supplied the necessary labour to meet this emergency. Transport was somehow scraped together to perform the lift, and fortunately the railway from Anzio to Rome was quickly rehabilitated.

---

[1] The 'specialist' divisions were the following (number of officers in brackets): Finance (8); Legal (9); Black Market (3); Public Safety (23); Intelligence (1); Public Health (2); Welfare (1 plus 7 Red Cross workers); Labour (2); Economics and Supply (9); Transportation, Communications and Utilities (20); Petroleum Products (4 civilians); Property Control (4); Refugees (1); Displaced Persons (1); Monuments, Fine Arts & Archives (2); Education (2). The Civil Affairs Branch consisted of 12 officers and General Hume's H.Q. of 4. Coordination with the Army Staff branches were as follows: G-1 (Personnel)—Legal, Finance, Black Market, Public Health, Refugees, Displaced Persons, Welfare and the Civil Affairs officers; G-2 (Intelligence)—Intelligence, Public Safety; G-3 (Transportation)—Fine Arts, Education, Property Control, Public Safety, Communications & Utilities, Labour; G-4 (Supplies)—Economics, Transportation, Accounting.

The experience of Naples had shown clearly the necessity of protecting the monuments and archives of the capital, not only from public vandalism but also from mishandling by the occupying troops. Not merely were arrangements made to put guards over the principal national monuments, but care had also been taken to furnish units beforehand with a list of historical monuments. It was laid down that the requisition of museums, etc., by Allied military officers would not be permitted without the consent of the Monuments, Fine Arts and Archives Division. This Division worked in very close contact with the Intelligence branches of 'S' Force, and the Archives officer, on inspecting the *Viminale*, discovered the complete archives and correspondence of Mussolini's personal secretary—a collection of unique importance.

The actual events which took place on the occupation of Rome are perhaps worth recording in some detail, though they do not illustrate the typical combination of problems with which A.M.G. had to deal on entering large towns. Apart from anxiety concerning the feeding of the population, swollen by refugees to close on two million persons, the occupation of Rome offered few difficulties to Allied Military Government. Arrangements had been made by Marshal Badoglio, with the approval of the Allied Control Commission, for General Bencivenga, one of the 'underground' representatives of the Army who remained in the city during the German occupation, to take civil and military control of the capital during the interval between the departure of the Germans and the entry of the Allied troops. But that interval had been so short that he had hardly been able to get into his stride when the Allies entered. The last Germans, who drew out on the night of 5th June, were closely followed by Allied troops. The first A.M.G. officer actually to enter the capital was the S.C.A.O. of II Corps, who managed during the afternoon of 4th June to penetrate some distance into the city and to post proclamations in the *Via Toscolana*, but fire from enemy snipers prevented further progress. It was not until seven o'clock the next morning that he was able to post them on the Capitol (*Campidoglio*), the seat of the *Governatorato*. An hour later Lieut.-General Mark Clark, accompanied by Brig.-General Hume, arrived at the Capitol, where they were met by General Bencivenga. As a temporary measure both A.M.G. and the Rome Area Command set up their offices in the traditional seat of the city's government.

The contrast between the conditions found in the capital on entry and those encountered in Naples was described by General Hume in the following words.

> Naples was largely in ruins, Rome was little hurt. Naples had suffered numerous and highly destructive air attacks by the Allies but Rome had not been fired upon by us, except for some of the

> suburban quarters and the railway yards. Naples was crowded with refugees in dire want and all but starving. Rome had a two day supply of food when we came in. Refugees there were . . . but they were of a considerably better class, as a whole, than were the poor found in such number at Naples . . . In Naples the Germans, before their retreat, had done everything conceivable to wreck the city and all its modern conveniences. In Naples there were no telephones, electric light apparatus, gas, street-cars, automobiles (except a few at first hidden), no lamps or candles, no food and no fuel. None of these things were absent in Rome, though many were in very short supply . . . Naples, having been exposed to German propaganda, expected the worst of Allied troops. Rome, having been re-assured, awaited us as liberators.

Though this picture proved perhaps, as we shall see, a little optimistic, it meant that A.M.G. had at any rate time to settle in before being overwhelmed by a multitude of simultaneous crises.

The first problem to be dealt with was that of Public Safety. The disarmament and disbandment of the neo-Fascist police force, *Polizia Africa Italiana*, of some 1,250 members was effected in six hours after the first interview between A.M.G's Chief Public Safety Officer and its commander. A more delicate task was the disarming of the police forces of the partisans, who had been armed largely by weapons secretly furnished by the Allies. The leaders of the six parties, who formed the underground Committee of National Liberation (C.L.N.), were therefore called into the conference. It was explained to them that the Allies intended to restore the *Carabinieri*, and they were requested to disband the partisan police formations and to surrender their arms. All the parties, except the Communists, immediately co-operated in disbanding their forces, but a police-raid on Party headquarters was required to bring the latter into line. But the general surrender of weapons ordered in connection with Proclamation No. 2 was not so easily accomplished. The number of firearms surrendered by the civilian population within the first ten days was comparatively small[1] and, as will be seen later, the quantity of weapons remaining in the hands of the public was a continual menace to public safety long after the responsibility for maintaining it had been handed back to the Italian Government. The re-organisation of the police forces of the capital was quickly accomplished. Over 3,000 ex-*Carabinieri* reported, many of whom had come out of hiding, and though a considerable number of the other police forces (Public Security Agents and *Metropolitani*) had to be dismissed, the mobile cadres both of *Carabinieri* and Finance Guards

[1] The actual numbers were 180 machine guns and 'automatics', 1,745 rifles, 570 revolvers, 210 sporting guns and 2,500 hand grenades.

brought in by the Allies enabled the Public Safety Division to perform this task without endangering the maintenance of public order.

A new municipal administration for the capital was immediately installed, the choice for 'Lord Mayor' falling upon Prince Doria Pamphili, after discussion with Signor Bonomi, a former prime minister now chairman of the Committee of National liberation. The title of the 'Lord Mayor' was changed from the Fascist *Governatore* to the traditional *Sindaco*. To assist him a *Giunta* was set up composed of two members of each of the six political parties constituting the Committee of National Liberation, the parties being requested to submit nominations. The investiture of the new *Sindaco* took place on 13th June in the Capitol, the 'Mansion House' of the Eternal City, which had several days before been vacated by General Hume and General Johnson, commander of the troops in Rome area.

A start was immediately made on the 'defascistisation' of the existing municipal administration by the application of the laws passed by the Badoglio Government. These now included the punitive provisions mentioned in the last chapter against 'collaborators' as well as Fascists. A directive had been issued by the Allied Control Commission dividing officials into three classes, the first to be arrested and sent to Salerno, the second to be arrested and held in Rome, and the third merely to be removed from office. But, as General Hume remarked, this directive could not be applied strictly—'one person who would under the directive have been removed and sent to Salerno for trial went there, as a matter of fact, as a Cabinet Minister'. The Fifth Army A.M.G. confined its purging activities mostly to the officials of the *Governatorato* and to the judges; the central administration could be dealt with adequately only by the Italian Government and the headquarters of the Control Commission. But a beginning was made by Colonel Poletti, when he took charge of Rome Region, on the lines adopted in Naples. A committee of twelve persons of unblemished reputation was appointed by him to initiate a preliminary purge.

Before A.M.G. was effectively installed orders had been issued by General Bencivenga for the removal of a number of officials, all of whom were subsequently found to be on the S.C.A.O's list for removal. But Fifth Army A.M.G., which was responsible for governing Rome only for ten days (5th–15th June), had little time to go very deeply into the epuration even of the *Governatorato* and, with the exception of the Governor of the Bank of Italy, Dr. Azzolini[1], no

---

[1] Dr. Azzolini was arrested and subsequently tried under the legislation introduced by Signor Bonomi, on the charge of having been an accessory to the removal by the Germans of the gold reserve of the Bank. He received a heavy sentence, but the charge was ultimately, on appeal, proved to be unfounded.

official of the higher rank was removed, since nearly all of these had left the capital, though over eighty persons of middle or lower rank were dismissed. About 250 officers of the Fascist militia, including several generals, were also arrested.

All the law courts were closed by A.M.G. in accordance with the usual practice. The process of eliminating the judicial officials considered politically undesirable was immediately set in hand. It was found that, with the exception of three sections of the Court of Cassation, whose judges had left the city, all law courts were in a position to function normally. On 24th June the Minister of Justice officially reinstated Dr. Ettore Casati, who had crossed the German lines to join the Badoglio Government, as First President of the Court of Cassation. All courts were in operation before the end of the month, by which time seven Allied Military courts had been constituted, five Summary and two Superior, which between them were disposing of about ninety-five cases a day. As at Naples, the Germans before leaving had wantonly released a large number of criminals from the prisons, but the Public Safety Division was able to improve on its performance in that city. Before ten days were up more than half of them had been recovered.

Though very little destruction had occurred in the city except in the outskirts, during the course of occupation those public utilities whose sources lay outside its confines, were considerably damaged. Water supply installations had suffered severely. Of the two systems supplying Rome, one, the Marcia aqueduct system, had been broken in several places, and the main junction between the water mains and the aqueduct at Tivoli was still in enemy hands when the Allied forces entered Rome. This was promptly sabotaged by the Germans with the result that the higher portions of the city of the seven hills were practically without water. But though the damage done at Tivoli was serious, local resources, with the timely assistance of the engineers of the Rome Area Command, enabled temporary repairs to be quickly undertaken. Close collaboration between the two supplying companies soon permitted water to be supplied to the whole city by means of an ingenious system of inter-connections, by dividing it into four zones and rationing them by rotation. Meanwhile the auxiliary water supplies of wells and cisterns were chlorinated to avoid the danger of contamination. Power distillation units were set up and water carts used for distribution to various points in the higher parts of the city. But it was not until the end of September that supplies were beginning to approach normal levels.

The supply of electricity was not so easily restored. The great hydro-electric network to the north and east, which furnished the capital's normal supply, had been cut off, so that the only available source was from two standby (diesel and coal) thermal plants in the capital and some small hydro-electric installations in its vicinity, which were quickly repaired and put back into operation. Civilian consumption had therefore to be severely rationed for many months. Civilian consumers had to content themselves during the early days with four hours of power supply every two days, though Allied military installations and Italian hospitals received a continuous service. Arrangements were also made to supply hospitals with gas, which had not been distributed for several months under German occupation. Although telephone services had been interrupted by the Germans before leaving, damage to these was much less than in Naples. By the evening of 6th June the chief military centres were in touch with each other by telephone. In a short time the general service was restored to the level which had been permitted under German occupation. The main post offices were found to be intact—in Naples they had been destroyed—and, once security considerations permitted, limited postal services were resumed on 1st July.

The normal bread ration allowed under the German occupation was only 100 gms (less than a quarter of a pound) per day, but this had been increased by a complicated system of extra allowances for special categories of persons, varying from 75 gms for children to 450 gms—about a pound—for those engaged in specially heavy labour for the German forces. These extra allowances covered a considerable percentage of the ration-card holders. But a black market was flourishing in which prices before Allied entry were as high as 240 lire per kilo. As soon as it was known that the Allies were approaching, prices fell to 100 lire, in anticipation, no doubt, of plentiful Allied supplies—an anticipation which was doomed to severe disappointment. A.M.G. found itself unable during the early days either to increase the basic ration or to maintain the German extra allowances. This meant that many people were subjected to a considerable reduction, but they were able to draw some comfort from the fact that the Allies distributed imported white flour, a commodity which the Italian public had not seen since the beginning of the war. On 21st June the bread ration was increased to 150 gms and four days later to 200 gms, but before long difficulties in transporting the necessary supplies, amounting to some 300 tons a day, made it impossible to distribute this quantity for some months with any regularity. Throughout the winter the feeding of the capital caused acute anxiety.

In other respects the immediate impact of Allied occupation on food supplies was also unfavourable, owing to the initial unwillingness of the Allied Commander, Rome Area, to place restaurants out of bounds to Allied soldiers. A.M.G. had suggested that this should be done immediately, and that special restaurants should be opened exclusively for troops and supplied with food from military sources.

The proposal was eventually accepted, and, though it did not wholly prevent the consumption of civilian food by Allied soldiers, it did greatly reduce the number of meals served from civilian sources. But it was not until November that the prohibition originally suggested by A.M.G. was enforced. Nor was the initial task of A.M.G. made any easier by the posting of a bulletin by the Psychological Warfare Branch on the walls of the capital, without previous consultation with General Hume, announcing that the bread ration was to be increased to 300 gms (nearly 11 oz.). The general supply situation had improved sufficiently to enable the Allied Control Commission to risk an increase in the ration in southern Italy. This step had been taken as a desperate effort to ensure the success of the *ammassi*, renamed *Granai del Popolo*, and to curb the appalling activity of the black market in Naples. But it entailed the diversion southwards of grain which would normally have gone to feed the capital from Ascoli Piceno and Macerata. Difficulties both of supply and of transport made it impossible to apply this increase to central Italy until the spring of 1945, scarcely two months before the conclusion of hostilities. This difference was a constant source of embarrassment to A.M.G. and led to a great deal of discontent.

Transport was everywhere the limiting condition in the distribution of supplies, both of the limited quantity of imported, and of the much larger volume of indigenous, produce. Fifth Army A.M.G. at the time of the occupation of Rome had under its command two truck units, one Italian, equipped with 140 vehicles in 'class B condition', and a British unit of thirty vehicles. This limited equipment had not only to supply Rome at the rate of some 300 tons a day from the dump at Anzio, but also to meet the growing forward requirements of A.M.G. Fifth Army for feeding areas north and west of the capital, so rapid was the advance of the Allied forces. In the first ten days or so of the Allied occupation about 1,000 truckloads of food, principally flour, were transported from Anzio to Rome, amounting to just short of 3,000 tons.[1] The total shipped in the period 27th May to 7th July, when the Anzio depot was closed, amounted to 10,000 tons of goods, shipped in approximately 3,000 truck-loads with a known loss of only two trucks. Later the chief port through which supplies were shipped from Naples was Civitavecchia.

Immediate steps were taken to mobilise the available transport resources of the capital A General Order was posted on the first day of occupation requiring the registration of all motor vehicles,

---

[1] Actual quantities were: flour, 2,500 tons; sugar, 125 tons; olive oil 150 tons; meat and vegetables (M & V) 75 tons; and soap 25 tons. Total 2,875 tons.

parts and accessories. New licences issued by A.M.G. were made obligatory, so as to restrict vehicles to essential services, permits to draw petrol being strictly limited to licensed vehicles. A start was made to put into operation existing road transport concerns, whose vehicles had in many cases been buried in order to preserve them from seizure by the Germans. Later all vehicles were pooled under an *Ufficio Trasporti di Roma*. The number of trucks under control by the end of August amounted to some 800, and by the end of September to about 2,300, of which only about 1,500 were in serviceable condition, largely owing to the lack of tyres. Smaller pools were formed in the provinces of the Lazio—Umbria Region. By these means it was possible to keep the supply of imported foodstuffs, chiefly flour, at the level of about 300 tons a day, and of other produce from the surrounding countryside at approximately 700 tons a day. This figure was however not much more than half the normal quantity. Though it would be an exaggeration to talk of starvation, there was certainly malnutrition, especially among the poorer classes, which manifested itself statistically in a definite increase in the incidence of tuberculosis.

The shortage of transport was not confined only to road vehicles Sea-haulage from the base depot in Naples was also limited by the restricted carrying capacity of the balance of Italian coastal craft (schooners) placed at the disposal of A.C.C. for civilian transport. The quantity of rail transport made available for civilian purposes by the military authorities was also extremely small, and, it must be confessed, not always fully or discerningly employed by the Allied Control Commission's Supply Officers. And though it was recognised, in principle, that in Army areas the distribution of essential civilian supplies was in the last resort a military responsibility, it is not surprising that the Armies, in hot pursuit of the enemy, should have been reluctant to part with any more than they could help of their resources for civilian purposes.

In these circumstances the flourishing of a black market was scarcely to be avoided. Immediately on entry A.M.G. published a list of prices for a large number of commodities, and, in order to ensure the marketing of various farm produce from the surrounding country through regularly ordained channels at controlled prices, established a series of control posts on all the roads leading to the capital. These measures for a while appeared to meet with some success but, in order to encourage the bringing of fruit and vegetables into the capital at a time when transport was desperately short, the Economic Section of A.C.C. decided to permit civilians to bring in fifteen kilos of foodstuffs without control in horse-drawn carts. This greatly weakened the whole system. The control posts were finally abolished by the Italian Government soon after Rome and

Lazio reverted to their administration. This, of course, gave an enormous stimulus to the 'black' markets. Meanwhile the efforts of the Black Market Section were poorly supported by the Italian courts in the cases of the small offender. The chief commodities involved in the black market operation were flour and potatoes.

During the summer and autumn life for civilians in Rome was certainly far from easy, and the absence of fuel and the seasonal decline in the supply of vegetable products made things even more uncomfortable in the winter. In these circumstances the genuine enthusiasm with which Rome had welcomed her liberators soon began to wear a little thin; the comment was not unfrequently heard that Rome had been better off under the German occupation. And though by this time the administrative responsibility for feeding the city had been handed back to the Italian Government, public opinion naturally blamed the Allies in general and the Regional Commissioner in particular.[1]

One of the aggravating causes of the severe shortages in Rome was the presence of an enormous number of refugees. A first estimate showed them to be about 100,000 in number, but later calculations brought the figure to between 200,000 and 300,000. Many of these were people who had fled to the capital to escape the heavy fighting in the Alban hills and in Lazio, while others were persons hiding from the German labour-drafts, among them a large number of disbanded soldiers. In connection with refugees A.M.G. had a double task, first to help the military authorities to prevent refugees blocking the roads, by stopping any more of them from entering Rome from the north, and by confining exits to the south to unimportant side roads; and, secondly, to evacuate them from the city, and to hold and feed them in staging camps pending their dispersal to their homes in the south. The Germans had already established a refugee camp, where several thousands of persons were found in a starving state, living under appalling sanitary conditions. Conditions here were immediately improved and a large holding camp set up at Cine Città (Cinema City) a suburb of the capital. Cine Città was also used as a reception camp for displaced persons. In view of the food scarcity arrangements were made to supply Allied nationals with additional rations and medical assistance, over 5,000 persons being assisted during the month of July.

The presence of a large number of refugees was known by A.M.G, before entering Rome, and it had been expected that emergency feeding on a large scale would be necessary. Arrangements were therefore made to coordinate the work of the various charitable

---

[1] Cf. the refrain of the song produced in one of the theatrical reviews—'*Charley Poletti, Charley Poletti, Meno ciarle e più spaghetti*, (Less talk and more spaghetti!)

institutions sponsored by the Church with other public feeding organisations. Three truck loads of meat, vegetables and biscuits were included in the first convoy into Rome. Immediately on entry contact was made with the Vatican committee which had been supplying, through various religious organisations, over 200,000 meals a day in popular and industrial kitchens, and the truck-loads were delivered to their warehouse. The work done by this committee was beyond praise, and by its active help in the early days much severe suffering was prevented. The supply of food-stuffs for these popular kitchens was during the autumn a constant problem. By the end of November, thanks to the evacuation of refugees, the number of meals served in popular kitchens had somewhat diminished, but it was still in the neighbourhood of 250,000 a day.

Post offices and banks were closed in accordance with Proclamation No. 4, though a few of the latter had actually opened on 5th June for business. 600 million lire from the *Banca d'Italia* in Naples and 240 million Allied Military lire were brought in and deposited in the *Banca d'Italia* on 5th June—a very necessary precaution, since cash reserves had been considerably depleted by withdrawals in the days preceding Allied entry. Actual cash in the twenty-six commercial banks in the city amounted to only 346 million lire against sight deposits of 8,680 million lire. The banks on consultation decided that they needed about 130 million lire to supplement their reserves before opening business. In order to provide an ample margin of reserves a further sum of 450 million lire was brought up from Naples, and deposited with the *Banca d'Italia*, on 12th June. Banks were opened for business without restrictions on 14th June, just a week after closing, as compared with six weeks in Sicily and four in Naples. In the first three days of business, the excess of deposits over withdrawals amounted to fourteen million lire.

The pursuit of the rapidly retreating Germans by the Allied Armies was so swift that scarcely two weeks had passed before rear army boundaries had already advanced beyond Rome. On 15th June Rome passed out of the control of Fifth Army A.M.G. and became an Allied Military Government Region. This arrangement only lasted a month, since it was imperative that the new Italian Government of Signor Bonomi should be established in the capital and that Rome should be included in Italian Government territory at the earliest possible date. The transfer of the Italian Government from Salerno took place on 15th July, when the headquarters of A.C.C. were also transposed from Naples to Rome. A month later Rome, together with the provinces of Frosinone and Littoria, was added to Italian Government territory, which had already been enlarged on 20th July by the transfer of Region III, all but the commune of Naples. Naples, like Leghorn and Ancona later, remained under the control of A.M.G., on account of the extreme military importance of the port as a supply base for the Allied Armies. Rome Region, whose Commissioner was Colonel Poletti, transferred from Region III, took over practically unchanged the staff which General Hume had brought to Rome, and was combined with Region IV. This had originally included, besides Lazio, the Abruzzi, and was reconstituted as the Lazio-Umbria Region, made up of the following provinces, Rome, Frosinone, Littoria, Viterbo and Rieti in Lazio and the two Umbrian provinces of Terni and Perugia, which passed out of Eighth Army A.M.G. control in September. Region IV thus became a 'mixed' region, since in three of its provinces, Rome, Frosinone and Littoria, Military Government no longer prevailed, as they had been transferred to Italian Government territory, whereas the four provinces to the north of Rome were still subject to Allied Military Government.

With the rapid advance of the Armies beyond Rome, Allied Military Government began to undergo certain changes both of *tempo* and of character. The territories overtaken by the 'spearhead' Civil Affairs organisation grew so rapidly that provincial teams could not be assembled sufficiently quickly to take over the provinces as they were liberated, with the result that the degree of control which could be exercised became much attenuated. It therefore became necessary to hand over at the earliest possible moment more and more responsibility to Italian officials on the spot. Yet the existing officials had been serving the neo-Fascist government and were therefore *prima facie* open to suspicion. Hence the need for their rapid elimination, and for the provision of immediate substitutes.

At the same time account had to be taken of the Committees of National Liberation, which had created a formidable underground movement under the German occupation. Their leaders had in some towns assumed control of the administration before the actual entry of the Allies. These local committees had been federated on a 'compartmental' basis, and after the liberation of the capital the Tuscan C.L.N. and those of the more northern regions tended to look for guidance more to the co-ordinating committee for the North set up in Milan, the *Comitato di Liberazione Nazionale per l'Alta Italia* (C.L.N.A.I.), than to the Central Committee in Rome. This made it all the more urgent to reconstruct the representative organs of local government in accordance with the law passed by the Badoglio Government, so as to direct their energies into channels which would give them some foretaste of the re-establishment of democratic institutions. 'Defascistisation' and the reconstruction of local administration thus became one of the immediate tasks of the Army A.M.G's.

With regard to the former, conditions were now much more complicated than those that had to be met in Sicily on the invasion of an enemy territory. There, apart from the elimination of Fascist organisations and of prominent Fascists in the state and communal administrations, the only practical policy for AMGOT had been to continue in office those officials who were willing to serve under its instructions. But now a double complication had to be envisaged as a result of the events which had taken place since the armistice. The presumption now was that at any rate the chief officials to be met with in the advance northwards had actively collaborated with the neo-Fascist regime of the Social Republic, and had therefore automatically incurred the penalties attached to treasonable conduct by the King's Government.[1] Moreover Allied Military Government of liberated territories was now envisaged as merely a transitory interlude, pending the return of their administration to that of the legitimate Italian Government. Traitor-officials had therefore to be handed for judgment to the Italian Government; and the substitutes appointed by A.M.G. had, as far as possible, to be men who would meet the approval of the Italian Government when it came to take over.

It had been agreed that the Italian law of 'defascistisation' should be appllied in Military Government territory, since only chaos could have resulted from the application by A.M.G. of principles of 'epuration' different from those enacted by the Italian Government. As a result of the more drastic measures initiated by Badoglio's six-party government and developed by its successor, the different classes of Fascists subject to automatic dismissal were enormously increased. Besides the categories of *Squadrista*, *Sciarpa Littorio*, etc., originally specified by AMGOT, they now included a long list of different classes of the hierarchy. And to this list was added another, of officials of the Social Republic, quite independent of their party ranks. All these persons were now liable not only to dismissal but to criminal prosecution as well. Hence the instructions, already noted in the account of the occupation of Rome, that, besides Fascist party officials, certain office-holders of the Social-Republican Government should be arrested. These included Prefects in charge of provinces, or in the service of ministries, Mayors of all communes of a population of more than 50,000 inhabitants, officers of any rank in the Fascist militia, Inspectors-General of Public Safety and a number of high judicial officials, the Governor and Vice-Governor of Rome and the Directors-General of all ministries. A second class of officials who were to be dismissed from office automatically included Vice-Prefects, Chiefs of Cabinet of Prefectures, Financial-Intendants of

[1] See above, p. 148, and below, pp. 206-07.

Provinces and Provincial Superintendents of Studies. These instructions were subsequently modified as the new legislation for defascistisation introduced by the Bonomi Government was brought into force in A.M.G. territory, and they were always qualified by a saving clause, to prevent complete breakdown in administration.

It was found almost everywhere that the chief provincial officers, Prefects and *Questori* (Chiefs of Police), had fled, and often many subordinate officials, so that the number of arrests to be made by A.M.G. was very small. Moreover the security authorities of the Armies had their own black lists. Though their cooperation with A.M.G. was now on much more satisfactory lines, security objections often led to the dismissal, if not to the physical internment, of officials whom A.M.G. might have been prepared to allow to remain at their posts. In these circumstances it was found advisable to create pools of available officials to be sent forward into liberated territories, a task which devolved upon the Interior, now called Local Government Sub-Commission. In order to preserve administrative continuity, a list was agreed with the Italian Government of the officials to be sent forward. After the liberation of Rome these pools were used to select provincial teams, e.g. Prefect, two Vice-Prefects, Secretary, Councillor and Chief Accountant, which were sometimes called forward as a unit. In other cases only one or two members of the team were required. In Army territories the S.C.A.O., and in A.M.G. Regions the Regional Commissioner, retained the power to make his own appointments in case of urgent administrative necessity, but in most cases Prefects for liberated provinces were sent up from Rome at the request of the S.C.A.O. by the Local Government Sub-Commission. Sometimes however, as in Lucca, a suitable candidate, though not a career official, was elected on the spot by the S.C.A.O. of the Army A.M.G. from the local leaders of the Committee of National Liberation. As the liberating armies advanced up the peninsula, it became more and more difficult to find suitable career officials uncompromised by Fascism. The necessity was therefore impressed upon the Italian Government of looking outside the ranks of permanent civil servants for its appointments. Substitutes for displaced mayors of communes and communal secretaries were generally found locally, though it was not always easy to discover suitable candidates. To meet this need, too, the Local Government Sub-Commission, in collaboration with the Ministry of the Interior, created a 'pool' of *Sindachi*, since it had been decided to dismiss all existing mayors and, the post of *Sindaco* being unpaid, it was not always easy in some of the smaller communes to persuade suitable candidates to accept it.

The reorganisation of local government, both provincial and communal, had been dealt with by the Badoglio Government in a decree-law (RDL of 16th April 1944) which embodied the principles of the changes already introduced by AMGOT, described in Chapter II. The provisions of this decree were applied in Military Government territory, being extended as far as was practicable to territories under Army A.M.G's. In the forward areas the responsibility for appointing the new Mayor and Communal Secretaries (town clerks) lay usually with the 'spearhead' Civil Affairs officer, who was sometimes too hard pressed to find an immediate substitute for the existing mayor, but was generally able to do so. Such a substitute was not necessarily looked upon as a permanency, and his appointment became subject to revision when provincial government under a Prefect was organised, since under the new local government law appointments to the post of Mayor were to be made by the Prefect—subject, of course, to A.M.G./A.C.C. approval.

As soon as conditions permitted after liberation, the A.M.G. Provincial Commissioner, in consultation with the Prefect, undertook the reconstruction of the most important local organisations on the pattern existing before the Fascist regime, which had been based on the principle of popular election namely, the *Deputazione Provinciale*—the executive committee of the elective Provincial Council, which appointed the unofficial members of the Provincial administrative board (*Giunta Provinciale Amministrativa*)—and the *Giunta Comunale*.[1] The appointments to these bodies were made by the Prefect subject to A.M.G. approval. The numbers of both these bodies were regulated by the population of the province or commune, but in order to secure adequate representation of the local C.L.N. the statutory numbers were sometimes exceeded, and care was taken in selecting the membership to give representation to local interests other than the purely political, so as to include elements to represent labour and agriculture as well as industry and commerce. Provincial and municipal decrees and orders were now issued, not in the name of Allied Military Government officers, but by Prefects and Mayors—with the *visto* of the A.M.G. officer concerned—an important step towards the rehabilitation of the prestige of the Italian Government.

During the retreat of the Germans from the Tiber to the Arno the Army A.M.G. had to take over a very large amount of territory in a few weeks. Rome had been entered on the night of 4th June, and taken over on the 5th, Orvieto and Terni were captured on the 14th and Chiusi on the 20th. Siena was taken on 3rd July, Volterra on the 9th July and Arezzo on the 16th. On the Adriatic coast the movement was equally quick. Pescara and Chieti were taken between the 8th and 12th of June and Ancona on 18th July, the same

---

[1] For a short description of Italian Local Government bodies see above, pp. 61-62.

day as Leghorn. One result of this rapid advance was that, with certain notable exceptions, the towns south of the line Arezzo-Leghorn were not severely damaged—much less so than those in the Cassino plain and the provinces of Frosinone and Littoria. But just south of the Arno German resistance stiffened. The southern half of Florence was not entered until 4th August and it was about a fortnight before the northern half of the city was cleared of the enemy. Pisa was not wholly in Allied hands until 1st September.

The southern part of Tuscany, Umbria and the Marches were on the whole well supplied with food, the latter region in particular producing some surplus which could help in the all-important task of feeding Rome, within the limits imposed by the shortage of transport. The ports of Civitavecchia and Piombino were quickly brought into action by the Navy, which helped to solve the problem of bringing up imported supplies by sea from the main base in Naples. But the northern part of Tuscany offered much more difficult conditions. The normal population of Florence was in the neighbourhood of 330,000—increased by refugees to over 400,000—and the surrounding hilly country produced comparatively little food. Leghorn had a normal population of about 125,000, though most of these had fled and some had been evacuated by the Germans, while Pisa, Lucca and Pistoia were towns of some 70 to 80,000 inhabitants. There was thus a large industrial population to feed, while industry itself was at a standstill owing to the systematic destruction by the Germans of the large hydro-electric installations of Umbria and Tuscany. Moreover the amount of destruction in the Arno valley and in the eastern vicinity of the Gothic Line between the Apennines and the Po valley was enormous. There was thus a very pressing refugee problem, which was emphasised by evacuations on military grounds at the time of the regrouping of the Allied Armies, which took place before the first attack on the Gothic Line.

Under these conditions the administrative arrangements of the Control Commission were put to a severe test, since it had to take over in a hurry large territories in central Italy, while at the same time holding itself prepared, in the event of the assault on the Gothic Line proving decisively successful, to undertake the military government of the Po basin. The halting of the Allied advance on the Winter Line of the Apennines enabled these preparations, which will be described in Chapter IX, to be made in some detail and afforded the opportunity for handing over more responsibility to the Italian Government. But with the limited 'ceiling' on the man-power of the Commission it is not difficult to imagine the chaos that might have resulted had the Commission been forced to assume the military government of northern Italy in the autumn of 1944.

As it was, the man-power of the Commission was stretched to its utmost and the enlargement of liberated territory which in fact took place showed very plainly that the detailed degree of control over Italian administration, which the Allied Commission had been planned to execute, was quite impracticable. Small wonder then that the rapid improvisation of provincial teams to take over the ever growing number of provinces in A.M.G. territory in the rear of the Armies did not always work very smoothly. The regional organisation of Region VIII (Tuscany) was particularly unfortunate, since its headquarters were shifted from place to place—

Map 8

Orvieto, Siena and Lucca—before it could be settled in its regional capital, Florence; indeed it only enjoyed control of its entire Region for a few days. Since parts of Tuscany remained in the Army area till a very late stage, Regional headquarters had to take over the administration of its provinces piece-meal. A large number of its provincial teams remained for a long time under command of Eighth and Fifth Armies. Thus Grosseto province was handed over to the Region on 8th August, Siena and Livorno on 8th September, Arezzo in the middle of October, Pisa at the end of November, and Florence, Lucca, Apuania and Pistoia not till 5th May 1945, a few days before hostilities in Europe were ended, and only five days before the three southern provinces of the Region, Grosseto, Siena and Arezzo, were handed back to the Italian Government. Moreover the provincial teams working under Army A.M.G's had their tasks complicated by the fact that, in Leghorn, Pisa and Florence, they had to take over large portions of their respective provinces many weeks before the provincial capital fell into Allied hands.

In addition to the usual problems of feeding and caring for the population in devastated areas, a new series of problems was now set to A.M.G. by the Resistance movement in central and northern Italy. It was not until the liberation of Rome that the problem of patriots and partisans began to obtrude itself in any marked degree upon the attention of the High Command in Italy and the Allied Control Commission.[1] The Resistance movement had of course started much earlier, as soon indeed as the armistice divided the country into German- and Allied-occupied portions, and from the very beginning it had been inspired as much by hatred of the Germans as by detestation of Fascism. Hence it was immediately encouraged and assisted by Allied military agencies, who started to repatriate selected anti-Fascist leaders for this purpose directly after the Salerno landings, and also to begin the dropping of supplies of arms and radio transmitters.[2] During the winter of 1943–4, when the Allied line was more or less stationary just north of Naples, a number of partisan bands had formed themselves south of Rome in the Abruzzi and in the hills of Lazio, but these were practically wiped out after the failure of the Anzio landing to lead to an immediate

---

[1] The two terms appear originally to have been synonymous. The members of the first bands, which came into being directly after the armistice, were, it seems, generally called by the public 'rebels', later 'patriots', and finally 'partisans'. Cf. Leo Valiani, *Tutte le strade conducono a Roma*, p. 200. If any distinction between the two terms can be said to have existed, it would appear that the term 'partisan' was restricted generally, to the organised military bands while the term 'patriot' was sometimes used in a wider sense embracing the whole Resistance movement.

[2] For an account of the repatriation of one of these, see Valiani *op. cit.*, Chapters 1 and 2, where the author describes his own journey from America via Algiers to southern Italy. Also M. Salvadori, *Resistenza ed Azione*, Chapter 5. Captain, later Colonel, Salvadori, of No. 1 Special Force, was for some months attached to the Patriot Branch of A.C.C.

capture of Rome. The Resistance movement attained a higher degree of organisation in Tuscany, Umbria and the Marches, though its main strength lay further north, in Piedmont, Lombardy and Venetia. As the Allies advanced north of Rome they overtook an increasing number of 'patriot' bands, armed formations of a semi-military character, and the problem presented by these to the Allied military authorities, to A.M.G. and to the Italian Government, became extremely urgent.

Patriot bands, like most guerilla formations, were of a very mixed nature as to size, efficiency, character and composition. The elements comprising the movement included anti-Fascists of all the old political parties. Many of these had maintained for years an underground opposition to Fascism. Most of their leaders had spent years in prison, from which they were finally released by Badoglio in the 'forty-five days'. Besides these political elements, reinforced by many civilians of all classes of society imbued with hatred of Mussolini's Teutonic allies, there were nuclei of the dispersed army who had taken to the hills, reinforced by a large number of workers threatened with deportation to Germany for forced labour. An extraneous element was provided by Allied prisoners of war, including Yugoslavs and even Russians, who had escaped from internment, often with patriot and peasant assistance, and joined the partisan bands in active operations against the German forces. These sturdy elements were not without less reputable attachments.

The bands and 'action squads' in and about Rome and in the Apennines north and south of the capital fell into two categories, those dependent on the Committee of National Liberation's military Committee, and those dependent on the Army's underground resistance organisation, which sprang up after the flight of Badoglio and the King from Rome on 9th September. Of this General Bencivenga had been belatedly appointed head by the Brindisi Government. The directing spirits of these two patriot organisations were called into conference by A.C.C. very soon after the liberation of the capital. A special section had been constituted at A.C.C. headquarters to deal with the 'patriots', which was subsequently absorbed into the Local Government Sub-Commission. This section worked in close collaboration with 'Special Force' (the Allied military organisation working with the Resistance movement), the Italian War Office and the patriot organisation later set up by the Italian Government, as well as with the Land Forces Sub-Commission (M.M.I.A.), in the endeavour to work out an agreed policy with regard to their treatment and disposal.

As the advance of the Allied Armies north of the Tiber liberated successive stretches of territory, more and more partisan bands were uncovered. The problem was how to get them back into civilian occupations. For, with certain exceptions connected with special operations, these guerilla troops were at first not wanted by the Armies, though later their military potentialities were recognised, when it became known, for example, that during the occupation of Florence they had performed some very useful work. The existence of armed civilians, however, was an obvious menace to public order, and the surrender of civilian arms had been from the invasion of Sicily onwards one of the first demands of A.M.G. Moreover the arms of partisan bands, which had largely been supplied from Allied sources, were required to be used again by the partisan units still fighting further north, to whom they were supplied by air. Arrangements had therefore to be made to persuade the partisan bands as they were 'uncovered' to disband, and to surrender their arms—no easy matter in many cases—and then to find suitable occupation for persons who had risked their lives in fighting for liberation, and often those of their families left behind in German occupied territory. With this end in view an address, signed by General Alexander, was posted up in communes on liberation, thanking the partisans for their services to the United Nations and exhorting them to assist in the re-establishment of their country and to co-operate with the Allied Military Government, which required them to furnish certain information—including names of active neo-Fascist collaborators—, and explaining to them the arrangements made by the Italian Government to assist them through Patriot Committees.[1]

Certificates of merit signed by the Commander-in-Chief were also issued to all those who could prove actual service in partisan bands. Representatives from the two Italian co-ordinating organisations, the *Giunta Militare* of the C.L.N. and the *Comando Bande* of the Italian War Office, were sent to Army A.M.Gs. Their function was to help the Army Civil Affairs officers to identify the leaders of patriot bands, to select certain suitable 'partisans' out of the bands to assist A.M.G. in local government, to produce a complete list of 'patriots' in the area, in order to enable certificates to be issued to all genuine partisans, and to assist in the setting up of Communal Patriot Committees. The communal committees were constituted normally on the following lines—the *Sindaco* was chairman and of the other members four or more were chosen by and from the patriots and two were either members of the *Giunta Comunale* or selected from respected local residents.

The first function of these communal committees was to distinguish genuine from 'bogus' patriots, and then to classify them according to their prospective occupations. There were a considerable number, perhaps even a majority, who wanted to go on serving

[1] The full text is given in the Annexe to this Chapter.

as partisans, but this was ruled out for military reasons. The regular soldier had, to begin with at any rate, little use for 'private armies', though a few were selected by 'Popski' (Lieut.-Colonel Peniakoff), the commander of a 'special force' working behind the enemy's lines, for certain services.[1] But there was an alternative for those who wished to continue on active service. Arrangements were made by which partisans of military age, instead of waiting for the calling up of their class, could enlist as volunteers, and considerable encouragement was offered to them to do so. There was, however, only a very poor response, since partisans wanted to be kept together as bands serving under their own officers, and refused to volunteer as individuals to serve in an army which only a few months before had been deserted by its chiefs and allowed to disintegrate. For those who opted for civilian employment a certain amount of work was offered by the Allied Armies, such as urgent work on bridging and road repairs, dock clearance, etc. An attempt, not wholly unsuccessful, was also made to enlist 'patriots' into special squads to be trained for mine clearance.

But to many of those who had sacrificed so much for the sake of fighting the Teutonic enemy these employments as 'hewers of wood and drawers of water' could not fail to appear below the dignity of a 'patriot', even if A.M.G. was sometimes able to offer rather more congenial employment as special police or motor-lorry drivers. It was usually possible to provide work on the spot for any local partisan who sought it, but there were many who had come from German-occupied Italy, and some from Sicily and the South. For these it was not so easy to find suitable jobs. For though during the harvest season there was a heavy demand for labour on the land and priority was everywhere given to patriots in all forms of employment, there remained a hard core which could not or would not be employed locally. These had to be given hospital treatment where necessary, maintained, and provided with clothing, pending their despatch to Italian Government territory. The provision of transport, rations and clothing for disbanded patriots was a constant source of anxiety to A.M.G., always desperately short of food and consumption-goods. It was only after prolonged discussion that assistance in these matters could be elicited from reluctant military supply authorities, not unnaturally concerned with husbanding their limited resources. And it was not until the attention of the Supreme Allied Commander was directed to the military as well as the political importance of the Resistance movement in northern Italy, that arrangements were made to secure more satisfactory treatment for the liberated 'patriots'.

[1] See Peniakoff, *Private Army*, pp. 449–460.

The first contact of A.M.G. with the Resistance movement had been made in Naples, where certain elements of the civilian population and some detachments of Italian soldiers had fought against the retreating Germans. But at the time of the Neapolitan 'four days' the patriot bands had not yet been organised. Rome was liberated without any struggle in the city itself, and A.M.G. was in charge of the capital for too short a time to complete the disarmament of the various resistance groups. But in the liberation of Florence it was for the first time faced with the problem of dealing with organised patriot bands on a substantial scale. During the operations leading to the capture of the city two patriot 'divisions' had come into action under the orders of the Allied Command, the '*Potente*' Division, composed almost entirely of Communists, and the *Giustizia e Libertà* division composed mostly of members of the Action party, with a 'Brigade' of ex-*Carabinieri* who had taken to the mountains after the armistice. Tuscan patriot formations played an important part in the street fighting, lasting several days, which took place north of the Arno, and in harassing the retreating Germans in the outskirts.[1] When the fighting was over their disbandment and disarmament was one of the most serious problems confronting the military government of the city.

The delicacy of this situation had been foreseen by Group-Captain Benson. On 18th August he had recommended that a senior Patriot Officer should be sent up from A.C.C. headquarters to take charge of the situation. This idea was adopted by his successor, General Hume —Florence had come under the Fifth Army on 21st August—and after a personal visit of inspection by Colonel McCarthy, head of the Patriot Branch, a special team, headed by a British police officer, Lieut.-Colonel Bye, the Regional Public Safety officer of the Emilia Region not yet in action, was sent to deal with the problem.

Fighting on the outskirts of the city was over by 1st September and an order was issued by A.M.G. directing patriots to hand in their arms by mid-day 7th September. This order was not issued through the commanders of the patriot formations. Before the time of expiry —on the morning of the 7th—the patriots, about 3000 in number, were paraded and inspected by the Commander of XIII Corps, Lieut.-General S. C. Kirkman, under whose command they had been fighting during the operations leading to the capture of the city. The General thanked the patriots for their assistance and handed to their divisional commanders the 'Alexander' Certificates of Merit for distribution. But by mid-day the arms handed in were

---

[1] These were reckoned, according to the official C.L.N. patriot source, to have reached by September the figure of 6,000 men, though at the beginning of August they were estimated by the Chief of Staff of the Tuscan Military Command at rather less than 3,000. A.M.G. estimates were much lower.

comparatively few, a large number of pistols in particular being retained by the disbanded patriots. The retention of arms was attributed in the main to the Communists, for political purposes. Though several patriots were arrested for transgressing the proclamation enacting the surrender of arms, by no means all the arms were recovered.

After 7th September the majority of the Tuscan partisans returned to their homes, but there was left over a core of some 350 men domiciled in other parts of Italy, who had to be maintained. Arrangements were made for these to be housed at the refugee centre until circumstances permitted them to be convoyed to their homes through refugee channels. An offer was also made to enlist them into the Italian Army, but during the first week only thirteen took advantage of this. Nor were efforts to persuade them to accept work at wages offered by A.M.G. much more successful. Thus, when a hundred men were wanted to clean out a school for the accommodation of refugees, not a 'patriot' came forward to volunteer. The reason given for refusing to work for the armies was the shortage of the civilian workers' ration. In general the patriots refused to work for anything lower than the Italian army ration. But even this was not sufficient inducement for enlistment.

From the partisan point of view the arrangements made to look after members of the bands who had been incorporated in liberated Italy were anything but adequate, considering the promises, definite or implied, made by Allied missions and propaganda directed by P.W.B. As Admiral Stone pointed out to the Supreme Allied Commander:

> Our reports from Allied Military Government Officers . . . have shown that patriots expect better and different treatment. They are dis-illusioned at their reception. Those that have really fought in bands and companies have expressed the desire to fight in the same formations. The meagre supplies of food and clothing that we have been able to give do not in their opinion fulfil the promises made to them by Allied missions with whom they have been operating.

The policy of attempting to make good civilians of the partisans by restoring them to their normal vocations, which had devolved on A.M.G. officers, had met with little success. This was due in part to the desperate shortage of material, equipment, food, accommodation and clothing at the disposal of A.C.C., but even more to the failure of the Italian Government to satisfy the moral aspirations of the partisan rank and file. Nor could the disillusionment be confined to liberated Italy. For this type of 'intelligence' the security lines of the armies constituted no iron curtain. The military authorities responsible for 'special operations' appear to have received definite evidence that the news of treatment received by 'patriots' in liberated Italy was having a damping effect on the enthusiasm of the 'patriots' north of the Gothic Line.

The presence of large numbers of armed persons, who had formed part of various partisan units, made the problem of policing towns as they were liberated of great importance. The *Carabinieri* had been dissolved by Mussolini though many of them had continued in service in the new police force, the *Guardia Nazionale Repubblicana* (G.N.R.), which formed part of the neo-Fascist party militia, and, though the Agents of Public Security had been left intact, there was an immediate need for reorganisation of the existing police forces. This, thanks to the mobile *Carabinieri*, offered no serious difficulties. The *Carabinieri* who had refused to serve the Social Republic and had taken to the hills quickly returned. By employing partisans, where necessary, as an auxiliary police force, C.A.P.O's were able—after screening the Agents of Public Security and dismissing certain elements—to put together an *ensemble* of police forces which, whatever its deficiencies, was able to preserve a reasonable degree of public order. The *Questore* had in practically every case decamped with the Germans, but a *vice-Questore* was usually present, and could be relied upon, where he was not eliminated by the Field Security Services, to carry on until such time as he could be replaced, if his Fascist past was at all compromising, from Rome. Apart from some crimes of violence and robberies by genuine or so-called 'partisans', there was no great increase in crime. The record of central Italy in this respect was much better than that of Sicily and the South. Nor were there many serious infractions of the proclamations. It was not until the autumn that the absence of food began to cause serious unrest, leading to popular demonstrations in Florence, Pisa and Pistoia, and even to a certain amount of rioting.

In rural areas one of the chief pre-occupations of the Army A.M.G's was the gathering in and amassing of the harvests into the *Granai del Popolo*. Fortunately the harvest of 1944 in central Italy was a good one, but there were two factors which greatly impeded its collection, the lack of transport and of petrol, oil and lubricants which interfered both with reaping and with threshing, and the presence of very large minefields laid by the Germans over extensive rural areas—wherever, in fact they had succeeded in holding the Allied advance for any length of time, such as the Cassino Plain, the Anzio beach-head, the Arno valley and the plain between the Adriatic and the Apennines on the east coast, north of Pesaro. The Armies could not make themselves responsible for the removal of these minefields except in the immediate proximity of roads, and the responsibility for their removal was naturally placed upon the Italian Government. In the forward areas, however, it was

A.M.G. which had to take such steps as were practicable to clear the countryside.

An attempt, not wholly unsuccessful, was made to enlist partisans in this work, and the Italian Army placed two pioneer companies trained in mine clearance at the disposal of the Commission; but the severely limited 'ceiling' placed upon its numbers by the Allies, and the more urgent military tasks on which the limited number of Italian troops were engaged, prevented the employment of more Italian troops for this purpose. Moreover the absence of mine detectors made it necessary at first to resort to the highly dangerous method of prodding. The Control Commission in the early autumn of 1944 was however able to arrange for the training of some Italian soldiers in the latest methods of mine clearance, and these in turn were allocated to two schools for training civilians. Eventually some detectors were supplied by the Armies and the work was speeded up. In the meantime, however, casualties to civilians were very heavy, and the reaping of the harvest was delayed in many cases until the corn had begun to sprout. In spite of these difficulties the amassing of the harvest in central Italy was rather better than had at first been expected.

Of great logistical importance to the Armies was the capture of Leghorn, the largest port on the western Italian coast between Naples and Genoa, which shortened by some hundreds of miles the overland transport from Naples to the front line. Scarcely less significant was the capture on the same day of the smaller port of Ancona on the Adriatic coast, which greatly relieved the congestion at Bari and Taranto, and also shortened very considerably the line of communications. The port of Leghorn had been doubly damaged, by the Allies and by the Germans, who in November had evacuated the entire population from the coastal and port areas of the old city. On Allied entry on 18th July only 35,000 out of a normal population of about 120,000 were to be found. This greatly simplified the initial task of A.M.G. The town remained under fire from German guns for well over a week, and the water supply had been cut off, the main aqueduct remaining for a considerable time in German hands. General Clark decided to keep the closed zone evacuated, and to allow only a very limited proportion of the population to return. This meant that a large number of refugees who had settled themselves in the neighbouring communes had to be evacuated out of the zone. The partisans proved extremely useful to the Allied forces; they acted as guards, indicated mined areas and undertook police duties. At their request the communal secretary, though a former Fascist, was retained in office. The provincial officials were not found in the city, but they began to return in the first days of August. The Prefect, the *Questore* and the First Secretary failed to make their appearance and substitutes were consequently brought up from Rome. After about a month the return of some of the population was permitted, since the water supply had to some extent been restored, and the labour demands of P.B.S., which took charge of the port and city, began to grow rapidly.

The military government of Florence offered many new problems, both administrative and political, to A.M.G. Eighth Army, to which fell the initiation of its planning and installation. A separate team, under Lieut.-Colonel Benton-Jones as S.C.A.O., was formed to undertake the government of the city independently of that of the province—a temporary arrangement which had also been followed in Rome. But the occupation of Florence was in other respects very different from that of the capital. Whereas the Germans slipped out of Rome practically without firing a shot, they and their neo-Fascist allies did not evacuate the part of the city north of the Arno without considerable fighting, in which the partisans played a conspicuous role in harassing the retreating enemy. The southern portion of the city south of the Arno was occupied without any struggle, but even here enemy snipers caused a great deal of bother. It was several days before the portion north of the river could be occupied, since the Germans had destroyed all the bridges across the Arno, except the Ponte Vecchio, and had heavily mined both its exits which were blocked by extensive demolitions, so that it was some time before the bridge could be used for even a limited volume of light wheeled traffic.

The first A.M.G. detachment set up its headquarters south of the Arno on 4th August. All electricity supplies were cut, there was practically no water—barely enough for drinking purposes—and all supplies had been removed by the Germans, who up to the time of evacuation had been distributing a bread ration of 200 gms a day and some oil. A.M.G. brought in a convoy of ten trucks of supplies on the night of 5th August and continued to bring up supplies from Siena by night convoy—day convoys not being yet permitted—with the object of building up a reserve for the northern portion of the city, which was reported to be very short of food. The feeding of the population living south of the Arno was thus carried out without grave difficulty, but the need of water was more pressing. This shortage was, however, successfully met, so far as drinking water was concerned, by the arrival of three tank wagons. But the burying of the dead raised a special problem. Civilian casualties from snipers and machine-gun fire across the Arno were fairly numerous, and the cemeteries remained for some time under enemy fire, so that a special cemetery had to be consecrated in the Boboli Gardens.

It was not until 13th August that Army A.M.G. was able to establish itself across the river, though a detachment had crossed on the afternoon of the 11th. Meanwhile a message had been sent over from the north side by the Archbishop, Cardinal della Costa, that the food situation there was very serious, particularly with regard to flour and milk for babies. A.M.G. therefore arranged for an immediate supply of eight tons of flour and one ton of milk to be manhandled across the Ponte Vecchio. The organisation of the transport of supplies across the river by this primitive technique was a considerable achievement. Before the bridge could be opened even to the lightest vehicular traffic, the daily volume of supplies so transported reached nearly forty tons. On entering the northern part of the city it was found that conditions with respect to supplies were not quite so bad as had been anticipated. The Germans had distributed a bread ration of 200 gms a day until about five days before the Allies arrived at the outskirts of the city and 100 gms a day until they actually evacuated, and they left behind about three weeks' supplies of breadstuffs. There was thus no difficulty in instituting a distribution of 200 gms a day from 14th August. But for some time the position of civilians in the no-man's-land beyond the canal was extremely bad, and in many places there was evidence of severe malnutrition, even in some cases of starvation.

South of the Arno A.M.G. on entry found the partisans organised into two bands, one almost 600 strong, well disciplined and co-operative, under Italian army officers; the other, much smaller in number, was made up, to quote Group-Captain Benson's description, of 'the usual type, who have taken up arms at the last minute when the fighting was over'. The latter were however kept under control. There was at this stage no outbreak of crime or disorder, and for this fact the partisans themselves were largely responsible. Their policing was admirable, though A.M.G. was forced to intervene when they attempted summarily to execute two men suspected of looting. The disarmament of the partisans south of the Arno caused no difficulty, but conditions north of the river proved very different. South of the Arno the most immediate problem was that of refugees, of which there were about 8,000, who needed immediate care, most of them being *sfollati* from across the river. The Palazzo Pitti was used as a refugee centre, and arrangements for evacuation into holding camps were made within a few days. The hospitals south of the river were found entirely without supplies, but, within three days, three tons of these were brought in by A.M.G.

On crossing the Arno, A.M.G. for the first time came up against the political problem of the Committee of National Liberation. The Tuscans were much more politically self-conscious than the inhabitants of southern Italy. Under the German occupation the Tuscan Committee of National Liberation (C.T.L.N.) in Florence had organised a powerful underground movement which had constituted a clandestine local government to take over the administration of the city when the Germans departed. When A.M.G. moved into the centre of the city, it found a provisional administration functioning as the unchallenged municipal and provincial authority. The committee, which represented only five of the six parties, that of *Democrazia del Lavoro* not having been constituted, had appointed a *Sindaco*, in the person of the eighty-three year old Socialist ex-deputy, Professor Gaetano Pieraccini, one of their members, and a *Giunta Comunale* as well as a *Deputazione Provinciale.* They had put the questorship in commission and made appointments to various other offices, including an *Ufficio Trasporti* to list all means of transport available for the provisioning of the city, and had set up various committees, including one of defascistisation, to supervise the administration of the city and the province. Their attitude to the Allies was to begin with most cooperative, but when A.M.G. appointed a Prefect from the outside—a career official who had only just been made Prefect of Ancona—the trouble began.

Meanwhile, quite apart from politics, Allied Military Government had its hands full enough of administrative problems, and at an early date it was made to change horses in mid-stream. A.M.G. Eighth Army had hardly established itself on the north bank of the Arno, when, owing to a change in army boundaries, the city and province were transferred to Fifth Army A.M.G.—a change which was accomplished without any discontinuity of administration. The administrative problems with which A.M.G. had to deal were those normally met with in a large town which had been the scene of nearly three weeks of fighting, where electricity was non-existent and water for some time practically confined to cisterns and wells. Mines and booby-traps were plentiful, in removing which the local air-raid precaution service, *Unione Nazionale Protezione Anti-Area* (UNPA), rendered valuable help, and deliberate demolition, especially on the river bank, where much of the mediaeval city had been destroyed, was very extensive. Sanitary conditions were dangerous since, besides human excreta in unflushed sewers, a hundred tons of miscellaneous refuse was accumulating every day and the transport promised by the Allied garrison failed to materialise, except for the two days' loan of one lorry. The burial of the dead was complicated by the absence of wood for making coffins, those available often having to be used two or three times. The Royal Engineers established emergency water points and early rains fortunately helped to clear the sewers. The work of restoring the damaged mains was also undertaken by Army engineers, but a month after the occupation of the northern part of the city water supply was still only a little more than a third of the normal flow; not till the beginning of October were supplies beginning to approach the normal level.

The milling of flour was impeded by the absence of electricity for practically a whole month, and the operational situation made the supply of vegetable foodstuffs from the surrounding country very difficult. And though in the first few weeks it had been possible to build up a small reserve of breadstuffs, the expansion of A.M.G's responsibility to Lucca, Pisa, Prato and Pistoia soon made it impossible to supply Florence on more than an extremely unsatisfactory hand-to-mouth basis, the limiting factor being, as everywhere transport. And, as winter drew on, the absence of fuel began to be felt even more severely, for the same reason. These conditions were continually contrasted by the public with the promises of Allied propaganda, and the humouring of public opinion was not rendered any easier by President Roosevelt's allusions to the 300 gm ration.[1] A number of rather angry food demonstrations took place but no rioting occurred. A.M.G. had reorganised the police forces of the city by importing 360 *Carabinieri*, and these, together with reliable elements discovered on entry, prevented any serious public disorder from this source.

The Tuscan Committee of National Liberation (C.T.L.N.) found it rather difficult to adapt itself to Allied Military Government. The *de facto* administration which it had set up could only receive very partial recognition. Both the Committee itself and its various *Giunte* had no constitutional authority and much resented being deprived of the executive powers which they fancied they had earned. Their predominantly left-wing orientation, in which the Communists and the Party of Action were the most active elements, made them extremely impatient of the more cautious procedure of the Prefect and A.M.G., especially in the matter of 'defascistisation'. The opposition of the C.T.L.N. to the Prefect threatened to create serious trouble in the administration, and the position was not improved by visits from Signor Togliatti (amongst other party leaders) from Rome. His support of the Communist element on the Committee and a subsequent speech made in Rome against the Prefect were far from helpful. The Committee accused the Prefect of being a Fascist and sent a deputation to Rome demanding the transfer of a wide measure of authority from the Prefect to their local committees, as well as the dismissal of the Prefect himself. Signor Bonomi refused to take any action, pointing out that the Prefect was an A.M.G. appointment and could only be dismissed by the Control Commission. Some satisfaction was however given to their aspirations by the appointment of the *Commissione di Controllo*, which had been set up before A.M.G's arrival to run the questorship, to function as the Tuscan Commission for Epuration under the new defascistisation

---

[1] See below, p. 245.

law, and by the confirmation of the Committee's candidate as mayor in the person of Signor Pieraccini. The selection for the membership of the communal *giunta* was not however altogether to the liking of the left-wing parties. Two of the members selected belonged to the *Partito Democratico del Lavoro*, reconstituted after liberation, whose entrance into the Tuscan C.L.N. had been refused, although this party had from the beginning formed part of the C.L.N. in Rome. After the visit of its representatives to the capital, the opposition of the C.T.L.N. to the Prefect diminished, and, though certain Field Security authorities reported in favour of his dismissal as an ex-Fascist, A.M.G. continued to uphold his administration, which now entered upon a period of comparative calm.

Apart from food, partisans and politics, perhaps the most pressing problem in Florence was that of refugees and displaced persons, which aggravated the existing shortage of houses resulting from enemy demolitions. Though the number of Allied troops quartered in the city was reduced to a minimum, Florence, like Rome, was used as a rest and recreation centre. This demanded the requisitioning of a considerable amount of accommodation. Thus not only were a large number of Florentines homeless owing to destruction and requisitioning, but the population of the city had also been greatly increased by refugees, among whom were a considerable number of 'displaced persons', some of Allied, others of neutral nationality. Many of these refugees and displaced persons had to be evacuated to the south, and A.M.G. was obliged to organise a holding centre to maintain them until the necessary transport could be arranged. Moreover, as the military situation became more or less established in certain sectors north of the Arno, refugees in large numbers began to sweep downwards from behind the German lines, and military considerations made it necessary to resort to large-scale evacuation of the civilian population in the forward areas.

The stabilisation of the line in the Apennines also produced another problem for the Public Safety Division not unconnected with refugees—the identification and apprehension of enemy agents. This was primarily the responsibility of the military security authorities, but the assistance of A.M.G. in the maintenance of road blocks and the checking of civilian movements was also required—a task to which the *Carabinieri* made a useful contribution. Large numbers of partisans also came through the line, and a Patriot Branch was created at Fifth Army A.M.G. to deal with this problem. Two large reception camps were set up, one at Pescia and one in Florence, to hold the partisans until they could be disbanded and dispersed.

The final occupation of the northern half of Pisa at the beginning of September stretched still further the limited resources of Fifth Army A.M.G. The southern part of the city had been largely demolished and was completely empty, and the bridges across the Arno had been destroyed. The northern part, less severely damaged, contained on occupation only about 15,000 inhabitants and was practically without water, since a portion of the main aqueduct remained for some time in the hands of the Germans, who had destroyed the pumping station which supplied both Pisa and Leghorn. Hence the first task of A.M.G. was to prevent the return of the majority of the inhabitants to their houses. And after water supplies had been assured by the Fifth Army engineers and the inhabitants could be allowed to return, the problem of supplying them with food became increasingly urgent. Conditions in the town were made more difficult by the presence of mines and booby-traps in large quantities, by desultory enemy shelling which lasted practically till the end of the month, and scarcely less by the large-scale requisition of what buildings remained by the Allied forces. After the occupation of Pisa city the provincial administration was fairly rapidly restored. A prefect sent up from Rome proved a very efficient officer. His energetic conduct in meeting the emergency prevented serious disorder when, later in the autumn, the Arno overflowed its banks and flooded the town as well as the surrounding countryside, which consisted largely of reclaimed land.

In order to economise on imported supplies and to encourage the gathering in of the harvests, a ration of 200 gms was only distributed in the larger cities like Pisa and Florence. In the remaining communes only 100 gms were distributed, until such time as they had gathered in their corn to the *Granai del Popolo*. This system worked fairly satisfactory in some of the rural communes. But the provisioning of the larger towns became increasingly difficult during the autumn, since a large part of the harvest in the district had been lost owing to military operations, and the distribution of the 200 gm ration was apt to be interrupted at intervals for several days at a stretch owing to lack of transport.

Lucca, Pistoia and Prato were also occupied during the autumn. Lucca was only slightly damaged; the provincial administrative machine (with the exception of the Prefect and the *Questore*) was virtually intact. The local C.L.N. had established a *sindaco* and the communal administration was running, law and order being preserved by the partisans until the arrival of the Fifth Army mobile *Carabinieri*. On the proposal of A.M.G. the president of the local C.L.N. was appointed Prefect. Conditions in Pistoia on the other hand were most uncomfortable. The town was for a long while under enemy shell-fire, the provincial administration had dispersed, and the partisan situation was extremely delicate owing to the antagonism between two rival bands. This trouble was however quickly solved. Most of the partisans were disarmed, but the feeding of the town was extremely difficult, war and weather having destroyed much of the harvest in the province. Before autumn had passed into winter, there was real hunger which finally led to active unrest and demonstrations. Hunger also threatened Prato, occupied in the second week of September, where there had been no distribution of bread since 22nd August. Here the water supply, too, had been destroyed and the population had to depend on wells and springs, often contaminated, with the result that there was a considerable outbreak of typhoid fever. Real hunger was encountered on entering Viareggio which had been badly damaged, especially in the harbour area. Here there was practically no local production of foodstuffs because the surrounding country had been either mined or flooded. Water and electricity supplies had both been cut off, but the essential needs of the population were met by transporting water from outside in a motor fire-engine.

The towns of northern Tuscany were the first industrial area to come under the administration of A.M.G. since the occupation of Naples. Textiles—cotton and wool—were the principal industries. Owing to the absence of electric power, sabotaged by the Germans—to say nothing of the absence of raw material—both were completely at a standstill for several months. It was not possible, except in a few factories, to restart production before hostilities were ended, and in many others not till long after. Thus a distinct problem of unemployment arose, which could not immediately be solved. Road repairs, bridging and clearance of debris afforded some scope for unskilled workmen, but skilled work was practically non-existent, and though the Army at Leghorn was eventually able to offer employment to all who could be brought into the city, absence of transport and housing accommodation limited the numbers which could be imported, while in other towns the Allied forces were by no means able to absorb the whole of the employable population.

But the problem of unemployment was trivial compared with that of food supply and distribution. At the beginning of September General Hume sent a message to A.C.C. headquarters pointing out that his food stocks amounted to no more than sufficient to feed half a million people—and Florence alone contained about 400,000—for about ten days, and that, unless larger supplies were immediately made available, he would be unable to feed communities as fast as they were liberated. The military implications of this position were 'tremendous and appalling' in as much as it might become necessary to employ combat troops to keep order, 'thereby stultifying the entire concept of military government'. He also emphasised that this situation would give a most dangerous handle to the propaganda of the enemy, besides convincing them that their policy of destroying food stocks, utilities, bakeries and transport had been successful in making Allied Military Government in this area ineffective. In the middle of October General Mark Clark actually sent a personal message of protest to General Alexander:

> Civilian food situation throughout Fifth Army area is critical and will become increasingly so as we advance. The 100 grammes of bread distributed daily are inadequate. Widespread unrest is manifest in Lucca and Pisa, while actual public demonstrations have occurred in Pistoia and Florence. Unofficial sources of information indicate that more serious incidents may develop. If such occur, combat troops may have to be diverted to maintain law and order. I am informed that enough imported food supplies are not in sight to permit adoption of a ration sufficient for health and efficiency in accordance with assurances lately given in Washington. An inseparable part of the food problem is the provision of sufficient road transport for the movement of imported or local supplies to the centres of consumption. Recommend that the urgent matter of providing adequate food and transport be given immediate consideration.

It was certainly fortunate, from the point of view of A.M.G. at least, that the halt on the Winter Line helped to ease the strain on the Fifth Army's transport.

So by only a very narrow margin was serious trouble avoided. Throughout the winter the bread ration in the Tuscan towns was maintained at 200 gms a day with a small fortnightly distribution of pasta, but supplies other than bread-stuffs were extremely short. Sugar for months was not available and salt was sufficient only for current human consumption, none being available for the curing of pig-meat. Soap was in constant deficit, with resultant outbreaks of scabies, and for several months there was no distribution of olive oil. It was scarcely surprising in these circumstances that Allied popularity was short lived in the Arno valley. As Admiral Stone observed:

> Except in areas where gunfire is audible the people are less friendly with the Allies. The contrast in the attitude between the Arno valley and a village within a few miles of the Germans is very striking.

The regular distribution of the bread ration during the winter did something to improve public morale, but the delay in implementing the 300 gm ration, which had been introduced in the South, continued to cause a great deal of bitterness.

At the end of December, owing to the initial success of an enemy attack in the Serchio valley, A.M.G. was compelled to cede to the enemy the commune of Barga in the province of Lucca. This was the first time since the Salerno landings that a commune had been lost after Military Government had been established. The commune was soon retaken, but not before an unconsciously ironical comment on the food situation in A.M.G. territory was received from the enemy. A Fascist radio was heard broadcasting a fond message of thanks to A.M.G. for the civilian food which the enemy had found in the village. This had only been delivered there two days before its capture.

Before passing on to the story of A.M.G. in the Eighth Army area, a brief paragraph on 'Welfare' work behind the lines can scarcely be omitted. On the welfare side the work of the British and American Red Cross field representatives with the Army A.M.Gs, in dealing with refugees and with the care of the sick, generally, and of mothers and infants in particular, was extremely valuable. Entering newly liberated towns with or very soon after A.M.G. spearhead officers, they made an immediate survey of the most pressing medical and welfare needs, planned the reorganisation of hospital facilities, and arranged for the distribution of clothing supplied by the American Red Cross to local committees. Their early surveys of the incidence of infectious diseases often enabled serums against typhoid and diphtheria to be promptly supplied and so prevented the outbreak of many serious epidemics. The work of Fifth Army A.M.G. in the assistance of Italian hospitals during the campaign was summed up in a report by the American Red Cross supervisor, Mr G. L. Bickel, in the following figures: 380 hospitals were surveyed, of which 296 were supplied with medicines, 247 with clothing, and over fifty reconstructed or repaired.

After the advance of the Fifth Army to the Apennines north of the Arno at the end of August, the Eighth Army succeeded in piercing the extreme eastern end of the Gothic Line, and began its advance into the south-eastern corner of the plain of the Po valley, thus turning the corner of the Apennines, near Rimini. Compared with those of northern Tuscany, the problems confronting A.M.G. on the Adriatic coast were comparatively easy. Speaking generally, the area was self-sufficient in bread-stuffs and vegetables though not in oil. Salt too was at first unobtainable for the curing of bacon, but the capture of Cesena furnished a fairly adequate supply for this purpose, so that eventually it was possible to distribute some animal fats. The nightmare of starvation which haunted the Civil Affairs officers in the large Tuscan towns for many months was fortunately not experienced. Nor did the problem of partisans or the Committee of National Liberation give rise to any trouble. Transport was short, but in emergencies the Army was able to give assistance, and there was no crisis like that experienced in Fifth Army area. Refugees were a constant problem, but the methods of dealing with these, which had been evolved during the progress up the Adriatic coast, were adequate; though, as the Army advanced, it was often impossible to get the requisite road and rail transport facilities to evacuate them southwards according to plan, and congestion rendered more formidable by the bad weather sometimes caused anxiety.

In addition to refugees and the ordinary administrative problems confronting the government of an area where the towns were largely devastated, A.M.G. was faced with special difficulties caused by the flooding by German sabotage of large tracts of reclaimed land near the Adriatic coast. Another difficulty was that of supplying communes in the Apennines in the winter, when the roads were in very bad condition and bridges had been destroyed. Moreover many of the Bailey bridges installed by the Army had been removed as the line advanced. In certain cases it was found necessary to stock these Apennine communes before the onset of winter with sufficient food to enable them to subsist until the spring.

In Forli province the problem of food distribution had been rendered somewhat easier by the action of the Italian authorities under German occupation, who had distributed to nearly three-quarters of the population quantities of grain ranging from 150 to 200 kilos before Allied entry, no doubt owing to difficulties of warehousing it in a dry state, in the hope that consumers would dry and store their individual allotments. In two provinces further south (Pesaro and Ancona) A.M.G. had also found difficulties in collecting and warehousing the harvest. Much of the grain was still lying unthreshed in the wet fields, while damage to warehouses and lack of insecticides made it almost inevitable that a large proportion even of such grain as was gathered in to the *Granai* would be spoiled. Authorisation was consequently given to issue a year's supply of grain to individual consumers, against the surrender of their ration cards, milling cards being substituted. A good deal of the harvest in the provinces of Pesaro and Forli was lost, but some 2,000 tons of grain from the latter were sent to relieve shortages in Florence. No such distribution had taken place in the province of Ravenna, where the harvest had been gathered in before the Germans flooded the land. Work was at once started on re-habilitating the drainage pumps sabotaged by the Germans, and on repairing and cleaning the drainage canals. It was possible, thanks to the timely assistance offered by the Royal Engineers of the Eighth Army, to reduce considerably the flooded areas before the spring.

Public health also presented a problem in the typhoid epidemic which originated in San Marino and later spread to Rimini. The occupation of this neutral republic by Allied forces took place for the following reason. General Alexander had issued an order that Allied troops would not enter the territory except, as permitted by international law, in direct pursuit of the enemy. The Germans had violated the neutrality of that independent Republic by retreating through it; the Eighth Army was compelled in consequence to do likewise on 21st September. An A.M.G. officer was sent up with the occupying troops as liaison officer, but out of respect for its neutrality Military Government was not proclaimed. Proclamations Nos. 1 and 2 were, however, shown to one of the Captains-Regent by Group-Captain Benson and the Republic was requested to enforce curfew. The Captain-Regent objected to this, on the grounds that it had been imposed by the Germans, though it was pointed out to him that the measure was really in the interests of the civilian population, in order to avoid incidents with the troops after dark, there being no electricity. Curfew was in consequence dispensed with. It was also made clear that the Republic would be evacuated by all Allied troops as soon as the military situation permitted. The Germans had taken all the motor transport of the Republic except one truck, and destroyed the electrical pumps which supplied the capital from the foot of the hill on which it stands, as well as the power station outside its boundaries which provided its electricity. Food conditions, in spite of the very large number of refugees who had entered the Republic, were not too bad, but A.M.G. arranged to send in immediately some forty tons in twelve trucks which were lent to the Republic.

The refugees greatly outnumbered the normal population of the Republic. They included, besides a large proportion of the inhabitants of Rimini, which had been very severely damaged and was found completely empty on entry, persons from Florence, Bologna and Milan, as well as from towns in the south. These had been housed in the capital, in two small villages and in the tunnels of the railway line from Rimini. Considering the circumstances, sanitary conditions did not appear to be bad, but some of the wells on which the refugees had to rely for drinking water became contaminated and a serious epidemic of typhoid fever broke out. Before this had become known, it had been decided to repatriate a number of them to Rimini for labour to assist the Army and to maintain essential services. With the returning refugees typhoid cases began to appear in considerable numbers, over 400 occurring within four months. The presence of refugees from northern Italy in the middle of a battle zone raised an important security problem. A cordon of *Carabinieri* was therefore formed round the Republic, and maintained until the battle had moved further north.

Ravenna was occupied on 5th December. There was slight damage by bombing, but nearly all the important monuments were intact. Disorganisation was much less than in most of the Adriatic towns, and the administration was soon functioning smoothly and well. Light and power and water supplies were cut off, but there was no shortage of food, and water from artesian wells was adequate. The local C.L.N. had been very active before the arrival of the Allies and proved very willing to help. As in Forli, the new Prefect, a career official from Sardinia, went in with the provincial team of Military Government officers, an arrangement which contributed greatly to the early establishment of the administration. A *Giunta Comunale* was immediately installed. It is also pleasing to record that no acts of vandalism by the troops occurred in a town second only to Rome and Florence in the importance of its artistic heritage.

To hasten the rehabilitation of the areas geographically in the Emilia Region (Region IX) but still under the administration of Eighth Army A.M.G., an arrangement was put into force in December under which a special administrative headquarters was set up, composed of staff officers of the Region working under S.C.A.O. Eighth Army. While the Regional and Army staffs retained their separate identity, they in fact worked as one team. The Eight Army A.M.G. officers acted mainly in the capacity of liaison with other branches of the Army staff, while the Emilia Region officers were charged with the administration of the civilian population. By this means full use was made of certain regional specialist officers who were not normally included in the mobile Army headquarters.

After the advance into the northern Apennines, the military importance of the Resistance movement in the North became increasingly appreciated. A modification of the patriot policy laid down after the liberation of Rome became imperative. The armies in the field had not been slow to recognise the military value of partisan bands, not only for special operations, but also for reconnaissance, and 'operations in areas inaccessible to regular troops', of which the Apennines, with the peaks running up to over 7,000 feet, provided plenty. The employment, maintenance and equipment of a limited number of partisans was therefore regularised. A patriot battle-zone was established, and only behind this zone was disarmament enforced. Within the zone British formations, in December 1944, were empowered to employ in the field up to 1,200 patriots,—1,000 in Eighth Army Zone and 200 in Fifth Army Zone, with a monthly turnover up to 600. Analogous arrangements had already been made for the American contingent of the Fifth Army. After some protest from M.M.I.A., it was also arranged that partisan casualties, which had previously been sent to civilian hospitals, often desperately short of beds, to say nothing of food and drugs and other equipment, should be evacuated to Italian military hospitals.

Partisans not employed as combatants by the Armies had to be screened, and their ultimate destiny, as volunteer recruits in the Italian army, as workers for the Allied Armies, or as ordinary civilians, had to be determined. For this purpose patriot centres were established behind both the Fifth and Eighth Armies by Army A.M.Gs., in the first instance, at Pescia and Florence, and Ravenna and Forli, respectively. Here partisans were fed up to thirty days by the Armies on Italian Army rations, after which their maintenance became the responsibility of the Allied Commission. Each camp was in command of an Allied officer, assisted by an Italian partisan of officer status, the detailed running of the camps being left to the partisans themselves. Attached to each camp was an Italian officer representing the Ministry of War. Fifth and Eighth Armies were made responsible for collecting, disarming and transporting patriots to these reception camps, after which their subsequent movements, except those of recruits to the Italian army depots, devolved on the Allied Commission. The Commission was empowered to issue to all partisans destined for civilian status, clothing, blankets and certain other equipment. The clothing, owing to the Commission's shortage of salvaged military material, on which M.M.I.A. maintained a first charge, had in the first place to be supplied by M.M.I.A.

These arrangements, though they did something to improve the material condition of partisans passing into liberated territory, did nothing to remove their main grievance, that they were not allowed to continue to fight for the liberation of their country in their own units, and under their own officers. The idea of incorporating patriot bands as units with the Italian army was at first strongly opposed, not only by M.M.I.A. but also by a large proportion of the professional element in the Italian army, an opposition which was greatly strengthened by the inflexible Allied attitude on the maximum number of Italian forces, limited by a rigid ceiling. For the existence of a number of semi-independent armed forces under the control of the Communist, or indeed any other party, could not fail to be a dangerous precedent. Nor was it easy to introduce guerilla-trained elements into the Italian Army Combat Groups, fitted out with all the modern technical resources of a professional army and conditioned by many months of specialised training. But the alternative danger of clandestinely-armed party-elements, and ultimately civil war, was even greater.

As the result of strong pressure from Admiral Stone and certain other quarters at A.F.H.Q., the more narrow military considerations were transcended. Before the end of February a modified policy was adopted which permitted the introduction of five patriot 'Reconnaissance Companies' into the Italian army, having the same status as the *Gruppi di Combattimento*. These Reconnaissance units were formed by patriots 'comprising their own bands and under their own officers'. They were not considered as an integral portion of the Combat Groups and were employed wherever the army commands considered desirable. In consequence the 'F' Reconnaissance Patriot Squadron of the Fifth Army and the *Banda Maiella* operating with Eighth Army, as well as certain other units like the 'Bulow' Partisan band, which was being used as an integral part of the Cremona Group, were incorporated into the Italian Army before the final advance into the Po valley. Before the end of March nearly 3,000 patriots were so enlisted. As a result of this new policy, partisans in this Adriatic sector provided few problems; since they were for the most part operationally employed and rendered conspicuous services to the Army. Those no longer required were dealt with in patriot centres set up at Forli, Faenza and Ravenna, where a considerable quantity of arms was surrendered.

To conclude this chapter, a note must be added on the Military Government of Elba. The island was occupied on 17th–20th June 1944 as the result of the operation 'Brassard'. This operation was not undertaken under General Alexander's command, but was carried out under General Wilson by French forces from the island of Corsica. But since Elba was a part of Italy, it was arranged that General Alexander should be its Military Governor, the Commander of the French forces, Brig.-General Magnan, being appointed Deputy Military Governor, and made responsible to General Alexander for the performance of this function, though operationally not under his command. In order to assist him in these duties, a team of Allied Military Government officers under an S.C.A.O. was attached to him by the Allied Control Commission. It was expected that the French troops would evacuate the island fairly soon after its effective occupation, and that the Military Government would then pass into the hands of Region VIII. The evacuation was, however considerably delayed. Arrangements had been made for the withdrawal of the French garrison on 20th September, but the shipping to effect this was not made available for nearly three months and the garrison only left the island on 11th December. The administration of the island passed to Tuscany Region on 20th December.

ANNEXE

General Alexander's Proclamation to Patriots

TO PATRIOTS OF ITALY NOW FREE CITIZENS OF ITALY

By your courage, skill and endurance you have hastened the liberation of your country. The United Nations, and Italy, thank you.

You have played your parts nobly and in accordance with the finest Italian traditions. But your task is not ended by the departure of the

Germans from Italian soil. There is much for you to do for your country and there is no time to lose. A new Italy has emerged from the crucible of war—an Italy which needs rebuilding—an Italy whose soil must be made to produce its utmost—a new Italy which above all needs you.

You have fought to free Italy. You must now help to rebuild the Italy you have helped so gallantly to free.

With the expulsion of the German invaders the shooting and killing are over, and new tasks lie before you. Behind the fighting Allied Armies comes the army of reconstruction and rehabilitation—that is the Allied Military Government—whose first responsibility is the maintenance of law and order. Your first task is to assist the Allied Military Government in its duty to relieve by every available means the suffering caused by war and by the savage brutality of the Nazis and Fascists.

The Allied Military Government will never hold truck with Fascist traitors. Apart from this it is not in any way concerned with politics in Italy. Its only object is to help the Italian people to help themselves.

Italian Patriots and all good citizens can be of great assistance to the Allied Military Government by working through their Representative Committees which will meet the Allied Military Government officers as soon as possible.

They must be prepared to report fully on conditions in their communities under the following headings:

1. Cases of destitution or extreme hunger.
2. Lists of medicines urgently needed.
3. Lists of available foodstuffs abandoned by Fascists or Germans.
4. The state of the public services.
5. Lists of arms, ammunition and explosives in Patriot hands.
6. Names of Fascists who have been active collaborators with the Germans; also names of other criminals and traitors, especially those who have denounced their compatriots to the Germans or to the Republican Fascists.
7. Complete lists of the names of those who have fought in Patriot bands and helped them. These should be prepared by the band leaders.

It is expected that Italian Patriots who, with arms in their hands and under the inspiration of their ancient tradition of valour, have played a heroic part in the liberation of their country, will be above all others ready to cooperate with the Allied Military Government. An Italian Patriot Committee has been formed under the Presidency of the Prime Minister of Italy with branches reaching down through Regions and Provinces into every Commune. It is the task of these Committees to assist the Patriots in every possible way and to enable them, where possible, to join the Regular Armed Forces, or to establish them in civilian occupations.

The Allied Military Government desires to leave the administration of the community in the hands of good citizens who are no longer under the yoke of Fascist tyrants.

H. R. ALEXANDER
General
Commander-in-Chief of Allied
Armies in Italy.

CHAPTER VII

SIX PARTY HARMONY[1]

On 5th June King Victor Emmanuel, in accordance with the undertaking he had given, signed at Ravello the document creating the Prince of Piedmont Lieutenant-General of the Realm—thus entrusting to his son the full power of all the Royal prerogatives, including the signing of Royal Decrees. Though in form this document was not actually an abdication, it was its virtual equivalent. From the moment of its signing King Victor Emmanuel III passed out of Italian history. On the following day Marshal Badoglio, in accordance with pre-arranged procedure, handed in the resignation of his Government to the Lieutenant-General of the Realm, who requested him to form a new government, to include the political leaders in the capital. On 8th June the Lieutenant-General of the Realm made, in accordance with arrangements previously agreed with the Allied Control Commission, a brief entry into the capital. Marshal Badoglio also flew from Naples to Rome taking with him seven members of his Cabinet—one from each of the six parties—and Count Sforza. He immediately held a conference with the Roman Committee of National Liberation in the presence of General Mason-MacFarlane. Signor Bonomi brought with him a representative of each party in the Central Committee including Signor De Gasperi (Christian Democrat) and Signor Nenni (Socialist). It very soon emerged from the discussions that the Roman group of politicians would maintain their unwillingness to serve under the Marshal. Badoglio consequently placed his resignation into the hands of the Lieutenant-General of the Realm and advised him to send for Signor Bonomi—which he did.

On the following day—9th June—Signor Bonomi formed his Government on a six-party basis, very much on the same plan as the last Badoglio Government, with seven Ministers without portfolio and nine in charge of Ministries. The Prime Minister, in accordance with a well-established Italian tradition, combined the premiership with the Ministry of the Interior and, in accordance with the wishes expressed by General Mason-MacFarlane, also the Ministry of Foreign Affairs, for which the most obvious candidate would have been Count Sforza. It appears that General Mason-MacFarlane

[1] I am indebted for the idea underlying this title to Signor Andreotti, whose brief volume *Concerto a Sei Voci* gives a description of the crisis which caused the dissolution of Signor Bonomi's first post-Fascist Government.

took it upon himself, without any instructions from the Combined Chiefs of Staff, to express the opinion that the appointment of Count Sforza as Foreign Secretary 'would not meet with much approval on the part of the Allied Governments'[1], a step which provoked protest from Washington to London on the part of the Acting Secretary of State who complained, with every justification, that his Government had not been consulted. The United States Government, indeed, later went so far as to request General Wilson to inform Signor Bonomi that General Mason-MacFarlane's views did not represent those of the Government of the United States, to which the appointment of Count Sforza as Foreign Minister would be entirely agreeable.[2]

The new Prime Minister was a veteran pre-Fascist statesman, then seventy-three years old. He had been Prime Minister from June 1921 to February 1922, in which office he was the immediate predecessor of Signor Facta, who held the premiership at the time of the March on Rome. Several Ministers were taken over from the last Badoglio Government, including the Minister of the Navy, Admiral De Courten, (who had held office continually since the fall of Mussolini), Togliatti and Croce, the last of whom resigned on account of age and infirmity on the transfer of the Government from Salerno to Rome. Other Ministers without portfolio were Signor Cianca (Action Party), Signor De Gasperi (Christian Democrat), Signor Ruini (Labour Democrat), Signor Saragat (Socialist), and Count Sforza (Independent). The Ministries were distributed among the six parties. The Service Ministers, for whose appointments the special agreement of the Allied Military Command was required, were as follows: Admiral De Courten retained the Ministry of the Navy, General Piancentini, Chief of Staff of the Air Forces, combined this office with the Ministry for Air, and a civilian, Count Casati, a Liberal, was appointed Minister of War. At the insistence of the Allies, Dr. Fano, Under-Secretary for Posts and Telegraphs, and General di Raimondi, Under-Secretary for Railways in the last Badoglio Government, retained their posts.

During the negotiations for the formation of the new government, both General Mason-MacFarlane and Signor Bonomi tried to persuade Marshal Badoglio to accept a post in the Cabinet, but the Marshal was determined to retire from the political scene. The negotiations were carried out by General Mason-MacFarlane on his own responsibility, without the assistance of either Sir Noel Charles, the British High Commissioner, or Mr Kirk, the American delegate to the Advisory Council, neither of whom accompanied

[1] Words used by General Mason-MacFarlane in describing the negotiations to General Wilson.

[2] See Cordell Hull *op. cit.*, Vol. II, p. 1563.

him to Rome, and without any formal consultation of the Council itself. It would appear that he was anxious to avoid any semblance of Allied interference with the normal constitutional procedure in pre-Fascist days, which might have been interpreted, particularly in America, as an unwarranted curtailment of the freedom of the renascent Italian democracy. He therefore did not consider it necessary to consult the Allied Governments during the various stages of these negotiations, in spite of strong representations made to him before his departure for Rome by Sir Noel Charles not to allow any definite steps to be taken before such consultation. Both Allied Governments were thus presented with a *fait accompli*, which aroused considerable indignation in London, since Mr Churchill had throughout been a strong supporter of Marshal Badoglio on account of his influence with the Italian armed forces, and had felt little respect for the self-appointed political 'ghosts' of the pre-Fascist era. Nor was the State Department much better pleased, though in Washington the Committee of National Liberation was looked on with much greater respect, and the importance of Badoglio to the Allied war effort estimated to be of much smaller value.[1] In the circumstances it was hardly practicable for the Allied Governments to repudiate the action of their representative. They therefore took a formal step to reassert their influence by withholding confirmation of the new Italian Government, pending consultation with the Advisory Council. It was finally agreed by the Council that the Bonomi Government should be allowed to take office subject to two conditions: first, that the new Government should formally express their readiness in writing to accept all obligations towards the Allies entered into by former Italian Governments since the conclusion of the armistice, including the 'long' armistice terms, with which every member of the new administration should be personally acquainted; and secondly, that it should undertake not to reopen the constitutional question until such time as the whole of Italy had been liberated and the Italian people should be free to express their views. These conditions were accepted without reserve by Signor Bonomi, whose administration was thereupon confirmed in office, ministers being sworn in on 18th June by the Lieutenant-General of the Realm under a new form of oath designed to meet the objections of the anti-monarchist members.

In view of the attitude taken up by the Roman Committee of National Liberation, it is difficult to see how, even with the strongest Allied support, Badoglio could have maintained himself in office, since most, if not all, of his former colleagues would probably have

---

[1] For an American account of this divergency in the standpoints of the British and American Government on the resignation of Badoglio, see Cordell Hull, *op. cit.*, Vol. II, p. 1564.

refused to continue to serve under him, and though, as a matter of form, there can be no doubt that the Allied Governments ought to have been consulted before the formation of a new Cabinet was undertaken, the final result could scarcely have been different.

The formation of the new Government almost coincided with a change in the headship of the Allied Control Commission. General Mason-MacFarlane, whose health had been far from good, went to London at the end of June to explain his actions. On his arrival in England, he was forced to undergo lengthy treatment for a spinal injury, which compelled him to resign his position. He was succeeded as acting Chief Commissioner by his deputy, Captain Ellery Stone (U.S.N.R.), whose acting rank was not confirmed until 10th November. The choice of Captain Stone reversed the principle, which had been agreed by the British and American Governments with General Eisenhower, that the Chief Commissioner should be of the same nationality as the Supreme Allied Commander. The Assistant Chief of Staff G-5 at A.F.H.Q. (Brig.-General Spofford) was also American. But this did not lead to any international dis-equilibrium, since it was interpreted as redressing the balance in the Commission, which under General Mason-MacFarlane's leadership had been considered in certain American circles as rather heavily over-weighted on the British side, both the Chief Commissioner and the Executive Commissioner being British.

The new Government, though formed in Rome, did not take office in the capital but in Salerno. Its separation from Rome, which immediately replaced Naples as the political centre of gravity, greatly hampered its efficiency, no less than the administrative work of the Control Commission. The inclusion of Rome in the Fifth Army area lasted scarcely a fortnight, owing to the rapid progress of the Allied Armies. General Mason-MacFarlane was therefore able to recommend an early transfer of the Government to the capital and, following the precedent set up when Badoglio's Government was transferred to Salerno, a simultaneous enlargement of Italian Government territory to include Rome. Both recommendations were submitted to the Advisory Council, which, though unanimous on the necessity of immediately transferring the Italian Government and itself to the capital, was less impressed with the necessity for an immediate transfer of territory. It was therefore arranged that the Government and Council should be transferred on 15th July, though the city remained subject to Allied Military Government for another month. The transfer of territory was made in two instalments. On 20th July the provinces of Naples, Benevento, Avellino, Foggia and Campobasso were transferred, but not the Commune of Naples, which was maintained as a military zone subject to Allied Military Government throughout the campaign. On 15th August the provinces of Rome—including Rome City—Littoria and Frosinone were also added to Italian Government territory.

One of the first actions of the new Government while still at Salerno was to pass a decree/law, No. 151 of 25th June, concerning the convocation—after the liberation of the whole of Italy—of a Constituent Assembly to decide the form of the constitution. According to a communiqué issued on 23rd June, the measure provided that after the liberation of the national territory the constitutional question should be decided by the Italian people, who for this purpose would elect by universal direct and secret ballot a Constituent Assembly. The wording of the decree seemed to imply that the actual decision of the issue, Monarchy or Republic, would be made by the elected assembly, thus excluding the alternative procedure of a referendum—a procedure which, in the opinion of Captain Stone and his advisers, would be more likely to guarantee a fair decision. On enquiry he was assured by the Prime Minister that the decree in question did not exclude the possibility of a referendum, and that the Government had not yet decided, and had no intention of discussing, whether the decision should be made by direct referendum or by the delegates to the Constituent Assembly.

The anti-monarchist politicians strongly favoured the plan that the Constituent Assembly should be called upon to decide the issue, and this no doubt was the reason for Prince Humbert's statement made to the correspondent of the *New York Times* in November that, in his view, a more accurate expression of the popular will on this issue would be secured by a referendum. The news of the publication of this statement in America aroused violent resentment. The parties of the Left proposed a resolution to be adopted by the Council of Ministers in which the Lieutenant-General of the Realm was severely criticised. The Cabinet, however contented itself with a resolution reaffirming its solemn pledge to decide the constitutional issue through the vote of a Constituent Assembly. Here once more the issue of Constituent Assembly *versus* referendum appeared to have been pre-judged, but Signor Bonomi again assured the acting Chief Commissioner that the law in question did not preclude the holding of a referendum. He admitted that the parties of the Left were strongly against a referendum, because they felt more certain of attaining their republican objective through the medium of the Assembly, but he added that in any case there was nothing to prevent the adoption of a decree embodying the referendum at a later stage. He also expressed his personal wish that the Allied Governments should ask that such a referendum be held. The question was eventually, as will be shown later[1], submitted to a direct popular vote.

---

[1] See below, p. 362.

The question of 'defascistisation' was the next preoccupation of the new Government. The last Badoglio administration had already laid down the general lines which were to be followed by its successor, in respect of both the purging of the public services and the punishment of Fascist crimes. But the legislation passed so far had been somewhat piecemeal: it already amounted, when the Badoglio Government fell, to twenty-eight decrees and ministerial orders. At the end of July the Bonomi Government passed a new coordinating decree (DLL 159) on Sanctions against Fascism, which divided these measures into four separate categories, namely, the punishment of Fascist crimes, the purging of the administration, the disposal of the profits made by Fascists, and the confiscation of Fascist party properties. It also reorganised the office of High Commissioner for Sanctions against Fascism by creating an assistant High Commissioner to supervise each of the four categories of sanctions.

In recasting the anti-Fascist legislation the Bonomi Government adopted the principle, which had been incorporated in the last measure of Marshal Badoglio, of making retroactively criminal the creation and the maintenance of the Fascist regime. The first part of this decree aimed at defining two categories of criminal offences—Fascism, and collaboration with the Germans. The definition of the former contained in the last Badoglio decree was widened. Under Article 2 of the new version, members of the Government and high ranking members of Fascism guilty of annulling the guarantees given under the constitution, of destroying the liberty of the people, of creating the Fascist regime, of compromising and betraying the fortunes of the country and bringing it to its present disasters, were to be punished by penal servitude for life and, in cases where the responsibility was greater, by death—in spite of the fact that the death-penalty, which had been reimposed by Mussolini, had once more been abolished. Persons coming under this category were to be tried by a special High Court of Justice. Smaller fry, organisers of Fascist squads, promoters and directors of the 'revolt' of 28th October 1922, promoters and directors of the *coup d'état* of the 3rd January 1925 and 'those who have since by relevant action contributed to maintain the Fascist regime in power', were to be tried by a Court of Assize. The political character of this retroactive legislation seems tacitly to be admitted in the constitution of the tribunals constituted to try these cases. The special High Court of Justice was not to be exclusively judicial in its composition, but to be comprised of a president and eight members chosen by the Council of Ministers from among high ranking judicial officials, serving or retired, and 'other persons of unquestionable rectitude'. The Courts of Assize were also given a mixed composition, being constituted by two judges and five laymen chosen by lot from special lists of 'citizens of umblemished moral and political behaviour', the presiding officer being in all cases a judge.

But sanctions were not confined to specified Fascist crimes. Article 8 contained an omnibus clause which permitted the punishment of Fascists on an even wider basis. Any person

> who for Fascist reasons, or by taking advantage of the political situation created by Fascism, has committed acts . . . , which while not being offences in the eyes of the law are nevertheless contrary to the rules of social and political integrity, shall be subjected to temporary disqualification from holding any public office or to loss of political rights for a period of not more than ten years. Whenever such a person is deemed to be a danger to society, he may be sent to an agricultural colony or a labour institution for a period of not less than one or more than ten years.

The trial of such cases was entrusted to a Provincial Commission presided over by a judicial official and composed of two lay members.

Collaboration with the Germans after the 8th September was summarily disposed of in an article (No. 5) laying down that whoever, whether a member of the armed forces or not, 'has committed a crime against loyalty and the military defence of the State, by any kind whatsoever of action, collaboration, help or assistance to the German invader', should be punished according to the provisions of the military penal code of war, members of the armed forces being tried by court martial and civilians by the ordinary courts.

The same article also contained a paragraph aimed at the members of the legislative assemblies who by their votes or actions contributed to the maintenance of the Fascist regime. These were subject to dismissal from their office by sentence of the special section of the High Court of Justice constituted in Article 2. It was under this clause that the 'epuration' of the Senate was undertaken. Very few members escaped the ordeal and most of the existing senators—life appointments of the Crown—were dismissed. Even Marshal Badoglio was deprived of his senatorship.

The criterion for 'epuration' of the public services departed somewhat from that originally laid down by AMGOT in Sicily concerning the automatic dismissal from office of all persons in the category of *Squadrista*, *San Sepolcrista*, etc., which had been maintained in the earlier decree-law of the Badoglio Government promulgated in December 1943. Dismissal was now only obligatory if the person in question was proved guilty of Fascist partisanship or improper conduct. If not so guilty, he might be awarded less severe punishment. But the definition of those liable to dismissal was considerably widened by including any person who had 'participated actively in the political life of Fascism or by showing himself a consistent apologist of Fascism, had proved that he was unworthy of serving the state', or obtained appointment or promotion through favouritism of the Party or its officials, or had been 'guilty of Fascist bias, incompetence or corrupt practice'. The applicability of sanctions was extended to officials of private concerns controlling public utility undertakings or concerns having a nation-wide interest, and to all officials who, after the armistice, had moved to north Italy with the neo-Fascist Government or pledged allegiance to it or in any way collaborated with it.

To hear 'epuration' proceedings in the first instance commissions were established in every ministry. Among institutions to be 'epurated' centrally from Rome were included cultural institutions such as the universities and the various academies, as well as the large joint stock banks and industrial concerns of nation-wide scope. For local government services commissions were to be appointed by the Prefect.[1] The professions were also included in this portion of the decree. Commissions were set up to purge all professional associations.[2] Both the High Commissioner for Sanctions against Fascism and the party concerned had a right to appeal to a central commission appointed by the Prime Minister and composed of a president, two judicial officers, two officials of the central administration, and two members nominated by the High Commissioner.

The new decree was immediately implemented in A.M.G. territory. But before the machinery for doing this could be brought into action, a preliminary epuration by A.M.G. was necessary. This was done by the automatic dismissals or suspensions already described in the last chapter. In order to guide A.M.G. in this rather delicate task of elimination in the large Tuscan towns, a list was prepared, after consultation with the High Commissioner, of prominent citizens of reliably anti-Fascist antecedents whom the Civil Affairs officers were instructed to consult. These consultations were however to take place secretly and the names of the consultants were not to be made public, the responsibility for the decisions remaining with A.M.G. Appeals to the High Commission were allowed by persons dismissed or suspended.

The vague and unprecise terminology of this legislation—passed by a Government of self-constituted party leaders under the control of a foreign power—creating retroactively a number of criminal offences and exacting punishment for actions alleged to have been committed, in some cases, nearly thirty years before, can hardly

[1] This arrangement was altered in November 1944, when the appointments were transferred to the High Commissioner.

[2] The commissions of first instance were 'mixed' containing nominees of the Prefect, the professional association or the minister concerned, as well as of the High Commissioner, but the president was in each case a judicial officer.

create an altogether favourable impression on the judicially minded. Indeed a protest against the principle of retroactive legislation was immediately made by a number of eminent Italian professors of law belonging to very diverse political persuasions. But it would be a mistake to regard it merely as a piece of anti-Fascist party vindictiveness. For though it is true that, owing to the deplorable disunion, weakness and inefficiency of the democratic politicians after the First World War, Mussolini, in creating the Fascist State, was able to preserve all the constitutional formalities, the fact remains that the spirit of the constitution was perverted. And even when all allowance has been made for the desire of individual politicians to get their own back on the authors of their humiliation, the determination to punish those responsible for this perversion of justice cannot be dismissed as mere vengeance. But good morals, like hard cases, often make bad law, and sometimes worse politics. And an historian cannot help asking the question whether the amnesties granted by the House of Savoy in Piedmont after the fall of Napoleon might not have provided a happier precedent.

But with regard to 'epuration', there can be no doubt that action at the top was necessary, whatever juridical objections may be urged against the precise form in which the purge was carried out. That some injustice was done has to be admitted. It is the tragedy of politics that injustice breeds injustice. Nor can it be denied that a good deal of care was taken to avoid the judgements of the various tribunals involved becoming a mere expression of popular vengeance. Hence the insistence on the inclusion of a judge (later a senior barrister) as president of every tribunal of first instance, and the humane and relatively tolerant instructions issued to members of the judging commissions by Count Sforza, summed up in the injunction 'act quickly, strike the "high-ups" and let off the smaller fry'[1], not always, unfortunately, observed.

The assistant Commissioner in charge of epuration was the Communist Signor Scoccimarro—a choice which did not contribute to party harmony within the Cabinet. It was soon suspected that he was using his influence to get rid of any official who would not prove in varying degrees amenable to the future actions of the Party. Signor Bonomi was compelled to demand his resignation—one of the circumstances which precipitated the final crisis which led to the breaking up of the six-party Government. For with its diversity of ideological traditions the coalition was anything but a harmonious combination. Party intrigues and manoeuvres reverberating in the loud-speaker of a renascent press soon made any semblance of unity impossible.

---

[1] *Far presto, colpire in alto, perdonare in basso.*

The first sign of disintegration manifested itself as soon as the new Government had taken office, in the form of a sort of polarisation towards the Left and the Right. It soon became apparent that only three of the six parties, the Socialist, the Communist and the Christian Democrats, could look forward with any confidence to obtaining the support of the masses of a still somewhat indifferent population. The Action Party, strongly republican and indeterminately 'leftist', was essentially a party of the intellectual *élite*, while neither the Liberals nor the Labour Democrats commanded any large following. The first 'polarising' movement was the action taken by the Socialist and Communist parties to form a private alliance, no doubt with a view to eventual elections. On 9th August the two parties announced their intention to associate together as close allies in the fight for the liberation of the country and for the total destruction of Fascism. A few days later a much smaller party fusion was announced on the Right.[1]

But whatever the difference within the Bonomi Cabinet in internal politics, there was one subject on which all parties agreed, the necessity of obtaining more favourable treatment from the Allies. Signor Bonomi as early as 22nd July had addressed a memorandum to Mr Cordell Hull, pointing out that the clauses of the armistice represented a situation historically and politically out of date and hinting that the time had come to substitute Allied status for cobelligerency. The Allies had laid down that the modification of the armistice terms would be dependent on Italy's contribution to their war effort. But hitherto Italy had been prevented from participating adequately in the liberation of her national territory. The Italian people felt that they were being kept in quarantine, since the request for adherence to the Atlantic Charter had never been answered, while that for participation in the International Labour office had been indefinitely postponed, and the demand for participation in the Bretton Woods Monetary Conference had not been welcomed. On the economic side Signor Bonomi pointed out the enormous costs of occupation, the vast issues of Allied military currency and the low rate of exchange which were bleeding the Italian people, and requested economic help from the Allies, more particularly the inclusion of Italy in the countries to which the Lend-Lease legislation could be applied.

He also demanded a drastic change in the functions of the Allied Control Commission, which should be relieved progressively of at least three-quarters of its duties, and directed towards a system less oppressive and less patently designed to interfere in all sectors of

---

[1] Between the Liberal Party (*Partito Liberale Italiano*) and the Democratic Liberal Party (*Partito della Democrazia Liberale*).

Italian life. It was not possible for a country to carry on under the administration of two governments and equally impossible for a civilised people like the Italians to be indefinitely subjected to a state of tutelage. He also suggested that the members of the Advisory Council should be turned into something like an Ambassadors' Conference, to take the place of the Control Commission. This was certainly plain speaking, much plainer speaking than Marshal Badoglio had ever found occasion to indulge in, though none of the themes were exactly new.

This move on the part of Signor Bonomi, which looked uncommonly like an attempt to drive the thin end of a wedge into what he fancied was a split in Allied policy towards Italy, received no encouragement from Washington. Mr Cordell Hull's reply, delivered nearly a month later, was a model of diplomatic repartee. He pointed out that in practice the armistice terms were being applied by the Allies solely for the purpose of furthering the prosecution of the war against Germany. If the Italian Government had any specific proposals to make with regard to their amendment, the U.S. Government would be glad to receive them. As to more active participation in the war against Germany, the limitations in the way of equipping and supplying a large force were emphasised, and, while sympathy was expressed with the Italian desire to participate in the various international organisations, it was pointed out that atonement for the crimes of Fascist Italy against many of the United Nations would require patience, understanding and hard work. As regards Italy's economic difficulties, these had been the subject of constant and careful study by the Allied Governments ever since the beginning of the liberation of Italian territory, but the limitation placed on the employment of Lend-Lease funds rendered it impossible to consider Lend-Lease aid as a solution to Italy's economic problems. It was hoped, however, that some satisfactory formula for helping Italy would be evolved in the near future. With regard to the Control Commission, until the Allied armed forces and their co-belligerents had achieved a final victory, it was essential that the Allied theatre commander should retain the authority that he exercised through this body, in order to enable him to prosecute the war to a successful conclusion. The composition of the Commission was, however, being studied by the Allied Governments in the light of the increasing emphasis on civilian problems, and their desire to return liberated areas to Italian administration as soon as military conditions permitted, had recently been manifested in the return of the Capital and several provinces to Italian administration.

After the visit of Mr Churchill to Italy (11th–28th August) it had become apparent, to British no less than to American eyes, that considerable changes were needed in the conduct of Allied military administration in Italy. The Italian situation was discussed by the Prime Minister and the President during and after the second Quebec Conference, and a joint statement generally known as the Hyde Park Declaration, emanating as it did from President Roosevelt's home, announced to the world on 26th September a further stage in the progress of Italy's political rehabilitation, which will form the subject of the next chapter. It was however, several months before the concessions implied in this policy could be worked out, and Signor Bonomi lost no occasion to press the Allies on the two main objectives of Italian foreign policy, ever since the conclusion of the armistice, namely the winning of the status of ally and the liberation of Italian prisoners of war. While the Yalta Conference was still sitting he took the opportunity on 7th February 1945 of addressing a note on both these matters in identical terms to President Roosevelt, Mr Churchill and Marshal Stalin.

The retention of the status of prisoners of war by men who were actually cooperating with the Allied armed forces had never been understood as anything but an insult by the Italian public, and Signor Bonomi was no more ready than Marshal Badoglio to agree to the Allied proposals in the matter. Marshal Badoglio, as has already been noted in Chapter V, had made a formal protest objecting, as a matter of principle, to the Allied policy of organising Italian prisoners of war into units under Allied command in all theatres of operation. Signor Bonomi on 23rd June repeated the substance of Marshal Badoglio's note, to which the Supreme Allied Commander replied that, while individual Italian prisoners of war might be released from time to time, no change in their general status was contemplated. A concession was however made to the Italian point of view by releasing the 65,000 Sicilian prisoners of war who had been placed on parole by General Alexander. The Italian Government had appointed a High Commissioner for Prisoners of War, who had been permitted, ever since the negotiations for the Prisoners of War Agreement had been broken off, to inspect the conditions under which Co-operator units were working, and satisfactory arrangements had been made for their welfare, which were in many respects considerably better than those enjoyed by the Italian Army.

Apart from 'defascistisation' the legislative activity of the Government included few measures of any political importance. Its chief business was concerned with the re-direction of the activities of the central government departments in Rome, the administrative problems concerned with food production and distribution, and the passing of a number of measures to implement various policies on economic matters which had already been discussed by the previous Government with the Control Commission, such as the blocking of agricultural products and the regulations for their sale at controlled prices, a new decree for the amassing of oil, a law imposing heavier penalties for the failure to supply due quantities of corn to the *Granai del popolo*, legislation abolishing the Fascist syndicates, and the repeal of Fascist racial laws in the educational sphere—which had already been abolished by A.M.G. during its progress up the peninsula.

Conditions in Sicily caused both the Italian Government and the Control Commission a good deal of anxiety. The Separatist movement appeared to be gaining strength, and though the appointment of Signor Aldisio, a Christian Democrat who had been Minister of the Interior in the last Badoglio Government, as High Commissioner to replace Signor Musotto, the former Prefect of Palermo, strengthened the hands of the central authorities, it did not immediately enable the Government successfully to counter the movement. Economic troubles too were impending, owing to the failure of the local authorities to amass more than a comparatively small portion of the grain harvest, which finally compelled the Allies, much against their will, to introduce a supply of imported grain. The tide of unrest caused by shortage of food and rising prices led to a nasty incident in Palermo on 19th October, when Italian troops opened fire on a crowd from which, apparently, a bomb had been thrown, and serious casualties occurred, 26 civilians being killed and over 150 wounded.

Nor were public disturbances in Italian Government territory confined to Sicily. In Rome itself in September, Caruso, the Chief of Police in the capital under the Social-Republic, was tried for Fascist crimes, the chief of which was collaboration with the Germans by handing over fifty prisoners for summary execution in the massacre of the Ardeatine caves. This trial led to the lynching of one of the witnesses by a mob, which broke through the police lines, invaded the Palace of Justice in search of Caruso, and, being unable to discover him, contented itself by seizing one Carreta, a former Governor of the Regina Coeli prison, dragging him to the centre of the Ponte Umberto, after practically tearing him to pieces, and throwing him into the Tiber. When the victim showed signs of reviving in the water, members of the crowd got hold of a boat and finally despatched him, dragged his body from the river and tied it to the grating of a first-floor window of the gaol. The mob was apparently urged on to commit this outrage by the relatives of the 300 victims murdered by the Germans. The *Carabinieri* present were few, and wholly unable to control the mob; but since Rome was Italian Government territory, Allied troops were not called out to restore order. Allied military police were however sent to the gaol, in order to prevent certain 'security' prisoners held there being liberated.

Fortunately this disturbance was only an isolated event, so that no special measures had to be taken by the Allied Command to preserve public order in the capital.

But the prestige of the Government in the eyes of the public was certainly lowered, and its internal dissensions soon worked themselves up to a climax. Behind the formal unity of the Cabinet, whose practical policy was, if not dictated, at any rate in a large part suggested by the Control Commission, the six parties and their newly liberated press made little pretence to disguise their mutual differences. A series of intrigues and manoeuvres on the part of the parties of the Left—in which the hand of Count Sforza was also plainly discernible—and their attempt to gain a preponderance in the more important Cabinet Office, finally induced Signor Bonomi on 26th November to tender his resignation to the Lieutenant-General of the Realm.

Immediately after receiving Signor Bonomi's resignation on 26th November Prince Humbert, in accordance with constitutional practice, consulted with Signor Orlando and Signor Toretta—who had been appointed by the Bonomi Government as Presidents, the one of a non-existent Chamber of Deputies, the other of a not yet purged Senate—and with the heads of the six parties. Meanwhile, the Party leaders had met together as the Committee of National Liberation of the capital without their Chairman Signor Bonomi, who had voluntarily absented himself, and elected Count Sforza to take his place. The outcome of this meeting was a note to Signor Bonomi, to the effect that the representatives of the six parties forming the C.L.N. wished him to inform the Allies that he would not be able to form a coalition government unless he entrusted the Ministry of Foreign Affairs to Count Sforza; in spite of the fact that Mr. Hopkinson, in the absence of Sir Noel Charles on a visit to the Eighth Army, had already informed the Marchese Visconti Venosta, the Under-Secretary for Foreign Affairs, that he hoped that it was fully understood that Count Sforza was not acceptable to His Majesty's Government as Minister for Foreign Affairs and still less as Prime Minister.

A delegation of three of the party leaders, Signor De Gasperi, Signor Saragat and Signor Cianca, all of whom had been members of Signor Bonomi's Government, thereupon called upon Sir Noel Charles on 28th November, to inquire whether British objections to Count Sforza's assuming the Foreign Secretaryship still held good. Sir Noel Charles informed them that, while His Majesty's Government had no wish to interfere in Italian internal affairs and had every desire to improve relations with Italy, this would be impossible if they insisted on Count Sforza becoming Foreign Minister. This action was, not without some reason, interpreted by Mr Cordell Hull as a

British veto on Count Sforza's appointment, and produced a protest from the State Department, in which regret was expressed that the Foreign Office, without prior consultation with them, had felt it necessary to intervene in an Italian internal political crisis and once more to veto Count Sforza's appointment.[1]

With the details of the various party manoeuvres during the crisis, which left Italy without a government from 26th November till 12th December, we are not here concerned[2], but it seems clear that the constitutional question largely determined the attitude taken both by the Socialist and by the Action Party. Both took the view that Signor Bonomi had put himself beyond the political pale by offering the resignation of the Government to the Lieutenant-General of the Realm instead of to the C.L.N. The Action Party also announced its refusal to take part in any government which did not give the post of Foreign Minister to Count Sforza. The Communists were much less intransigent, and finally decided to join the Christian Democrats in accepting office under Bonomi. Once more Signor Togliatti had succeeded in resolving a political deadlock, and in putting his party in a strong bargaining position—for his alliance with the Socialists remained unbroken, while he was able to command the sympathy of many patriotic non-Communists.

With the elimination of Count Sforza, the Socialists, and the Party of Action, Signor Bonomi's four-party Government, if not a model of internal concord, was a much more united body than his first Cabinet. The number of Ministers without portfolio was reduced to three—the Communist, Togliatti, and the Christian Democrat, Di Rodino, both Vice-Presidents, and a Liberal, Signor Brosio. Signor Bonomi retained the Ministry of the Interior, but the Ministry of Foreign Affairs was taken over by the leader of the Christian Democrats, Signor De Gasperi. With one or two exceptions the portfolios were held by men who had been Ministers in the previous Government. A new Ministry, that of Occupied Italy, was created, which was given to the Communist, Signor Scoccimarro, who was relieved of his position as Assistant High Commissioner for Epuration. Only one change was made in the Service Ministers. Signor Scialoia (Labour Democrat) replaced General Piacentini as Minister for Air, but Admiral De Courten and Count Casati continued to preside over the Ministries for the Navy and for War.

---

[1] Cordell Hull, *op. cit.*, Vol. II, p. 1568. Mr Churchill, on the other hand, strongly repudiated the suggestion that the action taken in Rome by the High Commissioner and his staff constituted a veto, or that it had in any way contravened the joint arrangements with the American Government, maintaining that H.M.G. had a perfect right to say that they did not have any confidence in Count Sforza. See also the Prime Minister's statement in the House of Commons, H. of C. Deb., 8th December 1944.

[2] For an interesting Italian account see Andreotti, *op. cit.;* also Tamaro, *op. cit.*, Vol. III, pp. 358-371.

In accordance with the precedents already established, the new Government gave the undertakings given by its predecessors, accepting all the obligations entered into at the armistice, and binding itself not to reopen the constitutional question. The appointments of the service ministers and officials were submitted for previous Allied approval and the Chief Commissioner was authorised to require the retention of Signor Fano and General di Raimondi. But in deference to the American point of view on non-intervention in purely internal Italian politics, it was decided that the names of other ministers and under-secretaries need not be submitted to A.F.H.Q. for approval. Count Sforza resigned his position as High Commissioner for Sanctions against Fascism. He was offered the post of Italian Ambassador in Washington, which he refused.

The formation of the four-party coalition was a personal triumph for Signor Bonomi. Politically it had two notable consequences. First, it greatly diminished the importance of the Roman Committee of National Liberation, a fact which was also reflected indirectly in an increase in the importance of the Milan Committee, a body which appeared at one time to be likely to dispute the authority of the central Government. In the second place, it gave the new Government a rather more Conservative complexion, and greatly increased the influence of the Centre, the Christian Democratic Party, which since the end of the war has continued to be the most influential political force in the country.

In dealing with the extremely difficult problem of inflation, which became month by month more acute, Signor Bonomi's second Government reversed the technique applied by its predecessors. The policy, hitherto applied under the guidance of the Control Commission, had been to try to hold wages at the level reached soon after the Sicilian occupation, which represented an increase of seventy to eighty per cent above the pre-invasion figure. This attempt, which had been weakened considerably by the higher level of wages paid by the armed forces, had not been wholly unsuccessful, though in many cases illegal wage additions had been paid by employers. Such success as it achieved had only been made possible by maintaining a heavy subsidy on bread, in the form of a 'political' price which bore little relation to the actual cost of production. The first Bonomi Government, at the insistence of the Control Commission, had in July fixed the 'political' price of bread at five lire a kilo—rather less than half the real cost—though it had itself been in favour of fixing an economic price.

The second Bonomi Government, in which Signor Soleri continued to hold the portfolio of the Treasury, found itself faced with a colossal budget deficit, estimated in December 1944 to amount to over sixty thousand million lire for the thirty-six provinces of Italian Government territory, of which something like half was due to the cost of the bread subsidy. It consequently decided to abolish the political price of bread, fixing new prices to include the full cost of grain sold to millers. The consequence of this measure was an increase in the retail price of bread to between sixteen and eighteen lire per kilo. To mitigate the effects of this increase on the family budget, a new monthly wage supplement (*caro pane*) of ninety-five lire was established, to be paid by employers to workmen and their dependants and by the State to public employees and registered unemployed. The attempt to hold wages had already been abandoned, since the first Bonomi Government at the end of October without consulting the Allied Commission—which had by this time lost the middle 'C' from its title—had, as the result of pressure from the resurrected General Confederation of free trade unions (CGIL), increased wages by a substantial amount in the form of the cost of living (*cara vita*) supplement amounting to between thirty and fifty lire a day. In this way a sharp turn was given to the inflationary spiral.

The Commission did not intervene in this change of policy. In the spirit of the 'New Deal for Italy,' which will be described in the following chapter, it left the Italian Government to take these measures on its own responsibility. But other steps were taken to bring Government receipts a little nearer the total of expenditures in order to limit the vicious spiral. These included the setting up of an economy committee to prune the budget, the revision of a number of tax schedules and the improvement of the process of tax assessment by local committees. War profits duty was also extended to agricultural incomes. Finally, an attempt was made to decrease the inflationary pressure by taking steps to withdraw superfluous monetary balances from the public: five-year Treasury bonds were offered for public subscription on 5th April 1945.

Anxiety about inflation had long been shared by the British and American Governments. Before the end of 1943 a special mission had been despatched by the Foreign Economic Administration of the United States Government, under Mr Adlai Stevenson, which devoted a good deal of its attention to this problem. The mission was inclined to lay emphasis upon the expenditure of A.M. lire by the Allied forces as the principal factor causing inflation: it also criticised by implication the rate of 100 lire to the dollar on the ground that it undervalued the lira. In May 1944 an Anti-Inflation Committee was set up at the Allied Control Commission's headquarters on which served special representatives of both the U.S. and U.K. Treasuries.[1]

[1] The committee was composed as follows: Captain Ellery Stone, Chairman: Colonel A. P. Grafftey-Smith and Colonel E. H. Foley, Jr., Joint directors of the Finance Sub-Commission; Mr Harold Glasser, of the Division of Monetary Research of the U.S. Treasury; Mr E. H. M. Lloyd, Economic Adviser of the British Minister of State's Office, Middle East; Colonel Upjohn; and Colonel N. E. Fiske, Deputy Executive Commissioner.

The pegging of wages was, according to the view of these experts, the critical point on which all hopes of arresting the progress of inflation depended. The programme was therefore envisaged of reducing the pressure on wages on all sides, (a) by ensuring that a minimum ration of prime necessities, clothing as well as food, should be distributed, where necessary, at subsidized prices, (b) by increasing revenue and keeping down expenditure, thus reducing the budgetary deficit, and (c) by mopping up superfluous purchasing power by taxation and borrowing.

On the financial side, the Committee had recommended measures for tackling the problem of the budget deficit on the lines which had already been worked out by the Finance Sub-Commission. These included proposals for a complete re-modelling of the antiquated machinery of taxes and of revenue assessment and collection.

The main weaknesses of the Italian fiscal system were summed up by the Finance Sub-Commission under three headings:

(a) a procedure of assessment unduly slow and highly inaccurate,
(b) a very costly system of collection which invited collusion and corruption of every kind,
(c) excessive reliance on *per quantum* as opposed to *ad valorem* consumption taxes.

Instead of a progressively graduated and unified income tax, there was a complicated system of fifteen separate taxes, income from different sources being taxed under different laws at different rates. Income from government securities was exempted from tax. The taxpayer was supposed to file an initial return of his income from different sources and then to submit returns in subsequent years in which there had been any change in the amount of his income. But the returns were used for information only, and not for self-assessment, and were in many cases never made at all. Tax officials made their own independent assessments and then bargained with the taxpayer. No attempt was made to ascertain what income the taxpayer actually received, but a theoretical earning-capacity was established by the use of arbitrary and complicated coefficients, and this was used as a basis for assessment.

There was an excess profits tax levied on commercial and industrial enterprises and based on the excess of income over the 1937/38 averages. This did not apply to incomes drawn from agriculture, which were exempt. Assessments were incredibly behindhand; in many cases those for 1940 and 1941 had not yet been fixed at the beginning of 1944. As an anti-inflationary measure the tax was useless. The turnover tax was equally unsatisfactory. Collusion between buyer and seller was widespread, and in most cases the tax was assessed in the retail trade by an *accordo* (agreement), under which estimated turnover was calculated by applying a co-efficient to the income tax assessment on the individual business, the coefficient being determined generally for each separate trade by the trade corporation in Rome.

Consumption taxes, on which communes depended for half their income, were incredibly expensive to collect, charges amounting in some cases to forty-five per cent of the proceeds. As a result of the scarcity of consumption goods, their gross yield had enormously diminished, since they were levied on quantity consumed at a flat rate, instead of being based *ad valorem* in order to take advantage of steadily rising prices. Last, but not least, the incredibly primitive system of farming out taxes for collection by public auction was, quite apart from collusion and corruption everywhere prevalent, absurdly expensive. The *aggio*, or premium charged by the *essatore*, amounted on state taxes to about seven per cent, whereas in the United Kingdom collection costs were estimated to be about 7.5 per mil.

To reduce expenditure two suggestions had been made which could be applied immediately. The first was concerned with an important inflationary item, the accumulated claims arising out of the unpaid bills of the Fascist regime and the requisitions of the Allied and Italian armed forces. These should only be met in cash where payment was necessary to enable a work or service to be continued which was in the interest of the Allied forces, or where it would obviate the necessity of incurring a different form of expenditure, such as relief. The second dealt with interest on the public debt. Charges on the floating debt should be reduced to 3½ per cent. It had also been recommended that the government deficit should be financed by the sale of relatively long term bonds.

To increase revenue the Committee had recommended certain emergency measures, including the arbitrary multiplication of the assessment of certain types of income by 'some figure from 2 to 6', a further raising of monopoly prices, and the increase of the property tax from ½ to 2 per cent. Finally, a scheme had been put forward for the impounding of excess purchasing power, either through blocking, or through taxation, in connection with a currency conversion. The question of troop expenditure was never mentioned in this report, a fact which elicited a pertinent comment from the Chief Administrative Officer, A.F.H.Q., who suggested that measures might be considered in Washington and London whereby such expenditure might be reduced.

It was perhaps too much to expect that a government, in the middle of a war, ruling over only about one-third, and that by far the poorer portion, of the population, should, at the point of a bayonet, undertake the immediate modernization of its inherited fiscal arrangements. The recommendations of the Anti-Inflation Commitee, which appear to have been made without any consultation of the Italian Government's wishes, included a number of long-range reforms which would seem to lie wholly beyond the scope of an Armistice Control Commission—a fact which was implicitly recognised by A.F.H.Q.[1] Nevertheless, under the gentle but constant pressure of the Allied Commission, the Bonomi Government was induced to make a creditable attempt, amidst quite exceptional difficulties, to carry out a programme of tax reforms, even if this was not as perfect as the financial advisers of the Commission would have wished.

A revision was made of the direct taxes. Rates on different categories of income tax were raised from two to eight per cent, and 'super tax' on large incomes from twenty-five to seventy-five per cent. Land tax was raised from five to ten per cent and the tax on profits from ten to twenty per cent. A serious attempt was also made to tighten up the methods of assessment and collection. The turnover tax, too, was revised. General rates were raised from three to four per cent and those on certain luxury goods increased from eight to twelve per cent. But the most important change was that of assessment and collection. The burden was put squarely on the purchaser, instead of being divided between him and the vendor. Prices of monopoly products, salt, tobacco and matches were repeatedly raised, though owing to greatly reduced production the additional revenue was not as large as had been hoped.

In the field of local taxation the taxes on articles of consumption (*imposte di consumo*) were placed on an *ad valorem* basis, thereby at last bringing the amount of tax charged into line with increased prices, and arrangements were made to reduce collection charges. Last but not least, a decree was under discussion with the Allied Commission, when the liberation of the North took place, which was to make compulsory the furnishing of an annual return of income by every individual and profit-making concern, with penalties for failure to comply—a reform which was finally adopted by the Italian Government after the end of the war.

Like its predecessor, the second Bonomi Government, whenever the opportunity arose, called upon the Allies to fulfil their promise of permitting Italy to work her passage by increasing the proportion of Italian combat troops. By this time the withdrawal of Allied troops from Italy for the invasion of Southern France had at length persuaded the Combined Chiefs of Staff to provide the necessary equipment for an equivalent of two divisions. But the martial spirit of the Italian people was not everywhere in evidence. The call-up,

[1] The Chief Administrative Officer pointed out in a pertinent comment: 'The implementation of the reforms of the Italian tax system must remain primarily a matter for the Italian authorities. Implicit in the developments of the policy of tax rates and exemptions are a number of broad social and political questions, which this headquarters does not undertake to appraise'.

or rather recall to the Italian Army, of the 1914-1924 classes in Sicily led to serious trouble. In Catania on 14th December demonstrations by students against the call-up led to severe rioting, in the course of which the *Municipio*, the Law Courts and the tax offices were burnt and gutted and other official buildings damaged. This outburst was followed by demonstrations throughout the island. Though the call-up provided the occasion for these disturbances there were other causes also at work. According to Admiral Stone's report to the Advisory Council, both Fascist and Separatist elements were in part responsible. And worse was to follow. In the province of Ragusa early in January a series of disturbances broke out amounting to something very like a rebellion. The disorder was finally repressed by the Italian military authorities without calling upon the aid of Allied troops, but not before the attention of both the Allied Commission and the Government had been called to the very narrow margin of safety afforded by the existing 'ceiling' of the *Carabinieri* establishments, which were included in the inelastic total assigned to the Italian Army. It was only with the greatest difficulty that the Combined Chiefs of Staff could be persuaded, on the eve of the final liberation of the north of Italy, to consent to any increase in the establishment of the main body of Italian police responsible for the preservation of public safety. In causing the disorders in Ragusa, as in Catania and elsewhere, both Separatist and Fascist influences appear to have been at work, the latter, it was believed, working under German direction. In Sardinia too some disturbances, though much less serious, occurred in connection with the call-up. These were easily suppressed and the final result of the call-up was much more satisfactory than in Sicily.

The suppression of the Ragusa rebels resulted in a steady decline in the influence of the Separatist party, thanks to the vigorous action taken by the High Commissioner, whose powers were considerably increased by the central Government, and in part also to the encouragement given by the Government to the idea of decentralisation involving a considerable degree of regional autonomy. The idea of regional autonomy had already been encouraged by the creation, by Signor Bonomi's first government, of a *Consulta*, an Advisory Council of twenty-four members representing a wide range of interests. A similar council was set up in Sardinia. But the Separatist party in Sicily continued to exist and to foment trouble. It was not until the arrest of Signor Finocchiaro Aprile by the Parri Government after the end of hostilities that its activities were virtually brought to an end.

Considerable progress was made in the arrangements for reconstituting at the earliest date the machinery of representative Government. The first Bonomi Government before it broke up had passed a decree ordering the preparation of electoral lists for the holding of local elections in the communes on the lines laid down in the pre-Fascist legislation of 1915. Under these arrangements women would have been precluded from voting. However, on representations made by Admiral Stone, the four-party Government in January 1945 decided to extend the vote to all women over the age of twenty-one. The plan already laid down was to have the lists ready in order to be able to hold 'administrative' elections i.e. those for communal and provincial councils, in the late spring. In fact these elections, as will be seen, did not take place until the spring of 1946 after the whole of Italy had been restored to Italian administration.

A further step was the proposal to create a National Advisory Council (*Consulta*) to perform some of the functions of a parliament, pending the possibility of electing the Constituent Assembly. This step had been viewed with some suspicion by the Socialist and Action parties in opposition as well as by the Communists, who preferred calling a congress of the Committees of National Liberation from all parts of the country. Signor Bonomi's four-party Government nevertheless decided to bring this body into being. An inter-party committee was appointed to draw up proposals for its composition and functions, in which representatives of the Action and Socialist parties participated. The final scheme was approved by the Government on 26th April, only a few days before the end of hostilities.

To return to 'defascistisation'. After the resignation of Count Sforza and the transfer of Signor Scoccimarro, though he was succeeded in the post of assistant High Commissioner for Epuration by another Communist, less was heard of the political abuse of 'epuration'. The criticisms now most frequently made were, first, that it was proceeding far too slowly, and secondly, that it was being applied only to the lower grades of public servants, whereas the important officials who had supported the Fascist regime were being left in office unscathed. That the machinery should work somewhat slowly was hardly to be avoided. The number of courts that could be set up without bringing the whole Italian judiciary to a standstill was limited. Moreover, since the offences for which officials were liable to be tried might have been committed over a period of twenty years, the collection of evidence and the assembly and examination of witnesses, with the country divided between the two belligerents, and the almost total lack of communications all made long delays inevitable, if conditions for a hearing with any appearance of fairness were to be maintained. Some acceleration of the process was, however, introduced on the suggestion of the Allied Commission, by widening the field for selecting the presidents of the commissions of first instance by including, besides magistrates, barristers and university professors.

The hearing of the cases of the top grades of the civil service took a great deal longer than had been expected and the necessity for reaching stability in the reorganisation of the various departments was very pressing. The first Bonomi Government had already felt itself compelled to adopt a special procedure in the case of the first four grades, which was embodied in a decree (DLL. No. 257) which gave power to the Prime Minister to dispense with the services of senior officers and officials who, though not ardent Fascists, had become hardened in the ways of Fascism, and to compensate them in some cases for the loss of office by adding a few years to their services to qualify them for a pension.

These provisions were a tacit admission of the inadequacy of the principles of the legislation upon which the whole process of 'epuration' had been based, though they did in fact considerably hasten the purging of the upper grades. But it was not until 24th March 1945 that the Government was able to announce the completion of the 'epuration' of the ninety-eight prefects in the territory under its administration. The purged prefects had all been appointed after the armistice, either by A.M.G. or by the Italian Government; but even so by no means all of them escaped sanctions. Rather over a third had been put on trial, and six had been dismissed. Although the purging of the local authorities, etc., by the provincial commissions had in many cases hardly started, considerable progress had been achieved with respect to the central administration. In all, over 25,000 cases had been referred to the various commissions. Of the higher officials (grades I-IV) 1,500 had been examined; 136 (or about nine per cent) had been dismissed, and 283 (nearly twenty per cent) retired under the provisions just described.

The interest of the Control Commission in speeding up the process of 'epuration' was very strong, because the dismissal of Fascists had been expressly included in the terms of the armistice and administrative efficiency required immediate action. With the sword of 'epuration' dangling over their necks, the morale of public servants, already enfeebled by the ravages of inflation, was sinking even lower. Strong, if not always wise, pressure was therefore constantly applied for thorough and speedy 'epuration' of the higher grades. No effort was made to control the Italian Government with respect to the lower. There were, however, occasions on which the pressure of the Control Commission was required to operate in the contrary direction, as for instance in the case of Count Pellegrini, the Director-General of the concern which controlled the telephone system throughout Sicily and southern Italy, who was first suspended from office by the Commission for 'Epuration' in Region III and later arrested by the Italian Government for collaboration with the Germans. Whatever truth there may have been in this accusation, this official had collaborated much more fruitfully with the Allies, having procured for them at no small risk to himself charts of the submarine cables terminating at Anzio and Fiumicino while Rome was still in enemy hands, thus enabling very important cable communications from Anzio to be established. The Chief Signal officer of A.F.H.Q. at once protested on the ground, explicitly stated, that without Pelligrini's help the restoration of main communications in Italy would have been an extremely difficult and tardy operation. Arrangements had consequently to be made with the Italian Government by which Signor Bonomi agreed that no action with regard to the 'epuration' or trial for Fascist crimes of technicians or experts employed by the Allies would be taken, except after consultation with the Control Commission.

In the punishment of Fascist crimes the Allied Commission was less interested, and the matter was left entirely to the initiative of the Italian Government. One of the trials is however worth mentioning for the light it throws on the conditions under the Bonomi Government, namely that of General Roatta, Assistant Chief of the General Staff of the Army at the time of the overthrow of Fascism, and therefore deeply implicated in the fall of Mussolini. The general was accused of organising a special section of the Intelligence division of the General Staff, which was used as an instrument of terrorism in the interests of Fascism. This trial led to serious disturbances. General Roatta, who was alleged to be suffering from heart trouble, had been transferred under guard of the *Carabinieri* from the Regina Coeli prison to the Virgilio military hospital. On the night of the 4th March 1945 he succeeded—how, was never discovered—in making his escape, and in spite of all the efforts of the Government to trace his whereabouts—including the offer of a reward of a million lire—he succeeded in remaining hidden, until some time after the Allied military regime in Italy was finished. The political repercussions of Roatta's escape were serious, since it was easy enough for the parties of the Left to see in it a reactionary Fascist plot; and, even if the complicity of the *Carabinieri* could not be proved, their gross inefficiency was almost equally disquieting.

Before leaving the subject of 'defacistisation' the historian may perhaps be permitted to indulge in a few general reflections. The introduction of the ideological issue into international warfare by the totalitarian party dictatorship would seem to have rendered out of date, or at any rate in need of far reaching reinterpretation, the convention of international law, under which an occupying power, in default of sovereignty, is only entitled to alter the laws of the occupied territory where this is specifically necessary to his military purpose. In the face of modern political phenomena like Fascism and National Socialism, the obligation to respect, "unless absolutely prevented the laws in force in the (occupied) country' would appear to stand in need of some qualification.[1]

With the conclusion of the armistice, the juridical basis for 'defascistisation' was of course changed, by the agreement of the Italian Government to the terms under which it agreed to take such steps as were demanded by the United Nations for the destruction of certain organisations and the dismissal and internment of Fascist personnel. The Control Commission thus found itself responsible for the action taken by the Italian Government for 'epuration'—a responsibility which could hardly have been avoided. But in virtue of the omnicompetent powers with which it was endowed, it also became responsible for the action taken by the Italian government in the punishment of 'Fascist crimes'—a much more controversial business. The legislation passed by the Bonomi governments was strongly criticised by a number of eminent Italian jurists of varying political complexions. And even if in this matter the initiative was in fact left to the Italian government, it is impossible to deny that the enactment of retroactive criminal penalties for actions extending back nearly a generation took place at a time when the Allied Control Commission still retained its middle 'C'. It is of course too early to pass any final judgement on this matter, but the question may already be asked, to what extent the historian of the future will endorse either the justice or the wisdom of these sanctions.

To complete this chapter, the relations of the Bonomi Governments with the Resistance movements in German-occupied Italy deserve a brief mention. On the occupation of Rome by the Allies, the centre of gravity shifted to Milan, to the *Comitato di Liberazione Nazionale per l'Alta Italia* (C.L.N.A.I.), which, besides coordinating the military action of the various resistance bodies, tended more and more to look upon itself as a kind of shadow-government, ready to assume office over the dead body of Mussolini's Social Republic the moment the German troops, by whose aid alone this puppet regime had been maintained, were driven from Italian territory. Soon after the liberation of Rome, the Milan Committee had succeeded in instituting at any rate the framework for a central military command of all the 'Volunteers of Liberation', as the partisan bands came to be called. Communications had been established with both the Allied forces and the Italian Government, by means of which arrangements were made for General Raffaele Cadorna, the Commander of the *Ariete* Division, who had distinguished himself in the abortive operations against the Germans during the three days following the

---

[1] Article 43 of the Hague Convention of 1907 concerning the Laws and Customs of War on Land. See above, p. 14, where the French text of the article is given in the footnote.

armistice, to be dropped by air into German-occupied territory as Military Adviser to the *Comando Generale* of the partisans, of which he was later to become the chief.

Meanwhile as early as July certain members of the Bonomi Government, notably Signor Palermo, the Communist Under-Secretary for War, were planning to gain control of the Resistance movement in the north. They wanted the partisans to be recognised as members of the Italian Army, and suggested that their operations should be directed by an Italian general from liberated Italy, and that the Italian Government should be consulted before the dropping of arms. A plan on these lines was put before the Cabinet by Signor Palermo but rejected. The Italian Government thereupon confined itself to setting up a National Committee, of which the Prime Minister himself was chairman. The creation of the organisation had been suggested by the Control Commission, which had, however, restricted its functions to the appointment of patriot representatives to work with A.M.G., the preparations of records of patriot activities, the payment to patriots of compensation and rewards, and the regular supply of information to the Patriot Branch. The opportunity was also taken to make it quite clear to the Italian Government that the Allied Commander-in-Chief reserved to himself the exclusive right to deal with all questions affecting patriots to the north of rear army boundaries.

But the attempt of the Italian Government to establish some form of control over the Resistance movement was not so readily abandoned. The second Bonomi administration decided to turn the Commission for Patriots into a full-blown ministry under a Minister for Occupied Italy. The former Assistant High Commissioner for Epuration, the Communist Signor Scoccimarro, was appointed to this new post and a plan for the constitution of the Ministry, incorporated into a decree, was submitted to the Allied Commission. The Ministry was to be divided into five sections, (1) General, (2) Military matters, (3) Assistance, (4) Liaison with the Ministry for Foreign Affairs, and (5) Press and Propaganda. Articles 3 and 4 laid down that the Minister should maintain contact between the Government and the C.L.N.A.I. and all clandestine activities, and direct the resistance of the population against the invaders, as well as developing relations with the 'Volunteers of Liberty' and providing for a uniform organisation to strengthen the partisans against the Germans. Under article 5 the Assistance section of the Ministry was to provide for every possible kind of assistance, moral and material, to Italians living in invaded territory and to receive and assist patriots in newly liberated zones and those who crossed the lines. The Liaison office with the Ministry of Foreign Affairs was to maintain contact with patriots outside national territory.

The reaction of the Allied Command to this plan was prompt and decisive. The Italian Government was informed that no communications between it and occupied territory or patriots abroad could be permitted, except through A.F.H.Q.; that this must be restricted to such subjects as A.F.H.Q. might determine; that rehabilitation of patriots in forward areas and areas under Allied Military Government could only be carried out through the Patriots Branch of the Allied Commission; and that the real work of the Italian Ministry should be confined to such subjects as the prevention of unemployment, the rehabilitation of the homeless, the provision of remuneration, the finding of employment, and the contribution of clothing for patriots through the agency of the Commission's Patriots Branch.

Before the final liberation of the North was undertaken the Ministry had agreed to assume all responsibilities for expenditures connected with Patriot Centres and to institute a uniform scale for payments to patriots and their dependants.[1] The assistance and re-employment of patriots in Italian Government territory was placed in the hands of a High Commissioner for Veterans, and two committees attached to the Prime Minister's office were appointed to examine the claims of individuals for recognition as patriots and to make recommendations for military awards. An organisation based on the pattern of the British Legion was also formed, called the *Associazione Nazionale Partigiani d'Italia* (ANPI), to look after the interests of patriots.

In the meantime important negotiations, to be described in Chapter X, were initiated between the Allied High Command, the Italian Government, and the C.L.N.A.I. concerning the arrangement to be made when the Allied advance should force the withdrawal of the German army from northern Italy.

---

[1] The scale originally fixed consisted of 1,000 lire demobilisation bonus, 5,000 lire gratuity to wounded patriots and 10,000 lire to the dependants of patriots killed in action. These sums, considering the enormous loss in the purchasing power of the lire due to advanced inflation, were certainly not excessive and had later to be increased.

CHAPTER VIII

NEW DEAL FOR ITALY

THE CONTRADICTIONS inherent in the improvised status of co-belligerency manifested themselves from the beginning. Allied policy tended to oscillate between two poles, which for convenience we may call 'defeated enemy' and 'ally'. And though it would certainly be misleading to describe these two poles as the respective lodestars of British and American policy, there is little use in attempting to disguise the fact that, generally speaking, British policy towards Italy was, quite naturally, somewhat 'tougher' than American in two respects. First, so long as the war lasted, the British were inclined to regard the Allied Governments as entitled to intervene more directly in the internal political development of the renascent democracy. This was clearly shown in the British insistence on submitting the change of Government and its composition after the resignation of Badoglio to the prior approval of the Advisory Council before the Bonomi Government was permitted to take office, as well as in the objections raised to Count Sforza. Secondly, the paramount interest of the British Commonwealth in the Suez Canal—to say nothing of the promises made by the British Government, while still at war with Italy, to the Senussi in Cyrenaica[1]—made it appear essential to guard against a repetition of the events of 1940, by preventing the return to Italy of her North African colonies after the war. This could not fail to make the British Government even more reluctant than the American to contemplate the grant to Italy of Allied status.

Nevertheless in the spring of 1944 it was the British, not the American, Government which entertained the proposal of superseding the armistice regime by means of a preliminary peace treaty, which would once and for all relieve Italy of her status as an enemy of the Allied powers. The idea of a preliminary peace treaty had its origin in the Foreign Office. It was prompted by Marshal Badoglio's request for Allied status. The Foreign Office had been impressed by the strength gained by the Italian Communist party as the result of the *volte face* executed by Signor Togliatti, which resulted in the solution of the constitutional crisis and the formation of Badoglio's six-party Government, and also by the granting of diplomatic

[1] That they would never again come under Italian domination, made by Mr Eden, in his speech in the House of Commons on 8 January 1942.

recognition to Italy by the Russian Government. While not in favour of granting Italy Allied status, it did not wish to adopt a completely negative attitude to Badoglio's request for improvement in this direction, and therefore proposed to tell the Marshal at the end of May 1944 that the Allies would be prepared to abolish the armistice regime and conclude a preliminary peace treaty as soon as they were satisfied that the military position permitted this and that the Italian Government had sufficient authority to speak on behalf of the whole Italian people. This preliminary treaty would make no concessions on ultimate issues to be decided at the peace conference when the war was over, nor would Allied rights under the armistice be surrendered. But enemy status would be abolished and Italy would become, if not an ally, at any rate an 'associated power'. Improvements in the economic situation of Italy were also envisaged, particularly an increase in the supply of imported consumer-goods, in the hope of strengthening moderate elements in the country, and so removing one cause of the dangerous drift towards Communism. It was also proposed to examine what concessions could be made in regard to the repatriation of Italian prisoners of war. Instructions were therefore given to Lord Halifax to consult the State Department on these proposals; but, by some departmental oversight, before the War Office had been consulted. The policy described above received full support from the Resident Minister at A.F.H.Q., Mr Macmillan. He reported at the beginning of June that both General Wilson and General Alexander would be prepared to see negotiations for such a preliminary peace started immediately. The Foreign Office, however, took the view, also shared by the War Office, that this was far too early, since the Allies only held one-third of Italy. The reception of the idea by the State Department was cautious rather than enthusiastic, and the matter was let drop—only to be revived at a later stage, as will be related below, by the State Department itself.

Meanwhile, the notion that some concessions to the Italian Government, in both the economic and the political sphere, were appropriate was not lost sight of. During his visit to Italy in the summer Mr Churchill discussed this question with Mr Macmillan and Sir Noel Charles at a meeting held in Rome on 22nd August. The conclusions there reached were summarised as follows. Without infringement of the existing powers of the Supreme Allied Commander, Italy should be regarded as a friendly co-belligerent and no longer an enemy state; she should be relieved from the applications to her of the Trading with the Enemy Act, and thus be permitted to revive her foreign trade. If possible, she should enjoy the benefits of U.N.R.R.A. The Allies should be guided by the principle that an increasing measure of responsibility should be gradually handed over to the Italian administration in the forms subsequently embodied in the Hyde Park declaration. The possible combination in Mr Macmillan of the two offices of Resident Minister and head of the Commission was also envisaged.

Italian affairs were discussed with Mr Roosevelt by Mr Churchill at the second Quebec Conference ('Quadrant') and also at the President's home, Hyde Park, in New York State. The results of these conversations were embodied in a joint statement, generally known as the Hyde Park Declaration, by the heads of the two Allied Governments, which was published on 26th September.[1] The announcement began by stating that the Italian people, freed from Fascist and Nazi domination, had in the past twelve months demonstrated their will to be free, to fight on the side of the democracies, and to take a place among the United Nations devoted to the principles of peace and justice. Notwithstanding the horror felt by the British and American peoples at the recent mob action in Rome, which had resulted in the lynching of Carreta, both the President and the Prime Minister felt they should give encouragement to those Italians who were standing for a political rebirth in Italy, and should afford the Italian people a greater opportunity to aid in the defeat of their common enemies, by placing a greater responsibility on the Italian people and its Government. An increasing measure of control would therefore be gradually handed over to the Italian administration—provided that it proved that it could maintain law and order and administer justice regularly. To mark this change, the name of the Allied Control Commission would be altered by dropping the word 'control' from its title, and the British High Commissioner in Italy, Sir Noel Charles, would assume the title of Ambassador—a title already conferred on the American representative on the Advisory Council, Mr Kirk. The Italian Government would also be invited to appoint direct representatives to Washington and London. Several important measures to improve economic conditions in Italy were also envisaged in the declaration. First and foremost, to relieve hunger, sickness and fear U.N.R.R.A. would send medical aid and other essential supplies. At the same time, first steps would be taken towards the reconstruction of the Italian economy—primarily with a military aim, in order to employ Italian resources to the fullest extent in the struggle against Germany and Japan. (With the latter country Italy was not yet at war; indeed war was not declared by Italy on Japan till after the conclusion of hostilities in Europe.) For military reasons the Allies would assist the Italians in restoring such portions of their electric power systems, their railways and motor transport 'as enter into the war situation', and would send engineers, technicians

---

[1] The full text is given in the Annexe to this Chapter.

and industrial experts to help in this rehabilitation. The application to Italy of the Trading with the Enemy Acts would be modified, so as to enable business contacts between Italy and the outside world to be resumed for the benefit of the Italian people. Finally, the declaration looked forward to the speedy arrival of the day when the last vestiges of Fascism would have been wiped out, and when free elections could be held throughout the country, so as to enable Italy to earn her proper place in the family of free nations.

The opportunity offered by this joint declaration—inevitably hailed by journalists as the New Deal for Italy—was immediately seized by the Italian Government to indicate the manner in which, in their opinion, it could best be implemented. In a memorandum sent to Commodore Stone, dated 4th October, by the Under-Secretary for Foreign Affairs, the implications of the announced change in the title of the Control Commission were set out with almost brutal frankness. The omission of the word 'control' should, in the opinion of the Italian Government, find its fulfilment in terms of cooperation, on the basis of solutions agreed by discussion between the parties, rather than in terms of guardianship (*tutela*) and authoritative control. The best and perhaps the only method of attaining this collaboration would be to introduce Italian representatives into the Control Commission headquarters, and into the sub-commissions. The Italian representatives would help to give to the activities of the Commission that unity of direction and co-ordinated action 'which at present is apt to be fragmentary, disconnected, and frequently contradictory'.

In the opinion of the Italian Government, all activities or functions exercised by the Commission which were not immediately connected with the war effort and its direct and concrete implementation should be handed back *in toto* to the administration of the Italian Government. Even those concerned with the war effort should be envisaged in a spirit of cooperation rather than coercion. With respect to the condition mentioned in the declaration, that the Italian Government must prove that it was able to maintain order and administer justice, the memorandum pointed out that the Italian Government must be in a position to do this without the obstacles that automatically arise from the superimposition of two governments. Allied intervention, therefore, in respect of law and order and the administration of justice should cease altogether; as well as, for example, in the matter of education.

The functions which should, either *in toto* or in part, be restored to the Italian Government, could be determined by a joint examination of experts specially appointed by the Allies and the Italian Government—an arrangement that would have the advantage of entailing a solution arrived at by free discussion. The same technique should be applied to the question of revising all the agreements concerning the transfer of territory to the Italian administration. In this connection, the Italian Foreign Office would be able to furnish full documentary evidence concerning all the specific Allied interventions and interferences in the various Government departments, which in the opinion of the Italian Government severely hampered the normal functioning of Italian organs of government.

The Allies should proceed immediately to reduce the number of the sub-commissions and of their officers in the provinces, especially those handed back to Italian administration:

> This superabundance of sub-commissions with their offices at the periphery seems to lead not only to an excessive fragmentation of work but also to the artificial creation of separate departments that . . . act independently of each other with grave prejudice to the comprehensive study of the different problems under consideration. It seems therefore necessary that corresponding to the limitation of the Commission's duties there should be a rapid 'demobilisation' (*smobilitazione*) of sub-commissions and offices. Unless this 'demobilisation' takes place rapidly, no doubt can be entertained that all those functions which it should today be decided to abolish would be reborn, thanks to the activity of offices and personnel permitted to survive, through the natural and automatic tendency inherent in all bureaucracies slowly to expand and increase.

This theme was developed in a further letter dated 16th November in which a gradual transformation of the Commission from a military to a civilian body was suggested. As to the sub-commissions, a substantial reduction in their number was advocated, and the elimination of those whose activities had no direct connection with the war effort, e.g. the Education Sub-Commission and the Legal Sub-Commission. This should be coupled with a progressive elimination of 'peripheral' (i.e. Regional and Provincial) offices, whose task was almost exclusively the control which it was intended to abolish. These should be done away with, and the functions of the Commission limited to direct cooperation at the centre on the highest level. The Commission should be concerned only with determining policies. Their execution should be left to the responsibility of the Italian Government, and all interference on the part of the Commission at the executive stage should cease. These interferences stifled the spirit of initiative and the sense of responsibility, 'besides reflecting in the majority of cases methods and habits that do not correspond to those of the Italian people and are therefore doomed to remain unproductive'. The letter also criticised the intervention of the Commission in the matter of appointments, transfers, promotions, etc., of Italian officials. These produced contrary results to those intended from the point of view of technical efficiency, and were politically superfluous as the result of the Government's determined measures of 'epuration.' The upshot of the reforms suggested was that the Commission should thus be transformed into a joint Italian-Allied body largely civilianised, and that the Allied officers attached to various Italian Ministries should be withdrawn. The service sub-commissions should be separated from it and organised as a military mission.

The proposals put forward in these two documents clearly went a long way beyond the policy contemplated in the Hyde Park Declaration. That declaration was so general in its terms that its detailed interpretation left considerable room for differences of opinion, and its embodiment in an agreed directive from the Combined Chiefs of Staff took a very long time—just over five months—to work out. In the meantime, as may well be imagined, the central direction of the Commission was seriously hampered by the absence of any clear delineation of policy. This confused situation was to some extent exploited by the Italian Government, which, for example, asserted its independence by abolishing the bread subsidy and increasing wages, against the advice of the Finance Sub-Commission.[1] It also illustrated clearly the dilemma constantly facing the Control Commission in Italian Government territory concerning the action to be taken, if the Italian Government should refuse to carry out the Commission's instructions or advice. Ultimately the only sanction that could be imposed would be to reinstate military government over the entire area of liberated Italy—a step which, for military as well as political reasons, could not have been contemplated, except in the case of the most deliberate obstruction of the Allied war effort.

Meanwhile discussions of the detailed arrangements flashed to and fro between London and Washington for month after month; there were, however, certain features of the new policy which could be implemented immediately. The title of the Commission was officially changed on 27th October, and arrangements were made fairly quickly to effect an exchange of diplomatic representatives between Rome, Washington and London. Even more significant was the announcement on 10th November of a change in the headship of the Commission. With a typical Anglo-Saxon disregard of verbal logic, Mr Harold Macmillan was appointed to the permanent headship of the Commission with the title of Acting President, the Supreme Allied Commander delegating to him his functions as President. His appointment, which made a civilian the effective head of the Commission, was no doubt intended to be interpreted as symbolising some relaxation of military control.

---

[1] See above pp. 216-17.

The exchange of diplomatic representatives between Italy and the United States and the United Kingdom brought out, with rather unfortunate clearness, a divergence of opinion between the two countries in respect of their policy towards Italy. Sir Noel Charles, though given the title of Ambassador, was not formally accredited to the Italian Government, since it was not considered proper to advise the King to accredit an ambassador to the court of a monarch with whom he was still at war. In practice, the difference in status of Sir Noel Charles and Mr Kirk had little significance, since both enjoyed direct relations with the Italian Government; but it was inevitable that this formal distinction should be interpreted as implying some difference in policy. This was accentuated by the fact that, in accordance with the agreement reached at the Pan-American Conference held in Rio de Janeiro in 1942, the Latin-American Governments had been consulted by the State Department about the renewal of diplomatic relations and that they had agreed that Italy should be recognised diplomatically in the conventional manner. Similar action was taken, as was only to be expected, by the Soviet Government, whose appointment of M Kostylev as Ambassador was announced on 28th October.

The appointment of direct representatives of Great Britain and the United States to the Italian Government at once raised the question of their relation to the Allied Commission, which since its inception had been regarded as the sole channel for the conveyance and implementation of Allied policy towards Italy, and had therefore been provided with a Political Section. In the reorganisation of the Commission, finally carried out in the spring of 1945, the Political Section was abolished, but this decision was not formally communicated by the Combined Chiefs of Staff till the end of January. In the meantime some method of distinguishing the matters to be handled through these two channels, diplomatic representatives and Allied Commission, had temporarily to be laid down, at General Wilson's request. He was consequently instructed on 21st November that the two diplomatic representatives would for the time being handle only political questions of 'specific' interest to their respective Governments, while the Commission would continue to deal with economic and administrative matters, as well as with matters arising out of the armistice terms. In cases of doubt the decision as to the proper channels of communication was to be decided by agreement by the men on the spot, Sir Noel Charles, Mr Kirk, and Mr Macmillan.

The renewal of direct diplomatic relations with the Italian Government by other Allied Nations also raised the question of what control or surveillance, if any, should be exercised by the Allied Commission over the negotiations with, and by, the Italian Government. A number of United Nations, for example Holland and Belgium, had already been permitted to establish consular officials in liberated Italy, but their dealings with the Italian Government had been channelled through the Political Section of the Control Commission. Once direct diplomatic relations had been established, it was no longer considered appropriate that the Commission should be interposed as the channel for their communications. All that was required was that the Commission should be kept fully informed of their activities. The United Nations were therefore permitted the normal cypher and bag facilities which had already been conceded to those who were members of the Advisory Council.

With regard to neutral countries, the Combined Chiefs of Staff had insisted that all negotiations between neutral missions and the Italian Government should be conducted officially through the Allied Control Commission, in spite of the fact that General Wilson soon after the liberation of Rome had expressed the opinion that this was neither necessary nor practical. They had, however, been prepared to allow unofficial contacts between neutral diplomatic officials and the Italian Foreign Office. Neutrals were now permitted to establish direct relations with the Italian Foreign Office, provided that the Allied Commission was kept informed of all negotiations undertaken by them. They were not, however, permitted to use cypher or bag facilities—with the exception of the Swiss, who were allowed a diplomatic bag—though representatives of those neutral powers which were represented at the Vatican continued to enjoy both these facilities from the Papal State.[1]

In formulating the measures required to implement the policy of the New Deal the most important part was taken by Mr Macmillan, whose views, as the new effective head of the Commission, naturally carried great weight in Washington no less than in London, and formed the basis of the directive finally issued to the Supreme Commander. The discussions over the draft of this directive in the Combined Civil Affairs Committee were even more than usually prolonged. With the details of these deliberations this volume is not concerned. Suffice it to say that the American members felt that the British proposals did not go far enough in the direction of relaxing Allied control. Their views were based on the fundamental idea that the armistice regime was by now out of date since Italy was co-operating actively in the war. They therefore proposed that the armistice regime should be superseded by a preliminary peace treaty, thus reviving the British proposal made in the spring of 1944. But the British Government at this stage were unwilling to agree to a

[1] Hence the very pertinent remark of Mr Macmillan that the attempt to guard against the leakage of military information in this way was trying to block a channel with a sieve.

step which they themselves had advocated only nine months before as a method of helping Marshal Badoglio. It was increasingly felt, as the end of the war was approaching, that the abolition of the armistice regime would prejudice the two cardinal issues of British policy for the post-war settlement, namely, the disposal of the Italian fleet and the refusal to return the North African colonies to Italian rule.

While no attempt was therefore made to modify the terms of the armistice, considerable progress was effected in mitigating their practical application by important concessions in the political sphere. The Political Section of the Allied Commission was abolished in the 'New Deal' directive received from the Combined Chiefs of Staff on 31st January 1945, which laid down that on political questions the Commission would receive advice from the British and American Ambassadors. It was, however, expressly stated that this did not imply any change in the responsibilities of the Combined Chiefs, who would continue to transmit directives on major policy and other matters falling within the scope of the Allied Commission. Control over Italy's internal arrangements, which had never been accepted by Italian public opinion, was considerably relaxed. The most important provision in this sphere was the abandonment by the Commission of its previous practice of approving all decrees issued by the Italian Government in Italian Government territory. The claim to exercise this control over all the actions of the Government, which the Allied Commission had exerted only imperfectly, was, as Mr Macmillan recognised, difficult to substantiate under the armistice terms, and in practice it had proved extremely difficult to enforce with any strictness. In abandoning it the Commission limited its dealings with respect to Italian Government territory to consultation and advice, but the Italian Government was told that the Commission should be informed of proposed decrees some time before their enactment, to enable the Chief Commissioner to consult with the Italian Government as to their application in A.M.G. territory, where, in his opinion, this was appropriate. The Italian Government was also relieved of the obligation of seeking the Allied Commission's approval for Italian appointments to national and local offices in Italian Government territory.[1]

The directive also laid down the withdrawal, as soon as possible, of all Allied Commission officers from the field in Italian Government territory. The Italian Government was informed by Mr Macmillan

---

[1] This dispensation was not however absolute. The appointments of the Service Ministers, the Under-Secretary for Telecommunications, the Director of Railways, and the chief Police officials, the Director-General of Public Safety, the Commanding-General and the Chief of Staff of the *Carabinieri*, the Commanding-General of the Finance Guards and of certain other commands in the Army, Navy and Air Force, had still to have the approval of the Allied Command before being made effective.

in a memorandum explaining the new directive, dated 24th February, that the regional offices for Sicily, Sardinia, the Southern Region and the Lazio–Umbria Region would be abolished. Allied Military Government was however continued in Naples commune. The right of the Allied Commission to send its officers into Italian Government territory 'when necessary' was also reserved, and it was arranged that certain specialist officers with economic functions would remain in Italian Government territory 'for a limited period'.

In order to emphasise the distinction under the New Deal between Allied Military Government and Italian Government territory, the directive laid down that officers of the Commission dealing with A.M.G. functions should, as far as was possible, be stationed away from the Allied Commission's headquarters. This segregation did not in fact prove practicable, because of the impossibility of separating the A.M.G. activities of the Commission from the remainder. With the same end in view the directive laid down that headquarter sections and sub-commissions (except the Service sub-commissions), should be progressively civilianised, to the full extent that circumstances permitted, except in so far as they 'exercised functions with respect to territories under Allied Military Government'. This exception, if literally interpreted, would in fact have prevented civilianisation altogether, since there was no sub-commission whose functions did not extend to Military Government territory.

In addition to the demobilisation of the regional offices in Italian Government territory, which had been epigrammatically recommended by Mr Macmillan on the grounds that 'at present these officers are insufficient to govern but sufficient to interfere', the directive emphasized a change in the function of Allied Commission headquarters, whose staff should 'occupy itself primarily with the consultation and advice to the Italian Government at high levels'. The directive also went a good way to meet some of the objections raised by the Italian Government to the activities of certain sub-commissions. Those of Education, Fine Arts and Monuments, Local Government, Legal, and Labour, were expressly limited. Not only were they restricted to an advisory function, but it was also laid down that advice in respect of Italian Government territory should only be given when requested by the Italian Government. Since the work of these sub-commissions was henceforward to be primarily concerned only with A.M.G. territory, their headquarters, according to the terms of the directive, should have been transferred from Rome to some place in A.M.G. territory, but this was not practical, since all of them were occupied with matters necessitating very frequent consultation with the Italian Government departments. The historian may perhaps be permitted to note the insistence in this directive on prescribing details of administrative procedure, without sufficient knowledge of the conditions in the field.

One more important concession was made to the Italian Government under the New Deal, though this was scarcely as far-reaching as Italian public opinion demanded. The status of Italian prisoners of war in Italy was to be terminated—under certain conditions. But there was no question of releasing Italian prisoners of war in other countries, Egypt, the Middle East, India, Great Britain and the United States, whose contribution to the war effort in various forms of labour was too valuable to be dispensed with. Mr Macmillan was impressed by the desirability of removing the stigma of the prisoner of war status, and opinion at A.F.H.Q. seems gradually to have crystallised in favour of this course.[1] The Combined Chiefs of Staff finally agreed that Italian prisoners of war in Italy should be released from this status, provided that their services were made available on terms satisfactory to the Supreme Allied Commander. But to arrive at agreement on these terms took a great deal of negotiation, and it was not until after hostilities had ended that they were finally released from their somewhat ambiguous position.

The first step in the re-establishment of democratic institutions was also included in the New Deal policy. The two Allied Governments agreed that, in accordance with the Moscow three-power declaration, it would be desirable to encourage the early holding of local government elections in Italian Government territory. Further, in order to counteract as soon as possible the effects of twenty years Fascist segregation from the intellectual production of the free world, the Italian Government was informed that it was the desire of the Allies to encourage free trade in knowledge and learning with the Italian people. The Allied Commission was therefore instructed to facilitate arrangements for the flow of books and other publications of a scientific, political, philosophical and artistic nature and for the movement of scholars, artists and professional men between Italy and the United Nations, so far as the exigencies of the military situation permitted.

While the New Deal policy only went part of the way to fulfil the aspirations of the more politically-minded sections of the Italian people, on the economic side, which deeply interested everybody, it held out a definite promise—it was not much more than that until hostilities in Europe were ended—of better things to come. It also brought with it one important improvement, the increase in the daily bread ration in liberated Italy north of the Garigliano from 200 to 300 gms (7 oz. to nearly 11 oz.) per head, for which General Wilson had been pressing for many months. In order to understand the

[1] In November the Prisoners of War sub-committee of the Supreme Allied Commander's Political Committee reported in favour of this step.

implications of the new proposals, it will be necessary to consider briefly the economic background of the Commission's activities. On the economic side the achievements of Allied military administration had been anything but brilliant, even judged from the purely military standpoint of exploitating Italian economic resources in the interests of the war-effort. This was due to a number of factors, among which perhaps the chief was the failure to recognise from the very beginning that neither indiscriminate seizure nor requisitioning by the advancing troops of transport and any other materials that could be made to serve an immediate convenience, nor the restriction of imports to the minimum quantity of consumer goods—almost entirely food and medical supplies—required to avoid disease and unrest among the civilian population, was in the long run consistent with a policy designed to make the best use of the resources of the country. It was perhaps natural enough that in the very early stages of the campaign, when a rapid advance at any rate to the line of the northern Apennines was expected, this simple conception of military requirements should have at first prevailed. But once it became plain that the advance up the peninsula would be hotly contested and therefore slow, and that military responsibility for the civilian economy of the country would be prolonged, the wider implications should have received clearer definition.

The problems raised for the Allied Commander-in-Chief became clear enough after the occupation of Naples and the halt on the line of the Garigliano. There could no longer be any doubt that he would be responsible for civilian supplies to Italy for an indefinite period, and that the quantity of goods which would have to be imported in the military programme in order to avoid disease and unrest would depend on the quantity of essential commodities which could be produced in liberated Italy. Thus quite apart from any political considerations—whether the Italian people were to be treated as ex-enemies or not quite friends—a much more comprehensive policy with regard to the Italian economy was required than one which confined itself merely to the importation of the minimum quantity of 'relief goods'. This fact was quickly appreciated at A.F.H.Q., as well as in Washington and London—more clearly perhaps than in the headquarters of the Allied Control Commission, whose economic planning appears to have been singularly defective and whose attention was at this period so largely occupied, as we have already seen, by political questions.

The chief cause of the weakness of the Allied Commission in the economic sphere was the absence of permanent leadership at the top. The first Vice-President of the Economic Section—a post allotted to an American Civilian, Mr Henry Grady—was appointed comparatively late, on 7th February 1944. Mr Grady only remained in the field for a short time, after which he went back to report to Washington, to return merely to hand over to his successor. Nor was his successor, Brig.-General O'Dwyer, any more successful. General O'Dwyer's occupation of the post was never intended to be permanent, and his gifts, energies and experience were not well suited to the particular type of economic planning which was required. He arrived in August 1944, and only stayed in Italy about six weeks. He then went back to Washington, with the expressed intent of 'hurrying things along' there. He never returned to resume his post, which in fact was not filled by a permanent appointment until March 1945. Thus the headship of this important section of the Commission was for most of the time filled by a *locum tenens* with all the disadvantages of mere acting rank. Moreover Mr Antolini, like General O'Dwyer, had no working knowledge of the combined economic arrangements and their planning in Washington and London—an acquaintance with which would appear essential for the leadership of the Economic Section. It was not altogether surprising therefore that its sub-commissions tended at times to pursue independent policies imperfectly coordinated with each other, that no clear policy for the Italian economy was ever evolved, and that a great deal of its work had to be revised in detail by G-5 at A.F.H.Q., involving long delays and often erroneous decisions.

The failure of the Control Commission to institute any programme for the systematic rehabilitation of the Italian economy with a view to producing the greatest contribution to the Allied war effort had been remarked in London and in Washington some time before the liberation of Rome. Neither the Combined Supply authorities nor the Combined Civil Affairs Committee appear to have been convinced that adequate measures were being taken to ensure that Italian production was being organised to produce the maximum output of essential commodities. The matter was finally brought to a head at the end of July 1944 in an unofficial letter addressed by General Hilldring, the head of the Civil Affairs Division of the American War Department, to General Spofford, in which he complained of the inability or unwillingness of the Control Commission to 'get into the business of making Italy self sustaining'.

This criticism was perhaps not altogether fair to the Control Commission, since it failed to take full account of the particular conditions under which its economic activities were being carried out. Three of these were particularly relevant. In the first place, the industrial potentialities of liberated Italy never came fully under the control of the Commission. Control of Italian economic resources lay in the last resort with the Commander-in-Chief of Allied Armies in Italy, since the military authorities were responsible for controlling the amount of fuel, both domestic and imported, allotted to civilian purposes, as well as the distribution of electricity, on which nine-tenths of industry in the south depended.[1] Next, the uncontrolled and often wasteful exploitation by troops of factory space and machinery left the Commission with very few resources, and those unpredictable; since it was never known beforehand how long a plant might be occupied by the military and how much of its essential machinery would either be removed or destroyed. Finally, such planning as could be done was rendered extremely difficult by the lack of communications and, until the capture of Rome, by the absence of Italian staff with the necessary knowledge and qualifications.

With the occupation of Rome and Tuscany the industrial resources of liberated Italy were considerably increased, though German destruction of the sources of power for many months prevented this increase from bearing any effective fruit. The acquisition of the records of the central government departments enabled planning of a rather more methodical nature to be undertaken, but the limiting factor of Allied military exploitation of Italian resources often rendered these plans more academic than practical. On the initiative of G-5 at A.F.H.Q., the Control Commission was asked to submit an integrated programme of industrial first-aid, indicating for each industry capable of contributing to the production of essential consumer-goods the supplies necessary to rehabilitate plants which could be put into operation without extensive reconstruction. The programme was to include the supplies required and the approximate production envisaged, and an estimate of its effect in reducing imports of food, clothing and medical supplies. This programme was still formally conceived within the framework of the 'disease and unrest' formula, but in drawing it up emphasis was placed by the Commission more on the necessity for an increase in the importation of consumption goods than on the reactivation of internal production. It had not yet been completed when President Roosevelt and Mr Churchill issued the Hyde Park Declaration.

Meanwhile General Wilson, after the liberation of the capital, had been impressed with the inadequacy of the abstract formula, 'prevention of disease and unrest', as a suitable guide for dealing with those areas of liberated Italy which were now outside the operational area. In a message to the Combined Chiefs of Staff, just before the middle of September, he called for a redefinition of Allied economic policy:

> As the battle line in Italy moves north and the operational phase in large portions of occupied territory is terminated I feel

---

[1] Their inability to allot power supplies, for example, to the nitrate factory at Crotone prevented the production of fertilisers indispensable for the increase of agricultural production.

> that the approach to problems of civilian supply and economic rehabilitation must be re-examined.
>
> . . . The Armistice Agreement under which the Allied Control Commission operates contains no commitments to the Italian people as to any measures of material assistance. However, there has arisen in Italy the expectation if not the assumption . . . that an additional measure of assistance and relief to the civil population would be forthcoming. Public utterances in both countries have tended to support this view.[1] Moreover, if the two Governments continue at this stage to consider only what is required in the interests of the war effort, they may lose the opportunity of insuring one of their long term interests, the establishment of a reasonably prosperous and contented Italy after the war.

In asking for new economic directives, General Wilson expressly mentioned the problem of inflation in such a way as to hint plainly enough that in his opinion the only way to counter it effectively was to increase the import of consumer goods. He had already defended the increase of the bread ration south of the Garigliano to 300 gms as the sole method in his power to counter the black market. He now wrote to the C.C.S. requesting authority to introduce the 300 gm ration throughout liberated Italy, even though this might entail, for the whole of Italy during the harvest year 1944–5, imports of no less than 1½ million tons, a million tons more than would be required by a 200 gm ration. The reasons given for this request were an interesting combination of economic and political considerations, namely, (a) the difficulty of approaching by any other means to the target figure of a daily intake of 2,000 calories fixed for liberated territories, owing to the low calorific value of available local resources, (b) the anti-inflationary argument already mentioned, (c) the under-nourishment of the population—a cumulative result of war years, (d) the fact that the armed forces were benefiting from local food-stuffs and forage at the annual rate of some 300,000 tons a year[2], and (e) the statement, made in some quarters though not endorsed by the Supreme Allied Commander, that conditions were now worse than under the German occupation.

It was not perhaps unnatural that, with an election in prospect, opinion in certain government circles in Washington had begun to think in terms of industrial rehabilitation for Italy in a way which appeared, to British eyes, to neglect the competitive claims of Allied nations who had been the victims of Italian aggression. Moreover, the whole question of civilian supplies for Italy became involved in an American departmental issue concerning their financing. The

---

[1] To say nothing of Allied radio propaganda which, ever since the invasion of Sicily, had been all too lavish in its promises.

[2] Almost entirely wine and surplus vegetables, see below, Appendix III.

War Department had, even before the occupation of Rome, been considering plans to divest itself of responsibility for civilian supplies in Sicily, Sardinia and southern Italy, on the ground that, since those portions of liberated territory were outside the area of military operations, the devotion of War Department appropriations to this object would be inconsistent with undertakings given to Congress. Since it was not considered practical, in the circumstances, to approach Congress for a specific appropriation for this object, the ingenious idea was conceived to try to make Italy financially self-supporting by crediting her with (1) the dollar equivalent of net troop pay—i.e. such part of the pay issued to American troops as was not remitted back to the United States or spent in canteens or in the purchase of American War bonds; (2) the proceeds of her exports to the United States; (3) the remittances of Americans to their relatives in Italy; and (4) the net earnings of the Italian merchant navy. The British Government was expected to follow suit.

This plan, which does not even appear to have been really carefully worked out, had no attractions for the British Government. In the first place, it was felt that there was no justification for releasing Italy from the costs of occupation at this stage, whatever remission of Italian indebtedness might later be made under the Peace Treaty. Secondly, it looked as if such an arrangement would result in Britain, which was taking practically the whole of Italian exports, actually accumulating a sterling debt to her ex-enemy. Thirdly, the implications of this arrangement, which had been first applied by both Allied Governments in North Africa, *vis à vis* the Free French Government, and was now the normal policy in other liberated Allied countries, were not such as to please the other European Allies. And, when the figures were looked into more carefully, it became quite clear that the sums credited to Italy in respect of troop-pay would not nearly meet the bill which the United States were paying for civilian supplies, even when added to the other credit items mentioned.[1] There was thus no hope of this ingenious device relieving the War Department of the responsibility of paying its share in the joint programme of civilian supplies for Italy, about three-quarters of which the United States had agreed to shoulder. Moreover, after investigation by a joint mission at A.F.H.Q., it was made plain to the American—no less than to the British—War Department, that it would be neither practicable nor desirable to have two different authorities responsible for the civilian supply programme of different portions of liberated Italy. It was therefore decided that the War

---

[1] The proceeds of U.S. net troop pay amounted only to $160 millions, whereas the total American share of the imports under the Allied Military Programme, July, 1943 to September, 1945, amounted to over $360 millions. See below, Appendix II.

Department should continue to finance the American share of the joint military programme.

It is against this background that the phraseology of the Hyde Park Declaration and its implementation in the economic policy of the 'New Deal' must be interpreted. The Hyde Park Declaration promised three things, more food, more transport, and industrial rehabilitation. The latter meant, besides more raw materials, more fuel and more materials for repairing war-damaged plant. Its implementation raised many problems for the Allied combined authorities, at a stage in the war when resources were narrowing and obligations increasing. How much could be allotted to Italy in view of the requirements of Allied nations now being liberated? And how, and by whom, were these increased supplies to be paid for? The first of these problems encountered, as we shall see, a large number of difficulties, but net-troop-pay dollar credits appeared to provide the answer to the second, so far as the United States Government was concerned.

On 4th October the President made a public statement in which he announced that steps were being taken 'to increase the bread ration in those areas in Italy where food supplies are below the standard necessary to maintain full health and efficiency' and that, to ensure the distribution of essential supplies, plans were being made to send 1,700 additional trucks to Italy—an announcement which appeared to promise in no doubtful terms the increase of the bread ration north of the Garigliano to 300 gms a day. On 10th October he announced that the United States would make available to the Italian Government the dollar equivalent of all lire issued as (net) pay to American troops in Italy. In addition, the dollar proceeds from Italian exports to America and remittances of private persons from the United States to Italy would be made available to pay for essential civilian supplies from the United States. It was explained to the Italian Government that the dollars so made available could be used for the procurement of such essential supplies as were not provided by the military programme of essential imports, and that a programme for the purchase of these supplies could be drawn up by the Italian Government, subject to the approval of the Allied Commission and of the Allied agencies concerned with the allocation of requirements in short supply and of transportation and port facilities. In these circumstances the British Government could scarcely refuse to bear a part, albeit a small one, in this supplementary programme; its contribution was limited to the proceeds of Italian exports to the United Kingdom. The unilateral gesture of American generosity with regard to net troop pay could hardly fail to strike Italian public opinion as confirming the contrast between American magnanimity and British austerity, even though, in explaining the policy to the

Italian Government, the United States Government, in order to go some way to meet British susceptibilities, had made it plain that the provision of these credits did not imply any surrender of American claims under the Peace Treaty.

Meanwhile for many weeks to come General Wilson had to wait for his directive on the economics of the New Deal. After the President's two announcements in October, the main implications of that policy became clear enough to permit planning based on certain assumptions to begin at A.F.H.Q. and the headquarters of the Allied Commission, under the leadership of Mr Macmillan. It was by this time fairly obvious that, however long the process of working it out in detail might take, the new policy would contain three essential features: a more liberal interpretation of the 'disease and unrest' formula to include *inter alia* the 300 gm bread ration, a first-aid policy of industrial rehabilitation, and a special relief programme to be administered by U.N.R.R.A. But at this stage of the war the implementation of such a policy was brought up sharp against an almost unsurmountable obstacle in the world shortage of shipping, which for many months delayed the implementation even of the first feature. The Combined Chiefs of Staff refused to allocate the extra shipping required to ensure the maintenance of the 300 gm ration, in spite of the publication of a letter from the President dated 31st October to the Secretary of War stating that he had 'determined to assume the responsibility of asking General Wilson to increase the ration to 300 gms'. The reproduction of this letter in the Italian press had naturally rendered Italians north of the Garigliano more impatient than ever. It was now plain to General Wilson that only an immediate increase would avoid unrest among the civilian population. But still the Combined Chiefs of Staff held out.

General Wilson, in a message of 19th October, had stated point blank that from the military standpoint the tranquillity of the Mediterranean theatre might be jeopardised if the 300 gm bread ration were not sanctioned, and had offered the C.C.S. a choice between two alternatives, namely, either to step up shipments to the level of 115,000 tons per month, or to use the existing stocks in the theatre, on condition that stocks so used would be replaced in full. On 30th November he pointed out that the situation in central Italy, particularly in Rome, Florence and Pisa, was deteriorating, and that the Chief Commissioner of A.C. had advised him that he could not much longer hold the population in line under the existing 200 gm ration and the shortage of other foods. In view of the widespread publicity given to the President's statement on the 300 gm ration he felt it to be imperative that he should be in a position to make an announcement on or before 1st December. The 1st December went by, and still no answer came.

Before the end of the year Field-Marshal Alexander, who had succeeded General Wilson as Supreme Allied Commander, returned to the charge. North of the Garigliano the combination of undernourishment and winter operational conditions was causing great distress and resentment, which had already led to disorders. His Army Commanders had again made forcible representations on the matter, and the necessity for preventing militarily serious disorders near and in the combat zone was patent. Meanwhile not only was the amount of wheat being shipped quite inadequate to fulfil President Roosevelt's promises, but cuts had recently been imposed in the form of a reduction of the shipments expected in January from 95,000 to 77,000 tons, which made it impossible for him to plan consistently for any uniform ration. He was prepared, if the C.C.S. found it impossible to meet the request for additional wheat without some contribution from, or deferment of, operational maintenance, to undertake to make this at the expense of military requirements, if this was operationally possible:

> It is my duty however to point out to you in terms which allow of no misunderstanding that I cannot administer those parts of Italy under my control in accordance with the policies . . . which are known to the Italians unless I am regularly provided with the means to do so. The alternative is an Italy embittered by unfulfilled promises, by hunger and distress. This, I believe, would be a grave handicap to our immediate war effort and a lamentable example to other nations of the justice of Allied dealing.[1]

In the face of such a protest the C.C.S. could no longer evade a decision. On 18th January 1945 they authorised SACMED to establish within liberated Italy the maximum basic ration he considered practicable, within the approved shipping programme, up to 300 gms. In deciding upon this maximum basis 'you should take into account the greatest contribution operationally possible from your military requirements'. This reply did not in fact enable Field Marshal Alexander to act immediately. On 26th January his stock position and advices of shipments for January still made it impracticable to order the increased ration at an early date. The actual arrivals of wheat in November, December and January had only averaged 70,000 tons instead of 100,000 tons. But February arrivals made up this deficit and the increased ration was made effective from 1st March.

---

[1] In view of these facts it is a little difficult to understand the statement made by Mr Stettinius in his account of discussions in Italy just before the Yalta Conference that SACMED was opposed to an increase in the Italian food ration—see Stettinius *Roosevelt and the Russians, the Yalta Conference*, p. 57–58, where he explains this opposition by an allusion to the British 'sensitiveness' to the shortage of shipping.

Nor was the implementation of the U.N.R.R.A. programme any easier. This was to consist of medical and sanitary supplies, of supplies for displaced persons, and of food for children and nursing mothers. It called for a monthly import of about 15,000 tons of dried milk, sugar, fats, flour and fish, etc., to be distributed by Italian Government agencies. U.N.R.R.A. had wished to begin operations in Italy in November, on supplies borrowed from the Allied Commission, but the Commission, desperately short itself, was unable to lend them. Hence a request was made by A.F.H.Q. for additional shipping for 5,000 tons in January which the Combined Chiefs refused to grant. Action was consequently taken by Governor Lehman, Director-General of U.N.R.R.A., at the highest level, and it was only by a personal appeal to the President and Mr Churchill that the small quantity of shipping required to enable him to start work in Italy was obtained. U.N.R.R.A. was by these means enabled to commence operations in the Naples area in the first quarter of 1945.

The implementation of the policy of industrial rehabilitation was not destined even to begin until after hostilities in Europe were over. After months of complicated negotiations, the new policy was at length defined and embodied in the 'New Deal' directive of 31 January 1945. This divided the programme of Italian imports into two categories, a military programme, for which the War department of both countries remained responsible, and a programme of industrial rehabilitation to be financed out of the reimbursement of net American troop pay, etc., and the proceeds of Italian exports to the United Kingdom.

The military programme was to continue to be based on the classical 'disease and unrest' formula, but, as Mr Macmillan insisted, the interpretation given to that formula was to be on rather more liberal lines, so as to include the extension to the whole of liberated Italy of the 300 gm bread ration. It was also to include, besides food, fuel, clothing, medical, sanitary and other agreed essential supplies, further categories of imports—namely (a) supplies such as fertilizers, raw materials, machinery and equipment, the importation of which, by enabling Italian domestic production to be increased, would reduce demands for the import of essential supplies required to prevent disease and unrest, and (b) supplies necessary for the restoration of such of the Italian power systems and transportation facilities as would further the military effort against Germany and Japan.

The industrial rehabilitation programme, which was to be drawn up by the Italian Government with the assistance of the Allied Commission, was not, like the military programme, to be subject to screening by Allied Force Headquarters, but was to be forwarded directly by the Commission, with its recommendations, to the Combined Civil Affairs Committee, for action by the appropriate civilian agencies of the United States and British Governments. The order of priority for industrial rehabilitation was to be determined by the Italian Government, except that industries for the production of munitions and other implements of war were to be rehabilitated only to the extent required by the Supreme Allied Commander or where it was decided by the Allies that this would further the military effort in other theatres. In respect of this industrial rehabilitation programme no commitments were to be undertaken as regards shipping.

In the meantime, pending the arrival of the 'New Deal' directive, the Allied Commission on 3rd November had requested the Italian Government to prepare a complete programme of essential imports other than food and medical supplies. This task had been undertaken by the Inter-Ministerial Committee for Reconstruction with the Assistance of the Allied Commission's Economic Section. It had been drawn up, without any anticipation of subsequent division into two categories, on the assumption that its portions formed an organic whole. But it had been compiled in haste, and had therefore to undergo considerable revision, quite apart from the separation of the military import programme from the supplementary programme. It was based on the following fundamental assumptions: (1) that imports of food, estimated at about one and a half million tons a year, would be sufficient to maintain a basic daily ration yielding 2,000 calories per head—a figure which, of course, implied the extension to the whole of Italy of the 300 gm (11 oz.) bread-ration, and that sufficient fertilizers and essential agricultural equipment would also be imported to ensure a maximum production of domestic food; (2) that a certain quantity of essential consumer goods, such as medical supplies, paper, shoes, clothing, household linen and blankets would be made available for the civilian population, and that the raw materials required to produce these, supplemented where necessary by finished products, would be imported; (3) that sufficient trucks, locomotives, wagons, etc., would be imported to place the Italian transportation system in a position to distribute the minimum rations of food and essential consumer goods, as well as the materials necessary for domestic production; (4) that the fuel and power required would be made available, in the form of domestically-produced and imported coal, petrol, oil and lubricants, and that sufficient materials for the Italian electric power systems would be imported to keep the power plants of the south running at half capacity, and those of central Italy, the output of which had been reduced by German sabotage to less than three per cent, at thirty-six per cent of their normal capacity.

The arrival of the 'New Deal' directive entailed a hasty splitting up of this unitary programme of requirements into two sections,

Category A items, to be included in the programme of military imports, with priority over Category B items, to be included in a supplementary programme of industrial rehabilitation. The division of the programme into these two categories proposed by the Allied Commission in the middle of March was drastically revised when the Category A items were submitted to A.F.H.Q. for screening by a committee composed of representatives of G-5 and the technical services, which eliminated many items by transferring them to Category B. Items for the rehabilitation of highway construction, tramways and private railways, and the whole programme of rehabilitating electric power systems were placed in Category B, as well as those required for rehabilitating the iron and steel, the pharmaceutical and certain other industries. Large portions of the transportation programme, which had been placed by the Allied Commission in Category A, were also transferred to Category B. The transportation items retained in the military programme, though greatly reduced, were still considerable. Tyres and spare parts formed a large part of these, sufficient quantities being included to get back into operation 23,000 vehicles and to maintain in operation 31,000 vehicles still running. New vehicles in considerable quantities were also included. The agricultural programme was also very substantially reduced by eliminating 300 Diesel motors for new fishing vessels—motors for the rehabilitation of existing vessels were included—and 300 pumps for draining land-reclamation areas in northern Italy, but a large amount of agricultural machinery, including over 2,000 tractors, was permitted to remain in Category A.

In its revised form the military import programme, though still bound by the classical 'disease and unrest' formula, contained a large number of items which would probably not have been included but for the New Deal policy. In addition to the increased food programme, the allowance for essential consumer goods was also proportionately larger, since with practically no domestic replacements possible hitherto, the need for the import of essential consumer goods had become incontestable, especially in the matter of clothing and footwear. In the matter of clothing, it was considered that the Italian textile industry south of the Apennines could not contribute much. The greater portion of the imports therefore had to take the form either of piece-goods or of finished articles. Clothing requirements had by this time been substantially increased by the needs of Italian refugees, who amounted in all to nearly two per cent of the population of liberated Italy. With the details of this military programme we need not concern ourselves any further. It was not until the end of April that the revised return of Category A items was transmitted to Washington, and, before work could be started on its implementation, hostilities in Europe were over. A table showing the items of commodities imported into Italy under the military programme will be found in Appendix II.

The 'New Deal' also envisaged, in a somewhat distant fashion owing to the shipping shortage, some resumption of Italy's foreign trade. The Italian Government was informed that the extent to which exports were to be stimulated and the development of the machinery to handle them were matters on which it was entitled to develop its own policy—subject to the limits imposed by 'certain shipping, military, financial and supply factors'. But the implementation of this policy was delayed pending the conclusion of negotiations by which the Italian Government was induced to accept the observance of the Allied 'black' lists. It was not until hostilities were over that Italian trade with neutral countries was permitted to develop. Finally, the 'New Deal' also implied proposals for giving the Italian Government greater responsibility in financial matters, but the negotiations for effecting this were not concluded until some time after hostilities in Europe were ended.

ANNEXE

The Hyde Park Declaration

The Italian people, freed of their Fascist and Nazi overlordship, have in these last twelve months demonstrated their will to be free, to fight on the side of the democracies, and to take a place among the United Nations devoted to principles of peace and justice.

We believe we should give encouragement to those Italians who are standing for a political re-birth in Italy, and are completing the destruction of its Fascist system. We wish to afford the Italians a greater opportunity to aid in the defeat of our common enemies.

The American and British peoples are of course horrified by the recent mob action in Rome, but feel that a greater responsibility placed on the Italian people and on its Government will most readily prevent a recurrence of such acts.

An increasing measure of control will be gradually handed over to the Italian administration, subject of course to that administration's proving that it can maintain law and order and the regular administration of justice. To mark this change the Allied Control Commission will be renamed 'The Allied Commission'.

The British High Commissioner in Italy will assume the additional title of Ambassador. The United States representative in Rome already holds that rank. The Italian Government will be invited to appoint direct representatives to Washington and London.

First and immediate considerations in Italy are the relief of hunger and sickness and fear. To this end we instructed our representatives at the United Nations' Relief and Rehabilitation Administration conference to declare for the sending of medical aids and other essential supplies to Italy. We are happy to know that this view commended itself to the other members of the Council.

At the same time first steps should be taken toward the reconstruction of an Italian economy—an economy laid low under the years of misrule of Mussolini, and supplies ravished by the German policy of vengeful destruction.

These steps should be taken primarily as military aims to put the full resources of Italy and the Italian people into the struggle to defeat Germany and Japan. For military reasons we should assist Italians in restoration of such power systems, their railways, motor transport, roads and other communications as enter into the war situation, and for a short time send engineers, technicians and industrial experts into Italy to help them in their own rehabilitation.

The application to Italy of the Trading with Enemy Acts should be modified so as to enable business contacts between Italy and the outside world to be resumed for the benefit of the Italian people.

We all wish to speed the day when the last vestiges of Fascism in Italy will have been wiped out, when the last German will have left Italian soil, and when there will be no need of any Allied troops to remain—the day when free elections can be held throughout Italy, and when Italy can earn her proper place in the great family of free nations.

CHAPTER IX

RE-ORGANISATION

THE RE-ORGANISATION of the Allied Commission entailed in the 'New Deal' was only the logical development of a process which had already been foreseen when the Control Commission was planned. It had originally been assumed that, as territories in rear of the Armies were handed back to the Italian Government, regional organisations would eventually be withdrawn leaving only a liaison officer in each prefecture.[1] But practice had lingered behind theory. Regional organisations in Italian Government territory were still firmly entrenched by the time that the New Deal directive arrived at the end of January 1945, even if the process of thinning them out had already begun.

Under the stress of the large increase in liberated territory, which occurred between May and September, a considerable thinning out of regional staffs in Sicily and Sardinia and the south of the peninsula had already taken place. The number of the Commission's officers in Sicily, which amounted to 180 at the time when Military Government in the island came to an end in February, had been reduced to fifty by the end of July and to about thirty-five by the end of October. A considerable saving in personnel had also been effected by the amalgamation, at the end of August, of Regions II, VII, (Calabria) and III into the Southern Region, which included the Allied Military Government of the Commune of Naples, and embraced the whole of the peninsula south of the northern boundaries of the provinces of Naples and Campobasso. The total staff of this consolidated Region appears to have been at the end of 1944 in the neighbourhood of 130 officers, of which the Commune of Naples accounted for about a third. The Lazio–Umbria Region, which by this time consisted almost entirely of Italian Government territory, had at the beginning of November an official strength of just over a hundred officers, and the Abruzzi–Marche Region, of which about half was by this time Italian Government territory, had an official strength of eighty-seven officers. The only Region in which a really drastic reduction of staff had taken place was Sardinia, which had never been under military government. Here the total

---

[1] See above, p. 75, 95.

strength had been reduced to thirteen officers, including mining specialists detached from the Coal Section of A.F.H.Q.[1]

In preparation for a possible advance into the Po Valley the establishments of the northern Regions had already been brought into action and assignments to them had already been made.[2] In the meantime, pending the actual advance north of the Apennines these large staffs—such as were not required for planning purposes—were not kept idle, being employed on temporary duty in the forward Regions. Of these forward Regions two were already in operation, with a large proportion of their staff infiltrated into the Army A.M.G's[3]. At this time the effective establishments of A.M.G. Fifth and Eighth Armies were respectively 71 and 74.

It is interesting to examine the relative importance of the various categories of officers in the field as shown in the November return. Civil Affairs officers in the Army A.M.G's and the Regions (both A.M.G. and Italian Government territory) amounted to just about 400, out of a total of some 1,075 officers. Of specialist officers the largest class was that of Police officers, amounting to about 130, of which over 90 were British. Next in number were the Supply officers, who accounted for about 100, closely followed by the Finance officers who accounted for 85.[4] The importance attached to Allied Military courts is shown by the numbers of Legal officers outside headquarters. These amounted to over 70. Transportation and Engineering and Public Health each contributed rather under 50 officers.

Staff at headquarters amounted to over 400, with a slight preponderance of American over British, thus reversing the proportion in the field, where British officers numbered 625 as compared with 450 Americans. The Transportation Sub-Commission, whose organisation was much criticised by 'Movements' at A.F.H.Q. was very heavily represented at headquarters with over 50 officers. Next in numbers came the Finance Sub-Commission with 34[5], followed by the Displaced Persons and Repatriation Sub-Commission which had just under 30. Compared with these figures the headquarter staffs of the Public Safety and Food Sub-Commissions were quite small—16 in each case—both Public Works (18) and Industry (20), now divorced from Commerce, being rather more heavily represented. Several Sub-Commissions confined their representation at headquarters to quite moderate proportions. Monuments

---

[1] Many of the sub-commissions were not represented in the island at all, their officers, the Regional Engineer among others having been withdrawn.

[2] Those for Liguria Region numbered 64, those for Piedmont 87, those for Lombardy 109 and those for Venetia 113 officers.

[3] Tuscany Region with an establishment of 119 officers and Emilia Region with 123.

[4] This figure does not include 16 Property Control officers who until the autumn of 1944 had formed a separate sub-commission.

[5] Not including four officers of the Property Control Division.

and Fine Arts (5), Education (4), Local Government (6), Agriculture (7), Commerce (9), Labour (9) and Legal (9) all had headquarters staffs numbering less than 10 officers.[1]

The exact application of the rule of parity in numbers between British and American appointments to the senior positions had not proved practicable. The post of Deputy-Chief Commissioner was not filled by a British appointment when Captain Stone became acting Chief Commissioner, but Brigadier Lush as Chief of Staff and Executive Commissioner was in practice the equivalent of a second-in-command. Of the Civil Affairs (Administrative) and the Economic Sections, the head of the former was British, Brigadier Upjohn, who had replaced Air-Commodore Lord Stansgate, while that of the latter was American—whenever this post was actually filled. Mr Grady had been succeeded after a comparatively short stay in Italy by Brig.-General O'Dwyer who arrived in July 1944 and returned to the United States in the autumn. It was not until March 1945 that his successor was appointed, and then only with acting rank, in the person of Mr Antolini, who had been Executive Director of the Section.[2] For many months before his appointment Mr Antolini was in fact acting head. He was assisted by Brig.-General MacKinley, who was appointed deputy Vice-President on 13th March 1945, but it was not until 20th April that General MacKinley was provided with a British colleague in the person of Brigadier Anderson.

The sub-commissions were fairly equally divided between the two nationalities. In the Civil Affairs Section the heads of the Legal, Education, Monuments and Fine Arts and Public Safety Sub-Commissions were American, those of the Displaced Persons, Local Government, and Public Health Sub-Commissions, British. In the Economic Section the heads of the Agriculture, Industry, Public Works and Transportation Sub-Commissions were American, those of Commerce, Food and Labour, British. The Finance Sub-Commission, which had absorbed the Property Control Sub-Commission, the head of which was originally British, was headed jointly by two Directors, one British and one American.[3]

Some changes had also been made in the Control Commission's organisations after General Mason-MacFarlane's reforms described in Chapter IV. After the transfer of Allied Force Headquarters from

---

[1] The figures quoted in the foregoing paragraphs do not, of course, include the Service Sub-Commissions.

[2] See above, Chapter VII.

[3] An interesting footnote is provided by the history of Russian representation, which (see above, p. 116) was initiated in quite a modest form. At the end of the summer of 1944 the Soviet Government increased the numbers of their representatives on the Commission, without any previous consultation, by appointing Major-General Susloparov, with four staff officers, to be assigned as observers to the various sub-commissions. These were quite separate from the special mission attached to the Displaced Persons Sub-Commission.

Algiers to Caserta in July 1944, the respective areas of command of Allied Armies in Italy and Allied Force Headquarters were redefined as the Operational Zone and Lines of Communications Area. The boundary between them was temporarily fixed on 10th September to follow the northern boundaries of the Provinces of Teramo, Rieti and Viterbo. At the same time the command of the Control Commission itself, which had originally been placed under General Alexander, was transferred to A.F.H.Q. This step was taken in order to relieve Field-Marshal Alexander[1] of the responsibility of day-to-day civil administration in large areas which now lay outside his command. He ceased to be the Military Governor of all occupied Italy—a responsibility which was assumed by SACMED. He was made Deputy Military-Governor of the operational zone with power to act for the Military Governor in all matters.

As a result of the transfer of A.C.C. to the command of A.F.H.Q. it automatically ceased to be the Civil Affairs Branch of Field-Marshal Alexander's command. There was therefore a staff *lacuna* to be filled at his headquarters. This was done by creating a forward echelon of A.C.C. at A.A.I. headquarters. Captain Stone, in his capacity as Chief Civil Affairs Officer, appointed a Deputy with a small staff composed of representatives of the Civil Affairs (formerly Administrative) Section, the Economic Section and the Food and Transport Sub-Commissions, to represent him at A.A.I. headquarters and to supervise the co-ordination of A.M.G. activities under A.A.I. The D.C.C.A.O. was given the title of Assistant Chief of Staff G-5 when A.A.I. in December was re-transformed into Fifteenth Army Group under the command of General Mark Clark.

The internal structure of the Commission was also reorganised at the beginning of October, so as to integrate the chain of command on American staff lines, by focusing it through a single channel under a Chief of Staff. (Under the arrangements made by General Mason-MacFarlane, the joint Vice-Presidents of the Political Section, Mr Reber and Mr Caccia, and the Vice-Presidents in charge of the Administrative and the Economic Sections, Mr Grady and Lord Stansgate, all had direct access to the Chief Commissioner, as well as the heads of the independent sub-commissions). The Regional Control and Military Government Section was transformed into the office of Chief of Staff to the Commission, a post which was occupied by Brigadier Lush, the Executive Commissioner, who was also given the status of Vice-President.

Under the Chief of Staff were organised five Vice-Presidents; the two joint Vice-Presidents of the Political Section, and three deputy Chiefs of Staff, in charge of the other Sections of the Commission,

---

[1] General Alexander was promoted Field-Marshal w.e.f. 4th June 1944.

namely the Civil Affairs Section—which absorbed the Displaced Persons and Refugees Sub-Commission and the Patriots Branch—the Economic Section, and the Establishments Section, from which depended the chain of command to the Regions and the Army A.M.G's. As the result of this 'streamlining' the number of officers at headquarters, which on 19th October still numbered about 420, was slightly reduced.[1]

Contemporaneously with these changes in the organization of the Commission there had been evolving a noticeable change in its manner of functioning. The theoretical transition from military government to 'advisory control' did not in practice deprive the officers of the Commission in Italian Government territory of all executive responsibility. It was still their business to ensure that the conduct of the Italian Government conformed to the requirements of an Allied base of operations, especially in matters of transportation and communications. This meant that in many instances Italian officials, both in Rome and in the provinces, had to be told what to do by officers of the Commission, even if the telling was formally couched in terms of advice. At the centre, the sub-commissions often posted officers to the relevant ministries for this purpose. Moreover certain essentially governmental functions continued for many months to be carried out by the Commission, such as the handling and distribution of imported supplies—food, medical stores, P.O.L. and coal. With regard to food, in particular, the responsibility for its distribution in Italian Government territory could not be handed over *in toto* to the Italian Government even after the liberation of Rome, since the feeding of Italian Government territory depended quite as much on Allied action as on that of the Government. For not only was direct Allied assistance needed and asked for by the Italian Government to secure the proper collection of the harvest, but the bread supply of Rome was dependent on the transfer to the capital in regular quantities of grain collected in A.M.G. territory.[2] Moreover, the ability to feed southern Italy on the scale laid down by the Allies was entirely dependent on Allied imports and Allied transportation. Industries in Italian Government territory manufacturing essential commodities, such as fertilisers, cement and soap, which the Commission was anxious to get into production, had also to be planned and supervised on the spot by its officers since electric power and a large number of indigenous materials were controlled by the Local Resources Board.

[1] The net result of these changes is shown in the chart in Annexe II to this chapter, which should be compared with those given in the Annexes to Chapter IV. One of the features was the transfer of the Security Division of the Regional Control and Military Government Section, commanded by Colonel Young, to the Public Safety Sub-Commission, of which Colonel Young became the Deputy-Director.

[2] See above, p. 168.

All this had meant maintaining a large number of officers in the Regions in Italian Government territory, though some attempt had been made after the installation of Signor Bonomi's Government to hand over progressively to Italian officials the responsibility for administering the policies laid down by the Commission. Under Allied guidance all phases of the supply and distribution of essential foodstuffs were concentrated under a separate food department in charge of a High Commissioner, and as early as 1st September the Italian Government began to take over the reception, warehousing, distribution and accounting of imported foodstuffs. But complete responsibility for the feeding of Italian Government territory had not yet been assumed by the Italian Government by the time that the New Deal directive arrived. The control of the distribution of medical supplies was also transferred to the Italian Government, which formed a National Association of Wholesale Druggists, *Ente Nazionale Distribuzione Medicinali Degli Alleati* (ENDIMEA) for the purpose, which started working at the beginning of November 1944.

In industry, too, some steps had been taken to transfer to Italian administration the responsibility for industrial controls. Arrangements had been made under which the Italian Government in the territories under its administration applied the measures laid down from time to time by the Local Resources Boards for the blocking of materials. The control of the hemp industry, which was of direct concern, not only to the Allied Governments on account of exports, but also to the Allied Navies for local production of rope, was also gradually handed over. But by the spring of 1945 officers of the Commission were still occupied in hemp control, as well as in supervising the timber production of Calabria, which was of direct interest to the Allied forces. By the end of September 1944 steps had been taken to transfer to the Italian Government's administrative control the fertilizer, soap-making, paper and cement industries. It was arranged that the Italian Ministry of Industry, Commerce and Labour should create small committees of experts, presided over by an official of the ministry, to be responsible for the transfer of control, the responsibility of the Industry Sub-Commission being progressively reduced to the screening and passing on, through A.F.H.Q. channels, to the Combined Chiefs of Staff of the demands compiled by the Italian Government for the necessary imports of raw and repair materials. The pace of this transfer of responsibilities was set by the enlargement of liberated territory, but the *vis inertiae* of a military bureaucracy—to say nothing of the reluctance of Italian officials to assume responsibilities—was not always easy to overcome. It needed the impact of the reorganisation carried through by Mr Macmillan to complete the process.

The New Deal directive gave a much-needed push to the completion of this process. It also entailed drastic changes in the way that the Commission worked. As has already been explained, the Political Section was abolished, its functions being in general assumed by the U.S. and British Embassies.[1] But the ultimate responsibility for action in all matters embraced by the armistice terms—which were originally designed to be as nearly all-embracing as possible—remained with the Supreme Allied Commander and his delegate, the acting President of the Commission. The chain of command from the Allied Governments through the Combined Chiefs of Staff was kept unchanged. Moreover, the Chief Commissioner was still in need of political advice in the day-to-day business of the Commission. This was provided by transferring the vice-presidents of the Political Section to the staffs of their respective ambassadors, and appointing them as political advisers to the Commission, where they continued to maintain an office.

The new directive did not entail any further modification of the actual structure of Allied Commission headquarters. It did, however, effect an important change in the field, through the withdrawal of nearly all of the Commission's officers from Italian Government territory. This resulted in the abolition of four regional headquarters, those of Region I (Sicily) and Region VI (Sardinia), the consolidated Southern Region (Regions II, III and VII) and Region IV (Lazio–Umbria), and in a reorganisation of Region V which shed the *compartimento* of the Abruzzi—wholly Italian Government territory after the beginning of April 1945—and took over Umbria from Region IV. The complete withdrawal of the Commission's officers ordered in the directive did not prove feasible. Quite a number of them were retained at the request of the various staff sections at A.F.H.Q., who were anxious to relieve the military commanders of as much responsibility as possible in the matter of relations with the Italian civilian authorities. The plans formed by the Commission for withdrawal were considerably delayed by A.F.H.Q., in consequence of the objections raised by other staff sections, with the result that it was not until April that the full programme of withdrawals could be executed.

The most complete withdrawal from Italian Government territory took place in Sardinia, where already by the beginning of December 1944 the total staff of the Allied Commission had been reduced to eleven officers. After the beginning of April only two A.C. officers, both mining experts, were left. Their functions were restricted entirely to advice regarding the output of the Sardinian coal mines, the only military interest which A.F.H.Q. still possessed in the

---

[1] See above, p. 237.

island. The Liaison officer of the Land Forces Sub-Commission (M.M.I.A.) with the Italian Military Command acted as the general liaison officer of the Commission on the island.

In the other Regions in Italian Government territory the Commission maintained only the minimum number of officers required to look after the interests of the Allied forces, in the form of Liaison officers assisted by a few specialists, e.g. Transportation, Accounting and Property Control officers. In Sicily two Liaison officers were maintained, one at Palermo to correlate the activities of the U.S. Naval base with the Italian authorities, and one at Catania to perform this office with respect to the British 204 Sub-Area. Only three specialist officers were retained on the island, a Transportation officer to regulate rail transport across the Straits of Messina to Reggio, a Property Control officer, and a Supply-accountant. In defining the duties of the Liaison officers great stress was laid on the point that they should avoid involving themselves in questions of Italian local government, and that, even if asked, they should refrain from giving official advice to Prefects and other Italian officials but refer them to their own ministries in Rome. Lampedusa and Pantellaria however continued to remain under Allied Military Government, and their C.A.O's were made to report to the Allied Commission's Liaison officer at Palermo.

Somewhat similar arrangements were made to replace the Southern Region; but Allied Military Government of Naples Commune continued, with a somewhat reduced staff of just over thirty officers, and three civilians representing the Industry and Public Works and Utilities Sub-Commissions.[1] The Commissioner for Naples Commune also acted as Liaison Officer with No. 3 District and P.B.S. A Liaison officer was appointed to Bari with similar functions in respect of the provinces on the Adriatic side of the Apennines.[2] He was given an assistant with special duties in respect of food, whose special function was to ensure that the arrangements by which surplus vegetables, fruit, etc., were placed by the Italian Government at the disposal of the Local Resources Board for feeding the Allied forces, worked smoothly and efficiently. A Food liaison officer was also provided on the west coast, at the port of Castellamare. The Liaison officer at Bari was also provided with a staff of six Transportation officers, located at Bari, Foggia, Campobasso, Reggio and Catanzaro, to co-ordinate the movement of essential supplies by rail

[1] The establishment laid down for A.M.G. Naples consisted of a Commissioner, and his deputy, 3 Civil Affairs officers, 3 Legal officers, 3 Public Health officers, 4 Public Safety officers, 5 Finance officers and 5 Transportation officers, as well as a Supply officer, 2 Commerce officers, a Public Works and a Communications officer.

[2] Liaison officer, Naples, was responsible for the provinces of Naples, Salerno, Benevento, Avellino Campobasso, Cosenza, Catanzaro and Reggio. Liaison officer, Bari, for those of Foggia, Bari, Brindisi, Lecce, Taranto, Matera and Potenza.

and road, and to supervise the pools of War Department trucks for which the Commission remained responsible until such time as they were officially handed over to the Italian Government. Certain officers in A.M.G. Naples Commune were also charged with liaison functions, notably the Medical officers and a Public Works and Utilities officer, who acted as liaison officer with H.Q. No. 3 District, to ensure that arrangements for the maintenance of roads in which the military authorities were interested were carried out smoothly by the Italian Public Works engineers. Thanks to these arrangements a considerable number of officers were made available for duty in the northern Regions. The number of Commission's officers in Sicily was reduced from nineteen to five; those in southern Region, including Naples Commune, from sixty-seven to about forty.

A very large saving of officers was also effected by the changes just as described in Regions IV and V. The Abruzzi–Marche and the Lazio–Umbria Regions between them still had by the middle of March an effective establishment of over 100 officers. With the elimination of Lazio and Abruzzi from this complex, the number of officers was reduced to less than half. Marche and Umbria remained under Regional control, but the Commission's officers left behind in Lazio and the Abruzzi were a mere handful, a Liaison Public Safety officer in Rome—a significant survival in view of the disturbances which had taken place in the capital—two Finance officers, one representing the Allied Financial Agency and one a Supply-accountant, a Property Control officer, a Transportation officer and a Communications officer. A Transportation officer was also retained for Teramo, Chieti and Aquila provinces, and one in Civitavecchia to keep in touch with the workings of the port. A Public Utilities officer was also posted to Civitavecchia, to deal with road maintenance.

ANNEXE I

Note on 'Civilianisation'

In Washington the opinion had been gaining ground during the early months of 1944 that the responsibility for administering Civil Affairs in the south of Italy should be transferred from the War departments to civilian agencies. Already at the end of July 1943 the War Department in Washington had begun to inquire when civilian agencies could enter Sicily to work under military command. But this idea obtained a negative response from A.F.H.Q., which insisted that so long as Sicily was enemy territory, a purely military government was necessary. Nor did the mixture of civilian agents with military officers appear to be a practicable proposition—though the admission of Red Cross personnel to work under A.M.G. orders was readily agreed on. In the opinion of General Bedell Smith, General Eisenhower's Chief of Staff, civilian agencies ought not to be permitted to enter the area until Allied Military Government had been brought to an end.

The armistice, and the handing back of Sicily and southern Italy to the control of the Italian Government, brought the question of civilianisation once more into the picture. The different forms in which the civilianisation was envisaged were the following:

(1) the handing over to civilian agencies of the responsibility for certain functions in Italy, such as the procurement and provision of civilian supplies, for all but the operational areas;

(2) the transfer to some civilian agency controlled by the Foreign Office, not the War Office, of the responsibility for supervising the administration of the territory restored to the Italian Government;

(3) the introduction into the Allied Control Commission of civilians without modifying the military chain of command.

The first of these methods had been from the beginning sponsored by the Civil Affairs Division of the War Department in Washington for two reasons: namely, the saving of military manpower, since the commitments for northern Europe were already taxing its resources to the uttermost; and the undertakings given to Congress concerning the War Department's appropriations mentioned in the previous chapter. The Civil Affairs division of the War Department, together with the State Department and the Foreign Economic Administration, had early examined the possibility of transferring to the latter the supply responsibility for Sicily, Sardinia and southern Italy. In July 1944 a small combined mission was sent out to A.F.H.Q. to explore the possibility of the transfer of this responsibility to civilian agencies. Its members were Major Keyes from the International Division of the U.S. War Department, Mr Dallas Dort of the State Department, Major Ellis of the Civil Affairs Directorate of the War Office, and Mr Workman of the Ministry of Supply. They asked themselves two questions. (1) Assuming that the Allied Commission remained responsible for supply of civil 'relief' and economic matters, should these responsibilities be detached from the Commission's other activities in order to be controlled directly, not by the Combined Chiefs of Staff, but by some combined civilian agency? For administrative reasons—the essential connection and dependence of the Commission's supply functions with and on activities controlled by A.F.H.Q., such as shipping, port facilities and transport—they decided that this would be most undesirable while fighting was still going on. (2) Could the responsibilities for the supply of civil relief for certain parts of Italy be taken out of the hands of the Commission altogether and transferred to some combined civilian agency operating on the spot? This was, also for administrative reasons, considered undesirable as long as hostilities were continuing. (In this connection it was pointed out that 'the evils of divided administration were clearly demonstrated during the few months when liberated Italy was under the control of independent A.M.G. and A.C.C. authorities.) As an alternative they recommended the introduction of civilians into the Economic Section of the Commission itself, noting that this had already to a considerable extent taken place. (The Section's staff at headquarters had already six civilians, while two of its sub-commissions, Transportation and Labour, contained four civilians each).

With regard to the second form, a much more radical proposal originated in London after the liberation of Rome. The Foreign Office had proposed at the end of June that the Chief Commissioner should be relieved of his responsibility for political decisions by their transference to the direction of the Advisory Council. The appointment of Mr Macmillan, British Resident Minister at A.F.H.Q. and responsible in this capacity to the Secretary of State for Foreign Affairs, as head of the Control Commission raised the issue in a more concrete form. The Secretary of State for War, impressed by the impossibility of separating responsibility for political from that for administrative questions, appeared at one moment inclined to hand over the responsibility for A.C.C.—though not, of course, A.M.G.—*in toto* to his colleague at the Foreign Office. In Washington, too, the question of the complete civilianisation of A.C.C. had been envisaged in connection with the further transfer of territory to the Italian Government after the occupation of Rome. The War Department also felt that the increasingly political complexion assumed by the Commission's activities afforded strong argument for the transfer from military to civilian control. At the end of June General Hilldring had already suggested that the Combined Civil Affairs Committee should consider the question with a view to fixing a target date for the transfer.

In fact civilianisation in neither of the above forms took place. It was decided after consultation with A.F.H.Q.

(a) that it would be a mistake to go back on the original amalgamation of A.M.G. with A.C.C. and that before hostilities ended no change in the existing chain of command was desirable;
(b) that it was impossible for administrative and military reasons to treat areas such as Sicily, Sardinia or the southern part of the peninsula differently from the rest of liberated Italy;
(c) that it was equally impossible to separate certain functions of the Commission, such as supply, from its other activities and hand them

> over to civilian agencies—though an exception to this rule was made in the case of the special relief programme for displaced persons and certain classes of Italians undertaken by U.N.R.R.A.

But the introduction of civilians into a number of posts, mostly in the Economic Section of the Commission, was accepted by A.F.H.Q., which itself suggested that military officers could gradually be replaced by civilian experts, in order to smooth the transition which would take place when hostilities were over, even if this involved a temporary loss of efficiency owing to the inferior prestige of civilians in Italian eyes.

The principle of introducing civilians into the Commission had already been accepted in principle in its original constitution, when Mr Grady, an official of the Foreign Economic Administration (F.E.A.), had been appointed vice-president of the Economic Section. This appointment had been followed by the introduction of another F.E.A. civilian, Mr Antolini, as executive director, and by the appointment of other civilians from F.E.A. By the beginning of October some forty American civilians had been introduced, but much fewer British, owing to the difficulty of finding suitable candidates whose services at home could be spared. A.F.H.Q. had accepted the introduction of those civilians on the understanding that they would be responsible only to the Commission, not to the civilian agency from which they came, and that they would report only through the regular Commission military channels to the Combined Chiefs of Staff. But the instruction given to them by F.E.A. did not altogether conform to this principle; cases occurred of direct correspondence with the American civilian agency. This was however, rectified on complaint being made by A.F.H.Q. to the C.C.S.

The proposals for civilianisation put forward by the American members of the Combined Civil Affairs Committee were much more drastic than those which were ultimately accepted by Mr Macmillan. The War Department wanted to civilianise the whole American contingent of the Commission's headquarters, except the Service Sub-Commissions and the Establishment Section, leaving only A.M.G. with a military character. They even went so far as to suggest the complete divorce of A.M.G. from the Commission. But this was not accepted by the Combined Chiefs of Staff, who left it to the discretion of the Supreme Allied Commander to determine the extent to which civilianisation was practicable. In fact the degree of civilianisation which had actually taken place before the cessation of hostilities was relatively small. In April 1945 the Commission was employing less than 100 Allied civilians—of whom only just over fifty were of officer status—as compared with over 1,400 military officers. By this time the Industry, Agriculture, Transportation and Labour Sub-Commissions had been placed in the charge of civilian directors. The first of these to be appointed was an American, Mr Vaughan, who succeeded a British officer, Colonel Todd, on 9th October, 1944.

CHAPTER X

PREPARING FOR THE NORTH

IN ORDER to understand the preparations for the Military Government of northern Italy, it will be necessary to consider certain factors of the operational planning for the last phase in the Italian campaign. For planning purposes Italy was divided into two areas, north-west Italy and north-east Italy. These were separated by a line running roughly north and south rather east of Milan, so that north-west Italy consisted of the *compartimenti* of Liguria and Piedmont, and portions of Lombardy—the provinces of Como, Milan, Varese and Pavia. The northern boundary of this area was the Italian frontier from Ventimiglia to a point on the Swiss frontier only about forty-miles west of the Stelvio Pass, where the frontiers of Italy, Switzerland, and what was till 1938 Austria, coincide. North-east Italy included part of the *compartimenti* of Emilia and Lombardy and all three Venetias.

This division was made because entirely different operational conditions were expected on the two sides of this north-south line. Once the Allied armies had broken into the Po valley the enemy would have very few lines of retreat, only the Brenner Pass and two or three passes from north-eastern Italy into former Austrian territory, since both the French and the Swiss frontiers were closed to him. He might indeed attempt to hold a line on the Adige, but, if that were forced, he would have no option except to retreat across the Alps through the Brenner and the passes to the east of it. Hence operations in north-west Italy would be small and brief. They would amount to little more than the mopping up of the odd pockets of resistance left after the enemy had extricated what forces he could into north-east Italy. This was to be the task of IV Corps. Static conditions would therefore rapidly supervene, the military requirements of which would very quickly be reduced to a small garrison of the strength of, say, two divisions. It was therefore arranged that the command of this area, after a brief operational phase (Phase I), during which any remaining German or Fascist formations would be eliminated, would pass (Phase II) from Fifteenth Army Group to A.F.H.Q. under the control of headquarters No. 2 District. This formation during Phase I would be acting as the administrative echelon of IV Corps, under the command of Fifteenth Army Group, and would locate itself at Alessandria. From the point of view of A.M.G. this meant that the control of Military Government which would be established by

A.M.G. Fifth Army would necessarily be brief, and that the Regional organisations, X (Liguria), XI (Piedmont), and XII (Lombardy), would have to be brought into army areas under command of A.M.G. Fifth Army (and IV Corps) during Phase I, and made to follow up close on the heels of the advancing spearhead teams. It also meant the division of A.M.G. Fifth Army into two practically independent units.

In view of the presumption that north-west Italy would become a 'hiatus area', the occupation of which would require only a few light mobile columns, it was decided that, though during Phase I all Military Government personnel would be under the command of Fifth Army and IV Corps, the planning of the organisation of Military Government, and the assistance to be given to A.M.G. by the military forces, should be arranged by A.F.H.Q. in collaboration with Allied Commission headquarters, the responsibility for executing these measures being delegated to No. 2 District. G-5, Fifteenth Army Group and A.M.G. Fifth Army were thus relieved of a good deal of work, in order to leave them freer for the task in north-eastern Italy.

In particular A.F.H.Q. made themselves responsible for providing all the resources required to clear and repair the port of Genoa up to the stage where 8,000 tons a day could be discharged and cleared. It was estimated that the maintenance of military forces in north-western Italy would not require more than 2,000 tons a day, so that civil supplies in an adequate volume, up to 6,000 tons a day, could be shipped by sea to this port. Plans were also made, pending the clearing of Genoa—which was calculated originally to require anything up to seven weeks—for the clearance of Savona and Imperia to enable some supplies for Liguria to be brought by sea. A.F.H.Q. also undertook to deliver civil supplies by road to a point north of the Apennines from the stockpile at Leghorn. The actual point of delivery and the quantity to be delivered were left to be determined later, but for the purposes of planning the point taken was Parma—roughly half way, as the crow flies, from Pistoia to Milan. The quantity which A.F.H.Q. undertook to furnish was 500 tons a day—an amount which A.M.G. planners considered too small.

A.F.H.Q. declared their willingness to provide civilian supplies, and vehicles to convey them, though their movement from rail-head was delegated to H.Q. Fifth Army. They also undertook to train Italian military drivers for all Allied Commission/A.M.G. vehicles which were required to deliver civilian supplies. Other responsibilities assumed by A.F.H.Q. which had direct bearing on A.M.G. were the rehabilitation of the electric power and water systems of Genoa and certain other places, and the provision of facilities for the construction and operation of bulk storage facilities for petrol, oil and lubricants, including a 4-inch pipeline from Genoa to Alessandria. The repair of certain railways and roads was also undertaken by A.F.H.Q. but responsibility for the work during Phase I was delegated to the Fifth Army.

An order of priority was laid down for the tasks to be undertaken by A.M.G. The first item was the provision of food. It was specifically stated that H.Q. Allied Commission would be responsible for providing an initial maximum daily bread ration of 200 gms. Next, A.M.G. was charged with providing civil resources for the military tasks to be undertaken by Fifth Army and A.F.H.Q., in the shape of civilian manpower and, wherever available, materials. With regard to these, close co-operation was to be arranged between A.M.G. and the Allied Forces Local Resources Board officers, who were to be established during Phase I at Fifth Army or IV Corps headquarters and during Phase II at Genoa, Turin and Milan. A.M.G. was made primarily responsible, as in southern Italy, for finding and preparing inventories of all types of materials, foodstuffs, plant, tools and equipment, as well as for the organisation of industries to manufacture essential products needed by the armed forces.

Finally, once military necessities had been provided for, the Allied Commission was to take charge of the economic rehabilitation of north-western Italy within the limits of the policies laid down by A.F.H.Q. First priority was given to the mobilisation of indigenous transport, the maintenance and repair of an adequate number of Italian vehicles, to be used for the transport of civilian supplies on a double shift basis. In view of the expected large-scale German sabotage (to say nothing of the systematic Allied air attacks on the enemy's lines of communication) the mobilisation of engineering resources for the reconstruction of such bridges, roads and railways as were not of direct military interest—to be co-ordinated with the Chief Engineer, No. 2 District, and the Director of Military Railway Services—was given second priority. This was followed, at long last, by the rehabilitation of such industries and public utilities as had no military interest.

A similar programme of Military Government objectives was laid down for north-east Italy, but here the normal sequence of administrative responsibilities which had been observed hitherto was left undisturbed. The telescoping of Phases I and II, which had been anticipated in the 'hiatus area' of north-west Italy, was not provided for, and the setting up of static headquarters (No. 1 District and P.B.S.) was planned in the normal manner, these taking over responsibility for the occupation troops as rear army boundaries moved forward. In the same way the responsibility for Military Government was to remain in the hands of the Army A.M.G's until

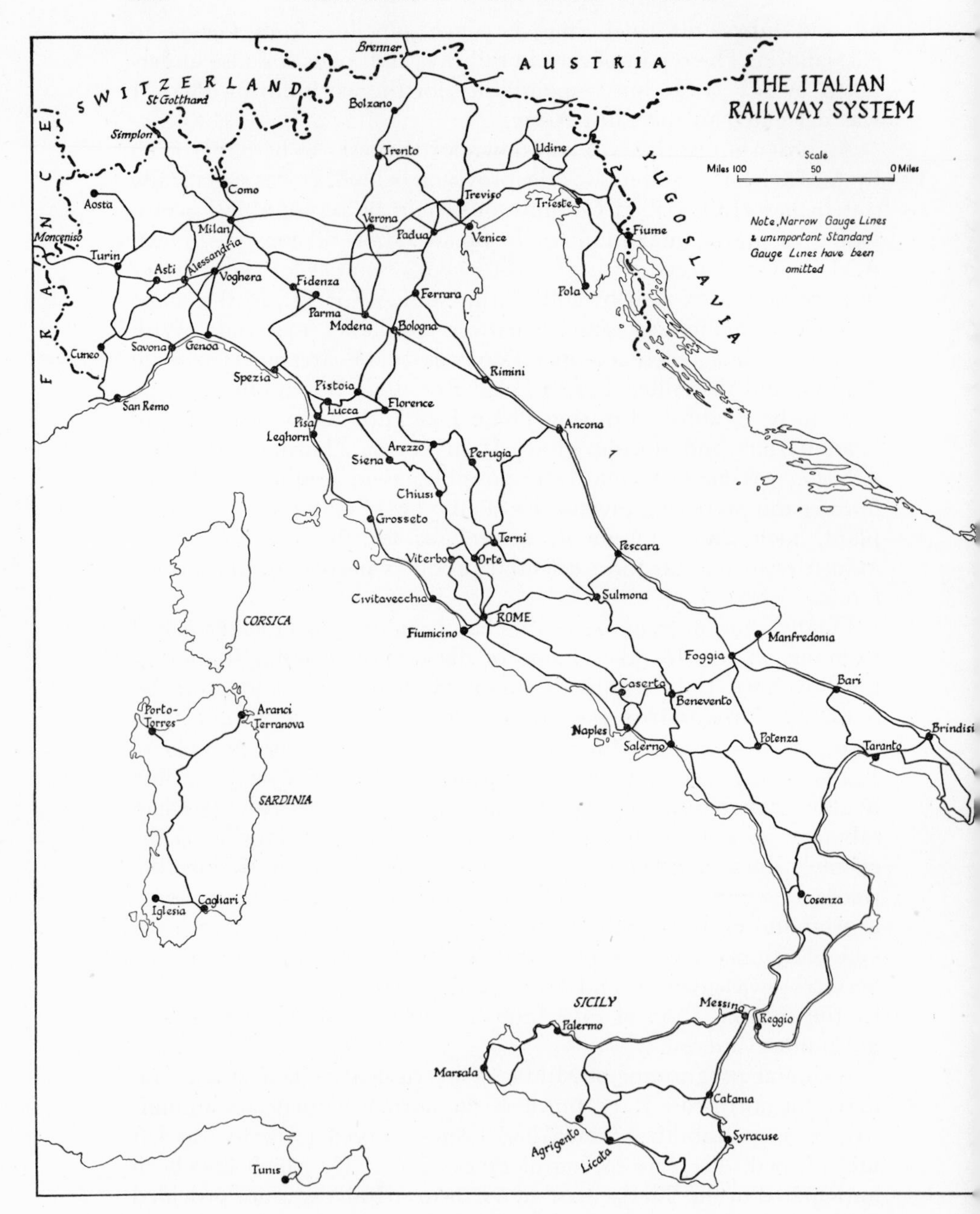
THE ITALIAN RAILWAY SYSTEM
Scale
Miles 100
50
0 Miles
Note, Narrow Gauge Lines & unimportant Standard Gauge Lines have been omitted
AUSTRIA
SWITZERLAND
FRANCE
YUGOSLAVIA
Brenner
St Gotthard
Simplon
Bolzano
Trento
Udine
Como
Aosta
Moncenisio
Milan
Verona
Treviso
Trieste
Fiume
Padua
Venice
Turin
Asti
Alessandria
Voghera
Fidenza
Ferrara
Pola
Parma
Modena
Bologna
Cuneo
Savona
Genoa
Spezia
Rimini
San Remo
Pistoia
Lucca
Florence
Pisa
Leghorn
Ancona
Arezzo
Perugia
Siena
Chiusi
Grosseto
Terni
Viterbo
Orte
Pescara
Civitavecchia
Sulmona
CORSICA
ROME
Fiumicino
Manfredonia
Foggia
Caserta
Bari
Benevento
Porto-Torres
Aranci
Terranova
Naples
Salerno
Potenza
Brindisi
Taranto
SARDINIA
Cosenza
Iglesia
Cagliari
SICILY
Messina
Palermo
Reggio
Marsala
Catania
Syracuse
Agrigento
Licata
Tunis

Map 10

THE ITALIAN ROAD SYSTEM
Scale
Miles 100 50 0 Miles
Only State roads with numbers, and Autostrade shown.
SWITZERLAND
AUSTRIA
YUGOSLAVIA
FRANCE
Brenner
Bolzano
Trento
Udine
Trieste
Fiume
Parenzo
Pola
Varese
Como
Aosta
Milan
Brescia
Verona
Padua
Venice
Turin
Asti
Alessandria
Piacenza
Rovigo
Parma
Ferrara
Cuneo
Genoa
Bologna
Forli
Spezia
Rimini
Imperia
Lucca
Pisa
Florence
S.Marino
Ancona
Leghorn
Siena
Perugia
Terni
Viterbo
Rieti
Aquila
Pescara
Civitavecchia
ROME
Avezzano
Vasto
Termoli
Vieste
CORSICA
Ceprano
Campobasso
Foggia
Terracina
Bari
Naples
Avellino
Brindisi
Salerno
Potenza
Taranto
Aranci
Terranova
Sassari
SARDINIA
Oristano
Muravera
Cosenza
Crotone
SICILY
Messina
Reggio
Palermo
Trapani
Marsala
Enna
Catania
Agrigento
Syracuse

Map 11

rear army boundaries moved forward, officers belonging to the Regional organisation being introduced, in the shape of provincial teams and specialists, pending the assumption of control by the Regional headquarters.

During Phase I the provision of supplies for the civilian population was to be the responsibility of the Armies, during Phase II, of H.Q. Allied Commission. In the event of a German collapse or surrender, the Armies (or the static formations behind them) were to assure the movement of civil supplies according to the following commitments—subject always to overriding operational requirements—namely, 350 tons per day to Padua, and 400 tons to Verona. The former was to be a British commitment to be undertaken in Phase I by Eighth Army and in Phase II by No. 1 District; the latter an American, to be undertaken by Fifth Army and P.B.S. The American Army Supply Services undertook to allocate the necessary resources for this purpose to the headquarters concerned. But the resources were subject to recall and were assumed to be available only for a period not exceeding one month. The British military authorities undertook to rehabilitate the port of Trieste, in preference to that of Venice. The opening and operation of Venice for the transhipment of civilian supplies was to be the business of the Allied Commission. The Armies also undertook to repair certain roads and railway lines.

North-eastern Italy comprised the whole area through which the Fifth and Eighth armies were to pass in their pursuit of the enemy to the Austrian frontier. The projected static areas were British No. 1 District and American Peninsula Base Section. P.B.S. was to extend from Leghorn through Bologna behind the Fifth Army, whose objective was to advance into Austria over the Brenner Pass. It was to form a U.S. corridor between the British No. 1 and No. 2 Districts as shown in the map opposite. No. 1 District was to extend behind the Eighth Army, the task of which was to occupy Venice and Trieste and to establish lines of communication from there by road and rail over the nearest routes from Udine and Trieste via Gorizia and Tarvisio, into the British zone of Austria, Carinthia. In view of the tension on the Yugoslav–Italian border it was expected that Venezia Giulia would remain in the operational zone for some time after rear army boundaries had been placed elsewhere upon the Italian frontiers. The policy had been laid down that Allied Military Government should be established everywhere within Italy's 1939 frontiers, so that the ultimate disposition by the Peace Conference of territories in dispute between Italy and her former enemies should not be prejudiced by any *fait accompli*.

It had originally been planned that the three Venetias should form a single Allied Military Government Region (Region XIII), not-

withstanding the very special conditions existing in Venezia Tridentina and Venezia Giulia, with their substantial minorities of Austrians, Slovenes and Croats. This decision had been based on the consideration that it would be wise to avoid any possible political reactions which might be aroused, both in the Italian public and in the minority populations themselves, as a result of the creation of separate administrative units. The two provinces of Venezia Tridentina, Bolzano and Trento, together with the purely Italian province of Belluno, were known to have been virtually annexed to the *Reich* under the German occupation, though in the event the actual administrative changes were found to be smaller than had been expected. They had been constituted as the *Alpenvorland*, and their civil administration had been placed under the *Gauleiter* of the Vorarlberg, who combined with this office that of *Reich* Commissioner of the Italian provinces. Venezia Giulia, together with the province of Udine, had also been organised as the special administration of the Adriatic littoral under the German military command.

It was considered advisable to make special arrangements in setting up A.M.G. in both these areas in order to avoid exacerbating minority feelings. The province of Belluno presented no problems since it was almost entirely Italian, nor did the problem of Trento, where the Austrian minority was quite small. Conditions in Bolzano were different. Here eighty per cent of the population were Austrian or German in sentiment, but the total population, almost entirely rural, was under 300,000, and the town of Bolzano itself was, in fact, still largely Italian. In these circumstances it was planned to restore the Italian system of administration in all three provinces, but to avoid importing Italian officials into German-speaking areas, and, where possible, to refrain from bringing in *Carabinieri* from southern Italy except for the mobile spearhead detachments. Gaps in the administrative machine of the province would be filled by the selection of local inhabitants. It was anticipated that A.M.G. might have to be maintained in Bolzano up to the conclusion of the Peace Treaty[1], whereas it was expected that the other provinces of northern Italy, except those of Udine and Venezia Giulia, would be handed back to the administration of the Italian Government quite soon after the conclusion of hostilities.

Venezia Giulia presented a much more difficult problem. The preliminary planning was concerted along the lines laid down in a memorandum by Captain Stone at the end of October. By the autumn of 1944 it had already become clear that the Yugoslav forces under Marshal Tito might have penetrated far into the territory

---

[1] Instructions to this effect were given by the Combined Chiefs of Staff as late as April, 1945.

before the Allied forces reached it, and that it might have become politically a 'hiatus area' under neither German nor Italian control, in which local Slovene or Croat partisans had established their own administration. If the regular forces of Marshal Tito had already occupied the area or part of it, the only solution to the problem would be to arrange an agreement by direct negotiation between Field-Marshal Alexander and the Yugoslav Commander-in-Chief. Such negotiations did in fact take place in the spring of 1945. Their story is told in Chapter XII. If, on the other hand, no regular Yugoslav forces were in occupation of the area when the Allies arrived, but local partisans had already taken control, there appeared to be a possibility of establishing A.M.G. without too much difficulty, provided that neither Italian police nor Italian officials were introduced into places where Yugoslav partisans had established themselves, and that any *de facto* administrative machinery which had been set up was made use of. Further details of planning arrangements for Venezia Giulia are given in Chapter XII. All that need be noted here is that the policy of keeping Venezia Giulia as part of Venetia Region had finally to be abandoned.

As was only to be expected, the feeding of the northern Regions was one of the chief preoccupations of the Commission. On the supply side an important feature of the planning was the estimation of the supplies required, and their stockpiling in strategic locations whence they could easily be transferred by the Armies to the principal foci of distribution, Parma, Verona and Padua. The general policy laid down by A.F.H.Q. was based on the following assumptions: an initial minimum ration of 200 gms of bread per day, to be increased, as soon as the local resources of wheat, rice or other grains permitted, to the equivalent of 300 gms a day. Maintenance plans were consequently made to bring in for the first month only the equivalent of 100 gms of bread per head per day, since it was estimated that the equivalent of another 100 gms could be procured locally.[1] Small quantities of other foodstuffs were also to be brought in—dried vegetables, tinned meat and soup, salt, sugar, powdered milk and olive oil or fats. These were only intended to be distributed to special classes, e.g. hospital patients and pregnant mothers, and inhabitants of large towns, who had few opportunities of getting hold of any local country produce. Special arrangements were planned to make extra food available to Army A.M.G's to meet the needs of devastated areas immediately on entry. Another commodity to be imported was soap—the absence of which had been much felt in the South, but owing to its extreme scarcity no general

[1] In all *compartimenti* except Liguria, where, on account of the absence of locally grown grains, quantity of imported bread-stuffs was to be equivalent to 200 gms.

issue in the North could be planned, regional allocations being intended solely to supply hospitals.

The estimated maintenance figures for the first month in the four northern Regions, Liguria and Piedmont, Lombardy, and the Venetias, excluding Venezia Giulia, are perhaps worth a passing glance. The estimated ration population was about fifteen million, and the amount of flour to be imported was rather over 26,000 tons, in addition to 1,200 tons of meat, 1,300 tons of dried vegetables, 2,200 tons of sugar, 1,500 tons of oils and fats, 800 tons of milk and 1,600 tons of salt.[1] The 'lift', to be provided by Eighth Army to Padua and Verona, left a slight surplus over these requirements, but that to be provided from Leghorn to Parma fell short of the required monthly figure by over 5,000 tons. In order to meet these food requirements the Allied Commission built up two stockpiles, one at Leghorn and the other at Ancona. This involved transporting considerable quantities of foodstuffs—nearly 20,000 tons—from Leghorn, where a surplus had accumulated, to the Adriatic side during the winter of 1944/5.[2]

Besides food, medical supplies and clothing were important items for which provision had to be made in order to prevent the occurrence of disease and unrest. For the supply of the former a depot had been established in Florence, which was subsequently to be moved to Genoa when liberated. Six months supplies for 1945 had been 'requisitioned' in August 1944 and were expected to arrive in May. Meanwhile, pending their arrival, at least two months supplies were on hand which could be drawn from the stockpile established at Naples. Supplies were calculated on a population basis, it being estimated that Liguria and Piedmont would require about 80 tons a month each, Lombardy 100 tons, Emilia 50 tons and Venetia about 100 tons. It was planned to establish ENDIMEA, the organisation created by the Italian Government for the distribution of imported medical supplies, as soon as areas were released to Regional control. No clothing for general distribution to the civilian population was provided, but arrangements were made to bring in special supplies for relieving the needs of refugees and other destitute persons. Most of these supplies had been given by private American charity—the American Red Cross and American Relief for Italy, Inc.—and they were to be distributed by the American Red Cross and the National Italian Committee for relief, *Ente Nazionale*

---

[1] Figures in metric tons. No figures for Emilia were included, as it was considered that this Region would be self-supporting from the beginning.

[2] By the middle of February total stocks accumulated on the Adriatic side amounted to about 18,000 tons of flour and 11,000 tons of other foodstuffs, while the quantity on the western side of the Apennines—chiefly Leghorn and Naples—amounted to 32,000 tons of flour and 5,000 tons of other foodstuffs.

Distribuzione dei Soccorsi per Italia (ENDSI) under the direction of the A.M.G. Public Health officers. By the end of 1944 a pile of about 100 tons of clothing, shipped by American Relief for Italy, had been accumulated at Leghorn, in addition to the other stocks of over 370 tons of clothing and blankets from miscellaneous sources (chiefly American Red Cross), which included some imported supplies. It was intended that American Red Cross clothing should meet the most pressing needs in the areas when first liberated, and that clothing provided by American Relief for Italy should subsequently be distributed by ENDSI, which had been equipped with fifty trucks by this American organisation.

Apart from the by this time only too familiar problem of civilian food supplies and transport, the most difficult question confronting Allied Military Government was how to deal with the Italian Resistance movement, which had been advertised in flattering terms in the press and the radio and deliberately somewhat inflated for propaganda purposes, in order to discourage the enemy and to support the 'patriots' in German-occupied territory. In addition to the obvious danger to public order of armed partisans, predominantly Communist in political complexion, there was a more fundamental issue concerned with the attitude which would be adopted on liberation by the underground Central Committee of Liberation in Milan, which at one time showed signs of intending to constitute itself the government of northern Italy, and a revolutionary government at that. The experience gained in the liberation of Florence had suggested that it was by no means a remote possibility that, before A.M.G. could appear on the scene in the 'hiatus area' of the northwest, the members of the Committee of National Liberation might have installed themselves in the most important executive positions; in which case they would be extraordinarily difficult to remove, and the obstructions that they could put in the way of any A.M.G. administration might be formidable indeed. Moreover, it seemed quite possible that the C.L.N.A.I. might have constituted itself into a government which refused to recognise the authority of the government in Rome.

The proposal was therefore made by Brigadier Lush, after consultation with the Operations Division of A.A.I. at the beginning of September, that three A.M.G. officers (with three P.W.B. officers) should be parachuted by S.O.E. into northern Italy to advise the Allied officers attached to the partisan forces and the Committee of National Liberation, in order to ensure the preservation of public order in the interval between the withdrawal of the enemy and the arrival of the Allied forces. The officers in question would have no executive powers, nor would there be any question of setting up A.M.G. before the arrival of the Allied troops. This proposal was not accepted by A.F.H.Q., but steps were taken to ensure that the Committee of National Liberation of Northern Italy would not only maintain public order, but also subordinate itself on liberation, first, to Allied Military Government and, later, to the Italian Government.

In November the Italian Prime Minister had written a letter to the Allied Commission drawing attention to the desperate situation of the partisans in the Alps resulting from the scarcity of supplies, and suggesting certain measures on the part of the Allies to overcome this. The Minister of Foreign Affairs also drew attention to their plight and asked for financial assistance. The Allied military authorities had for some time been helping the Resistance movement by 'infiltrating' Italian banknotes acquired and introduced through various channels, but the expenditure required to sustain partisan activity far exceeded the resources which could be made available in this manner. It was therefore felt that the Italian Government should be called upon to make a contribution.

The matter was brought to a head by a paper placed before the Supreme Allied Commander's Political Committee by Major-General Stawell, in charge of subversive operations in the Mediterranean theatre (SOMTO), who proposed a tripartite agreement between SACMED, the Italian Government and the C.L.N.A.I., under which the Milan Committee was to be recognised as the authorised representative of the Italian Government, while SACMED accepted General Cadorna, known under the pseudonym 'Valenti', as head of the military command of the C.L.N.A.I. Volunteers of Liberty. The general had been commander of an armoured division which had put up gallant resistance to the Germans on the two days following the signing of the armistice, and he had been dropped by parachute into northern Italy just after the liberation of Rome, at the request of the Milan Committee. During the period of enemy occupation the C.L.N.A.I. was to undertake to carry out the instructions of the Allied Command, directing patriots in their operations against the enemy; the Committee was also to exercise its best endeavours to maintain law and order and to safeguard the economic resources of the country during the interval between German withdrawal and the time when Allied Military Government took control. The Italian Government was to make a monthly contribution to the expenses of the C.L.N.A.I. during the period of enemy occupation: the sum of 100 million lire was to be paid at once, and subsequent monthly contributions were to be fixed according to the military and economic situation obtaining in each region. Incidentally General Stawell's paper proposing this draft agreement drew attention to the inadequacy of the arrangements for looking after patriots ont his side of the line, and the lack of resources and authority of the Patriot Branch of the Allied Commission.

Representatives of the C.L.N.A.I., among them Signor Parri, joint Deputy Commander of the C.L.N.A.I's military command, and the banker Pizzoni, were brought into liberated Italy on 14th November to discuss the position with the Italian Government and to sign an agreement on the lines just described. The idea of giving official recognition to the Resistance movement in the North, in which the Communist party was known to be predominant, was greeted by G-5 and the Allied Commission with little enthusiasm, in view of the recent Allied experience of resistance movements in Greece and Yugoslavia. The alternative of a bipartite agreement between SACMED and C.L.N.A.I. was therefore put forward, but SOMTO pointed out that C.L.N.A.I. were strongly of the opinion that recognition by the Italian government would give them a greater measure of control over the heterogeneous elements composing the Resistance movement, as well as greater protection from neo-Fascist reprisals, so that from the military point of view the value of the agreement would be greatly diminished if it were confined to a bipartite arrangement between SACMED and the C.L.N.A.I.

The crisis which put an end to the first of Signor Bonomi's Governments finally swung the balance against a tripartite agreement, since the delay in the formation of the new government made it impossible to agree on the terms of the document before Signor Parri felt himself obliged to return to Milan. A bipartite agreement was consequently made between SACMED and C.L.N.A.I. Under this agreement, the C.L.N.A.I. undertook to establish and maintain cooperation with all active elements in the Resistance movement, even if they did not belong to the committee. During the period of enemy occupation the General Command of the Volunteers of Liberty promised to carry out all instructions of the C.-in-C., A.A.I. The Committee also promised to do its best, on enemy withdrawal, to maintain law and order, to safeguard the economic resources of the territory against sabotage, and to hand over to Allied Military Government, immediately on its establishment, all the authority and powers of local government which it had previously assumed. It was also agreed that, as the enemy withdrew, all components of the General Command of the partisan forces would come under the direct command of the C.-in-C., A.A.I., and obey all orders issued by him or by A.M.G., including disbandment and disarmament when required. In return, SACMED undertook to give the Resistance movement the greatest possible assistance, including a monthly contribution not exceeding 160 million lire, which was to be repaid by the Italian Government.

This agreement was supplemented, on the constitution of the second Bonomi Government, by an agreement between the Government and the C.L.N.A.I., one of whose representatives had stayed behind in Rome to sign the document.[1] Signor Bonomi issued an Order of the Day on the 21st December 1944 in which he announced the recognition by the Italian Government of the C.L.N.A.I. as its representative, to which it had delegated the direction of the Resistance movement, and added that it had also been recognised by the Allied Command as the representative organ of all anti-Fascist parties in German-occupied Italy. This statement, subsequently corrected by the Italian Government, was, of course, inaccurate, since particular care had been taken to exclude any form of political recognition in the agreement between SACMED and the Milan Committee. In the agreement, as finally settled between C.L.N.A.I. and the Italian Government, equal care was taken to avoid phrasing which would in any way prejudice either the authority of A.M.G., which had already been recognised by C.L.N.A.I. in its agreement with SACMED, or that of the Italian Government. It was also found possible to include a reference to the armistice terms which was acceptable to the Milan Committee. The recognition of the C.L.N.A.I. by the Italian Government was severely restricted. The Committee was recognised as the organ of the anti-Fascist parties in German-occupied territory, and designated by the Government as its representative in the fight against Fascists and Germans. On the other hand, the C.L.N.A.I. recognised the Italian Government as the successor of the Government which agreed to the armistice terms, and as the sole legitimate authority in the portions of the country returned by the Allies to Italian administration.

The two agreements, the texts of which will be found in the annexe to this chapter, were completed by a third agreement made between General Alexander and the Italian Prime Minister on the 28th December 1944, under which the Italian Government undertook to make available to SACMED, through the Allied Financial Agency, the quantity of lire required to reimburse him for the payments already made by him to the accredited representatives of C.L.N.A.I., and subsequently such amounts as he might request, not exceeding 160 million lire a month.

Meanwhile plans were made upon a less exalted level for the treatment of partisans in the field. As a result of the experiences already met with by A.M.G., particularly in Florence, it had been realised that certain mistakes must be avoided and that a new procedure must be laid down, since in the advance to the north partisans

---

[1] During the discussion of this agreement the C.L.N.A.I. were asked to concur in a clause in which they fully accepted the government of the Lieutenant-General of the Realm as the sole legitimate government of that part of Italy not under A.M.G., and so worded as to bind them also to accept the terms of the armistice, an undertaking to which they at first objected. But the text as agreed on implied both these stipulations.

would be encountered in much larger numbers than had been come across hitherto. An operational instruction was issued by H.Q. Fifteenth Army Group, over the signature of General Gruenther, laying down the treatment to be given to partisans and patriots in some detail. The responsibility for carrying out the disarmament of partisans, 'as soon as this can tactfully and appropriately be accomplished', was laid fairly and squarely on the headquarters of Fifth and Eighth Armies and of IV Corps, the local responsibility for making the necessary arrangements being placed on A.M.G., 'with whom the local military commanders will be required to cooperate'.

The standard provision of the Proclamation forbidding the possession of arms by the civilian population, were not to apply to partisans in the initial stages. Every attempt was to be made to secure the confidence of their leaders and to conduct disarmament through them. Assistance in this matter was to be afforded by a number of Allied missions who were working in close liaison with the partisan bands; their aid was to be sought by local commanders and A.M.G. officers. These liaison officers, or the partisan commanders, were to be required to submit muster rolls of their formations and schedules of arms and warlike equipment to serve as a general check on the progress of disarmament. Every encouragement was to be given to partisans to hold ceremonial stand-down parades, which should appear as being held not by Allied orders, but at the partisans' own wishes. These stand-down parades were to be used as opportunities for affecting disarmament. The parades were to be conducted with as much ceremony as possible and the commander of the nearest Allied formation was to be present, to take the salute and to supervise the collection of arms. The handing in of arms was to be accompanied, where convenient, by the presentation of 'Certificates of Merit'. If these certificates, for any reason, could not be issued at the time of the parade, receipts were to be handed out for arms surrendered, which could subsequently be used as evidence for procuring a certificate.

If in any area the attendance at parade should be poor, or a substantial number of those attending failed to bring their weapons, the Allied officer concerned was to judge whether there was an innocent explanation or whether deliberate evasion of the order to disarm was being attempted. If the latter was the case, the partisan leader was to be informed, before the parade was dispersed, that all those who failed to hand in their arms at an appointed hour next day would be subject to severe penalties. If for any reason the holding of stand-down disarmament parades was not adopted and no satisfactory alternative method was proposed by the partisan commanders, an A.M.G. proclamation was to be issued on the lines of one used in Florence. This proclamation, after thanking the partisans for their services, pointed out that the normal rules laid down under the proclamation forbidding the possession of arms applied also to partisans. Thereafter any partisan found in possession of arms or explosives, without an A.M.G. permit, was to be brought to trial before an Allied Military court. While no time limit for disarmament was laid down, since any rigidity was undesirable so long as partisan leaders were offering cooperation, it was indicated that it should be possible to effect disarmament in approximately one week after the arrival of Allied forces in a given area, an unduly optimistic assumption, as will be shown in the next chapter.

It was estimated that there were about 100,000 partisans in northern Italy, 75,000 in north-west Italy of whom 50,000 were armed and active, and 25,000 in north-east Italy of whom 10,000 were armed. In view of the practically destitute condition of many patriots, the provision of food and clothing for 100,000 partisans for a maximum period of three months was to be undertaken as a military commitment, while pay and demobilisation gratuities would be forwarded by the Italian Government and issued by A.M.G. By offering partisans food, clothing and money, it was hoped that they could be induced to concentrate in convenient areas, as soon as supplies for them were brought up. They would then be disarmed, and a proportion of them would be enlisted in the Italian Army—the Italian Government had announced its willingness to accept partisans in the army at their equivalent rank up to that of Lieutenant-Colonel—while others would be formed into labour units for employment by A.M.G. and the Allied Forces. In general 'Patriots' were to be given first priority in all civilian employment. Those for whom no immediate employment could be found would have to be cared for at 'patriot' centres, until they could get a job, if they lived in the northern Regions; or, if they lived in the South, until they could be evacuated into Italian Government territory, where they would become the responsibility of the Italian Government. Arrangements would be made for partisans reporting at the concentration areas to be screened by members of their own organisation. Hospital treatment for those requiring it would be given by the Armies in military hospitals.

Authorisation for implementing these plans on the supply side had not yet been obtained when the North was liberated, though the Combined Chiefs of Staff had been asked to approve them about the middle of February. Towards the end of April the C.C.S. informed A.F.H.Q. that owing to worldwide shortages no additional imports could be made available for the purpose of supplying food or clothing to partisans. If partisan needs could not be supplied from existing civilian supplies, the issue of military clothing from excess theatre stocks was authorised, after making all possible use of captured

German supplies. As a result of these instructions, though rations for partisans on the Italian army scale were in fact issued by the Armies, no authority had been received to adopt this higher scale. The Allied Commission was therefore placed under obligation to refund certain issues.

The task of dealing with patriots in the advance north of the Apennines was divided into two phases. In Phase I it was the responsibility of Army headquarters. During this phase Army A.M.G. H.Q. were to have attached to them a Regional Patriot officer, and an Italian Military Patriot representative for each Region to be occupied, and as many Italian Army officers nominated by the Ministry of Occupied Italy as might be considered necessary. In accordance with the general plan of deploying A.M.G. officers, they were to be moved forward with Fifth Army, IV Corps or Eighth Army to their future regions or provinces; when Army or Corps moved on they were to remain behind and continue their work. Patriot officers were to move forward with corps headquarters as soon as possible in order to make their contacts. Patriot centres, as already explained, were to be set up in appropriate positions near the concentrations of partisans. Their staff was to be enlisted from the patriots themselves and paid in accordance with the scale laid down by the Italian Ministry of Occupied Italy. During this phase it was anticipated that the work of screening and disarmament would be accomplished, that the most pressing needs of hospital treatment and clothing would be attended to, and that a beginning would be made of their dispersal to their homes, through refugee channels if no other means were available. Though maintenance at patriot centres was permissible for as long as three months from the time of reception and disarmament, it was hoped that all partisans would have been dispersed considerably sooner. Funds were to be made available through A.M.G. Finance officers to pay gratuities to patriots and their dependants.

In the second phase, when the control of the areas was taken over by (British) District or (American) P.B.S., the administration and rehabilitation of patriots became the responsibility of the Regional authorities, in conjunction with the Command of the District or P.B.S. Regional Patriot officers now came under the control of the Regional Commissioners. Equipment already installed at patriot centres by the Armies was not to be removed, but the Region now became responsible for the transport required for conveying patriots and stores to or from the centres. In order to equip the A.M.G. Patriot officers with the necessary knowledge to carry out these new directives, special training courses were arranged, which were attended by nearly thirty officers. These plans, which were a great improvement on any previous arrangements, were not, as we shall see, destined to be carried out *au pied de la lettre*. The sudden collapse of the German armies in the north and the insurrection of the C.L.N.A.I. made strict adherence to them impracticable.

After the signature of the agreements referred to above, contact was maintained by both A.F.H.Q. and the Italian Government with the C.L.N.A.I. and the *Comando Generale* of the *Corpo Volontari della Libertà*. At the end of March General Cadorna and Signor Parri were both brought into liberated Italy for conversations with A.F.H.Q. and H.Q. Fifteenth Army Group. The subjects discussed included the eventualities of a German surrender, as well as the disarmament of partisans. With regard to the former the Allied Command made it quite clear that German troops would be expected to surrender and consign their arms to the Allies, not to the partisans, and that outlying German detachments would be required to remain where they were with their arms, until they could surrender to Allied troops. But the possibility in certain cases of local surrender agreements between partisans and German local commanders, perhaps with the intervention of Allied officers, was recognised. It was also made clear that the Allies intended to treat not only the regular units of the Social-Republican Army, but also the special neo-Fascist forces like the X Mas, the militias and the Black Brigades, as prisoners of war—though General Cadorna and Signor Parri would enter into no commitment on this subject on behalf of the C.V.L.[1]

The Allied scheme for concentration and disarmament in a number of partisan centres was also explained to the General and Signor Parri, who appear to have agreed on the necessity for the immediate dissolution of the last-minute 'patriots', and on the early demobilisation of the large body of real partisans who would wish to return to their homes. They made it clear, however, that, in their opinion, the immediate demobilisation of all the partisan forces would probably be impossible, owing to the likelihood of the neo-Fascists carrying on guerilla warfare, and urged the need, in the absence of any adequate police force at the Allies' disposal, for maintaining selected partisan police detachments under arms. They also insisted on the absolute necessity of avoiding any decisions in the matter of disarmament, *decisioni brusche autoritarie ed unilaterali*, without previous consultation with the representatives of the movement. As to the enlistment of partisans into the Italian army in integrated

---

[1] See the account of these conversations submitted by General Cadorna to the C.L.N.A.I., which is printed in his book *La Riscossa dal 25 Luglio alla liberazione*, pp. 237–244. In a decree passed just before liberation the C.L.N.A.I. laid down arrangements for the surrender and disarmament of the forces of the Social Republic. A distinction was made between conscripts and volunteers. Of the former, 'other ranks' on surrender and disarmament were to be allowed to go free; not so officers and non-commissioned officers, who were to be interned. Of the latter all ranks were to be interned.

units, the Allied Command appear to have adopted a somewhat reserved attitude, owing no doubt to the Allied policy of a fixed ceiling but the Minister of occupied territory, Signor Scoccimarro, strongly supported this idea.[1]

General Cadorna in his account of the conversations stresses the emphasis laid by the Allied Command on the measures to be taken by the partisans in protecting industrial plants and public utilities from German sabotage. After the severe sufferings inflicted on the partisans by the enemy during the previous winter, this would seem, reasonably enough from the Allied point of view, to have been regarded as their primary function—indeed the General rightly calls this the *Leitmotiv* of the Allied attitude to the partisan forces. It is interesting to note in this connection that both he and Signor Parri emphasised the limitations of the partisan resources for effective action in this matter, in the event of the Allied advance only making slow progress.

In the meantime the Italian Government through its intermediary, the under-secretary of the Ministry of Occupied Italy, continued to negotiate with the C.L.N.A.I. in Milan. In an agreement embodied in a declaration dated 29th March, the Committee undertook to administer the provinces and communes of northern Italy in accordance with the local government law of 1915, from the moment of insurrection until an Allied Military Government was installed, to which the powers exercised by the C.L.N.A.I. and its subordinate Regional, Provincial and Communal Committees were to be handed over.[2] It also undertook to recognise and to procure recognition for all orders and proclamations made by A.M.G. When requested by A.M.G. Regional Commissioners, the Regional C.L.N. would constitute themselves into Consultative Regional Committees, similar action being taken by the provincial committees. In communes the local C.L.N. would become the *Giunta Comunale*. The C.L.N.A.I. also undertook during the time that it was in authority to put into action a 'rapid and profound epuration' in the political, administrative, economic and financial fields.

The way was thus clear for the incorporation of the C.L.N.A.I. and its subordinate organisations into the structure of government in the northern Regions. The pre-Fascist representative organs of local administration were to be reconstituted with the assistance of the C.L.N's, subject to the limitations entailed by the impossibility of holding immediate elections, members being appointed by A.M.G.

---

[1] After liberation it would appear to have been General Cadorna himself who, as Chief of the General Staff of the Army, insisted on a rather restrictive system of entry. Cf. Cadorna *op. cit.* p. 292.

[2] Text in *Atti del C.L.N.A.I.*, pp. 41 seq.

according to the arrangements already described.[1] The Committees of Liberation were not to be permitted to set themselves up as alternative governments. But their advice was to be sought in the appointment of local bodies and of temporary officials. In regard to the latter, the problem was that of reconciling the claim of the Italian Government to appoint its officials in the north with that of the Committees to make their own nominations. It was anticipated that in a large number of cases, by the time the Allied Military Government officers had arrived, Prefects and Chief Constables (*Questori*) appointed by the Committees would already have been installed, whereas the Italian Government naturally wished to reserve its right to appoint career officials to these posts. It was therefore pointed out to the Government that any specific nominee whom they put forward for these posts would be considered by A.M.G., but that it would be quite useless to appoint any nominee who was not acceptable to the local C.L.N.

The following procedure was laid down. If on arrival the A.M.G. officer found a Prefect or *Questore* already appointed by the C.L.N.—a situation which did not appear to contravene the agreement between Field-Marshal Alexander and the C.L.N.A.I.—these appointments should not be confirmed immediately. Those found in office should normally be permitted to remain with acting rank pending the filling of the post by A.M.G. Nominations should then be invited from the C.L.N. and other prominent persons, e.g. the local bishop. The name of the Government's nominee would be supplied by headquarters, and opinion should be sought from the C.L.N. as to his possible acceptance. But the responsibility for the appointment remained with the Regional Commissioner or Army S.C.A.O., not with A.C. headquarters or the Italian Government. It was agreed that, wherever possible, a local nominee should be found, though it was emphasised that in the appointment of a *Questore* great importance was attached to the professional qualifications for this post of 'chief constable'. Purely political appointments were to be avoided. The Committees of Liberation were to be kept in being and consulted by both the Prefect and the A.M.G. Provincial Commissioner, but neither of these officers was in any sense bound to accept their advice, though it would be wise to do so, except where it conflicted patently with A.M.G. policy. If a member of the C.L.N. were appointed to an administrative position, it was considered better that he should resign from the Committee, though discretion was given in this matter to the Regional Commissioner.

The plans made for 'defascistisation' aimed at accelerating the somewhat dilatory procedure of the Italian machinery set up under

---

[1] See above, pp. 62-63, 174-75.

D.L.L.159 and its later modifications and amplifications. Three stages were envisaged: first the dismissal or suspension by A.M.G. of Fascists in key posts, already described in Chapter VI; next, the immediate setting up by A.M.G. of committees of three to five Italian citizens of integrity to conduct a preliminary 'epuration' of public offices, according to a list of essential priorities; and finally, the implementation of the machinery set up by the Italian Government under D.L.L.159, and its amplifications.

With regard to the preliminary purge by A.M.G., it was realised that not all of the higher public officials found in office could be classed as collaborators. Many of them had considered it their duty to their country to remain at their posts, and if some had taken the oath of allegiance to the Social Republic, others had, it was known, refused to take this oath to their own peril. Wholesale dismissals were therefore to be avoided wherever possible. Instructions were issued that only the heads of Service (or important business concerns) should be dealt with. Warnings were also given to Regional Commissioners against the hasty suspension of persons in important positions in administrations performing services essential to the Allied forces, and they were given powers to reinstate such persons where necessary.

It was realised that the preliminary process of 'epuration' would probably have been carried out by the C.L.N.A.I. and the partisans before A.M.G. arrived on the scene, and that dismissed persons might have already been replaced. In this case it was not considered advisable to remove the new holders from office. There would be no objection, if they were considered suitable, to the appointment of the same persons by A.M.G., provided that it was made plain that A.M.G. and not the C.L.N.A.I. was the appointing authority. If 'epuration' on a large scale had already taken place, personnel in the lower ranks should be recruited locally, since the number of minor officials which the Italian Government could supply was strictly limited.

Persons to be dismissed by the provincial commissioners to be set up by A.M.G. (General Order No. 35), included the classes of Fascists, neo-Fascists and collaborators enumerated in D.L.L. No. 159. They were divided into three categories; the first, called 'immediate' consisted of Civil Servants of the six highest grades, and directors, managers, and senior technicians of state-controlled public utility concerns; the second, called 'routine', comprised middle rank officials, as well as teachers of the lower ranks; the lower officials and other 'small fry' were placed in a third category, called 'postponed'. The jurisdiction of these Provincial Commissions was not final. They were merely to act as an interim tribunal, until such time as the regular Italian government machinery of 'epuration' could be organised. The principal qualification for membership was undoubtedly anti-Fascist antecedents, and they were to be appointed by the Provincial Commissioner after consultation with the C.L.N.

With regard to Fascist crimes, particularly that of collaboration with the Germans after 8th September 1943, the Allied Commission was inclined to leave the initiative to the Italian Government, but it could hardly avoid being responsible for what occurred in the northern Regions on liberation. It was realised that the Committees of National Liberation would almost certainly be found to have taken the law into their own hands. The problem was therefore to find some procedure which would satisfy the demand for retribution, and yet preserve the adherents of the defeated side from popular vengeance, or from the none too tender mercies of the informal tribunals set up by the partisans. With this end in view, consultations had been arranged between the Italian Government and representatives of the C.L.N.A.I. in Milan. An officer of the Allied Commission had also been sent to France to study the measures taken by General de Gaulle against collaborators. The results of these consultations were embodied by the Italian Government in a decree setting up an Extraordinary Court of Assize to deal with collaborators, which was immediately put into force in A.M.G. territory. This special court consisted of a judge and four lay members to be selected from a panel of 200 reliable anti-Fascists drawn up in each province by the C.L.N.

Wholesale arrests and imprisonment by partisans before A.M.G. appeared on the scene were considered highly probable. In these cases, it was decided that, unless prisons were intolerably congested, and provided that prisoners were not being obviously maltreated by their guards, it would be in the best interests of all concerned to leave persons arrested in prison, until the popular fury on liberation had evaporated. In accordance with the practice observed hitherto, the arrest and interning of Fascists considered dangerous to Allied military interests was to remain in the hands of the military security services.

It had been clear for some months that on liberation conditions might arise amounting almost to civil war. The arrangements for policing the north of Italy were therefore of the utmost importance. Yet in spite of this fact, it had not yet been possible, even on the eve of liberation, to obtain from the Combined Chiefs of Staff permission to raise the ceiling of the *Carabinieri* from 55,000 to 65,000, notwithstanding the serious disturbances which had broken out in Sicily in the winter. The numbers of the Italian army were reduced under the armistice to a comparatively small figure and a ceiling for the strength of the *Carabinieri* was fixed in the summer of 1944 by General Alexander's headquarters as 55,000, which was the pre-war establishment of the Corps. This figure was never accepted as reasonable by the Control Commission, since the responsibilities of this police force had been greatly increased after the occupation by extra tasks imposed. Such extra tasks were e.g. service with Allied and Italian military formations, the checking of civilian movement at the Army Control Line, the marshalling of refugees, the maintenance of block posts to prevent black marketing activities, the enforcement of the harvesting regulations (an important task which had not hitherto been undertaken by this Corps), as well as the joint patrolling of congested urban areas with the Allied military police—all this at a time when public discipline had been reduced in the wake of war and revolution, and in spite of the fact that the Fascist railway, port and street militias had been disbanded.

The practice of introducing *Carabinieri* from the south, which had been followed ever since the liberation of Rome, was to be continued. This was to be done in three stages. First, mobile *Carabinieri* were to accompany the occupying troops of the Allied Armies. These were to be followed by parties, previously brought well forward, and finally by reserve detachments designed to bring the strength of the northern Regions approximately to their pre-war figure with the re-enrolment of former *Carabinieri* reporting for duty. The Allied Commission had made plans for a 'spearhead' force of rather under 6,000 *Carabinieri* and an establishment in the new Regions (IX to XIII) of some 20,000. They therefore demanded an increase in the 'ceiling' from 55,000 to 65,000 with a permissive limit, in case of necessity, of 70,000. The occupation of central Italy had already put a strain on existing establishments, although arrangements had been made to transfer from prisoner of war camps in Africa and the Middle East nearly 50 officers and about 1,500 other ranks. A vigorous campaign for recruitment of *Carabinieri* was carried out and a percentage of army-conscripts was transferred to their ranks. By these means it was found possible to preserve public order, but without any margin for eventualities. Before the year 1944 had ended the establishment began to press heavily on the official ceiling.

The Allied Commission's request for a lifting of the *Carabinieri* ceiling from 55,000 to 65,000 had been supported by General Alexander at the beginning of November 1944, but proceedings at A.F.H.Q. were held up for several weeks. Nor did difficulties cease there. As the *Carabinieri* formed part of the Italian army, an increase in their ceiling would mean an increase in the size of the Italian army to be maintained by the Allies, a step which the Combined Chiefs of Staff, largely owing to American opposition on supply grounds, were unwilling to contemplate. As late as April 1945, in spite of the disorders in Rome, Sicily and Sardinia, the Combined Chiefs were still recommending that the *Carabinieri* needed for northern Italy should be obtained by the transfer of more members of their Corps from the South.

On the 28th April Signor Bonomi, who under the 'New Deal' had become solely responsible for maintaining order in Italian Government territory, approached the Commission for permission to pass a decree increasing the strength of the *Carabinieri* from 55,000 to 65,000. His request was strongly supported by Admiral Stone. SACMED on the 3rd May, though he had not yet received the authorisation from the Combined Chiefs of Staff, instructed the Allied Commission to inform the Italian Prime Minister that there was no objection, while at the same time making it clear that he was unable to enter into any commitments for the rations or the clothing of this additional 10,000. Authorisation from the C.C.S. to increase the *Carabinieri* ceiling from 55,000 to 65,000 was not obtained until the 15th May—a week after hostilities in Europe were over.

Since at the beginning of April the *Carabinieri* ceiling had not yet been lifted, it was decided that the disbanded members of this force reporting for duty could only be re-enlisted (after due screening) if an equal number of (over-age) *Carabinieri* in southern Italy were retired. But the need in Italian Government territory was so great that no reduction in their numbers there could be contemplated. *Carabinieri* returning to duty in the north would therefore have to be taken on in many cases only as auxiliary police. The position was rendered even more difficult by the fact that nearly a thousand members of the corps had to be seconded to police the French, Swiss and Austrian frontiers—an Army, not an A.M.G. responsibility.

The Republican National Guard and the neo-Fascist militias and police forces were to be immediately disbanded, but it was decided to employ, after due screening, the local Public Security Agents. This decision was inevitable, since it would not have been possible to bring in from the south a sufficient number of trained *agenti* without seriously endangering public order. And although it had been found in the south that this force had been more seriously infected with Fascism than the *Carabinieri*, their employment in liberated territory had proved indispensable. Under the command of a *questore* loyal to the Italian Government they had proved reasonably reliable. Indeed without their assistance the repression of crime would have become impossible. Similar considerations pointed to the employment of the Finance Guards. On liberation it was discovered that quite a number of senior officials of both forces, to say nothing of the lower ranks, had secretly assisted the partisans, or at any rate turned a blind eye on their activities. The critical question was the replacement of the neo-Fascist *Questori*. It could not be assumed that the selections made by the C.L.N.A.I. would in every case be acceptable. The Italian Government therefore was asked to form a pool of senior Public Security officers for transfer to the North, if and where needed.

The control of the frontier was a clear Army responsibility, though the Commission was consulted in its planning. In Fifth Army area—which extended to the Italian frontiers with France and Switzerland and part of Austria, including the Brenner—the Counter-Intelligence Corps, and in the Eighth Army area Field Security Services, were in charge of this function. Against the Allied Commission's advice, G-2 at A.F.H.Q. decided to suspend all the Italian frontier police agents discovered *in situ*, many of whom, it was discovered later, had been actively helping the partisans, and to replace them with detachments of *Carabinieri* and Finance Guards brought from the south, though these lacked what might have appeared indispensable, an intimate knowledge of the geography of the frontier. The withdrawal of these essential police agents embarrassed, as already noted, not only the Italian Government but also A.M.G.

The general plan during the early stages of the occupation was to close frontiers completely, but this did not prove very practicable, either on the borders between Piedmont and France, where the ordinary daily occupations of the inhabitants necessitated frequent passage of the frontier line, or on the Austrian frontier where an uncontrolled and uncontrollable movement of displaced persons took place immediately after the end of hostilities. The general arrangements for controlling civilian movements were planned as follows. A frontier zone was to be established in the form of a belt twenty-five kilometres wide round the 1939 frontier. All civilian movements of more than ten kilometres within this zone, and permission to enter or leave it, were to be controlled by the issue of passes by A.M.G. Nor were civilians to pass from Fifth Army to Eighth Army areas without a pass signed by an A.M.G. officer. These regulations, as we shall see, proved quite impossible to enforce.

The problem most intimately connected with frontier control, was that of refugees and displaced persons. There were still a considerable number of Italians in France and Switzerland and an enormous number in Germany. These, of whom there were thought to be about a million, consisted of civilian workers who had been transported for forced labour into Germany and ex-soldiers and ex-prisoners of war.[1] In addition, it was estimated that there would be found in northern Italy at least 30,000 displaced persons who were not Italians. During Phase I every effort would have to be made to impose a standstill. Meanwhile, a network of reception centres would have to be organised in order to deal with the wholesale repatriation which would take place in Phase II. It was assumed that during the

[1] Italian civilian workers in Italy at the end of the war appear to have numbered about 350,000, in addition to the six-to-seven hundred thousand soldiers interned there, who after July, 1944, were gradually reclassified as 'free' workers. See *Survey of International Affairs, 1939-1946*. Hitler's Europe, pp. 322–324.

occupational phase the principal problem would be the care of Italian war-refugees displaced by the Armies and of such nationals of the United Nations as might be liberated. For this purpose the system of refugee centres already organised in and behind the Fifth and Eighth Army areas would be sufficient, supplemented by the organisation of mobile forward groups. Allied nationals in large towns would also be cared for by the forward representatives of the Displaced Persons and Refugees Sub-Commission who would accompany 'spearhead' A.M.G.

In Phase II the systematic repatriation of these large masses of persons would have to be undertaken. Arrangements were to be made with the Italian High Commissioner for Refugees to assist in sorting them out. After the initial examination of the repatriates, who were to be 'screened' by Allied security authorities before crossing the border, former Italian soldiers or ex-prisoners of war would be handed over to the relevant military organisations, while the remainder would have to be dealt with by the Displaced Persons and Refugees Sub-Commission and the Italian High Commissioner for Refugees.

It was planned to set up an advanced repatriation headquarters in Milan, to control a number of collecting and transit centres (about twenty in all), with a capacity of 5,000 persons each, to be filled from a number of frontier repatriation posts. Italian Red Cross personnel were to assist in running the centres. Each frontier collection post and reception centre was to be provided with a certain amount of hospital equipment, medical stores being supplied through the Public Health Sub-Commission. Feeding was to be on the Italian refugee scale, from bulk supplies sent up to the Regions. The method of transport for refugees envisaged as normal was back-loading of Army and Allied Commission vehicles, but, as this was considered to be insufficient, a request was made to A.F.H.Q. for one G.T. company comprising 100 vehicles and ten ambulances and ten water carts for each Group headquarters. Allied nationals, using the term in its broadest sense, were also to be cared for in the refugee centres prepared, and in two additional centres to be established for them at Genoa and Trieste, each provided with a hundred-bed hospital.

Mention must be made, before closing this chapter, of a rather peculiar piece of economic planning, inspired by the hope of preventing inflation in the North, which unfortunately met with no success. This was the economic *cordon sanitaire* to be stretched across the peninsula along the line of the northern Apennines. It was believed that Mussolini and his German masters had been able to maintain a fairly strict system of wage and price-controls, and it was known that at the beginning of 1945 the general level of prices in the north was considerably below that obtaining in liberated Italy. The

Allied Commission therefore planned to stabilise both prices and wages at the official level in force on 3rd April 1945. In order to have any chance of doing this, it would be necessary to treat the five northerly Regions (Emilia, Liguria, Piedmont, Lombardy and the Venetias) as a separate economic unit, and, to insulate them completely from the contagion of the south.

It was realised that in many cases it might not be possible to hold wages at this level, owing to various disturbing influences, such as last-minute wage increases dictated by Mussolini or the Germans in order to create confusion, or the possible action of the workers

Map 13

themselves before Allied Military Government was installed. No changes in wages were, however, to be recognised until they had been submitted for examination to an Italian Joint Advisory Committee to be set up in each Region, consisting of representatives of industry, organised Labour, and the Italian Government. And all controlled prices in operation at the beginning of April were to be maintained, even if this meant a heavy subsidy on imported foodstuffs, the 'landed cost' of which might be very much above the official Italian price.

In order to prevent the sudden movement southwards of every kind of commodity, which would be attracted by the much higher prices prevailing in liberated Italy, it was decided by A.F.H.Q. to establish an Economic Control line running west to east along the northern boundaries of the provinces of Apuania, Lucca, Pistoia, Florence and Ravenna. This line was to be made effective by the setting up by the Armies of road blocks, where military police, assisted by *Carabinieri* and Finance Guards, were to examine all vehicles, military as well as civilian, to prevent the transport of practically all commodities across this line in either direction. The responsibility for setting up these road blocks was placed byA.F.H.Q. on the Armies, military formations being requested to cooperate with the Allied Commission in establishing an effective system of blocks and checks. In practice, as we shall see in the next chapter, this *Cordon Sanitaire Economique* was quite ineffective.

To conclude with a note on establishments. Responsibility for the Military Government of the whole of Italy north of the northern boundaries of Viterbo, Rieti and Teramo was destined to leave A.M.G. officers very thin on the ground. Though, as explained in the last chapter, there were not much more than about sixty officers left south of this boundary and in Sicily and Sardinia, the Umbria–Marche and Tuscany Regions occupied at least 150, and headquarters still close on 400 out of the total of about 1,500 officers, so there were only about 900 officers to undertake the Military Government of the five Regions north of the Apennines, with a population of about twenty million souls.

ANNEXE

Text of Memorandum of Agreement between The Supreme Allied Commander Mediterranean Theatre of Operations and the Committee of National Liberation for Northern Italy

1. The Supreme Allied Commander wishes the utmost military co-operation to be established and maintained among the elements which are active in the resistance movement. The C.L.N.A.I. will establish and maintain such cooperation as will bring together all active elements of the resistance movement whether they belong to the C.L.N.A.I. anti-fascist parties or to other anti-fascist organisations.

2. During the period of enemy occupation the GENERAL COMMAND OF THE VOLUNTEERS OF LIBERTY (being the military command of the C.L.N.A.I.) will, on behalf of the C.L.N.A.I., carry out all instructions of the Commander-in-Chief, A.A.I., acting under the authority of the Supreme Allied Commander. It is in general the wish of the SUPREME ALLIED COMMANDER that particular care should be given to all measures which will safeguard the economic resources of the territory against scorching, demolitions and like depredation of the enemy.

3. The Military head of the General Command of the Volunteers of Liberty (being the military command of the C.L.N.A.I.) must be an officer acceptable to the Commander-in-Chief, A.A.I., acting under the authority of the Supreme Allied Commander.

4. When the enemy withdraws from territory occupied by them the C.L.N.A.I. will exercise its best endeavours to maintain law and order and to continue the safeguarding of the economic resources of the country until such time as Allied Military Government is established. Immediately upon the establishment of Allied Military Government, C.L.N.A.I. will recognise Allied Military Government and will hand over to that Government all authority and powers of local government and administration previously assumed. As the enemy withdraws all components of the GENERAL COMMAND OF THE VOLUNTEERS OF LIBERTY in liberated territory will come under direct command of the Commander-in-Chief, A.A.I., acting under the authority of the Supreme Allied Commander, and will obey any order issued by him or by Allied Military Government on his behalf, including such orders to disband and surrender their arms, when required to do so.

5. During the period of enemy occupation in Northern Italy the utmost assistance will be given to the C.L.N.A.I. in common with all other anti-fascist organisations, to meet the needs of their members who are engaged in opposing the enemy in occupied territory; a monthly contribution not exceeding 160 million lire will be made on the authority of the Supreme Allied Commander to meet the expenses of the C.L.N.A.I. and all other anti-fascist organisations.

Subject to the general control of the Commander-in-Chief, A.A.I., acting under the authority of the Supreme Allied Commander, this sum will be apportioned to the following areas in the following ratio for the support of all anti-fascist organisations in those areas:

Liguria	20
Piemonte	60
Lombardia	25
Emilia	20
Veneto	35

The above sum and allocations will be subject to variation according to the requirements of the military situation: the maximum sum will be reduced proportionately as and when Provinces are liberated.

6. Allied Missions attached to the C.L.N.A.I., to the General Command of the Volunteers of Liberty, or to any of their components, will be consulted by them in all matters relating to armed resistance, anti-scorch and maintenance of order. Orders issued by the Commander-in-Chief, A.A.I., under the authority of the Supreme Allied Commander and transmitted through the missions concerned will be carried out by C.L.N.A.I., the General Command of the Volunteers of Liberty and their components.

Text of Agreement made between the Italian Government and the Committee of National Liberation for North Italy

The Italian Government recognises the Committee of National Liberation for Northern Italy (C.L.N.A.I.) as the organ of the anti-Fascist parties in the territory occupied by the enemy.

The Italian Government designates the C.L.N.A.I. as its representative in the struggle that the patriots have undertaken against the Fascists and Germans in that part of Italy not yet liberated.

The C.L.N.A.I. agrees to act towards this end as the delegate of the Italian Government which is recognised by the Allied Governments as the successor of the Government which signed the Armistice Terms and is the sole legitimate authority in that part of Italy which has already been or will later on be restored to the Italian Government by the Allied Military Government.

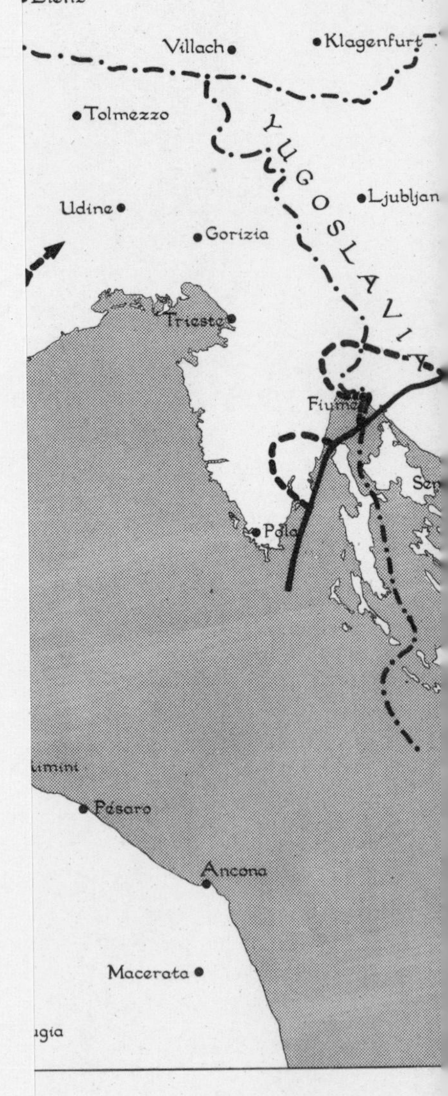

USTRIA
Lienz
Villach
Klagenfurt
Tolmezzo
YUGOSLAVIA
Udine
Gorizia
Trieste
Fiume
Pola
Pesaro
Ancona
Macerata

CHAPTER XI

LIBERATION

THE ESSENTIAL characteristic of the final phase of the Italian campaign was the extreme rapidity of events, which carried the Allied Armies from the Apennines to the Alps in little over a week. The main offensive opened on the evening of 9th April, Bologna was entered on 21st April, and by 1st May A.M.G. had already been established in Genoa, Turin, Milan and Venice. The next day hostilities in Italy were formally concluded, under the instrument of surrender signed at Caserta on 29th April, and within a week the war in Europe had ended with the final surrender of the remaining German armies. Thus the fundamental conditions under which Allied Military Government was to work were completely changed within a fortnight.

Hitherto the paramount problem facing A.M.G. in the forward areas had been how to keep the people fed—a problem dominated by the insufficiency of domestic and imported supplies and transport to distribute them. But in the North conditions in this respect were much easier. The harvest was due to begin to be gathered at the end of June, and existing supplies were sufficient to keep people fed, though not everywhere fully, till the new harvest was in. There was thus never any real danger of starvation or of serious prolonged shortages, even in the large cities like Genoa, Turin and Milan; though conditions during the first few weeks entailed some anxiety, when it was not found possible to distribute the 200 gm ration laid down by A.F.H.Q. as the minimum. In respect of other essential civilian supplies, except coal, the position was also much easier. Motor transport, though far from plentiful, was nothing like as short as it had been in southern Italy. The railway system was comparatively undamaged and, thanks to the continued supply of electric power, could promptly be put into operation. The expected destruction of the great hydro-electric installations never took place, so that within a comparatively short period transmission lines could be repaired, where they had been interrupted, and no shortage of power for current needs was generally felt. Other public utilities too were much less damaged. Telephone services were quickly restored, water supplies were for the most part reasonably adequate, and tramway and railway services were soon put back into operation. In some places they had never been completely interrupted.

In this last phase, the problem which caused A.M.G. most anxiety was public safety. With the collapse of the German army and the disappearance of the neo-Fascist regime, control of the administrative machine had everywhere passed into the hands of the C.L.N. before A.M.G. arrived on the scene. The *Guardia Nazionale Repubblicana* (G.N.R.), the police forces of the Social Republic—an amalgam of ex-*Carabinieri* and various neo-Fascist security-militias—had been dissolved by the C.L.N.; and though the other two regular police forces, the Agents of Public Safety and the Finance Guards, continued to function under the command of officers appointed by the C.L.N. they were almost powerless in the face of tens of thousands of armed partisans. The C.L.N. had constituted a police force from the partisan ranks, but the existence of miscellaneous bodies of armed men, of which the most powerful were Communists, was an obvious menace, since, in addition to the regularly militarised and comparatively well-disciplined military bands, the number of partisans had been enormously swollen on liberation by last-minute 'patriots', who had seized a large quantity of German and neo-Fascist arms.

The danger of civil war between patriots and neo-Fascist forces never took actual shape. The Allied Command very wisely decided that all irregular neo-Fascist forces, even the Black Brigades, were to be treated as prisoners of war, and such of them as were still found in existence after the Allied forces appeared on the scene surrendered to Allied units wherever they could. Moreover the mere fact of Allied occupation made anything like civil war or a revolution impossible. But clandestine executions resulting from the vengeance of partisan groups on their neo-Fascist enemies, which on more than one occasion resulted in the breaking open of prisons and the massacre of prisoners, were a constant menace to public order, to say nothing of the very large numbers of murders inspired merely by private vindictiveness, as well as blackmailing exactions and robberies carried out by ex-partisans. This danger could only be eliminated by the effective disarmament of all partisans—a process which needed very tactful and delicate handling, if recourse to a large scale intervention of the Allied armed forces was to be avoided.

Behind this problem of public safety lay the even more delicate political question of the C.L.N.A.I. and its relations, not only to Allied Military Government, but also to the Italian Government in Rome. The measures described in the last chapter did in fact lead to an orderly solution, but in the first days after the insurrection it sometimes looked as if the issue was still hanging in the balance. In the event, relations with Rome provided little difficulty. Nor did the transfer of powers by the Committees of National Liberation to A.M.G. lead to any serious complications. Though the Committees of National Liberation were nearly everywhere in effective control of the administrative machine when Allied troops arrived, and during the first weeks it was not always easy for A.M.G. to make it clear to them that executive action was no longer their responsibility, no conflict of any importance arose, even if here and there a considerable amount of obstruction was encountered. The acceptance by the Committees of their advisory role was rendered much easier by the fact that in nearly every case A.M.G. was willing to confirm the administrative appointments made before its arrival, and by the elevation of one of the most distinguished leaders of the Resistance Movement to the post of Prime Minister. In general too the Regional teams confined their intervention in the work of the administrative machine to the barest essentials. The end of hostilities made it plain, to A.M.G. no less than to Italian officials, that the transfer of administrative responsibility to the Italian Government would not long be delayed. A.M.G. therefore made no attempt to impose the system of detailed control which had been considered necessary in southern Italy. Nor indeed could such an attempt ever have been successful. The war was over, and the northern Italian officials were much more self-reliant than those in the South. Moreover, A.M.G. officers were thinner on the ground than ever.

The points at issue between the C.L.N.A.I. and the Italian Government in Rome were quickly brought to a head. It had always been assumed that on the liberation of the North the Bonomi Government would resign, and that either Signor Bonomi or some other political leader would then form a new administration including representatives of the more powerful half of the community. The selection of Signor Parri as the new premier successfully resolved the potential tension of North *versus* South, even if his administration was destined to be merely transitional. Once the Parri Government took over the controls, the influence of the Committees of National Liberation over the public opinion quickly faded out. The unity of these Committees, made up of members of renascent political parties inspired by profoundly differing ideals, had only been achieved in the days of clandestine warfare under the pressure of German and neo-Fascist violence. It had often been very far from perfect, and, now that the gaze of each party was focused upon the contest of elections for the Constituent Assembly, the Committees as such soon ceased to have any meaning or coherence.

To return to the campaign. The first Allied troops entered Bologna shortly after six o'clock on the morning of 21st April. A.M.G. officers of II Corps established themselves in the *Municipio* about mid-day. They found that the C.L.N. had already designated a Socialist Prefect and a Communist Mayor, both of whom proved admirably cooperative. Conditions were stated to be unusually satisfactory. There was no shortage of food and thirty days' supply of grain and potatoes were reported. Though there was no electricity from normal sources available, since the principal power station was still in German hands and power lines from the north had been cut, it was possible to keep a small thermal plant in action to pump water and supply light for all hospitals and some public buildings. The city was crowded with refugees, numbering well over 50,000 according to the first reports, and later found to be considerably more. The refugees had packed into the town from the surrounding countryside and installed themselves and their animals in such houses as they could find. The water system, owing to war-damage outside the city, was only working at about half capacity and the sewage system was severely injured with the result that sanitary conditions in many portions of the town were very bad. The telephone exchange had also been destroyed. But apart from this, damage to the main part of the city, with the exception of the railway station and the marshalling yards, was not as great as had been expected, though several important monuments, including the famous sixteenth century anatomical theatre, known as the *Archiginnasio*, had been wrecked.

Three 'brigades'[1] of partisans totalling nearly 4,000 were discovered in the city and their leader Dario, a Communist, agreed to do everything he could to assist disarmament. Owing to traffic congestion the 230 *Carabinieri* dispatched from Florence arrived only at midnight on the day of entry. But thanks to the C.L.N. it had been possible to 'screen' a city police force before taking the city. Police wearing an A.M.G. arm band were on the streets two hours after the first troops entered. The ceremonial parade for the distribution of Alexander certificates was held in the main square on the afternoon of 25th April, the day on which Crown Prince Umberto also visited the city and was well received. It was attended by General Mark Clark, commander of Fifteenth Army Group, Brig.-General Hume, commanding A.M.G. Fifth Army, and several other general officers. But much less than 4,000 weapons were handed in after the parade, and those only of the oldest types. The more efficient arms had been retained—an experience which was everywhere to be repeated in the other northern Regions. At Modena the disbandment parade was more successful, being attended by about 9,000 partisans. The number of weapons handed in in here, in Reggio Emilia, and in Parma was proportionately rather greater than in Bologna, though in these towns too the retention, chiefly by Communists, of the more efficient arms left food for thought.

[1] Care must be taken not to compare the size of partisan units with those of regular army formations with the same name. Sizes of partisan units varied enormously, but some idea of their real military equivalent may be gained from the fact that a partisan battalion was normally commanded by a first lieutenant, a 'brigade' by a major or lieut.-colonel.

Partisans continued for some time to present a considerable danger to public order. The *Carabinieri* imported by A.M.G. from the South were insufficient in number and poorly equipped, and the partisans at first had little respect for them. Nor were the ex-*Carabinieri* who reported for duty numerous enough for some time to build up a force adequate to deal with the crimes committed in the city and the surrounding country by 'patriots' who had for many months been outlaws. Partisan vindictiveness and private cupidity combined to create a formidable 'crime wave'. During the weeks following liberation a large number of crimes were committed not only in the cities but all over the surrounding country—assault and robbery, blackmail, illegal execution, mysterious abduction and assassination—the product of clandestine partisan-justice, as well as of private murder. Local C.L.N.'s also took the opportunity to demand large ransoms from rich landowners, Emilia being one of the chief areas of *latifondo*.

It would appear, from early Psychological Warfare Branch reports, that the C.L.N.'s, in which the Communists predominated, were in many cases none too eager, in spite of the efforts of the Christian Democrats, to come out into the open and call upon the partisans to quell these disorders, though they certainly did make some attempt to prevent the worst excesses of irregular justice. The C.L.N., in accordance with plans made before liberation, had appointed a special commission immediately after liberation, to bring to justice all Fascists and 'collaborators' who had been put into prison, except those held by the Allied authorities.[1] All persons apprehended were to be taken to the San-Giovanni-in-Monte prison. Most of them however, never reached it, but were tried by improvised tribunals and clandestinely executed. Three persons who were examined by this judicial commission, and released because they were found not-guilty, were discovered next day mysteriously killed.

The first task of A.M.G. was to suppress these irregular tribunals. The authority of the C.L.N. Commission as a judicial body could not be recognised, but use was made of it in the collection of evidence. With the setting up of the extraordinary courts of Assize, which came into action during the first days in June, in accordance with the Decree-Law published by the Italian Government on the day following the capture of Bologna, these manifestations of popular and private vengeance began to die down, but the number of crimes of violence committed both in the town and in the country continued to be appallingly high, and increased somewhat after the handing over

---

[1] The members of this Commission were a professional lawyer (Communist), a police Commissioner approved by the Communist party, and a Christian Democrat.

of Emilia to Italian Government administration at the end of July. But apart from this crime-wave public order was preserved.

After liberating Bologna, the victorious Allied Armies swept across the Po valley to the Alps. Modena was entered on 23rd April, Reggio Emilia, Parma, Mantua and Verona on the 25th, Piacenza on the 28th, Padua on the 29th and Venice and Milan on the 30th. Meanwhile IV Corps had advanced no less rapidly, occupying Genoa on the 27th and Turin on the 30th. Conditions at the installation of A.M.G. in the principal towns of the North were determined in nearly every case by the fact that a general insurrection of the partisans had occurred some days before A.M.G. arrived, and that the C.L.N. had managed to re-organise the administration by dismissing the chief officials of the Social Republic and placing substitutes of their own selection, Prefects, Mayors and *Questori*, at the head of the various departments.

In Genoa the patriots rose against the German garrison, apparently quite a considerable force, on 23rd April.[1] It would appear that the German commander, General Meinhold, had received orders from the German Higher Command to retire in the direction of Lombardy, and had endeavoured to obtain an agreement from the partisans through the intervention of the Archbishop to allow him to withdraw without fighting. But the intermediary whom he chose for these negotiations was a patriot; before going to the Archbishop's palace he divulged the secret to the partisans, who immediately rose in insurrection.[2] On the 25th the German Commander, apparently to the great surprise of the C.L.N.[3], surrendered to the partisans. The Allied forces did not appear on the scene until two days later. Apart from the destruction which had been caused by Allied air-raids—and this was very considerable—the city was not seriously damaged. The German plans to destroy the port appear to have been countermanded[4] or had miscarried, except for the mining of the harbour and its approaches and its blocking by sunken vessels, which caused many weeks' delay in opening it for civilian purposes. A considerable proportion of the dock installations were still in

---

[1] The first P.W.B. report after Allied entry reckoned the German garrison at between 6,000 and 7,000, but some Italian sources state that the German troops amounted to over a division. *Tamaro op. cit.* Vol. III, pp. 583–84.

[2] See Valiani, *Tutte le Strade Conducono a Roma*, p. 335.

[3] Cf. Tamaro, *loc. cit.*

[4] According to one Italian source (Silvestri, *Graziani, Mussolini e l'antifascismo*, p. 533), the installations of the port were spared by an agreement between General Meinhold and the Social-Republican General Farina. It would appear that General Wolff, the S.S. leader, in accordance with a pledge given during his negotiations for surrender with the representatives of the O.S.S. in Switzerland, had issued instructions that sabotage was not to be attempted. See Lanfranchi, *La resa delgi otto-cento mila*, pp. 261–63, who quotes the memoirs of Baron Parilli, one of the persons concerned with the negotiations.

action. Public utilities, except gas, for which there was no coal, were working almost normally.

But during the first days of liberation there was an acute food shortage, since stocks were exhausted. The roads had to be kept clear for Allied military transport, and all truck and car movements were stopped, to permit the systematic organisation of transport by A.M.G. Moreover restrictions imposed by the Allied Naval Command prohibited coastal fishing in the area. By 30th April A.M.G. had begun to bring flour in by road, and an initial daily distribution of 100 gms per head was inaugurated—the same ration as had been distributed just before liberation. But before the end of May this was increased to 150 gms, though the minimum laid down by A.F.H.Q. was not attained until July. Supplies for Genoa soon began to arrive by sea, but only in very limited quantities. Owing to the mining of the port entrance, they had to be unloaded on the beaches—a process which was sometimes interrupted by the weather. It was over two months before the port could deal with civil supplies in any volume.

Before Allied arrival the C.L.N. had installed as Prefect a member of the Liberal Party, a Christian Democrat Vice-Prefect, a Socialist Mayor, a Republican *Questore* and a Communist *Vice-Questore*, as well as certain other officials.[1] They had also set up popular tribunals and an elaborate machinery for 'epuration', embracing not only government departments and public utilities but also the whole of industry. This included committees in every workshop—a much more far-reaching system than had as yet been contemplated by the Italian Government. These committees were in most cases entirely dominated by left-wing ideas, and in many cases deliberately set about to expel managers and technicians, quite without regard to any Fascist associations. These factory committees had been set up by the C.L.N. only to make recommendations, not to take action, which was the responsibility of a central committee, but from the outset they took the law into their own hands. It was some time before the C.L.N. succeeded in curbing their excesses. These factory committees were found installed everywhere in the North and caused A.M.G. a good deal of trouble. Indeed, it was not until after the middle of June that the tangle was straightened out in a Regional Order adopted by all the northern Regions, which provided for the epuration of workmen and employees in private industry.

The Popular Tribunals for punishing Fascists and collaborators had already started a process of summary judgements and executions

---

[1] In Liguria the C.L.N. was formed by six parties, as also in Emilia, whereas the C.L.N.A.I. was composed only of five, since Labour Democrats were not represented in the North. The Republican party was a small group: its best-known leader was Piccardi, who had been Badoglio's right-hand man in his first government.

when A.M.G. arrived. They were immediately suppressed by agreement with the C.L.N., pending the setting up of the special Assize courts in accordance with the law just passed by the Italian Government. The result was that they went underground. The C.L.N. had promised in the first days of May to hand over all their prisoners to the normal police authorities, but found themselves unable to fulfil their promise. The partisan tribunals for many weeks continued to administer secret justice with summary executions, depositing the bodies of their victims by night in various places in the city and its suburbs. The number of persons executed in Genoa and the Ligurian towns probably amounted to several hundreds[1], and it was not until the special courts of Assize began to function in the beginning of June that these secret executions finally ceased.

Under these conditions imported Carabinieri, together with such Public Service Agents and Finance Guards as remained after 'epuration', were quite insufficient to guarantee the safety of life or property. It was therefore found necessary to supplement these regular police forces with auxiliary police recruited from the partisans. A force of 500 was recruited, 400 from the patriot bands and 100 from the smaller, part-time urban partisan units. These were finally incorporated with the existing regular police forces.

The adaptation of the Genoese C.L.N. to the new environment of Allied Military Government took a little time and gave rise to a good deal of disillusionment among the 'leftist' parties. In its clandestine period the Committee had compiled a scheme of legislation embodied in decrees dealing with social and economic measures besides 'de-fascistisation', under powers conferred on it by the C.L.N.A.I.[2]. These were intended to reinforce and supersede much of the legislation of the Government in Rome, considered as tainted with Fascist and Monarchist reaction. It therefore came as something of a shock when A.M.G., besides publishing its own legislation under proclamations and general orders, proceeded to introduce the legislation of the Central Government in Rome.[3] Nor was it easy to persuade the C.L.N. that its functions were now purely advisory. As late as 12th May the C.L.N. suggested to A.M.G. that all correspondence

---

[1] According to Simiani, *I Guistiziati dell' Aprile 1945*, the number was 1,500. It is impossible to arrive at any reliable figures for the number of persons killed in Northern Italy during the insurrection and the immediately following weeks. Estimates vary between 300,000—a fantastic exaggeration—and 1,732 the number given in 1952 by Mario Scelba, Minister of the Interior for the murders and disappearances between 25 April and 5 May. (See *The Survey of International Affairs, 1939–46*. 'The realignment of Europe,' p. 434). Simiani's figure (*op. cit.*) is 40,000.

[2] Under a 'circular' dated 30th August 1944, for the text of which see *Atti del C.L.N.A.I.*, pp. 44 seq.

[3] This was (theoretically) brought into force on 7th May by the introduction into Liguria of a truck-load of the back numbers of the *Gazzetta Ufficiale*.

between the Prefect and the Provincial Commissioner should pass through its hands.

The partisans continued for some time to give A.M.G. a good deal of anxiety with their summary executions and various acts of robbery, but there was no organised attempt to develop an anti-Allied or an anti-Rome resistance movement. Disbandment and disarmament however were not so quickly accomplished. A spectacular parade was held on 2nd May. The General commanding the 92nd U.S. Division invited the Regional commander of the partisan Corps of Volunteers of Liberty (C.V.L.) to take the salute with him, and though arms in considerable quantity were handed in, they were mostly of the obsolete variety. Disarmament of the population, as elsewhere in the North—A.M.G. proclamations notwithstanding—was a slow business. This was in part due to operational considerations. In Liguria certain partisan bands, amounting to about 1,800, were kept armed for some time in the mountains, in order to help IV Corps in the mopping up operations in the Ligurian hills, and in the frontier provinces the French attempts at occupation, to be described in the next chapter, rendered disarmament impracticable for some weeks. The regular full-time partisans, who had taken to the hills, were only one part of the problem. Much more difficult to deal with were the clandestine urban part-time 'special operation' squads and groups, SAP and GAP, to say nothing of the large number of bogus post-liberation 'patriots' who had acquired arms—a problem which reached even greater dimensions in Milan and Turin. In spite of these difficulties, the normal machinery of day to day administration continued to function reasonably well. Once the relations between A.M.G. and C.L.N. had been straightened out it was possible to proceed (rather belatedly) to the appointment of the various 'representative' bodies of local government, such as the Communal *Giunta*, and the *Deputazione Provinciale*, which gave active employment to many members of the C.L.N. and provided some administrative check on the actions of officials by giving voice to different currents of public opinion.

In Turin also the partisans had played an active part in driving out the enemy. The Piedmontese C.L.N., which, in the opinion of the British Partisan Liaison officer in Lombardy, was perhaps the most vigorous and efficient of the Regional Committees of Liberation, had set up its own administration some days before the arrival of A.M.G. It had also instituted a Partisan police force to maintain public order, after the National Republican Guard had been dissolved, and had carried out a drastic purge of the Agents of Public Safety and the Finance Guards. The 'liberation' of Turin had started with a series of general strikes—including one of magistrates —on 18th April. From that date the neo-Fascists and Germans lost control completely, and the workers entrenched themselves in the factories on 25th April. Fighting broke out on the following day, and the partisan bands from the surrounding country began to approach the city. The zero hour for the insurrection was 1300 hrs on the 27th, but GAP and SAP formations had already occupied many of the public buildings, including the police, radio and railway stations.

The Germans in Turin attempted to negotiate with the C.L.N. an unmolested withdrawal for their troops, but this was refused. A good deal of desultory street fighting took place, but the partisans were unable to prevent the withdrawal of German armoured detachments. The C.L.N. also refused a free passage through the city to General Schlemmer's forces, including two armoured divisions in retirement from the French frontier, and the General threatened to bombard the city, but this threat was not in fact carried out, apparently thanks to the intervention of Cardinal Fossati, the Archbishop of Turin.[1] The Germans consequently retired eastwards to the north of the city. For some days the Fascists put up a certain amount of resistance and a good deal of sniping took place. Meanwhile the partisans had occupied all the principal industrial and public-utility installations in and around the city. This certainly helped to save them from German sabotage, though in view of the collapse of the German army and the undertaking given by General Wolff during the negotiations for surrender in Switzerland, it is not at all clear to what extent plans of sabotage were actually on the point of execution, or to what extent they had been countermanded.[2] It was, however, discovered that one electric transmitter had been blown up at the last minute by a German officer.

Allied troops did not enter Turin until 30th April, and it was several days before A.M.G. could be properly installed. But the political advisers of the Commission, Mr Hopkinson and Mr Maclean, arrived by air from Milan on 3rd May and had an interview with the C.L.N., which was administering the area with the advice and assistance of the British Liaison officer attached to the Piedmontese partisan command. Although there were still a few German snipers in the town, all public services were running, and the provincial administration had already been reconstituted. Public order was extremely well preserved. The C.L.N.A.I. in a decree passed on 25th April 1945[3], the day before its formal assumption of power, had made arrangements for the punishment of Fascists and collaborators, setting up Commissions of Justice in each province to act as public prosecutors for the trial of persons before Partisan military tribunals

---

[1] Tamaro, *op. cit.* Vol. III, p. 611.

[2] It is interesting to note that General Cadorna lays great stress on the fact that, if the Germans had intended to carry out sabotage on an extensive scale, the partisan forces would have been quite insufficient to prevent them. See *op. cit.* p. 239.

[3] The text is given in *Atti del C.L.N.A.I.* p. 21 seq.

and People's Courts of Assize. The former were to function only during the state of emergency of the insurrection, when the province was placed under a sort of martial law. In Turin and other parts of Piedmont drastic action was taken during the state of emergency by the military tribunals. A large number of persons were executed. But General Trabucchi, the Commander of the Piedmontese C.V.L., defends, or at any rate extenuates, the actions of these courts-martial, not altogether unreasonably, on the ground that it was only by displaying great initial severity that he was able to prevent a real massacre.[1] During these days of insurrection there was not a single case of looting. On 3rd May the state of siege was ended by a prefectoral decree and People's Courts of Assize were substituted for the military tribunals. These popular courts, which included workshop tribunals dominated by Communists, were, of course, formally dissolved by the C.L.N. under orders of A.M.G. But in Turin too, as in Genoa, they went underground. A considerable number of secret killings took place, though not as many as in Milan, and before the end of the third week in May they had ceased entirely. The number of persons executed by the partisans appears to have been quite large. No accurate figures have been published, but General Trabucchi estimated that 2,000 were executed in Piedmont during the days of insurrection. The process of purging had also been taken in hand, and a Central Commission set up, the members of which were subsequently confirmed by A.M.G. But the establishment of miniature soviets in the principal factories, labelled 'C.L.N' and dominated by Communists, led, as in Genoa, to a good deal of confusion at first, owing to their practice of expelling wholesale members of the technical and managerial staffs.

The establishment of A.M.G. in the first days of May put an end to the administration of the Piedmontese C.L.N., which was perhaps rather quicker than that of Lombardy to understand that its executive functions had terminated. On 8th May it issued a formal resignation of its powers into the hands of A.M.G. and acknowledged its new advisory role, constituting itself as *Giunta Consultativa*. But it took a good deal longer to unlearn the habits of command, and for its various local subordinate organs to accustom themselves to their new purely consultative functions. Meanwhile the occupation of Piedmont was complicated by quite a different problem in the shape of the French penetration into the Val d'Aosta and other frontier territories, which will be dealt with in the following chapter.

Before describing conditions in Milan, the political centre of gravity of the North, it may perhaps be convenient to record some of the conditions discovered by A.M.G. Fifth Army in its advance to the Brenner and by A.M.G. Eighth Army on its way to the British zone

[1] Trabucchi, *I vinti hanno sempre torto*, p. 214.

in Austria. The difficulties which had been anticipated during the planning stage in the administration of Venezia Tridentina, in connection with the German minority population, did not in fact materialise. Though the Germans had administered the two provinces of Trento and Bolzano as well as that of Belluno under a special regime dependent upon the *Gauleiter* of Austria, they had not had time to alter the administrative system to any great extent. Beyond the infiltration of a considerable number of German civilian settlers and officials and the reinstatement of the old Austrian place-names, they had taken no measures of annexation to the *Reich*, except in the neighbourhood of Brunico (Bruneck), where a few communes appear to have been reorganised on the German administrative system. There had been no attempt to Germanise the province of Trento, except in a few communes, parts of which had been transferred by the Germans to Bolzano. The province was thus predominantly Italian. And even in the province of Bolzano there was a substantial Italian majority in the capital. The Austrian population was thus practically confined to the high Alpine area.

A.M.G. officers only reached Bolzano some days after the cessation of hostilities. The special Liaison officer of A.C. headquarters with Fifth Army A.M.G., who arrived in Bolzano on 5th May, reported that the C.L.N. before the arrival of A.M.G. had nominated their president, Signor De Angelis, as Head of the Administration—an emergency title created *ad hoc* to enable him to give orders to the Prefect. He was subsequently appointed Prefect by A.M.G. His appointment as Head of the Administration had been recognised by the Commander-in-Chief of the German forces in Italy, General Vietinghoff, and counter-signed by him. The Prefect in office was an Austrian by birth who had held the post for seven years and was generally liked by both Italians and Austrians. The town, which had been the headquarters of the German Supreme Commander and had therefore been packed with German troops, was under control of the C.L.N. and public order was being kept by joint patrols of Germans, still under arms, though they had surrendered, and a Partisan police force into which a large number of local ex-*Carabinieri* had been absorbed. The German patrols were, of course, done away with as soon as A.M.G. with its mobile *Carabinieri* arrived, but in the meantime the city presented the rather curious spectacle of armed Germans and armed partisans patrolling the streets, while Allied officers were walking about unarmed. Most of the provincial services were being run by joint committees representing both nationalities and the C.L.N. itself had coopted two ex-Austrian members. (A number of Austrian 'patriots' had incidentally been infiltrated by the Russians).

Relations between Italians and ex-Austrians were, considering the circumstances, good. The complete restoration of the normal Italian administrative machinery, under the able administration of Signor De Angelis, presented few difficulties. The immediate problems were the disposal of the surrendered Germans and the feeding and despatch southward of the stream of Italian refugees which soon began to return over the Brenner. The friendly relations that had grown up between Austrians and Italians in the first flush of liberation did not long survive the strain. But no really serious inter-racial trouble was experienced by A.M.G.

In Venice insurrection had broken out on the night of 26th April. On the 28th the neo-Fascist authorities, including the commander of a Black Brigade, made their unconditional surrender to the partisans, and the government of the C.L.N. was installed. The commander of the German garrison refused to surrender, and threatened at first to bombard the city from the mainland and the Lido, in spite of the orders which he was said to have received through the intervention of Herr Rahn, the German ambassador to the Social-Republic, that the city was to be spared all destruction and that fighting within its boundaries was to be avoided. An agreement was however subsequently made with the German Commander, at the suggestion, it would appear, of the British Liaison Officer with the partisan command, under which he was permitted to withdraw his troops unmolested, on condition that he abstained from all destruction. German troops withdrew on the night of 28/29th; the first Allied troops arrived from Mestre on the 30th. A few days before this agreement had been reached, the Germans had attempted to block the harbour by sinking certain ships, but their attempts appear to have been foiled by partisan initiative.

The establishment of military government provided no peculiar difficulties. The President of the Regional C.L.N. was particularly helpful, and little time was lost in making arrangements for the setting up of the special Courts of Assize to try Fascists. The report of the Regional Commissioner for May makes no mention of any clandestine executions in the city, such as those which took place in Turin and Milan, though many did occur in other portions of the Region, notably in the province of Padua where seven prisoners were taken out of gaol at Solesino on 9th May. Their bodies were discovered next day—a foretaste of the large scale massacre of prisoners which took place at Schio early in July. It was only by prompt action in setting up the extraordinary courts of Assize that serious trouble was avoided.

Though Venice itself was practically undamaged and nearly all the hydro-electric installations in the Region had escaped sabotage, destruction in certain cities, such as Vicenza, was heavy. An urgent problem was presented by the damage caused to the embankments of the Po, Adige, Brenta and Piave rivers by German demolitions and

Allied operations which had involved cutting through the banks to give access to Bailey bridges. The rivers were due to rise about the middle of May and to remain in flood until July. Immediate steps were therefore taken by the *Genio Civile* under the command of A.M.G. to make this safe. The Eighth Army also took a hand. Engineers put a large force to work to raise the approaches to the Bailey bridges and fill in the cuts, and the Army provided a million sandbags to assist the A.M.G. Regional Engineer in doing essential repairs.

Owing to the swift move of its formations into Austria following the German surrender, A.M.G. Eighth Army handed over provinces to Regional control at a very early date. Regional headquarters was established at Padua on 5th May and the provinces of Rovigo, Padua, Venice and Treviso were passed to Regional control on 8th May. A.M.G. was set up in Udine on 2nd May and the province was placed under Regional control on 11th May for administrative purposes, though it remained operationally under A.M.G. Eighth Army. The remainder of Venetia proper and Venezia Tridentina was under the control of A.M.G. Fifth Army.

It had been laid down by the Combined Chiefs of Staff as a matter of general policy that A.M.G. would be established in all territories within the Italian boundaries of 1939, including Venezia Giulia. But a large portion of this territory had been occupied some time before the arrival of the Allies by Yugoslav forces—Marshal Tito's army and partisans. Hence the negotiations with the Marshal to be described in the next chapter. Pending the outcome of these discussions it was considered impossible to set up military government in Trieste and practically the whole of Italy's formerly Austrian territory, though it was immediately established by the Eighth Army in a few communes on the Isonzo river, through which passed the road from Udine to Austria via Tarvisio. This and the railway line Udine–Tarvisio–Villach formed the main axis of communications of the Eighth Army into the British zone of Austria.

Yugoslav penetration had extended well beyond the limits of the old Austrian frontier and appears to have been directed towards the annexation of the territory between the Isonzo and Tagliamento rivers. It had been encouraged by the action of some of the Communist Italian partisan formations—for example, the *Natisone* division of the local *Garibaldini*—who had placed themselves in the winter of 1944 under the operational command of Marshal Tito's IV Corps. Not all the Friulian partisans however shared these Communist and pro-Tito sympathies. The non-party Osoppo division had assumed a more nationalist attitude, with the result that there had developed open rift between the two partisan forces, resulting in some killings of the Osoppo leaders. The Allies, on their arrival in

Udine, thus faced two mutually suspicious, if not hostile, Italian partisan formations, in addition to a considerable number of Yugoslav troops and partisans who had penetrated west of the Isonzo. The position was further complicated by the presence in the province of some Chetniks, about 8,000 of whom had fought their way against both Tito and the Germans into Gorizia. The Yugoslavs systematically commandeered foodstuffs and transport and every kind of commodity from the Italian inhabitants of the province. This for a while caused A.M.G. acute anxiety. When they finally retreated east of the Isonzo they carried away with them a great deal of loot, including cattle. But by the end of May nearly all the Yugoslav troops had been withdrawn. A.M.G. had been set up in the whole territory west of the Isonzo, though it was not fully established in Venezia Giulia west of the Morgan Line until about the middle of June.[1]

The official entry of Allied troops into Milan was made by the American 34th Division on 30th April, though small parties had managed to enter the outskirts of the city the previous day. Here too they found all public services working, since there had been no German demolitions. An efficient administration had also been installed by the C.L.N. As in Turin, the insurrection ordered by the C.L.N.A.I. on 25th April had been preceded by a widespread strike, during which various leaders of the Social Republic had made the attempt to negotiate with the Resistance movement, including Mussolini himself, who got into touch with General Cadorna and the C.L.N.A.I., through the historically appropriate intervention of the successor of St. Ambrose, Cardinal Schuster. During the insurrection itself there was a certain amount of street fighting and sniping by neo-Fascists, but by this time neither the Germans nor the Social Republicans had much stomach left for the fight. The actual scale of the fighting does not appear to have been at all heavy. Moreover the enemy, besides being demoralised by the departure of Mussolini, was also taken by surprise. The losses of the patriots were consequently very light.[2]

Allied Military Government was set up in the city on 30th April. The German commander had surrendered, but there were still about a thousand Germans in the city, of whom 150, with several German W.A.C's, had barricaded themselves in the Post Office building. The commander refused to surrender until he had received orders to do so, and threatened to blow up the telephone building if attacked. Meanwhile, an A.M.G. Communications Officer appears to have

[1] See below, p. 345.

[2] See Longo, *Un popolo alla macchia*, p. 437.

been working quite happily in the same building! But during these hectic days confusion was by no means confined entirely to the enemy. Of this the installation of A.M.G. provided an interesting example. Colonel Poletti, Regional Commissioner of Region XII (Lombardy), and his deputy, Colonel Hancock, who had been instructed to accompany the Senior Civil Affairs Officer of A.M.G. IV Corps into Milan, managed to arrive in that city the day before Allied troops actually entered it. The D.C.C.A.O. Fifteenth Army Group had met them in Florence and suggested that they should fly with him to Milan so that he could present them to the S.C.A.O., but on account of the weather they decided to proceed on their way by road. They thus arrived in the city on 29th April, the day before the S.C.A.O. of IV Corps, who insisted on their immediate withdrawal. The Regional organisation was not established until 13th May.

The officials installed by the C.L.N.A.I., whom A.M.G. discovered *in situ* on entering Milan, were after a lapse of some time confirmed by General Hume, S.C.A.O. Fifth Army, who was engaged in arranging the administration of Venezia Tridentina. They included a *questore* who had been a regular army officer on the Military Intelligence staff (S.I.M.) and three *Vice-Questori* two of whom were political appointments, but the third was a regular police officer who had been continued in office for technical reasons. The National Republican Guard (G.N.R.) had been dissolved, and the chief guardians of public order were a special partisan auxiliary police force, into which the *Questore* managed within a few days to introduce a nucleus of ex-*Carabinieri*. The Agents of Public Safety—after summary epuration—had been left in being, as well as the Finance Guards, who had played an important part in the liberation of the city.

Though there was no public disorder in Milan, the actions of the patriots, especially the last minute patriots, caused a good deal of anxiety to the A.M.G. Public Safety officers. It was estimated that the number of armed men in Milan numbered about 60,000. As in Turin and Genoa, the patriot justiciary, the military tribunals and the People's Assize Courts had resorted to executions on a considerable scale. Estimated number of victims varied between 500 and 2,000 during the first few days of occupation. And, though on 1st May the Prefect issued an order to suspend their activities, and A.M.G. on 5th May promulgated the law setting up the special Assize courts, summary executions still continued. Indeed, it was not until the end of May that they began to cease, after the special courts had actually started working, and the police measures organised by A.M.G. with the assistance of Allied Military Police for the suppression of this kind of violence had become effective.

On the arrival of A.M.G. the C.L.N.A.I. made no formal difficulty about handing over the reins of Government, but it took some time before its members, and those of its subordinate organisations, could be made to understand the real meaning of their purely consultative functions. Thus as late as 14th May the C.L.N.A.I.—whose new chairman was a citizen of Turin—passed a decree investing the Prefect of Aosta with powers to take the first steps towards the granting of autonomy to the Val d'Aosta by establishing both French and Italian as official languages, by revoking the Fascist Italianisation of local place-names, and by revising communal boundaries to bring them back to their pre-Fascist arrangement—all this without any reference to A.M.G. or to the Government in Rome.

The legislation passed by the C.L.N.A.I. during the interim period between the insurrection and the taking over of the controls by A.M.G. is of some interest. Perhaps the most significant was the decree annulling the socialising legislation of Mussolini's Republican government. This did in fact keep in being most of the essential features of the Duce's last desperate bid for left-wing support, such as the inclusion of workers' representatives in the councils of management, the limitation of profit-sharing—though the workers' share was diverted by the C.L.N.A.I. into a national workers' welfare fund—and the prohibition to dismiss surplus personnel, which had been introduced in the vain hope of preventing expatriation to Germany of Italian labour. This interim legislation, which was confirmed by A.M.G., set the pattern of Italian economic policy, not only during the early months following the end of hostilities, but also for a considerable time to come.

One feature of this legislation was the transformation of the neo-Fascist workers' representatives into the Shop-Committee of Liberation (C.L.N. *Aziendale*) whose activities in the field of 'epuration' have already been noted. This presented A.M.G. with a rather delicate problem, since in the matter of the purge its general policy was to put into force the existing legislation of the Italian Government. The measures taken by the Italian Government in Rome to 'epurate' private industry were considered inadequate by the C.L.N.A.I., whose representatives at their first contact with Rome had insisted that this should be carried out more thoroughly. But the crisis which resulted in the resignation of Signor Bonomi had prevented action being taken to this end.

Special importance was attached by the Allied Commission to the 'epuration' of the large industrial and commercial concerns in the North, on account of their business affiliations and connections with central Europe and the Balkans, which were regarded as potentially dangerous to Allied economic policy. A.M.G. felt consequently compelled to institute an industrial purge on lines designed to meet the popular demand in the North, while at the same time putting an end to the pernicious activities of the factory committees. This purge followed in general principles the methods already adopted for the public services, namely, preliminary suspension by A.M.G. of the heads of important concerns which had been seriously compromised by their Fascist past, and the appointment of a *Commissario* to administer the business. The *Commissario* was made responsible for the suspension of Fascist employees, and committees were appointed to hear charges of Fascism and collaboration, with powers of suspension or dismissal; arrangements were also made for the constitution of a committee to hear appeals.[1] All persons dismissed or suspended by factory committees since liberation were given the right to appeal to these committees for a reconsideration of their case. The damage done by the wholesale dismissals under Communist influence of technicians and managers was thus to a large extent repaired.

Meanwhile, in spite of opposition here and there from local committees, the relations between A.M.G. and the triumphant Resistance movement developed satisfactorily. A good deal of patience and tact on the part of A.M.G. was required in order to prevent early misunderstandings leading to a serious clash or fatally compromising the authority of military government. For once the war was over A.M.G. was naturally regarded by a large number of northern Italians as an anachronism. An arrangement was reached towards the end of May under which the C.L.N.A.I. issued a directive that all Regional and Provincial Committees of Liberation were to become advisory councils. An instruction had already been issued by General Hume that all decrees issued by the C.L.N.A.I. and its subordinate organs, committees and agencies, should cease to have effect as from 28th May, unless specifically ratified by A.M.G., on the perfectly legitimate ground that Allied Military Government was the only authority empowered to issue decrees and orders or to make appointments; but this pill was considerably sweetened by an arrangement made by Colonel Poletti that all decrees and appointments emanating from the Committee since Allied occupation should remain valid until superseded by A.M.G. orders. After this no serious political opposition to A.M.G. was felt, and, as already explained, with the installation of the Parri Government the importance of the C.L.N.A.I. rapidly faded.

Once the war was over, the whole apparatus of military government with its proclamations and general orders, designed originally for the occupation of an enemy territory during military operations,

[1] The President of these committees were appointed by A.M.G., and of the two other members one was appointed by the workers of the firm and the other by the employers in the industry in which the firm was engaged.

began to look a little out of date and place—especially in those sections of the country which had done so much to liberate themselves. This was indirectly recognised by General Crittenberger, the Commander of IV Corps, Fifth Army, who on 14th May issued a memorandum to his Civil Affairs officers which envisaged early modifications in standing procedure. The various restrictions imposed on civilian behaviour, like the curfew and the restriction on movement, were never really effective once all fighting had ceased. The ban on political assemblies in Army areas was strongly resented, especially by the parties of the Left. On 26th May Signor Nenni, then still a strong candidate for the premiership, was arrested at Vercelli by an over zealous Provincial Commissioner and charged with an offence under Proclamation No. 3 for having attended a public meeting which had not been authorised. Though he was very quickly released, the indignation aroused in political circles all over the country was very great.

Nor did the economic *Cordon Sanitaire*, which had been so carefully planned, prove practicable. Owing to the unexpectedly rapid advance of the Armies, the traffic barriers were in many places never set up by the Allied formations, and in others were quickly removed. This attempt to preserve the North from the inflationary contamination from the South does not appear ever to have been really feasible, and had it proved practicable its political repercussions might have been anything but desirable. In fact conditions in the North were not so far different from those in the South as had been supposed. Though prices and wages on Allied arrival were substantially lower than those in the South, conditions of suppressed inflation had already existed for some time. Liberation bonuses, the embargo on dismissing workmen and the influx of Allied military lire, soon equalised price levels in both sections of the country. The attempt to hold prices and wages at the level of 3rd April was no more successful than a similar endeavour had been in Sicily immediately after invasion.

The arrangements made for feeding the population of the North, on the other hand, worked out rather more easily than had been expected, in spite of some initial shortage of transport. For the first time since 1943 A.M.G. in its advance was not haunted by the nightmare of starvation. Except in some of the mountain areas, food supplies were sufficient to meet immediate necessities and the distribution of the stocks accumulated by A.M.G. in advance of operations made it possible to counter local shortages. Nearly everywhere the initial distribution on Allied entry was above the equivalent of 100 gms of bread-stuffs. In the Fifth Army zone 125 gms was generally the initial ration, in Eighth Army area mostly 150 gms, and in view of the imminence of the 1945 harvest it was possible in many places to raise this to the equivalent of 300 gms before July, thanks to the existing stocks of maize and rice, both grown plentifully in the valley of the Po.

Conditions in Milan on entry were, however, far from easy, and scarcely any easier in Turin. The normal bread-ration which was being distributed in Milan when the Allies entered was only 150 gms (5 oz.) a head per day of maize-flour, wheat-flour being entirely reserved for supplementary ration-card holders. These, however, included a very large proportion of the working population. Thus in the city and province there were only about 470,000 normal ration-card holders, whereas holders of supplementary cards amounted to more than 1,160,000. Some improvement was quickly made in the quality of the bread distributed to normal holders, thanks to the importation of wheat flour, and it was possible to continue the existing ration scale for other foodstuffs without interruption except for a while in the matter of meat. By the beginning of June it was possible to make the improvement of adding a second dish to the meal distributed at the Communal restaurants—a war-time improvisation much relied on by the Social Republic and very extensively patronised by the working population—first three and then four days a week. A request made by Colonel Poletti to increase the normal ration to 200 gms at the beginning of June was, however, refused by Allied Commission headquarters, because of the large-scale distribution of supplementary rations. But before A.M.G. withdrew it was found possible to introduce a uniform normal ration scale over the whole country equivalent in bread and other cereal foodstuffs to 300 gms (nearly 11 oz.) a head.

During the first three months after occupation, before the 1945 harvest had been made available, the feeding of the larger towns met considerable difficulties. Road transport was very short, though some help was obtained from the Armies and from German and Italian service vehicles. A breakdown in distribution was only avoided because the railways north of the Po could quickly be brought back into operation for the carriage of civilian goods. Though the supply of Piedmont via Genoa was badly held up by the impossibility of using the port, it was found possible to concentrate large supplies of foodstuffs at Forlì, which were transported by road to Cremona, a railhead from which distribution to the whole of north-west Italy could be effected.

With the details of A.M.G.'s economic arrangements following the cessation of hostilities we are not concerned. But a brief account must be given of the one really crucial problem—the disarmament of the 'patriots'. Mention has already been made of the only partially successful attempts at disarmament made in Emilia. In the regions beyond the Po the situation was much more complicated. Instead of 150,000 patriots, for which arrangements had been planned, the numbers actually discovered in arms was much greater[1]—over 300,000—a large proportion being last minute adherents of the days of popular insurrection. Moreover the sudden surrender of the German forces left many isolated pockets of the enemy still under arms, especially in the mountain districts. This was also true to a lesser extent of the neo-Fascist regular and irregular forces, though most of these had largely dissolved themselves spontaneously.

Further, the French intrusion into the Val d'Aosta and other districts in Piedmont and Liguria and the Yugoslav infiltration into eastern Venetia would have made it impossible to persuade the partisans in those areas to hand in their arms. Hence the immediate disarmament of all partisan forces according to the planned timetable proved quite impracticable. As Mr Hopkinson of the British Embassy—one of the Allied Commission's political advisers, who was in Milan in the first days of May—was able to observe, ceremonial parades in these circumstances could not be expected to produce more than a very small proportion of the arms in circulation. In fact neither in Milan nor in Turin was it possible to hold parades immediately at which any substantial measure of disarmament could be effected.

On the entry of Allied troops into Milan arrangements were immediately concerted by General Crittenberger and General Cadorna—sometimes without the knowledge of the Patriot officers of A.M.G.—by which orders to disarm were issued through the military command of the partisans. On 3rd May a special message was sent by Field-Marshal Alexander to the Chairman of the C.L.N.A.I. asking him to convey his admiration and gratitude to General Cadorna and his subordinate commanders and commenting upon the efficiency which the Committee of National Liberation had shown in restoring civil administration. Ceremonial parades attended by the most senior general officers of the Allied forces were held in Milan and Turin at the end of the first week of May, at which partisans were thanked for their services and exhorted to hand in their arms and return as quickly as possible to civil life. The handing in of arms was started immediately afterwards, but with varying success.[2]

---

[1] The number of Alexander certificates issued was about 300,000, but the actual number of genuine partisans and patriots is not easy to determine with any accuracy. Longo, the Communist leader, gives the total number who took arms in all Italy as 462,000, (*Un popolo alla macchia*, Chapter 12), a figure which is probably an over-estimate.

[2] At Verona, for example, on the 5th May, a parade of partisans was held at which General Hume was present. About 5,000 attended and a large quantity of arms were collected. At Venice there was a considerable difficulty in persuading partisans to hand in their arms. The first attempts were met with a blank refusal. At Padua, though partisan bands, some 4,000 strong, handed in rifles, no other arms were collected.

Another problem, that of the reflux of Italian and other refugees, caused A.M.G. a good deal of trouble. Once hostilities were over the attempt to make refugees 'stay put' proved quite impracticable, and arrangements, which are described briefly in Appendix VI, had to be made quickly, in conjunction with the Armies, for regulating this perishable traffic.

CHAPTER XII

FRONTIER PROBLEMS

IT WAS REALISED at an early date that on the north-eastern frontier of Italy political problems arising out of the claims of the resurgent Yugoslavs to Trieste and Venezia Giulia would cause dangerous complications. But it was only near the final stages of the campaign that in the north-west another frontier problem developed. After the armistice in September 1943 and the melting away of the Italian military forces which had occupied south-eastern France, partisan movements against the common enemy came into being on both sides of the Franco-Italian frontier. Contact was established in 1944 between the Italian partisans and the French *Maquis*. The entire liberation of France anticipated that of northern Italy. All German forces had withdrawn from the French side of the Italian border some months before the final Allied advance from the Apennines. During the autumn and winter of 1944 the Italian partisans were hard pressed by the combined forces of Mussolini's Social Republic and the German occupying forces, and many of them had retreated into French territory. The furnishing of Allied supplies by air, owing to weather conditions and enemy action, became increasingly difficult. Arrangements were consequently made by SACMED with General Eisenhower's headquarters for S.O.E. and O.S.S. to supply Italian partisans from bases established in France, at Annecy, Nice and Grenoble.

As a result of communications thus established, rumours reached both A.F.H.Q. and the Italian Government that plans were brewing in France for the annexation of the Val d'Aosta and certain other territories on the Italian side of the border. Some of this evidence definitely connected the *Direction Génerále des Études et des Recherches* (D.G.E.R.)—the French equivalent of S.O.E. and O.S.S.—with plans of this nature. Reports began to flow in during the winter of the massing of French forces—including Moroccan formations—along the Italian border. The Foreign Minister, Signor de Gasperi, drew the attention of Admiral Stone to these reports in a memorandum dated 9th February 1945, in which he deprecated the occupation of any portion of northern Italy by French troops, particularly in view of the fact that he was attempting to re-establish cordial relations with France through the resumption of normal consular and diplomatic relations. The establishment of the Army Detachment of the Alps, under General Doyen, along the border at first aroused considerable misgiving at A.F.H.Q. and at Fifteenth Army Group headquarters, where the advisability of French troops penetrating the Italian frontier was seriously doubted. SACMED at first refused permission for French troops to cross the Italian border, but this policy was subsequently modified; definite restrictions were, however, placed on the depth of French penetration.

The fears expressed by Admiral Stone concerning the repercussions of the use of French troops across the Italian border were shared by both the British and the American ambassadors in Rome, and scarcely less by Field-Marshal Alexander. But since Fifteenth Army Group had only a small superiority in number of divisions over the enemy, it was clear that the success of the major operation of the advance into northern Italy from the Apennines would be much more certain, if French troops could hold the German divisions as long as possible on the Franco-Italian frontier. He therefore inquired if General Eisenhower could help him 'by using deception methods and active operations by troops under his command' on his Italian border. Operational benefits to be derived by holding German divisions in north-west Italy over-rode political objections to the employment of French troops east of the Italian border. At the beginning of April permission was given to the French troops to patrol to a distance of twenty kilometres beyond the border, but a line was laid down beyond which the French Alpine Front Command was not to conduct operations into Italy.[1] There was never any question of permanent occupation of Italian territory by French troops. It was decided that immediate withdrawal of all French troops from Italy would be requested as soon as German resistance had come to an end, and that A.F.H.Q. would establish frontier control along the Italian side of the border.

In the event, thanks to the policy deliberately pursued by General Doyen (with the full backing, it would appear, of General de Gaulle), French penetration into Italy was far deeper than had been anticipated, and it was not confined to the normal activities of military occupation. A definite attempt was made to seduce the civil population from Italian allegiance and to make them express a desire to be annexed to France as a prelude to immediate annexation. French troops managed to penetrate as far east as Ivrea in the Val d'Aosta, Rivoli, only about twenty kilometres west of Turin, and even into Savona on the Ligurian coast. Owing to the swiftness of the German collapse, the French troops had in most places advanced far over the border some time before the troops of the Fifth Army could reach the vicinity. In view of the feeling of the partisans the situation was obviously extremely delicate, and armed clashes between them and the French troops appeared almost inevitable.

---

[1] See Map 15, on p. 322.

Field-Marshal Alexander lost no time in requesting S.H.A.E.F. to order the withdrawal of all French troops behind the frontier. On 28th April General Doyen was ordered by General Devers, commanding Sixth Army Group, who had led the Allied invasion of the south of France, to halt his offensive and to prepare to withdraw into France, as soon as the military situation permitted. He refused to obey these orders without obtaining the previous consent of his government. S.H.A.E.F. accordingly, on 7th May, sent a letter to General Juin, Chief of Staff for National Defence, requesting instructions for withdrawal to be issued to General Doyen. After delay of nearly a fortnight a reply was received in the following terms:

> I desire to present to you the point of view of the French Government on this subject. Operations in the Mediterranean theatre, as in the western theatre, being now completed, movements and stationing of French troops of the Alps are henceforth questions which no longer fall within the strategic sphere, but which should be examined by the interested governments. Consequently the question of withdrawal of the Army detachment of the Alps to the Franco-Italian frontier of 1939 can no longer be handled directly between the Supreme Command and the French Command, and should be dealt with on the diplomatic plane. While awaiting study by the interested governments, the Army detachment of the Alps will continue to remain in the area which it is now occupying.

Meanwhile Field-Marshal Alexander had reported the position to the Combined Chiefs of Staff, with the pertinent observation that it appeared unlikely that S.H.A.E.F. would be able to enforce French withdrawal without Government backing, and requested them urgently to provide this. Pending the exercise of governmental pressure, General Mark Clark, the Commander of Fifteenth Army Group, had given orders to General Truscott, commanding Fifth Army, to advance as rapidly as possible to the frontier, taking all practicable steps to encourage the French to withdraw, but in any case to establish frontier control. If hostilities were threatened by this action, he was instructed to order his troops to stand fast and to make an immediate report to Army Group H.Q. Nor was any modification made in the policy of setting up A.M.G. in all Italian territory, whether French-occupied or not, though in practice every precaution was taken to avoid the possibility of an armed clash. In order to reinforce A.M.G. IV Corps on the frontier, General Crittenberger transferred a considerable number of officers from combatant units for temporary duty as C.A.O.s in the French border territory. The suggestion of General Clark that French troops in occupation of northern Italy should be put under the operational command of Fifteenth Army Group, in order to facilitate A.M.G. and produce a more orderly state of military affairs, was not accepted by Field-Marshal Alexander, on the ground that such action might convey the impression that the French occupation of northern Italy had been ordered by the Allies, and so prejudice the action taken by both Allied Governments to secure an immediate withdrawal.

Personal relations established with General Doyen and his staff were correct, and relations between American and French troops on the ground extremely cordial; but progress was slow, on account of passive interference from the French, who had organised road blocks for this purpose on key routes. Nor was it always easy or even possible to establish A.M.G. in the face of French opposition, for example in the province of Cuneo. Here the attempt by Colonel Marshall to set up A.M.G. evoked a veiled threat from General Doyen, who sent a letter to General Crittenberger, commanding IV Corps, on 30th May containing the following message:

> I have been ordered by the Provisional Government of the French Republic to occupy and administer this territory. This mission being incompatible with the installation of any Allied administrative agency in the same region, I find myself obliged to oppose it. Any insistence in this direction would assume a clearly unfriendly character, even a hostile character, and could have grave consequences.

On 29th May Colonel Jordan, deputy Regional Commissioner of Liguria, was refused permission by the French local Commissioner to post proclamations in western Imperia, establishing Allied Military Government in that area. And worse was to follow. On 2nd June General Doyen sent the following message to General Crittenberger:

> I beg to let you know that I have been notified of the full approval given by the Chief of the Provisional Government of the French Republic. (to the policy laid down in the letter just quoted) General de Gaulle has instructed me to make as clear as possible to the Allied Command that I have received the order to prevent the setting up of A.M.G. in the territories occupied by our troops and administered by us, by all necessary means without exception.

The reaction of Field-Marshal Alexander to this threat was a telegram to the Combined Chiefs of Staff recommending that he should be directed by them 'to complete the occupation of north-west Italy and to establish Allied Military Government there, using force if necessary'.

Fortunately diplomatic action proved effective in avoiding the necessity for the use of force A strong personal message was sent by President Truman to General de Gaulle, stating that unless French forces withdrew immediately from north-west Italy all supplies to the French forces, with the exception of rations, would be stopped. The effect on General de Gaulle's policy was decisive, and immediate steps were taken to evacuate Italian territory.[1] On 11th June an agreement was reached for the withdrawal, by sectors, of all French troops behind the 1939 frontiers by 10th July, but not before the difficulty of disarming partisans in Piedmont and Liguria had been enormously increased.

The policy of encouraging a Separatist movement in the Val d'Aosta was made to appear more reasonable by the fact that the inhabitants' native language is French, and their attachment to their mother tongue, and all that that implies, had been severely offended by Mussolini's attempt at 'Italianisation' and the elimination of the French language from the schools. There was in the Val d'Aosta a definite demand for a considerable degree of autonomy, but of a real Separatist movement there was little question. The Val d'Aosta had for centuries formed part of the dominions of the House of Savoy. Indeed, the incorporation of Savoy, as well as Nice, into France was a comparatively recent event—the price paid by Victor Emmanuel II for the alliance with the Emperor Napoleon III, which enabled him to defeat the Austrians in the war of liberation of 1859. But recent local history had given some opportunities for an attempt to create a Separatist movement. The local C.L.N. in the valley had been relatively independent of the C.L.N. in Turin. In August 1944, on the arrest of one of the two local commanders by the Socialist Republican Government, the appointment of a successor (made by Turin) had aroused a certain amount of jealousy, which encouraged a few disgruntled partisans to try to work up a movement in favour of union with France.

It is perhaps worthwhile recording in some detail the background of the Allied Military Government established in the frontier provinces of Piedmont after the conclusion of hostilities. In the north, the centre of interest lay in the province of Aosta, which contains the most northerly of the important road-passes between Italy and France, the little St. Bernard. The district, which had belonged to the house of Savoy since the eleventh century, had enjoyed a Charter of Franchise granted in 1191, and had inherited a tradition of autonomy since feudal times which neither the centralised despotism of the eighteenth century nor the constitutional monarchy of the nineteenth century had wholly availed to destroy. The French language is the native tongue of its peasants, who speak an unmistakably French patois. The tradition of the French language has also remained among the aristocracy and the bourgeoisie, in spite of repeated attempts at Italianisation long before the days of

[1] For an account of these negotiations, see Winston Churchill, *op. cit.* Vol. VI, pp. 493–4.

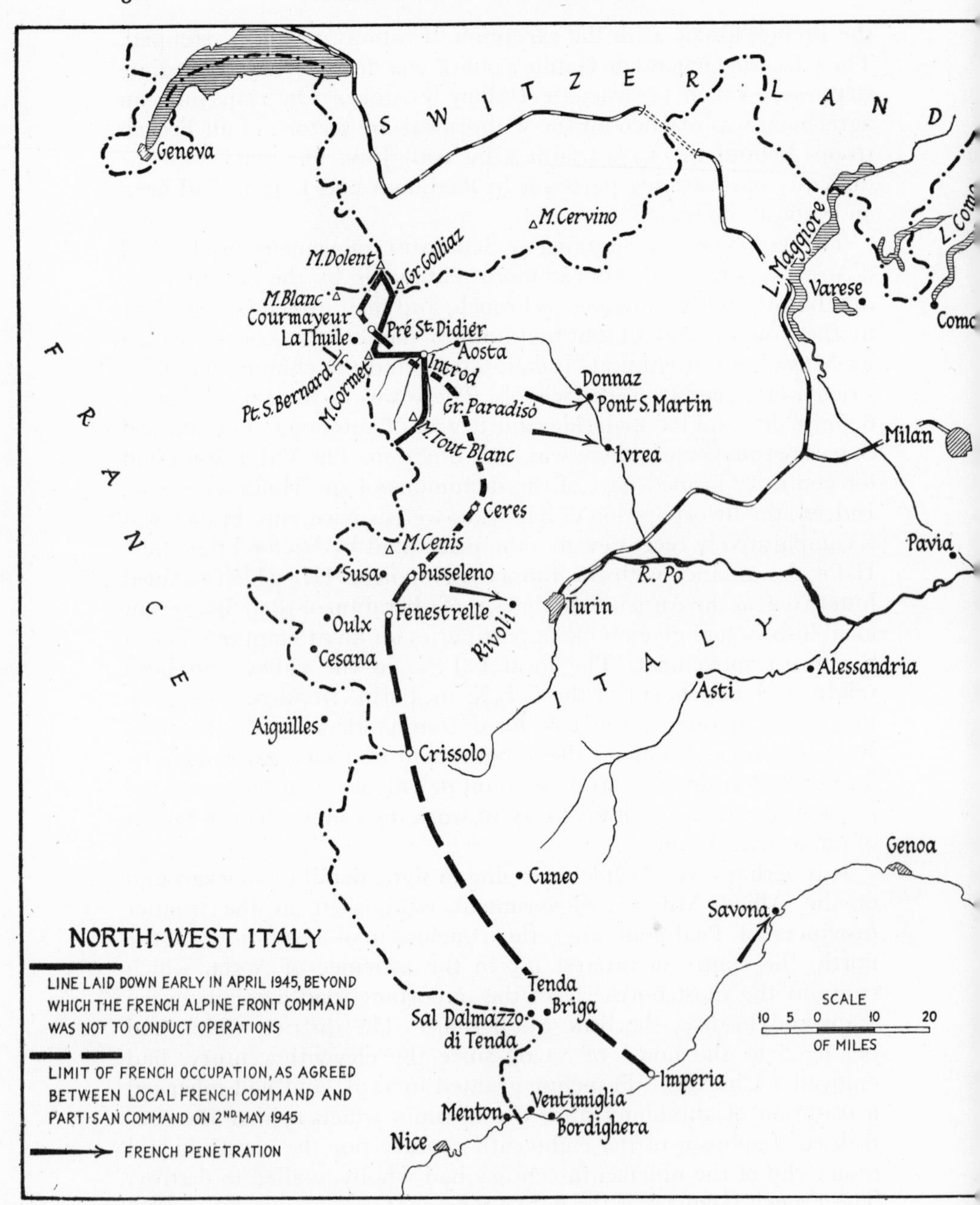

SWITZERLAND
FRANCE
ITALY
Geneva
M.Cervino
M.Dolent
Gr. Golliaz
M.Blanc
Courmayeur
La Thuile
Pré St. Didier
Aosta
Introd
Pt. S. Bernard
M.Cormet
Gr. Paradiso
M.Tout Blanc
Donnaz
Pont S. Martin
Ivrea
L. Maggiore
Varese
L. Como
Como
Milan
Ceres
M.Cenis
Susa
Busseleno
Fenestrelle
Rivoli
Turin
R. Po
Pavia
Oulx
Cesana
Aiguilles
Crissolo
Asti
Alessandria
Cuneo
Genoa
Savona
Tenda
Briga
Sal Dalmazzo di Tenda
Imperia
Menton
Ventimiglia
Bordighera
Nice
SCALE
10 5 0 10 20
OF MILES
NORTH-WEST ITALY
LINE LAID DOWN EARLY IN APRIL 1945, BEYOND WHICH THE FRENCH ALPINE FRONT COMMAND WAS NOT TO CONDUCT OPERATIONS
LIMIT OF FRENCH OCCUPATION, AS AGREED BETWEEN LOCAL FRENCH COMMAND AND PARTISAN COMMAND ON 2ND MAY 1945
FRENCH PENETRATION

Map 15

Mussolini. In 1919 four newspapers were still published either in French or in the two languages, French and Italian.[1] The attempt at 'Italianisation' had been renewed and intensified in a much more objectionable fashion by Mussolini, but without much real success. It was not therefore altogether surprising that French influence should have been strong enough even among the partisans to enable them to get together a 'quisling' secessionist committee of liberation. But events were soon to show how little genuine support lay behind this manoeuvre.

During the last few days of April 1945 an agreement was reached by the German troops in the valley with the Partisan command, that they should be allowed to retire unmolested, provided that they quitted the valley without committing any damage. On 28th/29th April French patrols began to cross the frontier, but the weather was so bad and the snow so deep that they were not able to come across in great strength. But their penetration created a profoundly antagonistic reaction among the partisans, now led by an Alpini officer of Valdôtain extraction, whose resolute action quickly eliminated all secessionist influences, so that there was a distinct danger that these would combine with the neo-Fascist forces to oppose them. Indeed, negotiations to this effect were in fact on the point of being concluded.

Fortunately this complication was avoided. A verbal agreement was reached between the local French commander and the Partisan command on 2nd May, by which the French occupation was to be confined to a line running fairly close to the frontier.[2] The occupation was to be purely military to ensure the security of the frontier, the Partisan General Command was to withdraw to Aosta town, and French troops were not to penetrate any further over the border. This agreement was arrived at at a meeting attended by the British liaison officer with the Partisan command, but apparently it was never embodied in any signed document. Nor was it kept by the French. Advance parties entered Aosta and a French officer with his headquarters at Prè St. Didier assumed the title of Military Governor of the Val d'Aosta and demanded accommodation in the provincial capital for his troops on a very considerable scale. The Prefect appointed by the C.L.N., Count A. P. d'Entrèves, attempted by various devices to put him off, and succeeded in delaying his entry until a few hours after the arrival of an American occupying force, which immediately set up A.M.G. Thus the quartering of French troops in the town as the sole occupying force was avoided;

---

[1] See the article signed 'A.P.E.' in *The World To-day*, June 1946, entitled 'Autonomy in Val d'Aosta', which initials denote Count A. P. d'Entrèves, now Serena Professor of Italian Studies at Oxford, mentioned below.

[2] See map 14.

but French troops as well as civilian agents penetrated as far east as Ivrea and Pont St. Martin. These endeavoured, through the 'quisling' committee of liberation, to persuade the Valdôtains to demonstrate in favour of annexation to France by means of specious promises and a distribution of certain foodstuffs, including salt—a vital commodity in exceedingly short supply.[1]

It was perhaps fortunate that the weather conditions, with very late snowfalls, rendered routes across the frontier difficult to cross. The little St. Bernard pass was not fully open to traffic until the middle of June. This prevented the penetration of French troops in any large formations, and by 12th May, when the Allied occupying troops had already arrived in the valley in considerable numbers, the total French troops in the Val d'Aosta were reported to number only about 1,000.[2] But the situation was extremely delicate, as armed clashes with partisans were certainly to be expected, and Allied occupying troops were too thin on the ground to prevent them. In fact no such clashes occurred, but feeling for some weeks continued to run very high, and the occurrence of minor incidents, like the arrest and deportation to France of a partisan alleged to have struck a French corporal—in spite of the fact that A.M.G. military courts were functioning—and the killing of another at Introd by French occupying troops, did not reassure the public or make things any easier for A.M.G.

The intense propaganda in favour of annexation to France, though it caused a great deal of anxiety to A.M.G., did not however succeed in seducing the *Valdostani* from their Italian allegiance. The Prefect when presented with a request for a 'plebiscite' on 18th May refused to countenance such action. As a counter-measure it was decided to send a deputation to Rome, representing the real 'autonomist' movement in the valley. Its demands were for the most part accepted by the Italian Government, which agreed to grant a considerable measure of regional home-rule, including 'cultural autonomy' in the teaching of the French language.

The position in the Val d'Aosta, so far as A.M.G. was concerned, was a good deal easier than that in certain districts further south, since French military occupation, except in a small area, had not

---

[1] For example, in the commune of Donnaz the tax collector reported that taxes were not being paid because of French propaganda. Farmers had been told not to pay taxes and promised that if they became French citizens they would not have to pay taxes for three years. In the province of Aosta, according to a report by the Provincial Commissioner, exemption was promised for at least ten years. Another inducement was the promise that within three years a tunnel would be made through Mont Blanc linking up Courmayeur with Chamonix.

[2] On 25th May Fifteenth Army Group estimated the French forces in the valley at about five infantry battalions with stronger forces further south, namely six battalions in the Susa valley and eight battalions between Cuneo and the coast.

become effective before the arrival of Allied troops. In the Susa valley leading down from the Mont Cenis Pass, where transport conditions were less difficult, French forces crossed the frontier in much greater numbers. No attempt was at first made to take over the civil administration, though the frontier was fixed some seven miles on the Italian side of the pass. But, later, definite opposition to the performance of their duties by A.M.G. officers occurred in many places in the valley. The role of A.M.G. in French occupied areas was particularly delicate. On one occasion, at Fenestrelle, A.M.G. was actually driven to apply for French help in maintaining public order, when the local Italian police chief had been killed by a civilian. The precedent thus established was distinctly unfortunate, in view of official policy.

In the districts of Tenda and Briga, where the frontier fixed after the cession of Nice to France in 1860 was defined so as to include in Italy a portion of territory on the French side of the watershed of the Alps, which had been a favourite hunting domain of King Victor Emmanuel II, the action of the French Army was more frankly annexationist. Tenda and Briga had been occupied by Italian partisans who had expelled the Germans during the last few days in April. Their arrival was followed in a day or two by French troops, who forced them to withdraw. The occupiers set up pro-French communal committees—composed largely of French citizens of whom there were a considerable number in the district—and a 'committee for the re-attachment of Tenda and Briga' to France. So called 'ballot' papers were distributed for signature, as in the Val d'Aosta, to give the impression of a plebiscite; but the papers did not contain alternatives to vote for, they merely expressed the desire of the signatory to opt for French nationality. Italian ration cards were abolished: French ration cards bearing the superscription of the 're-attachment committee' were introduced, and rations brought in from France. By this means pressure was brought to bear on the inhabitants, for ration cards of those who did not opt for France were endorsed 'not voting' so that rations might not be issued to their holders. Italian flags were taken down and French flags substituted and French currency substituted for the lira. An official visit was paid by the Prefect of Nice to Briga and its name was changed from Briga Marittima to Briga de Nice. Steps were also taken to drive out of the district all those who refused to opt for French citizenship. The French also took control of the important hydro-electric stations in the valley of the upper Roya, disconnected them from the Italian grid, and linked them with the French electricity system, in order to supply the area of Nice, thus diverting current from the source which normally supplied power for the railways Ventimiglia–Genoa and Genoa–Turin.

In these circumstance the setting up of military government in the Briga–Tenda area was practically impossible. It could not have been accomplished without strong military backing, which implied a very grave danger of hostilities. An A.M.G. officer had arrived in Tenda on 31st May and had begun to constitute a local Italian administration there and at Briga, posting A.M.G. Proclamations. These were however torn down, and various French posters substituted. Orders were, apparently, given by the French higher command on 5th June to expel the Italian administrations set up by A.M.G. and to ask A.M.G. officers to refrain from interfering with the administration of the area occupied by French troops. On 2nd June Colonel Marshall, the Regional Commissioner, held a conference at Tenda with the French Commander, who stated that he was under orders to prevent the continuance of Allied Military Government, using whatever force was necessary. In view of the orders issued by General Crittenberger on 2nd June that under no circumstances should armed clashes be permitted to develop between French and American troops, Colonel Marshall directed all A.M.G. officers to withdraw from the *Municipio*, but they continued to reside in the town to observe events.

A somewhat similar situation arose in Liguria, where the French occupied a considerable portion of the province of Imperia—containing fourteen communes, including Ventimiglia—up to the River Nervia, though in this case the pretext of a large number of French or French-speaking inhabitants could scarcely be brought forward. The same technique of 'persuasion' which had been employed further north was used, in the form of 'plebiscites', assisted by the supplementary ration card in exchange for a French identity card, and the distribution of food—including American canned foods supplied to the French military authorities. The town of Ventimiglia had been very badly damaged by Allied bombing, and when the French entered on 25th April there were only about 2,000 inhabitants on the spot, but they soon returned in considerable numbers. The French consequently set in motion a vigorous policy of reconstruction. Here, too, a separatist movement, in the shape of propaganda for an autonomous Italian and French free zone, was encouraged. The distribution of rations was arranged on a fairly generous scale—more generous than the rations actually distributed in some of the Allied-occupied parts of the province—and for the first few weeks the French occupation enjoyed some popularity.

A.M.G. was rather later in appearing on the scene, and some time was needed to set up its administration in the towns between Genoa and Bordighera. On 26th May orders were received from IV Corps to establish Military Government right up to the Italian frontier. On 28th May Colonel Jordan, the deputy Regional Commissioner, called upon the Commander of the French troops in the western part of the province to arrange for the establishment of A.M.G. The latter informed him that he had no instructions to permit its establishment, but that he would communicate with higher command who would have to get instructions from General Doyen. He agreed, however, to the posting of proclamations, in order to enable the Provincial Commissioner to comply with his orders, provided that no further action was taken pending General Doyen's decision. The following day Colonel Jordan and his assistants set out to post the proclamations. On their way they were overtaken by the French Commander, who told them that he had tried to get in touch with them during the night, to tell them that General Doyen was unable to envisage a change in the administration in west Imperia at this juncture.

In accordance with the policy of avoiding all possible occasions for armed clashes between the French and the Allies, the attempt to set up A.M.G. in this section of the Italian Riviera was temporarily abandoned, but not for long. Diplomatic action at the highest level quickly brought about a reversal of French policy. The following arrangements, agreed by General Morgan with General Carpentier on 11th June, worked on the whole very smoothly. French forces were to be withdrawn behind the 1939 frontier, being relieved by Anglo-American forces according to the following schedule. All French troops were to be evacuated from the Val d'Aosta by 28th June, from Susa–Oulx–Cesana by 1st July, and from Tenda–Ventimiglia by 10th July. The French transit camp at Susa for prisoners of war and displaced persons was to be maintained as long as required. All propaganda in the areas occupied by French troops was to cease immediately. As long as Allied troops were available, no troops of the Italian Army were to be stationed within fifteen miles of the frontier, but *Carabinieri* and customs guards were to be employed in the normal manner. Freedom of movement across the frontier on the part of local inhabitants on the scale normal in the years before development of Franco-Italian tension was to be permitted.

Special care was taken to save the face of the French Government, by ensuring that the movement of French troops to the west of the 1939 frontier should not be given any publicity, and that the public use of the term withdrawal should be avoided. SACMED also agreed to recommend to the British and American Governments that no official announcement of the withdrawal should be made—a precaution not wholly successful, since the news leaked into the Allied Press very quickly. The question of electricity from the Upper Roya Valley was also settled in the agreement. It was agreed in principle that the supply from the power house at Basse Roya to Nice and Menton should be continued, but the allocation of quantities was to be decided by A.F.H.Q. in relation to Italian demands.

This agreement did for the time being solve the question of the French frontier. French troops were withdrawn according to schedule, though French liaison officers, whose activities were not unnaturally regarded with some suspicion by the Allied military authorities as well as by the Italian Government, were left in a few strategical localities. And though it could hardly be affirmed that French propaganda 'ceased immediately', its intensity and effectiveness was enormously diminished. But it left an indirect legacy for A.M.G., whose efforts had to be directed, after the departure of the French troops, to the prevention of reprisals by the local authorities on those who willingly or unwillingly had lent themselves to the support of French pretentions.

That Yugoslavia would claim all the territory which had been added to north-eastern Italy under the peace settlement following the First World War was a foregone conclusion. By the summer of 1944 the Yugoslav resistance movement, which was strongly supported by Allied resources, had made such progress that it was more than probable that, when Allied forces came to occupy northern Italy, they would find Yugoslav partisans or troops in occupation of large parts of the territory of Venezia Giulia, which contained the largely Croat Istrian peninsula, as well as territory to the north of it whose inhabitants were mostly Slovene. The precaution was therefore taken by General Wilson of informing Marshal Tito in August 1944, on his visit to Italy to meet Mr Churchill, that it was his intention to set up Allied Military Government, thus automatically suspending Italian sovereignty, over the whole territory on the mainland which before the war had been under Italian rule, pendings its ultimate disposition between the Governments concerned. This direct Allied Military Government was necessary to safeguard Allied bases and lines of communication to central Europe. Since Allied troops would be supplied through the port of Trieste, they must have secure lines of communication protected by British troops on the route through Ljubljana–Maribor–Graz.[1]

This decision was also communicated to the Yugoslav Prime Minister and was discussed at a meeting on 13th August between Mr Churchill, Marshal Tito and Dr Subâsic. Both demurred at the proposal. But Marshal Tito agreed in principle that the Supreme Allied Commander should exercise general operational control throughout the region, including the port of Trieste, and that the

[1] The full text is given in Churchill, *op. cit.* Vol. VI pp. 81–2, whose account of these negotiations illuminatingly supplements the A.F.H.Q. records.

stationing of Allied troops in the area would be necessary in order to protect SACMED's lines of communication with Austria and Hungary. He considered, however, that the local civil and military administration should be conducted by his own civil and military authorities, since his National Liberation Movement already controlled many of the disputed areas. This view was of course entirely contrary to Allied policy, but it was agreed that the Marshal and Dr Subâsic would submit a memorandum on Istria suggesting ways and means of associating Yugoslav authorities with the administration of the territory—a document which never made its appearance. On 11th September the Italian Government was informed by Captain Stone that it was the intention of the Supreme Allied Commander to set up A.M.G. in the provinces of Bolzano, Trento, Fiume, Pola, Trieste and Gorizia; but that the final disposition of these territories would 'naturally be a matter of post-war settlement'.

As the year ended, with the Allies preparing to force the line of the Apennines and the Yugoslavs pushing back the evacuating Germans on the eastern side of the Adriatic, the question of the arrangements to be made in territory separating the Allied and Yugoslav armies and the safeguarding of Allied military lines of communication into Austria became more important than ever. Field-Marshal Alexander, who had now succeeded Field-Marshal Wilson as SACMED, decided to pay a personal visit to Marshal Tito to discuss military arrangements; but these were so bound up with political issues that prolonged consultations between the Combined Chiefs of Staff and the American and British Foreign Offices were necessary before any definite policy could be laid down.

On 27th November SACMED sent a message to the Combined Chiefs of Staff informing them of his intention to establish A.M.G. in Venezia Giulia on the usual pattern, except that it would be made clear at the outset that control of the territory would not revert to the Italian Government, but would remain in Allied hands until otherwise determined. Special arrangements were to be made to ensure impartial administration as between Slavs and Italians. Insofar as trustworthy local administrations responsive to local public opinion were found on Allied entry, they were to be maintained, so as to preserve the *status quo* between Italians and Slavs, and only indigenous officials were to be retained in office. Restraint was to be observed in the use of Italian *Carabinieri* and a special police was to be recruited locally. The basic law was to be Italian, but all legislation discriminating against persons of Slavonic origin was to be excluded and recourse to higher courts in Rome suspended. It was also suggested that local advisory committees of indigenous Italians and Slavs might be formed, which the A.M.G. authorities might consult at their discretion. It was foreseen that difficulties both political and military might be encountered in the imposition of A.M.G. over the whole area, unless Yugoslav agreement was secured in advance; it might therefore be advisable to undertake negotiations at a governmental level.

In principle the British view coincided with that held by the American State Department, that the control of the European pre-war Italian territories in dispute should be held by the Allies pending their ultimate disposition in the post-war settlement; but experiences in Greece had led to severe doubts as to how far such control was practical. SACMED was therefore asked by the British Chiefs of Staff early in 1945 whether, during operations into Austria, or, subsequently, for the maintenance of occupational troops there, A.M.G. would be required in the whole of Venezia–Giulia or in part of it; or, alternatively, whether his needs could be met by an agreement with the Yugoslavs for Allied military control of certain areas.

Field-Marshal Alexander's view was that, from the purely military point of view, all that was absolutely necessary was the control of the area of Allied lines of communication to Austria from Trieste and of the port of Pola. Hence the division of Venezia Giulia by a fixed military boundary would meet his needs, provided that the area west of it came under complete Allied military control and that all Yugoslav troops to the west of it came under his command. But the political disadvantages of such a solution were obvious, since they could hardly fail to be interpreted both by the Yugoslavs and by the Italians as a recognition of Yugoslav sovereignty over the area east of the demarcation line. The best course would be to establish A.M.G. under tripartite control with Yugoslavia as one of the partners, the area being made a British zone analogous to the British zone in Austria. By associating Russia fully with the establishment and operation of Allied Military Government in the area, it should be possible to overcome any objections raised by Marshal Tito. If it were not possible to secure American and Russian agreement to this arrangement, the next best course would be to divide Venezia Giulia and negotiate with the Yugoslavs for a provisional boundary on lines indicated—a solution which had been suggested by the Foreign Office. West of the 1914 frontier Allied Military Government would be established on the same basis as in the remainder of Italy.

A note was consequently delivered by Mr Eden at the Yalta conference to his American and Russian colleagues, Mr Stettinius and Mr Molotov, asking them to agree to establish some body to work out a provisional line of demarcation between the area in Venezia Giulia to be controlled by Marshal Tito and that over which SACMED should establish military government. H.M.G. would attempt to obtain Marshal Tito's acceptance of this arrangement, but in doing so they would like to be able to state that both the United States and Russia agreed with the proposal. No reply to this note was received at the conference.

Time was pressing: it was essential for SACMED to reach some sort of understanding. It was therefore arranged that Field-Marshal Alexander should try to reach a direct agreement with Marshal Tito on the military boundary between Allied and Yugoslav forces. The boundary meeting SACMED's military requirements would be a line running south and east of Trieste, at a radius of approximately fifteen miles from the city, and then running more or less north to north-west to the east of the road through Aidussina, Gorizia and Caporetto to Tarvisio and the Austrian frontier. But by the time fixed for Field-Marshal Alexander's conference with Tito at Belgrade on 21st February the State Department had not varied its instructions to press for the application of A.M.G. to the whole of the territory belonging to mainland Italy in 1939. Field-Marshal Alexander consequently decided not to put this proposal to Tito at this meeting, but to confine himself to an endeavour to ascertain his intentions.

In opening his discussion with Tito, the Field-Marshal stated that, when the forces under his command occupied Austria, the control of his line of communications to Trieste demanded the control of all the territory west of the 1939 frontier between Italy and Yugoslavia. In his reply Marshal Tito accepted the idea of Allied Military Government within the zone of Field-Marshal Alexander's communications, provided that his civil administration already installed in the area in question was retained, since unless this was allowed to function chaos would ensue, and he was prepared to agree that his civil authorities should be responsible to Allied Military Government. But he did not think it necessary for the Allies to occupy the Istrian peninsula, in order to protect their lines of communications to Austria. He also offered the Allies an additional line of communication to Austria through Ljubljana, though this, of course, ran mostly through Yugoslav territory.

By this time it was clear that the Slovenes were determined to extend their influence over as large a portion of Italy as possible, in order to make a case for Yugoslav annexation. East of the Isonzo the Yugoslav Army of National Liberation was in complete command of all territory not under effective German control, and great efforts were being made to extend their influence as far west as the Tagliamento, embracing practically the whole of the Friulano (province of Udine). Among other methods used for extending their influence was the subversion of Italian partisan brigades—of which the Communist were in the majority—by only permitting those brigades to operate in the area which were pledged to support Yugoslav claims.

The crucial question resulting from these conversations was therefore how to find an arrangement which would avoid both the appearance of prejudicing the final settlement to be made at the peace conference, and the outbreak of armed conflict between Allied and Slovene or Yugoslav forces. If the policy laid down of extending Allied Military Government to the whole of Venezia Giulia was not to be modified, even in the face of the probable extension of *de facto* Yugoslav (or Slovene) control over the whole region before Allied forces had time to arrive, then, Field-Marshal Alexander suggested that the Allies should make a virtue of necessity and invite the provisional Yugoslav Government—as soon as it was formed—to participate as an Ally in the Military Government of Venezia Giulia, and to send its representative to consult with his staff in formulating plans for A.M.G. Arrangements should be made for Allied troops to occupy the lines of communication area, and perhaps also Fiume and Pola; Yugoslav forces in other parts of Venezia Giulia should come under the orders of the appropriate Allied commander; and A.M.G. officers should be associated with such existing civil authorities as might be found functioning in the territory. He also expressed the opinion that the acceptance of this plan would depend entirely on its approval by the three great powers before it was proposed to the Yugoslav Government.

This message from SACMED virtually crystallised the practical issue into a choice between two alternative plans, (1) to divide Venezia Giulia into two operational zones, leaving the eastern one under Marshal Tito's control, and (2) to establish Allied Military Government over the whole of the region, with Yugoslav participation. But feeling in the State Department was strongly against a demarcation line, and in a note on 21st March, in reply to the proposals submitted by Mr Eden at Yalta, the Department continued to uphold the principle that no unilateral action which would prejudice the final disposition of the disputed area should be permitted. This objective could be achieved best by the establishment of Allied Military Government throughout the whole of Venezia Giulia under the Supreme Allied Commander. The note further assumed that Marshal Tito had accepted the idea of Allied Military Government in Venezia Giulia, with certain reservations affecting his local administrations already established there. Mr Stettinius thus found himself unable to agree to the establishment of a demarcation line and expressed the hope that the British Government would withdraw the proposal.

The assumption that the Marshal would be prepared to allow the establishment of Allied Military Government over the whole of Venezia Giulia, including those portions of the *Compartimento* lying to the south and east of the area of SACMED's lines of communication from Trieste to Austria, did not in fact prove to be correct. With further details of the discussion between the British and American Governments on the alternative policies with respect to Venezia Giulia this volume is not concerned. But one crucial issue was raised by this divergence in policy. SACMED was obliged to ask whether, if the Yugoslavs opposed the setting up of Allied Military Government over the whole of Venezia Giulia, both the Allied Governments were prepared to use force to establish it? And to this question the Combined Chiefs of Staff could only return a belated and rather ambiguous answer. Steps were, however, taken to reinforce Eighth Army troops in this area by an American contingent in the shape of U.S. II Corps.

Meanwhile events in the north of Italy were moving with unexpected rapidity. Field-Marshal Alexander still found himself without any instructions from the Combined Chiefs of Staff. He therefore telegraphed on 26th April declaring his intention, unless otherwise instructed, to act according to the following plan. Anglo-American task forces were to be constituted to seize those parts of Venezia Giulia which were essential to his military operations, including Trieste and the communications leading to it and from it into Austria, and also to occupy Pola. In this area Allied Military Government was to be set up in the usual way in the wake of the occupational forces as a joint Anglo-American undertaking, recruited as far as possible on an equal basis from American and British officers. A.M.G. was to be part of the military government organisation controlling other parts of Italy, and was to work through such suitable local personnel, whether Italian or Yugoslav, as might be found on occupation. Before the task-force entered Venezia Giulia, he would inform Marshal Tito of his intentions, and explain to him that any of his forces remaining in this area must necessarily come under SACMED's command.

Two days later, on 28th April, the instructions from the Combined Chiefs of Staff to Field-Marshal Alexander arrived. In these he was ordered to set up Allied Military Government in the whole of Venezia Giulia, including Fiume and the Quarnarolo islands (but not in Zara), and in Tarvisio and the surrounding areas, which before 1919 had formed part of Austria. SACMED was informed that the Combined Chiefs of Staff were recommending that the forces required to back this plan, as well as the Civil Affairs officers required to implement it, should be provided jointly by the American and British Governments, and that Soviet concurrence would be sought in requesting the Yugoslav Government to withdraw all their forces from Venezia Giulia. If any Yugoslav forces in the area failed to cooperate with the plan, the Field-Marshal was instructed to communicate with the C.C.S. before taking further action. He was also instructed 'to try to ensure' that the interim administration of Zara and certain other Adriatic islands acquired by Italy after the First World War, and now claimed by Yugoslavia, should be conducted in the name of the Allies; though it was recognised that in practice it might be necessary to permit Yugoslavs to perform the actual function of administration. In this message the Combined Chiefs emphasised the fact that the success of this policy depended upon Soviet co-operation and informed SACMED that the American and British Governments were considering the 'best method of seeking such co-operation and subsequent Yugoslav agreement to the plan'; but he was at the same time instructed to implement it, 'if military necessity so required', before Soviet and Yugoslav agreement had been obtained.

But by this time events had gone too fast and too far to make the policy practicable. The matter of supreme importance was to ensure that the Allied forces should arrive in Trieste before the Yugoslavs had succeeded in occupying it, and Field-Marshal Alexander took immediate action. On 30th April he telegraphed that he was about to enter Venezia Giulia. On 1st May the 2nd New Zealand Division made contact with elements of the Fourth Yugoslav Army at Monfalcone. General Freyberg met the Commander of the Fourth Yugoslav Army and informed him of his intention to advance to Trieste, and the following day (2nd May) the New Zealand Division entered the city about four o'clock in the afternoon. The German garrison, about 7,000 strong, which was still holding out, though Yugoslavs were already in occupation of a portion of the town, surrendered to General Freyberg shortly after his arrival. The New Zealand Division cleared up and occupied the dock area, leaving the remainder of the town to be taken over by the Yugoslavs, a decision which does not appear to have been altogether fortunate. The next day elements of the New Zealand Division also entered Gorizia, which had been occupied by local Yugoslav partisans. A few days later German troops everywhere had capitulated and hostilities in Europe were at an end.

During the next few weeks Field-Marshal Alexander and Marshal Tito each consolidated their positions in this area of Venezia Giulia, with the result that it was subjected to a double occupation of British and Yugoslav troops—a situation of considerable delicacy, as the Yugoslavs were intent on making sure of their claims by occupation as far west as the Isonzo and even beyond it. Thanks largely to the tactful precautions taken by the G.O.C. XIII Corps, Lieut.-General Sir John Harding, clashes between Allied and Yugoslav troops were avoided, but it was clear that the withdrawal of Yugoslav forces from the western part of Venezia Giulia would not be obtained, except by the exertion of considerable pressure, not excluding the threat of physical force. Meanwhile a series of messages passed between Field-Marshal Alexander and Marshal Tito which left no doubt that pressure on the governmental level would be needed to secure to SACMED even his essential military requirements.

On 30th April Field-Marshal Alexander sent a message to Marshal Tito informing him of his intention to occupy the areas already indicated, presuming that any of Tito's forces in these areas would come under SACMED's command, stating that he would set up Allied Military Government in the wake of his operational advance, which would function through such local authorities as were to be found in effective control, and asking Marshal Tito to communicate his plans. Marshal Tito replied to the effect that the situation had changed much since the Belgrade conversations: that, in order to liberate Yugoslavia and round up all enemy troops in the country as quickly as possible, he had made a plan, which was in fact being carried out, to liberate Istria, Trieste and Monfalcone and the territory up to the Isonzo river, and to advance up that river to the Austrian frontier. For Yugoslavia laid claims also to certain portions of Carinthia. The area of operation of the troops under his command would therefore be from the mouth of the Isonzo via Gorizia and Tolmino to Tarvisio. In accordance with the agreement reached at Belgrade, he was prepared for the Field-Marshal to use the ports of Pola and Trieste as well as the railway line Trieste–Tarvisio, part of which passed through Yugoslav territory. He also agreed that his 'regular' units and partisans operating to the west of the Isonzo line should come under SACMED's command.

On 3rd May Marshal Tito, on hearing of the Allied entry into Trieste, Monfalcone and Gorizia, sent a note of pained surprise to SACMED, protesting that Allied forces had entered these places—'cities which had been liberated by the Yugoslav Army'—without any previous notice, and asking for an immediate explanation. This message appears to have crossed with one from Field-Marshal Alexander to Marshal Tito congratulating him on the magnificent part played by his troops in the winning of these great victories, and informing him that the German garrison of Trieste had surrendered to General Freyberg's forces. These events had resulted in an overlapping of the operational areas of the Allied and Yugoslav Armies—a fact which need not cause any serious difficulties. SACMED's interests in Venezia Giulia remained exactly as had been explained in the Belgrade conversations, namely the 'effective control' of Trieste as a base for the large forces with which he intended to advance into Austria, and of the lines of communication from Trieste into Austria by road and rail. Provided that Yugoslav troops were immediately informed of the position the presence of troops of both armies in the same area need not give rise to inconvenience. He therefore requested Marshal Tito to instruct his local commander to get into touch with Lieut.-General Sir John Harding.

The receipt of Marshal Tito's protest on the entry of Allied troops into Trieste elicited a sharp rejoinder. Field-Marshal Alexander did not mince his words. He expressed his astonishment at Marshal Tito's 'apparent failure' to honour the agreement made in Belgrade, and informed him that he had ordered his troops to maintain their position in Trieste, Monfalcone and Gorizia. He also suggested that, since this question demanded an immediate solution, the Marshal should send his Chief of Staff to meet his own Chief of Staff (General Sir W. D. Morgan), and expressed his confidence that they could bring this conflict of views to a conclusion satisfactory to both.

Marshal Tito's reply made no attempt to conceal the political motives underlying his military penetration to the Isonzo. After expressing surprise at Field-Marshal Alexander's readiness to express his doubts as to the respect which he (Tito) had shown for the Belgrade agreement, he stated openly that he was not 'bound solely' by his military responsibilities, but that he was also Prime Minister, 'who must first of all take care of the interests of his country', adding that he was keeping his word, given in Belgrade, that SACMED might use the ports of Trieste and Pola as well as the lines of communication leading to Austria. On account of the truce which Field-Marshal Alexander had made with the German forces on the Italian front, the Yugoslav Army had been put into a difficult position because the Germans started to reinforce their troops on his front. Hence he had ordered his troops to occupy the communications leading towards Postumia from Fiume and Trieste, to attack the latter city, and, after the German capitulation, the town of Monfalcone and the lines of the Isonzo river, in order to protect the operations in Trieste and prevent the Germans from bringing reinforcements from the Italian front. Moreover the capitulation of German troops in the Tyrol, Carinthia and Styria, which had not been foreseen during the conversations in Belgrade, meant that SACMED had no longer before him a difficult military operation, but merely the occupation of these territories. The occupation of Venezia Giulia had 'not a purely military character' but also a political one, since it had been unjustly annexed by Italy in the peace treaty after the First World War. But he agreed to the meeting of the two Chiefs of Staff and suggested that General Morgan should meet his Chief of Staff in Trieste.

Field-Marshal Alexander replied that a quicker solution would be reached if the General went to Belgrade to discuss the question with the Marshal himself, and this was agreed. It now appeared quite certain to him that the policy of setting up A.M.G. in the whole of Venezia Guilia could only be carried out by the use of force; the essential thing was therefore to secure the vital Allied military interest—communications with Austria. He therefore sent General Morgan to Belgrade to offer the following terms of agreement, which were presented to the Marshal on 9th May:

> 1. As it is agreed that Field-Marshal Alexander requires the port of Trieste and the railways and roads from there to Austria via Gorizia and Tarvisio, to maintain his forces in north-east Italy and in Austria, the portion of the Compartment of Venezia Giulia west of the line on the attached map (later known to history as the Morgan Line) will be under his command.
>
> 2. All Naval, Military and Air Forces west of the line on the attached map will be placed under his command from the moment at which this comes into force.
>
> 3. Field-Marshal Alexander will govern this area using an Allied Military Government. Use will be made of any Yugoslav civil administration which is already set up and working satisfactorily.
>
> 4. To facilitate and simplify the working of the arrangements in paragraphs 1, 2 and 3 above Marshal Tito will withdraw the Yugoslav regular forces now in the portion of Venezia Giulia marked by a double line on the attached map by 11th May 1945.
>
> 5. Any irregular forces in this area will either hand in their arms to the Allied military authorities and disband, or will be withdrawn from the area.
>
> 6. In order to establish safe shipping lanes in the north Adriatic and particularly the approaches to Trieste, the port of Pola and the anchorages on the west coast of Istria between Pola and Trieste will be open to unrestricted use by Allied Naval forces.
>
> 7. This agreement is purely military and in no way prejudices or affects long-term policy regarding the ultimate disposal of the compartment of Venezia Giulia.

Pending the conclusion of an agreement it was quite impossible to establish any form of Allied Military Government in any portion of Venezia Giulia except two communes in the extreme west. Relations between Allied and Yugoslav troops were satisfactory in the sense that no disastrous incidents between them occurred, though throughout the western parts of the 'compartment' British and Yugoslav Armies were completely mixed. Indeed in some instances British and Yugoslav personnel were found by Mr Macmillan, on his visit to General Harding, billeted in the same house. But in Trieste special orders had been given to Yugoslav troops not to fraternise with Allied troops. The Yugoslav Commander had commandeered all large buildings and denied to Allied use all the seven barracks in the city. In general, the attitude of the local commanders was described as one of polite non-cooperation, pending settlement by higher authority of questions under negotiation. In places in the

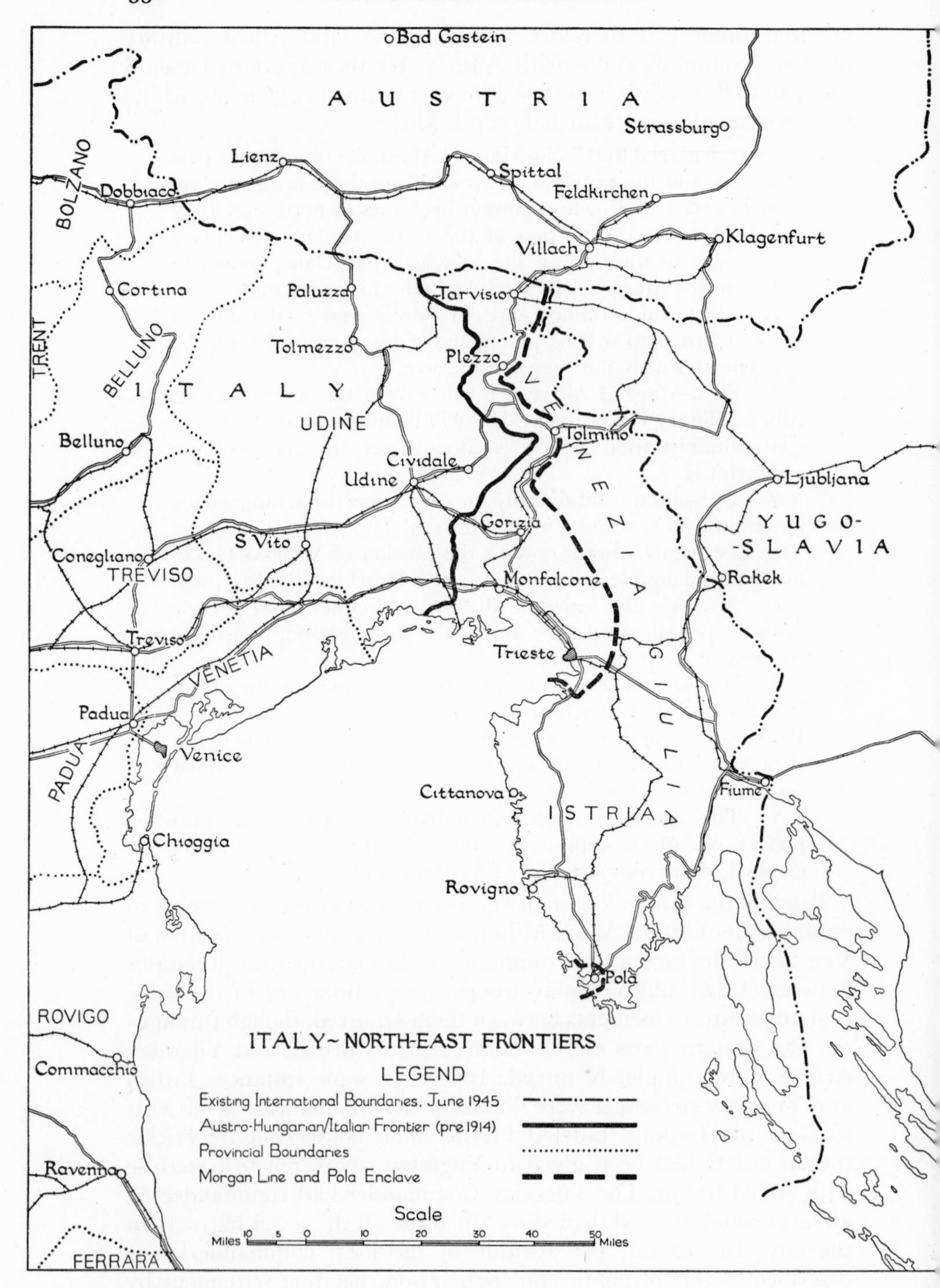
Bad Gastein
AUSTRIA
Strassburg
Lienz
Spittal
Feldkirchen
BOLZANO
Dobbiaco
Villach
Klagenfurt
Cortina
Paluzza
Tarvisio
TRENT
BELLUNO
Tolmezzo
Plezzo
ITALY
UDINE
Belluno
Tolmino
VENEZIA GIULIA
Cividale
Udine
Ljubljana
Gorizia
YUGOSLAVIA
S Vito
Conegliano
TREVISO
Monfalcone
Rakek
Treviso
Trieste
VENETIA
Padua
Venice
PADUA
Cittanova
Fiume
ISTRIA
Chioggia
Rovigno
Pola
ROVIGO
ITALY ~ NORTH-EAST FRONTIERS
LEGEND
Existing International Boundaries, June 1945
Austro-Hungarian/Italian Frontier (pre 1914)
Provincial Boundaries
Morgan Line and Pola Enclave
Commacchio
Ravenna
Scale
Miles 10 5 0 10 20 30 40 50 Miles
FERRARA

Map 16

western portion of the Friulano the Yugoslavs actually started to set up a Yugoslav civil administration, and their troops had penetrated into the British zones in Austria.

The negotiations with Tito on the military level did not reach any agreement. The Marshal refused to agree to Field-Marshal Alexander's proposals. While offering SACMED full use of the port of Trieste as a base, including such shore facilities as he considered necessary, and the communications that he desired, he insisted that civil government should be carried out by the Yugoslav National Liberation Committee. He refused to relinquish *de facto* sovereignty over the area, but he suggested that there should be set up a joint commission at Trieste which would coordinate with the Yugoslav civil and military authorities all military matters in Trieste and throughout the lines of communication, this joint commission to have over-riding powers over the civil and military authorities in matters pertaining to military interest. These terms were, of course, quite unacceptable. Field-Marshal Alexander informed Marshal Tito that his counter-proposals raised a political issue, and that the whole question must therefore now be referred to the British and American Governments. Meanwhile he proposed to use the port of Trieste to maintain his forces in north-east Italy and Austria and trusted that the Marshal would take steps to ensure that no regrettable incidents occurred.[1]

Pending the outcome of diplomatic negotiations between the Allied and Yugoslav Governments, SACMED maintained the *status quo*, though the civilian population in the areas occupied by Yugoslav partisans and troops soon began to feel the pinch of Yugoslav depredations. Gorizia and the province of Trieste were normally largely dependent for their food on the Po valley, and Yugoslav raiding parties were despatched over the Isonzo into Friuli to bring back food. Strict orders were issued that no A.M.G. supplies for the civilian population were to be sent east of the Isonzo and that the distribution in Udine province should be rigidly controlled, to ensure that none of them were appropriated by Yugoslav raiding parties who had been requisitioning supplies in the province. This requisitioning was to be prevented by all available means barring the use of arms. The official attitude was that hardship to the civilian population was deplored, but that the situation had arisen entirely through the action of the Yugoslavs, who by refusing the establishment of A.M.G. had prevented the distribution of Allied foodstuffs already earmarked and stockpiled. In the meantime the Yugoslavs

[1] How necessary such precautions were was shown very clearly a few days later when, on the advance of XIII Corps to Tarnova, the commanding officer of the 13th Yugoslav Division informed the commanding officer of 361st U.S. Infantry Regiment that he must withdraw 91st U.S. Division troops from Tarnova or he would force them out.

steadily built up their forces in the areas of Trieste, Monfalcone, Gorizia, Gemona and Cividale.

The policy of attempting to enforce Allied Military Government in the whole of Venezia Giulia, upon which the State Department had laid such stress, was in fact abandoned in the face of Yugoslav opposition. The question now was how to put pressure on Marshal Tito so as to secure Field-Marshal Alexander's control over the more limited area vital to his military line of communications. Even this might come to the point of actually using force. It would appear from Fleet Admiral Leahy's account that President Truman at first 'seriously contemplated taking a strong stand, even if it should result in hostilities between Anglo-American and Yugoslav troops';[1] and from Sir Winston Churchill's account, that as late as 12th May, President Truman was prepared to take strong action 'to uphold the fundamental principles of territorial settlement by orderly process against force, intimidation or blackmail', though it is not clear that this implied Yugoslav withdrawal from the whole of Venezia Giulia. Truman appears to have taken the view that the Allies should insist on Field-Marshal Alexander obtaining 'complete and exclusive controls of Trieste and Pola, the line of communication through Gorizia and Monfalcone, and of a big enough area to the east to ensure proper administration'.[2] Hence, although he was unwilling to commit himself to the use of force, unless American troops were attacked, he was prepared to bring strong diplomatic pressure on Marshal Tito from another quarter. It would appear that Fleet-Admiral Leahy, with President Truman's approval, actually sent a telegram to Stalin asking his assistance in these negotiations with Marshal Tito, and it may well be that the influence of Moscow was decisive, though no mention is made of this telegram in Sir Winston Churchill's account. The British and American notes presented the proposals for a demarcation line on 15th May.[3] Admiral Leahy states that on 19th May, the day before the telegram was sent to

---

[1] Leahy, *I Was There*, p. 430 (English edition). In this connection it is interesting to note Field-Marshal Alexander's appreciation of the implication of the use of force. The resources required to meet this threat would depend primarily on whether the Russians decided to back Tito, but even without their aid, so large a quantity of German resources had fallen into the Marshal's hands that it would require eleven divisions to meet Yugoslav resistance, five for Venezia Giulia, three to protect the Austrian–Yugoslav frontier and three to occupy the British zone in Austria. If the Russians decided to support Tito, it was impossible to estimate the resources which would be required; they would clearly be beyond any available in the Mediterranean theatre.

[2] Churchill, *op. cit.* Vol. VI, p. 483.

[3] This line which included Pola and the Istrian anchorages in A.M.G. territory was not accepted by Marshal Tito, who insisted on the line proposed earlier by General Morgan in Belgrade. A.F.H.Q. considered the demand for the occupation of Pola as both unnecessary and unwise, but President Truman had insisted on its inclusion, though SACMED was informed by C.C.S. that if Tito opposed the demand Allied forces would not be required to occupy the city.

Stalin, the American Ambassador in Belgrade informed his Government that Marshal Tito had declined to withdraw his troops or government from Venezia Giulia. On 21st May, however, he agreed to meet the essential Allied demands.

On that day the Yugoslav Foreign Office sent a note to the American and British Ambassadors in Belgrade announcing a reversal of the policy hitherto pursued. The Yugoslav Government now agreed to the establishment of A.M.G. under the authority of SACMED, on the basis of the demarcation line proposed by Field-Marshal Alexander, subject to certain minor modifications. In accepting this solution the Yugoslav Government considered the following conditions indispensable: first, that representatives of the Yugoslav Army should be included in the military administration of the area; secondly, that units of the Yugoslav Army should remain in it, though under the command of SACMED; and thirdly, that the Allied military administration should act through the civil authorities already set up in the area. The Yugoslav Government therefore proposed that the British and American Governments should start immediate negotiations in order to settle all questions in this connection. How far this *volte face* was dictated by Allied diplomatic pressure or by Russian insistence must be left for future historians to determine. But it is interesting to note that, on the same day that the Yugoslav note was handed to the Allied embassies in Belgrade, instructions were issued by the Combined Chiefs of Staff to Field-Marshal Alexander immediately to reinforce his troops in the disputed area, with the maximum available assistance from General Eisenhower, so that the Allied preponderance of force in those areas and the firmness of Allied intentions would be clear.

The new proposals from Marshal Tito were a great step forward, but the conditions laid down by him for the establishment of A.M.G. were not entirely acceptable. Field-Marshal Alexander refused to agree to Yugoslav officers participating in A.M.G., though he had no objection to a small mission being attached to Eighth Army H.Q. as observers; nor was he prepared to instruct his A.M.G. to 'act through the civil authorities which are already set up in the area'. A.M.G. must be empowered to use whatever civil authority they deemed best in any particular place, and to change administrative personnel at their discretion. They would however be instructed to use Yugoslav civil administrators wherever they were functioning satisfactorily. He was also prepared to agree that a Yugoslav regular detachment, not exceeding 2,000 all ranks, should occupy an area selected by him west of the dividing line, under his orders. He did not consider it desirable to include the town of Pola or the line of communication from Trieste to Pola in his own area, since his requirements were confined to the use of the port and the anchorages on the western coast of Istria. The American and British Governments however decided that Pola should be included in the agreement, thus increasing Allied military commitments by the setting up of A.M.G. in that city. It was however recognised that, if Marshal Tito should refuse to ratify the agreement, SACMED would not be required to occupy the town.

The terms of the agreement were consequently modified to combine Field-Marshal Alexander's essential requirements with the concessions he was prepared to make to Yugoslav demands. It was presented by the British and American Ambassadors and signed by Marshal Tito on the 9th June. In its final form the agreement contained seven articles. Article (1) placed the portion of Venezia Giulia west of the Morgan line and Pola under the command and control of the Supreme Allied Commander. (2) placed all Yugoslav military forces west of the Morgan line under SACMED's command, 'from the moment in which this agreement comes into force', and limited the Yugoslav detachment permitted to remain west of the line to 2,000. (3) stipulated that SACMED would govern the area west of the Morgan line (and Pola) through an Allied Military Government, and that use would be made of any Yugoslav civil administration which was set up and working in his opinion satisfactorily. A.M.G. would however be empowered to use whatever civil authorities they found best, and to change administrative personnel at their discretion. Marshal Tito was also empowered to attach a small mission to Eighth Army H.Q. as observers. The interpretation of this article, as we shall see, gave rise to considerable difficulty. Under Article (4) Marshal Tito agreed to withdraw all other regular Yugoslav forces from west of the Morgan line by 12th June; under (5) all irregular forces were either, according to SACMED's decision, to surrender arms or to withdraw to the east of the line. Article (6) stipulated that the Yugoslav Government would return all residents in the Allied area whom they had arrested or deported (except those who were Yugoslav citizens in 1939) and make restitution of all property that they had confiscated or removed. Article (7) laid down that the agreement in no way prejudiced or affected the question of ultimate disposition of the territories on either side of the line.

The stage was thus set for the installation of A.M.G. in the area west of the Morgan line, but the division of the *compartimento* into two zones, one under Allied, the other under Yugoslav, Government by a line fixed as the result of purely military considerations, at once raised a number of acute economic problems. In a supplementary agreement signed by the two Chiefs of Staff, General Morgan and General Jovanovic, on 20th June, concerning the detailed implementation of the Belgrade agreement just described, an attempt was made to ensure that the disturbance to the normal economic life of the inhabitants of Venezia Giulia should be reduced to a minimum. Telegraphic and telephonic communications between the two areas were to be uncontrolled and mail facilities undisturbed. No restrictions were to be placed on the movement within Venezia Giulia of persons either of Italian or Slovene origin normally resident in the territory, nor on the passage of such persons to and fro across the demarcation line. Railway communications were to continue uninterrupted, and a joint operating committee was established to ensure the equitable use of equipment and to regulate traffic. Normal economic movement across the line of demarcation was to be permitted to continue, subject only to such supervision as was necessary to prevent unauthorised movement of supplies. Detailed arrangements for the interchange of electric power, of water, and of the agricultural and industrial resources of both areas were to be worked out by a joint economic committee, and arrangements were to be made for the provision of funds by the principal financial institutions in centres in A.M.G. territory to post-offices and branch-banks east of the line.[1]

With regard to Article 3 of the Belgrade Agreement, the Yugoslavs attached to the Morgan–Jovanovic Agreement a verbal note on Allied Military Government, the principles of which were not accepted by the Supreme Allied Commander. This note stated that, since the population of the territory had 'compactly organised an armed resistance movement on the Allied side against the Italian Army, before the capitulation of Italy, and had built up and maintained until today' its own civil administration,

> the old system of Italian civil administration will not be renewed. Instead of that, the new organs of the already existing civil administration will be accepted, if they are working satisfactorily, according to the opinion of the Supreme Allied Commander. In case that A.M.G. is not satisfied with the work of the administrational personnel or any organs of the civil administration, the Regional National Committee, as the first subordinate organ of the civil administration to the A.M.G., is obliged, on request and to the satisfaction of A.M.G., to carry out immediate replacements.

The implications contained in this note were quite unacceptable, in view of the racial tension between Italians and Slovenes, which had been exacerbated not only by the form of military administration set up by the Yugoslavs on occupation but also by their manner of behaviour. The executive power of the Committees of Liberation

---

[1] It is interesting to note that in the course of these negotiations the Yugoslavs attempted to get the eastern portions of the province of Udine, which contained a Slovene majority, included in A.M.G. Venezia Giulia.

set up under Yugoslav occupation was even less compatible with Allied Military Government than that of the Italian C.L.N. in northern Italy.

During the short period of their occupation—the so-called 'forty days'—the Yugoslavs had begun to carry out extensive changes in the administrative machinery of the Slovene littoral. It would appear that a 'Slovenian National Government' was actually formed at Aidussina, at a meeting held on 5th May at which, among other persons, Lieut.-General Jovanovic and the Vice-President of the Central Yugoslav Government, M. Kardelj, were present, as well as British and American officers of the mission to the Yugoslav Army. The Italian system of prefectorial government had been suspended, though the Prefecture's staff was still kept on the pay-roll, and the administrative division of the province was altered. The 'Littoral' was divided into three 'districts'—Gorizia, the hinterland of Trieste and the autonomous city of Trieste, which was increased to include suburbs containing a substantial Slovene population. Each district was administered by an 'elected' Italo-Slovene Citizens Executive Committee (C.E.A.I.S.) with executive authority depending from the Regional Council of Liberation. The Prefecture had been relieved of all executive responsibility. Organisations such as the *Genio Civile*, SEPRAL (food distribution and rationing), and the *Consorzio Agrario* continued to function with Yugoslav-appointed chiefs, and the policing of the territory was put in charge of the Yugoslav-dominated Militia of Popular Defence, while sanctions against Fascism were carried out by People's courts, whose composition, with the help of the Italian Communists, was arranged in a manner satisfactory to the Slovene nationalists. Meanwhile in Trieste and Gorizia elements of the Italian C.L.N. were attempting to maintain an underground organisation.

The methods of military government employed by the Yugoslavs were hardly such as to please any but a small minority of Communist Italians. For example the attempt was made at Gorizia to conscript inhabitants into the ranks of the Yugoslav forces. News, often wildly distorted, of Yugoslav proceedings reached Rome, causing a great deal of anxiety to the Italian Government, which made repeated representations on this subject to the Allied Commission. But the Yugoslav Government, though oppressive and arbitrary, did not, in the words of an observer from Mr Macmillan's staff attached to XIII Corps, constitute a 'reign of terror'.[1]

[1] Subsequent evidence of happenings in Trieste and other places seem, however, to have shown that acts of violence against members of the Italian administration were widespread, and by no means confined to notorious Fascists. In other respects Yugoslav rule also left much to be complained of, such as the wholesale removal across the Morgan line of property belonging to Italian inhabitants, and the deportation of persons accused of 'Fascist crimes', whose restoration was specially included in Article 6 of the Belgrade Agreement.

In these circumstances it was hardly reasonable to expect A.M.G. to abandon the administrative system under which Venezia Giulia had been governed for a quarter of a century, in order to perpetuate a hastily improvised machinery of 'popular government' based on 'soviets' or committees under Yugoslav domination. Nor was it practicable to adopt a dual system, the Yugoslav committee system in communes with a Slovene majority, and the Italian system in those with an Italian majority. The only practicable step was to continue the Italian legal system as existing on 8th September 1943, with such subtractions as were required to purge it of Fascist features. This meant the abolition of the executive authority of the Yugoslav-sponsored councils and departmental committees of Liberation—a step interpreted by the Yugoslav Government as a contravention of the Belgrade Agreement which, in Article 3, expressly provided that 'use will be made of any Yugoslav civil administration which is already set up and which is working satisfactorily'. SACMED could only appeal to the saving qualification just cited. He was also able to point out that the policy of using Yugoslav 'administrations' was not practical, and that in the draft of this agreement submitted by him to the Combined Chiefs of Staff the word 'administrators' was used in place of the word 'administration', which appeared in the text actually presented for signature by the British and American ambassadors. In these circumstances there would appear to be some excuse for Marshal Tito's distrust of the Allied fulfilment of the Belgrade Agreement, and this goes some way to explain his unwillingness to fulfil most of the other clauses.

The agreement between Field-Marshal Alexander and Marshal Tito having been signed on 9th June, A.M.G. was set up in Trieste and the portions of Venezia Giulia west of the Morgan line without incidents on 12th June, under an American S.C.A.O., Colonel Monfort, who had been in charge of the first A.M.G. in the theatre, that of Pantellaria.[1] Some A.M.G. officers had been in Trieste as observers ever since its occupation by General Freyberg's troops. The headquarters of Venezia Giulia sub-region were established in Udine on 22nd May and provincial teams for Trieste and Gorizia Provinces were kept in readiness, pending the outcome of the negotiations with Marshal Tito. The Trieste team was actually introduced into the city on 25th May, with the strictest orders not to disclose that they were Military Government officers. Venezia Giulia was completely separated from Venezia Region and became a special unit, A.M.G. XIII Corps—later called A.M.G. Venezia Giulia—responsible to Lieut.-General Sir John Harding, commanding XIII

---

[1] See above, p. 33.

Corps, and subject only to technical direction from the Allied Commission.[1]

The form of Allied Military Government instituted differed in certain important particulars from that set up in the rest of northern Italy. For though the general system of Italian law and administration was applied, great care was taken to avoid all action which might appear to prejudice the ultimate disposition of the territory under the peace treaty. Thus there was no attempt to apply in this administratively fragmentary territory, consisting only of portions of three provinces, some of the legislation which had been passed by the Italian Governments since the fall of Mussolini. Italian law remained in force, except for Fascist legislation discriminating against Jews or other non-Italians. All enactments of the Fascist Republic, the Germans, and the Yugoslav military administrations were of course repealed. But though the courts continued to administer Italian law, appeals to the Court of Cassation in Rome were abrogated. In the same way all financial dependence upon Rome was avoided. Though Italian lire were recognised as legal tender, A.M.G. lire were used in preference wherever possible. The Finance Officer, H.Q. XIII Corps, was supplied with 150 million A.M.G. lire and a similar amount was held in reserve for Venezia Giulia by the Allied Commission in Rome, to be transported as required by XIII Corps, which provided the necessary armed guards. No other currencies were recognised nor any exchange rates, except that of the lira with the dollar and the pound sterling. And though the debt of the Italian Government was to be serviced in the usual manner, and the sale of postal savings-bonds and the acceptance of postal savings deposits continued, the issue of other Italian Government securities was suspended. The local machinery of the *Banca d'Italia* was employed for the financing of government and communal expenditure, such cash advances as were necessary being supplied in the form of A.M.G. lire by the A.M.G. Finance Officers. Existing banks were organised on an autonomous provincial basis, with the provincial branch of the *Banca d'Italia* acting as the lender of last resort, the necessary cash advances being made to the branch by A.M.G.

These arrangements were very similar to those made for AMGOT, Sicily, in 1943, except that the local *Banca d'Italia*, instead of the *Banca di Sicilia*, was used as the central bank. They were not, however, intended to be more than temporary expedients. The Yugoslavs lost no time in incorporating the portion of Venezia Giulia east of the Morgan line into Yugoslavia, and early in the autumn

---

[1] This arrangement was in theory similar to that of other Army A.M.G's, but later led to some conflicts of jurisdiction, since XIII Corps claimed the right to communicate on A.M.G. matters directly with A.F.H.Q. and to insist on controlling directly A.M.G. policy in all matters affecting law and order.

began to issue their own Military Government currency, in spite of a previous agreement to refrain from such an action. Financially the zone west of the Morgan line was consequently reunited with Italy. By this time the Italian Government had assumed the financial liabilities of the Allied Financial Agency, and undertaken to supply such funds as were required by XIII Corps for its own needs and for the financing of the Allied Military Government of Venezia Giulia.

The legal instruments establishing Allied Military Government in Venezia Giulia are perhaps worth a passing notice. Proclamation No. 1 established Military Government, defined war crimes and set up Allied Military courts. Proclamation No. 2 established property control, the legal tender and exchange rates (dollar and sterling) of A.M. lire, prohibited foreign trade transactions and continued the existing system of rationing and maximum wages and prices. Proclamation No. 3 dealt with the regulation of private means of communication (wireless sets), the prohibition of photography and declaration of cameras, etc., the regulation of newspapers and printed matter under licence from A.M.G., the prohibition of meetings and assemblies without a permit from A.M.G., and the display of flags, permitting the display of the Stars and Stripes and the Union Jack jointly on public buildings and prohibiting the display of any national flags except in the barracks or camps of the occupying troops, which included, of course, the Yugoslavs. Proclamation No. 4 enjoined the closing of financial institutions and the moratorium. Proclamation No. 5 dealt with 'epuration' and established special courts of Assize for the trial of Fascists and collaborators. An appeal from the special court of Assize was permitted to the court of Appeal in Trieste, but no appeal lay to the court of Cassation in Rome, and no sentence of death was to be executed unless or until confirmed by the Chief Civil Affairs Officer or such other officer, not below the rank of Brigadier or Brigadier-General, to whom this power was delegated by Field-Marshal Alexander. This Proclamation was rendered necessary by the immediate abolition of the People's courts set up by the Yugoslavs, whose procedure, as already mentioned, had resulted in executions of Italians on a large scale. Proclamation No. 6 dissolved the Fascist party and organisations affiliated to it, and dealt with the disposal of Fascist property, which was to be applied by A.M.G. to the benefit of the inhabitants of the Allied zone. These proclamations were supplemented by general orders on the usual A.M.G. pattern, dealing with the licensing of all motor vehicles, the collection of cereals, the repeal of anti-Jewish laws, the creation of labour offices and the creation of free trade-unions, the 'epuration' of public offices and private industry, etc.

In planning the Military Government arrangements for the occupation of Venezia Giulia it had been realised, as noted in

Chapter IX, that the arrangements for public safety would have to be adapted to meet the peculiar conditions of tension resulting from the presence of Yugoslav troops and partisans in the area. It was considered that the introduction of *Carabinieri* into Venezia Giulia would lead to trouble, while the police forces instituted by the Yugoslavs were even less likely to constitute impartial guardians of public order. The only way of meeting this difficulty would be to recruit a police force locally, from such suitable elements as could be found on the spot—a process which could not be accomplished in an instant. It was consequently decided that the Allied Military Police forces should take over the double function of civil and military policing, as well as the recruiting and training of an indigenous civilian police force. As a temporary measure the appointments of A.P.M. XIII Corps and S.C.A.P.O. A.M.G. XIII Corps were fused into that of Chief of Police, Venezia Giulia, directly responsible to G.O.C. XIII Corps, to whom both the military and civilian police branches were responsible. The force was modelled on the organisation of the Metropolitan police but, following the British colonial practice, the principal officers were Allied, mostly British, other ranks being recruited from local sources, such as indigenous ex-*Carabinieri*, members of the other Italian police forces who had joined the partisans, and also former members of the Yugoslav-dominated *Difesa Popolare*. Slovenes formed nearly a third of the total force.

The recruitment of this force was no easy matter in its earlier stages before the disbandment of the *Difesa Popolare*, which terrorised would-be volunteers. But after its disbandment, which took place on 24th June in the normal manner with ceremonial parades, recruitment became much easier. A force with a 'ceiling' of 3,500—afterwards increased to 6,000—was quickly raised and trained under A.M.G's Public Safety officer, Colonel Richardson, who in peace time had been an officer of the Metropolitan police. This force received its first test in action at the beginning of November, when hunger demonstrations took place at Trieste, first by Italians and the next day by Slovenes and Communists, and was completely successful in maintaing order—albeit with American and British military police in the background.

The disbanding and disarmament of the *Difesa Popolare* disposed of the partisan problem, which, as such, caused little trouble to A.M.G.; since the Yugoslavs had already disarmed most of the Italian partisans in Venezia Giulia who had not withdrawn into Udine before the Allied forces came on the scene, and after the disbandment the more bellicose elements among the Slovene partisans retired across the Morgan line. The Yugoslav troops remaining on the British side of the Morgan line, in accordance with the agreement, raised little real trouble after the disbandment of the *Difesa Popolare*, though they did for some time attempt in various ways to obstruct A.M.G. Slovene opposition to A.M.G. continued, encouraged by a free press; and strikes and demonstrations, often threatening to develop into armed violence, were frequent and very difficult to counter. The Communists showed much ingenuity in getting up these demonstrations. One of their favourite practices was the institution of the funeral, which entailed the digging up of the bodies of partisan 'heroes' and carrying them for re-burial in new locations by the longest possible route. That a good deal of 'private violence' was indulged in, by Italians no less than Slovenes, cannot be denied, but during the first six months of Allied Military Government in Trieste not a single life was lost in any public disorder.[1]

The attempt to associate Italians and Slovenes equally in the work of local self-government was much less successful. Under General Order No. 11, published on 11th August, A.M.G. had attempted to introduce a system of local government designed on Italian lines, provided with advisory councils to which representatives of all racial, political, and economic groups were to be appointed according to their respective local strengths. The province and the commune remained in essence unchanged, though the former was re-christened with the name of 'area', and the title of Prefect was abolished, the more democratic word President being used both for the chief official of the 'area' and for the mayors of the communes. The 'areas' were three, Trieste, Gorizia and Pola. The attempt was made to introduce Slovene elements into executive positions in the local administration as well as into the local advisory councils. To hold the balance fairly between Italian and Slovene interests both the Slovene and the Italian Committees of Liberation—of which the latter had been forced underground during the 'forty days'—were asked to nominate candidates for the administrative posts which needed filling after 'epuration' and for membership of the local communal and area councils. But the Slovene Regional Committee, acting presumably on orders from Marshal Tito, refused all collaboration and declined to submit any names for candidates either for local government councils or for the joint advisory committees on housing, agriculture, etc., to be appointed to assist A.M.G. in Trieste.

A.M.G., faced with this attitude of non-cooperation, decided none the less to proceed immediately with the setting up of machinery of local government. There was no difficulty in setting up the area

---

[1] See the article by Colonel Alfred C. Bowman, Senior Civil Affairs Officer of A.M.G. XIII Corps and Venezia Giulia from early in July 1945, in the *Military Government Journal*, the magazine of the American Military Government Association, for June 1948.

administration in Trieste, Pola and Gorizia, since in the area capitals the majority of the population was Italian. In about half of the communes it was also possible to appoint a mayor and communal council, but in nearly twenty of them, containing about fifteen per cent of the population of the Allied zone, the inhabitants refused to nominate either officials or counsellors. Not all of these communes were inhabited by a majority of Slovenes; in four of them the population was almost wholly Italian, but either Communist or overawed by Communists. In some of the non-cooperating communes a form of direct government under the C.A.O. had to be instituted, instead of the self-government envisaged in the General Order, and in certain cases it was far from easy, owing to Slovene intimidation, to get a communal or district administration started. But, while not prepared to cooperate under the General Order, the Slovene Committees in those communes did give some assistance in the performance of essential services, like the distribution of food and clothing. In spite of the lack of cooperation from the Slovene Committee of National Liberation, A.M.G. was able to put into effect certain measures which went a long way to satisfy reasonable Slovene opinion (which, notwithstanding Yugoslav political pressure, was by no means negligible) that A.M.G. as trustees of the disputed territory were maintaining a fair balance between the interests of the two nationalities. The Slovene language was made official, in the sense that it could be used no less than Italian in law courts, and a system of both elementary and secondary Slovene schools with their own programme was instituted.

The story of Military Government in Venezia Giulia belongs to political rather than to military history and cannot therefore be treated further in this volume. The Allied Zone continued under Allied military administration until the conclusion of the Peace Treaty with Italy, under which, except for Trieste, it became reincorporated into Italy, while the Yugoslav Zone as well as Pola was awarded to Yugoslavia. After the ratification of the treaty A.M.G. Venezia Giulia was reduced to A.M.G. Trieste, which remained in operation until the withdrawal of Allied occupying troops in October 1954.

CHAPTER XIII

THE END OF A.M.G.

IT IS NOT INTENDED to tell here the detailed story of Allied Military Government in the northern Regions after the end of hostilities, still less the later history of the Allied Commission, protracted for nearly two and a half years. The aim of this volume has not been to present an official history of the Allied Commission as such, but rather to give an account of the various military arrangements developed during the campaign for relieving the General in command of operations of as much responsibility as was practical for the behaviour and destiny of the civilian inhabitants of the country occupied by his troops. That these arrangements could be conceived in purely military terms, apart from wider political considerations, was impossible after the armistice; perhaps the chief interest of this story lies in the multifarious ways in which the political implications of the Italian situation bore upon the policy of the Supreme Allied Commander. But once hostilities have come to an end we pass from the narrow sphere of military to the wider scene of political history.

Once military operations were over and the Allied forces found themselves in a friendly and violently anti-German liberated territory, it might perhaps be supposed that the continuance of a foreign Military Government was quite unnecessary in order to ensure the military requirements of a no longer operational Allied Commander. But the situation was in fact not really quite so simple. Conditions on liberation, as we have noted, were anything but stable, and no one could tell how bitter or how complicated the consequences of partisan insurrection were going to prove. The existence of an armed Communist party of unknown dimensions, trained in the practice of guerilla warfare, must have seemed menacing enough to any Allied military commander, even before the 'Iron Curtain' had fallen. And though the talk of revolution, widely enough spread in the north, proved in fact to be little more than talk, there was a real danger of widespread civil disturbance, in spite of the negotiations, described in Chapter X, between the Allied Commander, the C.L.N.A.I. and the Rome Government. Colonel Salvadori, British liaison officer with the partisan command, informed the Allied Commission's political advisers as late as the beginning of May that the Socialists had until recently favoured a revolution, though they had decided later to change their objective to gaining control of the

Government in Rome by peaceful tactics, while the Communists had also been in favour of revolution. In these circumstances the continuation for a considerable period of Allied Military Government in the North was indispensable.

Fortunately the danger of civil war was avoided. It had always been understood that after the liberation of the North a reconstruction of the Government in Rome would be essential, just as it had been after the liberation of the capital. Arrangements were therefore made by A.M.G. for the immediate despatch to Rome of representatives of the C.L.N.A.I. After some weeks of rather involved negotiations Signor Bonomi resigned on 12th June. His place as Prime Minister was taken by Signor Parri, who had been one of the main pillars of the Resistance movement. In the formation of the new Government the unity of the six parties was restored, Socialists and Action party re-entering the coalition. On Admiral Stone's suggestion, the new Prime Minister had made this a condition of his assuming office. During the course of the negotiations a strong bid for the premiership was made by Signor Nenni who received the support of the Communists, but the opposition to his claims by the Christian Democrats was too strong. Their leader, Signor De Gasperi, was equally unacceptable. A compromise was finally reached by agreement on Signor Parri, who, though not a politician, was a member of the Party of Action. His appointment automatically disposed of the tension between Milan and Rome.

Of the new Cabinet of twenty ministers no less than fourteen had been born in the North, though seven had been members of the previous government; but the largest group, including Parri himself, were newcomers. The President of the Council was supported by two Vice-Presidents, the Socialist Nenni, who was placed in charge of the High Commission for Sanctions against Fascism as well as the organisation of the Constituent Assembly, and the Liberal Brosio, a member of the previous government, who was given charge of the *Consulta*, the quasi-parliamentary Advisory Council to be constituted to represent public opinion pending the elections to the Constituent Assembly. Signor Parri, in accordance with tradition, took over the Ministry of the Interior, but the Ministry of Foreign Affairs remained in charge of the Christian Democrat, Signor De Gasperi, and the Treasury in that of Signor Soleri. Admiral De Courten remained in charge of the Navy. The new Government, like its predecessor, was required to give an undertaking that it would observe Italy's obligation under the armistice, and refrain from raising the constitutional question, but the document embodying this declaration contained a paragraph stating that Allied rights under the Armistice and Instrument of Surrender with respect to the control over the Italian Government would be held in reserve in matters of day to day administration, subject only to overriding military needs.

Meanwhile on the organisational side the development of A.C./A.M.G. after the close of hostilities had not quite followed the pattern originally envisaged. The military plans for north-west Italy, involving the early transition from IV Corps to No. 2 District, did not work out as projected, owing to the intrusion of French forces into parts of Liguria, the Val d'Aosta and other districts on the Piedmont border. A.M.G. consequently remained under the command of the Fifth Army and IV Corps to administer regions with a population of over ten millions. And though the Regional organisations were set up, a good deal of confusion resulted from the fact that the Regional Commissioners were still under command of Fifth Army and IV Corps, and could communicate with A.C. headquarters on matters of policy only through G-5 IV Corps and G-5 Fifth Army, the staff of which had been designed on a 'spearhead' basis and was not adequate, either in size or in composition, to deal with the complicated economic and political problems which, since the close of hostilities, now formed by far the largest part of A.M.G.'s business. Communication facilities during these early weeks were far from adequate and messages from A.C. headquarters often failed to reach Milan.

At a conference held at Fifteenth Army Group on 24th May, the possibility of initiating Phase II was discussed, and the inconvenience of the present administrative arrangements for A.M.G. was pointed out by Brigadier Lush. It was however decided that no changeover could be made in the chain of responsibility through G-5 Fifth Army to A.C. headquarters. The conference did nevertheless result in some improvement in A.M.G's administrative arrangements through the setting up of a forward echelon of A.C. headquarters at Milan under Colonel Fiske; the staff of which was drawn from the Economic Section, in order to coordinate regional activities through Fifth Army. By the middle of June the dispute with the French over the occupation of Italian territory had been settled by the French withdrawal, and A.F.H.Q. directed that Phase II should come into force on 15th July. On 4th August Emilia was transferred to the Italian government.

On the Eighth Army front the transition from Phase I to Phase II came far sooner than had been anticipated. The tension on the Yugoslav frontier meant that in Friuli and the Allied occupied portions of Venezia Giulia Allied Military Government remained under direct Army control, but Regional control of the Military Government of four provinces of Venetia proper had, as we have seen, been established early in June. At the beginning of July A.M.G. Eighth Army was finally dissolved. Its place had been taken in Friuli and Venezia Giulia by A.M.G. XIII Corps (later, Venezia Giulia) responsible directly to Lieut.-General Sir John Harding.

Once the political crisis had been solved by the formation of the Parri Government, it was agreed that the handing over of the northern Regions to Italian administration should be accomplished as quickly as possible. Indeed it was at one time expected that A.M.G.—except in the disputed territory on the Austrian and Yugoslav frontiers—would be terminated as early as September. On the recommendation of the Chief Commissioner SACMED had proposed, in spite of the risk of serious disorders, to hand back the Northern Regions to Italian administration as easly as 30th September, on the ground that a later transfer after almost all Allied troops had been withdrawn would entail an even greater risk, quite apart from the obvious political advantages of an early termination of A.M.G. This proposal led to protracted discussions between the two Allied governments, who found themselves unable to agree on this date, for reasons connected with the situation in Bolzano, where the Americans were at first anxious to maintain A.M.G. It was however eventually decided that this province should be handed back to the Italian government with the rest of the Northern Regions—except Udine and Venezia Giulia—on 31st December. This delay was fortunate, since it enabled the Allies to ensure that the Italian Government would be in a position to maintain public order by progress made in two directions, the disarmament of the partisans and the reorganisation of the police forces, neither of which had been fully accomplished by the end of the summer. It was also strongly felt in certain circles at the headquarters of the Commission that Allied supervision would be required to ensure the free expression of the will of the people on the constitutional question in a popular ballot. Now that the war was over, definite choice by popular vote between the monarchy and a republic could no longer be postponed. Though the Parri Government, as well as its successor, gave the formal undertaking to engage in no action which would prejudice the constitutional question, the interpretation of that pledge by individual ministers was, to say the least of it, somewhat elastic. Meanwhile the essential conditions for such an expression of the popular will were still unfulfilled. Electoral lists in Italian Government territory were still far from complete. During its last few months A.M.G. was actively occupied with the preparation of these lists: but it had already ceased to exist before it was possible to hold any elections.

As soon as hostilities were over steps were taken to enlarge the territory subject to the Italian Government. At the end of April its frontier stood only a little north of Rome. It was not until 5th May that the northern provinces of Tuscany, Florence, Pistoia, Lucca and Apuania passed from Fifth Army A.M.G. to the control of the Tuscany Region (VIII). Five days later the provinces of Siena, Grosseto and Arezzo, the *Compartimento* of Umbria, and that of the

Marche—with the exception of the commune of Ancona—were transferred to the Italian Government. The transfer had been submitted for approval in the normal manner to the Advisory Council and had been approved by the American, British and French delegates. Those of the U.S.S.R., Greece and Yugoslavia stated that they were without instructions, and the last-named objected to further transfers of territory so long as Italy objected to the handing over of Venezia Giulia to Yugoslavia. A.F.H.Q., nevertheless, informed the Combined Chiefs of Staff that 'unless instructed to the contrary' the transfer would be carried out on 10th May. When that date arrived no reply had been received from C.C.S. and the transfer was effected. Almost immediately afterwards instructions were received that the transfer should be deferred, but after representations from A.F.H.Q. it was allowed to stand. By 4th August all Tuscany, except Leghorn, and Emilia had been added to Italian Government territory, with the approval of the Advisory Council. Only Liguria and the Regions north of the Po, together with the three ports, Naples, Leghorn, and Ancona, were now left under Military Government.

Though public safety conditions in Emilia left a good deal to be desired the turnover to Italian administration took place without any disturbance. But the problem of disarmament north of the Po had still to be solved. The arrangements made by General Crittenberger through General Cadorna for the disbandment and disarmament of partisans had only proved partially successful. In spite of the fact that General Cadorna, who immediately after liberation was appointed by the Italian Government to the post of Chief of the General Staff of the Army, had issued orders to all patriots to hand in their arms, actual collections at patriot centres were disappointing. Though in many places they amounted to as much as one weapon per known 'patriot', they did not include anything like the total number of arms which the partisans had managed to secure, or, as has already been explained, more than a few of the more modern and efficient weapons which had been supplied through Allied sources. Moreover, once the Germans had surrendered and the Social Republic collapsed, the influence of the Partisan High Command, the *Commando Generale*, never at the best of times undisputed[1], rapidly declined. The Partisan High Command and the regional commands were all dissolved by the middle of June. The responsibility for the enforcement of the orders issued through General Cadorna had to be placed on the leaders of the political parties.

---

[1] See General Cadorna's own account in *La Riscossa*. (*op. cit.*) *passim*.

If one may credit General Trabucchi's admittedly prejudiced account[1]—he was a regular Army officer and in command of the Piedmont C.V.L.—the actions of the A.M.G. Patriot Officers and their Italian collaborators, the military patriot representatives, do not appear always to have been excessively tactful. In particular General Trabucchi complains that the plans he had concerted with his staff for the demobilisation of the Piedmontese partisans were entirely disregarded. It would appear that the Piedmontese Committee of National Liberation had discussed demobilisation plans with Colonel Stevens, the British Partisan Liaison Officer. They envisaged a gradual process which would not take place instantly, but only after the absorption of partisans into the police forces, the regular army and public and private employment, whereas A.M.G. insisted on immediate disarmament.[2]

After the tremendous 'boost' given to the partisan movement by Allied propaganda—which had already aroused a certain amount of misgiving in certain circles at A.F.H.Q., to say nothing of the Army A.M.G.'s—their brusque disarmament must have come as something of a shock to the 'heroic liberators', many of whom had for months run every conceivable form of risk on behalf of their country. And, apart from the honours of the ceremonial parades, there was little enough that the Italian, or Allied Military, Government could offer the demobilised partisan. The initial demobilisation gratuity of 1,000 lire was ridiculously small, when compared with the inflated price-level which on liberation had risen by leaps and bounds, and, though this was subsequently increased to 5,000 lire, there were often considerable delays before the Italian Government made the bonus money available. Nor were conditions in the partisan centres by any means sufficiently attractive to induce 'patriots' to surrender arms. Though their rations on the Italian army scale were in most places immediately provided, it often took some time before any clothing—and that mostly 'salvaged' uniforms—could be made available from excess military stocks, which had first of all to be dyed before issue.

The opportunities for employment offered were by no means plentiful. For selected elements the reconstitution of the police forces provided a livelihood, first as special police formations, and afterwards as Agents of Public Safety—a body which, after purging, needed recruitment on a big scale—and to a smaller extent as *Carabinieri*, whose ceiling was at last revised. Recruitment to the

---

[1] General Trabucchi in the last chapter of his book, *I vinti hanno sempre torto*, expresses considerable bitterness at his treatment by the Regional Commissioner of Piedmont and the A.M.G. Patriot Officer.

[2] See Paolo Greco's notes in *Aspetti della resistenza in Piemonte*, p. 153.

army on a very limited scale was also offered. The Italian Government agreed to demobilise some of the more senior personnel incorporated in their armed forces and to replace them, to the extent of one-third, by volunteers. General Cadorna applied for 10,000 vacancies for patriot volunteers. But here again the ceiling of the Italian armed forces came into question and M.M.I.A. was obliged to limit the official intake to 4,000. The employment offered by the Allied forces was soon to become a diminishing quantity, though priority for partisans was maintained. But the pay-rolls of their former employers afforded, if not work, at any rate a livelihood. Once the first fury of liberation was over and political tension on the French frontier had relaxed, demobilisation of the militarised bands proceeded more or less according to plan, faster in Piedmont than in Lombardy and Venetia. In Piedmont and Lombardy Partisan Centres were all closed by the middle of July, while in Liguria they were closed by the end of that month. In Venetia demobilisation was rather slower. For operational reasons partisan bands had been retained under arms a good deal longer than elsewhere, and it was not till 24th June that the ceremonial disbandment parade took place at Udine.

But while disbandment took place, disarmament did not follow suit. The date for the completion of the handing in of arms had been fixed by General Crittenberger for the IV Corps area as 7th June, and orders to this effect were issued by General Cadorna to all his units before the dissolution of the Partisan Command. But when that day passed disarmament was anything but complete. The Communists had led the way in secreting arms, and the formations belonging to other parties had naturally followed their examples. For though the immediate chance of revolution had passed—the occupation by Allied forces made that impossible—who could tell when it might not return? As experience in Greece had shown, underground resistance movements are not easy to disarm. To collect a substantial portion of the weapons of the regular full-time militarised units was comparatively simple. But to keep track of those employed by the numerous sabotage squads in the towns and factories, (SAP and GAP) was in best of circumstances almost impossible. The last-minute patriot, who had got hold of weapons during the insurrection, added greatly to the problem. Many of these, a band of whom once actually held up General Cadorna near Pallanza, were just gangsters.

With the formation of the Parri Government the political danger from the Resistance movement had ended, but the danger of the gangster still remained. During the early days of liberation conditions of insurrection made it quite impossible to collect arms from civilians by the normal method of A.M.G. Proclamation and General

Order, but with the disbandment of the partisan units this once more became possible. After 7th June the possession of arms by ex-partisans became a criminal offence, and the problem of disarmament was now just a police operation, no easy matter—even with an efficient and well armed police force. In the conditions existing after the days of insurrection it was doubly difficult.

If it had been left merely to its own resources in the carrying out of disarmament, A.M.G. would certainly have been too weak. It was only through the cooperation of the Allied military police that the raiding of secret arms deposits by *Carabinieri* under the leadership of A.M.G. Public Safety officers could be made effective. During the summer a large number of raids were carried out by concerted action. In a factory in Milan, for example, three lorry loads were found in July, belonging to the third Garibaldini Division, including mortars, machine guns and anti-tanks mines. In August over fifty raids were made in Piedmont, in about half of which weapons were discovered. Meanwhile heavy sentences were inflicted by A.M.G. courts on persons convicted of illegal possession of arms.

As a result of these measures and of the increasing efficiency, as protectors of public order, of the *Carabinieri* under A.M.G. leadership, the partisans themselves, despairing of the possibility of starting a revolution, began either to abandon the arms they had collected, or even to hand them in to the public safety authorities. Thus, in Venetia in August, a large number of piles of arms were discovered abandoned by their holders, while in Novara in September, following the discovery of arms in a church, the key of which was in charge of a well known partisan leader, the local A.M.G. Public Safety officer was able to come to an arrangement with him, by which he and his followers surrendered their arms on the condition that no prosecution for past offences should be made. Nevertheless at the end of September there must still have been a large number of arms in private possession.[1] But the success of the operation cannot be measured by the simple statistics of the number of arms recovered. Its real test lay in the fact that, after A.M.G's responsibility came to an end, no major outbreak of armed force had to be dealt with by the Italian Government.

One of the chief factors leading to the establishment of more normal conditions was the institution of the Special Courts of Assize, which did much to allay the vindictiveness manifested by the public against Fascists and collaborators. There was some delay in setting up these courts, since the number of judges and judicial officials required to deal with the enormous quantities of prisoners—

[1] About 215,000 rifles, 12,000 sub-machine guns, 5,000 machine guns, 760 anti-tank weapons, 217 cannon and 12 armoured cars had been surrendered, but only about 5,000 pistols.

there were at the end of May some 5,000 in Milan alone—proved a severe strain on the resources of the judicial community. Northern Italy, in the first flush of partisan 'victory', was very reluctant to accept judges imported from the South, and there was in the North an insufficient number of magistrates of the appropriate grade. Nor were there enough officials of the Ministry of Justice to cope with the enormous volume of work. After some hesitation, it was agreed to import judges from south of the Apennines and arrangements were made with the Ministry of Justice for local barristers to take the place of the Ministry's officials.

Trials by the Extraordinary Courts of Assize started in most provinces during the last week of May. Considering the composition of these courts and the violence of popular sentiment against the Germans and their collaborators, the number of death sentences awarded was comparatively small, though prison sentences were frequent and heavy. Popular pressure was at times very great and led no doubt to many miscarriages of justice, but it was soon recognised that popular clamour could be artificially aroused by the payment of persons to shout '*a morte*' at the price of 200 lire a day. Arrangements were made by which trials of bad offenders could be transferred to courts outside their 'home-town' (provincial capital). In most places, according to the Legal Sub-Commission reports, prisoners were given a reasonably fair hearing, though strange incidents some times occurred, for example at Brescia, where a *Carabiniere* recognised the accused man in the dock and proceeded to shoot him during the course of the hearing. The courts on the whole worked quickly, but at the end of July there were still 3,500 cases in Lombardy, 3,400 in Emilia and nearly 5,000 cases in Piedmont awaiting trial. In these however most of the defendants were only insignificant members of neo-Fascist organisations without any specific charges against them. Both in Liguria and in Venetia the persons awaiting trial at the beginning of September were comparatively few. As the more important cases were disposed of, public feeling began to grow much calmer, and the proportion of death sentences smaller. But even at the beginning it was never very high.

In the matter of Fascist crimes the chief interest of A.M.G. was to prevent outbursts of popular vengeance, and this was on the whole successfully accomplished. Before A.M.G. in northern Italy came to an end, the Allied Commission could record with some satisfaction that considerable progress had been made in canalising the political activity of the Italian nation into rather more normal channels. By a decree passed in October (DLL No. 625) the special courts of Assize created to try Fascist crimes under DLL No. 159 of July 1944 were transformed into a special section of the ordinary courts of

Assize, each court still retaining lay members chosen by the C.L.N., but the special mixed section of the Court of Cassation which had been set up to hear appeals was abolished, all appeals being transferred to the regular Court of Cassation, an exclusively judicial body.

It remains to record briefly the much less spectacular activity in the field of 'epuration'. Since everywhere the C.L.N. had been in power some days before the Allies arrived, the preliminary suspensions by A.M.G. were mostly found to be unnecessary as the work had already been accomplished. The provincial committees under General Order No. 35 were therefore rapidly set up and got to work quickly with the effective cooperation of the C.L.N. Once the machinery for the purging of private industry had been created this too worked reasonably quickly. Meanwhile, with its eyes on the elections, which were to follow as quickly as possible the completion of the process of national liberation, the Bonomi Government had passed a further decree aimed at the elimination of 'politically dangerous persons' (DLL No. 149 dated 26th April 1945). This decree—which was largely an elaboration of the provisions of Article 8 of DLL No. 159—created a further network of provincial commissions, as well as a central commission to hear appeals, and it explicitly disfranchised all persons who had held certain posts (*cariche direttive*) in the Fascist Party as well as other rather vaguely defined classes of Fascists. It also re-defined the persons whom the government was given power to intern as 'politically dangerous'.

This decree was passed without being previously shown to the Allied Commission, a fact which elicited a strong protest from Admiral Stone, who refused to apply it in A.M.G. territory. The Italian Government replied that under the Macmillan memorandum of 24th February 1945 it was no longer necessary for the Government to consult the Commission before passing a decree. The question was raised again in September by Signor Nenni, the new High Commissioner for Sanctions against Fascism in Signor Parri's Government. The Italian Government again requested the enforcement of the decree in A.M.G. territory, but Admiral Stone once more declined to comply. A compromise however was reached, under which the disfranchising commissions were set up, since failure to do this would have prevented the preparation of electoral lists.

By this time the Allied belligerent interest in enforcing 'defascistization' had grown much less urgent, since it was realised that the Italians must be left to work out their own destiny. Not so that of the Italian Government, which elaborated the existing corpus of legislation by still another decree, DLL No. 702, in the middle of November. This limited the purge with certain exceptions to the higher grades of public servants and administrators. It also contained a rather flexible saving clause on collaborators, which appears to have been intended to provide machinery for the readmission to the public service of persons who had been dismissed in the first flush of liberation.[1]

The chief collaborators and dangerous Fascists were now eliminated, and precautions had been taken to guard against any recrudescence of Fascism. One of the chief objectives of Allied policy, on which the three-power Moscow declaration had laid such stress, had thus been accomplished. But the guarantee given in the declaration, that the Italian people would be afforded the opportunity to choose freely their own form of government, still remained to be implemented. The restoration of a system of representative government could not be just a simple reversion to the *status quo ante* Fascism, since the Moscow pledge clearly seemed to imply some consultation of the people on the constitutional question. The convocation of a Constituent Assembly to settle the form of constitution had been agreed among all the parties and had already been legislated for by the Bonomi Government[2], but the question of holding a referendum on the question of monarchy *versus* republic still required decision. Agreement had also been reached on the holding of local elections; but it had not yet been settled whether these were to take place before or after the elections to the Constituent Assembly. On this point the opinion of the parties was divided; those of the Left were in favour of holding elections to the Constituent Assembly first, those of the Right in favour of first electing the local government bodies.

Meanwhile, as a first step towards the re-establishment of democratic institutions, all parties were agreed on the earliest possible convocation of the Consultative Assembly (*Consulta*). This was designed to represent a larger body of public opinion than the Committees of National Liberation and was composed, under the decree passed by the second Bonomi Government, of three elements. The largest consisted of the representatives of the six parties of the C.L.N.; to these were added some twenty members of parties not represented on that Committee. After consultation with the Allied Commission, six members were also included to represent Venezia Giulia. The second element, which was intended to provide a certain continuity with the democratic past, was to consist of all living senators and deputies who had not been compromised by Fascist antecedents.[3]

---

[1] In the end most of the 1,879 Civil servants who had been dismissed and the 671 who had been compulsorily retired were reinstated. See *Survey of International Affairs, 1939–1946*, The realignment of Europe p. 435.

[2] See above, p. 205.

[3] The degree of political purity was determined by the Government. Signor Nenni, at the end of August, decided to submit to epuration a batch of over seventy senators, including two of the leaders in the final overthrow of Fascism, Marshal Badoglio and Admiral Thaon di Revel. Badoglio requested the Allied Commission to get his name deleted from this list, but it was decided that Allied intervention would be inappropriate.

The third element was supplied by representatives of the labour unions and ex-service men. The *Consulta*, not being an elected body, was in forms purely advisory; but the Government was compelled to ask its advice on all financial and budgetary questions and on the electoral law for the holding of the Constituent Assembly, to which it proposed a number of amendments. It held its first meeting on 25th September and elected Count Sforza as its President. The manner in which the electorate was to be given the opportunity of deciding the constitutional question now pressed for decision. Were the people going to be allowed to express their opinion by means of a referendum? or was the decision to be made by their elected representatives in the Constituent Assembly? The opinion of the Allied Commission and of its political advisers, that a referendum—preferably under Allied supervision—would give the better chance of a fair decision, had not altered, though with the New Deal policy and the dropping of the middle 'C' the *locus standi* of the Commission was much less certain.

The question whether the Italian Government should be advised to this effect was therefore submitted to the Combined Chiefs of Staff. It was finally agreed by both Governments that direct Allied interference would do more harm than good. The decision to settle the constitutional question by referendum was taken by the Italian Government on its own initiative in March 1946. It was also decided that local elections should precede those for the Constituent Assembly. Communal and Provincial elections were held in March and April 1946; those for the Constituent Assembly, combined with the referendum on the institutional question, not until the beginning of June, when a majority—though not a very large one—voted in favour of a republic.

Meanwhile, before A.M.G. in northern Italy came to an end, another change of government had taken place in Rome. The six-party Coalition under Signor Parri was even less united than that of Signor Bonomi. Once liberated from the pressure of the struggle against a common enemy, party leaders could only look to the coming competition for votes in the national elections. The occasion of the break-up of the Parri Government was the secession just before the end of November of the Liberal party, whose complaint, also echoed among the Christian Democrats, appears to have been that Signor Parri permitted himself to be too much influenced by the Communists. After examining the possibility of a government under an independent premier in the person of one of the veterans, Signor Orlando or Signor Nitti, the Committee of National Liberation was finally induced to maintain the six-party coalition under a new leader in the person of the Christian Democrat, Signor De Gasperi. The new Government was in composition very similar to its predecessor. The Prime Minister retained the post he had held in the previous Government as Foreign Minister. Admiral De Courten also remained at his post as Minister of the Navy. The Government was required to give the same undertakings as its predecessor, in respect of adherence to the armistice terms and the constitutional question, though in view of the approaching elections it became every week more difficult to keep this out of politics.

The final phase of A.M.G. may be summed up in a few paragraphs. Generally speaking, the degree of control exercised by Military Government officers after liberation was for the most part exceedingly remote: as the autumn drew on, and as demobilisation took its toll of A.M.G. officers, it became even remoter. After the installation of the Parri administration, the control by the Roman Government was extended to the North as rapidly as possible. All that now needed to be done by A.M.G. was to ensure the proper liaison of the occupying troops with the Italian Government authorities, once the fundamental issue of disarming the partisans had been settled and no danger of any overt disturbance of public order was any longer probable.

On the economic side the only practicable policy to pursue was to distribute the dole on a scale which would have been considered alarming by the propertied classes of any country before the Second World War. The lack of coal and raw materials, for which the whole of liberated Europe was competing, made it quite impossible to provide employment for the working population found in the North on liberation, to say nothing of the soldiers and workers deported to Germany who came pouring back into Italy during the next three months. Under an agreement reached in Milan on 23rd June, and confirmed by the Italian Government, the policy, which had been originated by the Social Republic and enforced by the C.L.N.A.I. on liberation, of compelling firms to maintain surplus workers on their pay-roll was continued in a modified form, employers agreeing to pay seventy-five per cent of earnings for hours not worked, up to a total of forty-eight hours weekly. The employee under this agreement received full wages for hours worked and seventy-five per cent of what he would have earned for the hours not worked. The cost of these payments was met as to one-third by the employer, two-thirds being borne by the *Cassa Integrazione Salariale* financed by the unemployment insurance fund, *Istituto Nazionale della Previdenza Sociale*, whose deficit was the liability of the Government. By this method, which was of course highly inflationary, the greater evil of industrial unrest caused by starvation was avoided.

The C.L.N.A.I., already before liberation, had set up an economic committee which continued to function under A.M.G. The representatives of northern Italian industry worked out a plan, which was approved and put into action by the Allied Commission in July, to utilise the small stocks of existing resources to the best advantage of the public. Industries in the five northern Regions were to be controlled by a series of committees, one for each industry, on which representatives from all the Regions were to sit. The work of these committees was to be coordinated by a central body, called the North Italy Industrial Council—the chairman of which was to be appointed by the Italian Government—consisting of six members: one industrialist designated by the A.M.G. Regional Commissioner of each of the five northern Regions (excluding Venezia Giulia) and one appointed by A.C./A.M.G. on the recommendation of the labour organisations. In this way the attempt was made to render Italian industry as far as possible self-governing, and to leave behind a mechanism of self-administered controls, the levers of which had simply to be placed in the hands of the Italian Government when A.M.G. withdrew.[1]

Once hostilities were over, the war departments in both Allied countries were anxious to divest themselves of responsibility for civilian supplies for Italy as quickly as was practicable. Very early action was taken by the American Government. On 21st May President Truman informed the Secretary for War that no responsibility for civilian supply in any European country should continue to rest with the Army, except as required by the military situation, a proviso which exempted Venezia Giulia. It had been envisaged by both Governments that this responsibility would be assumed by the United Nations Relief and Rehabilitation Administration (U.N.R.R.A.), whose council meeting was not due till August. When the Council met, some opposition was shown by the Ethiopian, Yugoslav and Greek delegations to the placing of an ex-enemy country on the same footing with regard to rehabilitation as devastated Allied nations, but the proposal of the British and United States Governments was passed, authorising U.N.R.R.A. to undertake relief and rehabilitation in Italy on the same scale and with the same priorities as in other liberated areas.

By this time it had already been decided that Army responsibility for civilian supplies would cease with August loadings[2], even though U.N.R.R.A. was clearly not in a position to undertake its new responsibilities until the beginning of 1946. The War Office, while agreeing in principle to the earliest practicable termination of its

---

[1] It is interesting however to note that according to Colonel Poletti even at this late hour some of the Commission's officers appear still to have found it difficult to resist the temptation to keep their fingers in the pie. At first they appear sometimes to have been reluctant to recognise the authority of the Industrial Council and the Industrial Committees.

[2] All except P.O.L. and coal, responsibility for which was terminated a month later.

responsibility for civilian supplies, was inclined to continue this until such time as U.N.R.R.A. was in a position to take over. But the War Department had decided to cut the cable earlier, and it was not possible in the light of President Truman's decision to reverse this policy. It was therefore necessary to make some interim arrangements to ensure that, during the intervening four months before U.N.R.R.A. took over, the flow of food and essential raw materials should not be interrupted. The gap was filled by the Foreign Economic Administration, which used the machinery of the combined civilian agencies. The portion of the military supply programme taken over by F.E.A. was estimated to be about two-thirds of the whole. The Canadian Government continued to furnish its proportion, leaving the remainder to be undertaken by the Government of the United Kingdom. This was in fact limited to the procurement of coal from South Africa and a few items which the Combined Boards recommended to be supplied from the United Kingdom and the Colonies.

The programme of Italian imports for 1945 had, as was explained in Chapter VIII, been divided into two portions: Class 'A' items consisting of the consumer goods required to avoid disease and unrest, now reinterpreted in a rather more generous manner, and Class 'B' items consisting of goods needed for the rehabilitation of Italian industry, to be financed out of Italian resources of which the largest part was the dollar credit resulting from the refunding of the American troops' net pay. The termination of the military responsibility meant that all Class 'A' items, the shipment of which was outstanding at the end of August, were transferred to Class 'B', and to finance them F.E.A. included the sum of 100 million dollars in its budget. This left the Allied Commission with the task of co-ordinating, with the Italian Government and the Allied civilian agencies, a schedule of Italian imports for the last four months of 1945 and a programme for 1946, to be taken over by U.N.R.R.A.—a task in which the planning of the Central Economic Committee of the C.L.N.A.I. played an essential part. The final estimate for imports to be undertaken under the U.N.R.R.A. programme for 1946 amounted to 450 million dollars.[1] In drawing up this programme due regard was taken of the surpluses of Allied military stores and equipment remaining in the theatre, which it was not considered economic to ship back to the United States or the United Kingdom. These were made available to the Italian Government. Meanwhile the somewhat tardy acceptance by the Italian Government of the

---

[1] Italian imports in 1946 actually amounted to nearly 595 million dollars of which $379·5 were accounted for by the U.N.R.R.A. programme. See *Annuario della Congiuntura Economica Italiana* 1938–47, p. 455.

Allied Black Lists had opened the door to the resumption of private trade between Italians and inhabitants of neutral and liberated countries. The transition to peace time conditions was thus completed.

On 31st December 1945 the whole of northern Italy with the exception of Venezia Giulia and the province of Udine was handed back to Italian administration, and A.M.G. came formally to an end everywhere except in that disputed territory.[1] And with its disappearance all Allied financial commitments were also terminated. An agreement had been reached with Signor De Gasperi under which the Italian Government, through the agency of the Bank of Italy, was to become the issuing authority of A.M. lire to take over all these in circulation, and to make itself responsible for meeting all future currency requirements of the Allied Forces. The value of the total issue up to December 31st 1945, was just over a hundred thousand million lire. (£250,000,000 at the official rate of exchange).[2]

[1] It had previously been made clear to the Italian Government that the continuation of A.M.G. in the province of Udine—which lasted until the withdrawal of Allied troops from Venezia Giulia on the creation of the Free Territory of Trieste, after the conclusion of the Peace Treaty—did not imply the contemplation of any change in Italian sovereignty.

[2] According to the *Memorandum sulle Questioni Economico-finanziarie connesse col Tratato di Pace*, issued by the Italian Government in 1946, the total of A.M. lire issued to the Allied Forces up to 31 December, 1945, was 102,920 million lire.

CHAPTER XIV

LESSONS AND ACHIEVEMENTS

In this chapter it is proposed to summarise briefly what would appear to the historian to be the main achievements of the Allied Military Administration of Italy during the two years' campaign, and to sketch some of its lessons. For this purpose it will perhaps be found convenient to divide our considerations into two portions, those affecting Allied Military Government in its stricter sense, and those concerning the wider aspects of the Commission's work.

To deal first with achievements, some of these can be seen most clearly in the critical weeks following the invasion of Sicily, when the task of AMGOT was to govern a portion of occupied enemy territory. First to be noted is the success with which a completely integrated Anglo-American administration was created, in which the difference in nationality really became in practice irrelevant. The tradition initiated by AMGOT was continued in the much larger body of the Control Commission. This enabled the inevitably more complicated and therefore less satisfactory system of national zones to be avoided. This achievement was greatly facilitated by the arrangements initially adopted in AMGOT whereby the equal division of nationalities was modified in the A.M.G. detachments attached to the armies. The system under which the commanding officer and two-thirds of the officers were of the same nationality as the army commander, which was maintained in principle (though not in detail) in the Army A.M.Gs thoughout the campaign, worked very well.

Next, it must be recorded that in spite of all the initial difficulties described in Chapter II arising out of the ignorance of the fighting soldier of the nature, purpose and even the existence of Military Government, AMGOT managed to fulfil its prime task very satisfactorily. It did succeed in maintaining law and order behind the fighting front, in preventing the action of civilians from endangering or impeding the operations of the armed forces, and in ensuring that, with the few exceptions noted below, neither the resources nor the attention of military commanders were distracted by the necessity of attending to problems caused by civilian disease or unrest. This achievement was maintained by the Army A.M.Gs on the mainland, which were based on the AMGOT pattern. Only on two occasions was it necessary for an army commander to call the attention of the higher command to difficulties arising from the condition of the civilian population. On both occasions the trouble was due to lack of food. Thus General Patton, in November 1943, saw fit to complain to General Eisenhower of the dangerous situation arising in Sicily, while General Mark Clark in the autumn of 1944 drew the attention of General Alexander to the critical food shortage, which had led to disorder and might entail the diversion of combat troops to the maintenance of law and order.[1] But such cases were quite exceptional. On neither occasion was it necessary to have recourse to any diversion of combat troops, though at the end of November General Wilson reported to the C.C.S. that owing to the food situation, particularly in Rome, Florence and Pisa, he had found it 'necessary to take precautionary measures to avoid the possibilities of disturbance'. But the margin of safety was certainly too small to be comfortable. It is worth noting however that, in spite of hunger and revolution, on only one or two occasions was it necessary to ask for the assistance of Allied troops in the maintenance of law and order during the whole campaign, and then only for a very short time and on a very small scale. None of these requests were made in Army areas.

Besides relieving the operational commander of all pre-occupations concerning civilian disease and unrest, A.M.G. was also able to assist him in assuring the security of his troops by preventing numerous normal forms of civilian activity which might have been exploited by the enemy, to say nothing of direct attempts of civilian sabotage. The enforcement by A.M.G. of martial law under Proclamation No. 2.[2], though by no means perfectly successful in protecting the property of the Allied military forces, did unquestionably contribute substantially to the security of their persons. The number of offences committed against the persons of Allied soldiers, sailors and airmen was comparatively small. Such as were committed were often done under severe provocation. Except in the case of agents deliberately 'planted' by the Germans, crimes of anti-Allied intent there were practically none—a striking contrast to conditions in German-occupied Italy.

The administration of justice by Allied Military Government courts was in several respects a notable, possibly a unique achievement, which presented some rather interesting features.[3] Perhaps the first point of interest is the number of cases tried, which from the invasion of Sicily up to some months after the end of hostilities amounted to about 150,000, of which by far the greatest number, at least

---

[1] See above, pp. 46-47, 193.

[2] The text of this Proclamation is given in Appendix I.

[3] For a general account of the work of the Allied Military courts see the article by Colonel Ian Campbell, at one time Chief Judicial Officer at A.C.C. H.Q., printed in the International Law Quarterly, Summer 1947 pp. 192–206 entitled '*Some Legal problems arising out of the establishment of the Allied Military courts in Italy*'.

140,000, were Summary court cases. The number of cases tried by Superior courts was about 7,000, of which more than 4,500 were tried in Sicily and the Southern Region. General courts only tried about 800 cases: these included, of course, all the trials of enemy agents for spying and sabotage, as well as all other really serious offences against the Allied Forces. On the technical side it involved an Allied experiment of great interest, in the public application of Anglo-Saxon rules of procedure in criminal cases, so very different from those of Latin countries. But from the point of view of the general public perhaps the most impressive feature was the procedure of permitting defence by enemy lawyers in a court-martial by an occupying force. The maxim laid down for 'Husky' that justice should not only be done, but be seen to be done, certainly made a deep impression on the members of the Italian bar who had occasion to come into contact with it. And even if the relaxation of the rules of evidence was sometimes such as would perhaps shock the legal purist, there can be no doubt whatever that, speaking generally, the trials conducted by Allied Military courts were scrupulously fair. It was clearly laid down that the duty of the prosecution was to present all material facts including those favourable to the accused, and that every accused person is supposed to be innocent until he is proved guilty and that he must be given the benefit of any *reasonable* doubt. If the prosecution did not succeed in proving its case beyond *reasonable* doubt, it was the duty of the court to acquit. Another case in point was concerned with confessions. The Italian police forces apparently did not suffer from any Anglo-Saxon scruples as to the means used to obtain them.[1] Hence the instructions, while not ruling out uncautioned or uncorroborated confessions, laid stress on the onus lying with the prosecution to prove the truth of confessions.

The rules of procedure finally codified by Colonel Ian Campbell contained elements derived from both British and American legal procedure, thus providing an interesting experiment in the application of Allied Military Government. Procedure was fairly elastic, a good deal being left to the discretion of the court. Hence the relaxation of the rules of evidence. The Rules were issued in a book in loose-leaf form, which made it possible, when a rule was amended, to substitute a new one without re-editing the whole book.[2]

---

[1] Campbell, *loc. cit.* In one case of alleged forgery of currency notes a confession was discovered to have been extorted by the police by actual torture. The court refused to admit the confession, and in the absence of other evidence the accused was acquitted.

[2] It is interesting to note that the Supreme Court Committee on Practice and Procedure, on which two former Legal Officers of the Allied Commission, Brigadier (now Mr Justice) Upjohn and Colonel (now Mr Justice) Willmer served, recommended in its second interim report that the new Rules of Court when brought into operation should be bound up in a similar loose-leaf form.

The arrangement by which all crimes against the Allied forces were tried by the Military courts of A.M.G., presided over in the case of graver offences by professional lawyers, worked admirably. It was one of the most important contributions of military government. The administration of military justice by laymen can never be wholly satisfactory, since the trial of enemy civilians by ordinary court-martial must almost inevitably appear to transgress too patently the maxim that no man should be judge in his own cause. But the very scrupulous procedure of the Allied Military courts during the occupation of Sicily produced even on the enemy public a profound impression of fairness. Nor was this sense of justice diminished when, after the armistice, the alien Allied occupants continued to administer a martial law based on their own very different legal system over co-belligerent civilians.

The trial by Allied Military courts of 'security' offences by civilians, including espionage and sabotage, entailed very close collaboration between the Field Security services of A.A.I. and the officers of the Public Safety Sub-Commission. For several months after the invasion of the mainland it was found that the evidence prepared by the Field Security authorities in these cases was frequently deficient, with the result that prisoners were acquitted who were almost certainly guilty. It was only after two experienced British police officers from the Commission were assigned to this task that a satisfactory procedure was evolved. On the other hand, the Legal Sub-Commission was particularly careful to maintain its judicial independence; it refused to be influenced by the inevitable pressure from the military commands for more severe sentences. In this connection a case, which cannot fail to be of interest to the international lawyer, is perhaps worth quoting. On evacuating Rome, the Germans left behind a group of Italian agents, provided with explosives and other devices, to commit sabotage against the Allies. The members of the group had attended a German sabotage course at the Hague at the beginning of the year, and signed voluntarily an undertaking to commit acts of sabotage on behalf of the Germans, from whom they had accepted money. They had been given a wireless transmission set for communicating with them, and had buried a large quantity of explosives in and about Rome. These were found by the Allied security agencies, who succeeded in arresting eight members of the group, intending to bring them to trial on the charge of conspiracy to commit sabotage against the Allied forces. The legal experts of the Commission refused to substantiate this charge, on the ground that the alleged acts of conspiracy had not been committed in Allied occupied territory, but in territory under the enemy's occupation, and could not therefore constitute a crime against the Allies. The agents were consequently only charged with failure to surrender explosives, for which crime, not the death penalty, but only the comparatively mild sentence of two to ten years imprisonment was imposed.

In maintaining its own regulations and those of the existing law of the land in the matter of controlled prices and the collection of agricultural produce A.M.G. was far less successful. The elimination of black markets proved wholly beyond its competence, and the attempt first made in Sicily to maintain the existing wage and price levels, and again in the North on liberation, appear to show that these may well be tasks which no Military Government can expect to accomplish. The lesson to be learnt here would appear to be that price-regulation should be applied only to a few essential commodities.

The success of the Army A.M.G's in re-establishing the elements of orderly administration in the forward areas, in devastated towns often under enemy shellfire for considerable periods after occupation, and in cajoling local officials into taking first-aid measures of self-help, such as the repair of public utilities and the reorganisation of hospital services, was everywhere, at any rate indirectly, of assistance to the combat forces. But the Armies also encountered two special problems, to the solution of which A.M.G. was able to make a valuable direct contribution, namely the control of civilian movements in general, and refugees in particular, and the disarmament and reabsorption into civilian life of the partisans.

As to the first of these, though the enforcement of the varying limitations imposed by military authority from time to time on civilian movements was far from perfect, the cooperation of the *Carabinieri* with the military police organisations was of very great importance. Without it the task of the Security services would certainly have involved the devotion of much larger resources of military manpower. The organisation of the arrangements for refugees (of whom a large proportion were persons evacuated from their homes for military reasons), their collection, marshalling, evacuation, feeding and care in hospital and in transit centres, up to the point when they were handed over to the charge of the Italian Government, was a service of great military importance successfully performed by A.M.G. after, it must be admitted, a good deal of initial confusion. It would otherwise have fallen on the Army commands, who were ultimately responsible, and did in fact provide most of the resources, including transport, required in the forward areas.

In the peculiar conditions resulting from the political division of Italy by a moving battle line, the responsibility of A.M.G. in dealing with the partisan movement was often delicate. On its handling of the situation depended in many cases the prevention of the outbreak of serious disorder, which could certainly have impeded military operations. Here too, in spite of the delays of higher authorities in providing much needed resources (of which some account was given in Chapter VI), A.M.G. succeeded in keeping the peace. And in the last stage of the campaign and the weeks following the end of hostilities it managed to prevent a good deal of bloodshed, mainly through the setting up of the Special Courts of Assize, often only in the nick of time.

Nor should the more humdrum contributions of A.M.G's to Army needs be neglected, particularly in the matter of labour. The organisation of labour exchanges in liberated towns enabled the armies to recruit all the different kinds of labour they needed without difficulty. In the vital matter of repairing damaged roads the organisation of the road maintenance gangs (*cantonieri*) as far forward as possible was particularly important. In the most forward areas it was not possible to recruit labour locally; labour gangs organised by A.M.G. had therefore to be transported to and from rear areas daily by the Armies. In this connection, the immediate repair of bridges was of the highest importance, since it enabled the temporary bridging erected by the Army engineers to be moved forward to meet the extending needs of the campaign. The organisation of this work by A.M.G. through contracts placed with Italian firms and by Italian labour was certainly of the greatest assistance to the Army engineers.

While in the forward areas the contribution of A.M.G. was certainly impressive, its general achievements in the economic sphere are much less easy to assess. This was, of course, chiefly due to the absence of resources, and the narrow limits of the military programme of imports. It would appear easy—perhaps a little too easy—to criticise higher headquarters for their slowness in accepting the proper equipment of A.M.G., especially in matters of transport, as an essential portion of their operational responsibilities. On the other hand it is difficult to avoid the conclusion that the weakness at the centre of the economic organisation of the Commission itself was responsible for a good deal of unnecessary confusion. Until its reorganisation at the beginning of 1945, the Transportation Sub-Commission appears to have been a conspicuous source of weakness. Moreover, in the Regional—as opposed to the Army—A.M.G's, the handling of supply and transport problems, especially in the early stages, was often far from satisfactory, chiefly because the number of officers with special training in these subjects was much too small.

As for the lessons to be derived from the experience of A.M.G. during the Italian campaign, the historian, who had some personal experience of its working and has had the opportunity of discussing its problems with many of those who were responsible for trying to solve them, may perhaps be permitted to formulate some tentative conclusions.

On the tactical side, the lessons concerning Military Government of occupied enemy territory were important. Most of these have already been described in earlier Chapters[1]; but one or two additional points will here be mentioned and some already mentioned underlined. First, whether the invasion be by sea or land, the necessity of teaching the task forces down to the regimental level, as early as possible during the training stages, the functions of military government and the ways in which it can assist tactical commanders. Secondly, the need to provide adequate transport and a minimum of office equipment, as well as an adequate staff of drivers, clerks, storekeepers, cooks, batmen and, above all, interpreters. In the initial stages in Sicily interpreters for A.M.G. were very deficient, and the attempts made by Civil Affairs Officers to procure them locally often resulted in the selection of most undesirable persons. It would appear to be preferable, where possible, to collect an adequate staff of interpreters before actual invasion of enemy territory. In invading certain countries the possibility of acquiring interpreters on the spot cannot be relied on under modern conditions in which 'collaboration' is liable to become a criminal offence. Moreover, when obtained locally, interpreters should be provided through the Field Security Services, who during this stage would be more competent to select suitable persons. Finally the allotment of due priority to Military Government personnel, transport and equipment in the transport programme of the phase immediately following the assault is of the utmost importance, particularly in a sea- or air-borne invasion.

To turn now to general administrative lessons. There can be little doubt that the decision to establish at the earliest moment an independent chain of command for Military Government through the C.C.A.O. direct to the Commander-in-Chief of the invading forces—who for the time being must act as Military Governor of occupied territory—was amply justified. Though it is, of course, essential that the mobile Military Government units should be under the command of the tactical commanders, it is almost equally important that, as soon as the wave of battle has passed over, the unity of command under the C.C.A.O. should be established, since Army A.M.G. headquarters must be kept small and mobile, and cannot therefore include the number of specialists required to govern Lines of Communications areas. Moreover the need for coordinating

---

[1] See above, pp. 63-66, 68, 82.

as soon as possible the practice of two or more Army areas, each of which must be concerned primarily with its own short-term operational problems, is obvious. The arrangements in Sicily worked admirably, but after A.M.G. Fifteenth Army Group was combined with the hypertrophied headquarters of the Control Commission, whose executive head, the Chief Commissioner, had become the C.C.A.O., the relations between Army A.M.G's and the higher echelon often became strained, as the observations made by General Hume and other responsible officers of the Army A.M.G's clearly show.

There can be no doubt that the Commission's headquarters often failed to recognise that when A.M.G. officers are attached to a field army they come fully and unreservedly under the orders of the Army Commander. The Commission often appeared to treat the Army A.M.G's in precisely the same way as the A.M.G's of the Regions behind Army boundaries, thus failing to realise the implications of warfare in the combat zone. The commanders of the Army A.M.G's seem only too often to have been placed in the position of having to choose between obeying either the orders of the Army Commander or those of the Commission's headquarters. And when the Army commander's orders were, as they always had to be, carried out, the Commission sometimes made things very difficult for the A.M.G. officers concerned. As General Hume pertinently remarked had there been more soldiers in the Commission's headquarters this might not have occurred.

One suggested solution to these difficulties, which General Hume appears to have favoured, was the formation of a complete G-5 section at Army headquarters with the 'same type of functions and responsibilities as other sections of the General Staff', and a similar G-5 section in the Lines of Communications Command. But it is difficult to see how this complication of the chain of command would really meet the problem, since Military Government cannot be equated with other military operations, and therefore needs a special form of organisation. The technical direction of Army A.M.G's from the centre was surely right in principle and could hardly have been avoided: all that can be said is that it might perhaps have been applied more intelligently.

The formation of permanent cadres of Military Government to accompany task forces throughout the campaign in the form of Army A.M.G's was unquestionably a success, and the gradual infiltration of the permanent regional staffs into the army areas, which was evolved in the course of the campaign, worked very well. The lessons learnt as to their composition should be applicable to future campaigns. The 'spearhead' detachments should consist principally of C.A.O's assisted by C.A.P.O's. The urgent necessity for guarding warehouses of essential civilian supplies from looting, experienced in the Sicilian campaign, suggests that where possible small guard detachments should form part of the 'spearhead'. Legal officers should also appear on the scene at the earliest possible date in order to enforce proclamations by military courts. While it may be admitted in principle that 'specialist' officers in the Army A.M.G's should be restricted to a minimum, they cannot be dispensed with altogether and some of them should follow as closely as possible on the 'spearhead' detachments, especially those concerned with civilian supplies and transport.

The assumption that, in the case of an agricultural community producing its own food supplies, no immediate importation of foodstuffs by the armies will be necessary, would not appear, judging by experiences in Sicily, to be always justifiable. Technical advances in the methods of destruction will almost certainly result in the production of devastated areas on a scale not experienced even in the Second World War. The conclusion to be drawn would appear to be that both welfare and supply officers will also be required to follow up 'spearhead' detachments at the closest possible interval, and that small stocks of foodstuffs and medical stores should be placed at strategic points as far forward as possible. The protection of civilian foodstuffs from looting at the early stages of invasion is also of the utmost importance. How far the local police can be relied on may be, at any rate in certain territories, unpredictable. It would probably be advisable wherever possible to have small detachments of military police attached to forward Military Government units. If conditions permitted the efficient employment of local police forces for this purpose, use could be made of these units to guard dumps of captured enemy war materials, (e.g. transport and P.O.L.), which operational troops had not time to secure. These were extensively pilfered in Sicily by civilians. Another lesson to be learned from 'Husky' is the immediate necessity of immobilising all civilian vehicles, and the blocking of all stocks of P.O.L. This should be done immediately on the occupation of any town.

With regard to the organisation of the mobile Military Governments, British experience would appear to suggest that headquarters should be attached to Army headquarters—not to any lower formation. Headquarters should be as small as possible, but must contain a number of specialist officers, Legal, Finance, Public Health, Supply and Transport, and possibly Welfare in largely devastated areas. The American system of attaching subordinate A.M.G. headquarters to corps and, under these, C.A.O's specifically to divisions also worked fairly well, but in a sea- or air-borne invasion the more flexible system employed by Eighth Army A.M.G. may be preferable, under which C.A.O's and C.A.P.O's are held in a pool to be distributed by the S.C.A.O. according to local needs, through the agency of Liaison Officers at corps headquarters. The system of mobile 'specialist' officers deployed by headquarters to follow up immediately behind the 'spearhead' detachments gave excellent results and would almost certainly be applicable to any future operations. These should include Finance, Legal and Supply, and perhaps Transport, Public Health and Welfare officers. The importance of establishing a permanent organisation corresponding to the local government divisions of the country in question as early and as near the front line as possible was most clearly proved, and the infiltration of regional officers into Army A.M.G. worked very economically, since it reduced the numbers of 'specialist' officers to be carried on the establishment of the mobile Military Governments. But the recall, without notice or consultation, by the Commission's Headquarters of specialist officers so 'lent' to Army A.M.G's led to frequent difficulties.

Another tactical lesson taught by Sicilian experiences was the need for a very close association of the 'spearhead' Military Government officers with the Divisional Field Security Section (F.S.S.). It should be possible to arrange that Civil Affairs and F.S.S. enter the captured towns together, and it has been suggested that they should set up their offices in the same building wherever practical. As Colonel Spofford noted, it is important to plan in advance some method of 'vetting' public officials in enemy territory, which can be put into operation immediately. The method of the *scheda personale* was too elaborate to be of any use in the tactical phase. Close collaboration with the Field Security Services both in the planning stage and in the field is required, so that objectionable officials can immediately be removed; but it should not be overlooked that the temporary retention of officials suspect to Field Security may often be indispensable.

The most obvious general lesson taught by experiences in Sicily and Italy is that, during the early stages after the tactical phase, the feeding of the civilian population is likely to be Military Government's most pressing task, at any rate in territories where no resistance movement is in existence. In Italy, A.M.G. was faced with two distinct groups of problems, the first arising out of the breakdown of the Fascist system of grain collection and rationing, the second out of the competition between civilian and military needs for limited resources of supplies and transport. In planning for 'Husky' the estimates of Italian agricultural production appear to have been somewhat optimistic, but they seem to have created an indelible impression. In spite of the fact that in Sicily and southern Italy the 1943 harvest was about one quarter below the average, the tendency to underestimate the need for imports persisted. The existence of an extensive black market was interpreted as a proof that what was required was not an increase in imports, but an improvement in the system of distribution. However true this may have been in theory, the fact remained that, though certain sections of the population were getting more than their legitimate allowances, the poorly paid masses in the large towns often could not afford to purchase sufficient to maintain an adequate standard of health and efficiency. And since a mere handful of A.M.G. officers, none of whom had any previous experience in solving problems of food distribution, was not able to make effective the weak administrative machine of the Italian government, the practical task of avoiding disease and unrest entailed a greater volume of imports than the theoretic minimum, the target very naturally envisaged in London and Washington.

The priority of military over civilian needs inevitably dominated the situation in the field. When it came to allocating limited resources of shipping, dock space and transport, it was natural that narrower operational considerations should prevail. Even when civil supplies were available, their transport encountered innumerable difficulties. Ships, for example, had to be loaded with mixed cargoes of military and civilian stores, and these might be diverted on military grounds to ports other than those at which the civilian supplies were most urgently needed. In all cases civilian necessities had to yield place to military needs. Hence, civil supplies demanded were frequently late in arriving, when they arrived at all. The position was aptly summed up by an American writer in the following sentences:

> Another major problem was that of fitting A.C.C. into the military picture as an integral part of military operations. Civil Affairs in occupied Italy was dominated by the fact that it was taking place in the rear supply area of the Allied Armies. Here military considerations were always paramount and the military tended to consider A.C.C./A.M.G. as 'marginal', the body which should bear the brunt of any unexpected difficulties.

The pressing problems of civilian supplies provided some lessons in military logistics which are worth noting. The implications of military reponsibility for assuring that the civilian population was adequately fed were very slowly learned. It needed a dangerous crisis, implying both disease and unrest in connection with the feeding of Naples in the autumn of 1943, to convince G-4 at A.F.H.Q. that circumstances could arise in which priority in procurement, shipping and transport had to be given to civilian imports over immediate operational requirements. Nor was this lesson perfectly assimilated, as the crisis which developed in the following autumn in Tuscany clearly showed.[1]

[1] See above, p. 192-93.

With regard to food, rural areas can probably be treated, at any rate for a very considerable time, as self-supporting; but large towns at once raise a problem, even in countries which normally grow sufficient foodstuffs to feed themselves. Quite apart from hoarding and black markets, the distribution of essential foodstuffs over different parts of the country may be very uneven. Moreover the districts providing the bulk of certain essential foodstuffs may be in enemy hands. Hence the importance of accumulating in military bases prior to invasion stockpiles of foodstuffs for civilian uses, which at a later stage can be diverted to military use if they prove not to be needed. The same principle applies to transport. This need not all of it be of the first rate quality or condition required for operational purposes, but it must be reasonably efficient, and provided with an adequate stock of tyres and spare parts.

In future operations it will be prudent to assume that, as in Italy, the railways will be fully occupied with military traffic. This will throw an enormous burden on indigenous road transport, which it may prove quite insufficient to shoulder. Transport and essential spare parts like tyres must normally be placed in the forefront of necessary civilian imports in any military programme. The logistical aspects of these two items of civilian imports may seem alarming to the fighting soldier, but experience in Italy showed clearly enough how serious food shortages may become, causing unrest which may interfere with military operations. Moreover, in the case of transport, the importation of a comparatively small quantity of A.M.G. vehicles, spare parts and tyres might even have led to ultimate logistical economies, since shortage of transport was undoubtedly one of the factors preventing the full 'amassing' of the harvests of 1943 and 1944, and the failure to distribute seed was certainly in part responsible for the small volume of the harvest of 1945.

The achievements of the Allied Military Administration of Italy as distinguished from A.M.G. are much more difficult to judge. What for example were the contributions of the Allied Commission to the success of the Supreme Allied Commander's operations? Where, and to what degree, did it fail to fulfil the purposes for which it was created? An adequate answer to these questions would entail a general examination of Allied policy towards Italy from the armistice to the peace treaty, which would certainly take us far out of the province of military history. Yet within that province certain tentative conclusions would appear to be indicated, though these too will take us beyond the scope of the Allied Commission's work, since in two important departments, the exploitation of Italian local resources and the re-establishment of a free Italian press, the controlling influence lay with other branches of A.F.H.Q.

The ultimate aim of Allied military administration in Italy, once the fact and status of co-belligerence were established, may for the sake of convenience be summarised under two main headings. First, the creation of internal conditions suitable for the maintenance of Italy as a base for the Supreme Allied Commander's military operations, and the exploitation of Italian military and civil resources in the interest of the Allied war effort; secondly—a more permanent 'objective'—the re-creation in Italy of democratic institutions capable of surviving after the withdrawal of the occupying troops.

Some of the achievements under the first of these headings have already been considered in our critique of A.M.G's achievements. The part played by the Allied Commission in its wider field remains to be assessed. As the organ responsible for seeing that the Commander-in-Chief's requirements were being met by the civil authorities in Italian Government territory, the Commission certainly performed a very useful function: as, for example, in ensuring that the various measures for 'blocking' materials in accordance with the policy determined by the Local Resources Board were observed by the Italian Government; in organising in A.M.G. territory, and supervising in Italian Government territory, systems of rationing electricity and P.O.L.—the latter with only partial success; in planning and supervising in conjunction with the Italian authorities the rehabilitation of the hydro-electrical systems in accordance with the instructions of the Electrical Reconstruction Committee; in supervising the works of the Italian authorities on road repair and maintenance and the rebuilding of bridges, in accordance with the priorities laid down by the Allied commands in the Lines of Communications zone—to mention only a few of the more conspicuous examples. On a lower plane, too, the existence of A.M.G./A.C.C. performed the very useful function of liaison between the Italian civilian authorities and the Allied military commands, by which a good deal of friction and misunderstanding was avoided.

It was perhaps inevitable that the Commission's paramount interest in the avoidance of 'disease and unrest' should have created some opposition between the points of view of G-4 and G-5, both in the matter of the limitation of civilian imports and in the military exploitation of local resources, but there are good reasons for supposing that in many cases the Commission's view provided a healthy corrective to the narrower outlook of some military authorities. The military method of exploiting local resources was often extremely wasteful. It is possible that the limited facilities of southern and central Italy might, under the control of the Allied Commission and the Italian Government, have been made to produce a considerably larger volume of goods, even, in some cases, of the kind that the Allied forces required. Yet on the whole military requisitions were carried out with very commendable restraint and with due regard to civilian needs, especially in the matter of foodstuffs. The machinery of the Local Resources Board, on which the Commission was able to represent civilian needs, worked well. But requisitioning of industrial plants and premises by the armed forces was, until near the end of the campaign, quite indiscriminate, with the result that factories for the production of essential civilian commodities were frequently put, and kept, out of action for trivial reasons. Though in the area of active operations no prohibitions can reasonably be imposed on the operating forces, the question must be asked whether behind the battle zone it might not perhaps be practicable to reserve the use of certain essential plants and premises for civilian purposes. This could, of course, only be done on the basis of reasonably well-informed economic planning—a matter in which the Allied Commission in Italy was certainly very deficient—and by the previous instruction of combat forces on the military importance of conserving certain civilian supplies.

Granted these premises, there seems some reason to believe that, at the cost of very little inconvenience to occupying troops, the need for importing commodities for essential civilian consumption might in certain circumstances be reduced. But it has to be admitted that in Italy, apart from coal, foodstuffs and machinery and materials for agriculture, civilian imports were very small. The only case where increased domestic production could certainly have reduced imports in any significant quantity was that of fertilisers. For the rest, where military authorities occupied or requisitioned facilities or goods deemed by the Allied Commission essential for civilian purposes, the civilian had mostly to go without. And it may perhaps be taken for granted that, if the military exploitation of local resources had in any way been made dependent on the consent of the Italian Government, the facilities placed at the disposal of the Allied forces would have been a good deal smaller.

For the wastefulness of military exploitation of local resources the Commission itself must bear a good deal of the blame. Until a very late stage in the campaign the Economic Section appears to have taken the Commission's membership of the Local Resources Board and its subordinate bodies very lightly. It seems to have attached little if any importance to the admittedly limited influence which the weight of its representatives on these bodies might have possessed. For reasons already explained in Chapter IX, the leadership of the Economic Section was far from satisfactory. It was repeatedly criticised, not without good reasons, both at A.F.H.Q. and by the Civil Affairs organisation of the War Departments in the two capitals. Hence the continual suspicion with which A.F.H.Q.'s demands for civilian imports were regarded by the Combined Civil

Affairs Committee and the various missions which it despatched to the theatre, and the elaborate duplication by G-5 at A.F.H.Q. of much of the Commission's work. It is difficult to avoid the conclusion that on the supply side some, at any rate, of this duplication might have been avoided by greater efficiency on the part of the Commission.

To the deficiencies, just noted, of the Economic Section one exception must be recorded. The leadership on the financial side was competent and efficient. The arrangements for the supply of currency to the occupying forces and to A.M.G. worked admirably and the Finance Officers succeeded in gaining the confidence of bankers and treasury officials, without which serious break-downs might have occurred. A larger proportion, perhaps, of the energies of the sub-commission's headquarters than was necessary was devoted to the attempt to work out long-term reforms in the system of Italian Government finance, but its contribution, especially in forward areas, to the smooth running of the administrative machine was very notable. There was however one task in which its success was only relative, that of coping with monetary inflation; though even here anything approaching a flight from the currency, which might have caused inconvenience to the armed forces, was averted. To attribute such inflation as did take place, as has been done by some Italian authorities, merely to the issue of an unbacked military currency is an over-simplification. Whatever the currency employed, the pressure of a large occupying force must inevitably lead to inflation.[1] And once inflation has begun, even if no open distrust in the currency is engendered, the stimulus given to 'black market' operations in every form may become irresistible. It would be quite unpractical to expect a military government to be able to control these, except by an enormous, and unjustifiable, expenditure of manpower. There is very little that an occupying power can do to keep in check inflationary tendencies, but two measures would certainly help to do so: first, the fixing of an exchange rate for the indigenous currency at a level which would diminish the quantity of military currency to be issued and discourage troop expenditure; and secondly, the restriction of the amount of troop-pay made available for private spending. The latter course would undoubtedly throw some burden on military resources by involving larger military imports of articles for canteens and requisites of army welfare organisations. But even this might result in an ultimate economy by restricting the volume of necessary imports.

Two questions naturally suggest themselves to the historian. Could inflation have been prevented? And, if not, was everything in fact

[1] It may be noted for example that the occupation of Iceland by Anglo-American troops also led to inflation, though the currency which they used was bought with sterling and dollars.

done which would reduce it to a minimum? The answer to the first question is clearly in the negative. The existing inflationary pressure in 1943, before the invasion, had already become irresistible. The system of price controls was rapidly becoming ineffective. Black markets were already in existence and price ceilings legally established were anything but watertight. Under these conditions the interruption and dislocation of the machinery of controls through the invasion, coinciding with the large increase in the circulating medium, made a considerable degree of inflation inevitable. The only debatable question is whether the amount of inflation might have been reduced had the exchange rate for the lira been fixed at a lower figure. As Professor Southard points out[1], at the time of the invasion the lira was under-valued at the official rate of exchange. This fact was implicitly recognised when the prices to be charged for imports into Sicily came to be considered, for it was found that to charge the equivalent of 'landed cost' at the official rate of exchange would bring them far above the existing level. There can be no doubt that on the basis of parity of purchasing power the lira at the moment of occupation was worth a good deal more than one cent.[2] The fixing of a lower rate would have meant that the amount of lire expended by the troops out of their pay and by the armed forces for labour and other services would have been smaller, but if it had been only half as much, as it would have been if the exchange rate suggested in Washington during the planning period of fifty lire a dollar had been accepted, a considerable degree of inflation would still have been inevitable. The inflationary pressure arising from the unbalanced budget would have continued unabated. Yet the historian finds it hard to resist the conclusion, official arguments notwithstanding, that the degree of inflation which actually occurred might have been reduced somewhat by an initial exchange rate giving greater value to the lira.

On the political side the achievements of the Allied Commission are much less easy to assess. During two critical stages the support of the Allied Commission was politically decisive. First, in the months following the King's flight to Brindisi, the initial recognition by the Allies of the King's Government provided an indispensable support for the continuity of the Italian State and therefore helped it to avoid many of the inconveniences caused by revolutions. Moreover, after Marshal Badoglio had, on Allied initiation, restored the freedom of

---

[1] See Southard, Frank, A., Jr., *The Finances of European Liberation*, p. 138.

[2] The figures quoted by Mr Foà from calculations made by the Bank of International Settlements seem to show that in 1943 equilibrium rates based on purchasing power parities would have been respectively 39.3 and 145 for the dollar and the pound. Bruno Foà *Monetary reconstruction in Italy* (Carnegie endowment for International Peace, New York, 1949, p. 117).

the Italian press, it is difficult to see how he could have maintained his administration, but for the Commission's active support, in the face of the hostile criticism of the self-appointed politicians. And much later, in the weeks following the end of hostilities, there would appear to be little doubt that the establishment of Allied Military Government in the northern Regions did help to avoid very serious trouble, which at one time looked like amounting to a revolution.

Once the representatives of the six parties had been brought into the Government—an achievement for which the Commission can claim no credit since it was only accomplished through the initiative of the Russian Government—Allied policy was inevitably bound to aim at a progressive liberation of the Italian Government from outside control. But some initial Allied tutelage was indispensable, and here the Commission unquestionably made an important contribution. On more than one occasion it was able to give a decisive direction to the turn of events. One of these was the holding of a referendum on the constitution question. Though the decision was finally taken without direct Allied intervention, the influence of the Commission had been exercised from the beginning in favour of this course, at a time when the majority of the renascent politicians were against it.[1] Another occasion was the framing of the new electoral law. The Bonomi Government had been at first inclined to a mere revival of the law as it stood before the Fascist revolution. It was due to the representations of the Allied Commission that women's suffrage—which had not existed in pre-Fascist days—was incorporated, as well as certain reforms in the traditional electoral procedure designed to eliminate possibilities of unfair political pressure.

One of the consequences of the policy of unconditional surrender formulated at Casablanca was in effect to place in the hands of the Supreme Allied Commander a kind of sovereign responsibility in the political sphere from which he was never able to divest himself. Under the 'Long' Armistice terms he was made the vehicle and the executant of Allied policy towards Italy. This no doubt then seemed essential in the absence of any possibility of diplomatic representation, owing to the continuance of the state of war. The directives of the Control Commission were consequently devised to give him powers of the most minute control over every department of national and local government. How far was this detailed system of control really necessary? There never was at any time the slightest danger of the Italian Government turning against the Allies. Both Marshal Badoglio and Signor Bonomi saw perfectly clearly that the only chance for their country was for Italy to 'work her passage'. Whether

[1] See above, pp. 205, 362.

Allied control in such detail was really the best way of helping her to do this may perhaps be doubted. At any rate it is difficult to resist the conclusion that all the military requirements of the Allied forces could have been met without it.

On the political side the results of this system of control were not altogether happy, in so far as, in the eyes both of the public and of the Italian officials, it made the Commission responsible for all the Italian Government's actions. To take only one example, much of the legislation on 'defascistisation' would appear in the more sober light of reason to be open to objection from the juridical point of view, and, though the responsibility for it rested in the first place with the Italian Government, the Allies could hardly escape being involved in some of the discredit attached by a serious body of liberal opinion to the more dubious punitive sanctions of this political purge[1], since, until the implementation of the 'New Deal' directive the consent of the Commission was formally necessary to all the Italian Government's acts. No doubt it was necessary, even from a strictly military point of view, to get rid of a small number of Fascist officials, but the historian cannot refrain from asking whether the general process of purging all the departments of national life was really one with which the Commander-in-Chief and a branch of his military staff should have had to concern themselves—to say nothing of the punishment of 'Fascist crimes' committed by Italians over a period of nearly a quarter of a century.

In exercising the Commander-in-Chief's sovereign authority, the Commission certainly showed moderation and restraint, and a quite disinterested desire to do the best that could be done for the Italian people. It also made a genuine effort—within certain limits—to foster the independence of the Italian Government. But, as we have already noted in Chapter IV, it was in fact impossible for it to remedy the defects of its original design. However strict the measures of control required in the early days of the Badoglio Government may have been, the installation of Signor Bonomi's six-party Government in Rome made such detailed degree of supervision quite superfluous, and its application a waste of valuable Allied manpower. Nor, in spite of the many defects of the Italian administration, did it always make for efficiency. For the members of this large Allied military bureaucracy did not always confine their activities within the limits commended by Gilbert for noble statesmen, and Italian public servants cannot always have found the intrusion of dignified amateurs into their administrative labours an incentive to self-reliance or a factor making for simplicity.

---

[1] See for example Croce, *op. cit.* pp. 124–6, and the protest of the Italian jurists mentioned above on p. 209; also Degli Espinoza, *op. cit.* pp. 199–200.

Yet it must be admitted that the Italian Government itself, even after the liberation of Rome, was on more than one occasion compelled to ask for administrative assistance. Nor can it be denied that the Control Commission did try to throw an ever-increasing degree of responsibility on to the Italian Government and its officials. But the fact remains that the original functions and structure imposed upon it at its birth were such as to render this attempt to a large degree self-defeating. A case could certainly be made out for the conclusion that without detailed Allied control in certain departments the Italian administration would have broken down in its essential tasks, particularly in the matter of food distribution. But this does not really invalidate the principal criticism which must be brought against the Commission's constitution and working, namely, that a very large proportion of its operations were concerned with matters which had only the slightest relevance, if any at all, to assisting the military task of the Commander-in-Chief. It is difficult to resist the conclusion that an extensive reduction in the size of the Commission and a much more drastic reorganisation of its functions would have made it a more efficient instrument.

The lumping together under one organisation of the three distinct tasks of executing the military terms of the armistice, of administering Military Government in the operational zone, and of exercising general political control over the Italian Government, only worked because in practice the task of 'enforcing' the military terms, or rather their re-interpretation in the light of the conception of co-belligerence, was undertaken quite separately by the 'independent' sub-commissions, while that of political control was progressively abandoned under the 'New Deal' policy. Once a government had been set up, which represented the politically active sections of the nation and was strongly anti-German, practically the whole machinery of control could have been demolished except in army areas, as was indeed rather belatedly attempted just before the campaign came to an end. Whether the function of such a political control as was necessary could have been left to the normal machinery of the Allied Foreign Departments, subject of course to the reserve powers of the Supreme Commander, is a matter in which opinion may well be divided, but there seems to be no reason to doubt that the administrative control required by the Commander-in-Chief in his military capacity could have been exercised through a small Military Commission in Rome, which would probably have worked most expeditiously with Italian officials through joint committees. And there is some reason for supposing that along these lines more effective Italian cooperation in the Allied war effort might have been obtained.

The only Allied political object of paramount importance was to ensure that, after hostilities were ended, adequate arrangements were made to give the Italian people the opportunity of deciding by a free vote the form and constitution of its future government. One cannot help asking whether this could not have been achieved without the elaborate machinery of the Control Commission. A Military Armistice Commission would at first sight appear rather a singular instrument for teaching democracy, but in fact it proved remarkably successful precisely in this respect. That the Commission did in fact achieve in the political sphere the main objects of Allied policy is not open to question. That does not, however, render irrelevant the consideration that it was a singularly clumsy and uneconomical instrument for achieving this purpose.

Nor is it possible to avoid asking whether it might not have been practicable to simplify the enormously complicated procedure by which the details of the Commission's policy were determined through the machinery of the Combined Civil Affairs Committee at Washington. The need for some central body to coordinate the actions of the Allied War Departments, their Foreign Offices, and Supply authorities, and to formulate general policies applicable to all theatres of war, is not open to dispute, nor is the value of the services rendered by Mr McCloy and General Hilldring, and by Lt-General G. N. Macready and his British colleagues, which will be treated in another volume. But at any rate at first sight there appear to be strong grounds for suspecting that the control which this committee attempted to exercise in Italy was too detailed and too dilatory. The frustration of the Allied Commission's headquarters staff at the delays in reaching any decision, even on quite minor matters, through the machinery of G-5, A.F.H.Q., and C.C.A.C., of which there is abundant evidence, cannot be just written off as mere 'grousing'. The delays, for example, in the issue of the 'New Deal' directives, the last of which, on financial matters, did not arrive until the war was over, certainly look like a striking example of bureaucratic dilatoriness. The international determination of decisions must inevitably be slow. There would therefore appear to be all the more reason to give theatre commanders wider discretion. In this connection it has been suggested to the historian by one commentator with first-hand experience of the problem, that a good deal of delay and misunderstanding might have been avoided if the Civil Affairs Departments in Washington and London had enjoyed more personal acquaintance with conditions in the theatre. For this purpose mere visits of high-ranking officers are not sufficient. It would seem desirable, where possible, to arrange temporary exchanges of officers in the middle ranks (G.S.O's 1 and 2).

The avoidance of duplication between the highest echelons is another matter which deserves careful attention. This problem during the Italian campaign was complicated by the fact that the two highest echelons were for about a year situated in different continents. At the earlier stages of an invasion the authority of the Commander-in-Chief of operations must obviously be paramount, while the task of the Supreme Commander's G-5 would appear to be principally concerned with supply matters. The question would appear to be whether—and, if so, at what stage and in what form—the Civil Affairs organisation operating in the field can be integrated with the Supreme Commander's G-5 staff branch, so as to avoid unnecessary duplication.

Finally a brief examination of the lessons learnt about staff may not be inappropriate. The importance of judicious selection was strongly borne out by the experience of the Control Commission which, as contrasted with AMGOT, was hastily improvised on an enormous scale, in circumstances which offered the different army services tempting opportunities to get rid of their weaker members, quite irrespective of any qualifications for their new tasks. The element upon which the success of Military Government mainly depends is the Civil Affairs Officer. It is impossible to lay down any exact qualification for this post, except decision, common-sense and some knowledge of the world. Knowledge of the language of the invaded territory is useful but not absolutely indispensable. Officers above military age, provided that their health is good, are suitable for jobs at headquarters, but would probably find the strenuous exertions often required by the post of C.A.O. too much for them. Some previous military service is very desirable. Careful selection and some previous training in local administrative conditions, history, etc., as well as training in their special duties, would appear to be indicated. The importance of Civil Affairs field training might perhaps be rather less in the case of certain 'specialist' officers, whose *métiers* are pretty well the same in any country, but it is certainly required for Supply officers, who should be practically acquainted with the workings of 'Q' and S and T. At Military Government headquarters it would be advisable, if possible, to have professional soldiers to do the work of 'A' and 'Q'. These activities are essentially linked to army services and a professional element would contribute greatly to smooth running.

On the staff side three weaknesses, which badly hampered the Allied Commission, may be mentioned. The first was the number of changes made in holders of high positions, particularly in the Economic Section, where it resulted in a conspicuous failure to plan and maintain any consistent policy. The second was the maintenance over many months of chief officers in merely acting rank. Thus even Admiral Stone had to wait from June to November for confirmation of his position as Chief Commissioner, a fact which could hardly fail to diminish his prestige in Italian eyes—to say nothing of the other branches of the Allied services. The same weakness was manifested even more strikingly in the Economic Section. Finally the absence of any uniform system of promotion in the services of the two nations gave rise to a great deal of ill-feeling of a kind which in an inter-Allied administration ought above all things to be avoided.

In conclusion a few words might be added on the subject of civilianisation.[1] This issue was raised early during the Italian campaign on account of the desire of the American War Department to rid its budget of the responsibilities for civilian supplies. During the period of hostilities, and for some time after, the ultimate responsibility for Military Government, and the maintenance of such controls as are necessary in a base of operations, must remain in the hands of the commander-in-chief of the theatre. This would suggest that the organisation responsible for these matters should be military. Civilians, even if they took charge of certain departments, would have to maintain military channels of command. And while the chain of command remains in military channels, it is difficult to see what advantage the injection of civilian elements would confer, whereas the disadvantages are obvious. In the first place, the inhabitants of the occupied territory would almost certainly be inclined to treat civilians with less respect. Secondly, it may be doubted whether civilians would not inevitably be placed in a position of inferiority *vis à vis* their equivalent ranks in the Armed Forces. Even in the democratic nations during wartime, especially in a theatre of operations, the sub-conscious military contempt for civilian authority cannot altogether be eliminated. The conclusion would appear to be that the position of 'Civil Affairs' as the Cinderella among the military services would certainly not be improved by partial civilianisation.

[1] See above, Annexe II to Chapter IX.

Appendices

APPENDIX I

Some AMGOT Proclamations

Note: In reproducing the text of these proclamations the preamble has been omitted in Proclamations 2, 4, 6, 7 and 11, and the article specifying their effective date, as well as, in certain cases, the articles concerning power to make orders and exact penalties.

Allied Military Government of Occupied Territory

Proclamation No. 1

TO THE PEOPLE OF SICILY:

WHEREAS in prosecuting their war against the Axis Powers, it has become necessary for the armed forces of Great Britain and the United States under my command to occupy Sicily.

WHEREAS it is the policy of the Allied Forces not to make war upon the civilian inhabitants of the occupied territory but to protect them in the peaceful exercise of the legitimate pursuits in so far as the exigencies of war and their own behaviour will permit, and

WHEREAS in order to preserve law and order and provide for the safety and welfare of my troops and of yourselves, it is necessary to establish Military Government in the occupied territory,

NOW, therefore, I, Harold R. L. G. Alexander, G.C.B., C.S.I., D.S.O., M.C., General, General Officer Commanding the Allied Forces in Sicily and Military Governor of the Territories Occupied, by virtue of the Authority vested in me by General Dwight D. Eisenhower, Commander in Chief of the Allied Forces in the North African Theatre of Operations do hereby proclaim as follows:

I

All powers of government and jurisdiction in the occupied territory and over its inhabitants, and final administrative responsibility are vested in me as General Officer Commanding and Military Governor, and the Allied Military Government of Occupied Territory is established to exercise these powers under my direction.

II

All persons in the occupied territory will obey promptly all orders given by me or under my authority and must refrain from all acts hostile to the troops under my command or helpful to our enemies, from all acts of violence, and from any act calculated to disturb public order in any way.

III

Your existing personal and property rights will be fully respected and your existing laws will remain in force and effect, except in so far as it may be necessary for me in the discharge of my duties as General Officer Commanding the Allied Forces and as Military Governor to change or supersede them by proclamation or order issued by me or under my direction.

IV

All Italian civil and criminal courts and all universities, schools and educational establishments will be closed until further order of the Allied Military Government.

V

All administrative and judicial officials of the provinces and communes, and all other government and municipal functionaries and employees, and all officers and employees of state, municipal or other public services, except such officials and political leaders as are removed by me, are required to continue in the performance of their duties, subject to my direction or the direction of such of my officers of the Allied Forces as may be deputed for that purpose.

VI

Further proclamations, orders and regulations issued by me or under my authority from time to time will specify what is further required of you, and what you are forbidden to do, and these will be displayed in court houses, police stations, or other public places.

VII

So long as you remain peaceable and comply with my orders, you will be subject to no greater interference than may be inevitable in view of military exigencies, and may go about your normal vocations without fear.

Proclamation No. 2

War Crimes

Article I

Offences Against the Allied Forces Which May be Punished by Death.

Any person who:

(1) Serves the enemy as a spy or harbors or aids an enemy spy;
(2) Communicates with the enemy or with any person within territory under their control in any manner or on any subject whatever;
(3) Sends to any person anywhere any communication giving any information whatever concerning the Allied Forces; or receives any such communication and fails promptly to report the same to the Allied Military Government;
(4) Bears arms against the Allied Forces;

(5) Has in his possession any fire arms, ammunition, explosives or similar war supplies after the date fixed by public notice, except in accordance with a permit of the Allied Military Government;
(6) Has in his possession any wireless or other apparatus for transmitting signals or other messages after the date fixed by public notice for their surrender;
(7) Wilfully misleads any troops of the Allied Forces in the performance of their duties;
(8) Assists a prisoner of war to escape or assists or conceals any prisoner of war after escape;
(9) Assists any of the enemy armed forces to evade capture;
(10) Enters or is found within any place or area designated as a forbidden area, either by the posting of a sign, or the presence of sentries, without a pass specifically authorizing him to be there;
(11) Steals any property of the Allied Forces or of any person belonging to the Allied Forces to the aggregate value of more than 10,000 lire;
(12) Removes, destroys or damages any war material belonging to the Allied Forces with intent to interfere with military operations or the safety of the Allied Forces;
(13) Interferes with communication by mail, courier, telegraph, telephone, cable, radio, or otherwise, or destroys or damages any facility of communication;
(14) Interferes with transportation by railroad, road, sea or air, or otherwise, or destroys or damages any facility of transportation;
(15) Interferes with the operation of any public service or utility, including water supply, electric light and power, gas, sanitation or similar services; or destroys or damages any facility or installation of any such service;
(16) Kills any member of the Allied Forces;
(17) Assaults any member of the Allied Forces with intent to kill or inflict serious bodily harm;
(18) Commits any act of plunder or pillage or robs the dead or wounded;
(19) Rapes any nurse or other woman serving with the Allied Forces or assaults any such nurse or other woman with intent to commit rape;
(20) Forges or alters any permit, pass, identity card or other similar paper addressed to or issued by the Allied Forces, or has in his possession any forged or altered permit, pass or identity card, knowing the same to be false;
(21) Incites any inhabitants of the occupied territory to insurrection against military authority, or organizes or leads any public demonstration or assembly for such purpose;
(22) Counterfeits any coin or note made legal tender by the Allied Military Government, or has in his possession any such coin or note knowing the same to be false; or
(23) Otherwise violates any of the laws of war, or wilfully does any act in aid of the enemy or hostile to or endangering the safety of the Allied Forces;

shall, upon conviction by a Military Court, be liable to punishment by death or by imprisonment, or fine, or both, as the court may determine.

Article II

Offences Against the Allied Forces Punishable by Fine or Imprisonment.

Any person who:

(24) Circulates in the streets or outside of his own house without a permit after curfew, which, until further notice, shall be from sunset to sunrise;

(25) Leaves the shore in any fishing boat or any other vessel or in any other manner except under such regulations as may hereafter be published;

(26) Gives false evidence before a Military Tribunal;

(27) Steals any property of the Allied Forces or of any member thereof of a value not in excess of 10,000 lire;

(28) Submits a claim against the governments of the United States or Great Britain, or of either of them, or any member of the Allied Forces, knowing the same to be false, fraudulent or exaggerated;

(29) Publishes or circulates or has in his possession with intent to publish or circulate, any printed or written matter in the interest of the enemy or its armed forces or hostile, detrimental, or disrespectful to the governments of the United States or Great Britain, the Allied Forces, or the Allied Military Government, or to the government of any other of the United Nations;

(30) Utters any speech or words hostile or disrespectful towards the United States or Great Britain, the armed forces of either, or any member thereof, or the Allied Military Government, or the government of any other of the United Nations;

(31) Assaults any members of the Allied Forces;

(32) Takes part in any public demonstration or assembly not authorized by the Allied Military Government;

(33) Falsely pretends to be acting under the authority of the Allied Military Government;

(34) Offers a bribe to or intimidates any person acting under the authority of the Allied Forces in order to induce him not to perform his duty;

(35) Interferes with the arrest or assists the escape of any person about to be arrested under the authority of the Allied Military Government;

(36) Acquires by gift or purchase any military equipment or war material belonging to the Allied Forces;

(37) Disseminates, by speech or writing, any false rumor calculated to excite or alarm the people;

(38) Knowingly makes any false statement to any member of the Allied Forces in connection with any matter of official concern;

(39) Removes or damages any notice, proclamation, or order posted under the authority of the Allied Military Government;

(40) Wrongfully receives or has in his possession property of the Allied Forces or any member thereof;

(41) Fails to have in his possession at all times an identification card issued pursuant to existing law;

(42) Issues any false identification card;

(43) Until further order of the Allied Military Government travels more than ten (10) kilometers beyond his own home without a permit issued by a Civil Police Officer;

(44) Wilfully disobeys any order given under the authority of the Allied Forces or the Allied Military Government where no specific punishment is prescribed; or,

(45) Does any act to the prejudice of good order or the safety or security of the Allied Forces or any member thereof;

shall, upon conviction by Military Court, be liable to punishment by such fine, or imprisonment, or both, as the court shall direct.

Article III

OTHER OFFENCES

Section 1. Conspiracy, advising or assisting violation. Anyone who conspires to do any act constituting an offense under this proclamation or any other proclamation or order issued under the authority of the Allied Military Government, or who advises, assists in or procures the commission of any such act, shall be punishable as a principal.

Section 2. Attempts. An attempt to do any act which constitutes an offence under this proclamation or any other proclamation or order issued under the authority of the Allied Military Government, shall likewise constitute an offense which shall be punishable to the same extent as though the act had been committed.

Article IV

VIOLATION OF ITALIAN LAW

Any person who violates any provision of Italian Law, may, at the direction of the Military Governor or under his authority, be brought to trial before a Military Court, and on conviction by such court, may be punished as provided by such Law.

Article V

COLLECTIVE FINES

Any mayor or other principal representative of any commune may be charged and tried as representing the members thereof with any offense for which such members are alleged to be collectively responsible, and in the event of his being convicted of such offense in his representative capacity, and collective responsibility being established, a collective fine may be imposed upon such commune.

Article VI

DEFENSES UNDER INTERNATIONAL LAW

It shall be a defense to any charge before a Military Court that the alleged offense was an act of lawful belligerency or otherwise privileged under principles of international law.

Article VII

ARREST AND DETENTION

Section 1. Arrest and search. Any authorized member of the Allied Forces may:

(a) Arrest or search any persons suspected of having committed or being about to commit offenses under this or any other proclamation or order;

(b) Enter and search any place and seize and take away any property for the purpose of investigating any such offense or arresting the offender, of preventing any such offense where there are grounds for believing that it is intended to be committed.

Persons arrested shall be brought to trial as soon as practicable before a Military Court convened in the locality, unless detained under the provisions of the next section.

Section 2. Detention. Any person suspected of committing or intending to commit a war offense or to engage in any political or other activity in the interest of the enemy or its Armed Forces or hostile to the Allied Forces or the Allied Military Government, may be detained pending further investigation, by order of any Senior Civil Affair Officer if in his opinion it would be prejudicial to the safety of the Allied Forces to permit such person to remain at large.

Whenever any person has been so detained, the Chief Legal Officer of the Allied Military Government shall be so informed, and he shall review the circumstances under which the detention was ordered. If the Chief Legal Officer certifies that he agrees with the opinion of the detaining officer, the detention may continue for a period of not longer than three months, subject to renewal for further periods of three months upon like certificates. If the Chief Legal Officer does not agree, then the question may be submitted to higher authority for decision.

Section 3. Provisions of this article not to apply to civilian internees. Nothing in this article contained shall prevent the internment of public officials or other civilians as civilian internees pursuant to the provisions of international law.

Proclamation No. 4
Allied Military Courts

Article I

CREATION OF ALLIED MILITARY COURTS

Allied Military Courts for the occupied territory are hereby established. There shall be General Military Courts, Superior Military Courts and Summary Military Courts, the constitution and competence of which shall be as set forth in Article III.

Article II

JURISDICTION

Section 1. Over Territory. Jurisdiction of every Allied Military Court shall extend to the whole of the territory occupied by the Allied Forces, and, as regards each part of the territory, from the time at which that part was first occupied.

Section 2. Over Persons. Jursidiction of every Allied Military Court shall extend to all persons in the territory except (a) members of the Allied Forces; and (b) persons who are treated as prisoners of war under the Geneva Convention of July 27, 1929.

Section 3. Over Offenses. Allied Military Courts shall have jurisdiction over:

(a) All offenses against the laws and usages of war;
(b) All offenses under any proclamation, order or regulation issued under the authority of the Allied Military Government;
(c) Any offense against Italian Law, provided the Military Government or an officer acting under his authority shall have ordered the trial of the case or class of cases by a Military Court.

Article III

CONSTITUTION OF ALLIED MILITARY COURTS

Section 1. General Military Courts. A General Military Court shall consist of not less than three officers of the Allied Forces appointed by or on behalf of the Military Governor at least one of whom shall be a Judicial Officer of the Allied Military Government. A General Military Court shall be competent to try all offenses within the jurisdiction of the Allied Military Courts, and to impose any lawful punishment.

Section 2. Superior Military Courts. Superior Military Courts shall consist of one or more officers of the Allied forces appointed by or on behalf of the Military Governor at least one of whom shall be a Judicial Officer of the Allied Military Government, if available. A Superior Military Court shall be competent to try all offenses within the jurisdiction of the Allied Military Courts and to impose any lawful punishment other than death or imprisonment for more than 10 years.

Section 3. Summary Military Courts. Summary Military Courts shall consist of one officer, who need not be a Judicial Officer, but may be any officer of the Allied Military Government if available, or otherwise any officer of the Allied Forces. A Summary Military Court shall be competent to try all offenses within the jurisdiction of the Allied Military Courts and to impose any lawful punishment except death or imprisonment for more than 1 year, or fine of more than 50,000 lire, or both such imprisonment and fine.

Section 4. Judicial Officers. For the purposes of this article every officer of the Allied Military Government who is a qualified lawyer is deemed to be a judicial officer.

Article IV

PROCEDURE

Section 1. Public Sessions. The proceedings of every Allied Military Court shall be public, except when otherwise ordered by the Chief Civil Affairs Officer or the Court.

Section 2. Rights of Defendants. Every defendant before an Allied Military Court is entitled:

(a) To have in advance of trial a copy of the charges upon which he is to be tried, if he so desires;

(b) To consult a lawyer before the trial and have a lawyer or other representatives of his own choosing defend him at the trial, except that the Chief Legal Officer or any Court may at any time prohibit any lawyer or other person from appearing in any Court. In any case, the Court may at the request of the defendant or otherwise, assign to him an officer to assist in the defense of the case;

(c) To apply to the Court for further time to prepare his defense, which application the Courts may grant or deny in its discretion;

(d) To bring with him such material witnesses as he may desire or have them summoned by the Court at his request;

(e) To give evidence on his own behalf at the trial, but he may not be compelled to do so;

(f) To have the proceedings translated for his benefit when he is unable to understand them otherwise.

Section 3. Rules of Procedure. The Chief Civil Affairs Officer shall make rules of procedure for the Allied Military Courts.

Section 4. Assessors. Every Military Court may appoint one or more assessors to sit with the Court. The duty of the assessor shall be to give such advice or assistance on any question as the Court may request.

Article V

IMPRISONMENT, FINES AND OTHER PENALTIES

Section 1. Previous Convictions. Before imposing sentence upon any person found guilty by an Allied Military Court, evidence of good or bad character, including any prior criminal records of the defendant before either military tribunals or the civil courts, may be received and considered by the Court in determining the sentence to be imposed.

Section 2. Fines. Where under any proclamation or order an offense is made punishable by fine, the Court imposing the fine may give such directions as appear to be just with respect to the payment of the fine and in default of payment of whole or part thereof may order the defendant to be committed to prison. Any such direction or order shall, for the purposes of review, be considered as part of the sentence.

Section 3. Order as to Residence. The General Miltary Court or a Superior Military Court, in lieu of or in addition to any other lawful punishment, may direct that the defendant establish his place of residence within a specified area.

Section 4. Confiscation. If under any proclamation or order a defendant shall be convicted of wrongful sale, purchase, use or possession of any article, a Military Court, in lieu of or addition to any other lawful punishment, may order restitution or compensation to the owner, or the forfeiture to the Allied Military Government of such article.

Section 5. Padlocking. If under any proclamation or order a defendant shall be convicted of an offense involving the sale of a harmful article or the operation of an improper place of business, a Military Court in lieu of or in addition to any other lawful punishment, may order that such place be vacated or closed for a fixed time.

Section 6. Suspension of a Sentence. A Military Court may direct that the whole or any part of a sentence of imprisonment imposed by it shall be suspended, on such terms as to good behaviour together with such other conditions (if any) as the court may impose. A subsequent conviction for any offense by an Allied Military Court shall have the effect of putting into operation any suspended sentence which the defendant may not have served, unless the Court otherwise directs.

Article VI

GENERAL POWERS OF COURTS

An Allied Military Court may make such orders and do all such acts and things as may be requisite for the due administration of justice and, without prejudice to the generality of the foregoing provision, may grant bail, accept and forfeit security therefor, make orders for the attendance of witnesses with or without documents, administer oaths, make orders for the disposal of exhibits, and punish contempt of court.

Article VII

REVIEW

Section 1. Right of Petition. Any person convicted by a Military Court, may, within thirty days after the imposition of sentence, file with the trial court or forward to the Chief Legal Officer, a petition, addressed to the Chief Civil Affairs Officer, submitting reasons why the conviction should be set aside or the sentence should be modified.

Section 2. Disposition of Record. Every record of trial by an Allied Military Court shall be transmitted to the Chief Legal Officer for examination and file.

Section 3. Powers on Review. The record of any case may on the recommendation of the Chief Legal Officer, and shall, in the event of a sentence exceeding two years' imprisonment or a fine of 50,000 lire, be reviewed by the Chief Civil Affairs Officer or by an officer of the Allied Military Government not below the rank of Lt. Colonel who may be appointed by the Chief Civil Affairs Officer for that purpose. The reviewing authority shall have power to set aside any conviction, to suspend, reduce or commute the sentence, or to order a new trial.

Article VIII

CONFIRMATION OF DEATH SENTENCES

No sentence of death shall be executed unless and until confirmed in writing by the Military Governor of the occupied territory, or by a specified officer not below the rank of Brigadier General or Brigadier to whom he may have delegated such power in writing.

Proclamation No. 6

Controller of Property

Article I

INTERPRETATION

In this Proclamation:

"Property" includes all forms of movable and immovable property and rights of property.

"Enemy State Property" includes all property owned, controlled or administered by any State at war with the United States or Great Britain and also property of companies, institutions or bodies in which any such State has any substantial interest, or over which it exercises substantial control.

Article II

APPOINTMENT OF CONTROLLER OF PROPERTY

The Chief Civil Affairs Officer may appoint an officer to be Controller of Property in the Occupied Territory, and also such Assistant Controllers and other Assistants as may be required. The Controller of Property and all Assistant Controllers and other assistants will carry out their duties as the duly authorized officers of the Allied Military Government.

Article III

POWER TO REQUIRE RETURNS AND ACCOUNTS

The Controller of Property may by notice in writing require any person to furnish returns, accounts and other information and to produce documents relating to any property, as the Controller considers necessary for the discharge of his functions.

Article IV

ALLIED PROPERTY

Section 1. Cancellation of Italian Measures Affecting Allied Property. All laws, decrees, orders or other measures taken by the Italian Government to sequestrate, block, confiscate or otherwise discriminate against property situated in the Occupied Territory, including obligations of debtors within the Occupied Territory, owned by the Governments of the United States or of any of the British Commonwealth of Nations or by the nationals of such States, or in which any such Government or nationals have any interest, are hereby abrogated.

Section 2. Declaration of property. All public officials of the Italian Government and all other persons in the Occupied Territory who have under their control or administration or in their possession or custody any property of the nature referred to in Section 1 shall:

(a) Forthwith declare such property by delivering to the Controller of Property a schedule or list describing the same;

(b) Upon demand of the Controller of Property, turn over such property or the control, possession, or custody thereof to the Controller or such person as may be designated;

(c) Upon demand of the Controller of Property, turn over all books, accounts, and records of the administration of such property during the period of Italian sequestration or other control to the Controller or to such person as may be designated by him.

Section 3. Maintenance and Care of Property pending Restitution. Until such time as they are ordered to turn over any property which is the subject of this Proclamation, all persons who are charged with the administration, custody or control thereof shall be fully responsible for the maintenance thereof and for taking all necessary measures for safeguarding and preserving the same. All such persons shall, as demanded by the Controller of Property, render regular reports as to the operations, custody and administration of the properties.

Section 4. Consent as to Certain Action. No persons so charged with the administration, custody or control of such property shall take or suffer to be taken any action which shall materially effect the value or the income therefrom, without the consent of the Controller of Property. Without limiting the generality of the foregoing, any such persons may obtain consent of the Controller of Property to the sale or mortgage of the property, or any portion thereof, and shall so give notice to him of any attachments of lien, termination of leases or other similar events.

Section 5. Extension to Property of other United Nations. The provisions of this Article may be applied by general or specific Order of the Chief Civil Affairs Officer, or any officer empowered by him, to the property situated in the Occupied Territory, including obligations of debtors within the Occupied Territory owned by any Government or any national of any of the United Nations not mentioned in Section 1 of this Article or in which any such Government or national has any interest.

Article V

ENEMY STATE PROPERTY

Section 1. Functions of the Controller of Property. The Controller of Property shall have power:

(a) to take into his control any Enemy State property not for the time being required by any other branch of the Allied Forces; and

(b) to assist all other branches of the Allied Forces to ascertain, secure and take possession of all Enemy State property which is susceptible of military use that they may require.

The Controller shall record and account for all Enemy State property which he takes into his control.

Section 2. Powers of Control. In relation to Enemy State Property which he retains in his control, the Controller of property may, subject to such special directions as he may from time to time receive from the Chief Civil Affairs Officer, exercise on behalf of the Allied Forces all rights and powers which they may have under international Law.

Article VI

OTHER PROPERTY

Section 1. Functions of the Controller of Property. The Controller of Property shall have power as directed by the Chief Civil Affairs Officer:

(a) to take into his control the private property of any company, institution, corporation, body or person whose activities are deemed by the Chief Civil Affairs Officer, or any officer empowered by him, to be prejudicial to the safety of the Allied Forces or public order in the Occupied Territory and whose said property might be used or applied, without such control, in furtherance of such activities;

(b) to take into his control any property, the control of which is, in the opinion of the Chief Civil Affairs Officer, essential to the needs of the Allied Forces or the inhabitants of the occupied territory; and

(c) to take into his control any private property whereof the owner or a representative of the owner, cannot be found present in the Occupied Territory and able to manage and protect the same.

Section 2. Powers of Control. In relation to property which he retains in his control under this Article, the Controller of Property may exercise all such rights and powers as may be conferred upon him from time to time by the Chief Civil Affairs Officer.

Article VII

DELEGATION OF POWERS

The Controller may delegate any or all of his powers to any officer appointed to be an Assistant Controller or other Assistant.

Article VIII

POWER TO MAKE ORDERS

The Chief Civil Affairs Officer may issue all such instructions and orders as may be requisite for the execution and carrying out of this Proclamation and may, without affecting the generality of the foregoing, make regulations for the recovery of fees, charges and expenses by the Controller of Property for any work done or services performed under this Proclamation in relation to any property.

Article IX

PROTECTION OF ALLIED MILITARY GOVERNMENT

The Allied Military Government and its officers shall be under no responsibility to the owner of any property taken into control under this Proclamation, or to any person interested therein, to make good any loss of or damage to such property, however caused, or to compensate any such owner or other person for any loss suffered directly or indirectly by reason of the taking of control of such property, but nothing in this Article shall relieve any officer of the Allied Military Government from any responsibility which he may be under to the Allied Military Government or to the Governments of the United States or Great Britain.

Article X

PENALTIES

Anyone who knowingly and without lawful authority:
(a) interferes with or obstructs the Controller of Property or any of his Assistants in the exercise of any of their functions hereunder;
(b) interferes with, removes, damages, conceals or makes away with any property which the Controller of Property has taken or is authorized to take into his control;
(c) interferes with, removes, damages, conceals or makes away with any property with intent to defeat, evade or avoid any responsibility, fine or punishment.
(d) withholds any information or any document which the Controller of Property is entitled to receive, or makes any false statement, or uses or refers to any false document in order to mislead the Controller of Property as to any of the matters which he requires to know for the purposes of this Proclamation; or
(e) violates any other provision of this Proclamation;
shall on conviction by an Allied Military Court be liable to imprisonment or fine, or both, as the Court may determine.

Article XI

POWER TO VOID TRANSACTIONS

The Chief Civil Affairs Officer, or any officer empowered by him, may by order direct that any transaction made at any time with regard to any property, movable or immovable, shall be set aside and held null and void if, in the opinion of the Chief Civil Affairs Officer or such officer empowered by him, the transaction was made to defeat, evade or avoid any provision of this Proclamation or any responsibility, fine or punishment, or to be imposed on any person or enemy government.

Proclamation No. 7

Dissolution of Fascist Organizations and Repeal of Laws

Article I

DISSOLUTION OF THE FASCIST PARTY

The organization known as the Fascist Party (P.N.F.) in the Occupied Territory is hereby dissolved and declared to be illegal. The property and assets of the said organization shall be taken by or delivered to officers of the Allied Military Government appointed for that purpose in accordance with directions which will be issued by the Chief Civil Affairs Officer.

Article II

ORGANIZATIONS AFFILIATED TO THE FASCIST PARTY

The Chief Civil Affairs Officer will from time to time issue Orders either dissolving the organization of any body or activity which appertains to, depends from, or is in any way affiliated to or controlled by, the Fascist Party, or declaring that the same or any branch thereof shall be carried on as being for the benefit of the people of the occupied territory but under such control or supervision and in accordance with such modification of rules, procedure and objects as the Chief Civil Affairs Officer may direct. Any such Order may make provision for the taking or safeguarding of the property or assets of any such organization and provide penalties for failure to observe and perform any provision of the Order.

Article III

DISPOSAL OF PROPERTY OF FASCIST ORGANIZATIONS

The Chief Civil Affairs Officer will make orders as to the disposal of any property acquired by the Allied Military Government under this Proclamation and may in his discretion as a part of any such order direct that the same property or any part thereof shall be applied by the Allied Military Government for the benefit of the people of the occupied territory in such manner or through such organization as he may direct.

Article IV

REPEAL OF LAWS

The Chief Civil Affairs Officer will by Order annul, amend or render inoperative any law in force in the Occupied Territory which relates to a Fascist organization or any dependent or allied organization thereof or which affects prejudicially the United States or Great Britain or their nationals or any other of the United Nations or their nationals and any law which discriminates against any person or persons on the basis of race, colour or creed, and he may also by any such order provide penalties for the failure to observe or perform the same.

Article V

OFFENCES

No person shall:

(1) promote assist or attend at any public or private meeting of the Fascist Party or any organization designed to replace it;

(2) use or permit to be used any building or other premises for the purposes of conducting any meeting, business or other affairs of the Fascist Party;

(3) print, publish or circulate, or have in his possession with intent to publish or circulate, any printed or written matter issued by or on behalf of the Fascist Party;

(4) wear or have in his possession any badge or insignia of the Fascist Party, or attire himself in such a manner as to suggest membership of the Fascist Party;

(5) make, collect or receive any subscription to the funds of the Fascist Party;

(6) take or receive any oath or give or receive any undertaking or promise to the Fascist Party;

(7) do any other act whatsoever intended or likely to promote or sustain the Fascist Party.

For the purpose of this Article the Fascist Party shall include any organization designed to replace it and any organization declared to be illegal under an order of the Chief Civil Affairs Officer made under Article II hereof.

Article VI

PENALTIES

Any person violating the provisions of this Proclamation shall, on conviction by an Allied Military Court, be liable to imprisonment or fine, or both, as the Court may determine.

Proclamation No. 11

General Police and Security Regulations

Article I

REGULATION OF PRIVATE MEANS OF COMMUNICATION

Section 1. Declaration of Radio Receiving Sets. Every person having in his possession any radio or wireless receiving set or equipment, or any parts, accessories, or material used in connection with wireless reception, or any private telephone wire or telegraph wire or any carrier pigeons, will declare the same within the time and at the place specified by official notice in each locality.

Section 2. Possession Unlawful. From and after the date fixed by such notice it shall be unlawful for any person in that locality to have in his possession or custody any of the articles above-mentioned which have not been declared as required by Section 1 hereof.

Article II

PROHIBITION OF PHOTOGRAPHY AND DECLARATION OF PHOTOGRAPHIC EQUIPMENT

Section 1. Photographing, Printing and Developing Forbidden. From the effective date of this order all persons in the occupied territory are forbidden:

(a) To take photographs of any sort, whether indoors or out-of-doors, and whether by still or cine or other type of camera;

(b) To develop or print any photographic film or plate of any nature, whether received from members of the Allied Forces or from any other person,

except with a written permit of the Allied Military Government.

Section 2. Declaration of Cameras, Photographic Supplies, Telescopes and Binoculars. Every person owning or having in his possession or custody any camera or any photographic supplies, or any telescope or binoculars, will declare the same within the time and at the place specified by official notice published in each locality. For the purpose of such declaration photographic supplies shall include:

Cameras—cine or still
Projecting apparatus
Developing and dark room equipment
Unexposed or exposed film, cine or still
Photographic paper and chemicals.

Article III

IDENTITY CARDS

Section 1. Possession of Identity Card. All persons must have in their possession at all times an identity card in accordance with the Italian law and must produce the same upon the demand of any member of the Allied Forces.

Section 2. Loss of Identity Card. If any person has lost or shall lose his identity card he shall report that fact both to the senior Civil Police Officer in his territory and to the official of the local government by whom the card was originally issued. A duplicate card may be issued to him providing the word "duplicate" is marked thereon.

Article IV

REGULATION OF NEWSPAPERS AND PRINTED MATTER

Section 1. Publication of Newspapers and Printed Matter Prohibited Without a Permit. No newspaper, magazine, book, pamphlet or circular may be published or printed without a written permit from the Allied

Military Government. Such permits will be either specific or continuing and will be issued by the Allied Military Government upon such terms and conditions as may be prescribed.

Section 2. Importation and Exportation of Printed Matter. Importation into and exportation out of the Occupied Territory of newspapers, magazines, books, or other printed matter is prohibited, except under permit issued by the Allied Military Government.

Article V

MEETINGS AND ASSEMBLIES

Section 1. Permitted Meetings and Assemblies. Meetings and assemblies for the following purposes may be held without permits:

(a) Meetings for religious purposes, including baptisms, weddings and funerals;

(d) Such courts of law as are authorised to function by the Chief Legal Officer of the Allied Military Government upon such terms and conditions as he may prescribe.

Section 2. Other Meetings and Assemblies Prohibited. Except for the foregoing, no person shall promote or attend any public meeting, theatrical, moving picture or other representation or performance, any public assembly or other public gathering, whether indoors or out-of-doors, or any parade or demonstration for which a written permit has not been granted. Such permits will be either specific or continuing and will be issued by or on the authority of the Commissioner of Civil Police of the Allied Military Government through the Civil Police Officer for the locality upon such terms and conditions as may be prescribed.

Section 3. Power of Civil Affairs Officer or other Officer to Disperse Assemblies. Notwithstanding the issuance of any permit, any Civil Affairs Officer or Civil Police Officer, if he has reason to believe that public disorder will ensue or that the safety of the Allied Forces is threatened, may order any meeting, performance, assembly, or parade to be suspended or terminated and require all persons present to disperse. Any such order will be complied with immediately by all persons present.

Article VI

FLAGS AND NATIONAL ANTHEMS

The public display of any flag or colours of Italy, or of any other country at war with Great Britain or the United States, and the public singing and playing of the national anthem and any other patriotic or political song or music of any such country are prohibited.

Article VII

"BLACK-OUT" REGULATIONS

All existing laws and regulations relating to "black-out" will be strictly enforced.

Article VIII

PENALTIES

Any person violating any provision of this Proclamation shall, upon conviction by an Allied Military Court, be liable to punishment by imprisonment or fine, or both, as the court may determine.

Proclamation No. 13

LEGAL RIGHTS OF THE ITALIAN PEOPLE

WHEREAS it is the purpose of the Allied Powers to deliver the people of Italy from the Fascist Regime,

NOW, therefore, I, Harold R. L. G. Alexander, G.C.B., C.S.I., D.S.O., M.C., General, General Officer Commanding the Allied Forces in Sicily and adjacent islands and Military Governor of the Occupied Territory, hereby proclaim as follows:

Article I

NO PERSON TO BE IMPRISONED WITHOUT TRIAL

No person shall be imprisoned by any Italian Official, unless he is duly charged with the commission of a specified crime.

No person shall be detained in prison without trial, which shall take place as promptly as conditions will allow.

Article II

ABROGATION OF POWERS TO IMPRISON OR FINE WITHOUT TRIAL

All powers to sentence any person to fine or imprisonment without trial vested in any Italian Official or official organization by the Law of Public Safety of 18 June, 1931, or by any amendments thereto, or by any law whatsoever issued under the Fascist Regime, are hereby abrogated.

APPENDIX II

Italian Imports under the Allied Military Programme
July 1943 to September 1945

Thousand tons

Commodity	*Procured by U.S.A.*	*Procured by U.K.*	*Procured by Canada*	*Total*
Grain and flour	1,050·1 }	632	382·8 }	2,464·1
Other foodstuffs	397·6 }		1·6 }	
Medical stores	10·0	0·2		10·2
Soap	8·1	5·2		13·3
Coal	1,337	1,954·2		3,291·2
Transport machinery	16·8			16·8
Other machinery for public services	0·4			0·4
Clothing footwear and textiles	12·2	2·1		14·3
Machinery and materials for agriculture	39·6	69·5		109·1
Machinery and materials for industry	3·1	1·2		4·3
Other machinery		0·2		0·2
Miscellaneous finished articles	13·8	0·3		14·1
Other miscellaneous products	1·6	10·5	3·6	15·7

The total value of the imports shown in this table was over $490 million, for which the United Kingdom was responsible for about $95 million, Canada for about $32 million, and the United States for about $363 million.

This table has been published in the *Annuario della Congiuntura Economica Italiana 1938–1947* by the *Istituto per gli studi di Economia* (p. 447).

Italian exports of foodstuffs to the United Kingdom from September, 1943 to March, 1945

		Quantity	*Value*
			£
Figs	Tons	10¾	377
Bitter Shelled Almonds	,,	11	1,401
Sweet Shelled Almonds	,,	324	44,475
Unshelled Almonds	,,	3,919	209,657
Filberts in Shell	,,	644¼	96,214
Lemons	Boxes	1,444,528	747,935
Bitter Oranges	,,	140,210	53,532
Sweet Oranges	,,	24,037	18,034
Lemon Oil	lbs.	321,166	228,104
Bitter Orange Oil	,,	8,519	4,687
Sweet Orange Oil	,,	32,468	17,046
Bergamot Oil	,,	107,077	88,339
Tangerine Oil	,,	5,692	5,692
Concentrated Lemon Juice	Galls.	378	217
Unconcentrated Lemon Juice	,,	67,217	8,043
Mustard Seed	Tons	93	2,324
Citric Acid	,,	1,360½	135,093
Argols	,,	665	69,603
Tataric Acid	,,	220	61,160
Wine Lees	,,	1,542	79,242
Wines	Galls.	98,081	95,961
Marsala and Sicilian Wines	Casks	774	21,000
			£1,988,136
			(a) 205,664
			£2,193,800

(a) Adjustment to correct previous credits to nett proceeds of sale.

Miscellaneous Italian Exports September 1943 – April 1945

(Tons)

Minerals and Metals:		*Chemicals:*	
Sulphur	29,803	Carbon disulphide	75
Pumice	263	Calcium tartarate	15
Talc	72		
Plastic chalk	30	TOTAL	90
Shingle	45		
Cement	500	*Miscellaneous:*	
Gypsum	30	Baskets	46
Salt	1,058	Briarwood	456
Cadmium	4	Cork	50
Mercury	180	Sumac	425
		Willow strips	101
TOTAL	31,985	Red squill	40
		Bentonite	15
Textile materials:		Books	2
Raw hemp	1,634	Sulphur retort	2
Hackled hemp	1,350		
Hemp and tow yarns	214	TOTAL	1,137
Cord and rope	1,161		
Silk and strusa	45		
TOTAL	4,404		

APPENDIX III

Military Exploitation of Local Resources

After the occupation of Naples a Local Resources Section was formed in A.F.H.Q., to deal with the procurement and allocation of local supplies, facilities and services, and an Italian Local Resources Board was set up on the mainland to work as an organ of the Advanced Administrative Echelon of A.F.H.Q. (FLAMBO) on 12th November, 1943. The functions of the Board were to coordinate all Army, Navy and Air Force requirements from local resources, other than rail and water transportation, coal and petroleum, and to allocate them to each branch of the Services. In exercising this function the Board was to work in liaison with A.C.C. and A.M.G., whose business it was 'to provide the Board with information regarding local resources of all kinds' and to 'state the minimum needs of civilian requirements'. But the determination of those requirements lay with the Board.

The Local Resources Board divided itself into a number of committees to deal with the allocation of certain commodities, namely Food Supplies, Engineering Materials and Forage, and a Miscellaneous Purposes Committee, which dealt *inter alia* with hemp and leather. A committee for the allocation of electric power resources was also set up, as well as one on prices and (later) on Industrial Coordination. Both on the main Board, the chairman of which was Lt.-General Sir Brian Robertson, and on the committees, the military services were represented by an overwhelming majority, representatives of the Allied Control Commission and A.M.G. being in quite a subordinate position.

The general method of procedure in controlling the use of local resources was as follows: commodities in short supply, in which the forces were interested, were 'frozen' by A.M.G. or A.C.C. on the request of the Board, that is, their purchase or procurement by civilians was prohibited. 'Frozen' commodities were divided into two classes, 'controlled' and 'restricted'. The allocation of 'controlled' items between all consumers, civilian and military, was made by the Board, whereas in the case of 'restricted' items only the surpluses remaining after the essential needs of the civilian population had been met were allocated between the Allied (and co-belligerent) Services. Schedules of 'controlled' and 'restricted' items were issued through command channels. Applications for these commodities had to be submitted by the interested branches of the Services to the Board monthly, together with an indication of priority, namely, 'urgent operational', 'normal maintenance', and 'stockpiling'. Bulk demands for civil requirements were submitted by the Control Commission.

On October 26th 1943 strict instructions were issued, prohibiting the procurement of local foodstuffs for consumption by the British and United States Armies, except known surpluses or perishable supplies. Of these surpluses, wine, fresh fruit and vegetables were the most important. The British forces, owing to their commissariat arrangements, which included much less tinned, dried, or dehydrated vegetables in their rations, relied much more on fresh vegetables than the Americans. British purchases of locally produced foodstuffs in fact amounted to nearly four times those of the American forces. They also included live animals, male sheep or goats, at the rate of about 1,000 a week for the feeding of Indian troops. In addition, the Services of both nations wanted to purchase fresh food—meat, fish, eggs, poultry, as well as fruit and vegetables—for patients in hospital. The purchase by troops of certain foodstuffs such as eggs, poultry, meat and fish was expressly prohibited. All foodstuffs except wine, which was super-abundant, were placed on the 'restricted' list, so that only surpluses remaining after civilian needs had been fully met were available for purchase.

The armed forces were also interested in forage. In the high Apennines, especially in winter, the supply of forward troops could only be maintained by mule. The demand for forage was met without any great strain on Italian civilian resources, in spite of a bad hay crop in 1944, reduced by drought. The quantities purchased by S. & T. were quite small. Total purchases from August 1944 to April 1945 amounted to only 60,000 tons.

For the first few months following the invasion of the mainland, the surpluses of fruits and vegetables were sufficient to satisfy service requirements to the full, but after the occupation of Rome and the advance to the northern Apennines, which brought very large urban populations into liberated territory, the situation began to deteriorate rather quickly. Owing to the scarcity of rationed foodstuffs the civil population was forced to rely to a far greater extent on vegetables. The Regions, especially those in Italian Government territory, were reluctant to part with surpluses and so failed to declare them. The Control Commission was consequently forced to cut drastically the estimates of surpluses available for purchase by the services. These shortages did not, however, affect the export of citrus fruit (chiefly lemons) from Sicily which, as shown in the table on p. 410, attained quite a large volume.

The principle was laid down clearly in September 1944 that the civilian population had prior claims on locally produced foods which were readily stored or transportable, like dried fruits, hard fruits, roots and certain green vegetables, but an exception was admitted in the case of the two latter items. Where these were bidden for by the armed forces, and no declared surplus was available, they might still be procured by military supply authorities, in exchange for their equivalent in dried or preserved vegetables. This worked for a short period, but both American and British supplies of preserved or dried vegetables soon gave out. The surplus of vegetables available for the troops, apart from hospital patients, was therefore cut down to nil.

In spite of these restrictions on army purchases, the total tonnage saved by foodstuffs from local resources was considerable. The total amount of foodstuffs obtained by the Allied forces through local procurement amounted to something like 300,000 tons. Using the official conversion-factor of two to one this meant a saving in ships' tonnage on foodstuffs alone of about 600,000 tons. From the point of view of saving ships' tonnage, engineering and building materials, such as cement and steel, fuel and timber, made a much greater contribution. Immediately on occupation the engineering services of both Armies took over such factories and workshops as were either undamaged, or capable of repair within a reasonable period, and started operating them for military account. With the cooperation of A.M.G./A.C.C. availability lists were drawn up of almost every conceivable item which could possibly be put to any use by any branch of the Services. These lists were then submitted to the Local Resources Board for allocation between the different branches. Meanwhile the items, which were mostly placed on the 'controlled' list, were 'frozen' by A.M.G., to prevent not only civilian purchase, but also irregular procurement by interested service branches. These lists were kept as flexible as possible, and additions or subtractions were made frequently as the supply situation altered.

Cement was at first not placed either on the 'controlled' or the 'restricted' list. At the beginning of December 1943 three large plants were being operated by the military, which had a capacity considerably greater than the Service requirements, which were then estimated at 7,250 tons a month. But before long military requirements expanded rapidly and cement was placed on the controlled list in February 1944. By the summer Service requirements were running up to 20,000 tons a month and the Control Commission was requesting that its allotment should be increased. After the occupation of central Italy the situation became much easier and cement was taken off the controlled list. During the nine months ending April 1945 the British forces consumed about 90,000 tons of locally produced cement.

Another structural material, on which very appreciable savings were made in Allied shipping, was timber. The two main areas producing this somewhat scarce commodity in southern Italy were the Gargano peninsula on the Adriatic coast and the Sila forest in Calabria. The Armies needed timber for two main purposes, constructional work of various kinds, especially bridges, and the more humble, but hardly less essential, purpose of firewood. Both American and British forces reserved to themselves the exploitation of certain areas in the Sila forest, from which the bulk of their timber requirements were drawn. The cuttings were done entirely in accordance with the rules of the Forestry Guards, with one out of five trees of merchantable size left standing, and though complaints were made from time to time about excessive exploitation, judged by the war-time practice of this country it was certainly not unreasonable. In between September 1944 and April 1945 some 150,000 tons, mostly pine, silver fir, and beech, were taken for military purposes, and nearly sixty saw-mills were continuously employed.

The entire output of the steel industry remained under military control. Before the advance beyond Rome, liberated Italy only contained two comparatively small centres of steel production, the larger in and around Naples, which was badly damaged, and the smaller near Bari. After the occupation of Central Italy, portions of the plant at Terni, containing furnaces and rolling mills, which had suffered considerable damage, were put into operation, but throughout the campaign there were practically no blast furnaces which could be repaired on a short-term programme. Steel making had therefore to rely almost entirely on scrap. Output was thus extremely small. The total quantity of steel produced from August 1944 to April 1945 was barely 40,000 tons. Among the varieties produced at Naples and Bari were sections, sheets, including tin-plate for canning, and back plates for the manufacture of cookers. At Terni, steel for 'Flambo' bridges—a semi-permanent variant of the Bailey Bridge—was manufactured.

Bricks were another structural material, the local procurement of which resulted in some saving of shipping. Local resources were sufficient to meet Service requirements without the imposition of any controls. The forces took over a large proportion of existing brick-works, and though there was a shortage of bricks for the reconstruction of war-damaged premises, this was not due so much to consumption by the Services, as to the shortage of fuel and transport which prevented brick-works from operating.

Another commodity of importance to the Engineering services, obtained in some quantity by local procurement, was paint, which was 'controlled' from the beginning, as well as its chief ingredients, pigments, linseed and linseed oil, of which all available stocks were allocated to Service use.

Sulphuric acid was put on the 'controlled' list in January 1944. At the time of occupation no plants in southern Italy producing it as an end-product were in operation, but it became available as a by-product in the manufacture of super-phosphate fertilizer. This before the war had been produced by the Montecatini concern at several plants. It was not at first considered economical to start these plants working on sulphuric acid production alone, but as considerable delay was being experienced in procuring phosphate-rock from North Africa and existing stocks of sulphuric acid were on the point of exhaustion, the Barletta and Portici plants were started on acid alone in June and July, 1944. Between them they produced a good deal more than military requirements.

A source of some economy in shipping was the provision from local resources of industrial gases. Their production was regarded as so important that a special sub-committee of the Engineering Materials Committee was formed to take charge of this. The two gases whose allocation was controlled were acetylene and oxygen, the former being in great demand by the Allied Navies for welding, and the latter also for breathing by the Allied Air Forces. With regard to acetylene, calcium carbide was placed on the 'controlled' list in October 1944. This was manufactured on a large scale at Terni where stocks amounted to 1,000 tons.

After the establishment of Foggia airbase at the beginning of 1944 there was great difficulty in producing locally sufficient oxygen of the right quality for breathing purposes, and it was not until the beginning of 1945 that local production began to catch up with service requirements. At the beginning of January 1944 production was over two million cubic feet a month short of requirements. A great step towards the bridging of this big gap might have been taken at an early date through the rehabilitation of the partially damaged plant at Crotone, which had been carefully surveyed and reported on by the Industry Sub-Commission of the Control

Commission. But its requirements of electric power were very large and discussions between the various service authorities involved hung fire, so that in the end this project was never carried out. Meanwhile the advance towards the Gothic Line added three important plants, two in Rome and one at Terni, whose output went a long way towards covering the deficit. The capture of Florence made further plant available. By October total production of stationary plants had reached over ten million cubic feet, which, when added to about seven million cubic feet produced by the Services' own mobile plants, more than covered total service demands.

Leather and all leather goods were put on the 'controlled' list in January 1944, but the control was limited to shoe leather and leather belting, the output of the latter being allotted almost entirely to the forces. Leather was in very short supply. Owing to the removal by the Germans of Italian domestic animals, slaughter of cattle had to be restricted, but the greatest bottleneck was the shortage of tanning materials. Almost all the factories producing these were in German-occupied Italy. During the first half of 1944 an appreciable amount of shoe leather was allotted to the forces for the repair of boots, very little being left for civilian consumption, but the pressure of civilian needs became so great that A.F.H.Q. was compelled in September 1944 to change the original order of priority, and to allot only the surplus, if any, after civilian requirements had been met, to the Allied military forces.

Of much greater importance to the Allied war effort was the contribution made by the Italian hemp industry: southern Italy produced an appreciable quantity—about 100,000 tons. This was considerably above the capacity of the manufacturing plants, concentrated chiefly in the Naples area. Arrangements were therefore made for the export of the surplus to the U.K. The hemp products most in request by the armed forces were ropes, canvas, sacks and sewing thread for shoemakers. Hemp and its products were placed on the 'controlled' list from the beginning. The control of the industry was taken over in January 1944 by the Allied Control Commission which set up a special hemp control office. In July 1944, when Campania (Region III) was handed over to the Italian Government, this control had to be relinquished, but steps were taken for an Italian organisation with compulsory powers to take its place.

The manufacture of ropes had attained before the end of the year an output of about 400 tons a month, most of which was devoted to types needed by the services, though a certain amount of inferior quality rope was also produced for agriculture and civilian purposes. Production of canvas, heavy, medium and light, at the beginning of 1945 exceeded 250,000 square metres a month. Most of this was devoted to service needs, but of the light varieties the Allied Commission received small amounts for civilian purposes, these being used as a substitute for cotton and linen. The manufacture of sacks was also important, as there was great competition for the limited output between the military authorities and the Control Commission, which needed them for harvesting. Production at its highest was about 140,000 sacks a month, but this rate could only be attained by cutting down the output of canvas. Some preference at harvest time was given to agricultural needs.

By the spring of 1945, supplies of raw material to maintain this output ran seriously short, owing to the dilatoriness of the Italian Government in fixing a price sufficiently high to facilitate the collection of hemp through legitimate channels. Black market and hoarding reached serious proportions and the export of hemp to the U.K. had to be suspended. But on the occupation of Emilia, the largest producing area, considerable quantities were found on farms. The liberation of the North disclosed ample supplies of rope and canvas, and service demands could easily be met in full. The prohibition on the export of raw hemp was withdrawn in July.

The distribution of electric power was placed under the control of the Local Resources Board, whose Electrical Power Committee made bulk allocations to Districts and Base Sections and to certain industries, e.g. hemp, chemical fertilizers, railways, etc., the division of the bulk allocation of each District and Base Section being the responsibility of the military commander. In central Italy in the first period after liberation the Allied forces were consuming at least three-quarters, and sometimes even more, of the total electricity generated, a percentage which was of course lowered as additional capacity was restored to operation. But even at the end of 1944 military users in Rome were consuming about thirty-five per cent of the total output, and in the Terni, Ancona, and Civitavecchia areas direct military consumption was still between seventy-five and eighty per cent of the total. In southern Italy the percentage consumed by the Allied forces was, in general, a good deal lower.

In spite of the poverty and lack of resources of southern Italy the total figures of local procurement by the Allied forces were quite large. In addition to nearly 300,000 tons of foodstuffs they included 1,215,000 tons of other commodities, of which the American services accounted for about 440,000 tons and the British close on 775,000 tons. The grand total of all commodities procured, including food, amounted to about 1,500,000 tons.

In these circumstances it was inevitable that a conflict of opinion should arise between the Military Government Section and the operational branches of the Supreme Commander's staff, a conflict the logistical merits of which, as well as its political implications, had sometimes to be determined at the highest command level. For the military method of exploitation of existing resources was often extremely uneconomical. Operational requirements, when the line had become static, were often interpreted to mean little more than immediate local convenience. Requisitions were consequently apt to be reckless and indiscriminate, R.E.M.E. being one of the worst offenders in this respect. Plants and tools were often requisitioned without being used; frequently the only use made of the former was to remove some key tools, making the rest of the plant worthless. Moreover the requisitioning of factory premises, to accommodate troops, or for dumps, without any inquiry into their civilian use, was bound to lead to many anomalies. Plants of critical importance to the civilian economy, to say nothing of military requirements, were sometimes put out of action, e.g. a plant for producing tanning extract, a critically short item needed for the production of belting and shoe leather both used by the armies; a repair shop for railway rolling stock, an impregnating plant for creosoting railway sleepers, and a phosphate-fertilizer plant, the output of which might have directly helped to decrease the imports of foodstuffs.

The issues between the Control Commission and the Local Resources Board were brought to a head by the report of the Anti-Inflation Committee of the Allied Commission, which recommended the creation of an Allied Economic Council with preponderant Allied Commission membership—the Chief Commissioner was to be chairman—to allocate resources and facilities of every kind when there were conflicting claims between military and civilian users and exports. This proposition was not accepted by General Alexander, who refused to surrender the principle that in the last resort civilian requirements must, with the exception of foodstuffs, be determined by the urgency of military needs. Something was however done by A.F.H.Q. to increase the Allied Commission's influence. The Commission's representative was made chairman of the Food Supply, Labour and Wages, and Prices Committees. Machinery was also set up in the shape of the Industrial Coordination Committee, of which the Chief Commissioner of the Allied Control Commission was chairman, for the constant review of military requisitions of factories and workshops.

The document laying down the procedure of this committee called the attention of all ranks to the importance of civilian requirements:

> All ranks must, even in the stress of active operations, remind themselves that whenever it is possible to achieve a military object by a choice of means otherwise equal, the method which damages least the essential needs of the civil economy is to be preferred and adopted. Care must be taken by the responsible commander that except in definite emergencies he neither occupies a premise essential to the civil economy nor dismantles or removes by purchase or requisition the equipment therein.

It was also laid down that in the planning for the occupation of an area the military planning authorities would consult with the Allied Commission on the anticipated military and civilian requirements affecting local resources, and that they should elaborate their plans, as far as practicable, to include any proposals agreed as the result of such consultation. It was, however, admitted that such agreements must of necessity be tentative, and depend upon the physical condition of the area and the military situation. The definite reservation so far as practicable of certain facilities for military, and others for essential civilian requirements was also recommended. In the immediate execution of operational plans, the decision of the Army Commander was, of course, to govern, but if the Allied Commission was of the opinion that the military use of any facility would cause undue harm to the civil economy, and local agreement could not be reached, it might, 'without interrupting the operational plan or its immediate execution', inform the Army Commander that an appeal would be made against his decision.

APPENDIX IV

Notes on Public Health

EPIDEMIC DISEASES[1]

TYPHUS

The technical details of the outbreak of typhus which occurred in Naples in the winter of 1943 have been described in two papers, *Typhus: Experiences in the Central Mediterranean Force*, (British Medical Journal, 29th June 1946, Vol. I and 6th July 1946, Vol. II) by Colonel Chalke, R.A.M.C., formerly Senior Hygiene Officer, A.A.I., and *Typhus Fever in Italy, 1943–1945 and its Control with Louse Powder*, in the American Journal of Public Hygiene Vol. 45, No. 3, May 1947. This note deals with certain aspects and activities which concerned A.M.G. For a brief account of the Public Health activities of AMGOT and A.C.C., see two articles by Colonel G. M. Frizelle, which appeared in the August and September numbers of *Public Heatlh* in 1956.

From the moment of first occupation conditions in Naples were ripe for an epidemic. The lack of cleanliness of the poorer quarters of the town and its inhabitants had been notorious for generations; Allied bombing and German sabotage completed the sanitary devastation by most extensive damage to the sewage system. Between twenty and thirty thousand of the population were living more or less permanently in tunnels, air-raid shelters and caves, destitute of any sanitary facilities, and a large part of the population was louse infested.

The necessity of guarding against an outbreak of this disease had already been foreseen at Allied Force Headquarters, for a large-scale epidemic, of dimensions far greater than anything that actually developed in Naples, had for two years been affecting the Arab population of Algeria. Two American organisations had been engaged since early in 1943 in studying typhus problems in Egypt and in North Africa, namely the U.S. Army Typhus Commission and the typhus team of the Rockefeller Foundation, whose experiments in mechanical dusting with insecticide powder practically revolutionised the technique of anti-typhus precautions. Before the end of September 1943 the head of the Rockefeller team, Dr. F. L. Soper, had been in touch with General Holmes in Algiers with a view to organising the prevention of typhus by 'delousing' in threatened areas, and it was agreed early in November that the Rockefeller team should be put into American Red Cross uniform and operate under the control of A.M.G. Fifteenth Army Group.

Immediately after occupation, the Italian head of the Public Health service in Naples city declared that there was no typhus. This optimistic

[1] In preparing this note I have had the privilege of consulting certain unpublished MS notes lent me by Colonel Chalke.

statement was very far from being true. Civilian cases had been reported in the vicinity of Naples as early as March 1943 in Castellamare and in Aversa, where eight cases, all in the same family, occurred about the end of April. In July cases were reported in Naples from a bathing establishment used by soldiers, and from the Poggioreale prison. The first cases were patients in the Military hospital, one a soldier returned by train from the Russian front, and three others, men brought by hospital ship from North Africa; twelve cases also occurred among Yugoslav prisoners. From Poggioreale prison the disease spread to four other prisons, including that of Pozzuoli. Before leaving Naples the Germans opened the doors of Poggioreale and Pozzuoli prisons and emptied their occupants into the streets. Many of these potential carriers of disease probably sought refuge in air-raid shelters. In September already twenty-two cases among civilians had been reported, and in October thirty-six. During the second half of November numbers began to rise rapidly to thirty-two in the third and forty-six in the fourth week.

By this time it had become abundantly clear that Neapolitan public health authorities were quite incapable of coping with the problem, partly owing to the complete lack of disinfesting equipment, of soap, fuel, transport and general facilities—not to mention the occupation by an R.A.F. maintenance unit of the hospital for infectious diseases, which had also been rather severely damaged by Allied bombing. The system of reporting contagious diseases had nearly broken down under the stress of war and occupation, and the rather loose employment among Italians of the word '*tifo*', which is used for both typhoid and typhus, added to the confusion. In these circumstances the Allied military authorities decided to take action. The Rockefeller team from Algiers was brought in to operate a programme of disinfestation, at first under the operational control of A.M.G. Region III and later under that of the U.S. Army Typhus Commission, headed by Brigadier-General Fox, who before the end of December was placed in charge of typhus control at Naples, operating directly under A.F.H.Q. FLAMBO set up a Typhus Control Board under the chairmanship of the D.D.M.S., of which the Director of Public Health, A.M.G. Fifteenth Army Group, and the Director of the Public Health Sub-Commission of A.M.G. were among the members, to coordinate all available resources for the military and civilian measures. Under this worked a local Typhus Committee under the chairmanship of the A.M.G. Regional Public Health officer.

Partly owing to the inertness of the Neapolitan public health authorities, A.M.G. was slow in realising the seriousness of the incipient epidemic—some sharp criticism on this point was made by General Fox—and a considerable time was allowed to elapse before the Rockefeller team arrived in Naples. In the meantime the military medical authorities had rendered very valuable assistance in the provision of disinfestors and disinfesting powders—the American M.Y.L. and the British A.L. 63—for civilian use. A.M.G. had also stimulated the local public health authorities to improve the method of finding cases and establishing contacts, and had arranged with FLAMBO for the evacuation of the hospital for infectious diseases.

The technique of combating the epidemic may be summarised as follows. First, the finding and isolation of cases. This had to be organised by the help of Italian physicians, assisted by the priesthood. Once cases were treated, the next step was to follow up their contacts and delouse them, beginning with the immediate family and, whenever possible, persons who lived in the same or contiguous buildings, or who worked in the same factory—'Spot' delousing. But this was not considered sufficient to prevent the spread of infection. It was therefore decided to embark on mass delousing, which was started at the end of December, by the opening up of over thirty stations, each of which at the height of its activity dealt on an average with some 1,500 persons daily. In general the public response to delousing was very satisfactory and most people were glad to submit themselves to a process of disinfestation, but it became evident that a certain portion of the population was not being reached, since typhus continued to occur in certain blocks within walking distance of the delousing stations. Special dusting crews were therefore instituted who systematically attacked whole blocks.

Special efforts, at first only partially successful, were made to prevent the spread of the disease to the surrounding communes and the remainder of the peninsula, by insisting on the delousing of all passengers leaving Naples by train, and by prohibiting all egress by road to persons not in possession of a certificate showing that they had been deloused. Flying delousing squadrons were also sent into the surrounding communes, where typhus cases were suspected, and extensive house to house delousing was carried out in some of the suburbs. Inoculation played only a very secondary part in combating the epidemic. It was, at the critical phase, practically confined to doctors and nurses and persons in very close contact with the Allied armed forces.

During the second half of December the number of new cases rose rapidly, reaching 227 in the last week of the month. By the second week in January the figures already began to show a sharp decline to 137 and in the fifth week had fallen to 64, thence declining continuously to 9 in the last week of February. By the third week of April, new cases in Naples had dropped to one, and after that no more fresh cases occurred in the city. The total number of cases recorded in Naples from 9th July 1943 to the end of April 1944 amounted to just over 1,400, and those outside Naples to about 500, practically all of which occurred within a twenty-five mile radius of the city.

The new technique of disinfestation, which had been worked out by the American Typhus Commission and the Rockefeller team in Egypt and North Africa, consisted of the dusting of persons fully dressed by mechanical methods, by means of dust guns, disinfesting not only the person but the clothing. Previous methods of delousing, though reasonably efficient, were much more complicated, involving complete undressing of the person, cleansing, and manual disinfestation, both of the person and of each piece of clothing separately—a process requiring a good deal of time, which could never have been accomplished on the colossal scale required. In Naples alone during the first fifteen days of January over 630,000 dustings were performed, the numbers treated on 10th January amounting to over 72,000. The total number of dustings administered between 19th December 1943 and the end of May 1944 totalled over three millions.

The working out of the new technique of disinfestation coincided with the discovery of the insecticidal potency of D.D.T. But the initial dusting in the Naples anti-typhus campaign was done almost entirely with M.Y.L., or with the British A.L. 63, as D.D.T. had not yet become available in sufficient quantities. The back of the epidemic was in truth broken by these disinfestants, of which the former was mostly used for the early contact dustings. The employment of D.D.T. on a large scale only took place when the mass dustings were started towards the end of December. The publicity given to mass dusting has somewhat obscured the very important part played by earlier insecticides in mastering the epidemic.

Special measures had to be taken to protect the Allied armed forces from becoming infected. At the beginning of January Naples was placed out of bounds to all members of the Allied forces, other than those on essential duty, and troops were forbidden to enter certain parts of the town and to use public vehicles or restaurants. All dock workers and civilians employed by the armed forces in officers' messes and workshops were dusted weekly. Only one British soldier, a deserter, and two Americans caught the disease. Steps were also taken to initiate the Italian armed forces in the new technique of disinfestation and to supply them with A.L. 63 and vaccine.

The responsibility for ensuring that the health of the civilian population does not imperil military operations is formally one of the chief tasks of military Government, though the protection of the troops from disease is the direct responsibility of the tactical commander. In this case A.M.G. was clearly incapable of meeting the emergency, having neither the personnel nor the special medical material required at its disposal. It was therefore inevitable that the military medical authorities in the shape of the American Typhus Commission should take control, though the essential ground-work for breaking the back of the epidemic was actually accomplished by the Rockefeller health team working under A.M.G. Though the organisation made responsible for controlling the outbreak was the American Typhus Commission, on a lower level the work done was an admirable example of cooperation among the various authorities concerned. Thus the Armies, quite apart from providing insecticide powders and disinfesting apparatus for civilian use, ambulances, transport and in certain cases supplementary rations for patients, made available an important element of the medical staff working under the Typhus Commission. A British research team took over the fifty beds at the reconstituted hospital for infectious diseases, where twelve British army nurses volunteered for this duty and a detachment of the Friends Ambulance Unit also assisted. An important part in the delousing campaign was also played by various army malarial control units. The medical staff of A.M.G. Region III provided valuable service in arranging meetings of local practitioners and in coordinating the work of the Neapolitan public health authorities.

On 19th February the Typhus Commission retired and for the remainder of the campaign the typhus control organisation was placed under the direction of A.M.G./A.C.C. In order to inculcate the lessons gained in combating the Naples epidemic, a typhus demonstration unit was set up by the Public Health Sub-Commission, and arrangements were made with the Ministry of the Interior for this unit to visit all the provinces of liberated Italy and to give demonstrations instructing provincial health officers in the technique of typhus control.

The influx of refugees which followed the cessation of hostilities provided another field for mass disinfestation. The danger of introducing typhus was obviously considerable. Dusting was instituted at all the frontier camps between Lake Como and Udine, but, since in the earlier stages a large number of incoming refugees had managed to evade passing through any of the camps, a second dusting screen was instituted at railhead and port camps, such as Bologna, Forli, Venice and Genoa.

SMALL-POX

An outbreak of small-pox made its appearance in Naples and the surrounding communes early in 1944. The general level of immunisation from vaccination was very low and a large number of cases in the province and city developed, though as the outbreak was of a very mild type, the deaths which occurred were very few, a fact which made it much harder to enforce isolation and precautionary measures. Up to the end of July 1944 870 cases were recorded and in October and November the number of cases was 360 and 317 respectively. From that point figures began to decrease, but it was not until hostilities were over that the epidemic in Naples was finally extinguished. In the autumn it had spread to Benevento. Cases of small-pox also occurred in Avellino and Salerno provinces. A campaign for vaccination was immediately inaugurated. Though, with the exception of Naples commune, the remaining area was in Italian Government territory, a medical officer from the Commission headquarters was despatched to take charge of the campaign. Vaccines from Palermo, and later from Rome, as well as supplies imported from the U.S.A., were employed. It was about a year before new cases were reduced to negligible proportions. From the onset of the epidemic in April 1944 till the end of February 1945 over 900,000 people were vaccinated in Naples commune and over 2,220,000 in Naples province, 150,000 in Avellino province, nearly 100,000 in Benevento province, and 90,000 in Salerno province. A small outbreak was also recorded in Palermo, but the prompt action of the public health authorities soon brought it to a close.

TYPHOID

In Benevento a small outbreak of typhoid occurred during March and April 1944, sixty-two cases being reported, with eight deaths. This subsided during May and June, but later began to assume epidemic proportions with thirty cases and six deaths in July and seventy-two cases and twenty-one deaths in August. There were ninety cases in September with twelve deaths and then the number dropped sharply in October to fifteen and in November to six. The chief causes of this outbreak were contaminated water supply, war damage to sewers, and general absence of public latrines. Very valuable help in combating this epidemic was received from British Army Medical Officers in the neighbourhood.

In October 1944 a sharp epidemic of typhoid fever occurred in San Marino. The normal population of this little republic, amounting to about 14,000, had been swollen by an influx of refugees from the northern Italian towns and from Rimini, where the disease was endemic and had simultaneously broken out. Some 810 cases occurred in the Republic, the outbreak being traced to a fault in an aqueduct, and 340 cases were also reported in Rimini. Total mortality amounted to ninety-three persons. Thanks to the cooperation of the army medical authorities, who took over control of the civilian hospital in Rimini, and the assistance of the American and British Red Cross nurses, the epidemic was suppressed before the end of the winter. Mass immunisation during the actual outbreak was not attempted, since a large number of persons had been exposed to the infection some weeks before control measures were undertaken and contacts were consequently dispersed over a very extensive area.

The outbreak at Prato, a commune of 80,000 inhabitants, was due to damage by the enemy to the aqueduct supplying the town, the absence of any piped system of sewerage and the pollution of surface wells. Typhoid appears to have been endemic in the town, but in the last three months of 1944 began to assume epidemic proportions, 145 new cases developing between the middle of December and the early days of January. Altogether between September 1944 and February 1945 nearly 500 definitely confirmed cases were recorded. Prompt action by the Allied army medical authorities and the American Red Cross enabled the epidemic to be arrested, and the mass immunisation of the population to be carried out by six inoculation teams.

MALARIA CONTROL

War damage and deliberate sabotage by the Germans resulted in the flooding of large areas of reclaimed land, not only on the west coast but also on the Adriatic. Round Salerno the canals draining the reclaimed areas (*bonifiche*) of the plain to the south were many of them badly blocked. The *bonifiche* north of Naples had been sabotaged in September 1943, while the whole drainage system of the Pontine Marshes was put out of action before the advance on Rome. The Tiber delta (*Agro Romano*) had been flooded earlier in the year and water from the Tiber had been diverted into low-lying areas. Similar sabotage had taken place in the *bonifiche* in the vicinity of Grosseto and on the delta of the Arno. On the east coast considerable war damage to drainage canals had taken place in the highly malarious zone of Foggia, while the *bonifiche* in the vicinity of Ravenna and the country stretching up to the highly malarious delta of the Po had been deliberately sabotaged.

In these circumstances a virulent outbreak of malaria not only among the civilian population, but also among the Allied armed forces, whose casualties from the disease in Sicily had been exceedingly heavy, might have been expected. That it did not take place was due, first to an enormous improvement in the discipline of anti-malarial precautions in the armed forces, secondly, to the new methods of control evolved by the combined efforts of the army medical authorities, the Allied Commission and the Italian public health authorities. The lethal qualities of D.D.T., which had revealed themselves so strikingly in the Naples typhus epidemic, were now extended from the louse to the anopheline mosquito. A Malaria Control branch was set up in the Public Health Sub-Commission under Colonel Paul F. Russell of the U.S. Army Medical Corps. The branch was organised into two sections—an advisory unit, to advise the Italian Government and A.M.G. on the measures to be taken to make malaria control efficient in the light of newly developed technique, and a demonstration unit, constituted by members of the Rockefeller health team assisted by several Italian physicians and entomologists. The chief purpose of this unit was to demonstrate the methods of employing D.D.T. both as a larvicide and as an unparalleled means of destroying adult mosquito. These methods included spraying from aeroplanes, hand dusting and spraying of buildings.

The functions of the Control unit was to assist A.C.C. and A.M.G. Public Health officers to develop an effective civilian malaria control programme primarily in order to provide the best possible extra-cantonment protection to the Allied forces, and to prevent malaria among civilians. This involved the closest collaboration with the military, medical and sanitary authorities in the development and application of the use of D.D.T., which amounted to a revolution in the technique of malaria control. The flooding on a large scale of land reclamation areas raised an enormous problem of larvicide, until such time as the normal methods of drainage could be re-established. To this problem a solution was found by mixing D.D.T. with oil and spraying it from a tank slung below an aeroplane. This method was first tried out in an area south of the Volturno River. Dusting from aeroplanes with Paris Green, supplied from army sources, was also carred out in the Pontine Marshes, until later experiments showed the superiority of the method of spraying with oil and D.D.T.

These two methods of larvicide from the air were of great assistance in arresting the epidemic of malaria which had inevitably begun to develop in the flooded areas. But the really spectacular discovery of the virtues of D.D.T. was made through its employment as a method of killing the adult mosquito. Experiments carried out by the demonstration unit in the Volturno district showed that by spraying the insides of buildings, such as dwelling houses and stables, practically the whole of the adult mosquito population could be destroyed, as well as any subsequently arriving adults, the killing power of one spraying remaining in the building for about two months practically unimpaired. From the military point of view the importance of this discovery could hardly be over-estimated, since it provided a method of control which enabled fast moving forces to be protected in far-forward areas. From the civilian standpoint also it was of scarcely less importance.

With the limited resources available, it was decided to concentrate on the Tiber delta and the coastal plains west of Rome, where German sabotage had submerged an area about half as big as that inundated in the Pontine Marshes. A double campaign was therefore concerted of larvicide and adulticide. Between July and the end of September flooded areas near Ostia Antica and on the Isola Sacra were treated weekly with larvicide, Paris Green and D.D.T. mixed with Diesel oil, with the result that by the end of September the mosquito larvae were practically exterminated in the former and reduced to very small quantities in the latter. A vigorous onslaught was also made on the adult population of anophelines in the Lido di Roma, the Isola Sacra and the town of Fiumicino. In the latter town over 3,000 rooms were treated until by the end of September adult mosquitoes were practically annihilated. Houses, barns and pigsties in the Isola Sacra were also treated. This vigorous campaign was however too late to prevent the outbreak of a considerable epidemic of malaria during the summer, though this was very much smaller than that which took place in the province of Littoria, where these measures could not be applied.

In preparation for the malaria season of 1945 arrangements were made for a large scale spraying operation to be undertaken in the Tiber delta before the onset of the mosquito breeding season. All buildings within an area of seven miles from the town of Lido di Roma were sprayed, as well as those in the Maccarese plain. Two tons of D.D.T. concentrate from Naples were made available by the Typhus Control Board, and D.D.T. powder was also shipped into Italy by U.N.R.R.A. Measures of control were also undertaken by the Italian Government in the Pontine Marshes and three officers from the Allied Commission were made available to assist in this work. But the operations were greatly impeded by the lack of transport. By the time hostilities had ended, the work in the Tiber delta was nearing completion, some 4,350 buildings containing over 39,000 rooms having been treated in an area embracing approximately 120 square miles. By the time the spraying was completed in June, almost 5,800 buildings had been treated, containing in all some 47,000 rooms.

These results were only made possible by the closest collaboration with, and most generous assistance from, the Armies in the matter of raw materials such as Paris Green, oil and D.D.T., and mechanical appliances such as sprayers of various kinds. Suppressive drugs were also made available from Allied sources, fifty million atabrin tablets being placed at the disposal of the Italian Government by the Allied Commission and a further fifty million tablets provided by U.N.R.R.A. The immense larvicidal aerial spraying programme, initiated by the Allied military medical and hygiene authorities as soon as hostilities were ended, was so successful that in the malarious areas of the northern Adriatic coast, such as the Po delta and the coastal sector near the mouth of the Isonzo, the mosquito population virtually disappeared, to the great benefit not only of the occupying troops but also of the civilian inhabitants.

VENEREAL DISEASE

In spite of the system of regularised prostitution under licence in houses subject to medical supervision, the incidence of venereal diseases among the civilian population was, especially in Naples, high, and under the stress of a double military occupation it soared to alarming altitudes. The medical control of licensed houses of prostitution was notoriously lax, and the consequent decision of the Allied military authorities to place all licensed brothels out of bounds immediately raised the problem of clandestine prostitution.

Under Italian law, as then existing, soliciting was a criminal offence, venereal diseases were subject to compulsory notification, an infected person communicating syphilis was liable to prosecution, and the Prefects had power to forbid the exercise of their profession by prostitutes infected with venereal diseases independently of any reference to actual communication. Unlicensed prostitutes could also be made subject to compulsory medical inspection. On paper these provisions would appear adequate to afford sufficient protection if they were strictly enforced. It was their enforcement that proved the problem. This was the more difficult because of the absence of any provision in the law regarding the compulsory detention of infected women while undergoing treatment or while awaiting trial. The places which gave the military authorities most anxiety were the two 'leave centres', Naples and Rome, where the infection rate among troops reached an appallingly high figure.

The control of the unlicensed prostitute through the application of the existing law in Italian Government territory and the provision of hospital facilities for the diagnosis and treatment of women suspected to be sources of venereal disease became one of the most difficult problems with which the Control Commission was forced to grapple. A veneriological specialist, of the American Army Medical Corps, was appointed to take charge of this function in the Public Health Sub-Commission, but owing to the general shortage of medical staff attached to the Commission he had to be diverted to other duties in January 1945.

The provision of a sufficient number of hospital beds and bedding was everywhere a difficult problem. Nevertheless some progress was made and V.D. hospitals were set up both in Bari and Foggia. A mobile V.D. hospital was also organised by Eighth Army A.M.G. Before the occupation of Rome, there were already established nineteen of these hospitals in Italian Government territory, with a total of over 2,000 beds, of which 1,800 were in continual use, the turnover being about 3,500 patients a month.

After the occupation of Rome, the Bonomi Government was persuaded to set up a V.D. inspectorate and the active cooperation of the civil police in arresting suspects was obtained, but the number of cases brought in was soon too large to be dealt with by existing public health resources, both of hospital accommodation and personnel. The rate of infection of Allied troops using Rome as a leave centre became alarmingly big, and the Allied military authorities had to bring pressure to bear on the Italian Government, through the Allied Commission, to reinforce existing legislation. Vigorous action was taken by the police in the spring of 1945. Houses of clandestine prostitution were searched and over 250 persons put in jail. But the number of hospital beds available was continually insufficient.

Under pressure from the Public Health Sub-Commission the Italian Government did issue special instructions to Prefects of all provinces concerning the medical examination and treatment of infected prostitutes, but these were for the most part only observed with great laxity. The Inspectorate for Venereal Diseases was also much hampered by lack of adequate transport and insufficiency of drugs and competent medical staff. Quite apart from the inadequate diagnostic methods of many of the Italian doctors, there were undoubtedly cases of corruption by which medical officers received bribes from the women for the granting of health certificates. Conditions in this respect were particularly bad in Naples, where the director of the principal V.D. hospital and his chief assistant were arrested and tried by an Allied military court for receiving bribes, but were acquitted. This incident induced the D.M.S. of No. 3 District to offer to lend a British V.D. specialist to supervise and re-organise the running of the hospital. The offer of assistance, both in the matter of drugs and equipment and of staff from military sources, on condition that Allied military medical authorities would be allowed to exercise supervision, was at last accepted, but only after the conclusion of hostilities.

APPENDIX V

Note on the Italian Press[1]

Military Government was relieved of all direct responsibility for the control of the Italian Press, which was directed from an entirely separate centre at A.F.H.Q., the Information and Censorship Section (INC) and its organ, the Psychological Warfare Branch, whose directives emanated from the Political Warfare Executive in London. The relations between P.W.B. and AMGOT were covered by a general agreement that any matters affecting Military Government would be referred to the S.C.A.O., who would have a right of veto on any matter likely to cause administrative difficulty. In the event of a local conflict of opinion between AMGOT and P.W.B. it was laid down that the matter should be referred to the Force Commander and, through him, to A.F.H.Q. for decision. This arrangement worked well, and AMGOT made no attempt to control the contents of the two daily papers set up at Palermo and Catania as soon as possible after occupation.

P.W.B. officers landed on the Eighth Army beaches on 13th July (D+3), made their way to Syracuse and immediately produced an English–Italian news sheet, the Eighth Army News—*Corriere di Siracusa.* But owing to the shortage of newsprint it was decided that only two daily papers would be produced in the island, one in Palermo and the other in Catania. In Palermo the resources of two existing dailies were pooled, and a new paper named *Sicilia Liberata* started publication on 19th August. Among its prominent features was a column giving 'the background of the news and democratic perspective of events', based on copy supplied by P.W.B. from Algiers. In Catania a daily paper named the *Corriere di Sicilia* was also inaugurated. Later, a thrice-weekly paper, the *Notiziario di Messina*, and a twice-weekly, *Vita Siciliana*, at Caltanisetta, were also started. The circulation of these papers, owing to the lack of newsprint and the absence of transport facilities, was quite small. *Sicilia Liberata* only printed about 40,000 daily copies and the *Corriere di Sicilia* 25,000 in the spring of 1944. They were entirely produced and edited by Italians, news, except for local reporting, being provided free of charge from Allied sources.

The armistice introduced an entirely new element into the problem of Press control. Under Article 16 of the 'long terms' the Italian authorities undertook to 'conform to such measures for control and censorship of the Press and of other publications, as the Allied Commander-in-Chief may direct'. But this was not construed by Marshal Badoglio as depriving the Italian Government of its right to control its own press. In the early stages, when the renascent political parties were in violent opposition to the

[1] I am indebted for much of the information contained in this note to Lieut.-Colonel Ian Munro who was at one time Chief Press Officer, Italy.

monarchy and refused to cooperate with the Badoglio Government, this led to a certain amount of difficulty, since the freedom of expression encouraged by P.W.B. and the Control Commission was regarded with extreme suspicion by the Press Office of the Italian Government. But after the basis of Marshal Badoglio's Government had been broadened by the adhesion of the Six Parties, these difficulties largely disappeared.

When P.W.B. opened its Press Office at Bari, the only daily newspaper in existence in the Apulian portion of King's Italy was a single sheet called the *Gazzetta del Mezzogiorno*, which was being used as an instrument of Monarchist propaganda, by an acting-editor who was a notorious ex-Fascist. At the instance of P.W.B., he was replaced by a competent anti-Fascist, and the Press officer of P.W.B. began to exercise control over the paper in conjunction with the Press officer of the Italian Government. A number of weekly papers, in accordance with Marshal Badoglio's proclamation on the freedom of the Press, were also permitted to give free expression to the points of view of the different parties. By the beginning of November three of these had already made their appearance in Bari.

In Salerno P.W.B. had been early on the ground and succeeded on 14th September in publishing its first number of *Corriere di Salerno*. A special edition called the *Giornale di Napoli* was printed ready to take into Naples when the city fell. In the middle of the month a daily paper called *Risorgimento* was produced in Naples under the auspices of P.W.B. to replace the three dailies which had existed before the armistice. *Risorgimento*, while mainly a vehicle for conveying straight news provided by Allied sources, also attempted to act as a forum for the views of the different political parties. As at Bari, permission was given to the parties to publish their news in their own weeklies.

Publications were only permitted under licence, a limitation dictated not merely by political considerations, but by the acute shortage of paper. A special body called the Allied Publications Board was created to deal with both licensing and censorship, and the control and distribution of all supplies of newsprint, home-produced and imported. The chairmanship of this body was vested in P.W.B. and the censorship branch of INC was given separate representation, as well as G-2, and A.C.C. Its functions were exercised both in Italian Government and in A.M.G. territory. In the matter of political censorship in Italian Government territory, opportunity was given to the Prefect to register any objections he desired on page proofs of the political weeklies before publication, though the last word rested with the P.W.B. Press officer. Military censorship was exercised under Allied direction. In A.M.G. territory, page proofs, before publication, were submitted to a Military Government officer. These arrangements were however only temporary, since the policy of P.W.B. was from the beginning directed to the placing of responsibility on Italian editors. Before the advance on Rome pre-publication political censorship (as opposed to military censorship) of weekly or fortnightly political papers was abolished.

In order to combine the dissemination of Allied propaganda with the creation of a free Italian Press, a systematic plan was evolved by P.W.B. in the spring of 1944. In the large cities—Naples, Palermo, Catania and

Bari—P.W.B. assumed direct control of the single daily paper, whose primary object was to carry 'straight' news, based on the United Nations News service, and to aid the work of the civil administration as directed by A.C.C., for example in the campaign for the *granai del popolo*. With regard to domestic Italian policy these papers were to maintain 'a neutral and objective attitude' and their editorial policy was to be kept strictly in line with the directives issued by A.F.H.Q. In order to coordinate P.W.B. and A.C.C. policy, weekly directives were issued after a meeting with A.C.C. representatives, including the Vice-President of the Political Section. No attempt was made to conceal the supervision by the Allied Publications Board of these papers. But the free expression of political opinions was also encouraged by granting a licence to each of the political parties to publish a two-page weekly. In the capital and in Florence provision was also made for the publication of 'free' political dailies. But licences and circulation were strictly limited owing to the shortage of newsprint.

In the allotment of newsprint and circulation these dailies were given the first priority. The second priority was allotted to the political weeklies (or dailies) published in these centres—where initial maximum circulation was fixed at 50,000—sponsored respectively by the Italian Government and the six Parties of the National Liberation Front. In order to give the Government rather greater weight, after its translation from Brindisi to Salerno, its weekly organ was changed to a daily. In addition to the primary publication centres, with P.W.B. dailies, secondary centres were established at Salerno, Lecce, Taranto, Potenza, Cosenza, Nicastro, Catanzaro, Reggio and Messina, where a number of newspapers (mostly weekly or bi-monthly) were published, but also several dailies, not controlled directly by P.W.B. Sardinia had two independent dailies, one published at Cagliari and the other at Sassari. A third priority was allotted to any other paper which was regarded as 'useful for social development'. This category included, besides political publications not sponsored by any of the six 'official' parties, various religious papers as well as art reviews, 'youth' organs, trade union magazines, medical and legal reviews, women's magazines and even humorous papers. Before the occupation of Rome the number of papers authorised in liberated Italy had reached quite a respectable figure, including eleven dailies (of which only four were controlled by P.W.B.), eighty-eight weeklies and twenty-six monthly or fortnightly publications.

P.W.B. also acted as an Allied newsagency, collecting data from various Allied sources and assembling them into a daily bulletin, which was distributed to the editors of the various political papers and also embodied into posters, which were put up in towns and villages in the forward areas. This basic news was at first confined to Allied sources, but in the spring of 1944 Italian news was added.

The plans for the occupation of Rome were based on the publication at the earliest opportunity of a P.W.B. daily, the *Corriere di Roma*, and the announcement, during the first emergency period, of the suspension of all other papers. During the second, or provisional, phase the pattern of priorities followed in Bari was to be adopted, six newspapers accredited to the six National Front parties being authorised. The three 'Roman' papers, which had been of world-wide report before the advent of Fascism, *Giornale d'Ialia*, *La Tribuna*, and *Messagero*, were after the 'epuration' of their staff, to be re-issued. Owing to the intervention of General Hume this plan was not carried out quite according to directive. The P.W.B. *Corriere di Roma* was, indeed, issued at once. But the suppression of the three famous 'dailies' was suspended, by order of the S.C.A.O. Fifth Army, and for a few days they were allowed to appear. However, the impression produced by the appearance of these ex-Fascist journals roused the indignation of the Committee of National Liberation, and after one or two issues they were suppressed. Newspapers, till then clandestine, which had been on sale when the Allies arrived, were given provisional licences. By the end of June, Rome was provided with no less than eleven dailies including, besides P.W.B.'s *Corriere di Roma*, a daily sponsored by each of the six liberation parties. The supply of newsprint was not sufficient to permit anything but quite a small circulation to the daily papers other than the *Corriere*, which was given a circulation of 180,000. The circulation of the Party dailies varied from 42,000 (*Avanti*, Socialist) to 23,000.

In Florence the P.W.B. paper, *Corriere di Firenze*, was brought out only a few days after the complete occupation of the north bank of the Arno. A week later a second-priority daily was permitted to appear, sponsored by the Tuscan Committee of National Liberation and representing all the five parties on the committee. The C.L.N. paper's circulation was fixed at a much lower figure than that of the *Corriere*, according to the normal P.W.B. procedure. In order to prepare for the continuation of the *Corriere* when P.W.B. relinquished its control, its ownership was vested in the Commune of Florence—an arrangement probably unique in the history of Italian journalism.

The establishment of a six-party coalition government under Signor Bonomi made it possible to take several steps towards establishing the independence of the Press in Italian Government territory. The first had already been taken in April, when pre-publication political—as opposed to military—censorship had been abolished. But though direct censorship was thus removed, Italian editors were left in no doubt as to the reserve power held in the background by the Allied Publications Board, of suspending the licence to publish. This sanction was used very sparingly, but was occasionally applied with salutary effect.

The next step was to delegate the responsibility for the granting and revoking of licences to an Italian body, subject to ultimate control by the Allied Publications Board. The machinery of control adopted, at the suggestion of the Italian Government, was a Press Commission, under the chairmanship of the Under-Secretary of Press and Information of the Ministry of the Interior, the members of which included representatives of the Press. In this body was vested the power of granting licences for publication of all kinds of books as well as newspapers—a power which had hitherto been in fact exercised by the local committees of the Allied Publications Board set up in the principal publications centres. The decisions of this body were subject to confirmation by A.P.B., a representative of which attended its meetings. Italian Government representatives also attended the meetings of the Allied Publications Board as observers. Minutes and decisions of the Commission were sent to A.P.B. for approval, and it was laid down that any decision of the Commission not ratified by A.P.B. would be re-examined by the Commission in the light of A.P.B.'s objections.

The hand-over of responsibility for the control of the press in Italian Government territory took place on 24th July 1944 and became applicable to Rome on 15th August, when the capital was incorporated in it. The authority delegated to the Italian Press Commission to issue permits was made absolute before the end of the year, ratification by A.P.B. being declared no longer necessary. Nevertheless A.P.B. reserved to itself the right of intervention at the request of Allied authorities in matters concerning military censorship or undemocratic conduct, including the right to suspend or revoke licences through the channel of the Italian Press Commission.

The next step was to hand over to the Italian authorities responsibility for the distribution of newsprint in Italian Government territory, after the deduction of the amount required for the production of P.W.B. papers, which consumed nearly half of the total newsprint available. This gave rise to some misgiving, since it became known that Allied imports were finding their way to the black market, particularly in Naples, and that certain Roman publications were systematically exceeding the authorised circulation. Arrangements were however made at the end of the year for the Press Commission to distribute newsprint requirements of the Roman papers, but responsibility for distribution to the other publication centres in Italian Government territory was not handed over till the beginning of February 1945.

It was not long before the Italian methods of distribution began to break down under the pressure of shortage, rendered even more acute by the granting of a larger number of extra licences. By the end of January 1945, permits granted to dailies totalling 25 had more than doubled, and over 260 other periodicals in the capital had been authorised. The total number of periodicals in liberated Italy at this time amounted to 527, with a total circulation (including Sicily and Sardinia) of just under a million and a half. Imports of paper for civilian consumption did not receive a very high priority. They had been worked out by A.P.B. and A.C.C. in the spring on a comparatively modest scale, namely 650 tons a month for the second half of 1944 and 1,000 tons a month for the first half of 1945, making a total of just under 10,000 tons for the year. Nothing like this quantity was actually shipped. Total newsprint supplies shipped from the United States from July 1943 to 10th January 1945 were only 4,500 tons and from Canada up to 31st March 1945 just over 1,500 tons.

The abolition of direct political censorship and the delegation of licensing authority to the Italian Press Commission rendered the 'control' of the Press by P.W.B. rather a delicate task, to be accomplished by education and persuasion rather than by direct intervention. The line between political and military censorship had never been an easy one to fix, and the military censorship instructions issued by INC had been so widely drawn as to intrude, not perhaps without reason, to some extent on the political field. But in practice the restrictions actually insisted on by military censors were comparatively unimportant. And P.W.B. was only on very rare occasions forced into applying the sanction of suspension.

Two further steps were taken to liberate the Press in Italian Government territory from the shackles of Allied tutelage. In its function as the disseminator of Allied propaganda, the chief instrument of P.W.B. had been its monopoly in the distribution of news from the outside world. The news, collected by radio, telegraph or mail from a large number of sources, private agencies like United Press and Reuters, the Ministries of Information in Washington and London, and the Tass agency in Moscow, was submitted to INC for military censorship and then translated into Italian. Together with Italian news collected by P.W.B.'s Italian reporters, it was distributed free of charge.

This monopoly was, after the liberation of Rome, attacked from two quarters. The large private news agencies in America and Great Britain started pressing for admission to Italy, and the Italian press demanded, and began to organise, an independent news agency of its own, free from all government influence, as a safeguard against any recrudescence of Fascism. Private news agencies were allowed to operate in Rome from 15th January 1945. The agencies who availed themselves of this permission were the Associated Press, United Press, Reuters, Exchange Telegraph and International News Services. The Italian Press now found itself dependent for its news on two principal sources, the Allied private agencies enumerated above, and the Italian Agency, ANSA. The telegraph and telephone system of the Italian Government, though at first not very efficient in all centres, was considered adequate for their initial operations. Certain Allied radio equipment, used by P.W.B. to supplement Italian resources, much of which had been requisitioned by Allied military authorities, was also placed at their disposal. The distribution of news by private agencies, subject only to military censorship, was thus initiated at the beginning of March. The cessation of P.W.B.'s news-dissemination entailed the surrender of the editorial control of the daily newspapers which it had established in Rome, Naples, Bari, Palermo and Catania, with due precaution to ensure that their control would not pass into reactionary hands. By agreement with the Italian Press Commission, the circulation of the papers in their new form was reduced, since they could no longer merit any priority in paper supply over their competitors. The function of coordinating the relations between the Allied Ministries of Information with the newly liberated Italian press was taken over by the Embassies and their Press attaches. The dissemination of Allied propaganda over the radio by P.W.B. in Italian Government territory was also given up, and the Italian 'B.B.C.', under its 'de-fascistised' constitution, assumed independent operation.

For the 'liberation' of the north, plans were made on the general lines already evolved. On the liberation of any town or district all 'Fascist' newspapers were to be suppressed, and their place was to be taken by an emergency news sheet, *Corriere Alleato*, prepared and issued by P.W.B. 'combat teams' serving with the Armies—an Italian version of the army service newspaper which, in addition to news, carried A.M.G. proclamations, etc., as had been done, for example, in the early days of the liberation of Florence. It was known that in the north there was a large number of clandestine papers. These were to continue publication openly after Allied occupation, provided that they applied for a licence and submitted to military censorship. The important pre-Fascist dailies in the big northern cities, which had been perverted by the Fascist regime, were to be closed down temporarily on Allied entry. A *Commissario* appointed by A.M.G. was to take them over, and initiate the process of 'epuration' of their staff. As soon as this was completed, they were to be allowed to reappear under their old historic titles. P.W.B. was to start its own news sheets in the regional capitals, and P.W.B. placard News Bulletins were also to be issued as required. The plan was discussed with the Italian Government and the delegation from the Committee of National Liberation in Northern Italy. It was agreed that both in Milan and Turin the five parties comprising the C.L.N.A.I. should each have their daily, but opposition was expressed by the C.L.N.A.I. delegates to the revival of the pre-Fascist newspapers under their old title.

The Press plan in its earlier stages worked very much on the lines laid down. In Milan the P.W.B. daily was quickly established in the office of the *Corriere della Sera* under the title of *Giornale Lombardo*. Its initial circulation of 200,000 was soon raised to 300,000. Five party dailies, which had made their appearance before Allied entry, were given permits to continue, but owing to the shortage of newsprint their circulation, which had ranged from 200,000 to 360,000 copies, was cut down to 150,000, though it was afterwards raised. But the scheme to re-establish the *Corriere della Sera* after 'epuration' ran into difficulties. The C.L.N.A.I. was strongly opposed to its re-publication under the old title, though the Allied Commission insisted on its appearance. This dilemma was resolved by changing its title to *Corriere d'Informazione*, which made its first appearance on 22nd May. In Turin a somewhat similar situation developed. The P.W.B. daily, *Corriere del Piemonte*, was quickly established with a circulation of 150,000, as well as five party dailies with a circulation of 100,000, but the revival of the *Stampa* and the *Gazzetta del Popolo* led to the same difficulties which had been met with in Milan. Finally agreement was reached with the C.L.N. on a change of title, and the first of these journals appeared as *La Nuova Stampa* without further incidents. The title of *Gazzetta del Popolo* was also changed to *Gazzetta d'Italia*.

In Venetia things went more nearly according to plan. The revival of the pre-Fascist *Gazzettino* did not here present the same difficulties that had been encountered in Milan and Turin. A *Commissario* was appointed, according to plan, when it was discovered that most of the shares of the owners, the San Marco Company, had been purchased by the Christian Democrat party during its underground existence in September 1944. This party-ownership was considered a bar to its appearance as an independent organ. The difficulty was temporarily solved by appointing a commission of three to advise the editor. The *Gazzettino* was finally launched, the only pre-Fascist daily to be revived under its own name, on 17th July.

The limiting factor in the proliferation of a free Italian Press in the weeks following liberation was not, as some of the politicians of the parties assumed, the desire of the Allied occupational authorities to prevent the expression of opinion of the 'left', but the absolute impossibility of procuring the required quantity of paper. This entailed the temporary imposition of an order of priorities in which Allied propaganda needs still, for a short while, occupied the first place.

With the end of hostilities, the need for the control of the Italian press, even in the territories still under Military Government (except in Venezia Giulia), automatically disappeared. The establishment of complete freedom as the final legacy of Allied occupation was a consummation which could hardly be delayed. By the middle of July the functions of P.W.B. in northern Italy—except Venezia Giulia—came to an end.

APPENDIX VI

Note on Displaced Persons and Refugees

(a) DISPLACED PERSONS

For the purpose of this note, Displaced Persons may be defined as non-Italians forced by the war, or by the events of the last years preceding it, to reside in Italy, either as internees, or under some sort of domiciliary supervision. They included, besides the nationals of United Nations, Jewish refugees from central Europe who had become stateless persons, as well as Yugoslav refugees who had come or been brought to Italy after the armistice under Allied auspices. Speaking generally, the Italians on the outbreak of war did not confine Allied nationals in concentration camps, but for preference used the system of *confino libero*. The only concentration camp uncovered by the Allies south of Rome was at Ferramonte di Tarsia in Calabria, which housed Yugoslavs (mostly Jews), Poles and Czechs, Austrians and Germans, as well as some Jewish Yugoslavs deported from Italian-occupied territory. The number of Yugoslavs interned was quite small, amounting south of the Apennines to less than 4,000.

The problem of the immigrant Yugoslavs was essentially connected with 'special operations' in the Balkans, which were not the responsibility of Allied Armies in Italy, being a purely British affair conducted at that time under the Middle East Command. It was therefore only logical that A.F.H.Q. should look to the Middle East for assistance in solving it. Arrangements were consequently made for the immigrant Yugoslavs who had crossed the Adriatic to be shipped to the Middle East, where they were accommodated in Egypt. Their presence in Italy was thus purely transitory, but since a large proportion of them came over, not by regular process of evacuation, but by such other means as they could procure, it was not easy to plan arrangements for their reception, nor on arrival was it possible for the transient communities to organise their life to any great extent. Moreover in the course of time the composition of the immigrants showed very considerable changes. To begin with, they tended to represent a fair cross-section of society, but after the spring of 1944, when facilities for reception and evacuation were reaching near saturation point, efforts were made to restrict immigrants to the *bouches inutiles*, with the result that children and the aged of both sexes tended to predominate. Indeed they included a large colony of orphans, who were flown from Yugoslavia and finally settled at Santa Cesarea in the heel of Apulia, where some 1,300 Croatian children, whose parents were in the fighting forces in Yugoslavia, had been placed. There they remained until the end of hostilities, at Marshal Tito's request.

In December 1943 the population of certain Dalmatian islands was being systematically evacuated. Between 27th December 1943 and

9th January 1944 about 6,500 refugees arrived in Italy. By arrangement with No. 2 District, two reception or transit camps were established with facilities for disinfestation, one at Bari and the other, later, at Tuturano near Brindisi. From these camps the Yugoslav refugees were dispersed to several holding centres, e.g. watering places lying in the region of Otranto, pending their ultimate transfer to the embarkation camp at Taranto, whence they were shipped to the Middle East. Transport and hospital services were provided by the British Lines of Communication organisations and arrangements were made for issue of army rations on the prisoner of war (non-working) scale for a daily strength up to 20,000.

During this transitory period before embarkation the chief problems were disinfestation—seventy per cent of the arriving refugees were found to be lice-infested—hospital care, the provision of clothing and other necessities, welfare, and screening by the military intelligence authorities. Until the Displaced Persons Sub-Commission was organised, such medical assistance as was necessary was provided from army sources, but the abolition of the Prisoners of War Sub-Commission enabled some of its medical personnel to be transferred to the Displaced Persons Sub-Commission, and these, together with Yugoslav doctors and nurses taken from the refugees and some Italian help, gradually built up an organisation of medical services, with the assistance of the Friends' Ambulance Unit, which rendered the sub-commission independent of the Army. The condition of most of the refugees on arrival was anything but good, and the number needing medical attention became very high, especially after the summer of 1944, as the average age tended to rise and the percentage of pregnant women and children was increased. As regards clothing, a certain amount of army salvage was provided, but in the main minimum needs were covered by Red Cross issue. On the welfare side, the help given by the American and British Red Cross was invaluable, especially during the earlier period before the organisation of Yugoslav welfare services could be completed.

These administrative problems were complicated by political dissensions between the Communist-dominated partisans under Marshal Tito, the adherents of the exiled Government of the King, and the Chetnik followers of General Mihailovitch. Some hundreds of Chetniks had come over to Bari with the Italian army, which evacuated the Dalmatian coast after the armistice. In many cases these had collaborated with the Italians against the Tito partisans, before Italy abandoned the Axis, and on arrival in Italy they had set up an anti-partisan committee composed of members of the Chetnik bureau in Split, which had been formed during the Italian occupation. They indulged in anti-partisan propaganda of a violent kind, thus creating serious trouble, which threatened to prejudice gravely Allied relations with Tito's Partisans. The Royal Yugoslav Government naturally took an interest in this group, and counter-accusations were not lacking. The situation was particularly delicate as A.F.H.Q. had agreed to the attachment to the Displaced Persons Sub-Commission of a group of Royal Yugoslav officers in common with military representatives of other Allied nations. As early as 10th November, the Middle East Command had suggested that on grounds of military security all

Yugoslavs should be restricted to residence in suitable areas to be specified, leave to travel or reside elsewhere being subject to special permission—a system hardly differing from the Italian condition of *confino libero*—and that, in any case, Chetniks should be separated from Partisans. With the limited accommodation in the camps available to the Displaced Persons Sub-Commission this was easier said than done, but the Chetnik Committee was abolished and the most dangerous leaders of the Chetniks interned in a camp at Pisticci in the province of Matera. Some of the remainder were removed to holding centres in the Lecce area. But the progress of segregation of Chetniks and Royalists from Partisans was never completely successful. The Chetnik and royalist element were naturally regarded by the military authorities of No. 2 District—to say nothing of Force 133 in charge of special operations in the Balkans—as a continual embarrassment, but it was only after several months that the efforts to persuade the Middle East Command to accept 500 of them, in addition to the Dalmation refugees, were finally successful. Arrangements were consequently made in Italy for refugees to be allowed to choose whether they should stay with partisans, or be segregated, such choice being made before a properly constituted body consisting of British officers and Partisan representatives.

At the end of 1943, the Middle East Command had agreed to accept up to 20,000 Yugoslavs, in the shape of refugees from the Dalmatian Islands. By the end of January 12,500 had been received in Italy (of which 4,700 had been evacuated to the Middle East) and it was stated that 13,000 were yet to come. Middle East thereupon agreed to increase their intake to 25,500. Evacuation was accelerated, and about 10th February had reached a figure of 11,300. By the end of April nearly 20,000 refugees had been evacuated from Italy to the Middle East, leaving less than 6,000 to complete the quota, and arrivals in Italy were still averaging about 1,850 a week. Middle East were therefore requested to increase their quota to 40,000, which they agreed to do. This acceptance was made conditional on U.N.R.R.A. providing essential medical personnel, which was not forthcoming, and pending their arrival the quota was finally cut down to 30,000. But in fact even this figure was never quite reached, since arrangements were made with Marshal Tito in May to ensure that no transport to Italy would be provided for refugees. Before the end of the year the success of the partisans had been such as to enable repatriation to Yugoslavia to begin. Nearly 5,000 were so repatriated in 1944. Besides Yugoslavs, before the campaign was over, a number of Maltese resident in Tunisia were repatriated and nearly 100 Jews were given a temporary refuge in the U.S.A.

The end of hostilities produced a fresh problem in the considerable numbers of displaced persons from central Europe, including anti-Communist Poles, Czechs, Hungarians and Yugoslavs, who had to be housed and sorted out since they could not be repatriated, as well as a considerable number of Frenchmen.

The first problem was to sort out the various categories of persons by nationality and status. Those who were to be repatriated were divided among camps, known as repatriation centres. One of these, in Milan, was to accommodate French and northern Europeans—French were also held at Genoa—another, at Padua, was for Yugoslavs who were returning to Yugoslavia, and Austrians bound for Austria. Greeks (except those domiciled in Tripoli), Albanians and Near-Eastern and Eastern nationals were concentrated at Bari; Poles wishing to return to Poland at Reggio Emilia. Stateless Jews were concentrated in camps administered by U.N.R.R.A.—Ferramonte, Santa Maria al Bagno and Santa Maria di Leuca, while dissident Yugoslavs were concentrated, partly in Apulia, partly in the Ancona area, and partly in Emilia. The influx of Jews from Austria, Germany and Poland, etc., many of whom consisted of clandestine immigrants over the eastern Alpine frontier, finally led to a decision to concentrate all Jews in Apulia and to transfer dissident Yugoslavs (about 7,000) to a series of camps in the Ancona area. Dissident Poles (about 8,000) were placed in special camps under the administration of the Polish Corps. The number of displaced persons who were collected into the Allied Commission's camps was never very large, amounting to under 30,000. In addition to these, displaced persons living outside camps were about 20,000. Repatriation was carried out on a dual system, either by individuals or by groups. By the end of December 1945 about 12,000 displaced people had been evacuated on the group system and rather less than 2,000 as individuals.

(b) ITALIAN REFUGEES

Experience in Africa had already shown that the evacuation of civilian population in an area of military operations should be planned and regulated beforehand in every detail, from the collecting point in the battle area to the final dispersal in the Lines of Communications zone. But planning for the regulation of civil evacuations on the mainland was only undertaken after the emergence of a widespread and predatory civilian nomadism forced the Armies and the Control Commission to concert measures to deal with this new menace. Fortunately there were available in AMGOT a number of officers who had experience of handling these problems. In November 1943 a group of these was made available to A.M.G. Fifteenth Army Group. Though attached to the Control Commission's nascent Displaced Persons Sub-Commission, they came under the command of A.M.G.'s Public Health and Welfare Division. This was not an ideal organisation, since neither health nor welfare is more than a detail in the handling of refugees, but it was the only arrangement practicable in the administrative confusion which enveloped the emergency of the A.C.C. Military operations in both army zones entailed the evacuation of a substantial number of civilians, while many others were either driven over the lines by the Germans before they retreated, or else spontaneously took refuge in liberated territory.

The problem was one of leap-frogging many thousands of persons from the forward battle area, over a zone where troops were everywhere thick on the ground, to districts where there was sufficient room to house them without interfering with operational demands for accommodation. This entailed a threefold division of responsibility between the Army, the

Control Commission and the Italian Government. In the absence of any previous planning the exact division of responsibility between Army and Control Commission was for some time disputed, in respect of transport, food, and medical and welfare services. Such was the chaos attending the organisation of the Displaced Persons Sub-Commission, that the handling of Italian refugees from army areas to dispersal point was temporarily removed from its jurisdiction and placed under a special branch at the Control Commission's headquarters, directly responsible to the Executive Commissioner. It was not until September 1944 that the Refugee Branch was reunited with the Displaced Persons Sub-Commission. A lot of trouble would have been saved if the necessity of planning for a refugee problem had been realised earlier.

Evacuation of civilians from army areas being a military responsibility, Armies were made responsible for providing the necessary camp accommodation, transport and rations, till they arrived at reception areas in Italian Government territory. They were ordered to assemble in forward areas and there marshalled under control of the military police at collecting points, with a minimum of personal belongings. It was not easy to persuade the peasant to part with his domestic animals, and a considerable number of the inhabitants often managed to 'go underground'. The difficulty was sometimes surmounted, as in the Cassino area, by establishing a communal farm for livestock as far back as possible, putting a number of farmers in charge, and arranging for the nearest *sindaco* to make a register of owners and give them a receipt. At collection points refugees were 'embussed' in lorries or other army vehicles and were conveyed to forward transit camps (or to the nearest railhead) en route for one of the main reception centres, all of these being on the army supply-axis, in order to make the maximum possible use of 'empties', both M.T. and railway wagons. From main reception centres they were conveyed, usually by rail, to the dispersal centres. Journeys had to be staged through centres where meals were served, since it was found that the issue of rations on trains was neither economical or efficient.

Refugees had to be subjected to a number of essential operations, in addition to being fed and transported. Of these registration was not the least important. Next, a medical examination was necessary. The precautionary measure of delousing was also important, as many of the refugees had been unacquainted with soap for a considerable period. Finally, the business of security screening in order to prevent the introduction of German agents was indispensable. Many refugees also stood in need of special attention. Thus provision of clothing was often essential and special nursing care was needed by the aged and infirm, pregnant mothers, children, etc., as well as by battle casualties—services which in forward areas were organised by British and American Red Cross workers assisted by nuns, and further back, where Italian civilian movement was less restricted, by nurses and ladies of the Italian Red Cross. The reception camps were staffed by the Italian Army. Rations supplied were on the (army) prisoners of war scale, which was a good deal more generous than the diet enjoyed by the ordinary civilian. Arrangements were also made to provide milk for children and nursing mothers.

In the early days of improvisation, the condition in reception centres left much to be desired. Indeed they were described with brutal frankness by a Red Cross field worker as little better than a Balkan prison. Some 32,000 persons were moved from the battle area between October 1943 and January 1944, of whom 30,000 came from the Eighth Army area, before the evacuation of the civilian population from the Anzio bridgehead was begun. During the six months following the landings in southern Italy the cumulative total of evacuees amounted to about 80,000 persons, for whom new homes had to be found in King's Italy. In the last quarter of 1943, Apulia absorbed the bulk of these refugees, amounting to over 30,000, but after January 1944 they had to be spread over Lucania and Calabria. In April arrangements were made to transfer 20,000 refugees to Sicily and in order to facilitate this transfer a transit camp was established at Reggio.

In Rome a large number of refugees were found. Some 7,000 had been settled by the Germans in a camp at Cesano, under conditions of great squalor, without sanitation of any kind. Thirty-one of the forty-seven schools in the city were also found to be filled with refugees. Cesano camp was cleared up at once, medical supplies brought in and Red Cross sisters and doctors installed. A new reception camp was set up at Cine Città, a southern suburb of Rome. On the Eighth Army side the main reception camp was moved from Foggia to Ancona and forward camps were also established. Camps north of Rome and south of the Apennines were being maintained at the end of the year at the following places: Chiaravalle, Castiglione Fiorentino, Santa Maria degli Angeli, Riccione, Torretta Palimbino, Pesaro, Solvay Rosignano, Lucca and Florence. Evacuation, which had sometimes been resorted to indiscriminately as a mere convenience to provide accommodation for the troops, became less frequent and civilians were allowed to remain in forward areas. The practice of leap-frogging refugees into lines of communication zones was largely abandoned. Attempts were made to hold them whenever possible in army areas as near to their homes as practicable. Only those who could not be accommodated locally were evacuated to Italian Government territory. By February 1945 the number arriving as far south as Rome had been reduced to just over 2,000, mostly from Rimini area. An unorganised movement of repatriation northwards from Sicily and the South had begun to create embarrassment, especially in Naples, and the medical services were greatly concerned at the possibility of an epidemic. On another occasion No. 2 District complained that hundreds of refugees had arrived at Barletta attempting to go north, the majority of whom held Region II A.C.C. passes. In spite of repeated protests from headquarters passes, continued to be issued, mainly by *Sindachi* and other Italian officials but also by Allied Commission officers. But by the winter it was found possible to inaugurate some measures of official repatriation to certain places north of Rome, such as Grosseto, Pisa, Leghorn, Pescara and Chieti. Refugees with homes in the South, including quite a number from German-occupied Italy, were conveyed by train and truck to Rome, Naples or Bari. Here they were sorted out at the reception centres, whence they passed under the control of the Italian High Commission for Refugees.

In Rome the Italian Government established a number of transit camps, from which those domiciled in Lazio were dispatched onward to destination camps. Refugees from devastated areas were established in camps as near as possible to their home town, in the absence of housing accommodation. During the period February–December 1944 the total number of refugees received in reception centres amounted to 155,487, of whom 150,880 were dispersed.

At the beginning of 1945 plans had been prepared, in collaboration with the Italian Government, for the creation of a considerable number of collecting points along the frontiers, from which groups of incoming refugees from central Europe, Italians who had been sent to forced labour, as well as returning soldiers, could be despatched southwards to thirty-two reception and transit centres in or near Milan, Turin, Genoa, Verona and Venice and some towns further south.

As a result of the sudden collapse of Germany at the beginning of May, the *Völkerwanderung* of displaced persons had got well under way before it was possible for Allied forces in Italy to close the frontiers. About 50,000 people, of whom the majority were Italians, came pouring over the Brenner, while streams of various nationalities, including Balkan dissidents, swarmed over the passes into Venezia Giulia. To close the frontiers and persuade or compel refugees to stay put was quite impracticable. The only thing to be done was to arrange with S.H.A.E.F. to control the flow, in accordance with the amount of transport and accommodation available. The improvisation of camps on a much larger scale than had been expected was necessary. A.F.H.Q. authorised Armies to give all possible assistance, including the loan of administrative and medical officers, trucks and water carriers, tents for hospitals, messing equipment, blankets and sanitary stores, as well as the diversion of food and medical supplies. To deal with the problem of camps, Eighth Army at the end of May created a number of new formations called D.P. units, consisting of ten assembly centres for 3,000 refugees each, six control camps for 1,000 refugees each and four forward groups, complete with medical staff and equipment, transport, accommodation, stores etc. Fifth Army followed suit, with frontier assembly centres and ten control camps. D.P. Units were also borrowed temporarily from the Austrian Control Commission, which had been organised in Italy. Transport, in the first instance, was supplied by 'back-loading' army supply-trucks, and all lorries proceeding south from the Bolzano area had orders to pick up refugees. But south of the Po valley the limitation of railway capacity led to bottlenecks at Genoa, Bologna and Rimini and a further bottleneck occurred at Rome, where nearly 70,000 arrived in June and only 46,000 were sent south. Large transit centres were accordingly established in Emilia, at Bologna, Modena and Forli. In the middle of June a conference was held at Bolzano between representatives of A.F.H.Q. and S.H.A.E.F. to canalise the movement to and from central Europe of Italians and German ex-prisoners of war. Two main routes were established, one over the Brenner and the other through Switzerland via Bregenz–Chiasso.

The organisation of this complicated immigration threw an enormous strain upon the Displaced Persons Sub-Commission, which had been dealing with about 12,500 people a month up till April, and in May was called upon to receive and disperse some 75,000. At the beginning of April it was operating only eleven camps north of Rome: by the end of May there were added to these about forty in the regions north of the Gothic Line. By the beginning of July this number had increased to forty-six. The location and capacity of the camps, which were divided into six regional groups, was in July as follows: *Venezia Tridentina*—two at San Candido, three at Bolzano, one at Malles, three at Verona included for this purpose in the group of Venezia Tridentina, one at Spondigna, one at Vipiteno; *Piemonte*—one each at Novara, Cuneo, Moncalieri, Domodossola, and two at Turin; *Liguria*—two at Genoa and one at Bordighera; *Lombardy*—three at Milan, and one each at Cremona, Brescia, Varese and Como; *Emilia*—three at Bologna, four at Reggio Emilia, two at Modena, two at Forli, and one at Riccione; *Veneto*—one each at Padua, Udine, Pontebba, Gemona, Treviso, Mestre, and one in XIII Corps area. In the centre of Italy camps were established at Palombina, Fermo, Servigliano and Chiaravalle.

The Italian refugees who came over the Brenner were in the beginning able-bodied men, without women or children, who had recently been conscripted to work for the Todt organisation in building fortress works in the Alpine redoubt. They were succeeded by another influx of forced labour which had been in the Reich for some considerable period and returned, not only over the Brenner, but also over passes more to the east converging on Udine. Another element was provided by Italian prisoners of war who had been captured by the Germans after the armistice, and there were also large numbers of troops of the Social Republic, who had been sent to be trained in Germany. By the beginning of July, the movement of refugees from Germany and Austria over the Brenner pass and via Switzerland had been regularly canalized and during that month over 155,000 people, an average of about 3,000 a day, were repatriated by these routes. Before the end of the month three train-loads a day began to arrive over the Brenner route at Verona, two filled with persons domiciled in the North and one with persons for the South. In August arrangements were made to break bottlenecks of rail transport southwards and seventeen trains a week running southwards enabled refugees coming from Germany to be rapidly cleared. By the end of August nearly 500,000 Italians had returned from Germany and Austria.

APPENDIX VII

Note on Labour

In planning the invasion of Sicily, it was clearly laid down that the armed forces would be responsible for engaging, administering and paying what labour they required and that the functions of AMGOT in this connection would be confined to advice on wage scales, etc., and assistance in getting in touch with sources of labour supply. The Armies had no difficulty in getting all the labour they wanted. The temporary unemployment caused by the Allied invasion was for the most part quickly absorbed by the employment created by the Armies, except in the case of the sulphur mining industry. But the lack of uniformity in the wage rates paid by the forces and their high level threatened to undermine the foundations of the whole wage/price system in the island, as well as leading to countless anomalies. The Services themselves soon realised the futility of competitive bidding for labour at unnecessarily high rates and agreed, after consultation with A.M.G., to a standard scale, introduced at the beginning of October 1943.

The chaos resulting from different wage rates paid by the armed forces in Sicily was quickly appreciated at A.F.H.Q. When the Advanced Administrative Echelon (FLAMBO) was set up in Naples immediately after occupation the regulation of Service wages was entrusted to the Local Resources Board, which set up a special committee to deal with this and other labour questions. The rates established in Sicily for wages paid by the Services to the various categories of civilian labour were adopted in a modified form, and became known as the 'Naples basic rate', local variations in the downward direction being permitted, wherever the cost of living conditions made this possible. These rates were intended to be slightly above those paid by private industry, in order to give the Services a small preference, which would avoid any competition from civilian employers though in many cases they were, at any rate to begin with, a good deal higher.

But the real incentive to attract labour to the forces was not money but food. Already in Sicily the armed forces had finally been obliged to supply heavy workers with some food in addition to the official ration. On the occupation of the mainland, the food problem became even more acute, especially in the Naples area. Even before the occupation the Italian Government had found it necessary, from January 1943, to supply dockyard workers at Taranto with a midday meal, and this practice was continued. The Armies were compelled to follow suit, by providing extra rations or a 'mid-shift' meal for all heavy workers.

Nor could the supply of extra rations be confined to heavy workers employed by the Armies on military works. Heavy workers in public utility services and other industries essential to the war effort had also to be supplied with extra food. The Allied Control Commission also found it necessary to supply them with 'mid-shift' meals—a resort which was at first looked upon somewhat suspiciously by the military authorities. After some discussion between the Commission and the Local Resources Board, it was finally decided to fix two scales of additional feeding—one, Scale 'A', to be applied to heavy workers directly employed by the armed forces, or by contractors operating exclusively for them, and the other, Scale 'B', to heavy workers in industries essential to the war effort, or to those employed by contractors working only part of their time for the armed forces.

The decision to destroy the syndical structure of the Fascist Corporative State left an aching void in the field of labour relations which had somehow to be filled. By the time of the invasion of Sicily, the corporative sanctions of the Government had so weakened that the collective contracts were honoured by both parties more in the breach than in the observance. There was therefore obvious need to devise some *ad hoc* machinery for the modification of existing contracts, for the settlement of industrial disputes and for maintaining in force such collective contracts as were still being adhered to. These tasks were undertaken by the Regional and Provincial Labour offices set up in Sicily by the Allied Military Government. They worked on the whole so successfully that they were adopted by A.M.G. for all Regions on the mainland. Before the armistice nothing was done by A.M.G. to encourage directly the formation of any new labour unions, but the first Government of Badoglio had already taken steps to liquidate the corporative system. Special commissioners had been appointed to the nine 'confederations' of employers and workers, with the object of restoring the *status quo ante* by giving freedom to employers' and workers' associations and divorcing their activity from the sphere of governmental action.

In these circumstances it was imperative for the Allied Military Government authorities to adopt a more positive attitude to the revival of free trade unionism. Several unions had already been formed in Palermo, and in the middle of October General McSherry requested instructions from the Combined Chiefs of Staff whether employees in Sicily should be granted the right to organise and select representatives for the purpose of collective bargaining, and to elect shop-stewards on the lines already approved before the evacuation of Rome by the Badoglio Government. An affirmative reply was received at the beginning of December, and General Order No. 17 approving the right of Labour to organise in Regions I and II, was published in January 1944. In the meantime, the formation of voluntary trade unions had gone ahead, chiefly on a local basis. By the beginning of 1944 there were about fifty-five of these bodies operating in Sicily, Calabria, and Lucania, and another fifty in the Naples area. A considerable number had also been started in King's Italy and a nucleus for the revival of the General Confederation of Labour was formed by central committees in Naples and Bari.

The occupation of Rome immediately created a problem for the armed forces. Civilian wages in Rome were traditionally a good deal higher than those in Naples and collective contracts under the Fascist labour code, *plus* revisions agreed between employers and employees before occupation, had pushed them to a level in many cases higher than the Naples basic rate. Moreover the German army had employed large quantities of labour, and the Todt organisation, though it had paid wage rates slightly below the civilian level, had augmented these with a free distribution of food. In view of these facts, Major-General Johnson, the commander of the Rome Area, on 27th June fixed the rate of wages to be paid by the armed forces at some fifteen to twenty per cent higher than the Naples basic rate, without previously consulting the Local Resources Board. His decision was overruled by A.F.H.Q.

Meanwhile the whole question of army wages was submitted to study by the Allied Control Commission for the Local Resources Board. This study showed that, since the Naples basic rate had been instituted, inflationary pressure had brought about a great rise in the price structure in southern Italy, while civilian wages were 'crowding the ceiling' of the armed forces' wages scale. It was therefore decided, first, to raise the basic Naples rate by twelve to thirty-three per cent, according to different categories of employment, and, secondly, to establish a special rate in Rome. Scarcely had the army wage ceiling been lifted, when unilateral action by the Italian Government sent the wages/prices indices spinning still further.

Before the creation of the 'Fascist' syndicates, Italian trade unionism had not been tied exclusively to any particular party. It had been divided into two wings, a Catholic and a Socialist, and the *Confederazione Generale del Lavoro* had represented only the latter, the former being organised in a separate Catholic Labour Union. The three parties now decided to create a single labour organisation fusing both elements in a unitary body, which was called the *Confederazione Generale Italiana del Lavoro* (C.G.I.L.).

The General Confederation made rapid progress in the organisation of the new 'free' unions, and its bargaining powers with the employers' associations were appreciable. Many contractors working for the armed forces were making very large profits, so that they could afford in many instances to grant wages quite considerably higher than the maximum allowed by law. Employers and the C.G.I.L. put their heads together and, having reached agreement, began to exert strong pressure on the Government to raise wages, this time compulsorily, by a large cost of living bonus, which was to be added to existing wage rates, even where these were already above the legitimate level, the 'ceiling' fixed by army rates.

Early in August C.G.I.L., after consultation with the Employers' Association, submitted to the Minister of Industry Commerce and Labour the agreed proposal for a cost of living bonus of forty to fifty lire a day, which was accepted by the Minister and submitted to the Control Commission at the beginning of September for approval. This was not given. On 19th October the Government announced, without consulting the Commission, that agreement had been reached between C.G.I.L. and the Employers' Association whereby, in addition to the cost of living bonus an additional five lire a day would be added to the family allowances, already increased by half, for each dependant. In the circumstances the Allied Commission did not feel justified in imposing its veto.

The result of this action by the Italian Government was to render finally illusive any hopes that might still have been entertained of arresting the inflationary process. Before the spring another general increment had been added in the shape of yet another indemnity, this time a *caro pane* (dear bread) bonus imposed as a compensation for the abolition of the bread subsidy.

On 17th February 1945, the Ministry of Industry, Commerce and Labour agreed with employers' and workers' representatives that there should be negotiations to clarify the confused wage structure, with its multiplicity of 'indemnities' based on the wage level in force in September 1942, so as to fix new basic rates for the various classes and a sliding-scale cost-of-living element demanded by the C.G.I.L. In consequence, a general upgrading of wages in civilian industry was anticipated, which entailed frequent and irregular variation of army rates. These had been increased in November 1944 as the result of the *cara vita* bonus and again from the beginning of March 1945 by a sum equivalent to the *caro pane* bonus. Some anxiety was felt by the heads of the military labour organisation as to their ability to maintain the small differential over civilian rates on which they relied for obtaining universal priority.

But wages were not the only problem. There was also the question of social insurances and services. These under the Fascist regime had become extremely complicated, including, besides family allowances, insurances against unemployment, accident, old age, invalidity and tuberculosis as well as special benefits in connection with marriage and maternity. From the point of view of the weekly pay-packet family allowances were important. They were really a form of augmenting wages, but they were paid by the social insurance agency, *Istituto Nazionale della Previdenza Sociale*, from the proceeds of a twenty per cent tax on payrolls. The payment of the employer's contribution to these social services raised a difficulty in respect of the workers directly employed by the Allied armed forces, for it was impossible to concede the right of the Italian Government to levy taxes upon the Allied forces, nor were the Armies prepared to accept any arrangement which would multiply their already existing large volume of paper work. Moreover, for security reasons, they were not prepared to reveal to any agency of the Italian Government the size of their pay-roll. The Italian Government declared itself willing to assume the financial burden of the employers' contribution early in 1944, but the actual means by which this was to be effected took over a year to put into practice.

There was a good deal of unrest in certain localities, but the amount of active labour trouble was surprisingly small. The ordinary motives prompting demands for higher wages were considerably weakened by the absence of consumption goods. The only thing that mattered was food, and prices in the black market, on which the worker was forced to rely for a proportion of his consumption, were so high that he could not afford to forego wages by striking. Moreover, the newly created unions had no strike funds to support him. And, if he was a heavy worker, he lost not only wages but food as well. The Allied forces offered comparatively good wages and, what was more important, more food. At the same time the employers were ready to offer considerable increases in money wages. These, though they did not enable the worker to maintain even his low pre-war standard of living, did enable him to keep starvation from his door. And in A.M.G. territory the presence of a Military Government certainly helped to prevent any serious outbreak of trouble.

Most of such labour trouble as did occur was inspired by the desire to get more food or clothing. In the original King's Italy the obvious focus for discontent was the dockyards of Brindisi and Taranto which, besides looking after the Italian fleet, did a great deal of important work for the Allied navies. Threats of a strike did indeed occur at Taranto in February 1944. General Mason MacFarlane made arrangements to impose Military Government at Taranto in the case of trouble, but the Italian Government proved capable of controlling the situation and no strike actually took place. In the end the matter was settled on the basis of a distribution of supplementary rations. Further trouble occurred at the Tosi dockyard in June, which was settled by the Prefect and the Italian naval officer in charge, by the grant of an immediate (and illegal) advance in wages.

In Sicily trouble broke out in the sulphur mines in May 1944. Wages were low and managements were disinclined to apply the increases which had been permitted under the Military Government arrangements. Moreover, the labour of this industry was not represented by any organised body. The Labour Sub-Commission secured the appointment of a committee representing management, labour and the Regional Labour office to arrange a wage revision, and the strike which had broken out was stopped, after arrangements had been made for the distribution of supplementary rations to heavy workers.

The Sardinian coal industry was also the scene of labour troubles. In April 1944 a strike broke out involving a small loss in production, followed by a further strike in June on a reduction in the flour ration. This was terminated by an increase in wages, but unrest continued, and was aggravated by the insistence of the Food Sub-Commission on uniformity in applying the lower ration scale of the mainland. Serious trouble again broke out in January 1945, which reduced production by 15,000 tons at a time when the world situation both in coal and shipping rendered a maximum production of Sardinian coal essential. The Food Sub-Commission authorised an increased bread ration for miners, which helped to allay the unrest, though this continued and manifested itself once more by a further strike in March. This unrest was due not only to short rations but to general discontent with working conditions. The matter was finally taken up by the Italian Government, with the result that during the spring a definite improvement was affected.

Only one stoppage of any importance affecting workers employed by the armed forces took place during the campaign. This was a stoppage of four days involving 4,000 workers in R.E.M.E. and other base-workshops in Naples in March 1945. It was a protest against the delay in increasing the wage-scales paid by the armed forces, so as to keep them in step with those of civilian industry in the area.

APPENDIX VIII

Note on Property Control

In planning for 'Husky' the functions of the Property Custodian were envisaged somewhat differently from those which had been assigned to this officer in Italian Africa. There the Custodian of Enemy Property appears to have been charged with a sort of general mandate to ensure that the usages of conventions of international law with regard to the appropriation, seizure and requisition of governmental, municipal, and private property were observed by the military authorities, as well as with the actual custody of such government and municipal property as was not required by the army for administrative purposes, including the control of public utilities and 'parastatal' enterprises and monopolies. This entailed in many cases the rather delicate task of persuading military commanders that they had acted wrongly, and ensuring their co-operation in rectifying the wrong that had been done. (See, Rennell, *British Military Administration in Africa 1941–1947*, Chapter XVII). It was realised that intervention by AMGOT along these lines would not be tolerated by commanders in the field. The activities of the custodian with regard to governmental property were therefore strictly confined to property of the enemy government not in custody of some other branch of the Allied forces. Close liaison was however established with 'Claims and Hirings' and the American equivalent, and arrangements were made for the Controller of Property to take over custody of government buildings when vacated by the armed forces.

Like all belligerent countries, Italy on declaring war had taken measures to sequestrate the property of enemy aliens. Analogous measures had been taken in this country, all such property being placed in charge of a Custodian of Enemy Property. It was decided to annul all legislation taken by the Italian Government by proclamation, and to make the Property Custodian, whose name had been changed to Controller of Property, take custody of all property belonging to Allied Nationals. Under AMGOT Proclamation No. 6, the text of which is given in Appendix I, all laws, decrees, orders or other measures taken by the Italian Government to sequestrate, block, confiscate or otherwise discriminate against British and American property were abrogated. All persons having charge of such property were enjoined to declare it forthwith to the Controller of Property, but to continue to maintain and safeguard it, until he took it into his custody or transferred it to such persons as he might designate.

It can hardly be doubted that this procedure was of questionable wisdom, since it tended to interrupt the continuity of responsibility of the Italian Government, which it was important in this case to maintain. The formal taking into custody of properties by an Allied officer was really without meaning, and after the armistice in King's Italy something of an anomaly, since it implied the exercise of executive functions on the part of the Property Control officers. This was indeed realised by the legal authorities of the Allied Commission, but at too late a date. The legislation which they persuaded the Italian Government to pass, in the shape of a dissequestration decree which did not interrupt its continuing responsibility for Allied property, was held up by technical objections raised in London by the Trading with the Enemy Department of the Board of Trade until after the end of hostilities.

The conception of a custodian for Allied property was in fact quite unworkable. To exercise any adequate measure of control a very large staff of experts would have been required, which considerations of military manpower could never have justified. Property Control officers were, however, able to take some useful steps to protect Allied property. By making inquiries into the work done by Italian administrators they certainly helped to keep these up to the mark, but their most important function was perhaps the defence of these properties from abuse by the Allied armed forces. In order to prevent damage by advancing troops, the first duty of the Property Control officer in Army A.M.G. areas was to ascertain as soon as possible after a locality had been liberated the whereabouts of all Allied properties, and to ensure that these had posted upon them a notice signed by the Allied Commander-in-Chief stating that the property was under Allied protection and forbidding the entrance of unauthorised persons, and, where necessary, to have military or police guards posted. In cases where Allied properties were requisitioned by the Allied armed forces, some degree of protection could be given by a close liaison with the appropriate Hirings or Real Estate officers.

Index

INDEX

(*The suffix letter 'n' denotes a footnote*)

S.O. Code No. 63-111-2-8*